D1450240

Chapter 4

Computer
Hardware
Overview

Chapter 7

Computer
Programming

Chapter 5

Computer
Software

Part Three

Computer
Programming
and
Languages

Chapter 8

Overview of
Programming
Languages

Chapter 6

Modern
Computer
Systems

Computers in Business Management
An Introduction

The Irwin Series in Information and Decision Sciences

Consulting Editors

Robert B. Fetter
Yale University

Claude McMillan
University of Colorado

Computers in
Business Management

An Introduction

Third Edition   1982

RICHARD D. IRWIN, INC.
Homewood, Illinois   60430

ISBN 0-256-02609-2

Library of Congress Catalog Card No. 81–84838

Printed in the United States of America

1 2 3 4 5 6 7 8 9 0 H 8 7 6 5 4 3 2

To Sandi

Preface

Computers have become essential tools in the operations and management of modern business firms and other organizations. The computer's impact on business has been revolutionary and promises to be even more so with the advent of the microcomputer revolution. Therefore, it is imperative that students in business and management programs gain a basic understanding of computers and their application to the data processing requirements of business. This is the type of *computer literacy* that should be demonstrated by educated people in business.

DESIGN AND CONTENT OF THE TEXT

This text is designed for courses which introduce students to computers in a business management context; that is, it views the computer as a valuable tool and resource for business operations and management. The text recognizes that most students in collegiate business programs will be future *computer users,* not *computer specialists.* As future managers or staff specialists in computer-using organizations, students need a basic understanding of computers and how they can be applied to the operations and management of business firms. Therefore, this text is designed to introduce students to:

- The fundamentals of computers and electronic data processing.
- The wide range of hardware and software available to computer users.
- The process of computer programming and several widely used programming languages.

- Modern data and information processing systems.
- Common and specialized computer applications in business.
- Management information and decision support systems.
- The process of systems analysis and design.
- The management of computer resources.
- The impact of computers on management and society.

OBJECTIVES OF THE TEXT

The primary goal of introductory computer courses in business curriculums should be to help students become knowledgeable business users of computer resources, as opposed to knowledgeable technicians in electronic data processing and computer programming. This text provides a teaching-learning resource which supports the attainment by students of this goal. Specifically, students should be able to demonstrate:

- A basic understanding of computers and how they can be applied to the operations and management of business firms.
- A basic understanding of EDP concepts, terminology, and techniques in business.

In this text such understanding can be demonstrated by successful attainment of a majority of the learning objectives listed at the beginning of each chapter. Thus, instructors can tailor the course to their unique circumstances by selective use of these learning objectives.

FEATURES OF THE THIRD EDITION

This edition represents a significant revision of the second edition. It reflects the author's own ideas, as well as the suggestions of the consulting editors, reviewers, and many instructors who used the text. The following highlights of the third edition should be emphasized:

- The text has been updated to reflect major developments in computers and information processing technology. For example, substantial material on microcomputers, minicomputers, data communications, distributed processing, data base systems, word processing, and decision support systems has been included.

- A major reorganization of the contents of most chapters has been made in order to improve the structure and sequence of the presentation of topics in the text. In many chapters, the concept of a *system* composed of *input, processing, output, storage,* and *control* components is used as a conceptual framework to help students tie together the many facts and concepts involved in the study of data processing systems, computer systems, and information systems.

- The sequence of several chapters in the text has also been changed. For example, the first chapter uses the dynamics of the computer revolution as a motivating vehicle to introduce students to the current world of computers. It includes a chapter supplement which introduces students to the use of a computer terminal or personal computer. The opening group of three chapters (Part One) also includes chapters on data processing concepts and computer fundamentals and is followed by a second group of chapters (Part Two) which introduces students to computer hardware, software, and different types of computer systems. At this point, instructors may assign any other parts of the text or move on to instruction in computer programming, using the chapters on the programming process and programming languages (Part Three) and a supplemental programming language text. The chapters on EDP concepts, data communications, distributed processing, data base processing, and word processing (Part Four), and those on management information systems, decision support systems, and systems analysis and design (Part Five), are new or have been significantly revised and restructured.

- The application of the text material to "real world" situations has been significantly strengthened with the addition of several *real world applications* at the end of each chapter and four *integrative case studies* at the end of the text. The real world applications are short excerpts which illustrate the application of major chapter concepts to actual business situations, and they are followed by questions which ask the reader to demonstrate understanding of such concepts and their application. The integrative case studies are longer descriptions of the problems and opportunities faced by actual computer-using organizations. Their purpose is to allow students to integrate the knowledge gained from reading and studying the text material and apply it to situations faced by real world business firms and other organizations.

● A major attempt has been made to increase the use of examples, figures, and photographs to reinforce and illustrate important concepts in the text.

● This edition continues to be a *language-independent* text. Chapter 8, "Overview of Programming Languages," provides students with a survey of popular computer programming languages, (FORTRAN, COBOL, BASIC, PL/1, Pascal, APL, and RPG) but is not intended for teaching use of a language for computer programming. Thus the third edition can be used:

1. As the only textbook needed for courses that do not require extensive instruction in computer programming.
2. As the main text, but supplemented with the appendixes on BASIC and Pascal in the Student Study Guide. This can provide sufficient text material for courses which require a brief introduction to programming in one of these languages.
3. As the core text used in conjunction with a supplementary programming language text in courses that require significant instruction and assignments in computer programming. Many excellent paperback texts are available for this purpose.

● Each chapter begins with a *chapter outline* and *learning objectives*, and ends with a *summary*, a listing of *key terms and concepts, review and discussion questions*, and *real world applications*. The text begins with a detailed *table of contents* and ends with an extensive *glossary* of data processing terms, a *bibliography* of recommended reading, and a detailed *index*.

● A Student Study Guide has been developed for the third edition. It contains detailed chapter outlines, chapter learning objectives, chapter overviews, definitions of key terms and concepts, chapter test-yourself questions (true-false, multiple choice, fill-in the blanks, matching), answers to test-yourself questions, and short chapter assignments. It also contains introductory appendixes on BASIC and Pascal. The study guide should be a valuable supplement to the main text.

● An Instructor's Guide is available to instructors upon adoption of the text. It contains instructional suggestions, answers to chapter questions, an improved test bank of over a thousand objective test questions and answers, and transparency masters of chapter illustrations.

A PERSONAL NOTE FROM A COMPUTER USER

It has been many years since I first became a *computer user* as a new financial analyst in the financial management training program of the General Electric Company. With only a freshly minted MBA to my name, I was immediately given the unwanted job of overseeing conversion of manual and punched card financial and accounting systems to computer processing for each department to which I was assigned during several years of rotating job assignments. This baptism by fire as a computer user was even more valuable to my computer literacy than a subsequent assignment in the EDP department, where I first learned the trials and tribulations of computer programming, using an assembler language called 9-PAC designed for the department's second-generation large-scale IBM 7090 computer.

At the end of my three-year stay with GE, I was hooked on computers. Not even a few years with the Data Processing Division of the IBM Corporation could change my user orientation. A subsequent Ph.D. in Business Administration from the University of Oregon produced a doctoral dissertation which was published by Bankers Publishing Company as a book entitled *The Impact of Computers on Banking*. It was based in part on consulting experience with the EDP management of several large and small banks.

This *computer user* background was the reason for my dissatisfaction with available introductory computer texts and led to the writing of the first edition of the present text. The book was written as an introductory text for present and potential computer users in business and management, not for computer professionals. This edition continues this user orientation and hopefully improves on it, both in its technological content and in its teaching-learning style.

It has become fashionable to talk of today's computer environment as being *the age of the user*. I prefer to use a term I have been using since the first edition in 1975. This book has not been written for the third or fourth generation of computers, but for *the user generation*.

ACKNOWLEDGMENTS

The author wishes to acknowledge the assistance of consulting editors Robert Fetter of Yale University and Claude McMillan of the University of Colorado; reviewers Lynn Ganim of the Life Office Management Association, Marc Goodfriend of Loyola University of Chicago, G. Vaughn Johnson of the University of Nebraska, Phillip J. Lederer of the University of Virginia–Charlottesville, Laurence A. Madeo of the University of Missouri–St. Louis, Gary Wicklund of the University of Iowa, and Jack Wimer of Baylor University; and the many instructors who suggested improvements to the revised edition. In particular, I wish to acknowledge the contributions of my Eastern Washington University colleagues Ray Hamel, who wrote the sections on the Pascal language in the text and the Student Study Guide, and Susan Solomon, who wrote the integrative cases at the end of the text; James Helgeson of the University of Oregon, who coauthored the Student Study Guide; and Ann Simpson of the ISC Systems Corporation, who revised and expanded the test bank. Special thanks for her invaluable assistance goes to Marsha McDowell, who typed most of the manuscript on a word processing terminal. The contributions of computer manufacturers and others who provided photographs and illustrations used in the text are gratefully acknowledged. Finally, I wish to express my gratitude to the many other persons at Eastern Washington University and in the city of Spokane whose assistance and support made this edition possible.

A SPECIAL ACKNOWLEDGMENT

A special acknowledgment is due the many business firms and other computer-using organizations that are the subject of the *real world applications* at the end of each chapter. In order of appearance in the text they are:

Cabarrus Urology Clinic; Treasury Department–Commonwealth of Pennsylvania; Doe & Ingalls, Inc.; The Atlantic City Press; Federal Express; Hubert Distributors; Ingersoll-Rand Co.; Spectra-Physics, Inc.; Physicians Microcomputer, Inc.; the Social Security Administration; Blue Cross of Virginia; the Kula Onion; the Boeing Company; The Hartford Insurance Group; Armstrong World Industries; Searle Chemicals, Inc.; Automobile Club of Michigan; the Department of Defense; Commercial Office Products Company; The Reserve Fund; the University of Iowa; First Interstate Bank Corporation; IBM Corporation; Chase Manhattan Bank; Hewlett-Packard Company; the Veterans Administration; Eastman Kodak; Glass Containers Corporation; GTE Electronic Components Group; Shaklee Corporation; Gould Instrument Division; Citizens Fidelity Bank; GE Plant Services Division; W. H. Shurtleff Co.; Hamilton/Avnet; Rockford Paper Mills; Mattel Toys; Farmers

Insurance Group; Armco Incorporated; Spaulding Division, Merrimack Valley Pet Supply; Yorx Electronics; Wang Laboratories; Citibank, N.A.; Martin Marietta Corporation; and Cumberland Farms Dairy Corporation.

The real-life situations faced by these firms provide a valuable demonstration of the benefits and limitations of using computers in modern organizations.

James A. O'Brien

Contents

puter Services: *Careers in Systems Development. Careers in Programming. Careers in Computer Operations. Careers in EDP Administration.* Computer Resource Management: *Managing Systems Development. Managing Computer Operations. EDP Personnel Management.* Computer Security and Control: *EDP Controls. Data Processing Controls. Organizational Controls. Facility Controls. Auditing EDP.*

Computers in Business Management
An Introduction

PART
ONE

Introduction
to Computers
and Data Processing

1

CHAPTER OUTLINE

The Computer Revolution

LEARNING OBJECTIVES

The purpose of this chapter is to develop a basic appreciation for the electronic computer by analyzing the development and revolutionary impact of computers on data processing.

After reading and studying this chapter, you should be able to:

1. Explain the importance of computers and data processing in today's society.
2. Define the terms: *computer, hardware,* and *software.*
3. Explain why the development and use of computers is called a computer revolution.
4. Identify the major characteristics of each generation of computers.
5. Explain the impact of the microcomputer revolution in terms of (1) microcomputer technology, (2) distributed processing, (3) personal computing, and (4) smart products.
6. Use a computer terminal, or personal computer, and a prewritten program to solve a short problem similar to the example illustrated in the Getting Started in Computers supplement at the end of this chapter.

Terms such as *data processing systems, computer systems,* and *information systems* can easily evoke images of mysterious, complicated, and technically sophisticated activities. Understanding the concepts behind such activities would seem to be a difficult task. Nothing could be further from the truth. For as you begin to read these opening lines of the first chapter, you are engaged in data processing! In fact, several observations could be made concerning your present book-reading activity.

- You are gathering **data.**
- You are storing **information.**
- You are engaged in **data processing.**
- You are a **data processing system.**
- You are being affected by **computer systems.**
- You are part of an **information system.**

The purpose of this text is to explain the fundamental concepts that underly such observations. These concepts are essential to an understanding of the present and future uses of the computer. Such an understanding can be acquired without an extensive technical background. Computers, data processing, and information systems will be revealed as important but understandable tools in today's society.

WHY LEARN ABOUT COMPUTERS AND DATA PROCESSING?

Why is a basic understanding of computers, data processing, and information systems so important? Volumes could be written to answer this question. However, at this point in your reading, three major points should be made:

- **Information,** along with energy, and materials is a basic resource in human society. We must learn to harness this resource to benefit society—including finding ways to use information to make better use of our limited supplies of material and energy resources.
- A major, even revolutionary tool in the production and use of information is the **electronic computer.** The use of computers is widespread and vital to business, government, and society. It has become even more so due to the rapidly growing use of the *microcomputer.* We must learn to use this tool in order to properly harness the information resource in today's dynamic society.
- The proper flow of information is vital to the success of

any organization. Thus, *information handling* or **data processing** activities represent:

- A major cost of doing business.
- A major job responsibility for many employees of a business.
- A major factor in employee morale and customer satisfaction.
- A major source of information needed for effective decision making by the managers of an organization.
- A vital, dynamic, and expanding career choice for millions of men and women.

Computers, data processing systems, and information systems have become essential tools in the operation and management of modern business firms and other organizations. As a present and future **computer user,** you should learn how to use these tools in order to minimize their detrimental effects and maximize the benefits to be derived from their proper use.

THE COMPUTER REVOLUTION

The development of computers has been acclaimed as the most important technological development of the 20th century, a development that has caused a *computer revolution* that rivals the Industrial Revolution of the 19th century. This sweeping claim is supported by evidence that the computer has significantly magnified our ability to analyze, compute, and communicate, thereby greatly accelerating human technological progress. Thus the development of the computer is also called the information revolution, the electronic revolution, or the second industrial revolution. It has succeeded in vastly multiplying human brainpower with the same impact that the first industrial revolution had in multiplying human musclepower.

Many of us are unaware of the vital role played by computers in today's society. Computers make possible much essential activity in modern science, engineering, education, medicine, government, industry, and business. *For example:*

- Computers perform in seconds, millions of calculations and record-keeping functions that humans would take years to complete.
- Computers store and retrieve billions of items of data and information each day.
- Computers monitor and control physical, biological, and

industrial manufacturing processes with such accurate and split-second response that many such processes become feasible only because of the computer.

- Computers analyze masses of scientific measurements and solve long and complex mathematical problems, such as those needed for space flight navigation.
- Computers record and process sales, purchases, inventories, bills, payrolls, checks, bank deposits, and millions of other daily business transactions.
- Computers analyze volumes of data on business operations and distill them into relevant information needed by management decision makers.
- Computers allow government agencies to daily process billions of statistics about government spending programs, tax revenues, and the many indicators of economic activity.
- Computers allow hospitals to use sophisticated equipment to diagnose illness and monitor patients, as well as to maintain accurate medical records.

FIGURE 1–1 Computers in Action

Courtesy IBM Corporation.

Courtesy Apple Computers, Inc.

Courtesy NCR Corporation.

Courtesy Xerox Information Systems.

- Computers control electric power generation and transmission systems that spread over vast regions of the country.
- Computers make possible national and international television, voice, and data communication systems including earth satellite transmission systems.

FIGURE 1–2   Speed and Power of the Computer

In the computer, the basic operations can be done within the order of a

NANOSECOND*

One thousandth of a millionth of a second.

Within the half second it takes this spilled coffee to reach the floor, a medium-size computer could—

$\left(\begin{array}{c}\text{given the information}\\\text{in magnetic form}\end{array}\right)$

Debit 2000 checks to 300 different bank accounts,

and *examine the electro-cardiograms of 100 patients and alert a physician to possible trouble,*

and *score 150,000 answers on 3000 examinations and evaluate the effectiveness of the questions,*

and *figure the payroll for a company with a thousand employees.*

and a few other chores.

Courtesy IBM Corporation.

* Computer operating speeds that were formerly measured in **milliseconds** (thousandths of a second) are now being measured in the **microsecond** (millionth of a second) and **nanosecond** (billionth of a second) range, with **picosecond** (trillionth of a second) speed being attained by some computers. Such speeds seem almost incomprehensible. For example, an average person taking one step each nanosecond would circle the earth about 20 times in one second! Computers operating at such speeds can process several **million instructions per second** (MIPS).

Thus the term *computer revolution* reflects the rapid and enormous changes brought about by the widespread use and dependence on computers in modern society. See Figures 1–1 and 1–2.

WHAT IS A COMPUTER?

Before we briefly review the origins and development of modern computers, let us define what we mean by the term **computer**. There are several varieties of computers and each has a variety of characteristics. However, in electronic data processing, in the computer industry, and in the popular literature the term *computer* refers primarily to a particular type of computer: the *electronic, digital, stored-program, general-purpose computer.* Such computers are used for almost all business applications and are the subject of this book. We can therefore use this definition:

A computer is an electronic device that has the ability to accept data, internally store and automatically execute a program of instructions, perform mathematical, logical, and manipulative operations on data, and report the results.

As Figure 1–1 indicates, there are many types and uses of computers. In Chapter 6 we will see that there are digital and analog computers, special purpose and general purpose computers, microcomputers, minicomputers, and many large types of computer systems, including *supercomputers!* In the remaining chapters of this text, we will explore fundamental concepts of the hardware, software, programming, applications, and management of modern computers.

Hardware versus Software

Computer equipment and devices are known as *hardware,* while sets of operating instructions (called *programs*) that direct and control computer processing are called *software.* See Figure 1–3. Examples of **computer hardware** include equipment such as:

- The *Central Processing Unit* (CPU) of a computer system.
- *Computer Terminals* which use a keyboard for input of data and a video screen or printer for output of information.
- *Magnetic Disk Units* which can store millions of items of data as magnetic spots on circular metal disks.

Computer software includes all types of programs of operating instructions which direct and control computer hardware in the performance of data processing assignments. This might include:

- *System software* such as *operating systems,* which control and support the operations of a computer system, and
- *Application software,* which are programs that direct processing for a particular use of the computer, such as an *inventory program,* or a *payroll program.*

The characteristics, components, and functions of computer hardware and software will be covered in the next few chapters. Let us now take a brief look at how electronic computers developed into the vital and revolutionary tools they are today.

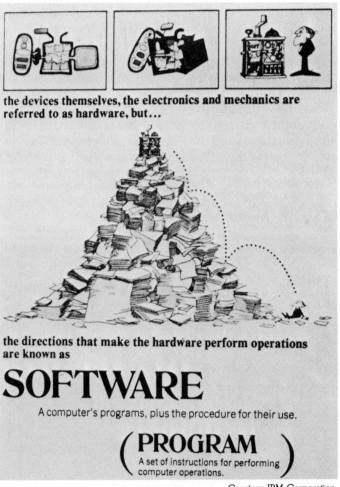

FIGURE 1–3   Computer Hardware and Software

the devices themselves, the electronics and mechanics are referred to as hardware, but...

the directions that make the hardware perform operations are known as

SOFTWARE

A computer's programs, plus the procedure for their use.

(PROGRAM)
A set of instructions for performing computer operations.

Courtesy IBM Corporation.

THE DEVELOPMENT OF COMPUTERS

Origin of Computing Machines

The electronic computer sprang from many origins, some well known, some lost in antiquity. Early manual computing devices and the use of machinery to perform arithmetic operations were important advancements. However, these and other devices were not computers, though they were important contributions to the development of machine computation.

The earliest data processing devices included the use of fingers, stones, and sticks for counting, and knots on a string, scratches on a rock, or notches in a stick as record-keeping devices. The Babylonians wrote on clay tablets with a sharp stick, while the ancient Egyptians developed written records on papyrus using a sharp-pointed reed as a pen and organic dyes for ink. The earliest form of manual calculating device was the abacus. The use of pebbles or rods laid out on a lined or grooved board were early forms of the abacus and were utilized for thousands of years in many civilizations. The abacus in its present form originated in China and is still used as a calculator. See Figure 1–4.

The use of machinery to perform arithmetic operations is frequently attributed to Blaise Pascal of France and Gottfried von Leibnitz of Germany for their development of the adding machine and the calculating machine, respectively, in the 17th century. (The programming language **Pascal** is named in

FIGURE 1–4 An Abacus

From an original in the IBM Corporation Antique Calculator Collection.

honor of Blaise Pascal.) However, the inventions of Pascal and Leibnitz incorporated some ideas similar to those used in the clockwork mechanism and the odometer, both of which has been developed as far back as the Greek and Roman civilizations. It must also be recognized that the calculators of Pascal and Leibnitz, and other early mechanical data processing devices, were not reliable machines. The contributions of many persons were necessary during the next two centuries before practical, working data processing machines were developed (See Figure 1–5).

FIGURE 1-5 Blaise Pascal

Courtesy IBM Corporation.

Electromechanical Punched Card Machines

The use of electromechanical machines for the automatic processing of data recorded by holes punched in paper cards was another major development in machine computation. Punched cards were developed in France by Joseph Jacquard during the 18th century to automatically control textile weaving equipment. However, their use in data processing originated with the work of the statistician Dr. Herman Hollerith during the 1880s. Dr. Hollerith was hired by the U.S. Bureau of the Census to develop new ways to process census data. The 1880 census report had not been completed until 1887, and it became evident that the processing of the 1890 census might not be completed before the 1900 census would get under way. Dr. Hollerith responded by developing a punched paper card for the recording of data, a hand-operated card punch, a sorting box, and a tabulator which allowed the 1890 census to be completed in less than three years.

Dr. Hollerith's work at the Census Bureau was supplemented by the work of James Powers who developed punched card machines that were used in the 1910 census. Both men left the Census Bureau to start business firms to produce their machines. The International Business Machines Corporation (IBM) is a descendant of Dr. Hollerith's Tabulating Machine Company, while the UNIVAC division of the Sperry Rand Corporation is descended from the Powers Accounting Machine Company founded by James Powers.

Mechanical and electrical improvements in punched card machines led to their widespread use for business and government applications in the late 1930s. These machines could "read" the data from punched cards when electrical impulses were generated by the action of metal brushes making electrical contact through the holes punched in a card. Data pro-

FIGURE 1-6 Electromechanical Punched Card Accounting Machine

FIGURE 1-6 Electromechanical Punched Card Accounting Machine

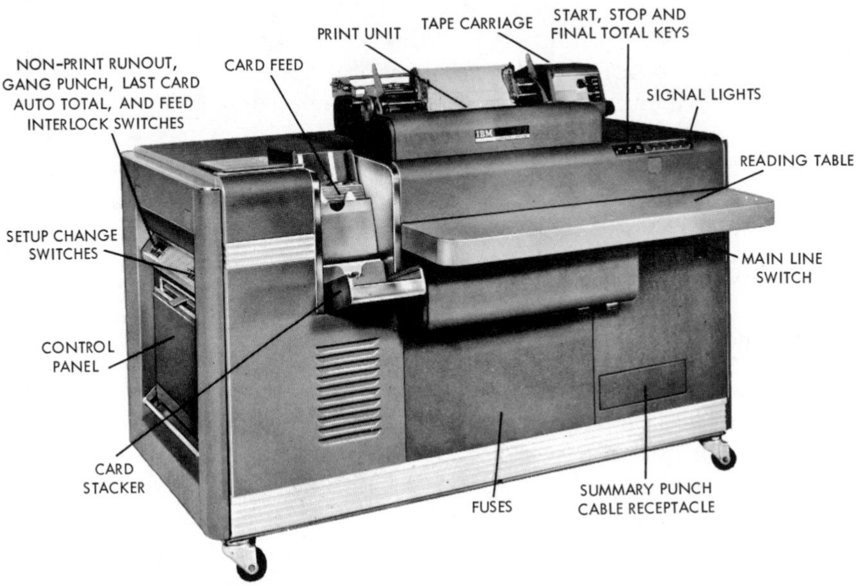

cessing operations were "programmed" by an externally wired removable control panel. Electromechanical punched card machines continued to be the major method for large-scale "automatic data processing" (ADP) in business and government until the late 1950s, when they were made obsolete by the development of electronic computers. See Figure 1–6.

Computer Pioneers

● Charles Babbage is generally recognized as the first person to propose the concept of the modern computer. He designed and partially built a steam-driven mechanical calculator called the "Difference Engine" with the help of a grant from the British government. In 1833, this English mathematician outlined in detail his plans for an "Analytical Engine," a mechanical steam-driven computing machine that would accept punched card input, automatically perform any arithmetic operation in any sequence under the direction of a mechanically stored program of instructions, and produce either punched card or printed output. He produced thousands of detailed drawings before his death in 1871, but the machine was never built. Babbage had designed the world's first general-

FIGURE 1-7   The Difference Engine

Courtesy IBM Corporation.

purpose, stored-program, digital computer, but his ideas
were too advanced for the technology of his time. See
Figure 1-7.

● Many of Babbage's ideas were recorded and analyzed by
Lady Augusta Ada Byron, Countess of Lovelace, the daughter
of Lord Byron, the famous English poet. She is considered
by some to be the world's first computer programmer. The
programming language **Ada** is named in her honor. See
Figure 1-8.

Almost a hundred years passed before the ideas outlined
by Babbage began to be developed. Highlights of this pioneering period include:

FIGURE 1–8 Augusta Ada
Byron

Culver Pictures, Inc.

• Dr. Vannevar Bush of the Massachusetts Institute of Technology (MIT) built a large-scale electromechanical analog computer in 1925.

• The first large-scale electromechanical digital computer was developed by Dr. Howard Aiken of Harvard University with the support of IBM in 1944. Aiken's Automatic Sequence Controlled Calculator, nicknamed MARK I, embodied many of the concepts of Charles Babbage and relied heavily on the concepts of IBM's punched card calculator developed in the 1930s.

• The first operational electronic digital computer, the ENIAC (Electronic Numerical Integrator and Calculator), was developed by John Mauchly and J. P. Eckert of the University of Pennsylvania in 1946. It was based in part on the work of John Atanasoff of Iowa State University, who had built a type of electronic digital computer in 1942.

The ENIAC weighed over 30 tons and utilized over 18,000 vacuum tubes instead of the electromechanical relays of the Mark I. The ENIAC was built to compute artillery ballistic tables for the U.S. Army; it could complete in 15 seconds a trajectory computation that would take a skilled person with a desk calculator about 10 hours to complete. However, the ENIAC was not a "stored program" computer and utilized the decimal system. Its processing was controlled externally by switches and control panels that had to be changed for each new series of computations. See Figure 1–9.

• The first stored-program electronic computer was EDSAC (Electronic Delayed Storage Automatic Computer) developed under the direction of M. V. Wilkes at Cambridge University, England, in 1949.

• The EDSAC and the first American stored-program computer, the EDVAC (Electronic Discrete Variable Automatic Computer), which was completed in 1952, were based on concepts advanced in 1945 by Dr. John von Neumann of the Institute for Advanced Study in Princeton, New Jersey. He proposed that the operating instructions, or *program*, of the computer be stored in a high-speed internal storage unit, or *memory*, and that both data and instructions be represented internally by the *binary* number system rather than the decimal system. These and other computer design concepts form the basis for much of the design of present computers.

Several other early computers and many individuals could be mentioned in a discussion of the pioneering period of computer development. However, the high points discussed

FIGURE 1-9   The ENIAC Computer

Courtesy UNIVAC Division of the Sperry Rand Corporation.

should illustrate that many persons and many ideas were responsible for the birth of the electronic digital computer.

The First Generation

The UNIVAC I (Universal Automatic Computer), the first general-purpose electronic digital computer to be commercially available, marks the beginning of the first generation of electronic computers.

Highlights of this generation included:

- The first UNIVAC was installed at the Bureau of Census in 1951. The UNIVAC I became the first computer to process business applications when it was installed at a General Electric manufacturing plant in Louisville, Kentucky in 1954. An innovation of the UNIVAC I was the use of *magnetic tape* as an input and output median.
- Another first generation computer, the IBM 650, was an intermediate size computer designed for both business and scientific applications. It had a *magnetic drum* memory and used punched cards for input and output.

FIGURE 1–10   The UNIVAC I

Courtesy Sperry-Univac.

- Computers developed before the first generation were special purpose one-of-a-kind machines, whereas 48 UNIVAC I's and almost 2,000 IBM 650's were built.
- The first generation of computers were quite large and produce enormous amounts of heat because of their use of **vacuum tubes**. They had large electrical power, air conditioning, maintenance, and space requirements. See Figure 1–10.

The Second Generation

The second generation of computers was introduced in 1959. Highlights of this generation included:

- Vacuum tubes were replaced by **transistors** and other *solid state, semiconductor* devices. Transistorized circuits were a lot smaller, generated little heat, were less expensive, and required less power than vacuum tube circuits.
- Second generation computers were significantly smaller and faster and more reliable than first generation machines.
- The number of computers in use grew rapidly, with the IBM 1400 series computers accounting for over 17,000 installations.

- The use of *magnetic cores* as the primary internal storage medium, and the introduction of removable *magnetic disk packs* were other major **hardware** developments of the second generation. Magnetic tape emerged as the major input/output and *secondary* storage medium for large computer installations, with punched cards continuing to be widely used.

The Third Generation

The introduction of the IBM System/360 series of computers in 1964 signalled the arrival of the third generation of computers. Highlights of this generation included:

- Transistorized circuitry was replaced by **integrated circuits** in which all the elements of an electronic circuit were contained on a small silicon wafer or *chip*. These microelectronic circuits were smaller and more reliable than transistorized circuits and significantly increased the speed and reduced the size of third generation computers.
- Significant improvements were made in the speed, capacity, and types of computer storage, and magnetic disk units came into widespread use.
- The *family* or *series* concept which provides standardization and compatibility between different models in a computer series was developed. Manufacturers claimed to have developed computers that could handle both business and scientific applications and process programs written for other models without major modifications.
- The emergence of *time sharing* (where many users at different terminals can share the same computer at the same time), *data communications* applications and the ability to process several programs simultaneously through *multiprogramming* were other features of the third generation.
- The third generation marked the growth in importance of **software** as a means of efficiently using computers. *Operating systems* of computer programs were developed to supervise computer processing, and high-level programming languages such as FORTRAN and COBOL greatly simplified computer programming.
- The first **minicomputer** was marketed by the Digital Equipment Corporation in 1965. These desk-top size minicomputers and other small computers had greater computing power than larger second generation systems and came into widespread use. This swelled the number of computers installed,

so that by the early 1970s, over 100,000 larger "main frame" computers were being used, and the number of minicomputers and other specialized computers also exceed 100,000.

The Fourth Generation

Changes of sufficient significance to merit the fourth generation designation were displayed by several computer systems beginning in the 1970s and continuing to the present time. Highlights of the present fourth generation include:

- The use of LSI **(large scale integration)** semiconductor circuits for both the *logic* and *memory* circuitry of the computer is a major technological development of the fourth generation. The use of LSI semiconductor technology enables thousands of electronic components to be placed on a tiny *chip* of silicon. For example, a chip less than a quarter of an inch square may contain between 10,000 to 500,000 transistors and other electronic circuit elements! See Figure 1–11.

- In 1972, several models of the IBM System/370 computer series became the first electronic computers with their main memories composed entirely of LSI semiconductor circuits. The use of such microelectronic **semiconductor memories** was a dramatic change from the *magnetic core memories* used in second and third generation computers.

- Main memory capacity of fourth generation computers increased dramatically. For example, a medium-size second generation business computer like the IBM 1401 had a memory of 4K to 16K—4,000 to 16,000 character positions of storage. In comparison, the fourth generation IBM 4341 medium-size computer has a main memory capacity of 4M to 16M—4 to 16 *million* characters of storage. The cost of such memory capacity dropped in the same period from about $2 per character to only a fraction of a cent per character of storage.

- The trend toward increased microminiaturization significantly reduced the cost, size and power requirements of fourth generation computers and greatly increased their processing speeds compared to third generation computers. Processing speeds in the nanosecond range and in millions of instructions per second are common. The decrease in computer hardware costs is reflected in the fact that the computing power of a $100,000 third generation business computer of 1970 can be purchased with a fourth genera-

Third Generation
Integrated
Circuits

Second Generation
Transistors

First Generation–Vacuum Tubes

FIGURE 1–11   Four
Generations of Computer
Circuitry

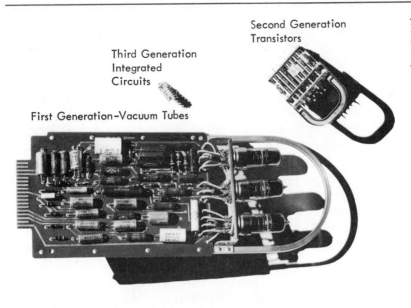

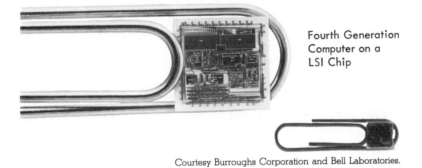

Fourth Generation
Computer on a
LSI Chip

Courtesy Burroughs Corporation and Bell Laboratories.

tion **small business computer** costing less than $20,000 in
the early 1980's.

● LSI technology led to the development of a **microcomputer**
in 1971 by M. E. Hoff of the Intel Corporation and Victor
Poor of the Datapoint Corporation. All of the circuitry for
the main processing unit of a computer was placed on a
single chip, called a *microprocessor!*

Other impressive fourth generation advancements, though
first developed in some earlier computers, are being used
extensively by fourth generation computer systems. They include:

- **Microprogramming**—the use of changeable *micropro-grams* of elementary control instructions which are stored in special memory circuits instead of being permanently "hardwired" into the control circuitry of the computer.
- **Firmware**—a development that involves permanently storing computer programs on semiconductor memory chips. Modules composed of these memory chips can be plugged into computer processing units to change their performance.
- **Virtual Memory**—a development that allows secondary storage devices such as magnetic disks to be treated as an extension of the main memory of the computer, thus providing the capability of a much larger main memory capacity.
- **Magnetic Bubble Memory**—introduced in the late 1970s, this form of electromagnetic storage chips fits between semiconductor memories and magnetic disks in price and performance.
- **Data Base Management Systems** (DBMS)—integrated sets of computer programs which greatly facilitate the control and use of data stored in the *data bases* or *data banks* of an organization.
- **Distributed Processing**—decentralization of electronic data processing tasks became possible through a network of microcomputers, minicomputers, *intelligent terminals* and other computers "dispersed" throughout an organization.
- **Word Processing**—where computers or intelligent terminals are applied to the automation of typing, text editing, and other office communications.
- **Structured Programming**—a highly structured programming methodology developed to increase programming productivity, accuracy, simplicity and economy.
- **User-Oriented Languages**—natural conversational languages developed to simplify the use of computers by *end-users* who are not extensively trained in computer programming.
- **Automatic and remote maintenance**—are capabilities built into the circuitry of fourth generation computers. Many equipment failure and error conditions can be automatically detected, logged, diagnosed, and corrected. Maintenance specialists of computer manufacturers can remotely monitor and direct maintenance from regional service centers.

All of these developments have greatly increased the usability, versatility and capacity of fourth generation computers and electronic data processing systems. Computers have come into such widespread use that by the early 1980s the estimated number of computer systems in use exceeded *one million!* Over one half of these computers were not larger "main frame" systems, but were smaller microcomputer and minicomputer systems purchased for scientific, educational, industrial, business and personal use. These estimates do not include the millions of microprocessors used in a wide variety

FIGURE 1–12 Computer Generation Characteristics

Major Characteristics	First Generation	Second Generation	Third Generation	Fourth Generation
ELECTRONIC CIRCUITRY	Vacuum tubes	Transistors	Integrated semiconductor circuits	Large scale integrated (LSI) semiconductor circuits
MAIN MEMORY	Magnetic drum	Magnetic core	Magnetic core	LSI semiconductor circuits
SECONDARY MEMORY	Magnetic tape Magnetic drum	Magnetic tape Magnetic disk	Magnetic disk Magnetic tape	Magnetic disk Floppy disk Magnetic bubble
INPUT MEDIA/ METHOD	Punched cards Paper tape	Punched cards	Key-to tape/disk	Keyboard/video data entry Optical recognition
OUTPUT MEDIA/ METHOD	Punched cards Printed reports	Punched cards Printed reports	Printed reports Video display	Video display Audio response Printed reports
SOFTWARE	User written programs Machine language	Packaged programs Symbolic languages	Operating systems High-level languages	Data base management systems (DBMS) User-oriented languages
OTHER CHAR- ACTERISTICS	Batch processing	Overlapped processing Real time processing Data communications	Time sharing Multiprogramming Multiprocessing Minicomputers	Microprogramming Virtual memory Distributed processing Word processing Microcomputers

Trend in Size of Computers
ENIAC computer . . . . House size (1,500 square feet!)
First generation computer . . . . Room size
Second generation small computer . . . . Closet size
Third generation small computer . . . . . . Desk size
Third generation minicomputer . . . . Desk-top size
Fourth generation microcomputer . . . . . From "chip" to typewriter size

Trend in Computation Speed of Computers
First generation . . . . 300 multiplications per second
Second generation . . . . 200,000 multiplications per second
Third generation . . . . 2 million multiplications per second
Fourth generation . . . . 20 million multiplications per second

Trend in Computation Cost of Computers
Average cost of doing 100,000 multiplications:
   1952 = $1.26   1958 = 26¢   1964 = 12¢   1974 = 1¢
Today, the cost is only a fraction of a cent!

FIGURE 1–13 Trends in Computer Size, Speed, and Cost

of industrial and consumer products. Figures 1–12 and 1–13 summarize major characteristics and trends of the fourth computer generation. Let us now examine more closely the fourth generation phenomenon that we call the "microcomputer revolution."

THE MICROCOMPUTER REVOLUTION

The development of the *microcomputer,* or "computer on a chip," is being heralded not only as a major development of the fourth computer generation, but as a major technological breakthrough that has started a "second computer revolution." See Figure 1–14.

> Now under way is a new expansion of electronics into our lives; a *second* computer revolution that will transform ordinary products and create many new ones.[1]
>
> We have been led—by natural inclination, by our accustomed notations for mathematics, and by technology—to develop a style of computing machines and a body of computing theory both of which are rendered *obsolete* . . . integrated circuit technology forces us into a *revolution* not only in the kinds of machines we build but also in their theoretical basis.[2]

Are such claims justified? It appears that they are. The microcomputer revolution can be described as a technological breakthrough that is bringing *computer power* to both *people and products.* The four major dimensions of this revolution are (1) microcomputer technology, (2) "distributed processing," (3) "personal computing," and (4) "smart products."

Microcomputer Technology

The development of microcomputers represents a major revolution in computer science and technology due to accelerating trends in microelectronics. See Figure 1–15. The microcomputer is a very small computer, ranging in size from a "computer on a chip" to a small typewriter size unit. Thus, computers of extremely small size and cost, but yet of great

FIGURE 1–14
A Microcomputer on a Chip

Courtesy Intel Corporation.

---

[1] "Here Comes the Second Computer Revolution," *Fortune,* November 1975, p. 135.

[2] Ivan E. Sutherland and Carver E. Mead, "Microelectronics and Computer Science," *Scientific American,* September 1977, p. 210.

Trend in Density
Maximum number of components per electronic circuit:
1959 = 1   1969 = 1,024   1979 = 1 million   1985 = over 50 million?
Maximum number of binary digits (bits) per memory chip:
1970 = 1,024   1980 = 65,536   1985 = over 500,000?

Trend in Speed
Speed of an electronic logic circuit:
Mid 1950s (vacuum tube circuit) = one microsecond
Early 1960s (transistorized printed circuit) = 100 nanoseconds
Late 1970s (integrated circuit chip) = 5 nanoseconds
Mid 1980s (integrated circuit chip) = 1 nanosecond?

Trend in Cost
Cost per integrated circuit chip:
1964 = $16   1972 = 75¢   1977 = 15¢   1985 = 1¢?
Cost per bit of integrated circuit memory chip:
1973 = 0.5¢   1977 = 0.1¢   1985 = 0.005¢?

Trend in Reliability
Reliability of electronic circuits:
Vacuum tube = one failure every few hours
Transistor = 1,000 times more reliable than vacuum tube
Integrated circuit = 1,000 times more reliable than transistor

FIGURE 1–15 Trends in Microelectronics

speed, capacity, and reliability are now a reality. Microprocessors and microcomputers are changing the design and capabilities of computer hardware and software. They are even being "embedded" into large computers to increase their speed and power!

An individual integrated circuit on a chip perhaps a quarter of an inch square now can embrace more electronic elements than the most complex piece of electronic equipment that could be built in 1950. Today's microcomputer, at a cost of perhaps $300, has more computing capacity than the first large electronic computer, ENIAC. It is 20 times faster, has a larger memory, is thousands of times more reliable, consumes the power of a light bulb rather than that of a locomotive, occupies 1/30,000 the volume and costs 1/10,000 as much. It is available by mail order or at your local hobby shop.[3]

Microcomputer technology requires a complex and delicate process for the production of microelectronic circuit chips. Crystals of pure silicon are grown in the laboratory and sliced into paper-thin *wafers*. Microscopic circuits are etched on the

[3] Robert N. Noyce, "Microelectronics," *Scientific American*, September 1977, p. 65.

silicon wafer in a series of layers in a complex photolithographic process. After testing the circuits on the wafer it is sectioned into several hundred chips. Defective chips are discarded and good chips are sealed with external wiring in individual packages. Since only a single speck of dust can ruin a chip, this entire process must be done in "clean rooms," where workers are dressed in surgical-type clothing and the air is constantly filtered. See Figures 1–16, 1–17, and 1–18.

Distributed Processing

Distributed processing is a new type of decentralization of electronic data processing made possible by a network of computers "dispersed" throughout an organization. Microprocessors and microcomputers now allow many data input, output, storage, and communication devices to become pow-

FIGURE 1–16 How Microelectronic Chips Are Made

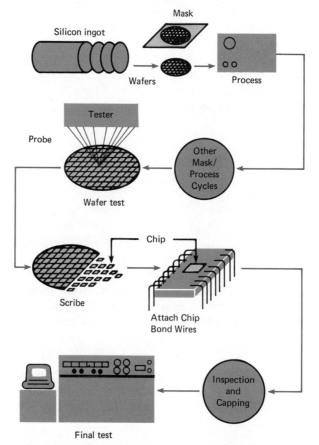

Source: Adapted from Monte Phister, Jr., *Data Processing Technology and Economics,* 2d Ed., (Bedford, Mass.: Digital Press, 1980).

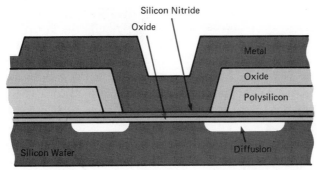

Silicon Nitride
Oxide
Metal
Oxide
Polysilicon
Silicon Wafer
Diffusion

Courtesy IBM Corporation.

FIGURE 1–17 The Layers of a Microelectronic Chip

erful "intelligent" processors or terminals with their own computer capability. Though started by the minicomputer, the microcomputer thus makes truly possible the "dispersion" of computer processing away from a central computer and out to the users in an organization. Distributed processing in branch offices, retail stores, factories, office buildings, remote locations, and other worksites is the result of this development. See Figure 1–19.

Personal Computing

Personal computing involves the use of microcomputers as "personal computers" by individuals for educational, recreational, home management and other personal applications. Thus, the power of computerized data processing is now finally available to everyone. Microcomputers are small, affordable, powerful, and easy to use. Hundreds of thousands of these computer systems are currently in use. Personal computing at home, at work, or at play is the result of this development. See Figure 1–20.

Smart Products

It is now economically and technologically feasible to utilize microcomputers to improve and enhance a host of present industrial and consumer products and create many new ones. *Smart products* with "intelligence" provided by built-in microcomputers or microprocessors which significantly improve their performance and capabilities are the result of this development. Smart consumer products range from electronic games and toys (some with "talking" microprocessor chips) to microwave ovens and automobiles with microprocessor intelligence, and even "smart cards"—credit cards with micro-

FIGURE 1–18 A Wafer Containing 64 Microelectronic Chips

Courtesy of Bell Laboratories.

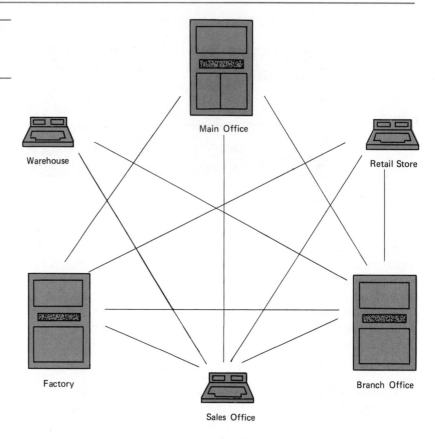

FIGURE 1–20 Using a
Personal Computer

Courtesy Apple Computer, Inc.

electronic memory chips embedded in them! Smart commercial and industrial products range from talking calculators and smart copying machines to industrial robots. See Figures 1–21 and 1–22.

A CONTINUING REVOLUTION

The developments of the fourth computer generation and the microcomputer revolution indicate the continued revolutionary impact of the computer on business and the rest of society. It is apparent that several major trends will continue into the foreseeable future:

- Computer hardware costs and size will continue to decrease steadily. This will result in the use of VLSI circuitry (very large-scale integration) and the development of extremely small *nanocomputers* and *picocomputers!*
- A *fifth generation* of computers will emerge with the probable development of supercomputers composed of super-

Smart Commercial and Industrial Products

Aircraft, cash registers, copying machines, data input—output—storage and communications devices, dictating machines, gasoline pumps, industrial robots, machine tools, measuring and testing instruments, scales, taxi meters, telephone switching systems, surveying instruments, traffic lights, TV cameras, whole-body scanners, vending machines, etc.

Smart Consumer Products

Automobiles, blenders, calculators, cameras, clocks, clothes dryers, cooktops, credit cards, dishwashers, electronic games and toys, fire and burglar alarm systems, heating systems, microwave ovens, pinball machines, radios, refrigerators, stereo systems, telephones, television sets, thermal ovens, washing machines, watches, etc.

Example: Automobiles—Microcomputerized Functions

Automatic emission control, engine control, braking and steering control, speed and skid control, collision avoidance system, vehicle performance analysis, vehicle diagnosis and maintenance analysis, accessory control, travel analysis, visual information display, etc.

FIGURE 1–21 Smart Products with Microprocessor or Microcomputer Intelligence

cold, superconducting *cryoelectronic* circuits called "Josephson Junctions" that must be immersed in liquid helium. These superfast *cryocomputers* with switching speeds of a few picoseconds (trillionths of a second) will be less than four-inches square in size but have computing power equivalent to today's supercomputers! Also on the horizon are computers with *optical processors* which use *photonic* rather than electronic circuits. They process data using laser beams instead of electronic pulses and operate near the speed of light.

● Use of microcomputers and microprocessors will continue to increase dramatically. Smart products will multiply as microcomputer intelligence is built into more and more consumer, commercial, and industrial products. Data processing devices of all kinds, as well as minicomputers and larger computers, will use microprocessors to increase their speed, power, and flexibility.

● The *office of the future* will become a reality by blending computerized word processing, electronic data processing, and telecommunications. Distributed networks of intelligent terminals and other computerized office devices will create *automated office* typing, dictation, copying, and filing systems, as well as *electronic mail* and message systems.

● Advanced information processing systems will merge the transmission and processing of data, images, and voices. This will involve extensive use of earth satellites, *fiber optics,* and *laser/video disk* technology in advanced telecommunication systems.

FIGURE 1–22   Smart Products

- Computers and computer terminals will become integrated into everyday business operations in offices, small business firms, wholesale and retail outlets, warehouses, and factories. Managers will rely heavily on computer-based management information systems (MIS) and decision support systems (DSS) to help them make better business decisions.

- Society as a whole will become increasingly reliant on computers in many areas. People will make every day use of computer-based systems such as *electronic funds transfer* (EFT) systems in banking, *point-of-sale* (POS) systems in retailing, and *computer-assisted instruction* (CAI) systems in education.

FIGURE 1–23   The Continuing Computer Revolution

THE COMING IMPACT OF MICROELECTRONICS

1980–85

Semiconductor chips are crammed with up to 500,000 transistors, giving each thumbnail-size chip the power of a mainframe computer.

All autos use microelectronic controls to boost engine efficiency.

Some 10% of homes have computers or terminals with access to remote data bases, mainly via telephone but also via two-way cable television and satellite communication.

1985–90

Semiconductor chips hold 1 million transistors. Each chip has the power of the biggest IBM System 370 computer.

All autos are equipped with microcomputers to warn when preventive maintenance is needed and automatically diagnose problems.

One-third of all homes have computers or terminals. In the office, electronic mail rivals paper mail in volume.

Robots and "smart" machines with microelectronic senses begin cutting into the labor force in factories.

Microelectronic implants begin controlling sophisticated new artificial organs, such as hearts.

Most doctors install computer-assisted diagnostic systems in their offices.

Most banks are interconnected through a computer network grid.

1990–2000

Chips contain 10 million transistors. Each chip has more computing power than installed today at most corporations.

"Smart" highways for semiautomated driving enter early development.

Most homes have computers. Data communications volume exceeds voice volume, and video phones enter the home.

Robots and automated systems produce half of all manufactured goods. Up to one-quarter of the factory work force may be dislodged.

Microelectronic implants restore sight, hearing, and speech.

Computer-assisted medicine extends into the home.

Schools turn to extensive use of computers.

Source: "High Technology," *Business Week*. Reprinted from the November 10, 1980, issue of *Business Week* (p. 96) by special permission. © 1980 by McGraw-Hill, Inc., New York, N.Y. 10020. All rights reserved.

All of these trends indicate that the computer revolution will be a continuing phenomenon in the future. See Figure 1–23. Therefore it is imperative that you gain a basic understanding of computers and how they can be best used and managed. This text is designed to help you achieve this important goal.

SUMMARY

- An understanding of computers, data processing, and information systems is very important today. They are major tools by which we can properly utilize information resources for the benefit of society and for the operation and management of business firms and other organizations.

- The development of computers is a revolutionary technological development of the 20th century. The computer revolution has succeeded in multiplying human brainpower with the same impact that the first industrial revolution multiplied human musclepower. Less than 20 years after it was commercially introduced, the electronic computer had revolutionized data processing in science, engineering, industry, business, and many other fields.

- The computer is an electronic device that has the ability to accept data, internally store and automatically execute a program of instructions, perform mathematical, logical, and manipulative operations on data, and report the results.

- Computer equipment and devices are known as "hardware," while the various sets of operating instructions, or programs that direct and control computer processing, are called "software."

- The ideas and inventions of many persons were responsible for the development of the electronic digital computer.

First generation computers were first produced in 1951 and were large devices that utilized vacuum tubes in their circuitries.

Transistors and other solid state devices were utilized in the *second generation* of computers which were introduced in 1959 and were smaller, faster, and cheaper than first generation machines. Magnetic cores were the primary internal storage medium, while magnetic tapes were widely used for input/output and secondary storage.

Third generation computers were introduced in 1964 and replaced transistorized circuitry with integrated circuits. The third generation also featured improvements in the speed, capacity, and types of computer input/output and storage devices, including the widespread use of magnetic disk units. Time sharing, data communications, operating systems, high-level programming languages, and minicomputers were other developments of the third generation.

The fourth generation began in the early 1970s with the introduction of computers which utilize such developments as large scale integrated circuits, microprogramming, virtual memory, and the replacement of magnetic cores with integrated circuitry for main memory. Distributed processing, data base management systems and the microcomputer are other fourth generation developments.

- The development of microcomputers in the fourth computer generation has been acclaimed as a second computer revolution because it is bringing computer power to both people and products. The microcomputer represents a major technological breakthrough in computer science and technology. Computer processing capability is being brought to the users in an organization through distributed processing and to everyone in society through personal computing and smart products.

KEY TERMS AND CONCEPTS

Computer	Computer generations
Hardware	Microcomputer
Software	Distributed processing
Program	Personal computing
Computer revolution	Smart products

REVIEW AND DISCUSSION QUESTIONS

1. Why is a basic understanding of computers, data processing, and information systems so important?
2. Why is the development and use of computers called a "computer revolution"? How has this computer revolution affected you?
3. What is a computer? What are hardware and software?
4. How are early computing devices related to the development of the electronic computer?
5. Who were some of the pioneers in the development of the computer? Explain the major contribution of each person.
6. What are some of the major characteristics of each of the four generations of computers?
7. What is the microcomputer revolution? How has it affected you?
8. The microcomputer revolution represents a major technological breakthrough which is bringing computer power to both people and products through distributed processing, personal computing, and "smart" products. Explain.
9. What have been some of the trends in size, speed, cost, and reliability due to the developments of microelectronics?
10. What are "smart" products? Provide examples of smart commercial and consumer products to illustrate your answer.
11. What are some of the major trends of the continuing computer revolution which are expected to continue into the future? Do these trends seem realistic? How will they affect your use of the computer?

REAL WORLD APPLICATIONS

1-1 Computers: Fad or for Real?

For a society that once banished science fiction writers to the pulp paperback kingdom, it's remarkable how easily the computer has slipped into the vernacular. Housewives know of chips, carpenters speak of microprocessors, mechanics replace bad boards along with cracked bearings, and workingmen hook computers to TVs so their kids can play ''Dungeons and Dragons'' with machines.

In just 25 years a citizenry that once chafed at the implicit scolding of a punched card's ''Do not fold, spindle, or mutilate'' has made of the computer and its electronic progeny the latest fad.

Products undreamed of when Nixon was president now talk to schoolchildren, translate foreign languages for tourists, and run warehouses without human intervention. Others play blackjack and ''Space Invaders'' with white-collar professionals in their offices.

In fact, though, the awakening in everyman to the excitement of computer technology is but icing on a cake baked over the last decade by business and industry. For if the populace now views the computer as fashionable, business and industry consider it heavy armament in a war against paper, inefficiency, and falling productivity.[1]

● Are computers a fad? Will their widespread use fade away? Or are they important weapons ''in a war against paper, inefficiency, and falling productivity''? Explain.

[1] Source: International Data Corporation, ''Computer Systems and Services for Business and Industry,'' *Fortune*, special advertising section, April 20, 1981, p. 40.

1-2 Computers in the Real World

● Manufacturing designers routinely use computers and computer graphics to design parts and generate the tapes for running numerically controlled machine tools. Now they are starting to use computers to tie design, manufacture, inventory control, and other functions into whole systems. The result: drastic drops in inventory-in-progress, quicker machine set-up times, more commonality of parts.

● As the nursing force dwindles, health care industries use computers in patient monitoring and drug dosage calculation; doctors are discovering the potential for computerized diagnosis assistance.

● Retailers reap benefits by capturing stock data electronically—for reorder, pricing, and merchandising, using electronic point-of-sale terminals.

● Automated teller machines allow banks to stay open around the clock. Competing banks even share machines in cases where one bank's business alone won't generate enough traffic.

● Publishers shove deadlines hours closer to print runs by computerization from original typing—through editing, revision, layout, and pasteup—to automated phototypesetting.

● Robots are used widely by auto makers in spray painting and other nasty applications; in Japan whole automated factories are on stream.

● Energy management is suddenly worth computerizing. Computers track the sun in solar installations, cycle thermostats in office buildings, and even heat buildings as a byproduct of operation.

● Artists play with computer imaging technology; animators use computers to make the repetitive drawings needed to produce cartoons.

● Offices everywhere are bursting with new automated typing equipment—word processors, microprocessor-based typewriters, small computers with text editing software—presaging an era where inte-

1-2 *(continued)*

grated word and data processing are commonplace, where voice, video, and data traffic all run on the same communications network.

The litany is endless. In every nook and cranny of the factory and the office, the computer—or some chip-based relative—is finding employment.[2]

- Can you think of other uses of computers than those mentioned above?
- Which is the most important or appealing to you? Why?
- Do any computer uses upset you? Explain.

[2] Source: International Data Corporation, "Computer Systems and Services for Business and Industry, *Fortune,* special advertising section, April 20, 1981, p. 42.

1-3   The Concorde, The Stagecoach, and Microelectronics

One hundred years ago the stagecoach was the principal mode of overland transportation. It moved at approximately 25 miles per hour and carried perhaps five passengers. We have come a long way in the last hundred years. Today the Concorde supersonic airliner is the most advanced vehicle of transportation available. It travels at 1,300 miles per hour, which is approximately 50 times as fast as the stagecoach. Concorde carries 200 passengers, which is 40 times the capacity of a stagecoach. If Concorde has 40 times the capacity of a stagecoach, and 50 times its speed, then in electronic terms, Concorde and the stagecoach are about the same, because in far less time electronics logic capacity has increased by a factor of one hundred thousand, and logic speed of operation has increased by a factor of one million. If Concorde could carry half a million passengers at 20 million-miles-per-hour it would then equal the rate at which microelectronics has advanced in the same time frame. And a ticket for a Concorde flight would have to cost less than a penny if it were to compare with the rate at which microelectronics has gotten cheaper![3]

- Why has the rate of progress in microelectronics been so great?
- Do you expect it to continue?
- What has been the impact of such progress on computers and their uses?

[3] Source: Adam Osborne, *Running Wild* (New York: Osborne/McGraw-Hill, 1979), pp. 162–63.

CHAPTER SUPPLEMENT

GETTING STARTED IN COMPUTERS

The easiest way to get started in computing is to learn how to use a computer terminal or a personal computer to carry on a simple *conversation* with a computer. *Conversational computing* is a type of *interactive* computer processing involving frequent interaction between a person and a computer. A user like yourself can explore and accomplish the solution to a problem with the assistance of a computer system. This frequently includes the use of *interactive programs* which are programs specifically designed for conversational computing. No actual programming is necessary when such prewritten programs are used, since it has already been accomplished by the system analysts and programmers who developed the programs.

An interactive program is designed to direct the computer system to request and wait for **input** from the user, who must only choose among the alternatives offered by the computer and provide it with **data.** Computer and user "converse" briefly and simply and a problem is solved for the user. The systems design and programming effort, the complex hardware devices, and the advanced software required are "transparent" to the user. All the user sees are the questions, comments, and responses that appear on the terminal as a solution to a problem is accomplished.

Let us use a brief example of conversational computing with a short interactive program to illustrate how simple the use of a computer can be. **No programming is necessary;** only a few simple entries and responses are required. The short program we will use is called BANK. It determines (1) interest charges, (2) monthly loan payments, and (3) savings account balances for a user.

First, a user must activate the computer or terminal by actions such as turning it on and/or dialing the telephone number of the time-sharing service or computer center. Once the computer or terminal is activated, it will begin to print or display messages. The user responds using the keyboard of the computer or terminal. (Most systems also require that a RETURN key be depressed after each entry.) Figure S1–1 shows the resulting conversation. It outlines the questions, comments, and responses of the computer (in capital letters) and the user (underlined). My comments are beneath each frame.

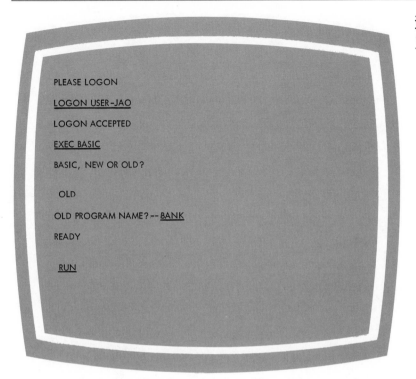

```
PLEASE LOGON

LOGON USER-JAO

LOGON ACCEPTED

EXEC BASIC

BASIC, NEW OR OLD?


  OLD

OLD PROGRAM NAME?--BANK

READY


  RUN
```

Frame 1:   You "LOGON" to the computer system by keying-in an identification code. After your LOGON is accepted, you ask the computer to execute a program written in the BASIC programming language. The computer asks if you want to use a previously written program (OLD) or write your own (NEW). You then indicate that you want to use a prewritten program called BANK. When the computer says it is ready, you ask it to begin processing (RUN) the BANK program.

FIGURE S1-1   *(continued)*

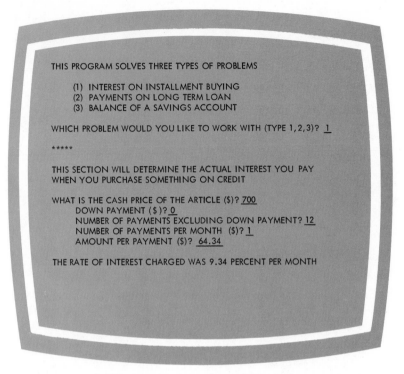

THIS PROGRAM SOLVES THREE TYPES OF PROBLEMS

    (1) INTEREST ON INSTALLMENT BUYING
    (2) PAYMENTS ON LONG TERM LOAN
    (3) BALANCE OF A SAVINGS ACCOUNT

WHICH PROBLEM WOULD YOU LIKE TO WORK WITH (TYPE 1,2,3)? 1

*****

THIS SECTION WILL DETERMINE THE ACTUAL INTEREST YOU PAY
WHEN YOU PURCHASE SOMETHING ON CREDIT

WHAT IS THE CASH PRICE OF THE ARTICLE ($)? 700
    DOWN PAYMENT ($)? 0
    NUMBER OF PAYMENTS EXCLUDING DOWN PAYMENT? 12
    NUMBER OF PAYMENTS PER MONTH ($)? 1
    AMOUNT PER PAYMENT ($)? 64.34

THE RATE OF INTEREST CHARGED WAS 9.34 PERCENT PER MONTH

Frame 2:   The computer explains what the BANK program does, and asks
you which type of problem you want to work. It then asks you for information
about an installment purchase and calculates the rate of interest you are
being charged.

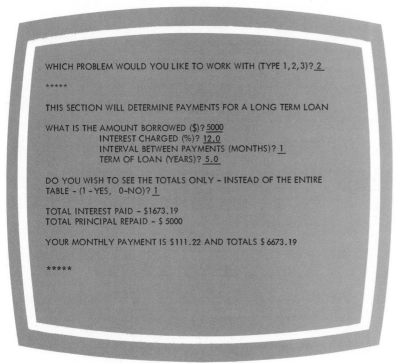

WHICH PROBLEM WOULD YOU LIKE TO WORK WITH (TYPE 1,2,3)? <u>2</u>

*****

THIS SECTION WILL DETERMINE PAYMENTS FOR A LONG TERM LOAN

WHAT IS THE AMOUNT BORROWED ($)? <u>5000</u>
        INTEREST CHARGED (%)? <u>12.0</u>
        INTERVAL BETWEEN PAYMENTS (MONTHS)? <u>1</u>
        TERM OF LOAN (YEARS)? <u>5.0</u>

DO YOU WISH TO SEE THE TOTALS ONLY – INSTEAD OF THE ENTIRE TABLE – (1 – YES, 0–NO)? <u>1</u>

TOTAL INTEREST PAID – $1673.19
TOTAL PRINCIPAL REPAID – $ 5000

YOUR MONTHLY PAYMENT IS $111.22 AND TOTALS $ 6673.19

*****

Frame 3: Here the computer uses information you supply to calculate your monthly payments for a proposed loan.

FIGURE S1–1   *(continued)*

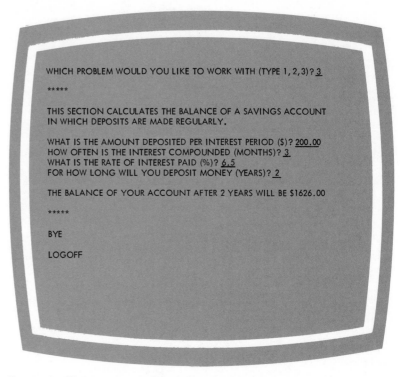

WHICH PROBLEM WOULD YOU LIKE TO WORK WITH (TYPE 1, 2, 3)? 3

*****

THIS SECTION CALCULATES THE BALANCE OF A SAVINGS ACCOUNT
IN WHICH DEPOSITS ARE MADE REGULARLY.

WHAT IS THE AMOUNT DEPOSITED PER INTEREST PERIOD ($)? 200.00
HOW OFTEN IS THE INTEREST COMPOUNDED (MONTHS)? 3
WHAT IS THE RATE OF INTEREST PAID (%)? 6.5
FOR HOW LONG WILL YOU DEPOSIT MONEY (YEARS)? 2

THE BALANCE OF YOUR ACCOUNT AFTER 2 YEARS WILL BE $1626.00

*****

BYE

LOGOFF

Frame 4: The computer calculates what your savings account balance
will be two years from now given information you supply. You then indicate
you are finished with the BANK program (with the command BYE) and
terminate your conversation with the computer (LOGOFF).

The BANK program used in this example is written in the
BASIC programming language. Part of it is shown in Figure
S1–2. Notice that many of the program statements are concerned with input/output, error, and exception routines, as
well as with appropriate calculations. As Figure S1–1 showed,
none of these *details,* were needed to use the computer to
solve the illustrated problems.

Assignment

This example should have demonstrated that anyone can
use a computer. Now it's your turn. Use a computer terminal
or personal computer and a prewritten program available
on your computer system to solve a short problem similar to
the example illustrated in this supplement. Good luck!

```
100 REM PROGRAM BANK
110 PRINT "FINANCIAL PROBLEMS"
120 PRINT
130 PRINT "THIS PROGRAM SOLVES THREE TYPES OF PROBLEMS"
132 PRINT
134 PRINT "      (1) INTEREST ON INSTALLMENT BUYING"
136 PRINT "      (2) PAYMENTS ON LONG TERM LOAN"
138 PRINT "      (3) BALANCE OF A SAVINGS ACCOUNT"
140 PRINT
142 PRINT "WHICH PROBLEM WOULD YOU LIKE TO WORK WITH (TYPE 1,2,3)";
144 INPUT Q1
146 PRINT
147 PRINT "*****"
148 PRINT
150 IF Q1>2 THEN 820
155 IF Q1>1 THEN 260
160 GOTO 590
260 PRINT "THIS SECTION WILL DETERMINE PAYMENTS FOR A LONG TERM LOAN"
270 PRINT
280 PRINT "WHAT IS THE AMOUNT BORROWED ($)";
281 INPUT A
285 PRINT "          INTEREST CHARGED (%)";
286 INPUT I
290 PRINT "          INTERVAL BETWEEN PAYMENTS (MONTHS)";
291 INPUT P
295 PRINT "          TERM OF LOAN (YEARS)";
296 INPUT Y
300 PRINT
360 PRINT "DO YOU WISH TO SEE THE TOTALS ONLY - INSTEAD OF THE ENTIRE"
361 PRINT "TABLE - (1-YES, 0-NO)";
362 INPUT P5
370 PRINT
375 IF P5>0 THEN 430
380 PRINT "          OUTSTANDING"
390 PRINT "          PRINCIPAL AT               PRINCIPAL"
400 PRINT "          BEGINNING     INTEREST DUE AT   REPAID AT"
410 PRINT "PERIOD    OF PERIOD     END OF PERIOD    END OF PERIOD"
420 PRINT
430 Z=(Y*12)/P
440 K=(I*(P/12))/100
443 I=(I/100)*(P/12)
446 E=(A*I*(1+I)**Z)/(((1+I)**Z)-1)
450 C=A
460 F=0
461 D1=0
470 T1=0
480 T1=T1+1
490 IF T1>Z THEN 554
500 B=T1
510 C=C-F
520 D=C*K
522 F=E-D
525 C=INT(C*100+.5)/100
530 D=INT(D*100+.5)/100
535 F=INT(F*100+.5)/100
541 D1=D1+D
548 IF P5>0 THEN 480
550 PRINT B;TAB(11);C;TAB(29);D;TAB(48);F
552 GOTO 480
554 IF P5<1 THEN 561
555 PRINT
556 D1=INT(D1*100+.5)/100
558 PRINT "TOTAL INTEREST PAID - $";D1
559 PRINT "TOTAL PRINCIPAL REPAID - $";A
```

FIGURE S1–2   Part of the
BANK Program

2

CHAPTER OUTLINE

Data Processing Concepts

LEARNING OBJECTIVES

The purpose of this chapter is to promote a basic understanding of data processing by analyzing (1) the fundamental concepts of data, information, systems, data processing systems, and the functions of data processing, and (2) the components, benefits, and limitations of manual and electronic data processing.

After reading and studying this chapter, you should be able to:

1. Give an example to illustrate the difference between data and information.
2. Explain the concept of a system as it applies to data processing and illustrate it with an example.
3. Give an example that illustrates the processing of data by each of the basic functions of data processing.
4. Outline how manual and electronic data processing systems differ.
5. Identify several benefits and limitations of manual data processing.
6. Identify the four basic advantages of electronic data processing.

INTRODUCTORY CONCEPTS

Data versus Information

The word "data" is the plural of "datum," though "data" is commonly used as both the singular and plural forms. *Data can be defined as any representation of facts, observations, or occurrences.* Data usually takes the form of numbers, words, or codes composed of numerical or alphabetical characters or special symbols. However, data can also take such forms as lines on a graph or other types of graphic representation.

The terms "data" and "information" are often used interchangeably. However, a distinction should be made between the two. Data should be viewed as the raw material which is *processed* into the finished product of information. *Information can be defined as data that has been transformed into a meaningful and useful form for specific human beings.*

Example. Names, quantities, and dollar amounts recorded on sales invoices represent data, not information to a sales manager. Only when such facts are properly organized and manipulated can meaningful sales information be provided, such as the amount of sales by product type, sales territory, or salesperson.

In some cases, data may not require processing before constituting information for a human user. However, data is usually not useful until it has been subjected to a process where its form is manipulated and organized and its content is analyzed and evaluated. Then it becomes information. See Figure 2–1.

FIGURE 2–1   Data versus Information

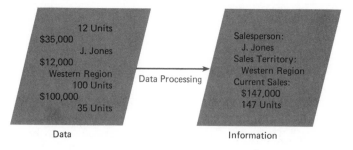

Data Processing

Data processing can be defined as the processing of data to transform it into information. Thus, data processing consists of any actions which make data usable and meaningful, i.e., transforms data into information.

Example. Your reading of this text is one type of data processing. Your eyes are transmitting the *data* of letters and words to your brain which transforms these images into *information* by organizing and evaluating them and storing them for later use.

The Systems Concept

The activity of data processing can be viewed as a "system." What is a system? A *system* can be very simply and broadly defined as *a group of interrelated or interacting elements.* Many examples of systems can be found in the physical and biological sciences, in modern technology, and in human society. Thus, we can talk of the physical system of the sun and its planets, the biological system of the human body, the technological system of an oil refinery, and the socioeconomic system of a business organization.

However, a more specific and appropriate concept of a system is utilized in data processing and computer technology. A *system* can be defined as *a group of interelated components that seeks the attainment of a common goal by accepting inputs and producing outputs in an organized transformation process.* Such a system (sometimes called a dynamic system) has three basic components:

Input consists of elements that enter the system in order to be processed.
   Examples. Raw materials, energy, data, human effort, etc.
Processing involves "transformation" processes that convert input into output.
   Examples. A manufacturing process, the human breathing process, data calculations, etc.
Output represents elements that have been produced by the transformation process.
   Examples. Finished products, human services, management information, etc.

These three basic components interact to form a "system."

Examples. A manufacturing system accepts raw materials as inputs and produces finished goods as output. A *data processing system* can be viewed as *a system which accepts data as input and processes it into information as output.* In this context, you as a reader of this book are a data processing system (see Figure 2–2).

The systems concept can be made even more useful by including two additional components: *feedback* and *control.* Figure 2–3 illustrates a system with feedback and control components. Such a system is sometimes called a *cybernetic* system, that is, *a self-monitoring and self-regulating system.*

Feedback is information concerning the components and operations of a system.

Control is a systems component that evaluates feedback to determine whether the system is moving toward the achievement of its goal, and then makes any necessary adjustments to the input and processing components of the system to insure that proper output is produced.

Examples. A familiar example of a self-monitoring and self-regulating system is the thermostatically controlled heating system found in many homes, which automatically monitors

FIGURE 2–2   Three Systems

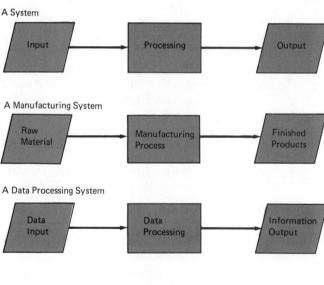

FIGURE 2–3   System Concept with Feedback and Control

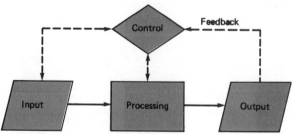

and regulates itself to produce a desired temperature. Another familiar example is the human body, which can be considered an adaptive cybernetic system that automatically monitors and adjusts many of its functions such as temperature, heartbeat, and breathing.

The feedback-control concept can also be applied to data processing systems. *Feedback* would consist of information describing the input, processing, and output activities of the data processing system. *Control* would involve evaluating feedback to determine if the system is operating according to established data processing procedures and producing the proper output. If not, the control function would make necessary adjustments to input and processing activities in order that proper information output would be produced.

Example. If *subtotals* of sales amounts in a sales report do not add up to *total sales*, then data processing personnel may have to change input or processing procedures to correctly accumulate all sales transactions.

Data Processing as a System

Figure 2–4 is a data processing system diagram that includes feedback and control components. It also introduces the storage function as a separate system component.

Storage is the data processing system function in which data and information is stored in an organized manner for further processing or until needed by users of the system.

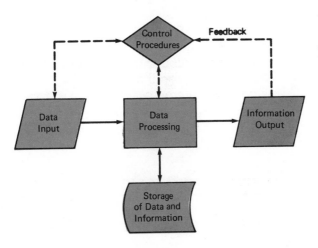

FIGURE 2–4 Data Processing System Concept

FIGURE 2–5   Data Processing
System Example: Sales Analysis

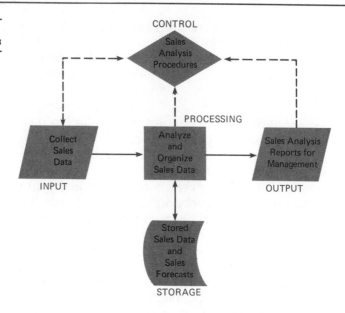

Example. Sales data is accumulated and stored for subsequent processing which produces daily, weekly, and monthly sales analysis reports for management.

Figure 2–5 illustrates the use of the data processing system concept with a simple business example which spotlights the following major system components:

Input.   Sales data describing individual sales transactions is collected and entered into the data processing system.

Processing.   The sales data is analyzed and organized in order to transform it into meaningful information.

Storage.   Sales data is stored and data describing previous time periods' sales as well as forecasted sales is provided for use in the processing component.

Control.   Correct processing of the sales data is accomplished according to specified sales analysis procedures. (Note that the **feedback** function is frequently included as part of the control function of a system.)

Output.   Sales analysis reports are prepared for the management of the business firm. Information concerning important trends in sales activity is provided.

DATA PROCESSING FUNCTIONS AND ACTIVITIES

Several common activities are performed by data processing systems. These activities can be grouped under the five

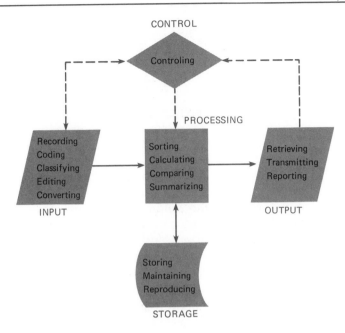

FIGURE 2–6   Data Processing Functions and Activities

basic system functions of **input, processing, control, storage** and **output**. This is illustrated in Figure 2–6.

Input

Before data can be processed into information, it must first be collected and entered into the data processing system by the **input** function. This function is also known as data collection, data capture, or data entry.

Recording.   Data must be recorded as events, transactions, and other phenomena occur and are observed. The recorded observations may take the form of a measurement, or some other numerical or verbal description of the observed activity. This data may then be recorded in tangible form on various types of **data media,** which are the tangible objects or devices on which data is recorded. Thus, data may be recorded on written **source documents** which are the original written records of an activity, such as purchase orders, checks, or sales invoices. Other more machine-usable types of data media may be utilized, such as magnetic disks or punched cards. However, it should be noted that data may be captured without the use of data media by devices such as the keyboard of a computer terminal, which allows direct entry of data (as electronic impulses) into a computer system.

Example: A sales person records the type of product and the amount of a sale on a written sales invoice or enters this data directly into the computer system by using an electronic "point-of-sale" terminal.

Coding. Data may be made more suitable for processing by assigning identification codes that consist of numbers, letters, special characters, or a combination of these.

Examples. A particular person could be represented by a *numeric* code, a Social Security number such as 575–34–3473; his academic performance by an alphabetic code, the letter grade *A;* his automobile by an alphanumeric code, the automobile license number *CJD-682;* and the amount of money in his possession by a code using both numbers and the special characters of the dollar sign and the decimal point, $1.42.

Classifying. Coding data is particularly useful when data requires *classifying,* i.e., arranging data into groups or classes with like characteristics.

Examples. Sales data may be classified according to customer, salesperson, and product. A business firm could assign numerical or alphabetical codes to each customer, salesperson, and product. Sales data for a particular time period could then be more easily grouped or "classified" by the customer, salesperson, or product involved.

Editing. The *editing* activity consists of checking the data for completeness and correctness. The objective of editing is to ensure that the collection and conversion of data is done correctly.

Example. Visually *verifying* that the codes and amounts on a sales invoice are correct.

Converting. The final activity of the input function in data processing may be the activity of converting the data from one data medium to another.

Example. The data may be transformed from written notations on a sales invoice into holes in a punched card, then transformed into magnetic spots on magnetic tape, and then transformed again into electronic impulses in the circuitry of a computer.

Processing

After data is collected and converted it is then ready for the processing function in which data is processed into information.

Sorting. First of all, data may be "put in order" in the *sorting* activity. This may involve arranging the data in a predetermined sequence or order, and grouping the data into several classifications. Sorting may also involve *merging* data, from several classifications into a larger classification, or *extraction,* where a particular group of data is selected out of a larger data classification.

Examples. Sales data could first be segregated by product classification; within each product classification, sales data could be grouped by customer; the customer groupings of sales data could then be sorted into an alphabetical order.

Calculating. The data processing activity of calculating refers to the *manipulation* of data by mathematical processes and the creation of new data.

Example. Multiplying the dollar amount of a sale by a discount percentage would produce a sales discount amount.

Comparing. The *comparing* activity performs comparisons on data in order to discover meaningful facts and relationships.

Example. Sales data may be analyzed in order to discover whether any of the sales made during a period exceed a certain dollar amount and thus qualify for a volume discount or whether any salesperson has failed to make the required minimum amount of sales during a period.

Summarizing. The *summarizing* activity condenses data by counting or accumulating totals of the data in a classification or by selecting strategic data from the mass of data being processed.

Example. The summarizing activity may be designed to provide a general manager with the sales totals by major product line, the sales manager with sales totals by individual salesperson as well as by product line, and a salesperson with sales data by customer as well as by product line.

Control

All data processing systems require a **control** component. This component includes the **feedback** concept which provides information describing the input, processing, storage and output activities of the data processing system.

Controlling. This function involves directing the data processing activities of the system according to specific instructions and procedures. It also involves evaluating feedback to determine if the system is operating according to established procedures and producing the proper output. If not, necessary adjustments to input, processing and storage activities must be made in order that proper information output is produced.

Example: The processing of sales data may be controlled by a series of manual data processing procedures or by a **program** of computer instructions in electronic data processing. Also, the sales amounts in all sales analysis reports would be analyzed to insure that the system is correctly accumulating all sales transactions, and that they are being correctly charged to the proper customer accounts.

Storage

The **storage** function is a major component of a data processing system. Stored data and information can be considered as an important foundation or base **(data base)** which supports every data processing system.

Storing. Data and information collected and produced by the data processing system is frequently stored for further use. Data and information can be stored temporarily between processing cycles or for longer periods and retrieved as needed by the users of the system. The storing activity includes the concept of storing data and information in an organized manner in order to facilitate its retrieval.

Example: Sales analysis information produced by the system is stored for later retrieval by management.

Maintaining. The quality of the data and information stored in the system must be maintained by a continual process of adding, deleting, correcting, and updating activities.

Example: The sales records of a business are updated to reflect the latest sales made by the firm.

Reproducing. Another aspect of the storage function is the *reproducing* of data. Data may be stored by simply reproducing or copying the data so that several copies of the data medium are produced.

Example. Duplicate copies of magnetic tapes representing sales data may be made. One reel of magnetic tape is then returned to the data processing system for further processing while the duplicate reel is used for data storage.

Output

The final data processing function is output. It involves the transfer of data and information produced by the data processing system to the prospective users of such information or to another data processing system.

Retrieving.   The *retrieving* activity involves the recovery of stored data and information.

Example.   Retrieving a copy of a sales invoice from a filing cabinet, or using a computer terminal to inquire about the sales activity of a particular customer.

Transmission.   The *transmission* activity involves the movement of data or information from one location to another so that it may be conveyed to its ultimate user or introduced as input into another data processing system.

Example.   Information is frequently transmitted by telephone circuits between computers and computer terminals installed at distant locations.

Reporting.   The *reporting* activity involves furnishing information produced by the data processing system to the ultimate users of this information.

Examples.   Information may be reported in the form of *printed* documents such as invoices, statements, and printed reports of all kinds. Information can also be reported in *graphic* form on charts, maps, and pictures. The reporting activity can also be accomplished by displaying information in *visual* form on *video display terminals* or in *audible* form by word of mouth or by computer *audio response* units.

MANUAL VERSUS ELECTRONIC DATA PROCESSING

There are many kinds of data processing systems. They range from a solitary human data processing system to large sophisticated systems using electronic computers. Materials as simple as a paper and pencil or equipment as advanced as the latest electronic computers can be utilized to process data into information. However, most data processing can be placed into two major categories: *manual* and *electronic* data processing. Figure 2–7 contrasts methods and devices that may be used to perform basic system functions in manual and EDP systems.

FIGURE 2–7 Manual versus Electronic Data Processing: Selected Methods and Devices

	Input	Processing	Control	Storage	Output
Manual Data Processing	Human observation Written records Typewriter Cash Register Calculator keyboard	Human brain Written calculations and analysis Calculators	Human brain Written procedures Calculator control circuitry	Human brain Written records Filing cabinets Microfilm Duplicating machines	Human voice Written reports Telephone Typewritten documents Calculator display
Electronic Data Processing	Data entry terminals Punched cards Magnetic diskettes Optical character readers	Computer processing units	Computer control unit Computer programs	Semiconductor storage circuitry Magnetic core, disks, drums, cards, and tape	Visual display, audio response, and printing terminals High-speed printers

Manual Data Processing

Manual data processing involves human use of such simple tools as paper, pencils, and filing cabinets to process raw data into information. Manual data processing may also utilize mechanical, electrical, and electronic devices such as typewriters and calculators as data processing tools. Use of such devices requires a combination of manual procedures and electro-mechanical equipment to carry out the basic functions of data processing. Data and instructions must be manually entered through a keyboard (such as a calculator or typewriter keyboard) and human intervention during the data processing cycle is required. Therefore, all nonautomatic data processing, even if it includes **machine-assisted manual** methods, can be classified as manual data processing.

Figure 2–8 illustrates the components of a manual data processing system. Data is received as **input** by telephone or mail. A calculator is utilized for **processing** by a clerk who **controls** the process according to written operating instructions. Data and information **storage** is provided by a filing cabinet. Typewritten reports are the **output** of this manual system.

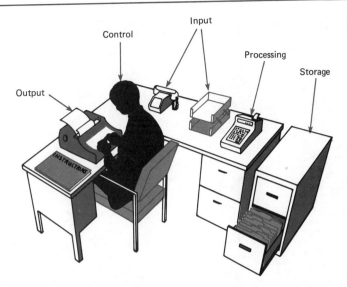

FIGURE 2–8 A Manual Data Processing System

Electronic Calculators.   Electronic calculators of various types are widely used in manual data processing. *A calculator can be defined as a data processing device suitable for performing arithmetical operations which requires frequent intervention by a human operator.* Electronic calculators have no moving parts and operate silently at almost instantaneous speeds. They carry out arithmetical operations and print the results on paper tape or display them electronically. They also provide automatic storage for constants and intermediate results that need to be retrieved periodically during a computation process. The size and cost of these calculators have been greatly reduced by the use of microminiature electronic circuitry. Thus, electronic calculators are extensively utilized in schools, homes, business firms, offices, and wherever there is a need for arithmetic computations in manual data processing systems.

Electronic calculators that can read data and operating instructions from various media, store data and instructions internally, and then produce several types of output are also available. Such calculators no longer have all of their mathematical capabilities ''hard wired'' into their circuitry. Instead, they can be programmed to carry out mathematical calculations by the insertion and storage of different types of instructions within the machines. These features indicate that such *programmable electronic calculators* can be viewed as special-purpose arithmetic microcomputers with limited input/output, processing power and storage capacity. See Figure 2–9.

FIGURE 2–9   Programmable Calculator with Magnetic Cards and Removable "Solid-State Software" Modules

Courtesy Texas Instruments Inc.

Benefits and Limitations. Manual data processing systems are beneficial to individuals or organizations if their information requirements are simple and the amount of data to be processed is limited. In manual data processing, transactions can be recorded easily in a human-readable form, and changes and corrections to such systems can easily be made. Manual data processing is also quite inexpensive at low volumes. As information requirements become more complex and the volume of data increases, the limitations of manual data processing begin to exceed the benefits of its use. Automated data processing systems become more efficient and economical. The major limitations of manual data processing include its inability to handle large volumes of work and its reliance on many cumbersome and tedious methods. It is also more susceptible to error and slower than other data processing methods because it requires human effort in most data processing activities. Therefore, electronic data processing systems are used by all organizations with complex or high-volume data processing requirements.

Electronic Data Processing

Electronic data processing (EDP) is the use of electronic computers to process data automatically. Human intervention in the data processing cycle is not necessary since an electronic computer can automatically execute a stored program of data processing instructions. The term **automatic data processing** (ADP) is sometimes used (especially by government agencies) because of this automation of data processing functions and activities caused by electronic computers. The term **computer application** is also used to describe such use of a computer to solve a specific problem or accomplish a data processing job for a computer user.

Figure 2–10 illustrates the use of electronic computers and related equipment to form an electronic data processing system. Notice that a "point-of-sale" terminal is used to capture sales data in the **input** function. Sales data is **processed** by an electronic computer under the **control** of a "sales analysis program" of processing instructions. **Storage** devices such as magnetic disk units are used to store the sales data and to provide additional sales data and sales forecasts required for sales analysis processing. Finally, managers utilize a video display terminal for the **output** of desired sales analysis information.

58

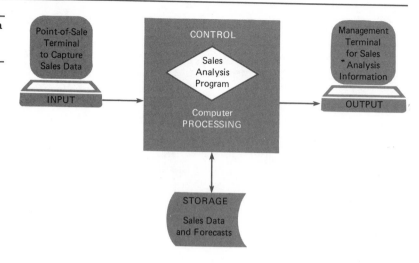

FIGURE 2–10 Electronic Data Processing System Example: Sales Analysis

Why Use Electronic Data Processing?

Today's business firms are faced with information require-ments of increased complexity and ever-increasing volumes of data to be processed. This is why so many firms, both large and small, have turned to electronic data processing. What has caused this growth in complexity and volume of data processing requirements? Three reasons stand out.

- Most business firms are faced with growth in the size, com-plexity, and scope of their operations. They are providing more products and services to more customers at more loca-tions with more employees.
- Business firms must respond to increased requirements for information from local, state, and federal governmental agencies. Such demands have become a major political issue as well as a major data processing problem.
- Managers and other users of information in the organization are demanding more kinds of information to support the management and operations of the business firm. The infor-mation demanded must be accurate, timely, and "tailored" to the needs of the manager or user.

The three reasons given above for the increased complexity of information requirements and data processing volumes are obviously interrelated and are all affected by the increased complexity and accelerated pace of social, political, and tech-nological change in today's society. What some have called an "information explosion" has occurred which emphasizes the need to automate data processing by the use of electronic computers. Why can electronic data processing meet the present and future information and data processing requirements of business firms? The answer lies in four basic advantages of EDP systems compared to manual data processing methods.

Speed.   We have previously mentioned the impressive speed of computers which are capable of executing millions of instructions per second. Thus, it takes a computer only seconds to perform millions of data processing functions that humans would take years to complete. This data processing speed of the computer allows electronic data processing systems to provide information in a **timely** manner to the managers and other users of information within a business firm. This is a major benefit of EDP systems. If an EDP system is not providing timely information, corrective measures must be taken by management to ensure that the speed capability of the computer is properly utilized.

Accuracy.   Computers can accurately process large volumes of data according to complex and repetitive data processing procedures. This is in contrast to manual data processing systems where the constant repetition of the same data processing tasks for large volumes of data by human beings becomes a cumbersome and tedious chore which is extremely susceptible to errors. This is not to say that computers always produce accurate information. However, computer errors are minimal compared to the volume of data being processed and are frequently the result of human error. For example, errors in management reports or customer statements are usually the result of incorrect data input supplied by humans, or errors in a computer program developed by a human programmer. Thus the term "garbage in, garbage out" (GIGO) is used by computer professionals to emphasize that incorrect input data or programs will result in incorrect output from the computer. It also emphasizes the importance of **control** procedures to ensure accuracy of EDP systems.

Reliability.   The accuracy of electronic data processing is directly related to the exceptional reliability of computers and their electronic circuitry. Modern computers consistently and accurately operate for long periods of time without failure. Their electronic circuitry is inherently reliable and includes self-checking features which insure accuracy and automatically diagnose failure conditions. Such built-in "diagnostics" and regular preventive maintenance checks help insure consistent reliability. Computers do "go down" or "crash" (stop working) but such *downtime* is only a fraction of one percent of the operating time of most systems.

Economy. The speed, accuracy and reliability of computers would be available to only a few large organizations if it were not for the very real economy of computer usage. An analysis of the costs of data processing at various volumes usually reveals that electronic data processing is more economically justifiable than manual data processing for most firms. See Figure 2–11. This cost advantage continues to increase as new developments in computer technology continue to drive down the historical cost of computer processing. (See Figure 2–12.) Of course, as in other areas of business activity, the

FIGURE 2–11 EDP is More Economical than Manual DP as Volume of Data Processed Increases

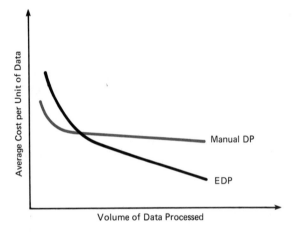

FIGURE 2–12 Decline in Cost of Computer Processing

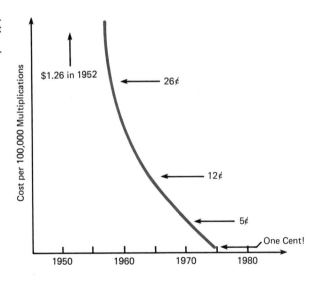

cost of EDP for a business firm can go out of control unless proper procedures are developed by management to control EDP costs.

The speed, accuracy, reliability, and economy of modern computers have made them an invaluable tool for most business firms and other organizations. Electronic data processing allows such organizations to operate more efficiently and effectively as they respond to the increased costs, complexity, and demands of the business environment. *For example,* a computer-using business firm can frequently reduce clerical costs, increase cash flow, or reduce investment in inventory. The computer can also help improve the quality of customer service and provide management with better information for decision making.

Of course for many firms, electronic data processing is an absolute necessity. *For example,* banks would not be able to process the millions of checks written each day; stock exchanges would not be able to process the millions of shares of stock traded each day; and airlines and travel agents would not be able to handle the millions of travel requests and reservations made each day. Thousands of business firms in many other industries would not be able to operate without the basic information concerning their customers, suppliers, inventories, and finances provided by their electronic data processing systems. Therefore, it is imperative that you gain a basic understanding of the "engine" that powers electronic data processing—the electronic computer.

SUMMARY

- A system is a group of interrelated components that seeks the attainment of a common goal by accepting inputs and producing outputs in an organized transformation process. Feedback is information concerning the components and operations of a system. Control is the component that evaluates feedback to determine whether the system is moving toward the achievement of its goal, and then makes necessary adjustments to the input and processing components to insure that proper output is produced.
- A data processing system accepts raw data as input and processes it into finished information as output. All data processing systems perform common system functions and activities. Data is first collected and converted to a form that is suitable for processing (input). Then it is manipulated or converted into information (processing), stored for future use (storage), or communicated to its ultimate user (output) according to data processing procedures (control).
- The two major types of data processing are manual and electronic data processing. Manual data processing systems are

simple and inexpensive if an organization's information requirements are simple and the amount of data to be processed is limited. As information requirements become more complex and the volume of data increases, the speed, accuracy, reliability, and economy of electronic data processing systems are required.

KEY TERMS AND CONCEPTS

Data	Data media
Information	Source documents
Data processing	Manual data processing
System	Calculator
Data processing system	Electronic data processing
Data processing functions: Input. Processing. Output. Storage. Control.	

REVIEW AND DISCUSSION QUESTIONS

1. Why are you a data processing system? Explain.
2. What is the difference between data and information? Use an example to illustrate this difference.
3. What is data processing? How is it similar to a manufacturing process?
4. What is a system? Give examples to illustrate your answer.
5. What are the basic components of a system? What roles does each component play in the operation of a system? Use a data processing system to illustrate your answer.
6. What are the two major types of data processing systems? Which type do you use most frequently?
7. Does all data processing require the performance of the basic system functions and activities described in the chapter? Explain.
8. Use an example to illustrate the processing of data by each of the five basic functions of data processing for both a manual and electronic data processing system.
9. Can electronic calculators be viewed as special-purpose arithmetic microcomputers? Why or why not?
10. What are several benefits and limitations of manual data processing?
11. How do the four basic advantages of EDP systems help managers of business firms cope with the increased volume and complexity of data processing requirements? Use examples to illustrate your answer.

REAL WORLD APPLICATIONS

2–1   Cabarrus Urology Clinic

The morning rush is on at the Cabarrus Urology Clinic in Concord, NC. Patients line the waiting room while nurses scurry about with charts and syringes and little vials. One doctor is busy with X rays, another with a consultation, a third is in surgery. The only person who doesn't have anything to do for the moment is the general secretary and computer operator.

Sherry Aldridge sits at her desk with a cup of coffee. Behind her, the clinic's 5110 computer is hard at work, keeping up with the enormous amount of paperwork generated by this busy three-doctor clinic. And while Ms. Aldridge isn't complaining about the time she now has available for other, routine tasks, she is still somewhat amazed at the difference the 5110 has made at the clinic.

"We billed almost $100,000 in insurance claims in just two days last month," she says. "It used to take one person—me—three or four weeks to file that many claims manually."

Going online with insurance claims has not only eased the load on the bookkeeper but also has improved both cash flow and patient services.

"We use the computer to store all the information on insurance claims," Ms. Aldridge explains, "and we also use it to print statements for both the insurance companies and our patients. The computer includes the correct procedure code for each item on a statement, which means we no longer get a lot of phone calls from the insurance companies asking us to explain the charges on a claim. Our turnaround time on insurance claims has gone from 90 days in some cases to about 30. The insurance companies are even paying more on some claims because the information is more specific.

"At the end of the month the computer prints a total register of all charges, all payments received and all insurance claims filed. The 5110 has even stopped us from having to pull patient charts when people call up to see if their insurance has been filed. We used to spend several hours a day on this—now we know at a glance."[1]

- What are some of the data processing system functions that you can identify in the example above?
- How does this example demonstrate the speed, accuracy, reliability, and economy of electronic data processing versus manual data processing?

[1] Source: "Results for Aircraft Consultant, Medical Clinic," *Viewpoint Magazine,* January/February 1979, p. 14. © 1979. Used with permission

2–2   Treasury Department—Commonwealth of Pennsylvania

The Treasury Department of Pennsylvania has a complete appropriation control and financial reporting system called TABS (Treasury Automated Bookkeeping System). It processes all daily commonwealth revenues and general disbursements.

The treasury uses a computer with over 20 terminals and a full range of peripherals. Treasury computer operations have progressed from the mere automation of check writing to the initial phases of a comprehensive data base-oriented information

processing facility supporting critical management systems. Information retrieval impossible before TABS is now an everyday occurrence.

Check production capability has increased from a maximum daily capacity of 20,000 to 30,000 checks to over 150,000 checks. In addition, normal processing time for vendors' bills was reduced from eight days to three days. This is from the time of submission of a bill to the issuance of a check.

2–2 *(continued)*

TABS replaced an antiquated manual ledger-card operation and increased processing capability by approximately 75 percent. At the same time, financial controls were strengthened over the processed transactions and the results of operations.[2]

- Identify the benefits of the EDP system described above compared to the manual system it replaced.

[2] Source: "Automated Bookkeeping System Saves State Treasury Time and Money," *Infosystems*, December 1980, p. 72. Copyright 1980, Hitchcock Publishing Co. Reprinted with permission.

2–3 Doe & Ingalls, Inc.

Describing the manual inventory system his company used until January of this year, Larry Liebman says that it ". . . was next to impossible to update, so we lived with its inaccuracies." Larry is president of Doe & Ingalls, a chemical distributor based in Medford, Massachusetts. With as many as 2,300 different items stocked in his 24,000-square-foot warehouse, ranging from one-gram bottles to industrial chemicals in 55-gallon drums, Larry's profit-making potential depends on a smoothly functioning system of inventory control. On a typical day, 50 or 60 orders involving several hundred items are filled and shipped to customers among the more than 600 who regularly buy from Doe & Ingalls. To keep them coming back, Larry strives for one-day service. "About 80 percent of our orders go out the next day," he says.

Before computerizing his inventory, this goal was not always easy to meet. The card-based manual system in use at D&I worked well, but the number of movements it was asked to monitor became so large that the office staff of five could not keep up with them. Late vendor deliveries went unrecorded. Standard practice assumed three weeks to restock after orders were placed with a vendor; but, in practice, as many as three months frequently elapsed between trigger point and resupply. Because of this, Larry's biggest problem with the system was ". . . not knowing what we had out on the floor." Some items were overstocked while others were sold out.

All this has changed, however. The new computerized inventory system provides exact inventory control, but does more as well. It prints orders, picking papers, and shipping documents. It writes invoices and prepares management reports. In short, it has taken over much of the burden of paperwork formerly borne by the office staff.

When an order is received, data is taken from the phone and logged onto a standard form. Order entry data includes customer number, product number, discount code, and quantity. Keying the product number into the machine brings up a CRT [video] display depicting case price and cost, unit selling price and unit cost, chemical nomenclature, and package type and size. The system then goes on to print a complete order, with appropriate prices, on a four-part carbon form. Shipping and picking papers are generated as part of the same package.[3]

- Identify the data processing system functions in the example above.
- Why do you think the manual inventory system was unsatisfactory?
- Why can the EDP system handle this situation?

[3] Source: *Distributor Benefits from Computerized Inventory Management*, Wang Laboratories, Inc.

3

CHAPTER OUTLINE

Computer Fundamentals

LEARNING OBJECTIVES

The purpose of this chapter is to promote a basic understanding of the electronic computer by analyzing (1) the functions and components of a computer system, and (2) the representation and organization of data in computers.

After reading and studying this chapter, you should be able to:

1. Identify the components and functions of a computer system.
2. Describe how a computer executes an instruction.
3. Explain why data representation is based on the binary number system.
4. Differentiate between a bit, byte, and word.
5. Explain how data is stored in computers, including primary and secondary storage, types of semiconductor storage, registers, and read-only storage.
6. Identify the impact of firmware and microprogramming on computer operations.
7. Explain the role of input/output interface devices in a computer system.

THE COMPUTER AS A SYSTEM

It is important to understand that the computer is not a solitary electronic data processing "black box," nor is it an unrelated grouping of electronic devices performing a variety of data processing activities. We must learn to understand the computer as a *system*, that is, as an interrelated grouping of components that accepts input and produces output in an organized process. An understanding of the computer as a **computer system** is one of the most important basic objectives of this text.

Like any *data processing system*, the computer can be viewed as a system which performs the basic functions of *input*, *processing*, *storage*, *control*, and *output*. If we apply these functions to computer equipment, or *hardware*, we can describe a computer system as being composed of the following system components:

Input. The input devices of a computer system include the keyboard of computer terminals, punched card readers, optical scanners, etc. They convert data into electronic form for input into the computer system.

Processing. The *central processing unit* (CPU) is the main processing component of a computer system. In particular, the *arithmetic-logic unit,* one of the major components of a CPU, performs the arithmetic and logic functions required in computer processing.

Storage. The storage function of a computer system takes place in the *primary storage unit* of the CPU and in *secondary storage* devices such as magnetic disk and tape units. These devices store data and program instructions needed for computer processing.

Control. The *control unit* of the CPU is the control component of a computer system. It interprets computer program instructions and transmits directions to the other components of the computer system.

Output. The output devices of a computer system include video display units, printers, card punch units, etc. They convert electronic information produced by the computer system into a *human-intelligible* or *machine-readable form.*

Figure 3–1 illustrates this concept of the functions and hardware components of a computer system. Figure 3–2 identifies some of the actual devices in a computer system. In order to fully understand the characteristics and capabilities of elec-

FIGURE 3–1   The Computer System Concept

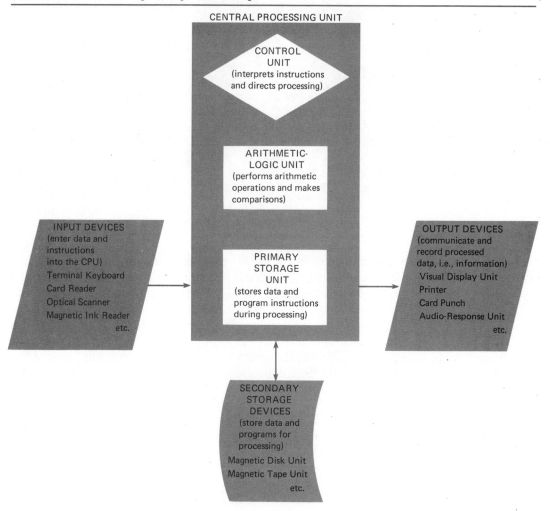

tronic computers, we must first gain a proper understanding of the components and functions of the computer as a system. Therefore, let us take a closer look at each of these system functions.

Input

Data and *program instructions* are entered into the computer in the *input* function. Data and instructions may be entered directly into the computer system (through the keyboard

FIGURE 3-2 Computer System Devices

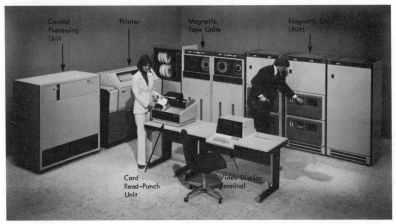

Courtesy NCR Corporation.

of a computer terminal, for example) or may first be converted into a machine-readable input medium such as punched cards or magnetic tape. In the latter case, "data entry" equipment such as card-punch machines convert data from source documents into punched cards which can then be entered into the computer system through an input device known as a card reader. Most computer systems automatically control the flow of data and instructions into the computer from various input devices. This contrasts with the manual keying of data and instructions of most calculators. Input devices convert program instructions and data into electrical impulses which are then routed to the primary storage unit where they are held until needed.

Processing

The processing function of a computer system is performed by the **central processing unit,** the most important hardware component of any computer system. This unit is also known as the CPU, the *central processor,* or the *main frame.* It is this unit that accomplishes the processing of data and controls the other parts of the system. The CPU consists of three subunits known as the *primary storage unit,* the *arithmetic-logic unit,* and the *control unit.* These are described below.

Arithmetic—Logic

The computer can perform the arithmetic operations of addition, subtraction, multiplication, and division. It can also identify whether a number is positive, negative, or equal to zero, and can compare two numbers to determine which is higher than, equal to, or lower than the other. This ability of the computer to make comparisons gives it a *logic capability*, for it can make logical changes from one set of operating instructions to another based on the results of comparisons made during processing. This ability of a computer to change the sequence of its use of instructions in a program is called *program modification*. For example, in a payroll program the computer can test if the hours worked by employees exceed 40 hours per week. Payments for such "overtime" would be computed using a different sequence of instructions than that used for employees without such overtime.

Calculation and comparison operations occur in the **arithmetic-logic unit** (or ALU). Depending on the application being processed, data may be transferred from storage to the arithmetic-logic unit and then returned to storage several times before processing is completed. The arithmetic-logic unit also performs such operations as shifting, moving, and temporarily storing data. Through its ability to make comparisons, it can test for various conditions during processing and then perform appropriate operations.

Storage

The computer can store both data and instructions internally in its "memory." This internal storage enables the computer to "remember" the details of many assignments and to proceed from one assignment to another automatically, since it can retain data and instructions until needed. The ability of the computer to store its operating instructions internally (the *computer program*) allows the computer to process data *automatically*, that is, without continual human intervention. This *stored program* concept differentiates computers from most calculators.

The storage function takes place in the *primary storage unit* of the CPU and in *secondary storage* devices. All data and programs must be placed in the **primary storage unit** (also called "main memory" or "main storage") before they can be used in processing. The primary storage unit is also used to hold data and program instructions between processing steps, and after processing is completed, but before release as output.

Primary storage is subdivided into many small sections called *storage positions* or *storage locations*. Primary storage is frequently compared to a group of mailboxes, where each mailbox has an address and is capable of storing one item of data. Similarly, each position of storage has a specific numerical location called an *address* so that data stored in its contents can be readily located by the computer. In most modern computers, each position of storage can usually hold one alphabetical or special character or two numeric digits.

Data and programs can also be stored in **secondary storage** devices such as magnetic disk and tape units and thus greatly enlarge the storage capacity of the computer system. However, the contents of such secondary storage devices cannot be processed without first being brought into the primary storage unit.

Control

Every other component of the computer system is controlled and directed by the **control unit**. The control unit obtains instructions from the primary storage unit. After interpreting the instructions, the control unit transmits directions to the appropriate components of the computer system, ordering them to perform the required data processing operations. The control unit tells the input and secondary storage devices what data and instructions to read into memory, tells the arithmetic-logic unit where the data to be processed is located in memory, what operations to perform, where in memory the results are to be stored; and, finally, it directs the appropriate output devices to convert processed data into machine or human-readable output media.

Output

The function of *output* devices is to convert processed data (information) from electronic impulses into a form that is intelligible to humans or into a machine-readable form. For example, output devices such as high-speed printers produce printed reports; card-punch units produce punched cards; and "CRT terminals" produce video displays as output. Most computers can automatically control a wide variety of output devices.

HOW COMPUTERS EXECUTE INSTRUCTIONS

Computer users should have a basic understanding of how a computer executes instructions. Such understanding helps users appreciate why a CPU contains the special-purpose circuitry and devices described in this chapter. It should also help users appreciate modern "high-level programming languages" which have simplified the task of writing computer programs. It is no longer necessary to write computer instructions utilizing complex "machine language" coding which describes in detail each step of the computer execution process described below.

Computer Instructions and Cycles

The specific form of a computer instruction depends on the type of programming language and computer being used. However, a computer instruction usually consists of:

* An **operation code** which specifies what is to be done (add, compare, read, etc.).
* One or more **operands,** which specify the primary storage addresses of data or instructions, and/or indicate which input/output and secondary storage devices will be used. See Figure 3–3.

FIGURE 3–3 Instruction Operation Codes and Operands

Operation Codes	Operand(s)
Start I/O	Channel 1, Device 191
Read	One Record into Storage Positions 1000–1050
Add	Quantity in Storage Location 1004 into Storage Location 2000
Subtract	Quantity in Storage Location 1005 from Contents of Register 10
Branch	To Instruction in Storage Location 5004

The operation code and operands of the instruction being executed as well as the data elements affected by the instruction are moved among the *registers* and other special-purpose circuitry of the CPU during the execution of an instruction. (**Registers** are high-speed storage circuits used for the temporary storage of an instruction or data element during the operation of the control and arithmetic-logic units.) A fixed number of electrical pulses emitted by the CPU's timing circuitry or *internal clock* determines the timing of each basic CPU operation. This period of time is called a *machine-cycle*. The number of machine cycles required to execute an instruction varies with the complexity of the instruction. During each machine cycle, electrical pulses generated by the internal clock energize special-purpose circuitry elements which sense and interpret specific instructions and data and move them (in the form of electrical pulses) between various subunits of the CPU.

The Instruction and Execution Cycles

The execution of an instruction can be divided into two segments, the "instruction cycle" and the "execution cycle." Simply stated, the **instruction cycle** consists of processes in which an instruction is *fetched* from primary storage and *interpreted* by the control unit. The **execution cycle** consists of *performing* the operations specified by the instruction which was interpreted during the instruction cycle. Figure 3–4 is a simplified illustration of what happens in a CPU during the instruction and execution cycles.

Notice the following operations within the **instruction cycle:**

1. First, the instruction is *fetched* from primary storage and temporarily stored in the registers of the control unit.
2. Next, the instruction is *interpreted* by the circuitry of the control unit. This involves decoding the operation code and operands of the instruction.

FIGURE 3–4 Computer Instruction and Execution Cycles

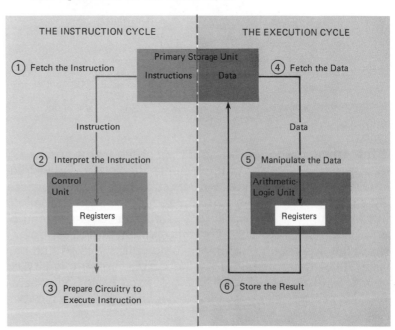

THE INSTRUCTION CYCLE | THE EXECUTION CYCLE

① Fetch the Instruction

Primary Storage Unit
Instructions   Data

④ Fetch the Data

Instruction

Data

② Interpret the Instruction

Control Unit

Registers

⑤ Manipulate the Data

Arithmetic-Logic Unit

Registers

③ Prepare Circuitry to Execute Instruction

⑥ Store the Result

3. Finally, the control unit prepares electronic circuitry "paths" within the CPU to carry out the required operations.

The operations taking place during the **execution cycle** consist of the following:

4. First, the data to be processed is fetched from its locations in primary storage and temporarily stored in the registers of the arithmetic-logic unit.
5. Next, the operations specified by the operation code of the instruction are performed (addition, subtraction, comparisons, etc.).
6. Finally, the result arising from the manipulation of the data is stored in primary storage.

The computer automatically repeats such instruction and execution cycles until the final instruction of a program is executed. Usually, instructions are sequentially executed in the order in which they are stored in primary storage. An "instruction counter" which automatically advances or "steps" in sequential order to the address of the next instruction stored in memory is used to indicate which instruction is to be executed next. Sometimes, a **branch instruction** is brought from storage whose operand indicates that the next instruction to be executed is in another part of the program. For example, a **test** or **comparison instruction** might specify a change in the sequential order of processing if the presence or absence of a specified condition is sensed. (Remember our previous example of a payroll program in which a different sequence of instructions is utilized for employees whose hours worked exceed 40 hours per week.) In such cases, the contents of the instruction counter will be reset to the address of a different instruction, and the CPU will "branch" or "jump" to that part of the program and begin executing its instructions.

Computer Execution Speeds

It should be noted that many computers execute more than a **million instructions per second** (MIPS). For example, several large computers have processing speeds in excess of 10 MIPS. Other measures of the internal operating speed of electronic computers are "machine cycle time" and "memory cycle time." **Machine cycle time** is the time necessary to complete one machine cycle while **memory cycle** time is the time necessary for a computer to recall data from one primary storage position. Machine cycle times are now *below 100* *nanoseconds* for many large computers, while memory cycle times of *several hundred nanoseconds* are common. Thus many modern computers would need only a few seconds to simultaneously:

- Compute the payroll for thousands of employees,
- Record thousands of sales transactions,
- Update the accounts of thousands of customers, and
- Adjust the amounts of thousands of items in inventory!

COMPUTER DATA REPRESENTATION

The letters of the alphabet in this book are symbols that when properly organized or "coded" into the English language will "represent" data that you, the reader, can process into information. Thus, we can say that words, numbers, and punctuation are the human-sensible code by which data is represented in this book. Similarly, data must be represented in a machine-sensible code before it can be processed by a computer system.

Data is represented in a computer by either the presence or the absence of electronic or magnetic "signals" in certain sections of its circuitry. This is called *binary* or "two state" representation of data, since the circuitry of the computer is indicating only two possible states or conditions. *For example,* transistors and other semiconductors are either in a conducting or nonconducting state, while devices such as magnetic cores can be magnetized in either clockwise or counterclockwise direction. Thus, we say that the electronic and magnetic circuitry of a computer operates in a "binary mode" since something is "binary" if it is made up of two parts or conditions. The binary characteristics of computer circuitry is the primary reason why the binary numbering system is the basis for data representation in modern computers.

Computer Number Systems

The binary number system has only two symbols, 0 and 1, and is, therefore, said to have a "base" of two. The familiar decimal system has a base of 10, since it uses 10 symbols (0 through 9). In the binary numbering system, all numbers, letters in the alphabet, and special characters are expressed as a sequence of either zeros or ones. The binary symbols 0 and 1 are called "binary digits" or more commonly "bits."

The *octal* (base 8) and the *hexadecimal* (base 16) number systems are used as a shorthand method of expressing the binary data representation within many modern computers. The binary number system has the disadvantage of requiring a large number of digits to express a given number value. The use of octal and hexadecimal number systems which are proportionately related to the binary number system provides a shorthand method of reducing the long "string" of ones and zeros which make up a binary number. This simplifies the jobs of programmers and computer operators who frequently have to determine the data or instruction contents of the computer.

Figure 3–5 shows the binary, octal, and hexadecimal equivalents of the decimal numbers 0 through 16. Using the relationships in Figure 3–5 you should be able to determine that the decimal number 17 would be expressed by the binary number 10001, the octal number 21, and the hexadecimal number 11, and so on. Several methods can be used to convert decimal numbers to a binary, octal, or hexadecimal form, or vice versa, but they are beyond the scope of this text.

Decimal	Binary	Octal	Hexadecimal
0	0	0	0
1	1	1	1
2	10	2	2
3	11	3	3
4	100	4	4
5	101	5	5
6	110	6	6
7	111	7	7
8	1000	10	8
9	1001	11	9
10	1010	12	A
11	1011	13	B
12	1100	14	C
13	1101	15	D
14	1110	16	E
15	1111	17	F
16	10000	20	10

FIGURE 3–5   Equivalents of Decimal Numbers

Computer Codes

Though the internal circuitry of the computer utilizes only binary ones and zeros, several coding systems have been devised to make the job of communicating with a computer easier and more efficient. These codes should be considered as shorthand methods of expressing the binary patterns within a computer. These computer codes can also be thought of as methods of organizing the binary patterns within a computer in order to more efficiently utilize its arithmetic, logic, and storage capabilities.

The most basic computer code would be the use of the "pure" binary number system as the method of data representation for all computer operations. Some scientific and special-purpose computers do utilize the pure binary code as their only method of internal data representation. However, most modern computers, though they may use a pure binary code for some operations, use special codes based on the binary, octal, or hexadecimal number systems.

Most common computer codes are versions of the *binary coded decimal* (BCD) coding system. In this system, decimal digits are expressed in a binary form using only the first four binary positions. Referring back to Figure 3–5 we see that the decimal digits 0 through 9 can be expressed by four binary positions. Therefore, any decimal number can be expressed by stringing together groups of four binary digits. For example, the decimal number 1985 would be expressed in BCD form as shown below.

Decimal Form	1	9	8	5
BCD Form	0001	1001	1000	0101

The *Extended BCD Interchange Code* (EBCDIC) is used by most current computers and can provide 256 different coding arrangements. The middle column of Figure 3–6 shows that this eight-bit code consists of four "numeric" bits (on the right) and four "zone" bits (on the left). The letters of the alphabet or special characters can be represented when combinations of zone and numeric bits are used. Another popular code is the *American Standard Code for Information Interchange,* which is a seven-bit code called ASCII. It is a standardized code developed primarily for data transmission devices but is also used by some computers. See Figure 3–6.

Most computer codes include an additional bit called the **check bit.** The check bit is also known as a "parity" bit and is used for verifying the accuracy or validity of the coded data. Many computers have a built-in checking capacity to detect the loss or addition of bits during the transfer of data between components of a computer system. For example, the

Character	EBCDIC	ASCII
0	1111 0000	011 0000
1	1111 0001	011 0001
2	1111 0010	011 0010
3	1111 0011	011 0011
4	1111 0100	011 0100
5	1111 0101	011 0101
6	1111 0110	011 0110
7	1111 0111	011 0111
8	1111 1000	011 1000
9	1111 1001	011 1001
A	1100 0001	100 0001
B	1100 0010	100 0010
C	1100 0011	100 0011
D	1100 0100	100 0100
E	1100 0101	100 0101
F	1100 0110	100 0110
G	1100 0111	100 0111
H	1100 1000	100 1000
I	1100 1001	100 1001
J	1101 0001	100 1010
K	1101 0010	100 1011
L	1101 0011	100 1100
M	1101 0100	100 1101
N	1101 0101	100 1110
O	1101 0110	100 1111
P	1101 0111	101 0000
Q	1101 1000	101 0001
R	1101 1001	101 0010
S	1110 0010	101 0011
T	1110 0011	101 0100
U	1110 0100	101 0101
V	1110 0101	101 0110
W	1110 0110	101 0111
X	1110 0111	101 1000
Y	1110 1000	101 1001
Z	1110 1001	101 1010

FIGURE 3–6 Common Computer Codes

computer may be designed to continuously check for an "odd parity," that is, an odd number of "binary one" bits (electronically "on" bit positions) in each byte of data that is transferred. In such cases, a check bit is turned on automatically to ensure that an odd number of electronically "on" bit positions is present in each byte of data in storage. Thus the check bit allows the computer to automatically determine whether the correct number of bit positions representing a character of data has been transferred.

Figure 3–7 concludes this section on data representation with an illustration of how data is physically represented in many modern computers. Assuming the use of the eight-bit EBCDIC code, Figure 3–7 reveals that one alphabetical or

FIGURE 3–7 Data Representation; EBCDIC Code

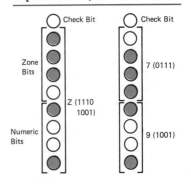

special character or two decimal numbers can be represented by an eight-bit code. The circles represent semiconductor circuit elements or other forms of primary storage circuitry. The shaded circles represent an electronic or magnetic "on" state, while the nonshaded circles represent the "off" state of binary devices. Thus, the first column of circles represents the letter "Z" while the second column of circles is called the "packed decimal" format, since two decimal numbers, in this case a seven and a nine, are represented by only eight bits. In both illustrations, the ninth or check bit is in an "off" state.

Computer Data Elements

The organization of data within a computer is a function of the internal design of the computer circuitry and the coding system utilized. Since most current computers are designed to utilize the EBCDIC coding system, we will confine our discussion to data organization based on that system. Computers that use other schemes of data organization differ in the size and names of the data elements used, rather than in the basic concepts required.

Bits. Figure 3–8 illustrates the hierarchy of data elements used by many computers. The smallest element of data is the *bit*, or binary digit, which can have a binary value of either zero or one.

Bytes. The grouping of eight bits required by such coding systems as EBCDIC is called a *byte*. Remember that a byte can contain either one alphabetical or special character, or can be "packed" with two decimal digits. The byte is the basic unit of data in most modern computer systems.

The storage capacity of most computers and storage devices is usually expressed in terms of bytes. Storage capacity is typically measured in **kilobytes** (abbreviated as KB or K) or **megabytes** (abbreviated as MB or M). Although "kilo" means one thousand in the metric system, the computer indus-

FIGURE 3–8 Typical Computer Data Elements

Name	Size
BIT	One binary digit
BYTE	Eight bits
WORD	Fixed word-length format: 8, 16, or 32 bits
	Variable word-length format: 1 to 256 bytes
PAGE	2K or 4K bytes

try utilizes K to represent 1,024 (2^{10}) storage positions. Therefore, a memory size of 64K, for example, is really 65,536
storage positions rather than 64,000 positions, but such differences are frequently disregarded in order to simplify descriptions of storage capacity. Thus, a **megabyte** is roughly one
million bytes, while a **gigabyte** is roughly one billion bytes
of storage, and a **terabyte** represents one trillion bytes of storage! Typically, computer primary storage capacities might
range from 4K bytes (4,096 bytes) for some microcomputer
memories to 40M bytes (40 megabytes or 40 million bytes)
of memory for a large computer system.

Words. The next major computer data element is the *word*.
The word is a basic grouping of binary digits, or bytes, that
is transferred by electronic circuitry between primary storage
and the registers of the arithmetic-logic unit or control unit.
Thus a computer with a 32 bit word-length usually transfers
data and instructions within the CPU in groupings of 32 bits
and can process data faster than a computer with a 16 bit
or 8 bit word-length. Word size varies with the type, size,
and manufacturer of a computer. For example, in the recent
past, microcomputers frequently used 8-bit words, minicomputers used 16-bit words, and larger computers used 32-bit
words. However, microcomputers are beginning to use 16
bit or 32 bit word-lengths, while minicomputers are moving
toward a 32 bit word-length, with some very large computers
using 64-bit words.

The size of a word also depends on whether the computer
is operating in a *fixed word-length* or a *variable word-length*
format. Computers operate in a fixed word-length mode when
each word consists of a fixed number of bits or bytes, while
in the variable word-length format, the size of a word varies
with the size of the data elements that are being processed.
For many computers, a word consists of four bytes (32 bits)
in a fixed word-length format and can vary from one byte
to 256 bytes in a variable word-length format.

Several other variations in word-length may be used by
modern computers. For example, computers with a word-size
of 32 bits might manipulate data and instructions in *half-words*
of 16 bits or *double-words* of 64 bits. Thus some present
computers use a double-word of 64 bits to move data in a
data path that is 64-bits wide within the circuitry of the CPU.
Also, some microcomputers utilize a *bit slice* design in which
data is moved in "slices" of two bits or four bits within the

elements of the microprocessor. These variations are designed to enhance the speed and efficiency of processing operations.

Pages. Finally, an important computer data element of modern computer systems is the *page*. The page is a computer data element that has been created due to the development of *virtual memory* in which secondary storage is treated as an extension of a computer's primary storage. Pages are transferred between primary and secondary storage in the virtual memory process known as *paging*. Pages of programs or data are continually transferred between primary and secondary storage in such virtual memory systems. For many computers, the page consists of 2K or 4K bytes.

PRIMARY STORAGE MEDIA

Semiconductor Storage

The primary storage of most modern computers consists of microelectronic semiconductor circuits. Groups of these circuits (each group representing eight bits or one byte, for example) make up each position of storage. Thousands of semiconductor storage circuits are etched on large-scale integrated (LSI) circuit *chips*. Each memory chip may be less than an eighth of an inch square and contain thousands of storage positions. For example, many current memory chips are 64K bit chips containing 65,536 bit positions for a storage capacity of 8K bytes. See Figure 3–9. Each storage position (cell) consists of a microelectronic switch or "flip-flop" circuit. The direction of the electronic current passing through each cell determines whether the switch is in an "on" or "off" position. Thus the binary digits 0 and 1 can be represented. The *state* of each storage position ("on" or "off") can be electronically sensed without altering that state. Since each memory cell can be individually sensed or changed in the same length of time, semiconductor storage is a *random access* or *direct access* storage medium. Figure 3–10 illustrates an eight-by-eight array that can store 64 bits (8 bytes).

Some of the major attractions of microscopic semiconductor storage are small size, great speed, shock and temperature resistance, and low cost due to mass production capabilities. Semiconductor memories use two basic types of LSI technology, *bipolar* and *metal oxide semiconductor* (MOS), with many variations of these two technologies being used. Bipolar circuits are faster but more costly than MOS circuits and are

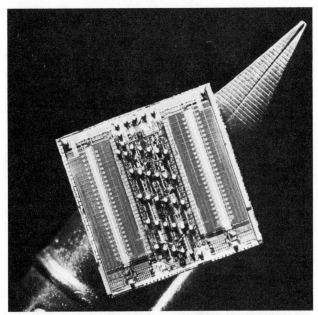

FIGURE 3-9   A 64K Bit Semiconductor Memory Chip

Courtesy IBM Corporation.

therefore used primarily for very high speed *buffer (cache)* storage, while most main memories use MOS type circuits. Access times for many bipolar memories are below 50 nanoseconds and into the picosecond range, while speeds of several hundred nanoseconds are common for MOS type memories. One major disadvantage of semiconductor memory used for primary storage is its *volatility*. Uninterrrupted electric power must be supplied or the contents of memory will be lost. Therefore, emergency transfer to other devices or standby electrical power is required if data must be saved.

The growth of semiconductor storage and microelectronic technology has caused the development of two basic types of semiconductor memory: random access memory (RAM) and read only memory (ROM). Variations of these two basic types are being used for electronic computers, calculators, and other devices requiring electronic storage of data or instructions.

RAM *Random Access Memory.* Used for temporary storage of data or programs during processing. Each memory position can be directly sensed (read) or changed (write) in the same length of time, irrespective of its location on the storage medium. This is a *volatile* memory.

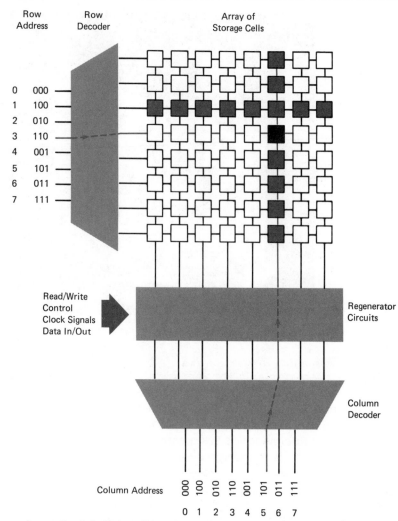

FIGURE 3–10 Diagram of a Semiconductor Memory Chip

Row Address

Row Decoder

Array of Storage Cells

0	000
1	100
2	010
3	110
4	001
5	101
6	011
7	111

Read/Write Control Clock Signals Data In/Out

Regenerator Circuits

Column Decoder

Column Address   000 100 010 110 001 101 011 111

0 1 2 3 4 5 6 7

Source: David A. Hodges, "Microelectronic Memories," *Scientific American*, September 1977, p. 136. Copyright © 1977 by Scientific American, Inc. All rights reserved.

ROM   *Read Only Memory.* This is a type of nonvolatile random-access memory used for permanent storage. Can only be read, not "written" i.e., changed. Frequently used control instructions (as in the control unit of the computer) and other more permanent programs such as programming language translators (compilers) and mathematical routines are permanently written into the memory cells during manufacture.

PROM   *Programmable Read Only Memory.* This is a type of ROM which can be programmed after manufacture. Several versions can only be written-in (programmed) once after their manufacture.

EPROM   *Erasable Programmable Read Only Memories.* These are a type of ROM that can be erased and reprogrammed indefinitely. Erasure of memory may require a special technique such as applying an extra large voltage or by exposing the circuits to ultraviolet light. These memories are useful for storage of contents that will be changed infrequently. Therefore PROMs and EPROMs are more flexible versions of read-only memories.

Other Primary Storage Media

Figure 3–11 illustrates the speed and cost of several alternative primary and secondary storage media. Notice the cost/speed tradeoffs as one moves from semiconductor memories to "moving surface" magnetic media such as magnetic disk and tape. Figure 3–11 also shows that MOS semiconductor and magnetic bubble memories are being used for both *primary* and *secondary* storage devices. At the present time, MOS semiconductor memories are being used primarily for primary storage though they are finding limited use in high speed secondary storage devices. Magnetic bubble memories are being used in numerous secondary "buffer" storage applications.

Magnetic Core. Magnetic core was a widely used primary storage medium in second and third generation computers. Magnetic cores are tiny doughnut-shaped rings composed

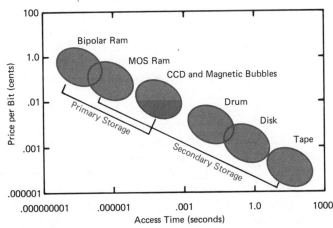

FIGURE 3–11 Storage Media Cost and Speed Tradeoffs

Source: Adapted from David A. Hedges, "Microelectronic Memories," *Scientific American*, September 1977, p. 138. Copyright © 1977 by Scientific American, Inc. All rights reserved.

FIGURE 3–12 Magnetic Core Plane

Courtesy IBM Corporation.

FIGURE 3–13 One Million Bit Magnetic Bubble Memory Chip with Associated Circuitry

Courtesy Intel Corporation.

of iron oxide and other materials that are strung on wires which provide an electrical current that magnetizes the cores. A string of several cores represents one storage position (eight cores plus one for a check bit for all computers using the EBCIDIC code). Thousands of cores strung on wires make up a core "plane" and several core planes make up a core "stack." See Figure 3–12.

Magnetic cores are a binary or two-state device, since they can be magnetized in a clockwise or counterclockwise direction producing the binary "on" or "off" state which is used to represent the binary digits 0 and 1. The direction of electric current in the wires running through the center of the cores determines their magnetic direction. This magnetic direction can easily be changed, though the magnetic core can retain its magnetism indefinitely if so desired. Thus, magnetic core memories retain their contents even when electric power is interrupted. The magnetic direction of each core can be individually sensed or changed at speeds in the nanosecond range. Magnetic core storage is therefore an extremely fast direct access storage medium.

Magnetic Bubble Storage. Magnetic bubble storage devices have been developed which utilize thin slices of garnet crystals on which tiny magnetized areas known as magnetic bubbles or "domains" can be generated. The data is represented by groupings of these magnetic bubbles which can be moved across the surface of the crystal slices by electrical currents or magnetic fields. Magnetic bubble chips with capacities of 32K bytes to 1 megabit (1 million bits) are now in use. Though magnetic bubble memory is slower than semiconductor memory, it has the important advantage of retaining data being stored even when electric power is cut off. While its use as a primary storage medium is limited at the present time, its use as a secondary storage medium is growing.

The first major applications of bubble memory have been in numerical control of machine tools, where dust and chemicals in the atmosphere make moving magnetic media unsuitable, and in portable terminals, where resistance to shock is important. It is being used as a built-in secondary storage medium in small computers and word processors and as "buffer" memory for devices such as programmable calculators and data entry terminals. Larger magnetic bubble devices that will replace some current magnetic tape or disk units for secondary storage are also being developed. See Figure 3–13.

Charge-Coupled Devices.   The charge-coupled device (CCD) is a slower "serial access" form of semiconductor memory which uses a silicon crystal's own structure to store data. Density of storage is similar to magnetic bubbles, but CCDs are faster. However, like other semiconductor memories, CCDs are a volatile storage medium.

Cryoelectronic Storage.   Cryoelectronic storage devices are being developed which will be much faster and smaller than semiconductor storage. Cryoelectronic devices consist of materials which become superconductors at extremely low temperatures. In Chapter 1, we described how a new generation of supercomputers using cryoelectronic circuits called **Josephson Junctions** are being developed. Such circuits (also called *super conductive tunnel junction circuits*) have demonstrated speeds in the 10 picosecond range. See Figure 3–14.

Laser Storage.   *Laser* storage devices (including devices called *holographic* memories) which utilize crystalline material to change the polarization of light are being developed. Changes in the polarity of light captured by these crystals would provide a binary storage device operating at the speed of light.

FIGURE 3–14   A Josephson Junction Circuit Chip

Courtesy IBM Corporation.

ADDITIONAL CPU CONCEPTS

Other CPU Components

The internal "architecture" of the CPU can be quite complex. A detailed knowledge of the circuitry and scientific principles involved is beyond the scope of this book. However it is important to understand the basic functions of the arithmetic-logic, control, and primary storage units of the central processing unit as they were described early in the chapter. In addition, you should understand that the CPU includes several types of special-purpose circuitry such as *registers, counters, adders, decoders,* etc. These electronic circuitry elements serve as temporary work areas, analyze instructions, or perform required arithmetic and logical operations. The number, function, and capacity of such circuits in a CPU depend on the internal architecture of each particular computer. Figure 3–15 summarizes some of these CPU components.

FIGURE 3–15 Other Central
Processing Unit Components

● **Registers.** High-speed storage circuitry used for temporary storage of an instruction or data element during the operation of the control and arithmetic-logic units.

● **Counters.** Devices whose contents can be automatically increased or decreased by specific amount, thus enabling them to "count" the number of particular computer operations.

● **Adders.** Circuits that perform the arithmetic operations of the arithmetic-logic unit.

● **Decoders.** Analyze the instruction code of the computer program and instigate the execution of instructions.

● **Internal clock.** Emits regular pulses at frequencies that range from several million to billions per second. The clock generates the electrical pulses that are used to energize the circuitry of the CPU and insure the exact timing necessary for its proper operation.

● **Buffer.** A high-speed temporary storage area for storing parts of a program or data during processing (also called a "cache" memory).

● **I/O interface or port.** Circuitry for the interconnection ("interface") required for access to input/output devices.

● **Bus.** A set of conducting paths (for movement of data and instructions) which interconnects the various components of the CPU. It may take the form of a cable containing many wires or of microscopic conducting lines on microcomputer chips.

● **Channels.** Special-purpose processors that control the movement of data between the CPU and input/output devices.

CPU Storage Areas

Several types of storage exist within the CPU depending on the particular storage function being performed. Figure 3–16 is a conceptual illustration of the types of storage that may exist within the CPU of modern computers.

Primary Storage Areas. The primary storage unit can be conceptually subdivided into input storage, output storage, program or instruction storage, and working storage. *Input storage* receives data from input devices, *program storage* contains program instructions, and *output storage* contains information waiting for transfer to output devices. *Working storage* holds information being processed as well as intermediate processing results. The primary storage units of many larger computers also include a small, very high speed **buffer** or **cache** storage area. It is sometimes called *scratch pad memory* because it is used to temporarily store data, instructions, and intermediate results during processing.

Arithmetic-Logic and Control Storage Areas. Other categories of CPU storage include *local storage* which consists of the high-speed *registers* of the arithmetic-logic unit and *control storage* which consists of the *registers* and *read-only storage*

FIGURE 3–16   Types of CPU Storage Areas

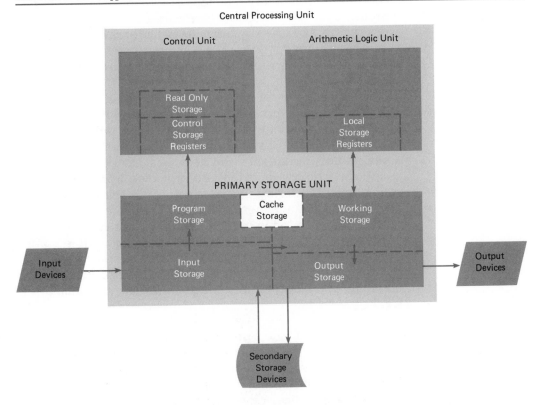

area of the control unit. **Registers** are high-speed storage circuits used for the temporary storage of an instruction or data element during the operation of the control and arithmetic-logic units. *General-purpose registers* carry out a variety of register functions, while special-purpose registers perform specific functions. For example, a *storage register* temporarily holds data or instructions taken from or being sent to primary storage. An *address register* may hold the address of the storage location of data, or the address of an input/output device or a control function. An *instruction register* contains the instruction being executed by the CPU. An *accummulator register* accumulates the results of arithmetic operations.

Firmware and Microprogram Storage.   The control units of many current computers contain ROM modules or other read-only storage areas where elementary machine instructions called *microinstructions* or *microcode* are stored. Sets of microinstructions (called *microprograms*) interpret the machine-language instructions of a computer program and decode them into elementary microinstructions which are then executed. Thus, elementary functions of the control unit that had formerly been executed by *hardware* (hardwired) *logic circuits* are now executed by **firmware,** which consists of *software* (microprograms) stored in ROM *memory circuits.* Thus *firmware* is a development that lies between *hardware* and *software.*

Many current computers load microcode into read-only storage areas of their control units by "writing in" microprograms from magnetic diskettes or cassettes. These read-only storage areas are not permanent ROM devices. Instead, they are semiconductor memory units that are protected from alteration of their contents during processing by electronic circuitry "locks." Deactivating these locks allows a different set of microprograms to be written into the read-only storage area. Thus, this type of ROM unit is frequently called *reloadable control storage* or RCS. Other forms of firmware use special semiconductor "memory circuit cards" or ROM semiconductor modules that are plugged into place in the control unit of the CPU.

Firmware and **microprogramming** (the use of microprograms) increase the versatility of computer systems by allowing various degrees of "customizing" of the *instruction set* of a CPU. For example, firmware enables one type of computer to **emulate** (act like) other types of computers and process programs written for them. The emulated computers are called *virtual machines* because they are not *real* computers. Remember, all of this is possible because firmware allows various control functions formerly performed by hardwiring to be performed by easily changed microprograms. Firmware is frequently used to enable newer computers to process programs written for older models, thus helping users **migrate** (move-up) from old computers to new ones.

The I/O Interface

Several computer system devices exist which are difficult to classify since they can be physically part of the CPU, a separate unit, or can be built into an input/output or storage device. The main purpose of devices such as *I/O ports, I/O busses, buffers, channels, and input/output control units* is to assist the CPU in its input/output assignments. These devices have been developed to provide a uniform, flexible, and efficient **interface** between the CPU and its input/output

FIGURE 3–17   Input/Output Interface Devices

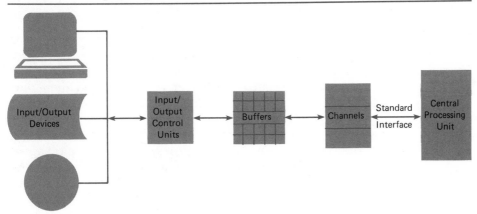

units. *(An interface is a connection or boundary between systems or parts of systems.)* They provide modern computer systems with the ability to carry out many input and output functions simultaneously, while at the same time allowing the CPU to carry out other processing functions, since it no longer must directly control I/O devices. See Figure 3–17.

Buffers. *Buffers* are high-speed storage units which are used for the temporary storage of input or output data in order to reduce the demands of input/output operations on the CPU. Buffers are sometimes built into the CPU or into the input/output device or may be housed separately in a peripheral unit. When buffers are used, the CPU does not have to wait for the input or the output of data but can initiate an input or output command and then return to other processing. Data can then move from the input device into the buffer or from the buffer into an output device without tying up the CPU. High-speed transfer of data occurs when an input buffer transfers data to a CPU or when a CPU can transfer data into an output buffer.

Channels. *Channels* are special-purpose microprocessors or miniprocessors which control the movement of data between the CPU and input or output devices. Channels are housed within the CPU or can be separate peripheral units and may contain buffer storage. Once the channel receives an input or output command from the CPU, it can control the operations of several input/output units simultaneously without disturbing the CPU. Only when the input or output operation is completed will the channel "interrupt" the CPU to signal the completion of its assignment.

There are two main types of channels, each of which can handle several input or output units. The *selector channel* selectively allows each input or output device temporarily to monopolize the entire channel in what is called the "burst mode" of data transmission. *Multiplexor channels* can control data input or output from several slower devices simultaneously in a *multiplex mode.* Most multiplexor channels can also operate in a burst mode in order to service high-speed input/output devices. Some multiplexor channels are called *block multiplexor channels* since they can transmit or receive data in "blocks" of several bytes of data, rather than one byte at a time. The high speed data transmission of these units is called "data streaming."

Input/Output Control Units. Channels are normally not connected directly to an input/output device but to an *input/ output control unit.* A control unit can be built into an input/ output device or housed as a separate unit (frequently called a *controller*) that controls several input/output devices. The job of the controller is to decode the input/output commands from the CPU or the channel and to control the operation of the appropriate input/output device, including the coding, decoding, and checking of data transmitted from the CPU. Buffer storage units are part of the controllers of some input/ output devices.

I/O Ports and I/O Busses. Microcomputers and minicomputers frequently use I/O ports and I/O busses as their input/ output interface. An *I/O port* consists of special circuitry designed to control and facilitate access to input/output devices. An *I/O bus* is a set of conducting paths which interconnects a variety of input/output devices with the CPU.

SUMMARY

- A computer system performs input, storage, arithmetic-logic, control, and output functions. The hardware components of a computer system include input devices, a central processing unit, storage devices, and output devices.
- The execution of a computer instruction can be subdivided into an instruction cycle (when the computer prepares to execute an instruction) and an execution cycle (when it actually executes the instruction).
- Data is represented in a computer in a binary form because of the two-state nature of the electronic and magnetic components of the computer. Most computers

utilize special codes based on the binary number system.

- Within the computer, data is usually organized into bits, bytes, words, and pages. In most modern computers, each position of storage can store one byte, and has a specific numerical location so that the data stored in its contents can be readily located.

- The major primary storage medium is integrated circuit semiconductor storage, with magnetic core, magnetic bubble, and other memories being utilized and developed.

- Besides the primary storage unit, the arithmetic-logic and control units contain small temporary storage areas called registers. Firmware microprograms are frequently stored in ROM modules or other read-only storage areas of the CPU. Firmware and microprogramming increase the versatility of a computer system.

- Input/output interface devices such as input/output control units, buffers, and channels provide a standard interface between the CPU and input/output devices, thus assisting the CPU in its input/output assignments.

KEY TERMS AND CONCEPTS

Computer system	Computer codes
Input devices	Computer data elements: bit, byte, word, page
Central processing unit	
Primary storage unit	Semiconductor storage
Secondary storage devices	Magnetic core memory
Arithmetic-logic unit	Magnetic bubble memory
Control unit	RAM and ROM memories
Output devices	Registers
Executing computer instructions	Read-only storage
	Firmware
Binary representation	Microprogramming
Binary number system	Input/output interface devices

REVIEW AND DISCUSSION QUESTIONS

1. Why is it important to think of a computer as a system?
2. What are the basic components and functions of a computer system?
3. What three major subunits make up the central processing unit of a computer? What are the functions of each of these units?
4. What is the difference in the functions of primary and secondary storage?
5. Do computers have a memory and logic capability? Explain.
6. Explain how a computer executes an instruction.
7. How fast do computers execute instructions?
8. Why do computers utilize binary number systems as the basis for data representation?

9. Explain how data is physically represented in the memory of a computer utilizing the EBCDIC code.

10. Differentiate between the bit, byte, word, and page computer data elements.

11. How much data can a typical computer hold in each position of storage? How can the computer readily locate the data in a specific location?

12. What are the major advantages and disadvantages of semiconductor storage?

13. What are the major types and functions of semiconductor memory?

14. If you were to design a computer, would you use magnetic bubble circuits for primary storage or secondary storage? Why?

15. Explain the functions of the various types of storage areas that exist within the CPU of modern computers.

16. Is firmware like hardware or software? Explain.

17. What is microprogramming? How does it increase the versatility of modern computer systems?

18. What are the functions of input/output interface devices such as input/output control units, buffers, and channels?

REAL WORLD APPLICATIONS

3-1 The Atlantic City Press

Like many other newspapers, The Atlantic City Press, Atlantic City, New Jersey, relies on computers. Dual computer systems support 24 editing terminals for local editors and reporters plus multiple terminals by which remote news correspondents can transmit news stories to the newspaper's main office.

When a story breaks, reporters gather the facts and enter their reports through individual keyboard terminals. Rewrite personnel go to work on the basic story via their own terminals. Last-minute details and additional facts are molded into the story and it begins to take its final form. Copy entered by the rewrite desk is recorded electronically and filed for retrieval on magnetic disk units. Each story file can then be called forth by the managing editor on a video terminal. While the managing editor reviews the story, high-speed line printers furnish printed copies for proofreading and editing; type corrections and changes can be entered through any terminal. Once this process is complete, the story file is automatically justified and hyphenated. Typesetting instructions are specified and the file is sent to production for printing on computer-controlled printing presses.[1]

● What computer system components and functions can you identify in the example above?

Source: *50,000 Computers Saving Managers Millions,* Digital Equipment Corporation.

3–2   Anatomy of a Computer System

The following computer system is a composite of features found in many current medium size computers.

- A central processing unit using advanced LSI semiconductor logic and memory circuits, and a 32-bit word length architecture.
- Microprogrammed control unit with 64 kilobytes of control storage.
- Four megabytes of main memory, with over 4 gigabytes of virtual memory.

- High-speed buffer (cache) storage of 128 kilobytes and sixteen 32-bit general purpose registers.
- Six channels (4 block multiplexer and 2 byte multiplexer channels).
- Machine cycle time = 200 nanoseconds. Memory cycle time = 500 nanoseconds.
- Up to 96 terminals, 16 magnetic disk drives, 4 line printers, 8 magnetic tape drives, and 6 communications lines can be supported.

- Can you identify the functions and explain the capabilities of the computer system components outlined above? Give it a try!

3–3   The Computer Memory Gap

The *primary storage* (main memory) of most modern computers consists of LSI semiconductor RAM (random access memory) circuits. Such semiconductor memory chips are fast, compact, tough, and relatively inexpensive. But their storage capacity is still limited, and they are volatile—their contents are lost if electric power is interrupted. Of course nonvolatile ROM (read only memory) semiconductor circuit modules are available but their use is limited to control unit microprogram storage, or infrequently changed program storage.

The *secondary storage* of most modern computer systems consists of magnetic disk and magnetic tape devices. These electro-mechanical, *moving-surface* memory devices use magnetic disks or tapes as their storage media. They are high-capacity nonvolatile memory devices, which magnetically retain their contents even if electric power is interrupted. But they are quite slow compared to semiconductor memories.

Enter *bubble memory*. Magnetic bubble memory stores and moves data magnetically as tiny magnetic spots—which look like bubbles under a microscope—on the surface of a special type of semiconductor chip. Bubble memory is slower than regular semiconductor memory, but it can be produced using conventional semiconductor manufacturing processes. Bubble memory chips can store much more data than semiconductor memory chips (1 million bits versus 64,000 bits, for example), and they are nonvolatile memory devices. Bubble memory is thus competitive with magnetic disk and tape memories in terms of nonvolatility, storage capacity, and price. It is also much faster and more reliable, since it has no moving parts, uses very little power, and is quite shock and temperature resistant. Thus magnetic bubble memory promises to fill the present computer memory gap.

- What is the computer memory gap?
- Why might magnetic bubble memories fill this gap in modern computer systems?

PART TWO

Computer Hardware, Software, and Systems

4

CHAPTER OUTLINE

Computer Hardware Overview

LEARNING OBJECTIVES

The purpose of this chapter is to promote a basic understanding of computer hardware by analyzing the physical and performance characteristics, functions, benefits, and limitations of major hardware devices.

After reading and studying this chapter, you should be able to:

1. Outline the functions, advantages, and disadvantages of several major hardware devices, indicating whether they perform input, output, or secondary storage functions and the type of media they utilize.
2. Visit the computer center of your school or business and identify and classify the various types of computer hardware being utilized. Also, determine the basic physical and performance characteristics of the major components of your computer system.

Categories of Computer Hardware

Computer hardware consists of the equipment and devices that make up a computer system plus input/output and storage *media* (such as magnetic tapes or disks) which are the tangible materials on which data is recorded. Computer hardware can be subdivided into three major categories:

Central Processing Unit. The CPU consists of the arithmetic-logic unit, the control unit, and the primary storage unit, and other special-purpose devices such as input/output interface devices. We analyzed this hardware category in Chapter 3.

Peripheral Equipment and Media. This hardware category includes all devices that are separate from, but are (or can be) **online,** that is, electronically connected to and controlled by the central processing unit. **Peripherals** include a wide variety of **input/output** (I/O) equipment and **secondary storage devices** which depend on a direct connection or communication link to the CPU.

Auxiliary Equipment and Media. This category includes equipment that is **offline,** that is, equipment that is separate from and *not* under the control of a central processing unit. Auxiliary equipment assists the input, output and storage functions of the computer system, and include: (1) **offline data entry** (input preparation) equipment such as keypunch machines which convert data from *source documents* into input media for later entry into a computer system, (2) **offline output** and **storage** equipment such as copiers and filing devices, and (3) **data processing supplies** such as paper forms which are used in operating a computer system.

OVERVIEW OF PERIPHERAL EQUIPMENT AND MEDIA

This chapter is an overview of the peripheral equipment and media categories of computer hardware. Before continuing any further, it is important to emphasize two major points:

- Many types of computer peripherals and media can be used for both input and output or for all three functions of **input, output,** and **secondary storage.** For example, magnetic disk equipment use magnetic disks as a data medium and perform all three functions of input, output, and secondary storage.
- Some peripheral equipment do not need to use *data media* for input or output. For example, many computer terminals consist of a keyboard to enter data directly into the computer

system and a CRT video screen to directly display visual output. Since such peripherals do not use data media, they are called *direct input/output* devices.

An overview of the major types of computer peripherals and media used today is shown in Figure 4–1. Major charac-

FIGURE 4–1   Overview of Computer Peripherals and Media

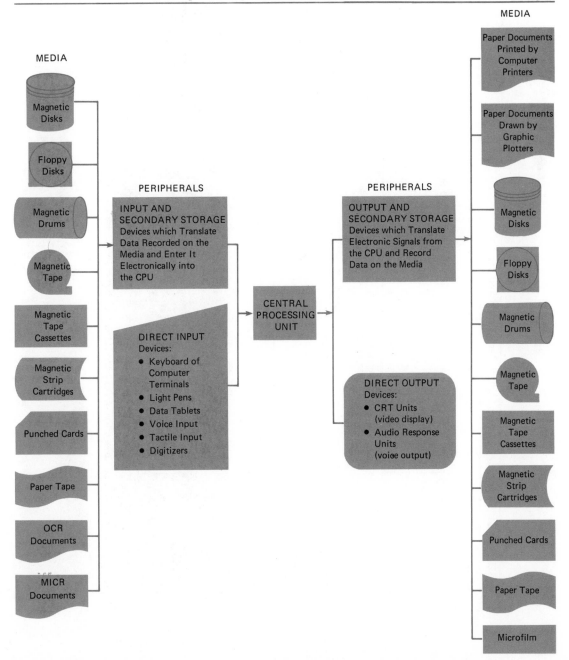

FIGURE 4–2 Overview of Input/Output Peripherals and Media

Peripheral Equipment	Media	Primary Functions	Typical I/O Speed Range*	Typical Storage Capacity	Major Advantages and/or Disadvantages
CRT terminal (VDT)	No tangible media	Keyboard input and video output	250–50,000 cps output	—	Convenient and inexpensive, but limited display capacity and no hard copy
Line and page printers	Paper	Printed output of paper reports and documents	200–3,000 lpm 20,000–60,000 lpm	—	Fast hard copy, but inconvenient and bulky
Character printer	Paper output	Printed paper output	10–400 cps	—	Low cost hard copy, but low speed
Card reader/punch	Punched cards	Input and output	Input: 150–2,700 cpm Output: 80–650 cpm	80 or 96 characters per card	Low cost, but slow speed and bulky media
Paper tape reader/punch	Paper tape	Input/output	Input: 50–2,000 cps Output: 10–300 cps	10 characters per inch	Simple and inexpensive, but fragile and bulky
Magnetic ink character reader (MICR)	MICR paper documents	Direct input of MICR documents	700–3,200 cps 180–2,000 dpm	—	Fast, high reliability reading, but documents must be preprinted and the character set is limited
Optical character reader (OCR)	Paper documents	Direct input from written or printed documents	100–3,600 cps 180–1,800 dpm	—	Direct input from paper documents, but limitations on input format

* Cps = characters per second; cpm = characters per minute; dpm = documents per minute; lpm = lines per minute.

teristics, functions, advantages and disadvantages, input/output speed, and storage capacity for *input/output* hardware are summarized in Figure 4–2. A summary of *secondary storage* hardware is shown in Figure 4–18, later in this chapter. These figures should be studied to give you a basic overview of the types of peripherals and media used by modern computer systems. A brief but more detailed description of these hardware devices is presented in this chapter.

SECTION I: INPUT/OUTPUT HARDWARE

Computer Terminals

Computer terminals of various types are the most widely used form of input/output hardware. Any input/output device that can use communications channels to transmit or receive data is a *terminal.* All such devices must be modified to include or be attached to special data communications interface hardware (discussed in Chapter 10) in order to have data communications capabilities. It should be emphasized that most terminals use a *keyboard* for direct entry of data into a computer system without the use of input media. The major categories of computer terminals are summarized below.

- **Visual Display Terminals.** Terminals which use a keyboard for input and a TV-screen for visual output are called *visual display terminals* (VDT), or more popularly, CRT (cathode ray tube) terminals. They allow the display of alphanumeric data and graphic images. They are the most widely used type of computer terminal.

- **Printing Terminals.** These typewriter-like terminals have a keyboard for data input and a printing element for output. They print one character at a time and are slower than visual display terminals or high-speed computer printers and so are usually connected to low-speed communication lines.

- **Intelligent Terminals.** *Smart* terminals have built-in microprocessors so that they can perform their own error checking and input/output communications control functions. *Intelligent terminals* are really microcomputers or minicomputers with input/output and data communications capabilities which can also act as *stand-alone* computers and independently perform some data processing tasks.

- **Data Entry Terminals.** These terminals typically use a keyboard for entry of data and a CRT screen so that data can be displayed and corrected before it is recorded on magnetic disks or tapes or entered into a computer system. These terminals differ from *transaction terminals* (see below) in that they may not be online to the main computer system and are typically used to convert data taken from source documents into computer-readable media (such as floppy disks) for later entry into a computer system. They are primarily used for data entry in *batch processing systems* where transaction data from source documents are grouped into *batches* before being processed by the computer.

- **Transaction Terminals.** These terminals are widely used in banks, retail stores, factories, and other work sites. They are used to capture *transaction data* at its point-of-origin. They typically use a keyboard for data entry and either a printer or video display unit for output, as well as a variety of other input/output methods and media. Thus, many transaction recorders might include a slot into which badges, plastic cards, inventory tags, or prepunched cards can be inserted for data input. Some terminals may use an OCR (optical character recognition) *wand* to directly enter printed data into a computer system.

FIGURE 4–3 Video Display Terminal

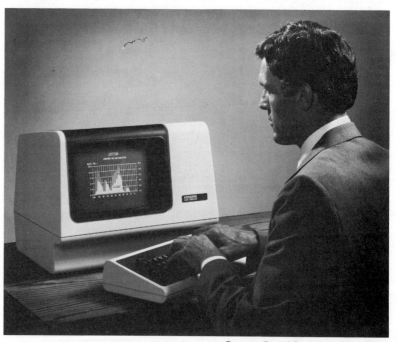

Courtesy Digital Equipment Corporation.

Examples. A transaction terminal in a factory could use an employee's plastic badge, prepunched cards and a keyboard to enter data directly into a manufacturing control system. Similarly, online *teller terminals* are used by banks and other savings institutions to update directly customer's savings account balances stored in the bank's computer system. *Point-of-sale* (POS) terminals connected online to a computer serve as electronic cash registers and allow instant credit verification and immediate capture of sales transaction data for entry into the computer system. Figures 4–3, 4–4, and 4–5 illustrate several types of terminals.

Visual Input/Output Hardware

Visual Display Devices. As we have just indicated, these devices typically use a cathode ray tube (CRT) similar to a television tube for the display of output, while a keyboard is used for most input. Thus keyed-in data can be displayed and corrected before entry into a computer system. Output is quickly and silently flashed onto the screen whenever requested.

Display Features. Most CRT units display a point-of-light called a *cursor* to assist the user in the input of data. The cursor may look like a *dot* or short *underline* or other shape that indicates the position of data to be entered or changed. Many other display features that an operator can control are available in more advanced (and more expensive) CRT units. These features include blinking cursors and characters, underlining displayed material, reversed video, split screen, scrolling, and of course multiple color displays.

- *Reverse video* is a feature which highlights areas of the screen where data is to be entered by having light characters on a dark background or dark characters on a light background. Usually the entire screen or just highlighted sections can be reversed in order to highlight specific information or to *format* the screen to assist operators in entering data.
- *Scrolling* allows the operator to move lines of displayed information either up or down the screen.
- *Split screen* or *split window* divides the screen into several sections or windows and allows different material to be shown in each section. See Figure 4–6.
- *Color* is a feature that adds multiple colors (like color TV) to CRT displays. Color displays are supposed to provide

FIGURE 4–4   A Printing Terminal

Courtesy Hewlett-Packard Co.

FIGURE 4–5   Point-of-Sale Terminal with OCR Wand

Courtesy NCR Corporation.

FIGURE 4–6 Split-Screen
Video Display

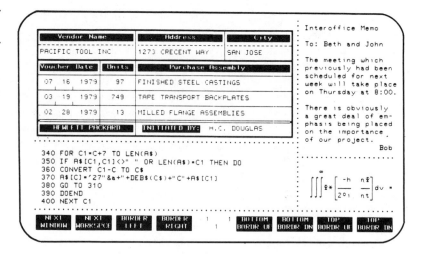

a more normal and natural people-computer interface. This should make using a video terminal a more attractive and comfortable experience and should result in fewer errors and more productivity. Color is a very effective way of categorizing displayed information. Color helps draw attention more easily to selected items and can be used to link related items in the display. Thus, if the terminal operator changes a data item that affects other data items in a display, the affected data items can be programmed to change color alerting the operator to the relationships that exist.

Data Entry Function. The display features mentioned above have made CRT terminals widely used *data entry* devices. Keyed-in data can be displayed and visually edited and corrected before input into the computer system. The terminal can be programmed to project a *formatted* screen which displays a document or report *format* on the CRT. An operator can then *fill out* this electronic form by using the keyboard to *fill in the blanks,* guided by the cursor. When both the computer and user agree the form is properly filled out, the data is entered into the computer system. See Figure 4–7.

Visual/Graphic Input. Advanced CRT terminals can accept *visual and graphic input* through the use of a variety of devices. They allow graphic or alphanumeric data to be entered directly into the computer system (and later changed or deleted) by "writing" directly on the CRT screen or the surface of other devices. Visual or graphic input has been used for many years in military applications, engineering and architec-

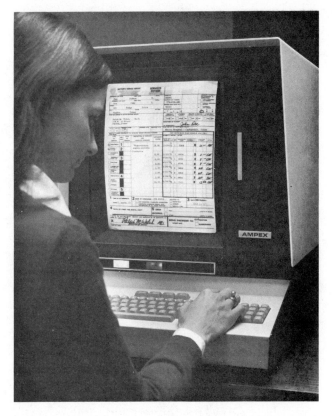

FIGURE 4–7   A Formatted Screen Assists Data Entry

tural design, scientific research, cartography (map making and analysis), and is now being used in many business applications.

- The **light pen** is a pen-shaped device which uses photoelectric circuitry to enter data into the computer through the CRT screen. A user can *write* on the CRT display because the light-sensitive pen enables the computer to calculate the coordinates of the points on the screen being touched by the light pen, even though the CRT screen may contain over one million points of light. See Figure 4–8.
- **Digitizers** of several types are used to convert drawings and other graphic images on paper or other materials into digital data and enter it into a computer system. Digital data can then be displayed on a CRT screen and processed by the computer system. One form of digitizer is the **graphics tablet** which has sensing devices embedded in a special tablet on which material to be digitized must be placed. A **graphics pen** (also called an electronic stylus) is pressed on the material placed on the graphics tablet to draw or

FIGURE 4–8   Using a Light Pen

Courtesy IBM Corporation.

trace figures which appear simultaneously on the CRT screen. A small hand-held device called a **cursor** with a small round viewing window with cross hairs etched on the glass, can be passed over the surface of a drawing or graphic image and convert it to digital data. Some graphic pens are *sonic digitizers* which use sonic impulses (sound waves) to digitize drawings laid on a graphics tablet. See Figure 4–9.

- **Touch-sensitive panels** are *tactile input* devices which allow operators to enter data into a computer system by touching the surface of a sensitized video display screen with a finger or pointer.

    Other Visual/Graphic Output.   Besides CRT terminals, other types of hardware are used to provide or support visual display of output.

- **Hard copy graphics devices** reproduce graphic computer displays on paper or other materials. This requires equipment such as printers, plotters, copying machines, or photographic devices. **Plotters** produce graphic displays using a pen-and-ink process, electrical inscribing, or electrostatic nonimpact techniques. The mechanical arm of the plotter includes a pen, and draws lines on the paper as directed by the computer. See Figure 4–10.

FIGURE 4–9 Using a Graphics Tablet and Pen As Digitizers

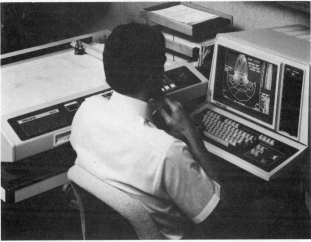

FIGURE 4–10 Using a Plotter and Graphics Terminal for Computer-aided Design

Courtesy Tektronix.

- **Liquid crystal displays** (LCDs), such as those used in electronic calculators and watches are also being used to display computer output in a limited number of applications, including small "pocket" computers and terminals.
- **Plasma display** devices are replacing CRT devices in providing visual displays in a limited number of applications. Plasma displays are generated by electrically charged particles of gas *(plasma)* trapped between glass plates. Plasma

display units are still quite expensive and not fully developed. However, they are being used in a limited number of applications where a compact, flat visual display is a critical factor.

Advantages and Disadvantages. Visual display units are much faster and quieter than printing devices and do not flood users with rivers of paper. A specific piece of information or an entire page of data can be displayed instantly in either alphanumeric or graphic form. The ability to correct or edit input data displayed by a CRT before entry into a computer system is a major benefit. The light pen and other digitizers provide a valuable method of visual/graphic input, while plotters produce hard copy drawings.

Visual input/output units are major advances in people-computer communication, but they do have several limitations. Special hardware circuits or software is needed to *refresh* the image of most CRT units or the data being displayed will fade away. Additional equipment is required to produce the hard copy that visual display units do not provide. In addition, there has been some controversy concerning the possible harmful effects of radiation generated by CRT units. Recent studies have shown that such radiation is minimal and not harmful, but research is continuing to investigate these and other complaints concerning the long-term use of visual display devices.

Computer Graphics

The use of *graphic displays* is part of the fast growing area of *computer graphics*. Most people find it difficult to quickly and accurately comprehend numerical or statistical data that is presented in a purely numerical form (such as rows or columns of figures). That is why charts and graphs are typically used in technical reports and business meetings. This graphics capability is now being offered in **graphics terminals** using CRT displays as well as *graphics plotters* and *graphics printers* which draw graphs on paper and other materials. Most computer systems now offer some degree of graphics capability including some of the less expensive microcomputer systems. However, advanced graphics features require additional hardware capabilities and special graphics software packages. Thus, advanced graphics terminals use special microprocessor chips called *display processors* and additional *buffer* memory. However, the rapid decrease in the cost of microprocessor and memory chips have moved computer graphics capabilities from large expensive computer systems down to the range of small, low-priced systems.

Computer graphics has been used for many years for complex engineering design applications called *computer-aided design* (CAD) used in the aircraft, automobile, machine tool, electronics, and other industries. Advanced graphics terminals and graphics programs allow operators to transform numeric data into graphic displays. Numeric data can be entered through the use of the terminal keyboard or retrieved from the memory of the computer system. Numeric data can be transformed into bar charts, pi charts, line graphs, three-dimensional graphs, or the multitude of drawings found in engineering design, architecture, and even *computer art!* Advanced graphics allows the operator to *zoom* in and out, to *pan* (turn) the drawing up or down, right or left in order to better analyze and modify the graphic display. This can be done with buttons on the terminal keyboard or by the use of a graphics control lever or *joystick.*

Computer graphics continues to assist engineers in designing complex structures, researchers in analyzing volumes of data, and process control technicians in monitoring industrial processes. However, its use to help managers analyze business operations and make better decisions is now being empha-

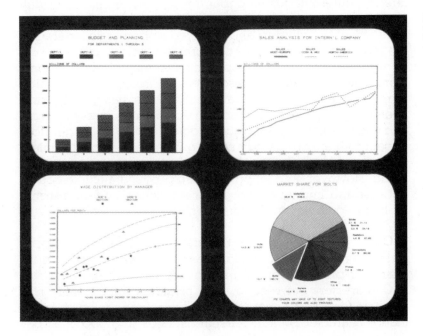

FIGURE 4–11   Business Graphic Displays

sized. Instead of being overwhelmed by vast amounts of computer-produced data, graphics displays assist managers in analyzing and interpreting data. Trends, problems, or opportunities hidden in data are easier to spot. For example, computer graphics would make it easier for a marketing manager to see complex market trends and analyze market problems and opportunities such as product line, sales outlet, and salesperson performance. Also, graphics displays can be done on an *interactive* basis and thus provide immediate *decision support* to management. These capabilities and developments indicate that computer graphics will be a management tool of growing importance in the years to come. See Figure 4–11.

Printing Devices

Most computer systems use printing devices to produce permanent (hard copy) output in human-readable form. Printers are used to produce printed reports and documents such as sales invoices, payroll checks, bank statements, and forms of all kinds. Printers can be classified as impact or nonimpact printers, character, line or page printers, and slow-speed and high-speed printers.

Impact and Nonimpact Printers. **Impact printers** form characters and other images on paper through the impact of a printing mechanism which presses a printing element (such as a print wheel or cylinder) and an inked ribbon or roller against the face of a continuous paper form. Multiple copies are produced by using carbon copy or other multiple copy forms. **Nonimpact printers** may use specially treated paper which forms characters by thermal (heat), electrostatic, or electrochemical processes. Other nonimpact printers use plain paper and inkjet or xerographic technologies to form an image. Nonimpact printers are usually much quieter than impact printers since the sound of a printing element being struck is eliminated. However, impact printers can produce multiple copies because the impact of the printing mechanism can transmit an image onto several layers of multiple copy forms.

Character, Line, and Page Printers. **Character printers** print serially (one character at a time) as typewriters do. Thus, most character printers print at the slow speed of between 15 to 150 characters per second. **Line printers** print an entire line at a time (up to 132 characters) and therefore are much faster than a character printer, reaching speeds of 3,000 lines per minute. **Page printers** print an entire page at a time and reach speeds exceeding 60,000 lines per minute.

Slow-Speed and High-Speed Printers. **Slow speed printers** are typically used in microcomputer and minicomputer systems and as slow speed printing terminals. They cost much less than high-speed printers and yet are fast enough for most small computer applications. Speeds of such printers range from 15 to 150 characters per second for character printers and up to 300 lines per minute for line printers. Slow-speed printers are usually character impact printers which use a rotating ball or wheel *(daisy wheel),* or a *dot matrix* printing element. The ball and wheel printing elements rotate to print a solid character. A dot matrix printing element consists of short *print wires* which are struck by a hammer to form a character as a series (or *matrix*) of dots. Solid character printing is usually of higher quality than dot matrix printing, but dot matrix printing is considered more reliable and versatile than solid type printing.

Other slow-speed printers include **ink-jet printers** which spray tiny ink particles from fast-moving nozzles against paper. Electrostatic charges placed on the paper attract the ink which forms characters of high-print quality. Ink-jet printers can print at speeds near 200 characters per second but are quite expensive. **Thermal printers** are nonimpact character printers which print a character on heat-sensitive paper by using heated wires to produce a dot-character similar to the dot matrix printing element.

High-speed printers can print at fantastic rates of speed. Line impact printers can print up to 3,000 lines per minute using a moving metal chain or cylinder of characters as the printing element. Costs for such printers depend on speed and print quality but can range from $3,000 to over $100,000. Nonimpact xerographic page printers use Xerox copier technology and microprocessor intelligence to print up to 4,000 lines per minute on plain paper. IBM, Xerox, and several other companies have developed high-speed **laser printers** which can print over 60,000 lines per minute. These page printers use laser beam technology and require a built-in minicomputer to control the printing process. Costs for such printers range from $150,000 to $300,000. See Figures 4–12 and 4–13.

Input Preparation Function. Computer output peripherals such as printers can also perform an *input preparation* func-

FIGURE 4–12   Using a Dot Matrix Character Printer to Produce Hardcopy of a Graphics Display

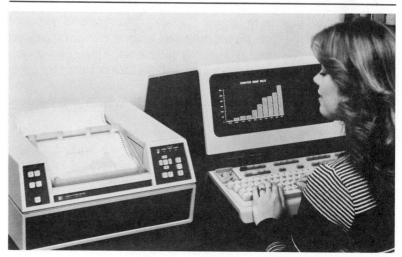

Courtesy Hewlett-Packard Co.

tion. High-speed printers can produce output in the form of documents printed in OCR or MICR characters. Forms produced in this manner are known as *turnaround documents* since they are designed to be returned to the sender. For example, many computer-printed invoices consist of a turnaround portion which is returned by a customer along with his or her payment. The turnaround document can then be automatically processed by OCR or MICR readers. Thus, the high-speed printer has performed an input preparation function.

FIGURE 4–13   A High-Speed Laser Page Printer

Courtesy Hewlett-Packard Co.

Advantages and Disadvantages.   Printing devices provide a computer system with the ability to produce printed reports and forms of all kinds. Printing of excellent quality can be done at high speeds. However, the speed factor is the cause of two contradictory problems. Computers can now produce printed reports so quickly that managers can be "buried" in mountains of paper. The ability of managers to use the information in computer-printed reports to assist their decision making is diminished by the rapid flow of volumes of paper. On the other hand, high-speed printers are not fast enough output devices for most computer systems, thus causing an "output-bound" condition. The data transfer rate of high-speed printers is over 4,000 characters per second, which is quite slow compared to over 300,000 characters per second for magnetic tape output. This problem is being solved by the use of visual display terminals, offline magnetic tape to printer operations, and microfilm output devices.

Punched Card Hardware

Card Readers and Punch Units. Punched card hardware was widely used in electronic data processing because of the prior use of the punched card in electromechanical data processing systems. Punched card peripheral equipment for computer systems includes *card readers* and *card punch units*. These units use photoelectric cells to sense the holes in the punched cards and convert the data into electric pulses which are then converted into the internal code of the computer. Cards are read by two different reading stations in card reader units as a check on the accuracy of the operation. Card punch machines punch output data into cards under the control of the computer, and include a reading station to check on the accuracy of the punching process. The *card read-punch* combines the functions of reading and punching into a single unit. See Figure 4–14. The reading speed of card reading devices varies from 160 to 2,700 cards per minute, while card punching speed varies from 80 to 650 cards per minute.

FIGURE 4–14   Card Read-Punch Unit

Courtesy IBM Corporation.

The Punched Card. The punched card used in many computer card readers and punches is the 80-column punched card also known as the "Hollerith" card. Up to 80 individual data elements such as alphabetic, numeric, and special characters can be punched into such a card, using the *Hollerith code* shown in Figure 4–15. Notice that numeric characters require the punching of only a single hole, while alphabetic and special characters require the punching of two or three holes in a column. Also widely used is a 96-column punched card. See Figure 4–16. Data is punched as round holes in

---

FIGURE 4–15 Punched Card Coding: 80-Column Card

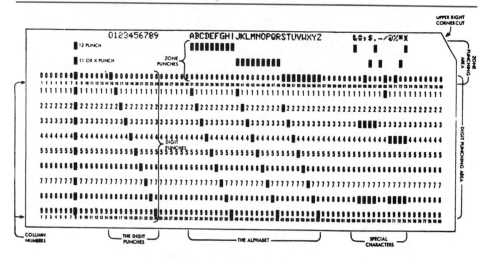

FIGURE 4–16 Punched Card Coding: 96-Column Card

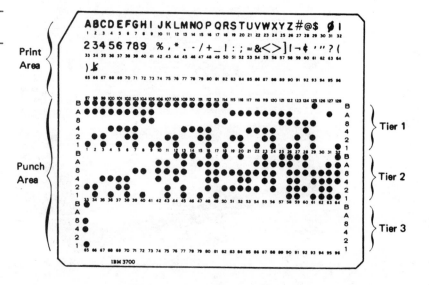

three sections of this smaller card, with each section containing 32 characters. This card uses the EBCDIC computer code.

Punched Card Data Entry Equipment.   The *keypunch* machine records data in punched cards by punching holes in the cards through the use of a keyboard similar to that of a typewriter. Accuracy of the punching process is checked by a *verifier* which is similar in appearance to the keypunch. Instead of punching holes it electrically senses whether a discrepancy exists between the keys being depressed and the holes punched in the card during the keypunching operation. If a discrepancy exists, a hole is punched in the top of the card above the incorrectly punched column. Machines called "card data recorders" are available which perform both the punching and verifying functions. See Figure 4–17.

Advantages and Disadvantages.   Punched cards are a familiar, inexpensive, and simple input/output and secondary storage medium. Data in a file of cards can easily be changed by adding, deleting, or repunching a card. Punch card output

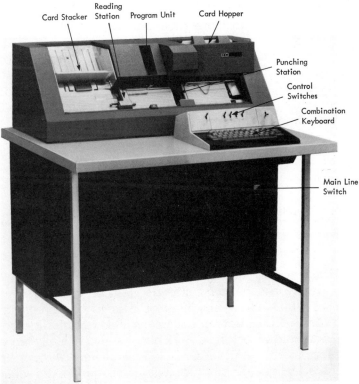

Card Stacker   Reading Station   Program Unit   Card Hopper

Punching Station

Control Switches

Combination Keyboard

Main Line Switch

FIGURE 4–17   Keypunch Machine

Courtesy IBM Corporation.

can be in the form of a human-readable document which can later be used as input to an electronic data processing system. Punched card paychecks and utility bills are familiar examples. However, cards are bulky, can hold only a limited amount of data, and provide a very slow method of computer input/output compared to magnetic media. For instance, an inch of high-density magnetic tape can hold as many characters of data as 80 punched cards, and magnetic tape input speeds range up to 350,000 characters per second compared to a maximum of about 2,500 characters per second with punched cards. Another major limitation of punched cards is the keypunching, verifying, and other *input preparation* activities that are required before data can be entered into the computer system. Thus the use of punched cards is declining.

SECTION II: SECONDARY STORAGE HARDWARE

Secondary storage hardware consists of media and devices which are used to store data and programs in support of the primary storage unit of the computer system. Thus secondary storage (also called *auxiliary storage*) hardware greatly enlarges the storage capacity of the computer system. However, as we have noted earlier, the contents of secondary storage devices cannot be processed without first being brought into the main memory of the CPU. Figure 4–18 summarizes the functions, speed, storage capacities, advantages, and disadvantages of secondary storage peripherals and media.

Direct versus Sequential Access

Secondary storage hardware consists of two basic types: *direct access devices* and *sequential access devices.*

● **Direct access storage devices** (DASDs) is the term used to describe secondary storage devices such as *magnetic disks* which allow any item of data to be *directly* stored or retrieved. **Direct access** means that each storage position has a unique address and can be individually accessed in approximately the same length of time without having to search through other storage positions. The direct access process is similar to directly selecting a specific song on a

FIGURE 4-18 Overview of Characteristics: Secondary Storage Peripherals and Media

Peripheral Equipment	Media	Primary Functions	Typical I/O Speed Range*	Typical Storage Capacity	Major Advantages And/or Disadvantages
Magnetic disk drive	Magnetic disk	Secondary storage (direct access) and input/output	Data transfer: 100,000–3,000,000 bps Access time: 15–200 ms	Over 300 million characters per disk pack and a billion characters per drive	Large capacity, fast direct access storage device (DASD), but expensive
Floppy disk drive	Magnetic diskette	Input/output (direct access) and secondary storage	10,000–20,000 cps	250,000 to 2,500,000 characters/disk	Small, inexpensive, and convenient, but slower and smaller capacity than other DASDs
Magnetic tape drive	Magnetic tape	Secondary storage (sequential access) and input/output	15,000–750,000 bps	Up to 180 million characters per tape reel	Inexpensive with a fast transfer rate, but only sequential access
Magnetic tape cassette deck	Magnetic tape cassette	Secondary storage (sequential access) and input/output	3,000–5,000 cps	1–2 million characters/ unit	Small, inexpensive and convenient, but only sequential access
Magnetic strip storage unit	Magnetic strip cartridge	Mass secondary storage (direct/sequential access)	Data transfer: 25,000–55,000 cps Access time: up to several seconds	Up to 500 billion bytes per unit	Relatively inexpensive, large capacity, but slow access time
Magnetic drum unit	Magnetic drum	Secondary storage (direct access) and input/output	Data transfer: 230,000–1,500,000 bps Access time: 10–100 ms	Up to 200 million characters	Fast access time and large capacity, but expensive

* Cps = Characters per second; bps = bytes per second; ms = microseconds.

FIGURE 4–19 Sequential versus Random Access Storage

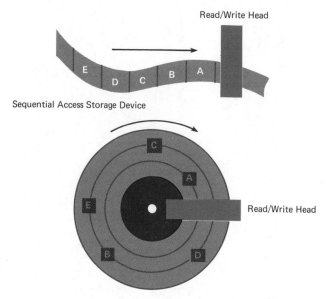

Read/Write Head

Sequential Access Storage Device

Read/Write Head

Direct Access Storage Device

phonograph record. Direct access is also called **random access,** which is the same storage capability possessed by *primary storage media* such as semiconductor *random access memory* (RAM).

● **Sequential access storage devices** use secondary storage media such as *magnetic tape* whose storage locations do not have unique addresses and cannot be directly addressed. Instead, data must be stored and retrieved using a *sequential* or *serial* process. Thus data is recorded one after another in a predetermined sequence (such as a numerical or alphabetical order) on a storage medium such as magnetic tape. Locating an individual item of data requires starting at the beginning of a tape and searching all of the recorded data until the desired item is located. This is similar to having to "fast forward" or rewind a home tape recorder to hear a specific song or conversation. See Figure 4–19.

Magnetic Disk Hardware

Magnetic disk media and equipment are now the most common form of secondary storage for modern computer systems. They provide a direct access capability and high storage capacities at a reasonable cost. The two basic types of magnetic disk media are conventional *(hard)* metal disks and flexible *(floppy)* disks. Several types of magnetic disk peripheral equipment are used as direct access storage devices (DASDs) in both small and large computer systems.

Characteristics of Magnetic Disks. Magnetic disks are thin metal disks which resemble phonograph records and are coated on both sides with an iron oxide recording material. Several disks are mounted together on a vertical shaft which typically rotates the disks at speeds of 2,400 or 3,600 revolutions per minute (rpm). Electro-magnetic *read-write heads* are positioned by access arms between the slightly separated disks to read or write data on concentric circular *tracks*. Data is recorded on tracks in the form of tiny magnetized spots to form binary digits arranged in serial order in a code such as EBCDIC. Thousands of bytes can be recorded on each track, and there are several hundred data tracks on each disk surface. Each track contains the same number of bytes because data is packed together more closely on the small inner tracks than on the large outer tracks.

Figure 4–20 illustrates some of the physical storage characteristics of magnetic disks. In this illustration there are 11 disks

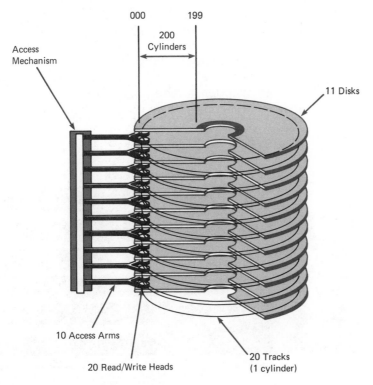

FIGURE 4–20   Illustration of a Magnetic Disk

which provide 20 recording surfaces since the unprotected top surface of the top disk and bottom surface of the bottom disk are not used to record data. An access mechanism with 20 read-write heads is shown, providing one head for each recording surface. This illustration shows a **moving-head** access mechanism which moves in and out between the disks in order to position the read/write heads over the desired track. Other types of magnetic disk units may use **fixed-head** (or *head-per-track*) access mechanisms which do not move because they provide a read/write head for each track of each disk.

Figure 4–20 also illustrates the concept of a *cylinder,* which is one of the basic methods of organizing data on magnetic disks. In this illustration, each cylinder is composed of the 20 circular tracks that are on the same verticle line, one above the other, on each of the 20 recording surfaces. Figure 4–21 illustrates a moving-head access mechanism which is attached to access arms that move all the heads together between the disks and position each over the 20 tracks that make up one cylinder. Thus a cylinder is sometimes defined as the collection of tracks that can be read when the read/write heads are stationed in a position between the disks. In Figure 4–20, each disk surface contains 200 tracks, which means that the disk units shown can store data in 200 cylinders.

When the cylinder method of organization is used, the location of an individual data record is determined by an address consisting of the cylinder number, the recording surface number, and an individual data record number. In another popular

FIGURE 4–21 Read/Write Access Arms of a Magnetic Disk Unit

method (called *fixed block architecture*) each track is divided into a fixed number of blocks or sectors. (In many current systems, a fixed block contains 512 bytes.) In this method, every block in the entire disk unit is given an individual number and data is found by using this number as the storage location address of data.

Types of Magnetic Disks. There are several types of magnetic disk arrangements including removable disk packs and modules as well as fixed disk units. The removable disk devices are the most popular because they can be used interchangeably in *magnetic disk units* and stored *offline* when not in use.

- **Disk packs** are easy to handle; one popular type contains eleven disks, each 14 inches in diameter, is about 6 inches high, weighs about 20 pounds and can store over 300 million characters. See Figure 4–22.

Courtesy Burroughs Corporation.

FIGURE 4–22 Magnetic Disk Pack in Container

- Magnetic **disk modules** (also called *Winchester* disk modules) combine magnetic disks, access arms, and read-write heads into a sealed module or cartridge. This design (called *Winchester* technology) reduces exposure to airborne contaminants such as smoke or dust and significantly increases speed, capacity, and reliability compared to regular *open* disk packs. One typical disk module contains four magnetic disks, each 8 inches in diameter and can store over 70 million bytes. See Figure 4–23.

- Some magnetic disk units use **fixed disk,** nonremovable magnetic disk assemblies. This allows higher speeds, greater data-recording densities, and closer tolerances

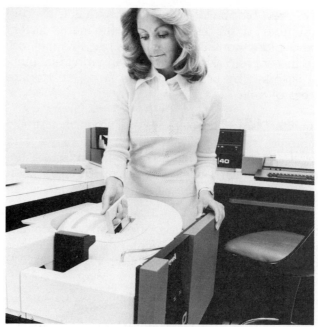

Courtesy Honeywell Information Systems.

within a sealed, more stable environment. Fixed disks typically use a fixed-head access mechanism (one read-write
head per track) and thus have great speed as well as high
storage capacity and reliability. One typical fixed disk unit
contains six 8-inch disks and has a storage capacity of more
than 500 megabytes.

Sealed disk modules and fixed disk drives have grown in
popularity because their control of the disk environment results
in a faster, more reliable operation and more compact, high-
density storage capacity, as well as very low read/write head
"flying heights." The read/write heads in magnetic disk devices "float" or "fly" on a cushion of air and do not touch
the surface of the disk. The clearance between the read/write
head and the disk surface is usually less than 50 microinches
(millionths of an inch). Thus all magnetic disk units have air
filtration systems to remove airborne particles such as smoke
or dust. Such particles could cause the read/write head to
come in contact with the disk (called a *head crash*) which
usually results in the loss of data on that portion of the disk.
This explains the increased use of both fixed and removable
Winchester-type disks, since they are sealed and filtered to
eliminate all particles greater than 17 microinches. Thus the

read/write head of many Winchester-type disk devices flies less than 20 microinches above the disk surface which improves the quality and density of its data recording capability. Figure 4–24 illustrates the size of airborne particles compared to the flying height of conventional magnetic disk devices.

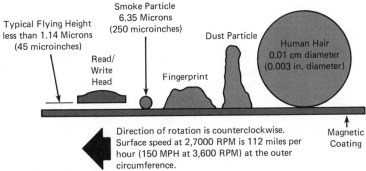

FIGURE 4–24   Comparative Size of Magnetic Disk Contaminants

Source: Adapted from Ronald Rosenberg, "Hard Disk Drives," *Mini-Micro Systems*, February 1979, p. 47.

Capabilities of Magnetic Disks. The speed of magnetic disk units is expressed by their *average access time* and *data transfer rate.* The average access time refers to the time it takes a read/write head to access a specific data location on a magnetic disk. The average access time of moving-head disks includes both the time required to move the read/write head into position over the track where the data is stored *(seek time),* and the time it takes the disk to rotate until the desired data is under the read/write head *(rotational delay).* Of course, since fixed-head disks provide a read/write head for every track on the disk, seek time is eliminated, so the average access time equals the rotational delay time. Average access times for moving-head disks range from about 30 to 60 milliseconds and from 15 to 30 milliseconds for fixed-head disk units. The data transfer rate of magnetic disk units refers to the speed by which data can be transferred between the disk unit and the CPU. Data transfer rates vary from 100,000 to over 3 million bytes per second (bps).

Storage capacity of *magnetic disk units* varies depending on the type, number, and arrangement of magnetic disks in a unit. Magnetic disk units may contain one or more *disk drives,* each of which accommodates one removable disk pack or module, or contain a permanent grouping of fixed disks. The storage capacity of individual disk packs, modules or

FIGURE 4–25 Large Magnetic
Disk Unit with Multiple Disk
Drives

Courtesy IBM Corporation.

fixed disk drives range from several million bytes to over 500 megabytes, while large magnetic disk units containing multiple disk drives can store several billion bytes (gigabytes). Recent development of read-write heads using microelectronic semiconductor technology has significantly increased magnetic disk storage capacity and performance. See Figure 4–25.

Floppy Disks. The magnetic *diskette,* or *floppy disk,* is a small, flexible magnetic disk that resembles a small phonograph record. It consists of a polyester film covered with an iron oxide compound. A single disk is mounted and rotates freely inside a protective jacket which has access openings to accommodate the read/write head of a floppy disk drive unit. Conventional floppy disks have an eight-inch diameter and have storage capacities of over 1 million bytes on disks which only record data on one side, and over 2.5 million bytes for double-density diskettes. *Mini-floppy* disks have a 5-inch diameter and provide over 250,000 bytes of storage. Average access times for floppy disks is about 100 milliseconds. Floppy disks have become a popular secondary storage and input/output medium for microcomputer and minicomputer systems. They provide an economical and convenient form of direct access storage with greater storage capacities than most magnetic tape cassettes and cartridges. They are also removable and interchangeable with other diskettes and can be conveniently stored offline when not being used. See Figure 4–26.

FIGURE 4–26 Floppy Disk
Data Entry Unit with Dual Disk
Drives

Courtesy Mohawk Data Sciences.

Magnetic Disk Data Entry. Magnetic disk and floppy disk systems can be used for the *data entry* function in which data from source documents (such as sales invoices) is recorded on the magnetic disk media. Large **key-to-disk** systems use many keyboard/CRT terminals which input data simultaneously to a central magnetic disk unit. These systems are usually offline from a large computer system but are connected to a minicomputer for control and support. Key-to-disk systems are expensive and can only be justified for applications with large volumes of data from many sources, in which immediate processing of data is not required. The major advantage of these systems over key-to-tape methods is that they do not require the merging and sorting of magnetic tapes that is characteristic of key-to-tape systems.

Floppy disks are also used for data entry by microcomputer, minicomputer, and small business systems. Data is typically entered via a keyboard, visually verified by display on a CRT and recorded on a diskette. Floppy disks provide an inexpensive data entry medium for such small computer systems.

Advantages and Disadvantages. The major attraction of magnetic disks is that they are superb direct access secondary storage devices. They are thus superior to magnetic tape for many current applications which require the immediate access capabilities of direct access files. Removable disk devices provide large storage capacities at a relatively low cost, and can be easily stored offline. One of the limitations of hard magnetic disks is their higher cost compared to magnetic tape. Thus a large magnetic disk pack or Winchester module may cost over $1,000 while a large capacity magnetic tape may cost less than $100. Of course, this limitation does not apply to floppy disks which cost only a few dollars. Magnetic disks may also be slower and less expensive than magnetic tape for applications where large sequential access files are used.

Magnetic Tape Hardware

Magnetic Tape. Magnetic tape is a widely used input/output and secondary storage medium. Data is recorded in the form of magnetized spots on the iron oxide coating of a plastic tape somewhat similar to that used in home tape recorders. Magnetic tape is usually subdivided into nine horizontal tracks or channels in order to accommodate a check bit and the eight-bit EBCDIC Code. Blank spaces known as "gaps" are used to separate individual data records or blocks of grouped records. Most magnetic tapes are ½ inch wide and 2,400 feet long and are wound on plastic reels 10½ inches in diameter. The density of the data that can be recorded on such tape is frequently either 1,600 or 6,250 bytes per inch. Thus, a reel of magnetic tape could contain over 180 million bytes, which is the equivalent of over 2 million punched cards. See Figure 4–27.

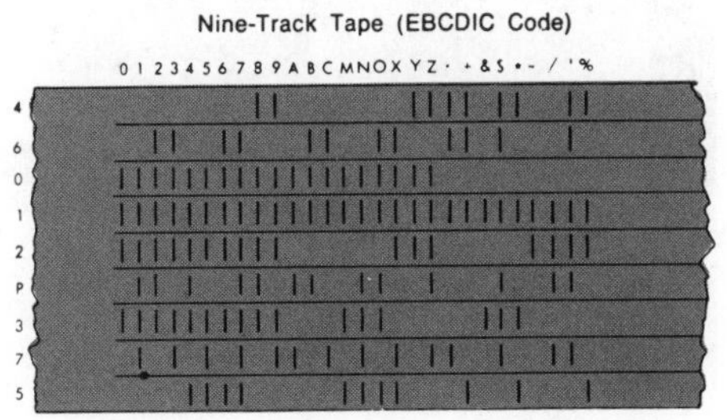

Nine-Track Tape (EBCDIC Code)

FIGURE 4–27   Magnetic Tape Data Storage

Magnetic Tape Cartridges and Cassettes. Magnetic tape also comes in the form of small *cartridges* and *cassettes* which are produced by magnetic tape typewriters and other devices that record data directly from a keyboard to magnetic tape. The small cartridge has a capacity equivalent to about 275 punched cards, while cassettes can store up to 2 million characters. Magnetic tape cassette decks are being used as low-cost input/output units for minicomputer and microcomputer systems and "intelligent" terminals.

Magnetic Tape Peripherals. Devices that can read and write data on magnetic tapes are called *magnetic tape drives*. Electromagnet read-write heads record data on each channel in the form of magnetic spots on the tape during writing operations. The read-write heads are also used in the reading operation to sense the magnetized spots on the tape and convert them into electronic impulses that are transmitted to the CPU. Reading and writing speeds range from 15,000 to 180,000 bytes per second using standard magnetic tape and up to 750,000 bytes per second for high-density tape. Small magnetic tape *cartridge readers* can read data at the rate of 900 characters per second while magnetic tape *cassette decks* can read or write data at speeds ranging from 300 to 5,000 characters per second. See Figure 4–28.

FIGURE 4–28 Magnetic Tape Drive

Key-to-Tape Devices. *Key-to-tape devices* enter data directly from a keyboard onto magnetic tape. The aim of such *data entry* devices is to bypass the process of first recording data into punched cards or punched paper tape and then converting these media into magnetic tape. These devices produce magnetic tape in the form of standard-size magnetic tape reels, small cartridges, and cassettes.

Data recorded on standard-size magnetic tape reels can be used by the magnetic tape units of a computer system, while small magnetic cartridges and cassettes require special computer peripheral equipment such as tape cartridge readers and cassette decks. However, keyboard-to-cassette or cartridge devices are small, portable, and less expensive than keyboard-to-standard magnetic tape devices. See Figure 4–29.

Magnetic Strip Hardware. *Magnetic strip* hardware combines the inexpensive high-capacity benefits of magnetic tape with the direct access advantages of magnetic disks and drums. These advantages are offset to some extent by a slower access time. Magnetic strip units offer "mass storage" capacity random access storage at a lower cost than magnetic disks and drums. They are used for applications that do not require fast access times, such as for a large inventory file in a batch processing system.

Magnetic strips are similar to magnetic tape but can be about 3 inches wide and up to 770 inches long. Several hundred strips are mounted in removable cartridges and stored in a "honeycomb-like" arrangement of "cells." The magnetic strip *mass storage system* allows the computer to select an individual strip, move it under a read-write head, and return it to its cartridge. Such units may store from 16 to 500 billion bytes of data! Access times are quite slow, however, ranging from a fraction of a second to several seconds. Data transfer rates vary between 25,000 to 55,000 characters per second. See Figure 4–30.

Advantages and Disadvantages. Magnetic tape is a high-speed input/output medium as well as a high-density secondary storage medium. In comparison to punched cards, magnetic tape is less expensive because one reel of tape can replace hundreds of thousands of cards, occupy a lot less

FIGURE 4–29   Keyboard-to-Magnetic Tape Device

Courtesy Honeywell, Inc.

FIGURE 4–30 Magnetic Strip Cartridge and Data Cell Unit

storage space, and can be reused many times because data can be easily erased and new data recorded. The limitiations of magnetic tape include the fact that it is not human-readable, that it is vulnerable to dust particles, and that it is a *sequential access* storage medium and thus slower than direct access media like magnetic disks.

Other Secondary Storage Devices

Several other secondary storage devices which are still being used or developed should be mentioned.

Magnetic Drums. Magnetic drums are still being used as direct access storage devices but are being replaced in many applications by fixed-head magnetic disk units which are faster and have larger capacities. Magnetic drum devices are similar to magnetic disk units except that the magnetic drum is a cylinder instead of a group of disks, and drums have fixed read/write heads for every track or *band* on the surface of the drum. A typical drum might rotate at 3,500 rpm and have 800 data tracks, store several million bytes, and have an access time of less than 10 milliseconds and a data transfer rate of over a million bytes per second.

Semiconductor Secondary Storage. In Chapter 3, we mentioned how magnetic bubble, charge-coupled devices (CCD) and other semiconductor storage technologies were being used as secondary storage media in some microcomputers and portable terminals. In addition, several firms offer semiconductor storage units as direct access secondary storage devices using CCD (charge-coupled device) semiconductor technology. In fact, these devices are marketed as competition for magnetic disk devices, and are called *semiconductor disk* or *solid state disk* units. They are significantly faster and less expensive than *electromechanical,* "moving surface" direct access storage devices such as magnetic disk units, but have smaller storage capacities. They are competitive with most fixed-head, fixed-disk devices which are needed for high-speed transfer *(paging)* of programs and data between primary and secondary storage devices in large computer systems using *virtual memory* capabilities. Data transfer rates range from 1.5 to 4 megabytes per second, and these units provide from 10 to 100 megabytes of storage.

Optical Disks. Research and development work is continuing on a new mass storage medium using optical disks (also called *videodisc* or *video disk*) technology. Video disks are being introduced commercially for entertainment and educational use in homes, schools, and industry. In these applications, video disks compete to some extent with video cassette systems, especially prerecorded educational and entertainment video cassettes for television viewing. (Video disks can hold several hours of high-quality television pictures and sound or the equivalent of over 50,000 35 mm photograhic slides. Thus an individual disk could contain the text and picture contents of the entire *Encyclopedia Brittanica!*) However, the use of optical disks as a secondary data storage medium in electronic data processing is still in the research and development stage. One version uses a laser to burn microscopic pits arranged in 54,000 circular tracks in a recording layer sandwiched between two transparent 12-inch plastic disks. This *laser-optical* system uses laser beams to read the information stored on the disk. Capacities in billions of bits are available with research continuing on the development of a *terabit* (one trillion bits) disk pack which would cost less than $200. One of the limitations of this medium is that data cannot be erased, so at the present time, it can be used only for long-term *archival* storage where historical files must be maintained.

SECTION III: SPECIALIZED HARDWARE

Voice Input/Output Hardware

Applications of voice input/output devices have been limited in the past but are now growing rapidly and should be widely used in the future. Rapid advances in microelectronic technology have developed *talking chips.* These are microprocessor chips that synthesize human speech and are being used to give **voice output** capabilities to everything from children's toys to telephone communication systems. **Voice input** hardware has not developed as fast as voice output devices. However, the use of voice input terminals with limited speed recognition capabilities is growing steadily in applications ranging from sales data entry to manufacturing quality control.

Voice Input. Speech is the easiest, most natural means of human communication. When voice input is perfected, it will be the easiest, most reliable method of data entry and *conversational computing.* Voice input of data into a computer system is now at the frontier of people-computer communication, but has become technologically and economically feasible for a variety of applications. **Voice data entry terminals** are now being used which allow the direct entry of data into a computer system by verbal communication of a human operator. A typical configuration might consist of one or more portable *voice recognition units,* microphones, and a CRT terminal for visual display of spoken input. This system can have over a 1,000-word vocabulary and support several users simultaneously. Other voice-recognition *modules* have all of the required circuitry on a single circuit board including a vocabulary of several hundred words and are being incorporated in visual display terminals and microcomputer systems. See Figure 4–31.

FIGURE 4–31 Using a Voice Data Entry System

Courtesy Interstate Electronics Corporation.

Voice input units rely on *voice recognition* (or *speech recognition*) microprocessors which analyze and classify acoustic speech patterns and transform them into electronic digital codes for entry into a computer system. The process is directed by speech recognition programs which compare the speech input to previously stored voice reference patterns that are kept on a secondary storage device such as a magnetic disk. Most voice input systems require ''training'' the computer to recognize a limited vocabulary of standard words for each individual using the system. Operators train the system to recognize their voices by repeating each word in the vocabulary about 10 times. Trained systems regularly achieve over a 99 percent word recognition. *Speaker-independent* voice recognition systems are being developed which allow a computer to understand a voice it has never heard before. Use of such systems would eliminate the need for training.

Voice input devices are now being used in work situations where operators need to perform data entry without using their hands to key-in data or instructions, or where it would provide faster and more accurate input. *For example,* voice recognition systems are being used by several manufacturers for the inspection, inventory, and quality control of a variety of products, and by several airlines and parcel delivery companies for voice-directed sorting of baggage and parcels. In another application, a major U.S. oil company uses a voice recognition system to receive oil exploration data over the telephone which are called in from exploration centers around the country. This application demonstrates that voice recognition technology can transform the telephone into a voice input terminal.

Besides data entry and computerized machinery control, other voice recognition applications include information retrieval from data banks, telephone network control, and *speaker recognition* systems. In speaker recognition applications, voice input to a computer is analyzed to verify the identification of a speaker. The speaker's voice is compared to a file of previously recorded voice patterns (sometimes called *voice prints*) in order to establish the identification of the speaker. Widespread use of this type of voice recognition is expected as the basis of identification and security measures required by *electronic funds transfer* (EFT) systems which should largely replace cash and checks as the primary method of payment in the future.

Voice Output Devices.   Voice output devices have changed dramatically as a result of the microcomputer revolution. Computer **audio-response** units have shrunk dramatically in size and cost. Some audio-response units store a prerecorded vocabulary of words, phrases, or syllables on magnetic disk or magnetic bubble units and use a minicomputer to assemble and transmit a verbal answer. However, microelectronic **speech synthesizers** are now being used which fit the devices necessary to synthesize human speech onto a single chip of silicon about one fifth of an inch square! Texas Instruments was the first to develop a "talking chip" and introduced it in 1978 with an educational toy called "Speak & Spell." It holds the patents for an integrated circuit that digitally synthesizes human speech, a speech synthesis filter that electronically models the human voice tract and a converter that drives the speaker so that audible speech can be generated. National Semiconductor produces a talking chip called "Digitalker" which breaks a human voice into "wave form" fragments and then patches these forms together into words to form synthetic speech. Several other semiconductor companies are producing such chips and they are rapidly being used to provide computerized speech for toys, games, consumer appliances, automobiles, elevators, and a variety of other consumer, commercial, and industrial uses. Such speech synthesizing microprocessors are also being used in electronic calculators, digital watches, and in hand-held computers and foreign language translators. See Figure 4–32.

Voice output devices allow the computer to verbally guide an operator through the steps of a task in many types of activities including data processing. They are widely used to allow computers to respond to inquiries and other input over the telephone. In many present applications, input of data is accomplished by pressing the buttons of a *Touch Tone* telephone while output is in the form of a voice produced by an audio-response device controlled by a computer system and transmitted over the telephone lines. This application is found in bank *pay-by-phone* bill-paying services, stock quotation services, and customer credit and account balance inquiries.

Advantages and Disadvantages. Voice input/output devices provide the quickest and easiest method of people-computer communications. Every telephone becomes a potential computer terminal. Voice output devices are small and inexpensive, while voice input devices are now feasible for many applications. Chief limitations concern the quality of synthetic

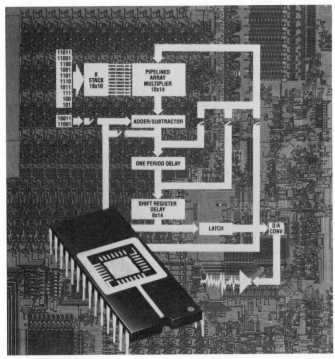

Courtesy Texas Instruments.

* Also shown is a diagram of the operation of the chip, with an enlarged view of the chip circuitry in the background.

FIGURE 4–32   A Talking Chip*

speech and the limited vocabulary and training required by most voice recognition systems. These limitations should be overcome with the continued development of electronic voice technology.

OCR Hardware

Optical character recognition (OCR) equipment can read alphabetic, numeric, and special characters that are printed, typed, or hand-written on ordinary paper. OCR is an attempt to provide a method of direct input of data from *source documents* into a computer system. The conversion of data into punched card or magnetic tape form is not necessary when OCR is used. There are many types of optical readers, but they all employ photoelectric devices to scan the characters being read and the convert reflected light patterns of the data into electronic impulses which are accepted as input into the computer system. Documents which contain characters which do not meet the character design standards of the optical reader are rejected. OCR devices can only read certain types of

```
ABCDEFGHIJKLMNOPQRS
TUVWXYZ0123456789.,
'-{}%?⌐⌐⌐:;=+/$*"&
```

printing or handwriting, though progress is continually being made in improving the reading ability of OCR equipment. A widely used character design for OCR is shown in Figure 4–33.

Optical character recognition devices can read preprinted characters and characters produced by typewriters, cash registers, calculators, credit card imprinters, and handwriting, providing the characters meet OCR standards. OCR equipment can also read pencil marks made in specific poistions of a form. This variation is called *mark-sensing.* OCR devices such as hand-held **wands** are being used to read data on merchandise tags and other media. See Figure 4–34. OCR devices can read documents that contain *bar coding* which is a code that utilizes bars to represent characters. Bar coding on packages of food items and other products has become commonplace since it is required for the *automated checkout* "scanners" being installed by the supermarket industry. See Figure 4–35.

FIGURE 4–34 Using an OCR Wand for Factory Data Collection

Courtesy IBM Corporation.

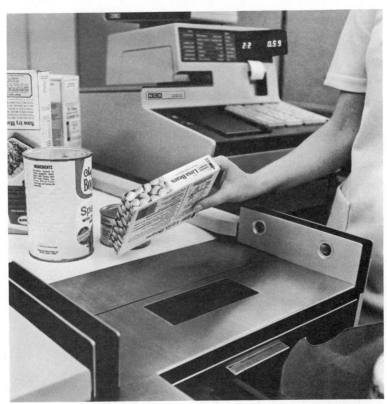

FIGURE 4–35   Supermarket OCR Scanner

Courtesy NCR Corporation.

The scanner emits laser beams, which are reflected off the Universal Product Code. The reflected image is converted to electronic impulses which are sent to the in-store minicomputer where they are matched with pricing information. Pricing information is returned to the terminal, visually displayed, and printed on a receipt. It all happens as fast as the item can be moved past the scanning window.

The Universal Produce Code (UPC) on the package (above and left) identifies the item as a grocery product (the 0 on the left) of the Green Giant Co. (specified by the 20000), which in this instance is a 10-ounce frozen package of baby lima beans in butter sauce (specified by the 12190).

Advantages and Disadvantages.   The major benefit of OCR is that it provides a method of direct input of data from a source document into a computer system. It thus eliminates much costly input preparation activity and increases the accuracy and speed of an electronic data processing system. OCR is extensively used in the credit card billing operations of credit card companies, banks, and oil companies. It is also used to process utility bills, insurance premiums, airline tickets, and cash register and adding machine tapes. OCR is used to automatically sort mail, score tests, and process a wide variety of forms in business and government. The major limitation of OCR has been its stringent character design requirements. Other major limitations for some applications were high document rejection and error rates. However, recently developed OCR readers can read typewriter, word processor, or computer printing of OCR characters with extreme accuracy.

MICR Hardware

Magnetic Ink Character Recognition (MICR) allows the computer systems of the banking industry to magnetically "read" checks and deposit slips and thus sort, tabulate, and post them to the proper checking accounts. Such processing is possible because the identification numbers of the bank and the customer's account number are preprinted on the bottom of checks with an iron-oxide based ink. The first bank receiving a check after it has been written must encode the amount of the check in "magnetic ink" on its lower right hand corner. The MICR system utilizes 14 characters (the 10 decimal digits and four special symbols) of a unique design. See Figure 4–36.

MICR characters can be preprinted on documents or can be encoded on documents utilizing a keyboard-operated machine called a *proof-inscriber*, which also segregates checks into batches and accumulates batch totals. Equipment known

FIGURE 4–36 A Check with MICR Encoding

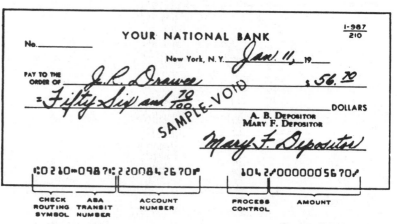

as MICR *reader-sorters* "read" a check by first magnetizing the magnetic ink characters and then sensing the signal induced by each character as it passes by a reading head. The check is then sorted by directing it into one of the pockets of the reader-sorter while the data is electronically captured by the computer system. Reader sorters can read over 2,000 checks per minute with a data transfer rate of over 3,000 characters per second. See Figure 4–37.

Advantages and Disadvantages. MICR processing has been tremendously beneficial to the banking industry. Banks would be hard pressed to handle the processing of checks without MICR and computer technology. MICR documents are human-readable as well as machine readable. MICR has proven to be a highly accurate and reliable method for the direct entry of data on a source document. Major limitations of MICR is the lack of alphabetic and other characters and the necessity

FIGURE 4–37   MICR Proof Inscribers

Courtesy NCR Corporation.

to encode the amount of the check in a separate manual processing step.

Micrographics Hardware

The use of computers in the field of *micrographics* involves:

- **Computer-output-microfilm** or COM, in which microfilm is used as a computer output medium. High-speed microfilm recorders are used to electronically capture the output of computer systems on microfilm, microfiche, and other *microforms*.
- **Computer-input-microfilm** or CIM, where microfilm is used as an input medium. CIM systems use OCR devices to scan microfilm for high-speed input of data.
- **Computer-assisted-retrieval** or CAR, in which special-purpose computer terminals or minicomputers are used as *micrographics terminals* to locate and retrieve automatically a microfilm copy of a document.

Micrographics hardware includes microfilm recorders, hard copy printers, microfilm readers, and micrographics terminals. See Figures 4–38 and 4–39.

Advantages and Disadvantages. Micrographics hardware is widely used to replace computer printing devices which are too slow and produce too much paper. COM Recorders can have a data transfer rate up to 500,000 characters per second and "print" up to 60,000 lines per minute which is much faster than most high-speed printers and equals or exceeds the output rate of magnetic tape or disk units. Microfilm output also takes up only 2 percent of the space of paper output.

Micrographic output thus is a lot faster and takes up much less space than paper output. The storage, handling, and retrieval of microfilm files is substantially easier and cheaper than paper documents. COM is used to sharply reduce the volume of computer-printed paper even though some COM users record *all* transaction data instead of merely producing printed "exception reports." Such users claim that they can provide better customer service and better information for management because the computer provides them with up-to-date microfilm records of all transactions, recording only exception items on paper. The major limitation of COM has been its high hardware cost, which limited it to high-volume applications or the COM facilities of computer service centers.

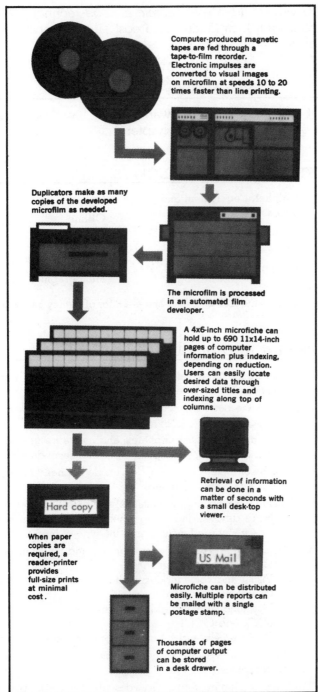

Computer-produced magnetic tapes are fed through a tape-to-film recorder. Electronic impulses are converted to visual images on microfilm at speeds 10 to 20 times faster than line printing.

Duplicators make as many copies of the developed microfilm as needed.

The microfilm is processed in an automated film developer.

A 4x6-inch microfiche can hold up to 690 11x14-inch pages of computer information plus indexing, depending on reduction. Users can easily locate desired data through over-sized titles and indexing along top of columns.

Retrieval of information can be done in a matter of seconds with a small desk-top viewer.

Hard copy

When paper copies are required, a reader-printer provides full-size prints at minimal cost.

US Mail

Microfiche can be distributed easily. Multiple reports can be mailed with a single postage stamp.

Thousands of pages of computer output can be stored in a desk drawer.

Courtesy of Datacorp.

FIGURE 4–38   How COM Works

**FIGURE 4–39
A Micrographics Terminal**

Courtesy Eastman Kodak.

However, advances in *microimage* technology have made micrographics much more cost effective and a fast growing area of computer use.

SUMMARY

Figures 4–1, 4–2, and 4–18 should be used to summarize the types of computer hardware which have been discussed in this chapter.

KEY TERMS AND CONCEPTS

Peripheral equipment and media

Auxiliary equipment and media

Computer graphics

Online

Offline

Direct access

Sequential access

Micrographics

Refer to Figures 4–1, 4–2, and 4–18 for other key hardware terms.

REVIEW AND DISCUSSION QUESTIONS

1. What are the three major categories of computer hardware? What types of devices are included in each category?
2. What is the basic distinction between online and offline devices? Give examples of each.
3. Can some computer peripherals and media be utilized for more than one basic function; i.e., input, output, and secondary storage? Explain.
4. Which computer peripheral devices do not need to utilize data media for input or output? Explain.
5. Outline the functions, advantages, and disadvantages of several major hardware devices, indicating whether they perform input, output, or secondary storage functions and the type of media they utilize.
6. Distinguish between the characteristics and functions of the following:
    a. CRT and printing terminals.
    b. Visual and voice input/output hardware.
    c. Character and line printers.
    d. Magnetic tape and disk hardware.
    e. MICR and OCR hardware.
    f. Direct access and sequential access storage devices.
7. What are the reasons for the increasing use of computer graphics and micrographics?
8. Which of the hardware devices described in this chapter do you personally use? Which devices are most widely used by people in organizations with whom you come into contact on a regular basis? Evaluate such devices from this personal perspective.

REAL WORLD APPLICATIONS

4-1   Federal Express

Fast delivery is what Federal Express is all about. So management could appreciate the ability of Tektronix Graphics to deliver information quickly and concisely. "Prior to Tektronix we'd draw a few graphs by hand," says analyst David White, "and they weren't exactly pretty. Most graphic reports we now provide routinely we never had time to do at all."

Graphics terminals and plotters are now in use throughout the company. They're in Flight Operations, helping clarify flight schedules. In Management Information and Market Analysis departments, turning statistical printouts into line graphs and pie charts. In Operations Research, helping draft more efficient intracity courier routes. Color graphics may soon move into the corporate boardroom.

Using Tektronix Easy Graphing software, secretaries with no previous terminal experience are producing graphic reports every day. Analysts are constructing multicolor, fine line graphs on plotters for final presentations.[1]

• What are the advantages of computer graphics to Federal Express?

[1] Source: Courtesy of Tektronix, Inc.

4-2   Hubert Distributors

After Michigan's third largest beer wholesaler acquired 25 battery-powered, hand-held Route Commander data-entry terminals, sales errors no longer surfaced.

"We wholesale about two million cases of beer a year," says Alice B. Shotwell, vice president and general manager of Pontiac-based Hubert Distributors. "With Route Commanders, we've virtually eliminated sales-ticket errors that previously averaged two per driver per day—or 250 per week—for our 25 routes."

Data stored on a magnetic tape cassette in each Route Commander are put into Hubert's in-house computer system when each of the 25 drivers check in; a complete report is available before the end of each business day. It shows total sales by dollars, total sales by product, where each product was delivered, how much cash was taken in, and a wealth of other information.

"Previously," says Shotwell, "we had to keypunch every sales ticket into our computer system, which took too much time. Normally, we wouldn't have figures for one day's business unit until about the middle of the following day—even though we were using computers."

Now the data from the Route Commander terminals is transferred to an IBM Series One computer, under control of a Lear Siegler CRT, which puts the information onto a diskette that goes into an IBM System 34 computer. When all the information is on one diskette, Shotwell can get an immediate daily report on one entire day's business.[2]

• Why is the use of hand-held data entry terminals better than the previous methods used by Hubert Distributors?
• What other types of computer hardware do they use? Explain what you think their functions are.

[2] Source: "Beer Distributor's Portable Computers Lift Accuracy," *Computer Decisions*, November 1980, p. 114. Copyright 1980, Hayden Publishing Company. Reprinted with permission.

4–3 Ingersoll-RandCo.

The giant Ingersoll-Rand Co., a manufacturer of heavy and energy-related equipment, uses COM to minimize the production and shipping expenses of engineering drawings. Since statistics can be fun, it is interesting to note that without COM, Ingersoll-Rand would be shipping the equivalent of seven railroad cars full of paper engineering drawings each month. Mailing costs for paper drawings would be three times as much as for their microfiche equivalents.

But more importantly, the company has found a way to combine graphical representations with alphanumeric data on microfiche. If paper drawings were prepared for ultimate use, at least 50 and maybe 100 people would be needed to combine the related numbers, letters and words with their respective graphics drawings. Ingersoll-Rand does this with one individual.[3]

- How and why does Ingersoll-Rand use COM?

[3] Source: Neil D. Kelly, "A Role in the Paperless Office," *Infosystems*, February, 1980, p. 54. Copyright 1980, Hitchcock Publishing Co. Reprinted with permission.

5

CHAPTER OUTLINE

Computer Software

LEARNING OBJECTIVES

The purpose of this chapter is to promote a basic understanding of computer software by analyzing the functions, benefits, and limitations of major software components.

After reading and studying this chapter, you should be able to:

1. Differentiate between the following terms:
   a. System software versus application software.
   b. Control programs versus service programs.
   c. Overlapped processing versus dynamic job processing versus multiprogramming.
2. Outline the functions and components of an operating system.
3. Identify the benefits and limitations of (a) data base management systems, (b) virtual memory systems, and (c) software packages.
4. Describe the role of programming language translator programs.
5. Determine the various types of system and application software used by your computer center. For example, determine the types of operating systems, programming language translators, service programs, and software packages that are utilized.

OVERVIEW OF COMPUTER SOFTWARE

Computer software includes all types of programs which direct and control *computer hardware* in the performance of data processing functions. It is often said that software "gives life" to hardware. Computer software can be subdivided into two major categories; *system software and application software.*

> **System software**—programs which control and support operations of a computer system, such as an *operating system* program.
>
> **Application software**—programs which direct the processing of a particular application, such as a *payroll* program, or *inventory control* program.

An overview of the major types of software is shown in Figure 5–1.

SYSTEM SOFTWARE

System software consists of computer programs which control and support the computer system and its data processing activities. As shown in Figure 5–1, system software includes a variety of programs such as operating systems, data base management systems, communications control programs, processing and control programs, and programming language translators. Each of these programs perform an important function in modern computer systems, and should be understood by knowledgeable computer users.

Operating Systems

An operating system can be defined as *an integrated system of programs which supervises operations of the CPU, controls the input/output and storage functions of the computer system, and provides various support services.*

The primary goal of the operating system is to maximize the productivity of a computer system by operating it in the most efficient and effective manner possible. An operating system minimizes the amount of human intervention required during processing by performing many functions that were formerly the responsibility of the computer operator. An operating system also simplifies the job of the computer programmer, since it includes control programs and processing programs which greatly simplify the programming of input/output

FIGURE 5–1 Overview of Computer Software

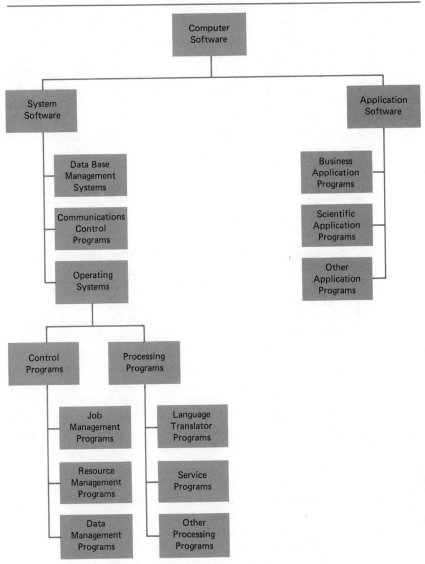

and storage operations and many other standard data processing functions. Operating systems have become indispensable for most computer systems in order to handle the demanding requirements of modern electronic data processing. Figure 5–2 illustrates the role of an operating system and its programs in serving as a **software interface** between computer system hardware and the application programs of computer users.

150

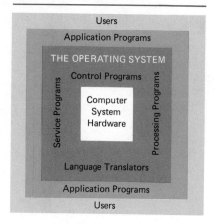

Most operating systems are designed as a collection of program *modules* which can be organized in several combinations to form operating systems with various capabilities. An operating system can therefore be tailored to the requirements of a particular computer system and user. Thus, a mix of operating system capabilities can be acquired to fit the processing power and memory capacity of a computer system and the type of data processing jobs that need to be done. Figure 5–3 illustrates some of the major program modules found in many operating systems. Let us examine some of these important programs.

Control Programs

Control programs perform three major functions in the operation of a computer system.

Job management—preparing, scheduling, and monitoring of jobs for continuous processing by the computer system. The job management function is provided by an integrated system of programs which schedules and directs the flow of jobs through the computer system. Job management activities include interpreting *job control language* (JCL) statements, scheduling and selecting jobs for execution by the computer system, initiating the processing of each job, terminating jobs, and communicating with the computer operator.

FIGURE 5–3 Programs in an Operating System

Resource management—controlling the use of computer system resources by the other system software and application software programs. These resources include primary storage, secondary storage, CPU processing time, and input/output devices.

Data management—controlling the input/output of data as well as its location, storage, and retrieval. In earlier operating systems, this was called the *input/output control system* (IOCS), since it is a collection of programs which performs all of the functions required for the input and output of data. Data management programs control the allocation of secondary storage devices, the physical format and *cataloging* of data storage, and the movement of data between primary and secondary storage devices. Since most business computer applicants require a great deal of input/output and secondary storage activity, the use of data management programs greatly simplifies the job of programming business applications.

The Supervisor. In some operating systems, the functions of resource management and job management are handled by a group of programs called the *supervisor* (also known as the *executive,* the *monitor,* or the *controller*). The supervisor directs the operations of the entire computer system by controlling and coordinating the other components of the operating systems as well as the activities of all of the hardware components of a computer system. Portions of the supervisor reside in primary storage whenever the computer is operating, while other supervisor segments are transferred back and forth between primary storage and a *systems residence* direct-access storage device. The supervisor monitors input/output activities and handles interrupt conditions, job scheduling and queueing, program fetching, and primary storage allocations. The supervisor also communicates with the computer operator through the computer console concerning the status of computer system operations, and records information required for proper job accounting.

Processing Programs

The **processing programs** of an operating system include programming language translator programs, service programs, and other processing programs.

Language Translator Programs. *Language translators* are programs which can convert the programming language instructions of computer programs into *machine language* instructions. Computer programs consist of sets of instructions written in programming languages like BASIC, COBOL, FORTRAN, or Pascal which must be translated into the computer's own *machine language* before they can be processed by the CPU. Most programming language translator programs are called either **assemblers** or **compilers.** Other types of language translators exist, such as *interpreters,* which translate and execute each program statement one at a time, instead of first producing a complete machine language program. (The major categories and types of programming languages are covered in Chapter 8.) The language translation process is called *compiling* when a compiler is used and *assembling* when an assembler is used. Figure 5–4 illustrates the typical language translation process. A program written in a language like BASIC or COBOL is called a *source program.* When the source program is translated into machine language it is called the *object program.* The computer then executes the object pro-

152

FIGURE 5–4   The Language Translation Process

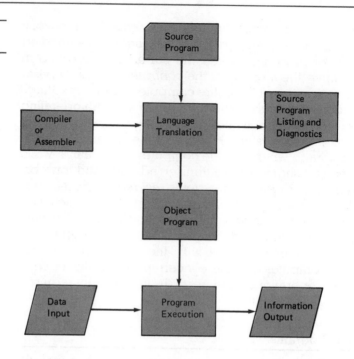

gram. Besides the object program, most compilers and assemblers also produce a listing of the source program and a listing of error messages, called *diagnostics,* which identify programming errors recognized by the translator program.

Service Programs.   *Service programs* are specialized programs which perform common routine and repetitive functions and are made available to all of the users of a computer system. For example, service programs, language translators, and most control programs and applications programs are usually maintained in *program libraries.* Therefore, an important service program usually provided is the *librarian,* which catalogs, manages, and maintains a directory of the programs that are stored in the various libraries of the computer system. Another service program is the *linkage editor,* which edits a program by defining the specific storage locations it requires and linking together parts of the program with required subroutines. *Sort-merge* programs are important service programs which perform the sorting and merging operations on magnetic tape or magnetic disk units which are required in many data processing applications.

Many operating systems provide special service programs for automatic program testing and *debugging,* which is the process of correcting errors (bugs) in a program. Finally, a major category of service programs is *utility programs* or *utilities,* which are a group of miscellaneous programs that perform various "housekeeping" and file conversion functions. Utility programs clear primary storage, load programs record the contents or primary storage (memory dumping), and convert a file of data from one storage medium to another, such as card-to-tape, tape-to-disk, etc.

Other Processing Programs.   Other processing program modules can be added to advanced operating system software. These include *application development systems* and *system performance monitors.*

Application development systems provide interactive assistance to programmers in the development of application programs. Software tools such as DEC's Adminis-11 *application generator,* or IBM's DMS (development management system) help simplify and automate the programming process. An application development system does this by providing programs which support interactive program editing, coding, testing, debugging, and maintenance by programmers using video display terminals. Figure 5–5 shows some of the program components of an application development system.

System performance monitors are programs which monitor the processing of jobs on a computer system. They monitor computer system performance and produce reports containing detailed statistics concerning the use of system resources such as processor time, memory space, I/O devices, and system and application programs. Such reports are used to plan and control the efficient and effective use of a computer system.

FIGURE 5–5   Programs of an Application Development System

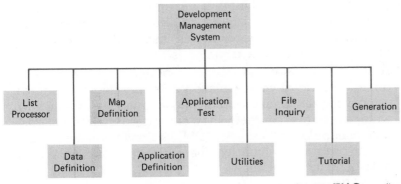

Courtesy IBM Corporation.

Data Base Management Systems

A *data base management system* (DBMS) is a set of computer programs which control the creation, maintenance, and use of the *data bases* of a computer-using organization. A DBMS is a fourth generation computer software development which is required for the use of integrated collections of data and information known as *data bases* which are essential to the efficient and effective use of computers in modern organizations. We will explore the concept and structure of data bases in Chapter 10, and their use in modern information processing systems in Chapter 11.

A DBMS automatically performs the following tasks:

Data base creation—defining and organizing the content, relationships, and structure of the data needed to build a data base.

Data base maintenance—adding, deleting, updating, correcting, and protecting the data in a data base.

Data base processing—using the data in a data base to support various data processing assignments such as information retrieval and report generation.

A data base management system controls all use of the data bases of a computer-using organization. It works in conjunction with the data management control programs of the operating system which are primarily concerned with the physical input, output, and storage of data during processing. Advanced computer systems may even use a **back-end processor** or *data base machine,* which is a special-purpose computer which contains the DBMS. Use of a DBMS has three important characteristics which are illustrated in Figure 5–6.

- End-users can use a DBMS by asking for information from a data base using a simple English-like **query language** or **report writer** and receiving an immediate response. No difficult computer programming is required.
- A DBMS facilitates the job of programmers because they do not have to develop detailed data-handling procedures using a conventional programming language each time they write a program. Instead, they can include several simple **data manipulation language** (DML) statements in their application programs which lets the DBMS perform necessary data handling activities.
- A DBMS removes the data base from the control of individ-

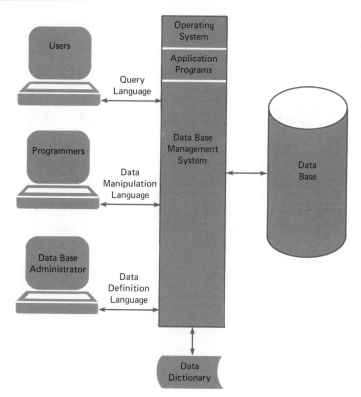

FIGURE 5-6   Role of a Data Base Management System

ual programmers and computer users and places responsibility for it in the hands of a specialist called a **data base administrator** (DBA). This improves the integrity and security of the data base. The data base administrator uses a **data definition language** (DDL) to specify the content, relationships, and structure of the data base and to modify it when necessary. Such information about the data base is stored in a special file called a **data dictionary** which is maintained by the DBA for use by the DBMS.

Figure 5-7 illustrates the use of a query language. Figure 5-8 lists some of the popular DBMS programs available today.

Communications Control Programs

Modern electronic data processing realies heavily on *data communication systems*, which provide for the transmitting of data over electronic communication links between one or more computer systems and computer terminals. This requires data communications software consisting of *communications control programs* stored in a main computer (called the *host*)

FIGURE 5–7 Using a Query Language

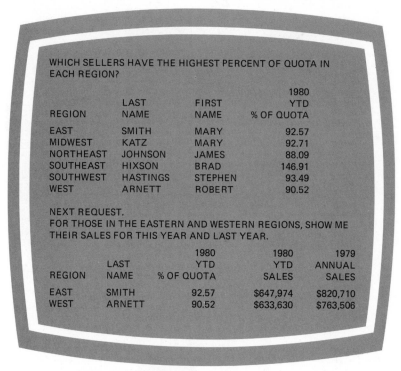

WHICH SELLERS HAVE THE HIGHEST PERCENT OF QUOTA IN EACH REGION?

REGION	LAST NAME	FIRST NAME	1980 YTD % OF QUOTA
EAST	SMITH	MARY	92.57
MIDWEST	KATZ	MARY	92.71
NORTHEAST	JOHNSON	JAMES	88.09
SOUTHEAST	HIXSON	BRAD	146.91
SOUTHWEST	HASTINGS	STEPHEN	93.49
WEST	ARNETT	ROBERT	90.52

NEXT REQUEST.
FOR THOSE IN THE EASTERN AND WESTERN REGIONS, SHOW ME THEIR SALES FOR THIS YEAR AND LAST YEAR.

REGION	LAST NAME	1980 YTD % OF QUOTA	1980 YTD SALES	1979 ANNUAL SALES
EAST	SMITH	92.57	$647,974	$820,710
WEST	ARNETT	90.52	$633,630	$763,506

Sample session with INTELLECT, courtesy of Artificial Intelligence Corporation.

FIGURE 5–8 Examples of Current Data Base Management Systems

DBMS	Supplier
ADABAS	Software AG
IDMS	Cullinane
IDS	Honeywell
IMS	IBM
IMAGE	Hewlett-Packard
MODEL 204	Computer Corp. of America
SYSTEM 2000	Intel
TOTAL	CINCOM

or in specialized communications control *front-end computers.* Communications control programs perform such functions as a connecting or disconnecting communication links between computers and terminals, automatically checking terminals for input/output activity, assigning priorities to data communications requests from terminals, and detecting and correcting transmission errors. They control and support the data communications activity occurring in a communications network, and work in conjunction with the operating system and data base management system of the host computer. (We will discuss data communications software in more detail in Chapter 10.)

APPLICATION SOFTWARE

Application software or *application programs* consists of computer programs which direct the computer system to perform specific data processing activities required for the solution of business, scientific, and other problems of computer users. Thus, application software is sometimes called *user programs* or *problem programs,* and is frequently subdivided into *business* application programs, *scientific* applications programs, and other applications program categories. Figure 5–9 illustrates how application programs are related to the major types of system software, including the operating system, data base management system, and communications control programs of a computer system.

A **computer application** *is the use of a computer to solve a specific problem or to accomplish a particular job for a computer user.* Computer applications are frequently subdivided into *business, scientific,* and *other* applications categories. Business applications involve the processing of business and administrative data, whereas scientific applications involve complex mathematical calculations and problem solving. For example, a computer program that directs a computer to process a payroll or update an inventory is called a *business application program,* whether it is used by a business firm, a government agency, or an educational institution. Likewise, a computer program that involves complex statistical analysis might be called a *scientific application program,* even though it is used by business analysts as well as by scientists and engineers. The *other applications programs* category covers a wide variety of applications in such areas as education, law enforcement, art, and medicine.

FIGURE 5–9 System and Application Software Relationships

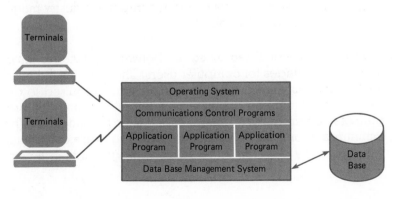

Software Packages

Computer software can be subdivided in two general categories:

User-written software—programs written by the users and computer programmers of a computer-using organization.

Software packages—programs supplied by computer manufacturers, independent software companies, or other computer users. Software packages are also known as *canned programs, proprietary software,* or *packaged programs.*

Software packages can also be subdivided into two distinct categories:

System software packages—control programs, processing programs, and service programs acquired from a computer manufacturer, dealer, or software company.

Application software packages—(also called *application packages*) consist of business, scientific, and other application programs. They can be purchased or leased from computer manufacturers, software companies, or other computer users. Figure 5–10 provides just a small example of the many kinds of application packages which are available.

Software packages usually come in the form of magnetic floppy disks or magnetic tape reels or cassettes, along with manuals and other printed material that describe and document the programs. Time-sharing service subscribers can use software packages by merely requesting that a specific program be made available to their time-sharing terminal. Information about software packages is available from computer manufacturers, software firms, time-sharing companies, and in the many advertisements found in computer industry magazines and other publications.

Advantages and Disadvantages. Software packages have several advantages for computer users. They reduce the need for the expensive and time-consuming effort required to develop user-written programs. The number of computer programers required by a computer-using organization can be minimized. Computer manufacturers and software companies can frequently develop more efficient programs than a com-

FIGURE 5–10 Examples of Business Application Packages

- *Accounts Payable.* Receives data concerning purchases from suppliers and produces checks in payment of outstanding invoices and cash management reports.
- *Accounts Receivable.* Receives data concerning customer invoices and payments and produces monthly customer statements and credit management reports.
- *Critical Path Scheduling.* Solves critical path or PERT networks of project activities.
- *General Ledger.* Produces the general ledger trial balance, income statement, and balance sheet of a firm, and various income and expense reports for management.
- *Inventory Control.* Receives data concerning customer orders, prepares shipping documents if the ordered items are available, and records all changes in inventory.
- *Investment Analysis.* Evaluates capital investments by projecting cash flows and determining expected rates of return for a proposed investment.
- *Lease-Purchase Analysis.* Compares leasing versus purchase of equipment.
- *Order/Transaction Processing.* Processes customer orders and sales transactions and produces receipts for customers and data needed for sales analysis and inventory control.
- *Payroll and Labor Analysis.* Receives data from employee time cards and other records and produces paychecks, payroll reports, and labor analysis reports.
- *Pro Forma Statement Analysis.* Projects up to five years of financial statements (balance sheet and income statement) for a firm.
- *Return on Investment.* Computes returns for an investment in common stock.
- *Sales Analysis.* Produces management reports analyzing the sales generated by each salesperson, customer, product, etc.
- *Transportation Linear Program.* Determines the least cost schedule for transporting goods from several sources to several destinations.

puter user can, because they are specialists in software development.

Of course, software packages do have their limitations. Some ready-made programs may be too generalized and have to be tailored to the needs of a specific user through extensive programming effort. Other packages may have been written for specific users, and require significant reprogramming before they can be used by others. It must also be emphasized that not all software packages are well-written, efficient, error-free programs. Most software packages are written by reputable professional programmers from computer manufacturers, dealers, and independent software firms. However, software packages may also be developed by inexperienced "kitchen table" programmers, whose expertise is questionable, and whose programs may contain errors and be quite inefficient. Many of these programs are aimed at the personal and small business computer market. Therefore users should carefully investigate the quality and "track record" of a software package and its supplier before making a purchasing decision.

Firmware Packages

In Chapter 3 we discussed the concept of *firmware*, which consists of microprograms (software) stored in ROM modules (hardware). Thus we concluded that firmware has characteristics of both hardware and software. This blurring of the line between hardware and software is accelerated by continuing developments in microelectronics. Many microcomputers and minicomputers use removable ROM modules in which major software functions have been permanently programmed into microelectronic memory circuitry. For example, ROM modules might contain:

- Language translator programs such as a BASIC *compiler,* or
- Common business application programs such as payroll programs.

It appears that firmware will continue to take over many current hardware and software functions. Electronic *logic* circuitry which is designed to accomplish a particular task (such as perform an arithmetic operation) can be replaced by microprograms stored in microelectronic *memory* circuits. Thus firmware is also called *solid-state software,* since machine language microinstructions are permanently stored in semiconductor memory circuits. Given the steadily decreasing cost of microelectronic memory circuitry, many experts are predicting that microelectronic firmware modules will continue to take over many functions now performed by both hardware devices and software packages.

SOFTWARE AND COMPUTER PROCESSING CAPABILITIES

Modern software can provide computer systems with several important processing capabilities, such as *overlapped processing, dynamic job processing, multiprogramming, virtual memory,* and *virtual machines.*

It is important that we gain a basic understanding of these capabilities, since they make possible the efficient and effective use of computers for business data processing. Figure 5–11 illustrates some of the computer processing capabilities provided by a modern operating system. Let us now briefly explore each of them.

FIGURE 5–11   Computer Processing Capabilities Provided by a Modern Operating System

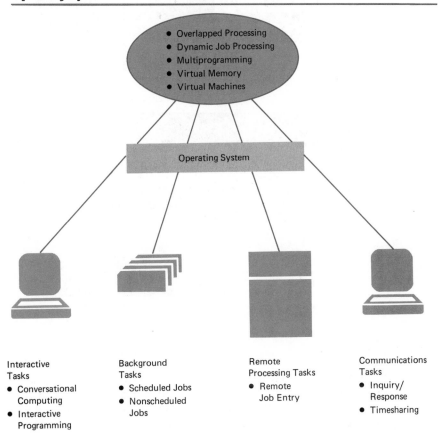

Interactive
Tasks
- Conversational
  Computing
- Interactive
  Programming

Background
Tasks
- Scheduled Jobs
- Nonscheduled
  Jobs

Remote
Processing Tasks
- Remote
  Job Entry

Communications
Tasks
- Inquiry/
  Response
- Timesharing

Overlapped Processing

A computer system with an *overlapped processing* capability can increase the utilization of its central processing unit by overlapping input/output and processing operations. *Input/output interface hardware* (buffers, I/O control units, and channels) and *system software* (data management programs) make such processing possible. Overlapped processing is the opposite of *serial processing,* where the processing function cannot take place until the input function is completed, and the output function must wait until the processing function is completed. Thus, the input, processing, and output equipment of a computer system are idle for large portions of the time necessary to complete a data processing assignment. A computer system is *input/output bound* if its CPU must

FIGURE 5–12 Serial and Overlapped Processing

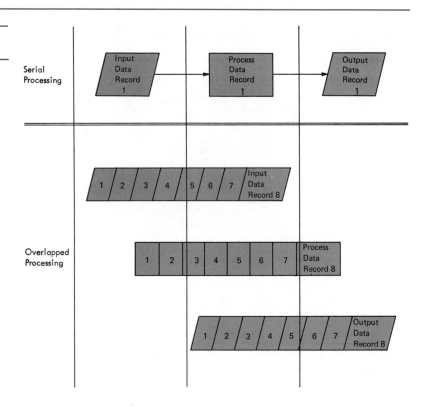

wait while its input/output equipment carries out its functions and is *process-bound* (or CPU-bound) if the input/output devices have to wait while the CPU is involved in computations and other operations. See Figure 5–12.

Overlapped processing was developed to help solve these problems and thereby to increase the *throughput* of a computer system. "Throughput" can be defined as the total amount of fully completed data processing occurring during a specific period of time. Thus, the efficiency of a computer system is gauged not by the speed of its input, processing, or output equipment, but by its throughput; that is, the amount of data processing completed during a period of time. The time it takes to complete a data processing assignment is called *turnaround* time. Overlapped processing greatly increases the throughput of most business computer systems and reduces turnaround time because most business applications require large amount of input/output operations.

Overlapped processing frequently involves an activity known as **spooling** (simultaneous peripheral operation online) which allows input and output operations to occur simultaneously with processing operations. Input data from low-speed devices is stored temporarily on high-speed secondary storage units to form a *queue* (waiting line) which can be quickly accessed by the CPU. Output data are also written at high speeds onto tape or disk units and form another queue waiting to use slow-speed devices such as a printer or a card punch. The operating system supplies a special utility program to control the spooling process.

Dynamic Job Processing

Some operating systems allow computers to perform **stacked job processing** in which a series of data processing jobs are executed continuously without operator intervention being required between each job. Necessary information is communicated to the operating system through the use of a *job control language* (JCL) consisting of various job control statements. JCL statements provide the operating system with such information as the sequence in which jobs are to be processed and the input/output devices required for each job.

Dynamic job processing is a term used to describe the constantly changing computer operations required by modern electronic data processing and provided by many current operating systems. In dynamic job processing, jobs are not processed sequentially in stacks but are processed according to a constantly changing *priority interrupt system*. A system of priorities is established for jobs, job steps, and various operational situations which indicates when the CPU can be "interrupted" in its processing and diverted to another task. For example, an error indication or a signal from the computer operator would have a higher priority than a payroll processing computation.

A priority interrupt system usually requires "time slicing," in which each job is allocated a specified "slice" of CPU time (frequently a fraction of a second) as measured by the electronic clock of the computer. Jobs are interrupted if they exceed their allocated time slice, are replaced with a waiting job, and are assigned another priority for later processing. A priority interrupt system usually results in a waiting line, or *queue*, of jobs that may be stored in primary storage or in direct access storage devices called "swapping" storage. Thus, dynamic job processing involves the *continual swap-*

ping of jobs and job steps between the primary storage and the swapping storage on the basis of a continually revised queueing and priority interrupt schedule maintained by the operating system.

Multiprogramming

Multiprogramming can be defined as the ability of a computer system to process two or more programs in the same period of time. This is accomplished by storing all or part of several programs in primary storage and then switching from the execution of one program to another in an interleaving process. The operating system does this by transferring entire programs or segments of programs and data into and out of main memory from secondary storage devices and by allowing arithmetic or logic operations for one program to be performed while simultaneously performing input/output or storage operations for several other programs. Only one instruction at a time is executed by the central processing unit. However, the operating system switches so quickly from one program to another that it gives the effect of simultaneous operation. (Also considered a form of multiprogramming is **multitasking,** which involves the concurrent use of the same copy of a program by several different *tasks.*)

A multiprogramming capability allows a computer system to better utilize the time of its central processing unit, since a large part of a CPU's time can be wasted as it waits between jobs. When dynamic job processing involves multiprogramming, the operating system must allocate portions of primary storage among various jobs and job segments. The operating system subdivides primary storage into several fixed or variable "partitions," or into a large number of "pages." This allows several programs to be processed during the same period of time.

Figure 5–13 shows the allocation of primary storage into three *fixed partitions:* one for the operating system, a "foreground" partition for high priority programs, and a "background" partition for low priority programs. Typically, *high priority programs* have extensive input/output requirements but require only small amounts of CPU processing time. *Low priority jobs* usually have extensive CPU processing requirements or are routine jobs which do not require immediate processing. For example, a time-sharing system with many

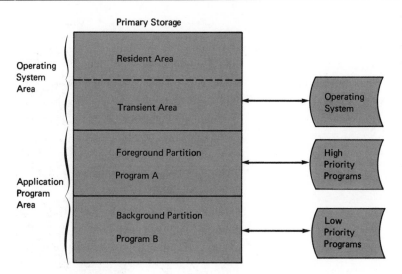

Primary Storage

FIGURE 5-13
Multiprogramming with Fixed Partitions

remote terminals may utilize the foreground partition, while stacked job processing might take place in the background partition.

Figure 5-13 shows that application programs and parts of the operating system are stored on direct-access storage devices such as magnetic disk units, so that they can be shuttled back and forth between primary storage and secondary storage devices. Notice that only part of the operating system "resides" continuously in the "resident area" of primary storage. Other programs of the operating system are transferred to a "transient area" of primary storage from a magnetic disk "system residence device" whenever they are needed.

Virtual Memory and Virtual Machines

Virtual memory is the ability to treat *secondary storage* devices as an extension of the *primary storage* of the computer, thus giving the "virtual" appearance of a larger main memory than actually exists. Data and programs are subdivided into *pages* which are transferred between main memory and secondary storage devices by the operating system so that it appears that the computer has a larger "real" memory than it actually does. Thus, the computer system can be utilized as if it had "virtually" unlimited primary storage. For example: one recent computer model with a real memory (primary storage) capacity of 512,000 bytes can act as though it has a memory size of 16 million bytes through its use of secondary

FIGURE 5–14 The Virtual
Memory Process

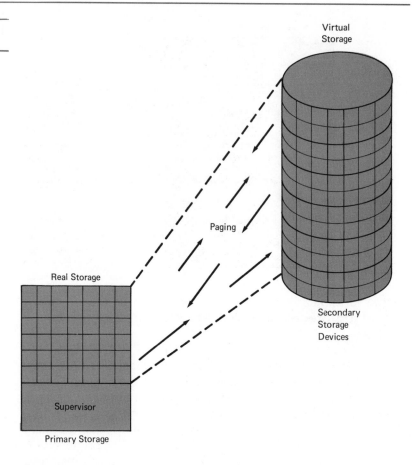

storage on magnetic disks and its virtual memory operating system. See Figure 5–14.

Virtual memory requires a form of dynamic relocation called **paging**. Primary storage is segmented into a large number of *pages* whose contents and location are automatically controlled by the virtual memory operating system and the use of special hardware registers. Programs and data are subdivided automatically into pages and moved to and from secondary storage devices and retrieved as needed. This paging is "transparent" to the computer user. A program may appear to be stored and processed in a single section of primary storage, when in reality it is subdivided into pages which are scattered throughout primary and secondary storage.

With virtual memory, large programs can be easily processed, since programs do not have to reside entirely in main memory and subdividing large programs into segments or overlays is no longer necessary. Efficient use is made of primary storage since pages of programs can be placed wherever space is available. Many more programs can be run simultaneously when paging is used. For example: the third generation multiprogramming operating system of one computer manufacturer allowed from 6 to 14 user programs to run concurrently. However, its fourth generation virtual memory operating system has a theoretical maximum of 250 concurrent users! This difference is primarily due to the fact that virtual memory systems require that only a few pages of a program being processed be in primary storage. Only those parts of a program containing the specific instructions and data actually being processed are required.

Virtual memory systems have several limitations which should be mentioned. Many users of virtual memory systems found that applications took longer to process and used more total memory space. Thus the easier programming of a virtual

FIGURE 5-15   Example of the Virtual Machine Concept

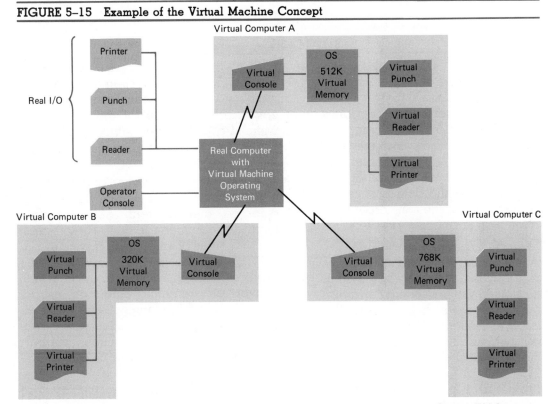

Courtesy IBM Corporation.

memory system seems to have been gained at the expense of some throughput time and some waste of the memory resources of the computer system. In some systems, the problem can become so acute that a *thrashing* condition occurs where the operating system must spend most or all of its time moving pages or segments between primary and secondary storage units. Proper systems and programming controls are needed to minimize the increase in "overhead" (i.e., time and memory space) that can result from the use of virtual memory systems.

The concept of virtual memory has expanded to include the concept of virtual computer systems or **virtual machines.** A combination of virtual memory operating systems and microprogramming is required. Several different configurations of computers can then be simulated by a single computer system. These simulated computers, called *virtual machines,* provide one or more computer users not only with virtual memory, but with complete virtual computer systems, including both virtual hardware and software. See Figure 5–15.

SUMMARY

- Computer software can be subdivided into the two categories of system software and application software. System software consists of computer programs which control and support the computer system and its data processing activities. Application software consists of computer programs which direct a computer system to perform specific data processing activities required for the solution of business, scientific, and other problems of computer users.

- A major category of system software is operating systems. An operating system is an integrated system of control and processing programs which supervises the processing operations of the CPU, controls the input/output of the computer system, and provides various support services. In modern computer systems, the computer user and the computer operator communicate with the computer through the operating system. Operating systems with multiprogramming, virtual memory, and other capabilities have become indispensable for most computer users in order to handle the dynamic job processing required by modern EDP systems.

- The control programs of an operating system perform the three major functions of resource management, data management, and job management. The processing programs of an operating system consist of language translators, and service programs. Language translator programs convert programming language instructions into machine language instructions. Service programs are specialized programs which perform common support functions for the users of a computer system.

- Data base management systems control the creation, maintenance, and use of the data bases of an organization. A DBMS simplifies the use of the data and information in a data base for both users and programmers. Communications control programs control and support the data communications activity between the computers and terminals in a data communications network.

KEY TERMS AND CONCEPTS

System software	Communications control programs
Application software	
Operating system	Computer application
Control programs	Software packages
Supervisor	Overlapped processing
Processing programs	Dynamic job processing
Language translator programs	Multiprogramming
Service programs	Virtual memory
Data base management systems	Virtual machine

REVIEW AND DISCUSSION QUESTIONS

1. What is the distinction between system software and application software?
2. What are the major categories of system software?
3. What are operating systems? What are the major components of operating systems and what are their functions?
4. What is a data base management system (DBMS)? What role does it play in the operation of computer systems?
5. What is the advantage of a DBMS to a computer user? A programmer?
6. Modern operating systems provide computers with capabilities such as overlapped processing, dynamic job processing, and multiprogramming. What advantages in electronic data processing are gained by each of these capabilities?
7. How does multiprogramming differ from multiprocessing?
8. What is virtual memory? What benefits and limitations are provided by virtual memory systems? By virtual machines?
9. Does every computer application require an application program? Why?
10. What are the benefits and limitations of software packages?
11. What is the function of communications control programs?
12. How has microprogramming, firmware, and developments in microelectronics blurred the line between hardware and software?

REAL WORLD APPLICATIONS

5–1 Spectra-Physics, Inc.

A manufacturer of high technology products (lasers and electro-optical instruments), Spectra-Physics, Palo Alto, Calif., has grown dramatically over the last five years, from $25 million to $140 million in sales, and growth continues at a rate of some 25 percent per year. The firm operates eight divisions, each having a separate production capability involving thousands of parts, assemblies, and operations, and many suppliers of components, ranging from nuts and bolts to microprocessors and rare gasses.

Company management realized that explosive growth required highly developed production control. Early in the growth phase, controls were centralized and handled by a small computer. As growth progressed, the firm learned that turnaround time was not responsive to fast-moving events. A corporate decision was made to decentralize operations, making each division an accountable P&L center, and to install divisional manufacturing information systems that are linked to an overall corporate management information system.

Roy Daheb was brought in as corporate director of MIS to design and install the system, which had to include not only manufacturing, but marketing and financial, as well. He considered this a challenge since it was mandatory for all production operations to continue unimpeded during MIS implementation and complete control of inventory and financial status had to be maintained during the changeover from old to new.

Daheb took an interesting approach to accomplish his goals. Rather than take on the huge task of developing all the elements of a complete MIS in-house, he opted to purchase existing packages and link them together with programs developed by his staff, such as an online, front-end module which allows terminal-independent linking of all present and future MIS modules. The catalyst for the direction taken was set by the selection of MAC-PAC/HP, a modular online manufacturing control package, jointly developed by accounting firm Arthur Andersen & Co. and Far-West Data Systems Inc. of Irvine, Calif.

The package runs on Hewlett-Packard 3000 computers operating in COBOL environments. With the decision to use MAC-PAC/HP came the requirement to operate the entire MIS in an HP 3000-COBOL environment. A McCormack & Dodge financial package was selected for the financial portion of the MIS and converted to HP3000-COBOL by Far-West Data Systems. The HP 3000 systems selected also use the multiprogramming executive (MPE) operating system, and the Image/3000 data base management system (DBMS).[1]

- Identify the system and application software packages selected by Spectra-Physics.
- What are the functions of these packages?
- Why didn't Spectra-Physics develop these programs themselves?

[1] Source: "Software Package Leads to Online System," *Infosystems,* November 1980, p. 92. Copyright 1980, Hitchcock Publishing Co. Reprinted with permission.

5–2 Physician's Microcomputer, Inc.

Dr. Greg Berlin of San Francisco wanted to buy a microcomputer system when he set up his practice, but couldn't find one he liked. "As I learned more about microcomputers," Berlin recalls, "I began to realize that most of the microcomputer systems available for physicians made the office more difficult to manage. They solved a few problems but introduced many others. There's no reason for computers to be that difficult to operate. It shouldn't take any training at all. You should be able to say,

5-2 *(continued)*

"This is how you turn the machine on, and this is how you insert a diskette,' and that's it. So I began to design software that teaches users as they go along, that makes it very difficult to destroy something or do something accidentally."

For four years, Berlin spent about half of his time working on a complete office-practice system. The program uses standard medical codes to keep patients' health records, does the billing, even processes insurance claims. To work the bugs out of it, Berlin invited friends to try to make the program "crash." He now markets his system, through Physician's Microcomputer, Inc., for under $25,000.[2]

- Why did Dr. Berlin develop his own software?
- Would you say that he has tried to develop software that: Is *user-friendly?* Is *well documented?* Has *built-in* controls? Explain.

[2] "The Data Game: Business and the Microcomputer," *Passages,* May 1981, p. 24. Reprinted with permission.

5-3 The Social Security Administration

The head of the Social Security Administration warned Congress recently that the $140 billion agency is facing a crisis with its 20-year-old computer system, which he described as patched together and in dire need of repair. "We do our job by brute force rather than by technology," Commissioner John A. Svahn told two House Ways and Means subcommittees.

Svahn said it would take up to $500 million and five years to replace the administrations' computers and to program them to keep track of wage records for 200 million Americans and benefits payments to 36 million others. He said the system has for years been patching "unwieldy and inefficient" software together to take on new tasks. The agency is not even able to document all its software, he said, adding that "in the system jargon, that means no one can figure out how they work."

It takes new programmers up to two years to learn how to work with the system, said Svahn, calling it "a rather bizarre situation." Svahn said Social Security has been saddled with more tasks than just writing checks, including draft registration and keeping track of workers' wages.

He also said he was not yet ready to propose a plan to Congress for new computers, although he told the subcommittees, "Over the past 10 to 15 years, because of new program demands . . . (we have) not been able to keep up with rapidly advancing technology. Today we face a crisis in systems operations."

A Reagan administration transition team warned last January 12 that there were problems with the computer systems, which it described as "antiquated . . . error-prone and cumbersome." Svahn said today that the agency's computers have been overloaded by benefits changes made by Congress. Instead of designing new systems to accomodate new programs, he said Social Security has been modifying its old computer systems.

He said this has "resulted in enormously complex, patchwork systems encompassing decades of different programming techniques . . . Over time (it) has been unwieldy and inefficient." He said it had taken nearly 600 computer programs, produced by programmers working for 20,000 hours, and 2,500 hours of computer processing time to make the changes necessary for benefits to be increased 11.2 percent in July.[3]

- What is wrong with the computer systems of the Social Security Administration?
- Is it just a case of antiquated hardware, or is software a major problem?
- Is a complete overhaul of Social Security software necessary? Explain.

[3] Source: Adapted from Christopher Connel, "Old Computer Bugging Social Security," *Associated Press,* May 21, 1981.

6

CHAPTER OUTLINE

Modern Computer Systems

LEARNING OBJECTIVES

The purpose of this chapter is to promote a basic understanding of the major types of computer systems in use today.

After reading and studying this chapter, you should be able to:

1. Identify the differences between the following:
   a. Analog and digital computers.
   b. Special-purpose, general-purpose, and dedicated computers.
   c. Scientific and business computers.
2. Outline the major differences between the various sizes of computers.
3. Explain the use of microcomputers and minicomputers as personal computers and small business computers.
4. Discuss the trend toward multiprocessor computer systems.

Now that you have covered the fundamentals of computers and their hardware and software, you are now ready to analyze the important characteristics of modern computer systems. Today's computer systems display striking differences as well as basic similarities. Differences in computer characteristics and capabilities have resulted in the development of several major categories of computer systems. Computer systems are frequently classified by *type* (digital and analog), *purpose* (general-purpose, special-purpose, business, scientific, and dedicated), by *processor architecture* (uniprocessor and multiprocessor) and by *size* (micro, mini, small, medium, large, and super computers). In this chapter, we will analyze these types of computer systems, concentrating on their hardware and software characteristics, cost, sources, and their primary application areas.

TYPES OF COMPUTERS

Analog and Digital Computers

There are two basic types of computers, the analog and the digital. The basic difference between these two types of computers is that the digital computer *counts* discrete units while the analog computer *measures* continuous physical magnitudes.

Analog Computers. The electronic analog computer performs arithmetic operations and comparisons by measuring changes in a continuous physical phenomenon such as electronic voltage, which represents, or is "analogous" to, the numerical values of the data being processed. Analog computers are used on a limited basis to process the data arising from scientific or engineering experiments, manufacturing processes, and military weapons systems. *For example,* the temperature changes of a chemical process can be converted by the analog computer into variations in electronic voltage and mathematically analyzed. The results of the processing could be displayed on dials, graphs, or TV screens or be used to initiate changes in the chemical process.

Digital Computers. Digital computers are the most common form of computers. A digital computer will perform arithmetic operations and comparisons on numbers (digits) and other characters that have been numerically coded. The accuracy of the digital computer is limited only by the size of its memory and the preciseness of its data input. The digital computer can process both numeric and alphabetic data, has internal storage, and has great flexibility because of its stored program characteristic. Digital computers are used for business and scientific data processing, industrial process control, and most other computer applications.

Special-Purpose, General-Purpose, and Dedicated Computers

Digital computers are frequently classified as either special-purpose, general-purpose, or dedicated computers. A **special-purpose computer** is specifically designed to process one or more specific applications. Some of these computers are so specialized that part or all of their operating instructions are built into their electronic circuitry. However, the use of built-in microprocessors and microelectronic memories makes it possible to easily customize computers for specific uses. Special-purpose computers have been built for both military and civilian applications (such as aircraft and submarine navigation, aircraft, missile, and satellite tracking), airline reservation systems, and industrial process control. Special-purpose computers are widely used as **front-end processors** for control of data communication networks and are beginning to be used as **back-end processors** for management of data base systems. Many computerized **word processors** for automatic typing and text editing are special-purpose computers found in modern offices. Several of these important special-purpose computer applications will be discussed in more detail in upcoming chapters.

A **general-purpose computer** is designed to process a wide variety of applications. For example, applications ranging from scientific and engineering analysis to business data processing are possible merely by changing the program of instructions stored in the machine. The variety of applications that can be processed is limited only by the size, speed, and types of input and output devices of a particular computer. The versatility of the general-purpose computer is achieved with some sacrifice of speed and efficiency, though this is more than offset by its ability to handle a wide range of applications.

A **dedicated computer** is typically a general-purpose computer that has been "dedicated" or committed to a particular data processing task or application, even though it is capable of performing a wide variety of other tasks and applications.

For example, general-purpose computers are frequently dedicated to performing such jobs as data communications network control, data base management, input/output control for larger computer systems, online banking, and automated manufacturing. The development of minicomputers and microcomputers has accelerated the trend toward the use of dedicated computers. It has become economically feasible to dedicate these small yet powerful computers to more specific data processing tasks such as word processing or small business accounting applications.

Scientific and Business Computers

Previously, computers were designed as fixed word-length machines for scientific data processing, or as variable word-length computers for business data processing. However, present general-purpose computers can be programmed to operate for either scientific data processing (using fixed-length words) or business data processing (using variable-length words). However, **scientific computers** are still being built for the high-speed processing of numerical data involving complex, mathematical calculations. Some scientific computers are large *supercomputers* while others are powerful, special-purpose processing units called *array processors* which can be attached to a CPU to vastly increase the arithmetic processing power of a computer system. Scientific computers are typically designed with limited input, output, and storage capabilities but have advanced "number crunching" computational power in order to handle the large amount of computations that are typical of scientific applications.

Business computers are general-purpose computers which can efficiently process the large volumes and variety of numeric and alphabetic data that is required by payroll, billing, inventory and other typical business applications. Such computers have extensive input, output, and storage capabilities but have slower numeric computation speeds than special-purpose scientific computers. General-purpose computers used for business data processing come in all sizes, from small microcomputers to powerful large-scale computer systems.

MICROCOMPUTER SYSTEMS

Microcomputers are complete general-purpose digital computers that range in size from a "computer on a chip" or a handheld "pocket computer," to a small typewriter-size unit.

Chapter 1 described how the small size, low cost, and computing power of the microcomputer has had a revolutionary impact on computer use.

Hardware

The heart of a microcomputer is a **microprocessor** (MPU) which is an individual microcomputer central processing unit (CPU) on a chip. A "single-chip" computer consists of a microprocessor along with primary storage and input/output interface circuits. However, most microcomputers are "single-board" computers which consist of a microprocessor chip (as the CPU) along with other integrated circuit chips for memory, input/output interface, and other special functions plugged into a circuit board. Most microcomputers use an 8-bit word-length in their processing operations. However, a trend toward microcomputers using a 16-bit world-length is evident and 32-bit microprocessors are emerging. Microcomputers use both ROM (read-only memory) and RAM (random-access memory) for primary storage. Permanently stored in the ROM units of many microcomputers are control programs and other programs, including language translators. The contents of these ROM units can only be read and cannot be altered by the microcomputer user. The RAM units of the microcomputer provide temporary storage of data needed during input/output and processing operations. Microcomputer primary storage capacity might range from 4K to 16K bytes of ROM, and 4K to 128K bytes of RAM. Memory capacities can usually be expanded by plugging in additional ROM or RAM modules. Figures 6–1 and 6–2 illustrate a complete computer on a chip. Figure 6–3 gives an inside look at the microprocessor, memory chips, and circuit board of a microcomputer.

FIGURE 6–1 Microcomputer on a Chip (center) Mounted on a Carrier

Courtesy Intel Corporation.

A variety of input, output, and secondary storage devices (known as peripherals) can be attached to many microcomputers to form a *microcomputer system.* Most microcomputers use a standard typewriter-like keyboard as their main *input* device, and a regular television set or a CRT unit for video *output.* In many microcomputers, the microprocessor memory and other circuit board devices are contained within the keyboard unit. A 10-key numeric pad can usually be added to the keyboard to facilitate entry of numeric data. A typewriter-quality printer can be added for "hard-copy" printed output.

FIGURE 6–2 Single-Chip Microcomputer: Enlarged View

Courtesy Intel Corporation.

A complete general-purpose digital processing and control system in one large-scale integrated circuit. The device combines a microprocessor, which would ordinarily occupy an entire chip, with a variety of supplementary functions such as a one kilobyte program memory, data memory, multiple input-output (I/O) interfaces, and timing circuits. The location of various computer functions are identified here, including the five basic functional blocks: control, memory, registers, ALU, and I/O ports. The upper-half portions of the chip represent the memory and I/O functions that transform the chip from a simple microprocessor into a microcomputer.

Keyboard

8-Bit Z-80
Microprocessor

16K RAM

Courtesy Tandy Corporation.

FIGURE 6–3   Location of the Microprocessor and Memory Chips of a TRS—80 Microcomputer

Courtesy Tandy Corporation.

Courtesy IBM Corporation.

FIGURE 6–4   Microcomputer Systems

Courtesy Tandy Corporation.

Courtesy Apple Computer, Inc.

Top, left to right: Radio Shack TRS-80 Model II with built-in floppy disk drive and video display unit; IBM personal computer system including dual floppy disk drives, video monitor, and thermal printer. Bottom, left to right: Radio Shack TRS-80 pocket computer; Apple II Plus microcomputer system with thermal printer, video monitor, and two floppy disk units.

Secondary storage devices include magnetic tape cassettes and cartridges or *floppy disk* units. A wide range of other peripheral devices is available including *audio response* and *voice synthesizer* units for audio and voice output, *voice recognition* units for voice input, and *graphic tablets* for graphic input. Microcomputers can also act as *intelligent terminals*. This requires an *acoustic coupler* as a telephone interface device which connects a microcomputer to data communication systems. Figure 6–4 illustrates a variety of microcomputer systems and peripheral devices.

Software

A wide variety of software is available for most microcomputer systems. Ready-to-use software *packages* include control programs, computer language translators, statistical, business, educational programs, and computer games. These software packages are available in the form of cassettes, cartridges, floppy disks, plug-in ROM modules, or may be built into the microcomputer's original ROM unit. For example, a BASIC interpreter might be stored in ROM, while application programs like a payroll program or computer games would come in the other forms mentioned. BASIC is the most popular programming language for microcomputers followed by other languages such as Pascal, FORTRAN, and COBOL. As mentioned in the previous chapter, care must be taken to acquire efficient and error-free software from reputable sources.

Cost

Microcomputer costs may range from less than $500 for a beginning microcomputer system with only a keyboard and black-and-white television monitor, to over $5,000 for an expanded microcomputer system with several peripherals such as floppy-disk units and hard-copy printers. However, microprocessor chips encased in a plastic and metal package cost as little as $10 to $20 per chip. Thus the cheapest part of a microcomputer system is the microprocessor and its related memory and control circuitry. Peripheral devices such as hard-copy printers may cost between $800 and $2,000 while floppy-disk units can vary from $500 to over $1,500. Software costs must also be considered, though the software permanently stored in ROM such as a BASIC interpreter might be included in the price of the microcomputer hardware. Additional software may run from $5 for a computer game to $50 for a simple payroll program on a magnetic tape cassette, to $500 for a more complex accounting package requiring several floppy-disk units.

Applications

In the first chapter we discussed how microcomputers and microprocessors are responsible for the development of *personal computers* and *smart industrial* and *consumer products.* Microcomputer systems are also used as *small business computers* to process applications such as payroll, accounts receivable, accounts payable, and inventory control. They are used as small office computers for computerized word processing and text editing. They are being used by professionals and managers to provide convenient, portable, personalized support for analysis and decision making. They are also used for industrial process control, in industrial robots, at construction sites, and in scientific laboratories. They are rapidly spreading into the classroom—from grade school through college—using programs for computer-assisted-instruction (CAI).

Sources

Microcomputer hardware and software can be purchased from many different sources. There are over a thousand specialized retail computer stores (such as Computerland) which sell many different brands of microcomputers and other hardware and software as well as providing educational and repair services. Over 7,000 Radio Shack consumer electronic stores have been successful in marketing several hundred thousand of the TRS–80 series of microcomputers. Heathkit stores and catalogs offer microcomputers in kit form as well as fully assembled models. Other highly popular microcomputer systems are the Apple II and Apple III manufactured by Apple Computer, the PET (Personal Electronic Transactor) by Commodore Business Machines and a variety of other microcomputers by Altair, Texas Instruments, Hewlett-Packard, Ohio Scientific and many other companies, including even IBM! In addition to the hundreds of microcomputer manufacturers who also sell software, there are literally thousands of independent software suppliers who market their products through computer retailers and by mail order. A good source for more detailed information on microcomputer hardware, software, and applications are the personal computing magazines such as *Creative Computing, BYTE,* and *Personal Computing.* Figure 6–5 is a brief buyer's guide to popular personal computers.

FIGURE 6–5 A Buyer's Guide to Personal Computers

Computer/ Price Range	Where to Buy It	Primary Applications	Advantages/ Disadvantages
Apple 2 $1,330–$7,000	Computer stores	Home, schools, small business, professionals	Lots of software, but not enough power for some business uses
Apple 3 $4,240–$5,810	Computer stores	Professionals	Not much software
Atari 400 $399–$720	Computer, department, and electronics stores	Home	Low cost and excellent graphics, but keyboard difficult to use
Atari 800 $1,080–$2,000	Computer, department, and electronics stores	Home, schools, professionals	Excellent graphics, but cannot expand into a large system
Commodore VIC $299–$550	Computer and department stores	Home, schools	Low cost, but not much software
Commodore PET $995–$2,885	Computer stores	Home, schools	Not supported well in field
Commodore CBM $1,495–$4,000	Computer stores	Small business, professionals	Not supported well in field
Hewlett-Packard 85 $3,250–$6,000	Computer stores, direct sales	Scientific/technical, professionals	Special features for technical users, but small screen
IBM $1,565–$6,000	Computer stores, direct sales	Home, schools, small business, professionals	Good field support, but availability could be limited
Osborne Computer $1,795	Computer stores	Professionals	Portable, but small screen
Radio Shack Model 2 $3,000–$8,000	Radio Shack stores	Professionals, small business	Lots of software, but no color
Radio Shack Model 3 $699–$4,000	Radio Shack Stores	Home, schools, small business, professionals	Low price, but no color
Texas Instruments 99/4 $525–$4,000	Department stores, catalogs	Home, schools	Low price, but limited software
Xerox 820 $3,195–$6,400	Computer stores, direct sales	Small business, professionals	Good support, but no color
Zenith Z89 $2,895–$9,000	Computer stores, Heath Electronic centers	Small business, professionals	Very reliable, but no color

Source: Reprinted from the September 28, 1981, issue of *Business Week* by special permission. © 1981 by McGraw-Hill, Inc., New York, N.Y. 10020. All rights reserved. (Data from Datapro Research Corp., Future Computing, Inc., and Gnostic Concepts, Inc.)

PERSONAL COMPUTERS

One of the great attractions of microcomputers is their use as **personal computers**. Such systems may consist of a type-writer-size unit with a keyboard costing only a few hundred dollars, which can be used with a home TV unit for video output and a small cassette tape recorder for secondary storage. This simplicity and low entrance cost as well as the many possible personal uses of the microcomputer have caused a tremendous boom in personal computing. Of course, additional increments of hardware and software can escalate the cost of a home computer system as personal computer users become more proficient and want additional computing power to expand and improve their systems' capabilities. The cost of such high-priced personal computer systems may be hard to cost-justify on the basis of personal pleasure and home applications. This is why many personal computer systems are being used for business and professional applications which can more easily justify their expense. In any event, there are a large number of uses for personal computers which we can group into *six major categories.*

- **Entertainment and Hobbies.** The availability of TV "electronic game" cartridges for first-time computers is a strong attraction for many personal computer users. Many users moved up to microcomputers after first trying their hand at "dumb" electronic TV game devices. Games range from Star Trek, Pong, and electronic football to more challenging games like electronic chess or backgammon or complex "fantasy" games like Dungeons and Dragons. Computer games can provide many hours of stimulating and creative individual and family entertainment. Personal computers can themselves become a personal hobby. Some hobbyists like to assemble their own microcomputers and purchase kits for this purpose. Other hobbyists enjoy developing new and unique uses for their microcomputers, and in continually testing and modifying such applications. Other people may use their personal computers to support their own hobbies. For example, ham radio operators may use their personal computers to calculate and keep track of the locations of their overseas contacts; amateur musicians might use a "music synthesizer" attachment to generate new musical scores; while amateur artists can use the graphics capability of their computers to draw electronic designs, pictures, and other visual art.

- **Personal Finance.** Personal computer systems can be used for financial recordkeeping, analysis, and planning. Financial data such as family budgets, taxes, mortgage and other installment payments, transportation, and other expenses and investments can be organized and stored for later retrieval and analysis. The personal computer can therefore help with personal and family budgets, income tax preparation, bank checking and savings account balancing, medical and other insurance claims processing, tracking the stock market, evaluating various investment opportunities, and other forms of financial analysis and planning.

● **Home Management.** Personal computers are versatile home management tools. They can help control home heating systems to conserve energy, run security alarm systems, control household applicances, maintain fire alarm systems, control home lighting, and automate lawn and garden sprinkler systems. They can also help with household recordkeeping such as maintaining an inventory of all major items in a home, a file of recipes and menus, or a file of names, addresses, and phone numbers. Personal word processing applications can use the microcomputer to automate letter writing and other correspondence, produce mailing lists, keep dairies, and prepare other forms of typewritten material.

● **Education and Personal Development.** Microcomputers are already being used for computer-assisted instruction (CAI) in grade schools, high schools and colleges. This trend has extended into the home as educational "programmed learning" software is used in microcomputer systems. The computer can tutor students (both children and adults) in almost any subject since many educational program packages are available on magnetic tape cassettes, cartridges, and floppy disks. Thus, personal computers can tutor students in everything from mathematics to music, from English and French to BASIC and Pascal. Program packages are also available for "personal development" applications such as relaxation therapy, self hypnosis, assertiveness training, positive thinking, and other forms of development. Software is even available which can direct the microcomputer to chart biorhythms and give astrological advice!

● **Professional Use.** Of course, many personal computers are used by scientists, engineers, attorneys, physicians, teachers, managers, and business people to support their professional activities. In these cases, the microcomputer is used to do recordkeeping, perform various types of analysis, store and retrieve data and information, do word processing and text editing tasks and even help managers make decisions! (The use of microcomputers for *small business computing* will be discussed in the next section.) Predictions are being made that many professional work activities will be distributed to the home, thus allowing individuals to work at home with personal computers tied into their organization's computer network.

● **Information and Communication.** Personal computers have become intelligent terminals that are tied into public

FIGURE 6–6 Home Computer Network Services

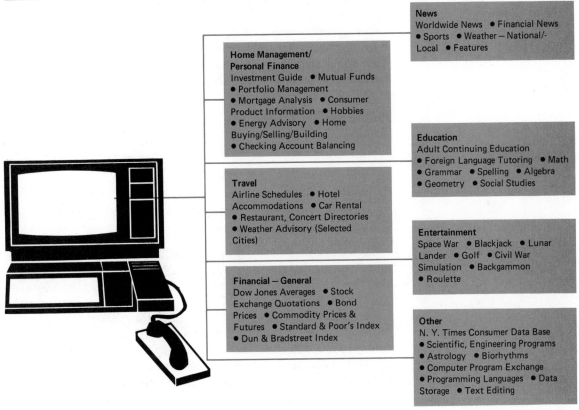

News
Worldwide News • Financial News
• Sports • Weather — National/-
Local • Features

**Home Management/
Personal Finance**
Investment Guide • Mutual Funds
• Portfolio Management
• Mortgage Analysis • Consumer
Product Information • Hobbies
• Energy Advisory • Home
Buying/Selling/Building
• Checking Account Balancing

Education
Adult Continuing Education
• Foreign Language Tutoring • Math
• Grammar • Spelling • Algebra
• Geometry • Social Studies

Travel
Airline Schedules • Hotel
Accommodations • Car Rental
• Restaurant, Concert Directories
• Weather Advisory (Selected
Cities)

Entertainment
Space War • Blackjack • Lunar
Lander • Golf • Civil War
Simulation • Backgammon
• Roulette

Financial — General
Dow Jones Averages • Stock
Exchange Quotations • Bond
Prices • Commodity Prices &
Futures • Standard & Poor's Index
• Dun & Bradstreet Index

Other
N. Y. Times Consumer Data Base
• Scientific, Engineering Programs
• Astrology • Biorhythms
• Computer Program Exchange
• Programming Languages • Data
Storage • Text Editing

Courtesy Texas Instruments.

computer-based information networks such as *The Source* by
Telecomputing Corporation of America and MicroNet by
CompuServe, Inc. These networks offer "viewdata" services
which allow two-way transmission of pictures and sound between a computerized home TV set and computerized national
data bank services. Figure 6–6 illustrates the wide variety of
services offered. Costs are presently about $5 per hour for
evening, nighttime, and weekend use of regular telephone
lines. The provision of such services by cable-TV companies
should further reduce the cost of home information and communication services.

MINICOMPUTER SYSTEMS

Minicomputers are small general-purpose computers that
are larger and more powerful than some microcomputers,

but are smaller and less powerful than most of the models of larger "main frame" computer systems. However, this is not a precise distinction, since high-end models of microcomputer systems are more powerful than some minicomputers, and high-end models of minicomputers are more powerful than some small and medium-size main frame computers. Minicomputers have a wide range of capabilities and characteristics such as:

- CPU speed and memory capacity.
- The number and types of peripheral devices that can be supported.
- Telecommunications capabilities.
- Ability to handle large numbers of CRT terminals.
- Ability to process several jobs at the same time.
- Their range of total costs.

In Chapter 1 we reported that the minicomputer was a development of the third generation of computers which began in the mid-1960s. Sales of minicomputers accelerated during the late 60s and 70s until minicomputers became the fastest growing segment of the computer market. The reasons for their great popularity are obvious. At one time, most computer manufacturers and DP managers believed that all of the data processing needs of an organization could be handled by conventional larger-scale computer systems. However, many *end users* in scientific laboratories, engineering

FIGURE 6–7 Minicomputer System

Courtesy Hewlett-Packard.

departments, manufacturing and industrial process plants, and many smaller organizations could not afford larger computer systems, or were dissatisfied with the level of service provided by large central computer installations. These users needed a smaller, less costly computer system which was still large enough to handle their data processing requirements. Since minicomputers were designed to handle a limited set of jobs and peripheral devices, they could be physically smaller and less costly than larger computers. Most minicomputers can also function in ordinary operating environments, and do not need special air conditioning or electrical wiring, and can be placed in most offices and work areas. In addition, since they are comparatively easy to operate, the smaller models of minicomputers do not need a staff of DP professionals but can rely on properly trained regular employees. Therefore, large numbers of users purchased and continue to acquire minicomputer systems. See Figure 6–7.

Hardware

Minicomputers can perform all of the functions of larger computers but are usually physically small, low-cost machines which usually have fewer registers, smaller word-length, slower processing speeds, smaller memories, and less input/output and data communication capabilities. Minicomputers typically have a 16-bit word-length but the number of 32-bit *super-minicomputers* is growing. Primary storage capacity might range from 16K to 512K bytes of semiconductor memory, though minis with *megabyte memories* are available. A wide variety of *miniperipherals* are available for minicomputer systems. Smaller minicomputers might be limited to a CRT terminal, slow-speed character printer, and floppy-disk secondary storage, while larger minicomputers use more peripherals such as multiple CRT terminals, larger capacity hard magnetic disk units, faster line printers and punched card and magnetic tape devices. Typically, CRT terminals are used for keyboard input and video displays, and printing terminals or small line printers are used for hard copy paper output. Magnetic floppy disks and removable disk packs are used to provide several megabytes of secondary storage. Smaller versions of standard magnetic tape and disk units, faster printing devices, and many other peripheral devices are available. Many minicomputers also have a data communications capability since they are widely used in *distributed processing networks*.

Software

Software is an important component of minicomputer systems. A minimal amount of software was available in the early years of minicomputer use. However, a wide variety of software packages are now available, including operating systems, several major programming languages, and application software packages developed for a large number of specific industries and types of business. FORTRAN, COBOL, BASIC and RPG and several other languages are available on minicomputers. Even data base management systems (DBMS) software are available for popular minicomputer systems. However, it must be emphasized that minicomputer software may be scaled-down versions of the software used on larger computers. For example, the full features of programming languages like FORTRAN and COBOL may not be available on minicomputer systems. Just as with microcomputers, software is available in the form of magnetic tape cassettes and floppy disks including many prewritten application packages which make it unnecessary for many minicomputer users to develop their own programs.

Cost

The wide variation of minicomputer capabilities is reflected in a wide range of prices for minicomputer systems. The majority of minicomputers cost between $5,000 and $50,000 though prices between $50,000 and $100,000 and even higher must be paid for some *super-mini* systems. Like microcomputer systems, the cost of input/output and secondary storage peripheral devices frequently exceed the cost of the minicomputer CPU. Each unit of software needed must also be purchased unless it is "packaged" along with the computer hardware.

Applications

Minicomputers are quite versatile. They are being used for a large number of business data processing and scientific applications. Minicomputers first became popular for use in scientific research, instrumentation systems, engineering analysis, and industrial process monitoring and control. Minicomputers can easily handle such uses because these applications were narrow in scope and did not demand the processing power of large systems. Minicomputers are now being used as *intelligent terminals* and *end user* computer systems in *distributed processing networks.* They serve as industrial process-control and manufacturing plant computers, where they play a major role in computer assisted manufacturing (CAM) and computer assisted design (CAD) applications. They are also being used as *front-end* computers to control data communications networks and large numbers of data-entry terminals. Also, many current *word processing computers* are either special-purpose or dedicated minicomputers or intelligent terminals. In addition, there is a fast-growing category of minicomputers known as *small business computers* which we will discuss in the next section.

Sources

The leading manufacturers of minicomputers include Digital Equipment Corporation (DEC), IBM, Honeywell, Hewlett-Packard, Data General, Wang Laboratories, Prime Computer, Basic-Four, Burroughs, and NCR. Minicomputers can be purchased directly from a local or regional office of the larger computer manufacturers or through independent distributors who represent one or more minicomputer manufacturers who do not sell directly to end users. Some of these dealers are called *original equipment manufacturers* (OEMs). They buy minicomputers from manufacturers and add peripheral equipment and software tailored to the needs of each user. Peripheral equipment and software can be purchased from manufacturers, independent dealers, and a large number of independent software development firms. Many minicomputers are available on a **turnkey** basis in which a complete system of hardware, software, and systems development needed by a user for a set of applications are provided by the minicomputer vendor. This even includes installing the computer system and training the employees of the user in its operation. Thus, supposedly, all an end user has to do is simply "turn the key" and operate the minicomputer system.

SMALL BUSINESS COMPUTERS

One of the fast growing segments of the computer market is known as **small business computers.** These small computers are specifically designed for the data processing requirements of offices and small business firms, or a limited number of business applications in large businesses and other organizations. The term "small business computer" is used quite loosely, since it is usually applied not only to *minicomputers* but also to larger *microcomputer* systems and smaller *main*

FIGURE 6–8 Small Business
Computer System

frame computers. Therefore, processing power, hardware devices, software packages, and costs will range widely over the spectrum from large microcomputers to minicomputers and small full-scale computer systems. What will not vary is the primary use of such computers for business data processing applications. See Figure 6–8.

Applications

Small business computers are usually dedicated to common business and accounting applications (discussed in Chapter 14) such as accounts receivable, accounts payable, inventory control, payroll, and general ledger accounting. Besides these *recordkeeping* applications, small business computers can also be applied to *operational* applications such as inventory control, sales order processing, and a variety of other applications that support the data processing needs of functional departments within a business organization. Small business computers are also used for *managerial reporting* and *data base applications,* which not only provide traditional management reports but allow users and management to make inquiries and use an integrated data base. Prewritten program packages are usually provided for the processing of such applications.

Small business computers are used not only as *stand-alone* computer systems, but also are connected by telecommunications links in distributed processing networks of computers.

This emphasizes the fact that small business computers are not only being acquired by small business firms, but are being purchased by larger business organizations to *disperse* business data processing capabilities throughout the departments of their organizations. From all indications, small business computer systems will continue to be a fast growing application area for small computers. Of course, it should be emphasized that many business people underestimate the amount of computing capacity needed to handle their business applications. For example, there are many cases where personal computers were used for business applications and were unable to satisfactorily handle the volume, diversity, and time requirements involved. In other cases, business applications quickly outgrow the capacity of personal computers and have to be replaced with larger minicomputer systems, thus forcing a firm to "start all over" because of differences in the computer systems used.

Sources

Business people are buying their small business computers from independent computer dealers, "system houses," and computer retailers as well as directly from computer manufacturers. In many cases, small business computers are purchased on a *turnkey* basis, including software packages. Additional software can be purchased from many independent software firms which specialize in providing business application software packages. System software such as operating systems and data base management systems is also available. Vendor maintenance and support services are not provided by many microcomputer and minicomputer manufacturers, though it is of utmost importance to insure proper computer system operation. Vendor maintenance contracts and other support services must be purchased from the manufacturer, the OEM, computer dealer, or retailer.

LARGER COMPUTER SYSTEMS

We have already indicated that the development of microcomputers and minicomputers has erased many of the traditional distinctions between small, medium- and large-scale computers. For example, some minicomputers are cheaper and more powerful than traditional small computers while many *super-mini* computers are frequently less expensive and more powerful than some medium-size computers. Though these developments have weakened the traditional size distinctions between full-scale computer systems, they are still widely used in the computer industry.

Small Computers

Most **small computer systems** are larger and more versatile than many minicomputers and have greater input/output and storage capabilities. Many of these small systems dislodged electromechanical punched card equipment from small business data processing installations during the 1960s. Thus, many small computer systems stressed the use of punched cards for input and output, and magnetic tape for secondary storage. However, these second generation peripheral devices and media are being displaced by CRT video terminals and magnetic floppy-disk and hard-disk units. Small computer systems can also support a large number of other peripheral devices including high-speed line printers, large capacity magnetic disk and tape units, and many data communications terminals. Since small computers are full-scale computers, they have a 32-bit word-length, with primary storage capacities ranging from about 128K bytes to several megabytes.

Like most modern computers, small computers may make heavy use of *firmware* and thus have much of their internal instruction sets written in *microprograms* or *microcode* which are stored in ROM or reloadable control storage units in their CPUs. Also, many full-scale computers are now using a *multiprocessor* design in which the CPU contains more than one processor. A more complete line of software packages is usually provided by the manufacturers of small computer systems, including operating systems, data base management systems, and specialized industry application programs. Therefore small computers are no longer limited to *batch processing* jobs where groups (or *batches*) of transactions are processed periodically, but can now also handle *realtime processing* applications where transactions are processed as they occur. Most of these small computers can also process a limited amount of data processing jobs at the same time, including servicing users at remote terminals.

Selling prices for small computer systems range from about $50,000 to over $250,000, while monthly rentals may vary from $1,000 to $5,000 per month. These wide variations in prices are of course primarily related to the amount of storage capacity and the number of input and output devices that are included in a particular system. Many small computers are manufactured by companies which also make a full line of larger main frame computers such as IBM, Honeywell, Control Data, DEC, Burroughs and NCR. Most of them provide a complete line of hardware and software products to support their small computer systems. Examples of some current small computers include the IBM System/38 and 4331, Hewlett-Packard's HP3000 series, DEC's VAX 11/780 and Burrough's B920. See Figure 6–9.

Medium-Size Computer Systems

As with other computer sizes, there is much overlap between the medium and large computer system categories. **Medium-size computers** are larger, faster and can handle more input/output and storage devices than small computers. Primary storage capacities range between 1 and 10 megabytes, with selling prices falling between $200,000 and $1 million, and monthly rental charges between $5,000 and $20,000 per month. These computer systems have secondary storage capacities of several *gigabytes* because of their use of many high capacity, online magnetic disk units. Like most full-scale computers, they usually take advantage of a *virtual memory* capability. Examples of medium-size computers include the IBM 4341 and the Burrough's B4700. See Figure 6–10.

Large Computer Systems

Large computers have even faster processing speeds, greater storage capacity, a wider selection of input/output devices and greater processing capabilities than medium-size computers. A typical large computer installation might include

FIGURE 6–9   VAX 11/780 Small (super-mini) Computer System

Courtesy Digital Equipment Corporation.

FIGURE 6–10   IBM 4341 Medium-Size Computer System

Courtesy IBM Corporation.

several tape drives and high speed printers, many high capacity magnetic disk units, a variety of specialized input and output devices, and a capacity to support hundreds of remote terminals. Operating speeds are in the low nanosecond range and processing speeds of at least several million instructions per second (MIPS) are common. Memory capacities range from 1 to 50 megabytes. Larger models may have a *multiprocessor design* including more than one CPU sharing a common memory. These powerful computing systems are used for large and complex data processing assignments in which the ability to handle hundreds of remote input/output terminals and process many applications simultaneously is required.

Large computer systems are used by large corporations and government agencies which have enormous and complex data processing assignments. For example, large computers are necessary for organizations processing millions of transactions each day, such as major national banks or the national stock exchanges. Large computers can also handle the great volume of complex calculations involved in scientific and engineering analysis and simulation of complex design projects such as the design of aircraft and spacecraft. A large computer can also act as a *host computer* for distributed processing networks that include many smaller computers. Thus, large computers are used in the national and international computing networks of major corporations such as airlines, banks, and oil companies.

FIGURE 6–11 UNIVAC 1100/ 60 Large Computer System

Courtesy Sperry UNIVAC.

Large computers are supported by a great number of sophisticated software packages including virtual memory operating systems and data base management systems. Such software gives them a *multiprogramming* capability where many programs can be processed at the same time. Thus many large *time-sharing* networks allow hundreds of users to utilize a large computer at the same time. Monthly rentals for large computer systems range from $20,000 to over $200,000 per month with purchase prices varying from about $1,000,000 to over $5,000,000. Examples of large computer systems include the IBM 3033 and 3081, the Honeywell 66/80, and the Amdahl 5860 and 5880. See Figure 6–11.

Supercomputers

The term **supercomputer** has been coined to describe a small number of extremely large computer systems. Supercomputers may be built under contract for a specific user such as the ILLIAC IV built by Burroughs for the University of Illinois at a cost of $24 million. However a small number of supercomputers are built each year for users such as large government research agencies, military defense systems, national weather forecasting agencies, and very large time-sharing networks. The leading maker of supercomputers is Cray Research which produces the Cray–I, the most widely used supercomputer. It has a 64-bit word-length, an effective machine and memory cycle time of a dozen nanoseconds, and weighs over five tons. Control Data is the other major manufacturer of supercomputers. The CDC Cyber 205 supercomputer is capable of 800-million arithmetic floating-point operations per second. Purchase prices for supercomputers are in the $5 million to $15 million range. These massive computer systems are extremely large and fast and advance the state-of-the-art for the entire computer industry. See Figure 6–12.

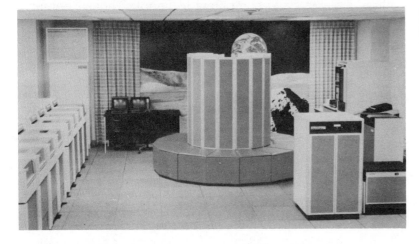

FIGURE 6–12   The Cray–I Supercomputer

MULTIPROCESSOR COMPUTER SYSTEMS

Many fourth generation computers can be classified as **multiprocessor computer systems** since they use a *multiprocessor architecture* in the design of their central processing units. Instead of having one CPU with a single control unit, arithmetic-logic unit, and primary storage unit (called a **uniprocessor** design), the CPUs of these computers contain several types of processing units. The two major types of multiprocessor architecture involve:

● **Support processor systems.** The key to this new multiprocessor design is the use of *microprocessors* to control the operations of several major processing functions, such as input/output, primary storage management, and data communications, thus freeing the main **central processor** (sometimes called the *instruction processor*) to do the major job of executing program instructions.

- **Coupled processor systems.** This multiprocessor design uses multiple CPUs, or CPU configurations consisting of multiple arithmetic-logic and control units which share the same primary storage unit.

In addition, there are two types of multiprocessor systems that involve the control and coordination of several *separate* computer systems.

- **Subsidiary Processing Systems.** One or more separate computer systems handle specific functions (such as input/output) for and under the complete control of a larger computer system. For example, a large *master* computer may utilize smaller *slave* computers to handle "housekeeping" chores such as input/output operations. In other cases, several computers may be interconnected in order to handle large processing assignments and to provide a *backup* capability that would not be present if only one large computer was used.

- **Distributed Processing Systems.** One or more cooperating but *independent* computer systems are physically and organizationally dispersed throughout a computer-using organization. (We will discuss such distributed processing systems in Chapter 11.)

Support Processor Systems

Figure 6–13 illustrates the *support processor* design of the IBM 4341 computer system. Notice how there are four separate processors: (1) the instruction processing unit, (2) the storage control unit, (3) the channel execution unit and (4) the service processor unit. The *instruction processing unit* consists of the control unit and the arithmetic logic unit and controls and directs the processing of the other processing units. Thus the other processing units are *support processors* for the instruction processing unit. The *storage control unit* manages the transfer of data and instructions from the primary storage and cache units to the instruction processing unit and the channel execution unit. The channel execution unit manages the input/output control functions of the *channels* of the computer system. The *service processor* handles a variety of functions including the operator console, a magnetic diskette drive

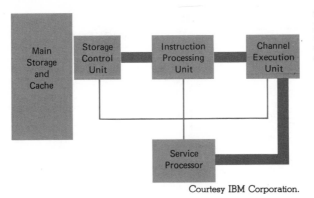

FIGURE 6-13 Support
Processor Design of the IBM
4341 Computer System

Courtesy IBM Corporation.

for loading microprograms and the circuitry for the computer's automatic and remote maintenance service functions.

Many other variations of the support processor design are used by modern computer systems. For example, the Burroughs B920 computer system employs from five to eight processor modules, each containing a microprocessor and its own buffer memory. In a B920 with five processor modules, there is one main *operating control module* (which serves as the control unit for the computer), while one module handles input/output functions, another manages primary storage, and two modules are *task processors* that compile and execute application programs. This design allows a task processor to be switched over to act as a storage management processor or system control processor in event of their failure. Also, the processing power of the computer can be substantially increased by the addition of more processor modules.

Coupled Processor Systems

The **coupled processor** design is illustrated by Figure 6-14 which shows two multiprocessor designs in the IBM 3000 large computer series. IBM calls this a *tightly coupled* processing design. In this configuration, two or more central processing units are interconnected so they can execute two or more instructions *simultaneously,* one in each processor. This ability of a computer system to execute several instruction simultaneously is known as **multiprocessing.** Notice that in the 3033 multiprocessor design, two CPUs share the same primary storage and are coordinated by a *multiprocessing* control unit.

The 3081 *processor complex* is a large computer system that IBM calls a *dyadic processor.* In this configuration, two

FIGURE 6–14 Tightly Coupled
Multiprocessor Designs

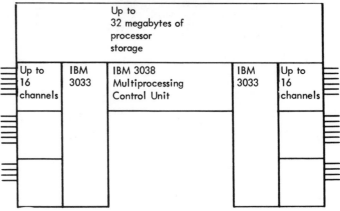

IBM 3033 Multiprocessor

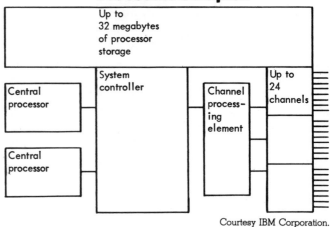

IBM 3081 Processor Complex

Courtesy IBM Corporation.

separate CPUs and a channel processing unit are coordinated by a system control unit and share the same primary storage. The *tightly coupled* processor design allows CPUs to share access to all available primary storage, and all CPUs are under the control of a single operating system. However, there are many other coupled processor configurations. In a *loosely coupled* design, processors are connected by channel-to-channel adaptors or system busses. For example, Figure 6–15 shows a multiprocessor design of Tandem Computers, in which multiple CPUs are interconnected by two independent

FIGURE 6–15   A Loosely Coupled Multiprocessor Design

DYNABUS™ (dual independent interprocessor busses)

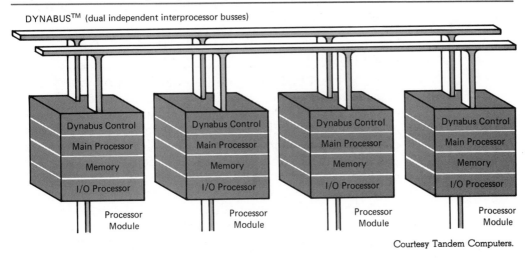

Courtesy Tandem Computers.

busses. Notice that each *processor module* has its own primary storage and I/O processor.

Reasons for Multiprocessor Systems

Computer manufacturers are now moving toward multiprocessor architectures primarily because of the availability of powerful, low cost microprocessors, which can be dedicated to handle specific CPU functions. Therefore, attaining the advantages of multiprocessing has become technologically and economically feasible. The benefits of a multiprocessor computer system include:

- Significantly greater and faster processing capability, especially when a true *multiprocessing* capability exists (when more than one instruction can be executed at the same time).
- Better utilization of primary storage since processors share primary storage.
- More efficient use of input/output and secondary storage peripheral devices.
- Increased reliability since multiple processors provide a backup capability as well as help to meet peak load processing.
- Reduced software problems since processors may share the same system control and service programs.

200

- A more economical arrangement than having several independent computer systems share processing responsibilities.

Multiprocessor Trends

It is evident that there is a trend toward the increased use of multiprocessor computer architectures. Many large computers are using microprocessors to handle subsidiary functions in support of the CPU. Other computer systems use the tightly coupled approach in which several CPUs are interconnected and share the same primary storage, operating system, and peripheral devices. Still others use the subsidiary approach where one or more separate computer systems handle specific functions for, and under, the control of a larger computer system. Computers are using and will increase their use of multiprocessor designs which might include components like the following:

- A **front-end processor** for data communications control.
- A **back-end processor** or *data base machine* for management of large integrated data bases.
- One or more **input/output processors** or *channel management processors* to manage the I/O channels and control units for input/output functions.
- An **arithmetic processor** or *array processor* to handle complex, large volume arithmetic "number crunching."
- **Language processors** which would allow direct execution of programs written in high-level programming languages (for example, a FORTRAN processor).
- **Control processors** which would accomplish functions presently done by the control programs of operating system software.
- **Service processors** which would handle many of the subsidiary service functions of present operating system software.

FIGURE 6–16 An Advanced Multiprocessor Computer System

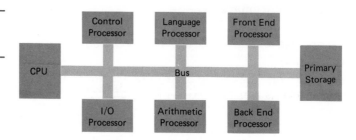

Figure 6–16 illustrates the architecture of a computer with such multiprocessing components. Many of these specialized processors are already being used by present computer systems. This has led some experts to predict that the computer of the future will not be a **computer system,** but will be a **system of computers.**

SUMMARY

- Computers are frequently classified by type (digital, and analog), purpose (general-purpose, special-purpose, business, scientific, and dedicated), by processor architecture (uniprocessor and multiprocessor) and by size (micro, mini, small, medium, large, and super computers).

- Analog computers measure continuous physical magnitudes, such as electronic voltage, while digital computers count discrete units (digits). A special-purpose computer is specifically designed to process a specific application, while a general-purpose computer is designed to process a wide variety of applications. Scientific computers are designed for the high-speed processing of numerical data involving complex, mathematical calculations. Business computers are general-purpose computers which are designed to efficiently process the large volumes and variety of numeric and alphabetic data that is characteristic of business data processing. A dedicated computer is a general-purpose computer that has been committed to a particular data processing task.

- Microcomputers are general-purpose digital computers that range in size from a computer-on-a-chip to a small typewriter-size unit. Microcomputers are being used in smart industrial and consumer products and as personal computers and small business computers. Personal computers are typically used for entertainment, personal finance, home management, education, and professional activities.

- Minicomputers are small general-purpose computers that are larger and more powerful than most microcomputers. They are being used for a large number of business data processing and scientific applications. They are being used as intelligent terminals and end-user systems in distributed processing networks, as industrial process-control computers, front-end data communications computers, intelligent terminals, word processing computers, and small business computers. Small computers specifically designed for the data processing requirements of offices and small business firms, or a limited number of business applications in large businesses are known as small business computers.

- Many fourth generation computers are multiprocessor computer systems which have CPUs which contain several types of processing units. Some computers use microprocessors to handle subsidiary functions in support of the CPU, while others involve several separate CPUs which are interconnected and share the same primary storage. Computer manufacturers are moving toward multiprocessor architectures because of the availability of powerful, low-cost microprocessors which can be dedicated to specific CPU functions.

KEY TERMS AND CONCEPTS

Analog versus digital computers

Special-purpose versus general-purpose computers

Dedicated computers

Microcomputer

Microprocessor

Personal computer

Minicomputer

Small business computer

Small, medium, large, and super computers

Multiprocessor computer system

REVIEW AND DISCUSSION QUESTIONS

1. How do the following types of computers differ?
    a. Analog versus digital computers.
    b. Special-purpose versus general-purpose computers.
    c. Scientific versus business computers.

2. How does a dedicated computer differ from a special-purpose or general-purpose computer? What are some of the uses of dedicated computers?

3. What are the major characteristics and uses of microcomputers and minicomputers? Distinguish between their use as personal computers, intelligent terminals, and small business computers.

4. What are the major differences in the capabilities and costs of small-, medium-, and large-scale computers? How has the development of "super-mini" computers begun to blur such distinctions?

5. Can owning a personal computer be cost-justified based on typical personal computer uses? Explain.

6. Are small business computers designed only for the computer applications of small business firms, or can larger organizations use such computers?

7. Are larger computer systems really necessary, given the power and versatility of modern minicomputers? Why or why not?

8. What are the major types of multiprocessor computer systems? Why is there a trend toward such systems?

9. Why have some experts predicted that the computer of the future will not be a *computer system*, but will be a *system of computers?*

REAL WORLD APPLICATIONS

6–1   Blue Cross of Virginia

"In terms of reliability and availability, it's by far the best new machine we've ever installed."

Leo Harris, technical operations manager for Blue Cross of Virginia, is referring to the organization's IBM 3032 Processor, which anchors a terminal network for interactive claims processing.

"We run the 3032 twenty-four hours a day, seven days a week," Mr. Harris reports. "During last August and September, we were averaging above 99.5 percent availability. If you look at how we're driving that machine, we're getting a lot of mileage."

Availability is important to Blue Cross, because the mainframe drives a 200-terminal network through which users in hospitals and doctors' offices enter medical claims. The interactive system prompts users on how to enter claims, notifies them of any errors in an online adjudication process, and informs them when they can expect payment.

Virginia Blue Cross is committed to a long range goal of achieving paperless processing, to lower operating costs and increase customer service.[1]

- Why does Blue Cross of Virginia need a large computer system?
- Is there still a need for such large systems in business? Explain.

[1] Source: "Big Processors at Work," *Data Processor*, February 1979, pp. 2–3. Reprinted with permission.

6–2   The Kula Onion

Bernie Eiting owns a delicatessen and specialty grocery store, the Kula Onion, in the Kula district of Maui, Hawaii, and a marketing company in Chicago. After looking at various machines, he bought a Z80-based Vector Graphic system.

"We use it in the managing of the little store," says Eiting. "We have the Peachtree accounting package. We're in the process of putting out a quarterly newsletter for the store. I use the word-processing program for that and for general business corre-

spondence. I also have a mailing-list program that merges with my word processing. Through our data-base management system, we can do some independent programming in English, without having to call in a programmer. I produce management indexes, such things as the kind of return I get on my investment and so forth." Eiting also does direct-mail advertising for himself and for clients of his Chicago company, Marketing Dynamics. Eventually he intends to upgrade his system with a hard-disk setup for mass storage.[2]

- List the ways Bernie Eiting uses his microcomputer.
- Is such versatility unusual for a microcomputer system? Explain.

[2] Source: "The Data Game: Business and the Microcomputer," *Passages*, May 1981, p. 21. Reprinted with permission.

6–3 The Boeing Company

Small companies aren't the only ones using microcomputers. Boeing, for instance, owns more than $400 million worth of computer hardware, including some of the most powerful machines in the world; it also owns several hundred microcomputers. Most are commercial machines, according to Ron Hougham, manager of Boeing's Systems Engineering Architecture Group in Seattle, but some are very simple personal computers.

"We generally have the policy that if a person can use an $800 Commodore Pet to do a particular job, and if that machine can do the same job as an $8,000 industrial-grade machine, then we classify that as an innovative use," Hougham explains. "We have several installations like that. Our Data Center in Kent, Washington, contains a number of IBM 3033 machines. Their performance is monitored and displayed on a graphics screen by a Commodore Pet. It opens some people's eyes to see an $800 machine monitoring a million-dollar machine, but it works very well."[3]

• How does the Boeing Company demonstrate that large corporations as well as small business firms can use microcomputer systems?

  [3] Source: "The Data Game: Business and the Microcomputer," *Passages,* May 1981, p. 21. Reprinted with permission.

Computer Programming and Languages

7

CHAPTER OUTLINE

Computer Programming

LEARNING OBJECTIVES

The purpose of this chapter is to promote a basic understanding of computer programming by analyzing (1) the functions of the six stages of computer programming, (2) the concepts and applications of structured programming, and (3) the construction and use of several program design aids.

After reading and studying this chapter, you should be able to:

1. Summarize the functions of the six stages of computer programming.
2. Outline several ways that structured programming affects program design, coding and debugging.
3. Briefly explain the purpose of structure and HIPO charts, layout forms, flowcharts, pseudocode, and decision tables.
4. Prepare simple system and program flowcharts.
5. Identify the basic types of computer instructions.
6. Identify several types of programming errors and describe some checking and testing activities of program debugging.
7. Discuss the purpose and content of program documentation and maintenance.
8. Discuss developments in interactive programming and their impact on the programming process.

Understanding the fundamentals of computers and their hardware and software is an important achievement. However, it is equally important that you have a basic understanding of how computers are *programmed* to do what we want them to do. That is the purpose of this chapter, the following chapter on programming languages, and any practice in actual computer programming that you may be required to do in an introductory computer course.

THE PROGRAMMING PROCESS

Computer programming is a process which results in the development of a *computer program,* the set of detailed instructions which outline the data processing activities to be performed by a computer. Business people, managers, and other computer users must understand the computer programming process if they are to communicate effectively with programmers concerning computerized solutions to business problems. In addition, the development of time-sharing terminals, micro- and minicomputers, and simpler computer languages make it possible for many computer users to be their own computer programmers. Also, for many computer users, the programming process will eventually involve the use of simple conversational languages in a "dialog" with the computer. Thus, a basic knowledge of computer programming is desirable for all present and potential computer users.

The Stages of Computer Programming

Computer programming is a process that involves more than the writing of instructions in a programming language. Computer programming may be subdivided into six stages, each of which is summarized in Figure 7–1. In this chapter, we will discuss the tools and activities needed to accomplish each of these programming stages. However, before going any further, we should introduce two important developments in modern programming known as **structured programming** and **interactive programming.**

Structured Programming

Structured programming is a programming methodology which is part of a renewed emphasis on **software engineering,** which involves the systematic design and development of soft-

FIGURE 7-1   The Stages of Computer Programming

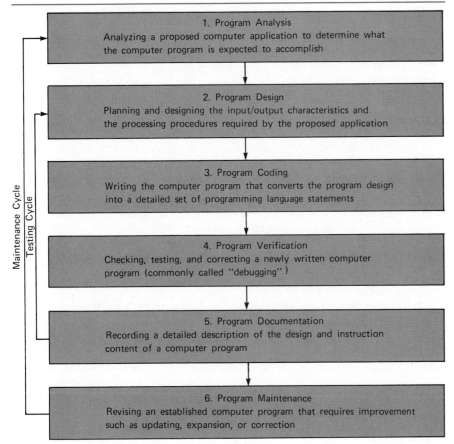

ware, and the management of the software development process. Software engineering views the development of a program as a coordinated activity involving people, tools, and practices, using modern design, development, and management methods in an integrated approach. Structured programming involves methods such as *top-down* program design and uses a limited number of *control structures* in a program, in order to create highly structured *modules* of program code. Structured programming includes program design, coding, and verification techniques such as *top-down design, modularity, stepwise refinement,* and *chief programmer teams.* It also includes tools such as *structure* and *HIPO charts, structured coding, pseudocode,* and *structured walkthroughs.* We will discuss the role of these computer programming techniques in this chapter.

Structured programming is an attempt to reduce the cost of developing and maintaining computer programs by standardizing program development and structures, thus increasing their simplicity and accuracy, and minimizing programming cost and maintenance. Software engineering and structured programming are methodologies which enable computer programming to become more of a *science* than an *art.* Traditional ways of programming rely on the creativeness of each programmer to write "efficient" programs that require a minimum of instructions, storage, and computer time to perform a specific data processing assignment. However, this flexible and creative environment frequently results in complex and difficult-to-read programs which require much testing before they are error free, and thus are costly to develop and maintain.

Structured programming, on the other hand, emphasizes a standardization of programming design concepts and methods, which significantly reduces program complexity. Therefore, structured programming can produce the following benefits:

● *Programming productivity*—programmers write more program instructions per day with fewer errors.
● *Programming economy*—The cost and time of program development and maintenance are reduced.
● *Programming simplicity*—programs are easier to write, read, correct, and maintain.[1]

Interactive Programming

For many users and programmers, computer programming is becoming an automated, interactive process. A computer user or programmer can design and code the processing logic of a computer program with substantial realtime assistance from a computer system. This involves using a computer or computer terminal to code, translate, test, debug, and de-

---

[1] H. D. Mills, *How to Write Correct Programs and Know It.* IBM Federal Systems Division, February 1973. Mills reports that IBM programmers utilized structured programming techniques in developing an online information system for the *New York Times.* The entire project produced over 83,000 lines of code with less than four errors per 10,000 lines of code, and only one error per manyear of effort!

velop alternatives for a new program in a realtime interactive process. Such *interactive programming* has become feasible through the use of software tools such as **application development systems** which provide interactive assistance to programmers (including menus, prompts, and graphics) in their development of application programs. Application development systems simplify and automate the programming process, just as *data base management systems* (DBMS) simplify and automate the creation, maintenance, and extraction of data and information from the data bases of an organization. They contain programs called *programming tools* which support interactive and automated program logic generation, editing, coding, testing, debugging, and maintenance. (Refer back to Figure 5–5 in Chapter 5.)

FIGURE 7–2   Programming Support Provided for Interactive Programming

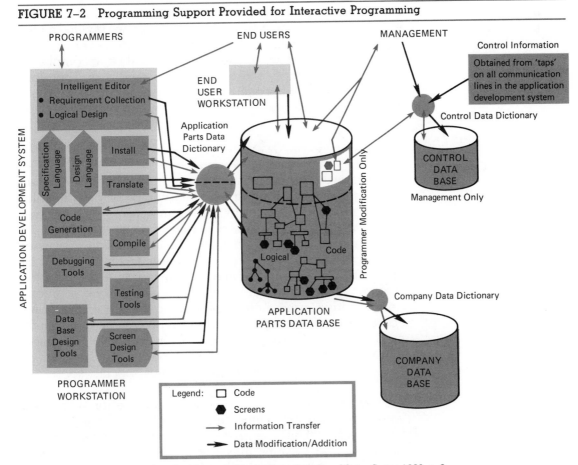

Source: Mitch L. Zoluker, "Editors Introduction," Adapted from *Data Base*, Winter–Spring 1980, p. 8.

Interactive programming relies on the concept of the *programmer workstation* (or *workbench*) which provides programmers with programming support (illustrated in Figure 7–2) which includes:

- *Hardware* support—a computer terminal with a keyboard and visual display unit.
- Programming *tools*—software (such as application development systems) to assist in the development of programs.
- Application program *parts*—standard program segments stored in an application parts data base.
- Data base management systems—resources for the real-time use of common data bases such as *data manipulation, report generator,* and *query languages,* and a *data dictionary.*

Continuing developments in interactive programming and structured programming will have a significant effect on the computer programming process in the future. Some experts even predict that such developments will one day make most current programming practices obsolete. However, it is still important to understand what activities must be accomplished in order to develop workable computer programs. Therefore, we shall now examine each of the basic stages of the computer programming process.

PROGRAM ANALYSIS

"What is the proposed program supposed to do?" *Program analysis* is an important first step in computer programming which answers that question. The amount of work involved is directly related to the type of application being programmed and the amount of *systems analysis and design* (discussed in Chapter 15) that has previously been accomplished. If the application to be programmed is viewed as a *problem* that requires a solution, then program analysis can be a process described by terms such as *problem definition* and *problem specification.* If the application to be programmed is considered a *system,* then program analysis might be described as a process that involves the determination of *systems objectives, systems requirements,* and *systems specifications.*

Program analysis may be relatively simple for short problems or for complex mathematical problems whose arithmetic form clearly defines the problem to be solved. Even complex problems and systems may not require extensive program analysis if a thorough job of systems analysis and design has been accomplished. If this is the case, then program analysis will consist of an analysis of the objectives, requirements, and specifications of the proposed program. Figure 7–3 details what a systems analyst might provide a computer programmer at this stage for a major programming project.

Whether the application to be programmed is simple or complex, and whether the proposed application has been

FIGURE 7–3 System Specifications for Programming Analysis

PROGRAM/PROJECT SPECIFICATIONS

Purpose	This should be a concise statement (one paragraph) of what is to be accomplished by the program/project.
Scope	This should describe in one sentence the extent of the program/project.
Input	This should describe the types of data to be processed, in detail. Included should be the *source, format, volume, codes,* etc.
Output	This should describe all information produced, in detail. Included should be *type, format, volume, codes, forms, sizes, copies, distribution.* . . .
Exceptions	This should describe any input or output to be handled but not processed by the program. An example of this would be where all records are read from a tape, but certain types or codes are to be ignored completely in the actual manipulation of data.
Processing	This should describe the actual steps to be followed to achieve the results required of the program/project. Normally this should be the largest section in the specifications, but every attempt should be made to make this area as clear and concise as possible.
Formulae	This should describe as clearly as possible the actual calculations to be performed in the processing. It should be shown separately so that examples can be included but should be referenced by the process section.
Decision Tables	This should show complex editing and control situations in an easily understandable way. The intention of the decision table would be to eliminate large amounts of writing in the process section by referencing the process to the decision table.
Controls	This should describe the internal and external controls to be incorporated into the program/project. Also included in this section would be any error messages to be generated by the programmer.
Comments	This should include any information that the systems analyst feels will clarify or make the programming easier.
Schedule	This should specify the normal frequency and running time of the program/project. Also, it should include the retention cycle of the tape or disks used in the operation.
Samples, Forms, Examples	This should include source documents, printer layouts, test data generated.

Source: Adapted from *Automatic Data Processing and Management* by Nathan Berkowitz and Robertson Munro, p. 245. Copyright © 1969 by Dickenson Publishing Company, Inc., Belmont, California. Reprinted by permission of the publisher.

subjected to an extensive systems analysis and design effort, the program analysis stage requires a preliminary determination of what the program is supposed to accomplish. Thus (1) the **output** required, (2) the **input** available, (3) the data held in **storage** that will be provided or updated, (4) the **processing** (mathematical, logical, and other procedures) that will probably be required, and (5) the **control** procedures that will be needed should be determined.

Once these preliminary determinations have been made, the final step of programming analysis is to determine whether the proposed application "can" or "should" be programmed. Is programming the proposed application possible and practical? A request for more information about the proposed application or a recommendation that the proposal be redesigned or abandoned may have to be made at this point.

PROGRAM DESIGN

The *program design* stage of computer programming involves the planning and design of the specific input/output characteristics and processing procedures required by the proposed application. As in the case of the programming analysis stage, the amount of effort required in the program design stage depends on the complexity of the application and the amount of systems analysis and design work that has previously been performed.

Program design requires the development of a logical set of rules and instructions that specify the operations required to accomplish the proposed data processing application. This aspect of program design is known in computer science as the development of an **algorithm**, which can be loosely defined as a set of rules or instructions that specify the operations required in the solution of a problem or the accomplishment of a task.

In the program design stage, one must first develop the general organization of the program as it relates to the main functions to be performed. The program is usually divided into several main subdivisions, such as a beginning *initialization* section, input, processing, and output sections, as well as an ending *termination* section. Most programs also have sections that deal with the testing and control of exceptional conditions such as errors or other deviations from normal processing requirements. The use of common *subroutines* that are available to perform operations required by any section of the program must also be considered during the design stage.

Computer programmers may use "structure charts," "HIPO charts," "flowcharts," "decision tables," and input/output and storage "layout forms" in the program design stage. We will discuss these analytical tools shortly.

Top-Down Design

Top-down design is a method of program design that is a major part of "structured programming." It entails the following steps:

- The programmer must define the *output* that is to be produced, the *input* required, and the *major processing tasks* that are necessary to convert input into output.
- The major processing tasks are then "decomposed" into independent *"functional modules"* which define the processing structure of the program.
- Finally, the processing "logic" or algorithm for each module is defined. The programmer designs the "main module" first, then the lower level modules.

Each program module in the top-down design is usually limited in its contents by the following restrictions:

- Each module should have only one entrance and one exit point.
- Each module should represent only one program function, for example, "read master record."
- Each module should not require more than one page of program code, which is about 50 lines of programming language instructions.

The purpose of these restrictions is to simplify and standardize the programming process, by making programs easier to read, test, and correct. Dividing a lengthy program into modules facilitates not only the design process, but coding, testing, and documentation as well.

Structure Charts

A program designed by a top-down method consists of a series of modules related in a hierarchical "treelike" structure.

FIGURE 7-4 Structure Chart Example For an Inventory Program

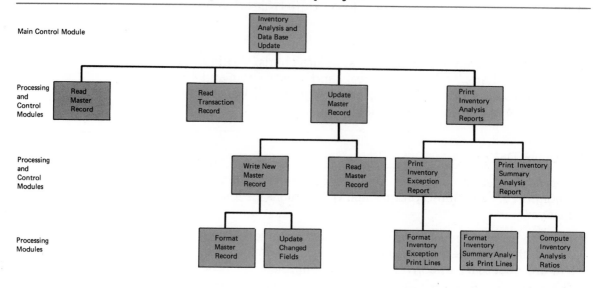

Main Control Module

Processing and Control Modules

Processing and Control Modules

Processing Modules

A **structure chart** may be used to show the program modules, their purpose, and their relationships. The structure chart thus shows the flow of logic in a program utilizing a "tree" of interconnected program modules. Figure 7–4 is an example of a structure chart for a simplified inventory system. The **visual table of contents** is related to the structure chart, but each module is numbered so that its position in the structure chart and its operations can be more easily referred to by other program documentation methods. See Figure 7–5.

FIGURE 7-5 A Visual Table of Contents

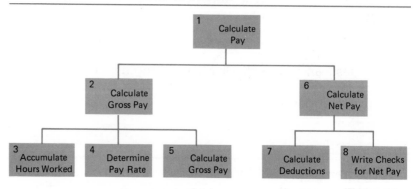

HIPO Charts

Another aid in top-down design is the "HIPO chart" or diagram (Hierarchy + Input/Processing/Output). It is used to record the input/processing/output details of the hierarchical program modules. The HIPO chart aids the programmer in determining:

- The *output* required—its format, media, organization, volume, frequency and destination.
- The *input* available—its source, format, media, organization, volume, and frequency.
- The *processing* needed—the mathematical, logical, and other procedures required to transform input into output.

A HIPO chart for the main program module (also called the "main control module") is done first and gives an overall view of the input/processing/output of the program. The HIPO charts or diagrams can then be constructed for the other lower level modules in the program. Figure 7–6 is an example of a HIPO chart for a gross pay calculation. (It is part of module-2 in the visual table of contents of Figure 7–5.)

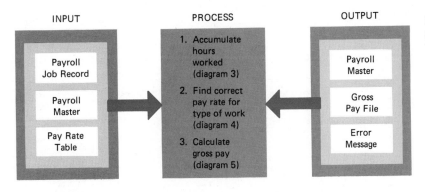

FIGURE 7–6 A HIPO Chart for a Gross Pay Calculation

Layout Forms

Layout forms are used to design the format of input, output, and storage media. They usually consist of preprinted forms on which the form and placement of data and information can be "laid out." Layout forms are used to design source documents, input/output and storage records and files, and output reports. Layout forms for punched cards, magnetic

FIGURE 7–7 Card Layout Form

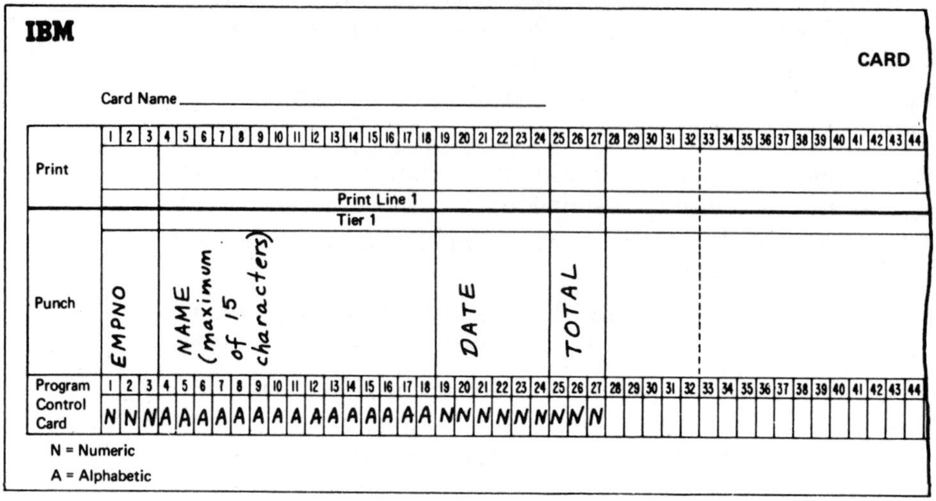

FIGURE 7–8 Printer Layout Sheet

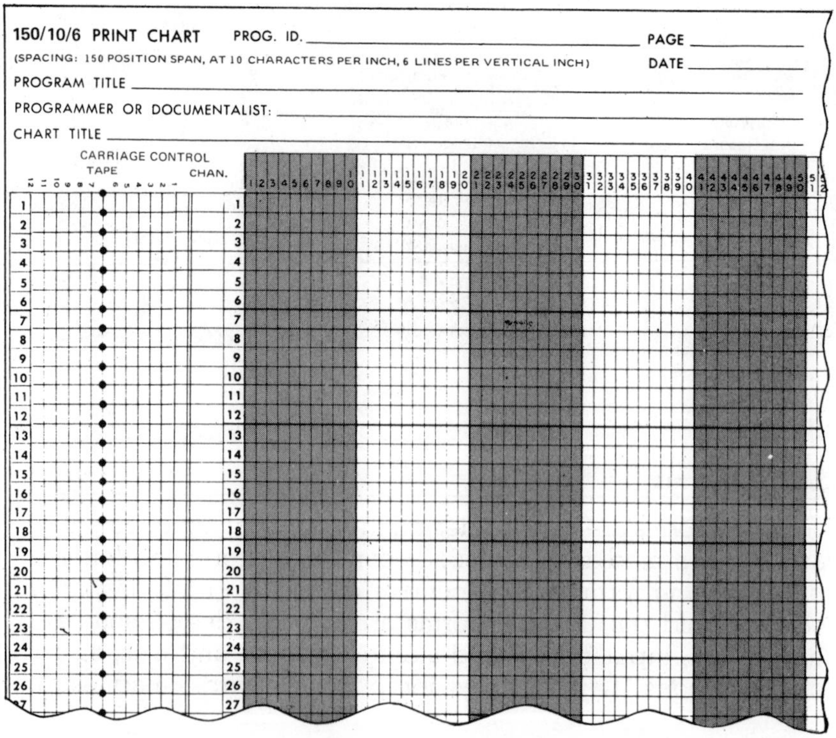

tape, magnetic disks, and printed reports are widely used. See Figures 7–7 and 7–8.

Flowcharts

The *flowchart* is an important tool for computer programming and systems analysis. A flowchart (also called a "flow diagram") is a graphic representation of the steps necessary to solve a problem, accomplish a task, complete a process, or it may be used to illustrate the components of a system. For example, Figure 7–9 humorously illustrates the many activities and decisions "Oscar" faces each morning. The flowchart illustrates the *order* in which a variety of *decisions* are to be made and *activities* performed in the *process* of Oscar's early morning *routine.*

In electronic data processing, there are two basic types of flowcharts, system flowcharts and program flowcharts. A *system flowchart* is a representation of the components and flows of a system. A *program flowchart* represents the data processing steps (algorithm) to be performed within a computer program. Commonly used system and program flowcharting symbols are illustrated and described in Figure 7–10.

FIGURE 7–9   A Flowchart of Oscar's Morning

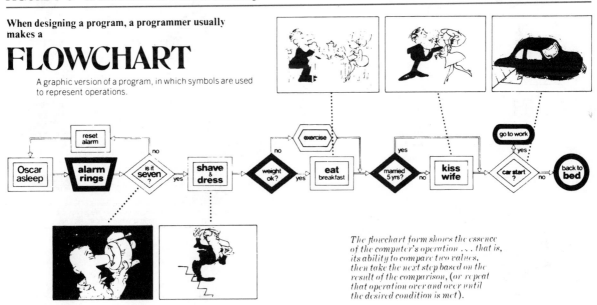

Courtesy IBM Corporation.

FIGURE 7–10 Flowchart Symbols

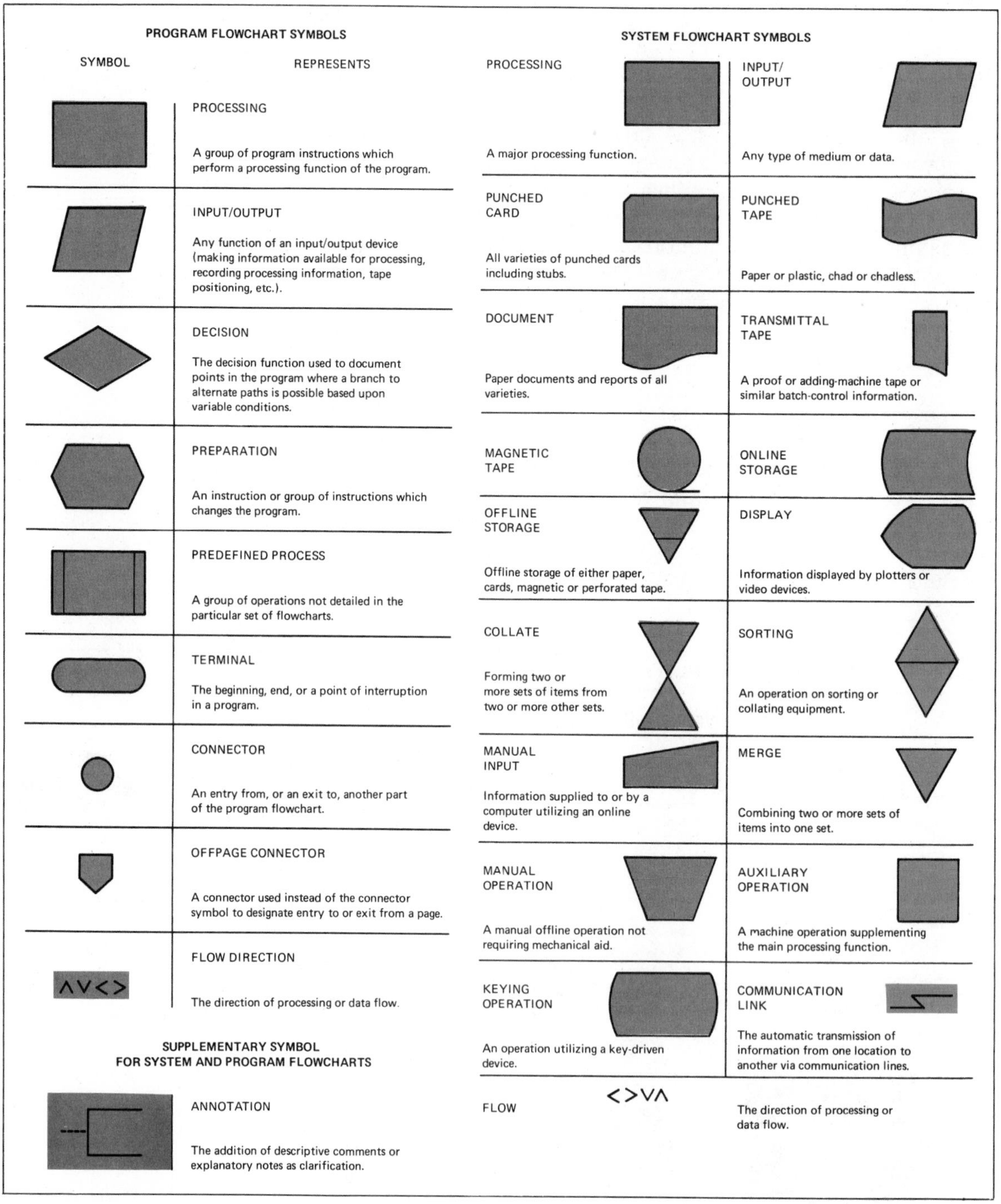

PROGRAM FLOWCHART SYMBOLS

SYMBOL	REPRESENTS
	PROCESSING — A group of program instructions which perform a processing function of the program.
	INPUT/OUTPUT — Any function of an input/output device (making information available for processing, recording processing information, tape positioning, etc.).
	DECISION — The decision function used to document points in the program where a branch to alternate paths is possible based upon variable conditions.
	PREPARATION — An instruction or group of instructions which changes the program.
	PREDEFINED PROCESS — A group of operations not detailed in the particular set of flowcharts.
	TERMINAL — The beginning, end, or a point of interruption in a program.
	CONNECTOR — An entry from, or an exit to, another part of the program flowchart.
	OFFPAGE CONNECTOR — A connector used instead of the connector symbol to designate entry to or exit from a page.
∧∨<>	**FLOW DIRECTION** — The direction of processing or data flow.

SUPPLEMENTARY SYMBOL FOR SYSTEM AND PROGRAM FLOWCHARTS

	ANNOTATION — The addition of descriptive comments or explanatory notes as clarification.

SYSTEM FLOWCHART SYMBOLS

PROCESSING	A major processing function.	**INPUT/OUTPUT**	Any type of medium or data.
PUNCHED CARD	All varieties of punched cards including stubs.	**PUNCHED TAPE**	Paper or plastic, chad or chadless.
DOCUMENT	Paper documents and reports of all varieties.	**TRANSMITTAL TAPE**	A proof or adding-machine tape or similar batch-control information.
MAGNETIC TAPE		**ONLINE STORAGE**	
OFFLINE STORAGE	Offline storage of either paper, cards, magnetic or perforated tape.	**DISPLAY**	Information displayed by plotters or video devices.
COLLATE	Forming two or more sets of items from two or more other sets.	**SORTING**	An operation on sorting or collating equipment.
MANUAL INPUT	Information supplied to or by a computer utilizing an online device.	**MERGE**	Combining two or more sets of items into one set.
MANUAL OPERATION	A manual offline operation not requiring mechanical aid.	**AUXILIARY OPERATION**	A machine operation supplementing the main processing function.
KEYING OPERATION	An operation utilizing a key-driven device.	**COMMUNICATION LINK**	The automatic transmission of information from one location to another via communication lines.
FLOW	<>∨∧		The direction of processing or data flow.

Courtesy IBM Corporation.

System Flowcharts

The *system flowcharts* used in information systems development show the flow of data among the components of a data processing system or information system. Such flowcharts were used several times in the preceding chapters of this book to illustrate components and flows of data in various systems. The system flowchart emphasizes how data moves in various forms through the stages of input, processing, output, and storage. It does not show the details of the processing that takes place in the computer program. System flowcharts can vary in their degree of complexity. For example, Figure 7–11 illustrates a payroll system, utilizing just the three basic flowcharting symbols that indicate input/output (a parallelogram), processing (a rectangle), and the direction of data flow (an arrow). A more detailed system flowchart of the payroll system is shown in Figure 7–12. Notice that the flowchart

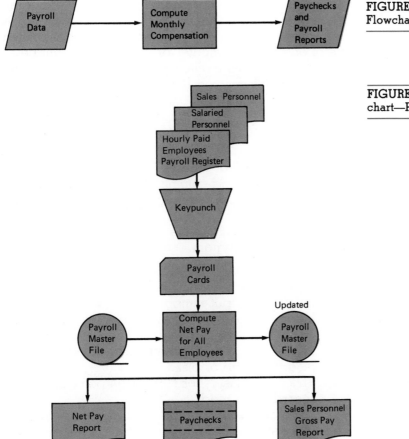

FIGURE 7–11   Simple System Flowchart—Payroll

FIGURE 7–12   System Flowchart—Payroll

illustrates the flow of data in the system and the input/output and storage media that are utilized and does not present the details of computer programs that will be required.

Program Flowcharts

A *program flowchart* illustrates the detailed sequence of steps required by a computer program. A program flowchart can be used to: (1) visualize the logic and sequence of steps in an operation, (2) experiment with various programming approaches, and (3) keep track of all processing steps, including procedures for alternatives and exceptions. Once final versions of the flowcharts for a program are completed, they serve as a guide during the program coding, testing, documentation, and maintenance stages of computer programming.

Program flowcharts can also vary in their complexity, ranging from "general" flowcharts to "detailed" program flowcharts. Figure 7–13 is a general program flowchart of a "sales personnel payroll report" program, which is a simplified example of one of the computer programs that might be required in a payroll system. It outlines the steps that result in the printing of the "Salesperson Payroll Report." This process would ordinarily be just a segment of a larger payroll program but has been modified to illustrate the use of program flowcharting symbols.

In the example of Figure 7–13, salesperson payroll data records are read and commissions and gross pay calculated and included in a printed report. Each symbol in the flowchart has been numbered so that we can explain the function of each symbol and show the flow of processing and control activities in this program.

1. This is the start of the program.
2. A salesperson payroll record is read as illustrated by the input/output symbol. It should contain data "fields" like the name, monthly salary, commission rate, and sales quota of each salesperson. The data record could be in the form of a punched card, or could be stored on magnetic tape or disk.
3. This is the "last record" decision point. Has the last data record been read?
4. If the answer is yes, the program comes to a stop.
5. If the answer is no, the processing symbol indicates that

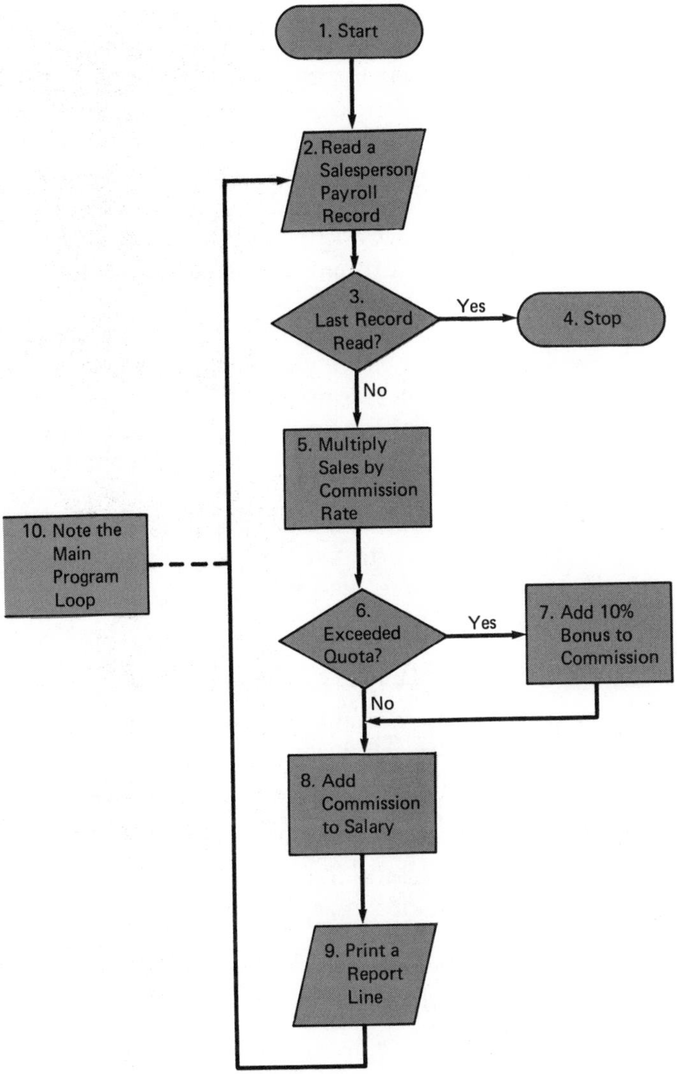

FIGURE 7–13   General Program Flowchart— Salesperson Payroll Report

the sales amount on this data record should be multiplied by the commission rate to compute the sales commission earned.

6. Another decision point. Has the sales made exceeded the sales quota set for this salesperson?

7. If the answer is yes, a 10 percent bonus (10 percent of the normal commission) is added to the commission earned.

8. If the answer is no (and also whenever completing step 7) the sales commission earned is added to the regular

monthly salary to compute the monthly "gross pay" for the salesperson.

9. A line on the Salesperson Payroll Report is printed. This would probably include the name, quota, sales, commission, salary, and gross pay for each salesperson.

10. This "comment" symbol points out the main "loop" of the program. A **program loop** allows any computer program automatically to repeat a series of operations. In this example, the main program loop of input, processing, and output operations is repeated until the last payroll record is read. The *looping* process is then ended by the program modification feature which allows computer programs automatically to modify themselves by *branching* to another routine. In this example, when the last record is read, the program *branches* to a stop. The looping process is shown in this flowchart by an arrow that connects the beginning and ending symbols of the loop, though two connector symbols (see Figure 7–10) could have also been used.

Structured Flowcharts

Structured flowcharts are another development of structured programming. They illustrate the steps in a computer program using basic program *control structures* (that we will cover shortly) and use a "box-within-a-box" format to show what is to be done and in what order. Many people find them easier to understand than regular flowcharts. Use of structured flowcharts is growing, since they emphasize the top-down and structured process within a computer program. Figure 7–14 is a compact structured flowchart revision of the traditional flowchart shown in Figure 7–13.

Decision Tables

Decision tables are another important tool of the systems analyst and computer programmer and are used in conjunction with, or in place of, flowcharts. Using flowcharts for the analysis and design of complex programs involving many specified conditions and decision paths becomes an extremely difficult and frequently unsatisfactory process. The flow of data and the logical sequence of the program or system become hard to follow, and errors or omissions may result. Therefore, decision tables may be used in such cases as a tool for the analysis and design of programs and systems involving complex, conditional decision logic.

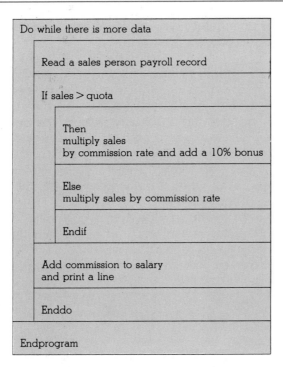

FIGURE 7–14 Structured Program Flowchart— Salesperson Payroll Report

A decision table is a tabular presentation of system or program logic. The general format of a decision table is shown in Figure 7–15. It shows that there are four basic parts to the decision table:

FIGURE 7–15 General Format of a Decision Table

Table Heading	Decision Rule Heading
Condition statements	Condition entries
Action statements	Action entries

- The *condition stub* which lists conditions or questions similar to those contained in a flowchart decision symbol.
- The *action stub,* which lists statements describing all actions that can be taken.
- The *condition entry,* which indicates which conditions are being met or answers the questions in the condition stub.
- The *action entry,* which indicates the actions to be taken.

Most decision tables also include a table heading and decision rule headings or numbers. The columns in the condition entry and action entry section of the table (called the "body" of the table) illustrate various **decision rules** since they specify that **if** certain conditions exist, **then** certain actions must be taken. Depending on the complexity of the decision logic, condition entries are indicated by a Y (yes), or a N (no), comparison symbols such as $< \leq = \geq >$, quantities, codes, or are left blank to show that the condition does not apply. Action entries are usually indicated by an X. When a decision table is completed, each rule indicates a different set of conditions and actions.

A simple example should help clarify the construction and use of a decision table. Figure 7–16 illustrates a decision table based on the payroll system and program examples flow-charted in the preceding pages. The decision logic has been made more complex than in the previous example in order to illustrate the usefulness of decision tables for the analysis of decision logic. Examine Figure 7–16 to see what actions are taken when various possible conditions occur.

For example: decision rule Number 6 concerns the case of a salesperson who has made sales for the month but has not exceeded his/her sales quota. Given these conditions, the payroll processing actions that must be taken are to com-

FIGURE 7–16 Payroll Decision Table

PAYROLL TABLE NO. 1		DECISION RULE NUMBERS						
		1	2	3	4	5	6	7
CONDITIONS	Hourly paid Employee	Y						
	Salaried Employee		Y					
	Executive Employee			Y				
	Unclassified Employee				Y			
	Salesperson					Y	Y	Y
	Made Sales?					N	Y	Y
	Exceeded Quota?					N	N	Y
ACTIONS	Compute Wages	X						
	Compute Salary		X					
	Compute Sales Salary					X	X	X
	Compute Commission						X	X
	Compute Bonus							X
	Salesperson Gross Pay Processing					X	X	X
	Net Pay Processing	X	X			X	X	X
	Go to Payroll Table Number:			2	3			

pute his/her salary and commission (but not a bonus), perform other salesperson payroll processing, and perform net pay processing common to all employees. The information in column 6 of the decision table can therefore be expressed in words by the following decision rule statement:

If an employee is a salesperson who has had sales for the month but has not exceeded his/her sales quota, **then** compute his/her salary and commissions, and complete salesperson payroll processing and all-employee net pay processing.

Pseudocode

Another tool in detailed program design that is part of the "top-down" design of structured programming is "pseudocode." *Pseudocode* is the expression of the processing logic of a program module in ordinary English language phrases. Like decision tables, pseudocode was developed as an alternative to flowcharts. In many programming assignments, flowcharts were found to be an unsatisfactory way of expressing the flow and logic of a program.

Pseudocode allows a programmer to express his or her thoughts in regular English phrases, with each phrase representing a programming process that must be accomplished in a specific program module (as detailed in a HIPO chart). The phrases almost appear to be programming language statements; thus the name "pseudocode." However, unlike programming language statements, pseudocode has no rigid rules; only a few optional "keywords" for major processing functions are recommended. Therefore programmers can express their thoughts in an easy, natural, straightforward manner, but at a level of detail which allows pseudocode to be directly convertible into programming language coding. Figure 7–17 provides an example of pseudocode for a simple listing of inventory items that might be a module in an inventory program.

Figure 7–17   Pseudocode Example

```
Open the files
Read an input record
DO-UNTIL no more input records
   Clear the output area
   Move the purchase date, name,
      stock number, and amount in
      inventory to the output area
   Write a line on the inventory report
   Read an input record
END-DO
Close the files
Stop
```

PROGRAM CODING

Program coding is the process that converts the logic designed during the program design stage into a set of programming language statements that constitute a computer program. The term "programming" is frequently used to refer only to the program coding stage, but, as we have seen, five other important steps are also necessary. Depending on the programming language used, coding involves a rigorous process which requires the computer programmer to strictly follow specific rules concerning format and syntax (vocabulary, punctuation, and grammatical rules).

Structured Coding

Structured coding is an important part of "top-down structured programming" which stresses that only three basic "control structures" should be utilized for program coding: (1) *sequence*, (2) *selection*, and (3) *repetition* (or loop). Using just these three basic control structures simplifies and standardizes program coding and makes the resulting programs easier to read and understand. Figure 7–18 illustrates the three basic control structures of structured programming in both traditional and structured flowcharts.

Sequence Structure. Expresses the fact that program instructions are usually executed in the order in which they are stored in the computer. Figure 7–18 illustrates that program statements in function A will be executed before those for function

FIGURE 7–18 The Three Basic Program Control Structures

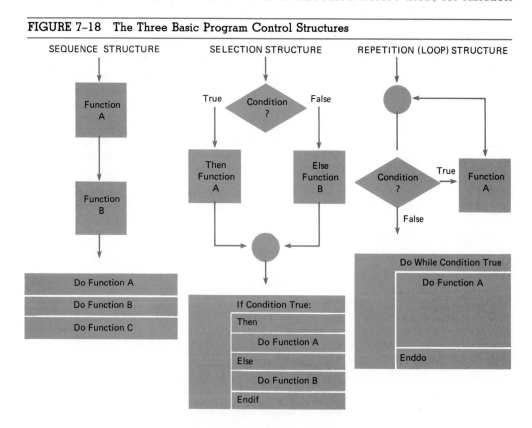

B. Thus we say that "control" flows from function A to function B.

Selection Structure. (Also called the *decision* or IF-THEN-ELSE structure.) Expresses a *choice* between two program control paths based on a *test* which results in either a true or false condition. Figure 7–18 shows that if the test is *true,* control will flow to function A and its statements will be executed; if the test is *false,* function B will be done.

Repetition (Loop) Structure. (Also called the DO-WHILE or DO-UNTIL structure.) Expresses the performing of a program function *while* or *until* a condition is *true.* Figure 7–18 shows the flow of program control which can be expressed as "do function A *while* the condition is true." The opposite control flow can be expressed by a variation of this structure which would say "do function A *until* the condition is true."

Structured coding can be implemented to some extent in many current programming languages. However, it is easier to implement in some languages (such as PL/1, Pascal, and COBOL) than in others (such as FORTRAN and BASIC). Structured "top-down" programming and coding are designed to simplify the flow of program control and eliminate or minimize "branching" forward and backward from the main flow of the program. Thus the main control module (also called the "mainline") should clearly show that control flows from the top down, i.e., top to bottom without being transferred to earlier program modules. The cause of much of this unnecessary branching is blamed on the "GO TO" statement found in many programs. Therefore, this aspect of structured programming is sometimes called "GO TO-less" programming.

Types of Instructions

The types of instructions available to a computer programmer for program coding depend on the program language used and the *command repertoire* or *instruction set* of the computer CPU. However, computer instructions can usually be subdivided into six categories: (1) specification, (2) input/output, (3) data movement, (4) arithmetic, (5) logical, and (6) control.

- *Specification instructions* are descriptive instructions which describe the data media to be used, the size and format of data records and files, the constants to be used, and the allocation of storage. Many of these instructions are based on the input/output and storage layout sheets completed during the program design stage. The "FORMAT" statement of FORTRAN or the "PICTURE" statement of COBOL are examples of specification instruction statements.

- *Input/Output instructions* transfer data and instructions between the CPU and input/output devices. "READ" or "PRINT" statements are examples of such instructions.
- *Data movement instructions* involve rearranging and reproducing data within primary storage. "MOVE," "SHIFT," or "STORE" instructions are examples.
- *Arithmetic instructions* are instructions which accomplish mathematical operations, such as "ADD," and "SUBTRACT."
- *Logical instructions* perform comparisons and test conditions and control some branching processes as illustrated in the decision symbol of program flowcharts. Examples are "IF, THEN," or "COMPARE" statements.
- *Control instructions* are used to stop and start a program, change the sequence of a program through some branching processes, and control the use of subroutines. "DO," "RETURN," and "STOP" statements are examples of control instructions.

Figure 7–19 shows a FORTRAN coding form with the statements and flowchart of a very simple FORTRAN program. The program reads values of Y and Z from an undetermined number of data cards, computes X = Y + Z, and prints the resulting values of X. Examples of simple programs coded in several widely used programming languages are included in the next chapter.

PROGRAM VERIFICATION

Program verification, more commonly known as "debugging," is a stage of programming that involves checking, testing, and correction processes. Program verification is a necessary stage of computer programming because newly coded programs may contain errors (bugs) which must be identified and corrected by a debugging process.

Programming Errors

Programming errors are of three major types: syntax errors, logic errors, and systems design errors.

FIGURE 7-19   Coding Form with the Statements and Flowchart of a Simple FORTRAN Program

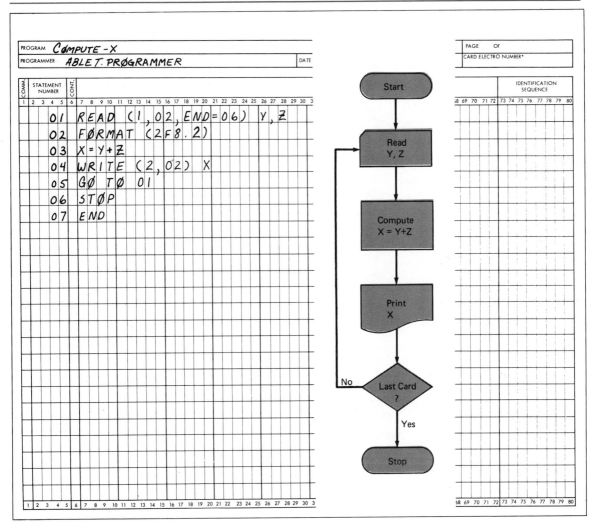

Syntax errors (also called clerical errors) are caused by violating the rules of the programming language in which the program is coded or by making mistakes in the organization and format of data. These errors can be as simple as a misplaced decimal point or comma and can be made by the programmer or be the result of an error made in the terminal entry of the source program.

Logic errors are errors that occur because of mistakes in the logical structure of a program. Necessary procedures may have been omitted or incorrect procedures included in a program. For example, a payroll program that did not distinguish between hourly paid employees and salaried employees or which used an incorrect commission for salespersons would produce logic errors.

Systems design errors are errors in the design of a computer application that result in a program that produces unsatisfactory results for a computer user. A program may be free of clerical and logic errors and still not meet all the requirements of a proposed data processing application. Such errors are caused by failures in communication between the programmer and the systems analyst or computer user.

Clerical errors are easier to detect than logic errors because they are usually identified during the language translation process when "diagnostic messages" identifying such errors are produced. Clerical errors may also cause the computer to "reject" a program during this process or later processing. Logic errors are harder to detect, since they will not be identified by the translator diagnostics, and the complete program may be processed by the computer without being rejected. The output of such a program, however, will be incorrect.

The incorrect and sometimes nonsensical results caused by program and input data errors are humorously referred to as "garbage." This is the basis for the phrase "garbage in, garbage out" (GIGO). It emphasizes that the computer will blindly process incorrect data and instructions and will willingly produce volumes of incorrect and useless results. Therefore, many control and testing procedures must be built into all EDP systems and computer programs.

Checking

Program checking must take place during the program design, program coding, and program verification stages. Checking should take place during and after the development of program design aids such as HIPO charts, pseudocode, flowcharts, and decision tables. The purpose of this procedure is to verify that all program requirements are being met and to determine that the design aids correctly represent the processing logic required by the program. Checking should take place at the completion of the program coding stage to ensure that the instructions correctly translate the logic of the flowcharts and decision tables and that any clerical errors have been identified. This "desk checking" process is facilitated if top-down design and structured programming have been used because they significantly simplify and standardize program logic and coding, thus making programs easier to read and correct.

The final checking process involves attempting to have the program or program module translated into a machine language program that is acceptable to the computer. During or after such a translation process, *diagnostic messages* will be printed, identifying mistakes in the program. The programmer makes necessary corrections to the program and then makes another translation attempt. This final checking process must be repeated until an error-free "pass" is accomplished and the resulting machine language program is ready for a test period.

Structured Walkthroughs

Structured walkthroughs are an aid to good programming design, coding, and debugging, and are one of the tools of structured programming. A structured walkthrough is a methodology which requires a "peer" review (by other programmers) of the program design and coding to minimize and reveal errors in the early stages of programming. Its aim is to promote errorless and "egoless" programming by having other programmers formally involved in any programming process. Thus structured walkthroughs may involve the "team programming" concept where several programmers are assigned to develop the same program under the direction of a "chief programmer." Team members review each other's design and coding at regular intervals as each program module is designed and then coded. Structured walkthroughs are an attempt to minimize the cost of program verification by catching errors in the early stages of programming, rather than waiting until the program has reached the testing stage where corrections are more difficult and costly to make.

Testing

A properly checked object program or program module is tested to demonstrate whether it can produce correct results utilizing "test data." This *testing* should attempt to simulate all conditions that may arise during processing. Therefore, test data must include unusual and incorrect data as well as the typical types of data which will usually occur. Such test data is needed to test the ability of the program to handle exceptions and errors as well as more normal forms of data. The programmer must have previously prepared the test data by manually (and carefully) calculating and determining the correct results. After the object program has processed the test data, the output is compared to the expected results. If correct results are produced, the program or program module is considered properly tested and ready for use.

In structured programming, the higher-level modules of a program are supposed to be coded and tested first. Since the lower-level modules are not ready for testing, "dummy modules" are created in their place so that each higher-level module can be tested. As lower-level modules are tested, higher level modules are tested again. This allows coding and testing modules separately and from the "top down." This process simplifies finding errors because errors can be isolated in specific modules, which are supposed to occupy only one page of program code. Then when even the lowest-level program modules are successfully tested, the program is considered fully tested.

The final phase of program verification is a temporary period in which actual data is used to test a computer program. If the program has been designed to replace an older data processing method, this procedure is known as "parallel processing." The parallel run allows the results of the new program to be compared to the results produced by the system it is to replace. If the results agree over a specified period of time the old operation is then phased out.

PROGRAM DOCUMENTATION

Program documentation is a process that should occur throughout all of the other stages of computer programming. Program documentation is the detailed description of the design and the instruction content of a computer program. Program documentation is extremely important in diagnosing program errors, making programming changes, or reassembling a lost program, especially if its original programmer is no longer available. Descriptive material produced in the previous stages of computer programming should be collected and refined, and new material developed. A "program documentation manual" should be assembled which might include contents as shown in Figure 7–20.

Program specifications.   Describe what the program is supposed to do.

Program description.   Consists of structure charts, HIPO charts, pseudocode, input/output and storage layout sheets, program flowcharts, decision tables, object program listing, and a narrative description of what the program does.

Verification documentation.   Includes listings of test data and results, memory dumps, and other test documents.

Operations documentation.   Consists of operating instructions which describe the actions required of the computer operator during the processing of the computer program.

Maintenance documentation.   A detailed description of all changes made to the program after it was accepted as an operational program.

FIGURE 7–20   Contents of Program Documentation

PROGRAM MAINTENANCE

The final stage of computer programming begins after a computer program has been accepted as an operational program. *Program maintenance* refers to the continual revision of computer programs that is required if they are to be improved, updated, expanded, or corrected. The requirements of business data processing applications are subject to continual changes and revisions due to changes in company policies, business operations, government regulations, etc. Program maintenance is therefore an important stage of computer programming, involving the analysis, design, coding, verification, and documentation of changes to operational computer programs.

Large computer users frequently have a separate category of application programmers, called *maintenance programmers,* whose sole responsibility is program maintenance. Theirs is a difficult assignment, since they must revise programs they did not develop. This should emphasize the importance of the structured programming approach since it provides simplified, standardized, and structured documentation which is easy to read and understand. Such documentation is essential for proper program maintenance. Inadequate documentation may make program maintenance impossible and require the rewriting of an entire program.

SUMMARY

- Computer programming is a process which results in the development of a detailed set of instructions which outline the data processing activities to be performed by a computer. Computer programming may be subdivided into the six stages summarized in Figure 7–1.

- Structured programming is a programming methodology which involves the use of a top-down program design and uses a limited number of control structures to create highly structured modules of program code. Structured programming includes program design, coding, and verification techniques such as top-down design, structure and HIPO charts, pseudocode, structured coding and structured walkthroughs.

- Program design aids such as structure charts, HIPO charts, flowcharts, pseudocode, and decision tables are important techniques used not only in program design but also assist in program coding, debugging, documentation, and maintenance.

- Once a computer program has been coded, it may be verified by a debugging process, documented with suitable program documentation, and revised when necessary by the program maintenance activity.

- Interactive programming involves the use of software tools such as application development systems and other hardware and software resources to make computer programming an automated, interactive process.

KEY TERMS AND CONCEPTS

Computer programming	Decision tables
Structured programming	Program coding
Interactive programming	Basic control structures
Program analysis	Types of computer instructions
Program design	Program verification
Algorithm	Debugging
Top-down design	Syntax errors
Program modules	Logic errors
Structure charts	System design errors
HIPO charts	Garbage in, garbage out
Layout forms	Program checking
System flowcharts	Structured walkthroughs
Program flowcharts	Program testing
Structured flowcharts	Program documentation
Program loops	Program maintenance
Branching	Application development systems
Pseudocode	

REVIEW AND DISCUSSION QUESTIONS

1. Why is knowledge of computer programming desirable for computer users?

2. Identify each of the stages in the computer programming process.

3. What is structured programming? What benefits are claimed for its use?

4. What is interactive programming? What hardware and software resources does it require? Will it make traditional programming methods obsolete? Why or why not?

5. What is top-down design? How is it accomplished? What benefits are supposed to result from its use?

6. What is the purpose of structure charts, HIPO charts, layout forms, decision tables and pseudocode?

7. What is the purpose of a flowchart? How do system flowcharts differ from program flowcharts?

8. Construct a simple system flowchart and a program flowchart that illustrate the flow of data and some of the processing steps required to accomplish some data processing task. Use a data processing task of your choice, such as the processing of payroll records, student grades, sales transactions, or mathematical computations.

9. What are the basic system and program flowcharting symbols which represent input, processing, output, decision points, etc.?

10. What is a decision table? Why are decision tables utilized?

11. How does a decision table show the decision rules that are possible in a given situation? Give an example.

12. What are the three basic control structures of structured coding? What benefits are supposed to result from their use?

13. What are the six basic types of computer instructions? What functions are performed by each basic type of instruction?

14. What is program debugging? What activities are involved?

15. Is program debugging always necessary? Explain.

16. Differentiate between syntax, logic, and system design errors. Which type of error is easier to detect?

17. What does the phrase "garbage in, garbage out" mean?

18. What are structured walkthroughs? How do they assist the program verification process?

19. Why is program documentation important?

20. What is the purpose of the program maintenance stage?

REAL WORLD APPLICATIONS

7-1   The Hartford Insurance Group

Several years ago, IBM suggested that The Hartford might improve the productivity of its 400-person Data Processing Systems Department by employing the recently formalized improved programming technologies: structured programming, top-down program development, chief programmer teams, development support libraries, Hierarchy plus Input-Process-Output (HIPO) diagrams, and structured walk-throughs.

At that time a major addition to the Total Group System was underway, with the next stage a system to handle Group Commission Administration. Mr. James Arend, assistant vice president in charge of the Systems Department, selected this as a pilot project. This pilot eventually produced 25,000 lines of COBOL code, including CRT edit modules, file maintenance, and report formatting routines. DL/I was used to handle the data base.

Mr. Arend says, "The improved technologies produced a better system than traditional methods, the project was better controlled, the functions better understood, and the testing less costly." He is particularly happy with the way the new techniques are spreading among his people, promising a continuation of these benefits.

Pershing Parker, project leader for group commission administration, analyzed the effect of the technologies on that project. His report lists the following specific benefits:

- *Improved Communications.* Users, analysts, and programmers used HIPO diagrams as a common document of understanding. Team members knew what was happening throughout the development cycle and could contribute to the solution of problems beyond their area of immediate concern.

- *Improved Project Control.* Team organization and the existence of a detailed written specification made project control straightforward.

- *Increased Productivity.* COBOL code written in the structured programming format consistently took fewer statements than the conventional code required to accomplish the same operation. Structured walkthroughs turned up problems in the design stage where they could be corrected more easily, rather than in the debugging stage. Specifically, of 650 errors found in the system, 450 were found in the design stage and only 26 in system tests, and all 26 were minor. Top-down program development enabled programmers to spot gross redundancies and to create a more compact logical design.

- *Shorter Development Times.* Early stages of design and coding take more manpower with the improved programming technologies than with conventional techniques, but this is more than offset by savings in subsequent activities. The group commission administration project finished two months ahead of a 12-month schedule, consumed 6 percent less than the estimated manpower, and used less than 2 percent overtime.

- *Improved Programmer Morale.* At first, management was concerned that people would resist the more rigid requirements imposed by the technologies, but people readily accepted them and became enthusiastic when they saw the results.

- *Less Machine Time.* System testing required less machine time because of the quality of the programs. Conservative calculations suggest the use of the technologies saved The Hartford 40 hours of system test time. The company expects structured programming and segmentation of code will save machine time in production.[1]

- How did The Hartford use structured programming technologies?
- What benefits resulted from using such techniques?

[1] Source: Adapted by permission from *Improved Programming Technologies at The Hartford* (pp. 3–4).© 1979 by International Business Machines Corporation.

7-2   Armstrong World Industries

Armstrong World Industries, Inc., Lancaster, Pa., a diversified manufacturer of home furnishing products, is implementing an advanced marketing information system to increase productivity and provide its top management with better control of the company's farflung operations.

In developing programs for the system, Armstrong personnel used IBM's Development Management System (DMS). This set of programs simplified implementation of programs using online 3270 display devices. Data base management, display management, and message handling functions provided by these programs make it possible to implement applications in the online environment with a minimum of programming.

"DMS has enabled us to get three to four times more productivity from programmers," says Mr. D. Dwight Browning (corporate vice-president and director of business information services),"because of the simplified process of developing display screens, the more orderly interaction with the data base, and because they can work at terminals where they get immediate results. In addition, the maintenance work on programs is significantly faster." The company's DMS library exceeds 350 programs. The Query-By-Example (QBE) program was also installed to simplify access to data by authorized management and staff. Data Language/I (DL/I) was employed to help create the system's data files.

"Several members of our executive committee," says Mr. Browning, "are heavily experienced in marketing and therefore are enthusiastic about getting data that was difficult to obtain previously when they were sales managers. DMS has helped us develop an effective corporate marketing information system. QBE simplified production of special displays for management with information that can really focus on ways to improve productivity."[2]

- What benefits does Armstrong derive from using application development software for computer programming?
- What other types of software are used to reduce programming effort by programmers and users?

[2] Source: Adapted from "For Better Sales Statistics," *Data Processor*, February/March 1981, pp. 2–3. Reprinted with permission.

7-3 Small Business Software Timebomb

The following short article on shoddy programming practices and their effect on small business computer software is destined to be a classic and is reproduced in its entirety. It should be required reading for all business computer users.

Beware of predictions when experts agree. Opinions aside, Titanics do sink and swine flu epidemics fail to materialize. Today's "everybody-knows-it" is that the golden age of small-business computing is nearly upon us. Rubbish. We're on the threshold of unprecedented confusion.

"Small-business computing" is the use of cheap, dedicated computers to automate the recordkeeping of companies with low dollar volume and few employees. Numbers for *low* and *few* vary with the user, but let's include Bertie's Button Boutique and exclude Chrysler.

The Problem

Writers and lecturers tell us that the availability of modestly priced systems makes it practical for small companies to rely on computers for accounting, freeing people to concentrate on managing. Sounds neat, eh?

The problem is that the accounting *is* the managing. Once you've got all those figures for factors like inventory, receivables, payables, and profit projections, management consists of doing what the bottom line demands. Oh yes, managers also hire help, select product lines, and decorate showrooms; but it's ignorance of that bottom line that leads to failure. That golden era we're approaching is actually one of automated ignorance.

The Timebomb

You see, it's the word "cheap" that represents the timebomb. The $5,000 disk-based computers are really good values. A competent commercial programmer (humor me and accept the abbreviation CCP) can convert them into systems from the experts' dreams. Most systems will be programmed instead by kitchen-table amateurs (KTA's).

The CCP recognizes that systems must be maintained. He prices his product to allow revisions whenever the governments change their reporting rules. He incorporates the true cost of money in his projections. He includes automatic file backup. He keeps an audit trail. He alters a record only after confirming the validity of the new item. He offers editing for data entry. He tailors the prompting messages to the operator's level. He generates paper records as a basis for manual accounting during unscheduled downtime. He documents exhaustively. These features and others all add to the initial cost of the CCP's product.

The KTA overlooks some of these niceties. It's enough for him that his inventory program calculate the number of marshmallows on hand. His program is cheap. Tick, tick, tick.

The Mad Bomber

There is no practical limit to the supply of bad programs, because our hobby is spawning a large cottage industry. I know a few programmers who genuinely promote computing. They conscientiously develop tight, fast, reliable packages which meet the user's expectations. These careful programmers are uncommon.

Many programs sold today are coded quickly, loosely, and carelessly. There is only superficial testing. No one confirms that every loop has been tried, every meaningful data mix injected. No one traces the calculations for possible loss of numeric significance. If it works once, it must be okay. Anyway, selling a few copies will yield enough money to buy a printer to check the coding.

Much of what gets published in computerist magazines promotes this attitude. It is tempting, isn't it? Form a company with a fancy name, sell a program, write off your equipment as a business expense, get rich. Everyone's doing it. Then you find out that the bottom has fallen out of the games market, so you turn to the next touted mother lode: small business. You borrow a book on accounting, dash off an implementation of your untested understanding, and rush to advertise. We'd all be horri-

7-3   *(continued)*

fied if anyone did that with a drug or a vehicle, but it's far more common in programming than you believe. Is injuring the means of someone's livelihood less reprehensible than injuring his body?

The Odds

Do you doubt that there are more bad programs than good ones? Look at what happened to radio discipline when CB became a toy. That's what is going on today in programming. Many suppliers teach programming. Very few stress responsibility and the need for self-discipline. With a stream of questionable programs reaching the marketplace, the chances of choosing a dangerous package are disturbingly high. The ratio of KTA's to CCP's is topheavy.

Who will warn the potential victim? Probably no one. If Bertie of button fame knows enough about the financial end of his business, he may cut through the mystique and be hardnosed about his specifications. He may ask about updates, fixes, revisions, warranty, and a maintenance contract. But if Bertie knows only buttons, he's apt to believe what he's told about small-business computing. Mostly, he's not hearing the whole truth.

The Consequences

Let's be fair. The manager intelligent enough to see the merit in the extra cost for the CCP's product will benefit and prosper. He probably would prosper in any case; the computer will merely enhance the prospects for success.

Now, you may object that a business run by someone ignorant of sound practices will fail anyway. Perhaps, but the computer is being promoted as insurance against such ignorance. Read the ads. The CCP and the KTA are making similar claims. Both promise to automate a crucial aspect of the enterprise. Neither lists the features omitted. Neither specifies what supplementary manual effort is required or what minimum knowledge the user must possess. The result of a wrong choice is that the

wasted investment in the KTA's system will hasten the failure of the weak business. Yet where do we read that the coming of small-business computing will boost the failure rate?

I wish I could tell you that the solution lies in buying software from the major hardware vendors. Sadly, some of them apparently employ their own KTAs. As an example, a mailing list program from a leading personal computer manufacturer takes 30 hours to sort a list of 150 names and addresses. I know a CCP whose version in the same Basic takes only 55 seconds.

How many small businesses could tolerate the day-long loss of inventory-ordering-, and accounting-capabilities just to update a mailing list? Guess what? The major vendor's software specifications don't mention this problem. Furthermore, if you trigger this sort, you'll have no clue about how the routine is progressing or when you might expect to get your system back.

Slothful perfomance has one benign aspect: the user can detect it. It may disqualify that particular system, but at least it's not fatal.

Sloppy data-handling, though, is a disaster. I've seen a program than can't abide a key's being struck during a file update. The consequence of such an innocent act is the substitution of that key's value for the one then being moved. There's no warning; the file is contaminated and accepted. That is a program's ultimate transgression.

If the manager is lucky, he will notice that an item makes no sense. Whether he will then be able to correct it is still an open question. Should the substitution go undetected, the timebomb has been armed and started. The computer may later order a wrong item, misaddress a shipment, report erroneous FICA data, overpay a supplier, underbill a customer, or erase the disk. Even a capable manager could lose a business with that kind of help.

Before you laugh, how does your system handle that situation? How do you know?

242

7–3 (concluded)

The Remedies

What recourse is open to the person whose business dies from contaminated data? Perhaps he can sue the KTA, but with what real hope of getting remuneration? Many KTA's are at least clever enough to include disclaimers about fitness, merchantability, and nonresponsibility for consequential damages. Realistically, there are no after-the-fact remedies.

Are there any safeguards for the prudent buyer? I usually offer this personal advice:

It's often wiser to buy your cheap computer from someone scaling his computers down, rather than up. I think your chances of success are better if you pay more to IBM than if you pay less to a fledgling concern known for TV games or calculators.

Never discontinue your manual practices until your computer has demonstrated that it can do as well. Run the manual and the automated operations in parallel for a while.

Ditch the computer if it doesn't perform from the beginning. Your initial dissatisfaction arises from only the bugs you've been able to detect. If obvious things are going wrong, don't risk assassination by the hidden bugs.

Never buy a computer package without first interviewing experienced customers. Talk to the computer operator as well as the company owner. Don't rely on hearsay testimonials. Remember that you're in an adversary relationship with the salesman. It's like buying a car.

Don't expect the system to compensate for your own ignorance. How will you know if it's working?

Find out whether the vendor is using this system in his own operations. It's no guarantee, but it's a devastating question to spring on the salesman.

The Prospect

Too few managers will demand rigorous proof of performance before committing their company's well-being to a computer system. We who relish the beneficial impact of computers on mankind will sustain bruises during the coming wave of disillusionment, as small-business computing too often betrays its promise.

You can lessen the blow by speaking out on the need for responsibility in programming.[3]

- What problems in small business computer software and programming practices are exposed by the author? What is the cause of these problems? What are some solutions?
- The author makes a point that programming business computer applications involves many important considerations and should not be taken lightly. Do you agree? Explain.

[3] Source: Paul F. Doering, "The Bleak Future of Small Business Computing," *Creative Computing*, November 1980, pp. 52–53. Copyright © 1981 by Creative Computing, 39 East Hanover Ave., Morris Plains, NJ 07950.

8

CHAPTER OUTLINE

Overview of Programming Languages

LEARNING OBJECTIVES

The purpose of this chapter is to promote a basic understanding of computer programming languages by analyzing the fundamental characteristics and use of several major types and widely used versions of programming languages.

After reading and studying this chapter you should be able to:

1. Explain the differences between machine, assembler, high-level, and natural languages.
2. Summarize several major characteristics, benefits, and limitations of FORTRAN, COBOL, BASIC, PL/1, Pascal, APL, and RPG.

TYPES OF PROGRAMMING LANGUAGES

Programming languages allow computer instruction to be written in a language that is mutually understandable to both people and computers. Many different programming languages have been developed, each with its own unique vocabulary, grammar, and uses. A brief description of several languages is outlined in Figure 8–1. We will briefly analyze several of these languages later in this chapter. However, let us first examine the four major types of computer programming languages:

- *Machine* languages.
- *Assembler* languages.
- *High-level* languages.
- *Natural* languages.

Machine Languages

Machine languages are the most basic level of programming languages. In the early stages of computer development, instructions were written utilizing the internal binary code of the computer. This type of programming involves the extremely difficult task of writing instructions in the form of coded strings of binary digits. Programmers had to have a detailed knowledge of the internal operations of the specific CPU they were using and had to write long series of detailed instructions in order to accomplish even simple data processing tasks.

Programming in machine language requires specifying the storage locations for every instruction and item of data used. Instructions must be included for every register, counter, switch, and indicator that is used by the program. These requirements made machine language programming a slow, difficult, and error-prone task. Depending on the internal code used by the particular computer being programmed, machine language instructions could be expressed in pure binary form, binary, octal, or hexadecimal codes, or even codes which utilize decimal numbers and/or alphabetical characters (which were then decoded by the circuitry of the CPU into pure binary form). For example, a machine language program that would add two numbers together in the accumulator and store the result ($X = Y + Z$) might take the form shown on page 248. Like many computer instructions, these instructions consist of an "operation code" that specifies what is to be done and an "operand" which specifies the address of the data or device to be operated upon.

FIGURE 8–1   A Summary of Several Major Programming Languages

Ada: Named after Augusta Ada Byron, considered the world's first computer programmer. Developed in 1980 for the U.S. Department of Defense as a standard "high order language." It resembles an extension of Pascal.

ALGOL: (ALGOrithmic Language). An international algebraic language designed primarily for scientific and mathematical applications. It is widely used in Europe.

APL: (A Programming Language). A mathematically oriented interactive language originated by Kenneth Iverson of IBM. It utilizes a very concise symbolic notation designed for efficient interactive programming.

APT: (Automatically Programmed Tools). A special-purpose language designed to describe and control the functions of numerically-controlled machine tools.

BASIC: (Beginners All-Purpose Symbolic Instruction Code). A simple procedure oriented language developed at Dartmouth College. It is widely utilized for interactive programming using time-sharing systems and has become a popular language for minicomputer and microcomputer systems for small business use and personal computing.

COBOL: (COmmon Business Oriented Language). Designed by a committee of computer manufacturers and users (CODASYL) as an English-like language specifically for business data processing. It is the most widely utilized programming language for accounting and other business applications.

FORTRAN: (FORmula TRANslation). The oldest of the popular compiler languages. It was designed for solving mathematical problems in science, engineering, research, business, and education. It is still the most widely utilized programming language for scientific and engineering applications.

GPSS: (General Purpose System Simulator). A special-purpose language designed to describe simulation procedures for computer processing of the mathematical simulation models of a wide variety of operations and processes.

Pascal: Named after Blaise Pascal. Developed by Niklaus Wirth of Zurich as a powerful successor to ALGOL, and designed specifically to incorporate structured programming concepts and to facilitate top-down design. Pascal has become a popular language for both small and large computers.

PL/1:   (Programming Language/1). A general purpose language developed by IBM. It was designed to combine some of the features of COBOL, FORTRAN, ALGOL and other special languages. It is thus a highly flexible "modular" general-purpose language that can be used for business, scientific, and specialized applications.

RPG: (Report Program Generator). A problem-oriented language which generates programs that produce reports and perform other data processing tasks. It is a widely utilized language for report preparation, file maintenance, and other business data processing applications of small computer users.

SNOBOL: A special-purpose "string manipulation" or "symbol manipulation" language. It is used to process "character strings" and symbols such as manipulating information in its own natural language form. It is an important programming language for applications such as text editing and abstraction, language translation, and information retrieval.

Operation Code	Operand	
1010	11001	(Replace the current value in the accumulator with the value Y at location 11001.)
1011	11010	(Add the value Z at location 11010 to the value Y in the accumulator.)
1100	11011	(Store the value X in the accumulator at location 11011.)

The three machine language instructions shown merely compute the sum of two one-digit numbers and store the results in a single storage location. Many more instructions would be needed in order to complete a computer program which would accept data from an input device, perform the addition operation, and transmit the results to an output device.

Assembler Languages

Assembler languages are the next level of programming languages and were developed in order to reduce the difficulties in writing machine language programs. The use of assembler languages requires the use of language translator programs called *assemblers* which allow a computer to convert the instructions of such languages into machine instructions. Language translator programs were discussed in Chapter 5.

Assembler languages are frequently called "symbolic" languages because symbols are used to represent operation codes and storage locations. Convenient alphabetic abbreviations called "mnemonics" (memory aids) and other symbols are used to represent operation codes, storage locations, and data elements. For example: the computation $(X = Y + Z)$ in an assembler language program might take the following form:

Operation Code	Operand	
LD	Y	(Load Y into the accumulator)
AD	Z	(Add Z to the accumulator)
ST	X	(Store the result X)

Notice how alphabetical abbreviations that are easier to remember are used in place of the actual numeric addresses of the data. This greatly simplifies programming, since the programmer does not need to know or remember the exact storage locations of data and instructions. However, it must be noted that an assembler language is still "machine oriented," since assembler language instructions correspond closely to the machine language instructions of the particular computer model being used. Also, notice that each assembler instruction corresponds to a single machine instruction so that the same number of instructions are required in both illustrations. This "one for one" correspondence between assembler instructions and machine instructions is a major limitation of some assembler languages.

Assembler languages are still widely used as a method of programming a computer in a machine-oriented language. Most computer manufacturers provide an assembler language which reflects the unique machine language *instruction set* of a particular line of computers. This characteristic is particularly desirable to *systems programmers* who program systems software (as opposed to *applications programmers* who program applications software) since it provides them with greater control and flexibility in designing a program for a particular computer. They can then produce more *efficient* software, i.e., programs that require a minimum of instructions, storage, and CPU time to perform a specific data processing assignment.

Macro Instructions

Many assembler languages have been improved by the development of a *macro instruction* capability which is also a basic concept in the design of high-level languages. A macro instruction is a single instruction which generates one or more machine instructions when it is translated into machine language. Macro instructions are provided by the software supplier or written by a programmer for such standard operations as arithmetic computations and input/output operations. The format and sequence of instructions that will be generated by the "macro" must first be defined, but from then on a single macro can be written each time the desired sequence of instructions is required in a program. The development of a macro instruction capability for modern assembler languages reduces the number of instructions required in an assembler language program, thereby reducing programming time and effort and the potential for programming errors.

For example: An assembler language with a macro instruction capability would probably include a macro for the process of addition. The computation of $(X = Y + Z)$ might then take the form of a single macro instruction which would later be translated into the three machine instructions required for addition. The macro instruction might take the form:

$$ADD\ Y,\ Z,\ X$$

Subroutines

Assembler languages were further improved by the development of the "subroutine" concept which is also used by all compiler languages. A *routine* is a sequence of instructions in a program that performs a particular data processing activity, such as an "input" routine, an "addition" routine, and "sort" routine. The term *subroutine* is used to describe a special-purpose routine or small program which can be made part of a larger "main" program in order to perform a standard data processing task. Subroutines eliminate the necessity of programming a particular data processing operation each time it is required in a computer program. For example, many input/output activities and mathematical and statistical calculations can be performed by using standard "preprogrammed" subroutines. Subroutines that check input data for errors or compute the square root of numbers are examples of the many types of subroutines that are frequently used.

A subroutine can be defined at the beginning of a program and then used whenever needed in the program by the use of a specific macro instruction which causes the program temporarily to "branch" to the subroutine, perform necessary operations, and then return to the regular sequence of the program. A more widely used method of using subroutines involves storing many standard subroutines in an online "subroutine library" that is available to all computer users. In this method, the main program of a computer user would "call" a subroutine by the use of a particular macro instruction whenever the subroutine was needed. The computer would then branch to the specific subroutine in the subroutine library, perform necessary operations, and then return to the main program. The subroutine is therefore a powerful tool which minimizes programming effort and provides different computer users with an efficient method of performing common but special-purpose data processing operations.

High-Level Languages

High-level languages are also known as *compiler languages.* The instructions of high-level languages are called *statements* and closely resemble human language or the standard notation of mathematics. Individual high-level language statements are really macro instructions since each individual statement generates several machine instructions when translated into machine language by a high-level language translator program called a *compiler*. Most high-level languages are designed to be *machine-independent,* i.e., a high-level language program can usually be processed by computers of different sizes or manufacturers, depending on the compiler used.

High-level language statements do not resemble machine or assembler language instructions. Instead they resemble the English language or mathematical expressions required to express the substance of the problem or procedure being programmed. The *syntax* (vocabulary, punctuation, and grammatical rules) and the *semantics* (meaning) of such language statements do not reflect the internal code of any particular computer but instead are designed to resemble English or mathematical expressions as closely as possible. For example, the computation $(X = Y + Z)$ would be programmed in the high-level languages of FORTRAN and COBOL as:

FORTRAN: $X = Y + Z$
COBOL: COMPUTE $X = Y + Z$

If we defined X as GROSSPAY, Y as SALARY, and Z as COMMISSIONS we could illustrate how close to the English language a high-level language statement can be with the FORTRAN and COBOL statements:

FORTRAN: GROSPAY = SALARY + COMMIS
COBOL: ADD SALARY TO COMMISSIONS GIVING
             GROSSPAY

Advantages of High-Level Languages. A high-level language is obviously easier to learn and understand. It takes less time and effort to write an error-free computer program or to make corrections and revisions that may be required. However, high-level language programs are usually less efficient than assembler language programs and require a greater amount of computer time for translation into machine instructions. These characteristics were considered serious limitations when high-level languages were first developed. However, the savings in programmer time and training, the increased speed and storage capacity of third and fourth generation computer hardware, and the efficiency and versatility of modern computer software have made high-level languages the most widely used programming languages for business, scientific, and other applications.

Since many high-level languages are machine-independent, programs written in a high-level language do not have to be reprogrammed when a new computer is installed, and computer programmers do not have to learn a new language for each computer they program. High-level languages have less rigid rules, form, and syntax, thus reducing the potential for errors. Compiler language translators include extensive diagnostic capabilities that assist the programmer by recognizing and identifying programming errors.

Types of High-Level Languages. High-level languages are frequently subdivided into "procedure oriented" languages and "problem oriented" languages. *Procedure-oriented languages* are general-purpose languages that are designed to express the "procedure" or logic of a data processing problem. Programmers do not have to concern themselves with the details of how the computer will process a program. Popular procedure-oriented languages are FORTRAN, COBOL, PL/1, and BASIC.

Problem-Oriented Languages are designed to provide an efficient programming language for specialized types of data processing problems. The programmer does not even specify the procedure to be followed in solving the problem but merely specifies the input/output requirements and other parameters of the problem to be solved. Such programming simplicity is possible because the specialized nature of the language allows the problem-solving procedure to be "preprogrammed." Some examples of problem-oriented languages are: RPG, which is used to produce reports and update files, GPSS, which is used for simulation applications, LISP, which is used to process lists of symbolic data, and COGO, which is used for the solution of civil engineering problems.

Natural Languages

Several types of programming languages have recently been developed which are very close to English or other human languages. Much research and development activity is still underway to develop computer programming languages that are as easy to use as ordinary conversation in one's *natural* language. Development of the complex language translator programs (sometimes called *intelligent* compilers) required to translate such natural languages into structured machine language programs is also involved. The term *natural language* is used to describe a variety of such languages. Other names used include: *very high level languages* (VHLL), *nonprocedural* languages, *actoral* languages, *application-oriented* languages, *user-oriented* languages, and so forth. Also related to these languages are the *query, report generator,* and *data manipulation* languages provided by most current data base management systems, which allow users and programmers to interrogate and access the data bases of a computer system using English-like statements. See Figure 8–2.

- Give me the top ten sales people in 1981.
- What is the average salary of accountants in the Rochester Division?
- Show me a histogram of the number of offices in the Northeast by district.
- Compare estimated production to actual production for all departments.
- Correlate salary to years of service for all supervisors over age 55.
- How many different policy holders carry uninsured motorist protection?
- What is the minimum age and salary by state, city, and store for all female employees?
- Report the base salary, commissions, and years of service of all sales clerks in New York and Massachusetts.
- Show the statistics for family income and size in Mississippi and Alabama.
- Compute the total ratio of 1982 estimated production to 1981 actual production for all products.
- List the sales managers with salary plus commissions + bonuses − deductions > $50,000.

FIGURE 8–2 Natural Query Language Statements

Courtesy Artificial Intelligence Corp.

Natural languages are called *nonprocedural* or *procedureless* languages because they do not require users to write detailed *procedures* that tell the computer *how* to do a *process*. Instead, natural languages allow users to simply tell the computer *what* they want. Most natural languages are designed to support interactive programming and conversational computing using a personal computer or online computer terminal. They are also more tailored to users and user applications. The languages are also called *very* high-level languages to differentiate them from conventional high-level languages. All indications are that such languages will one day make computer programming as easy as ordinary conversation.

Figure 8–3 illustrates the multilevel structure of programming languages, which ranges from microprogram machine

FIGURE 8–3 Levels of Programming Languages

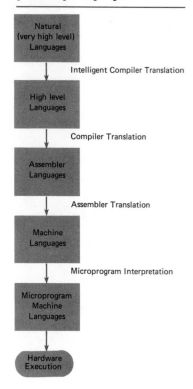

FIGURE 8–3 Levels of Programming Languages

Natural (very high level) Languages

Intelligent Compiler Translation

High level Languages

Compiler Translation

Assembler Languages

Assembler Translation

Machine Languages

Microprogram Interpretation

Microprogram Machine Languages

Hardware Execution

languages to very high-level languages. Notice also the types of language translation needed at each level.

POPULAR PROGRAMMING LANGUAGES

Hundreds of programming languages have been developed, many of them with humorous names ranging from FRED and LOLITA to STRUDL and SYNFUL! However, the seven high-level languages most widely used for the coding of business application programs are FORTRAN, COBOL, PL/1, BASIC, Pascal, APL, and RPG. A brief analysis and illustration of each language is presented in the remainder of this chapter.

FORTRAN

FORTRAN (FORmula TRANslation), developed in 1957, is the oldest of the popular high-level languages. As its name indicates, FORTRAN was designed primarily for solving the mathematical problems of scientists, engineers, and mathematicians. Therefore, FORTRAN programs use many mathematical statements utilizing words, symbols, and numbers in algebraic types of expressions.

Since FORTRAN cannot express certain input/output and nonnumeric operations, it is not suitable for many business data processing applications which require extensive processing of alphanumeric data files stored on many secondary storage devices. FORTRAN IV and FORTRAN 77, the latest versions of FORTRAN, are the most widely used programming languages for scientific and engineering data processing. However, FORTRAN is also utilized to program business computer applications which involve many mathematical calculations. For example, FORTRAN is frequently utilized to program quantitative business applications in operations research and management science that require such techniques as statistical analysis, mathematical models, network analysis and linear programming.

Many versions of FORTRAN have been developed by computer manufacturers, and large computer users have added special features to their FORTRAN compilers. For example, several versions of FORTRAN have been developed to simplify the teaching of FORTRAN in schools or to facilitate interactive programming in FORTRAN. One of the most noticeable features of some versions (such as WATFOR, WATFIV,

XTRAN, and FASTRAN) is that they allow "free form" input/output statements similar to the BASIC programming language.

FORTRAN now exists in two standard forms: FORTRAN and Basic FORTRAN. These standard versions were developed by the American National Standards Institute in cooperation with the computer industry. Basic FORTRAN is a shorter and simpler version of standard FORTRAN and is probably the most widely used form of the FORTRAN language. The full standard version of FORTRAN is an extension of Basic FORTRAN with advanced features and a greater variety of instructions.

FORTRAN Statements

There are five major categories of FORTRAN statements.

1. *Arithmetic statements.* Arithmetic operations to be performed are described by statements closely resembling mathematical expressions.
2. *Input/output statements.* Fundamental input/output words are READ and WRITE, which read or write the contents of specific data fields from or to a specified input/output unit.
3. *Specification statements.* The fundamental specification words are FORMAT and DIMENSION. FORMAT statements specify the "format" (size, type, number, etc.) of input or output data fields and records, while DIMENSION statements specify the dimensions (rows, columns, levels) of "arrays" of data items, and reserve the memory locations required to store each element in an array.
4. *Control statements.* Fundamental control words are GO TO, IF, DO, STOP, and END. GO TO and IF statements alter the sequential execution of program statements by transferring control to another statement, while DO statements command the computer to repeatedly execute a series of statements (a "program loop" or "DO loop") that are part of the computer program. STOP and END statements terminate a program.
5. *Subprogram statements.* Subprogram statements include CALL, RETURN, FUNCTION, and SUBROUTINE statements. Such statements allow programmers to develop and utilize the "preprogrammed" functions and subroutines that are stored in the "subroutine library" of the computer system.

Sample FORTRAN Program

Figure 8–4 illustrates the statements and flowchart of a short and simple FORTRAN program that computes the average (arithmetic mean) of the scores received on an exam by students in a class. Note that variable names like "COUNTR" are abbreviated due to one of the restrictions of FORTRAN. A brief analysis of the program reveals the following data processing activities:

1. Two values, a counter (COUNTR) and an accumulator, (TOTAL) are cleared to zero. (Statements 01 and 02.)
2. Input of exam scores (SCORE) is by a READ statement using the form specified by a FORMAT statement. (Statements 03 and 04.)
3. The counter (COUNTR) keeps track of the number of

FIGURE 8–4 Sample FORTRAN Program

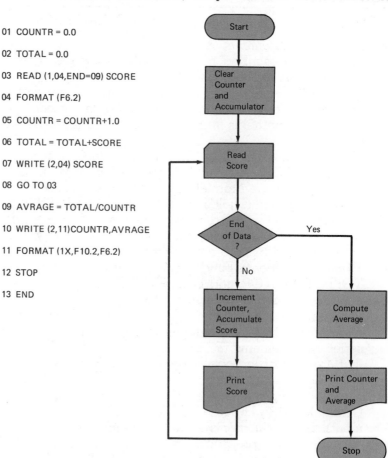

```
01 COUNTR = 0.0
02 TOTAL = 0.0
03 READ (1,04,END=09) SCORE
04 FORMAT (F6.2)
05 COUNTR = COUNTR+1.0
06 TOTAL = TOTAL+SCORE
07 WRITE (2,04) SCORE
08 GO TO 03
09 AVRAGE = TOTAL/COUNTR
10 WRITE (2,11)COUNTR,AVRAGE
11 FORMAT (1X,F10.2,F6.2)
12 STOP
13 END
```

scores being read, while a running total of scores is accumulated (TOTAL). (Statements 05 and 06.)

4. After each exam score is printed, the program "loops" back to read another score. (Statements 07 and 08.)

5. When the computer senses that it is out of input data (note the END = 09 in the READ statement) it will transfer control or "branch" to statement 09.

6. The average exam score (AVRAGE) is calculated by dividing the total scores accumulated (TOTAL) by the number of exam scores (COUNTR) tallied. (Statement 09.)

7. The average exam score and number taking the exam is printed as output and the program terminates. (Statements 10, 11, 12, and 13.)

COBOL

COBOL (COmmon Business Oriented Language) is the most widely used programming language for business data processing. It is an English-like language that was specifically designed to handle the input, processing, and output of large volumes of alphameric data from many data files that is characteristic of business data processing. COBOL was developed and is maintained by the Conference on Data Systems Languages (CODASYL) which is composed of representatives of large computer users, government agencies, and computer manufacturers. The specifications of the COBOL language are therefore subject to periodic revision and updating. The American National Standards Institute (ANSI) has developed standards for COBOL which recognize different "levels" and "modules" of COBOL. Standards for a "Minimum Standard" COBOL and "Full Standard" COBOL have also been developed.

COBOL's use of English-like statements facilitates programming, makes it easy for a nonprogrammer to understand the purpose of a particular COBOL program, and gives a "self-documenting" capability to COBOL programs. Thus, COBOL is widely utilized for business data processing and can be used by the computer systems of most manufacturers. Of course, COBOL does have several limitations. It is a "wordy" programming language which is more difficult for nonprofessional programmers to utilize than other languages such as FORTRAN or BASIC. Since it has a business data processing and batch processing orientation, it is limited in its applicability to scientific data processing and interactive processing.

The COBOL Divisions

Every computer program written in the COBOL language must contain four major parts called "divisions," which are summarized below.

1. *The Identification Division.* Identifies the program by listing such information as the name of the program, the name of the programmer, the date the program was written, and other comments which identify the purpose of the program.
2. *The Environment Division.* Specifies the type of computer and peripheral equipment that will be used to process the program.
3. *The Data Division.* Describes the organization and format of the data to be processed by the program.
4. *The Procedure Division.* Contains the COBOL statements (called "commands") which describe the procedure to be followed by the computer in accomplishing its data processing assignment.

COBOL Procedure Division Statements

The Procedure Division is the section of a COBOL program that is most like programs written in languages like FORTRAN or BASIC. The major statements in this division of COBOL can be grouped into the following four categories:

1. *Input/output statements.* The OPEN statement is utilized to prepare files to be read or written. The CLOSE statement terminates the processing of a file in a program. The READ statement reads a single record from a file that is named in the statement. The WRITE statement writes a single record that is named in the statement onto an open output file.
2. *Data movement statements.* The MOVE statement transfers data from one area of storage to another.
3. *Arithmetic statements.* The COMPUTE statement is utilized to perform arithmetic operations that are expressed in the form of a mathematical formula. The ADD, SUBTRACT, MULTIPLY, and DIVIDE statements perform the arithmetic computations indicated.
4. *Control statements.* GO TO and IF statements alter the sequential execution of program statements by transferring control to another statement. The PERFORM statement transfers control temporarily to another part of the program, while the STOP statement temporarily or permanently halts the execution of the program.

FIGURE 8–5 Sample COBOL
Program

```
1    IDENTIFICATION DIVISION.
2    PROGRAM-ID. SIX.
3    AUTHOR. STEVE RUNDELL.

4    ENVIRONMENT DIVISION.
5    INPUT-OUTPUT SECTION.
6    FILE-CONTROL.
7       SELECT CARD-FILE ASSIGN TO SYSIPT.
8       SELECT PRINT-FILE ASSIGN TO SYSLST.

9    DATA DIVISION.
10   FILE SECTION.
11   FD   CARD-FILE
12      RECORDING MODE IS F
13      LABEL RECORDS ARE OMITTED
14      DATA RECORD IS CARD-IN.
15   01   CARD-IN.
16      02 NAME-IN                PIC X(40).
17      02 SCORE                  PIC 999.
18      02 FILLER                 PIC X(37).
19   FD   PRINT-FILE.
20      RECORDING MODE IS U
21      LABEL RECORDS ARE OMITTED
22      DATA RECORD IS PRINT-LINE.
23   01   PRINT-LINE              PIC X(133).
24   WORKING-STORAGE SECTION.
25   77   STORE-NUMBER            PIC 999   VALUE IS ZEROS.
26   77   STORE-SCORE             PIC 99999   VALUE IS ZEROS.
27   01   PRINTER-LINE.
28      02 FILLER                 PIC X.
29      02 NAME-OUT               PIC X(40).
30      02 FILLER                 PIC X(5).
31      02 SCORE-OUT              PIC ZZ9.
32      02 FILLER                 PIC X(84).
33   01   AVERAGE-LINE.
34      02 FILLER                 PIC X(46).
35      02 AVERAGE                PIC ZZ9.99.
36      02 FILLER                 PIC X(81).

37   PROCEDURE DIVISION.
38   OPEN-FILES.
39      OPEN INPUT CARD-FILE.
40      OPEN OUTPUT PRINT-FILE.
41   READ-CARDS.
42      READ CARD-FILE AT END GO TO END-OF-JOB.
43      ADD SCORE TO STORE-SCORE. ADD 1 TO STORE-NUMBER.
44   MOVE-DATA.
45      MOVE NAME-IN TO NAME-OUT.
46      MOVE SCORE TO SCORE-OUT.   WRITE PRINT LINE
47      FROM PRINTER-LINE.   GO TO READ-CARDS.
48   END-OF-JOB.
49      DIVIDE STORE-NUMBER INTO STORE-SCORE
50      GIVING AVERAGE-SCORE.   MOVE AVERAGE-SCORE
51      TO AVERAGE.   WRITE PRINT-LINE FROM AVERAGE-LINE
52      AFTER ADVANCING 2 LINES.
53      CLOSE CARD-FILE.
54      CLOSE PRINT-FILE.
55      STOP RUN.
```

Sample COBOL Program

Figure 8–5 illustrates the statements of a simple COBOL program that computes an average exam score similar to the previous FORTRAN example. Notice the large number of statements required by the first three COBOL divisions. However, notice how easy it is to read the English-like statements that detail the data processing procedures required by the program.

BASIC

BASIC (Beginner's All-purpose Symbolic Instruction Code) is a widely used programming language for time-sharing applications and interactive programming. It is also being widely used by minicomputer and microcomputer systems for small business use and for personal computing. BASIC was developed in the early 1960s at Dartmouth College as a simple, easily learned language that would allow students to engage in interactive (conversational) computing utilizing a time-sharing computer system. BASIC resembles a shortened and simplified version of FORTRAN. With only a few hours of instruction, a computer user can solve small problems by "conversing" with a computer, utilizing a time-sharing terminal or small computer. BASIC has proven so easy to learn and utilize that it has quickly become a widely used programming language.

Several versions of BASIC have been developed. Such "extensions" of BASIC have transformed it into a more powerful language which can handle a wide variety of data processing assignments utilizing either batch processing or real-time processing. The extensions of BASIC have not been standardized, and differences exist in the BASIC compilers developed by many computer manufacturers and large computer users. However, the specifications for the most essential and widely used parts of BASIC (called Standard Minimal BASIC) were standardized in 1978. Versions with more advanced features (frequently called "Extended" BASIC) are more likely to contain differences in specifications and usage.

BASIC is widely used to provide a "conversational computing" or "interactive processing" environment for computer users at remote terminals or using minicomputer or microcomputer systems. Such an environment allows a BASIC program to be coded, debugged, and executed in "real time," frequently called *interactive programming*. An example of conversational computing using a program written in BASIC was provided in Chapter 1. However, this chapter will provide an example of a BASIC program written "from scratch" using a computer terminal or small computer with interactive programming capability.

BASIC is a "friendly" language that is easy to learn and use, for several reasons. Entering data is easy because input is comparatively "free form," i.e., no rigid input format is necessary. Output formats are also provided if desired. Most BASIC compilers are really interactive *interpreters* which translate each BASIC statement immediately after it is "typed in," and provide helpful "diagnostics" immediately if an error is sensed in a statement. Correcting an erroneous BASIC statement is also easy. Retyping the line number of such a statement and a corrected version of the statement is all that is necessary. All of these benefits must be balanced against the lack of a standard extended version of BASIC and its limited ability to handle large data base processing applications.

BASIC Statements

There are five major categories of statements in fundamental versions of BASIC:

1. *Arithmetic statements.* Arithmetic operations can be accomplished through the use of the reserved word LET followed by an equal sign and an arithmetic expression, such as LET X = Y + Z. Arithmetic expressions may also be contained in a PRINT statement.
2. *Input/output statements.* Fundamental input/output words are READ, DATA, INPUT, and PRINT. READ statements read the contents of specific data fields from input data provided by DATA statements. INPUT statements accept input data directly from the terminal, while PRINT statements type output onto a terminal.
3. *Control statements.* Fundamental control words are GO TO, IF . . . THEN, FOR, NEXT, and END. GO TO and IF . . . THEN statements alter the sequential execution of program statements by transferring control to another statement. FOR statements command the computer to repeatedly execute a series of statements (a "program loop") that are part of the computer program. NEXT statements are used to end program loops formed by the FOR statement, while an END statement terminates a BASIC program.

4. *Other statements.* Two other BASIC statements are frequently used even in simple BASIC programs. REM statements are not translated by the compiler or executed by the computer. They are merely remarks and comments of the programmer which help document the purpose of the program and only appear in the program listing. The DIM statement is utilized in BASIC to specify the "dimensions" (rows and levels) or "arrays" of data items. It reserves the memory locations required to store each element in an array.

5. *System Commands.* BASIC system commands are not BASIC program statements but are "commands" to the operating system of the computer. They control the use of the BASIC compiler and the processing of BASIC programs. Some examples are:

RUN	Tells the computer to execute a program.
LIST	A listing of the statements in the program is printed or displayed.
NEW	Indicates that the user wants to write a new program.
OLD	Indicates that the user wants to use a previously written or "canned" program.

Sample BASIC Program

Figure 8–6 illustrates the "real time" programming of a simple BASIC program that computes an average exam score

FIGURE 8–6 Sample BASIC Program

```
/EXECUTE BASIC
*BASIC OLD OR NEW? NEW
*NEW PROGRAM NAME? AVERAGE
 READY

*10    REM PROGRAM TO COMPUTE AN AVERAGE EXAM SCORE
*20    LET C = 0
*30    LET T = 0
*40    READ X
*50    IF X = -0 THEN 90
*60    LET C=C+1
*70    LET T=T+X
*80    GO TO 40
*90    LET A=T/C
*100   PRINT "AVERAGE SCORE IS";A
*110   DATA 64,87,43,95,66
*120   DATA 75,59,97,67,-0
*130   END

*RUN

AVERAGE SCORE IS 72.5555

*BYE
```

similar to the previous FORTRAN and COBOL examples. It outlines system commands of the user, responses of the computer, the statements of the BASIC program, the input data of exam scores, and the output of the computed average exam score. Student exam scores are contained in the two DATA statements used. The computer reads these one at a time until all are read and then automatically branches to statement 90 to compute the exam average, prints it, and terminates the program. Note how in many BASIC versions, the system command to terminate use of the BASIC compiler is the appropriate "BYE."

PL/1

PL/1 (Programming Language 1) was developed by IBM in 1965 as a general-purpose language which could be used by new generations of "general purpose" computers for both business and scientific applications. PL/1 was designed to include the best features of FORTRAN and COBOL as well as some of the capabilities of assembler languages and ALGOL. PL/1 is not as widely used as COBOL and FORTRAN, primarily because other software suppliers were slow to develop PL/1 compilers. However, growth in the use of PL/1 is expected to continue as more computer users adopt it as their primary programming language.

PL/1 has been criticized as being difficult to learn and inefficient to program. However, even its critics agree that it is a highly flexible "modular" general-purpose language which is better suited to the requirements of "structured programming" than many other languages. PL/1 attains its flexibility by providing features which support business, scientific, real-time, and systems programming applications and by utilizing a "modular" design and a "default interpretation" capability. Thus, PL/1 is organized into modules (or "subsets") which are tailored to specific applications or levels of complexity similar to the levels and modules of ANSI COBOL.

The default interpretation feature simplifies PL/1 programming, since it allows a programmer to ignore the specifications of the PL/1 modules not being used. The PL/1 compiler will automatically select the "default interpretation" for each specification that is required by a program unless it is specified by the programmer. Such "default specifications" are usually the specifications of modules that are utilized by programs that do not require the advanced features of PL/1.

The modular design and default interpretation features of PL/1 facilitate its use by former users of FORTRAN, COBOL, and ALGOL and by computer users with either simple or complex EDP requirements. PL/1 can also be utilized by both large and small computers, since PL/1 compilers are available in modules that are tailored to the various PL/1 language subsets.

Another feature of PL/1 that contributes to its flexibility and facilitates program coding is a *free-form format* for program coding. No special coding form is required, and more than one statement can be written on a line. Also, different "modes" of data (integer, real, etc.) can be mixed in an expression. The PL/1 compiler automatically performs the necessary conversions so that proper results are obtained. Finally, PL/1 allows free-form formatting of input and output (as in BASIC), though the format of the data can also be specified as in FORTRAN and COBOL.

PL/1 Statements

A PL/1 *statement* is defined as a string of characters terminated by a semicolon. A Pl/1 program consists of several statements which are grouped into "blocks" or "groups." One or more blocks make up a "procedure"; while one or more procedures make up a complete PL/1 *program*. Five basic categories of statements used in simple PL/1 programs are outlined below:

1. *Assignment* or *Arithmetic* statements assign values and perform arithmetic and logical operations.
2. *Input/output* statements transfer data between the CPU and input/output devices. When input/output is in the form of discrete data records in a file, the READ or WRITE statements are utilized. When input/output takes a "free form" FORMAT in the form of a continuous "stream" of characters, the GET and PUT statements are utilized.
3. *Control* statements (such as DO, GO TO, and IF-THEN statements) control the execution sequence of the statements in a program. They perform comparisons and test conditions, transfer control within a program through a "branching" process, and direct the repetitive execution of statements by forming "program loops."
4. *Data declaration* statements specify the mode and format of data variables. For example, DECLARE statements specify the number of rows and columns in "arrays" of data and the "levels" of data fields in a data record.

5. *Program structure* statements identify and specify the types of program segments being utilized. A procedure "label" identifies a procedure; for example, the label "PAYROLL" might be used for a payroll calculation procedure. The procedure statement: PROCEDURE OPTIONS (MAIN), identifies a program as a simple "main" program, as opposed to a complex program with several procedures (subroutines) and other options. The END statement is the last statement of a PL/1 program.

Sample PL/1 Program

Figure 8–7 illustrates a simple PL/1 program to compute an average exam score which is similar to programs in the previous programming language sections. Note the similarity of some of the statements to FORTRAN and COBOL. Also, a free-form "stream" format is used for input and output which is reminiscent of BASIC. Note also the use of the "DO WHILE" statement which forms a loop that is one of the basic program control structures of structured programming.

```
AVERAGE: PROCEDURE OPTIONS (MAIN);
    /* PROGRAM FOR AVERAGE OF STUDENT SCORES */
    /* END OF SCORES IS INDICATED BY A NEGATIVE NUMBER */

    DECLARE (AVERAGE, TOTAL, VALUE, SCORE, COUNTER)
      FIXED DECIMAL;

        COUNTER = 0;
        TOTAL = 0;
        GET LIST (SCORE);
        DO WHILE (SCORE > = 0);
          COUNTER = COUNTER + 1;
          TOTAL = TOTAL + SCORE;
          GET LIST (SCORE);
          END;
        AVERAGE = TOTAL/SCORE;
        PUT LIST ('AVERAGE SCORE IS', AVERAGE);
    END AVERAGE;
```

FIGURE 8–7   Sample PL/1 Program

PASCAL

Pascal is a general-purpose language named after the noted mathematician and philosopher Blaise Pascal (1623–1662), who invented a practical calculating machine at age 19. Pascal was invented in the late 1960s by Professor Niklaus Wirth of Zurich who was looking for an ideal language to teach the concepts of structured programming and top-down design.

The small number of types of Pascal statements and the simplicity of its syntax has enabled systems programmers to write very efficient and "bug-free" Pascal compilers which occupy a minimal amount of memory. This, together with its appeal as a logically complete and easy to learn language, explains the growing popularity of Pascal especially as implemented on microcomputers.

One of the major contributions of Wirth's work is his formalization of the concept of "type" as used in Pascal. Each item of data must have its *type* specified explicitly or implicitly in the module in which it appears. As data is passed from one module to another their type must not change and any attempt to write a program which violates this principal should result in an error message generated by the compiler.

The main disadvantages of Pascal in the opinion of many programmers are the lack of a variable dimension facility for arrays and the lack of flexible file handling capabilities. Some implementations of Pascal, however, have provided extensions to the language which overcome these deficiencies.

A notable achievement in the implementation of Pascal is a complete single-user software system for interactive use on microprocessors, developed by Kenneth L. Bowles of the University of California, San Diego, called UCSD Pascal.

Pascal Statements

A Pascal program consists of a program statement followed by declaration statements, which in turn are followed by executable statements. Statements are separated by semicolons and the program is terminated with a period. Declaration statements are used to assign constants to identifiers, to declare the "type" of each variable, and to define procedures and functions (which in turn contain declarations and executable statements). Executable statements are described below:

1. *Assignment* statements are used to assign a new value to a variable, usually as a result of a calculation.
2. *Input/Output* statements move data between variables and either external devices or internal files defined by the user. Files are declared specifying the "type" of data they are to contain. *Textfiles* represent data as a string of characters such as English letters or decimal digits. Other files may hold numerical data with internal (binary) representation.

3. *Compound statement*—a sequence of statements enclosed between BEGIN and END is considered to be a single statement in the logic of a program.
4. *Conditional statements* chose alternative flow of control based on the value of some expression. PASCAL includes the IF-THEN, the IF-THEN-ELSE and, for multiple alternatives, the CASE statement.
5. *Repetitive statements* repeat the execution of a statement or sequence of statements until some condition is met. These "structured statements" include the WHILE-DO, the REPEAT-UNTIL, and the FOR statement.
6. *GOTO statement*—there is rarely a need to transfer control from one place in a block of code to another using a GOTO, and it is considered poor programming practice to overuse this statement. Its presence often complicates attempts to verify the correctness of a program and violates structured programming concepts. However, the GOTO statement can be effectively used to abandon a section of a program from deep within a set of "nested" loops.

Sample Pascal Program

To illustrate Pascal programming Figure 8–8 contains yet another program which finds the average of exam scores. It should be apparent from studying this program that Pascal bears more resemblence to PL/1 than to the other languages we have discussed. When comparing with the PL/1 program note that the Pascal program uses the control structure REPEAT-UNTIL rather than the WHILE-DO and that the repetition is terminated by the use of the standard function *eof* which returns the value "true" when an "end-of-file" has been reached.

```
PROGRAM averagescore (infile,outfile);

VAR score, sum, average, count : real;
    infile, outfile : text;

BEGIN
    sum:=0.0; count:=0.0;
    REPEAT
        read(infile, score);
        sum:=sum + score;
        count:=count + 1.0
    UNTIL   eof(infile);
    average:=sum/count;
    write (outfile, 'Average score is', average)
END.
```

FIGURE 8–8   Sample Pascal Program

APL

APL (A Programming Language) is an interactive language originated by Kenneth Iverson of IBM. It is a sophisticated *problem-oriented* language designed for interactive problem solving. It uses a very concise symbolic notation representing a large number of built-in functions and operators which make it possible to write complicated programs in a simple, concise form. APL uses a special character set illustrated in Figure 8–9. This requires a terminal with an APL keyboard or APL character capability.

APL is a powerful language which can specify the processing of complex operations with just a few *operators* and variables. APL allows very efficient, interactive programming. Only a few operators are needed to define and manipulate large arrays of data. APL does not require the programmer to specify the detailed procedures needed to construct and control program loops that would be required in other high-level programming languages.

IBM has offered an APL compiler since 1968. APL compilers are also available for other computer systems, including one offered by the Digital Equipment Corporation. APL is especially popular in time-sharing systems, and thus is available from several nationwide time-sharing networks. APL's concise, symbolic notation make its programs difficult to read, and it requires a large amount of primary storage. However, it is not difficult to learn to use APL for many common mathematical operations. The availability of APL from time-sharing networks has increased its use as a programming language.

APL Statements

There are over 50 APL *operators* which can be used to construct APL statements. A few simple examples are shown in Figure 8–10.

FIGURE 8–9 A Typical APL Character Set and Keyboard

APL Statement	Function
A ← □	Provide input data for A
A + B	A plus B
A ⌈ B	Find the larger of A and B
A ← 1 2 3	Assign this list (vector) of numbers to A
3 2 ρ A	Create a 3 X 2 matrix or two-dimensional array from the vector A

FIGURE 8-10 Examples of APL Statements

Sample APL Program

Figure 8–11 illustrates a simple APL program to compute an arithmetic mean (average) of a group of numbers. As soon as the program was entered at a computer terminal, it asked for and was supplied with input data, and immediately computed the average.

```
        ∇AVERAGE
[1]     'ENTER NUMBERS'
[2]     X ← □
[3]     'THE AVERAGE IS'; +/X ÷ ρX
[4]     ∇

        AVERAGE
ENTER NUMBERS
□:
        2 4 6 8
THE AVERAGE IS 5
```

FIGURE 8-11 Sample APL Program

RPG

RPG (Report Program Generator) is a simple "problem oriented" language which was originally designed to generate programs that produced printed reports. However, several versions of RPG have been developed (such as RPG II and RPG III) which have made RPG a widely used language for report preparation, file maintenance, and other business data processing applications of small computer users. RPG cannot handle large complex applications which require a "procedure oriented" language (such as COBOL, FORTRAN, and PL/1) and a large computer system. However, RPG can easily handle many types of straightforward business applications and can be used with small computer systems that do not have the hardware and software capabilities required by many procedure-oriented languages.

Since it is *problem-oriented* rather than *procedure-oriented*, RPG does not require the use of statements which outline the procedure to be followed by the computer. Instead, a person using RPG fills out a few simple "specification sheets" which are used to describe (1) the form of the input data, (2) the input/output devices and data files to be used, (3) the format of output reports, and (4) the calculations that are required. Given these specifications, the RPG translator program generates a machine-language program that can perform the necessary data processing operations and produce required reports. RPG is comparatively easy to learn and simple to use, which adds to its popularity with small computer users. The RPG II version is widely utilized for business data processing applications by thousands of small business computers.

RPG Specification Forms

Programming in RPG usually involves the use of at least three of the four specifications forms described below.

- *File description specifications.* This form defines the data files to be utilized. It identifies a file as input and/or output, specifies its basic characteristics, and assigns it to a particular input/output device.
- *Input specifications.* This form specifies the format of data records contained in an input file. It identifies and describes the records in the file, and the data fields that make up each record.
- *Output specifications.* This form specifies the format of the output report. It identifies and describes output data records and their fields. It may also specify: (1) the use of titles and headings, (2) printer carriage control, (3) editing operations, and (4) the conditions which govern the writing of each type of output record.
- *Calculation specifications.* This form is utilized whenever a program requires mathematical operations, such as addition, subtraction, multiplication, and division. It specifies the mathematical operations to be performed and identifies the types of data which are to be utilized in each calculation.

The completed specifications forms represent the RPG "source program." Each line of a specifications form is recorded on punched cards or entered into a computer terminal.

The RPG compiler then translates the source program into an "object program" which consists of machine-language instructions that represent the data processing procedures required by the specifications forms. Thus, the RPG compiler has "generated a program" that can produce reports and carry out other data processing assignments when appropriate input data is entered into the computer system.

Sample RPG Program

We will conclude our introductory analysis of RPG by showing a simple RPG program that computes GROSS PAY as the sum of SALARY + COMMISSIONS. However, since many RPG compilers limit the size of data names and file names

---

FIGURE 8–12   Sample RPG Program

File Description Specification

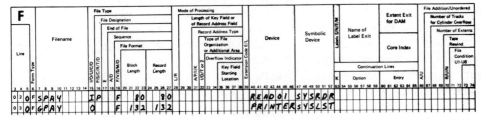

RPG   INPUT SPECIFICATIONS

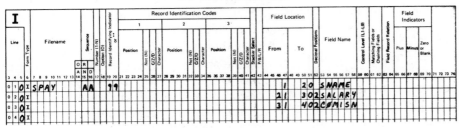

RPG   CALCULATION SPECIFICATIONS

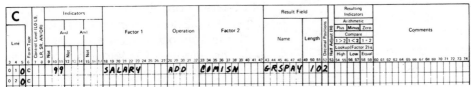

RPG   OUTPUT   SPECIFICATIONS

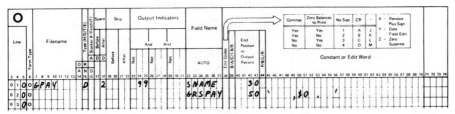

to six characters, data names are shortened to comply with such restrictions.

Figure 8–12 illustrates the specifications forms of a simple RPG program that (1) reads an undetermined number of "salesperson payroll cards" containing the name, salary, and commissions of each salesperson, (2) calculates GRSPAY = SALARY + COMISN, and (3) prints the name and gross pay of each salesperson.

SUMMARY

- Programming languages are a major category of system software. They allow computer instructions to be written in a language that is understandable to both people and computers. The four major levels of programming languages are machine languages, assembler languages, high-level languages, and natural languages. Language translators such as compilers and assemblers are needed to convert assembler or compiler programming language instructions into machine language instructions. High-level languages such as FORTRAN, COBOL, BASIC, PL/1, Pascal, APL, and RPG are the most widely used programming languages for business applications.

- FORTRAN (FORmula TRANslation) is the most widely utilized language for scientific and engineering data processing. However, it is also utilized to program business computer applications that involve many mathematical calculations.

- COBOL (COmmon Business Oriented Language) is the most widely utilized language for business data processing. It is an English-like language specifically designed to handle the input, processing, and output of large volumes of alphanumeric data from many data files that is characteristic of business data processing.

- BASIC (Beginner's All-purpose Symbolic Instruction Code) is a simple, widely used

programming language for time-sharing applications and interactive programming. It is also being widely used by minicomputer and microcomputer systems for small business use and for personal computing.

- PL/1 (Programming Language 1) is a general-purpose language designed for both business and scientific applications. It is a highly flexible, modular language which is better suited to the requirements of structured programming than many other languages.

- Pascal was designed specifically to incorporate structured programming concepts and to facilitate top-down design. It has become a popular programming language for microcomputers as well as larger computer systems.

- APL (A Programming Language) is a sophisticated problem-oriented programming language designed for interactive problem solving. It uses a concise, symbolic notation and is especially popular for time-sharing applications.

- RPG (Report Program Generator) is a simple problem-oriented language primarily designed to generate programs that produce business reports. RPG requires the use of "specification sheets" instead of program statements. The RPG II version is widely utilized by small business computer users.

KEY TERMS AND CONCEPTS

Machine language	FORTRAN
Assembler language	COBOL
High-level language	BASIC
Natural language	PL/1
Macro instruction	Pascal
Subroutine	APL
Language translators	RPG

REVIEW AND DISCUSSION QUESTIONS

1. How do machine, assembler, high-level and natural languages differ? Which type is easier to program and understand?

2. What is a macro instruction? How does it differ from a subroutine?

3. What are the advantages and limitations of high-level languages?

4. Will we ever be able to program a computer using a natural conversational language? Explain.

5. What is the purpose of language translator programs such as assemblers and compilers?

6. What are the major characteristics and uses of FORTRAN?

7. What are the major categories of FORTRAN statements? Give an example of each.

8. What are the major characteristics and uses of COBOL?

9. What are the functions of the major divisions of COBOL?

10. What are the major characteristics and uses of BASIC?

11. What are the major categories of BASIC statements? Give an example of each.

12. What are the major characteristics and uses of PL/1?

13. What are the major categories of PL/1 statements? Give an example of each.

14. What are the major characteristics and uses of Pascal?

15. What are the major categories of Pascal statements? Give an example of each.

16. What are the major characteristics and uses of APL?

17. How do APL statements differ from those of more conventional programming languages?

18. What are the major characteristics and uses of RPG?

19. How does programming in RPG differ from that required by the other languages described in this chapter?

20. Compare and contrast the major characteristics of the programming languages discussed in this chapter. Which language would you recommend for business data processing? Explain.

REAL WORLD APPLICATIONS

8-1 Searle Chemicals, Inc.

How does the research and development computer service of a large pharmaceutical company win very high user satisfaction, even though it is working with only half the staff and 30 percent of the budget it had two years earlier?

Searle's Research Services switched from time sharing on a batch-oriented mainframe to an online system built on several minicomputer systems. Research Services went on to a further innovation. It does a large part of its application programming in Digital's DATATRIEVE data management language.

The programmers, many of whom had minimal computer background, do jobs in days that would normally take months, and pull enthusiastic users into the design and use of new application systems in a way that would not have been possible before.

DATATRIEVE is a query language that automatically formats reports, but also stores and modifies data in a variety of data structures. DATATRIEVE also defines the formats and logical relationships among both hierarchical and relational data structures. It provides all these capabilities in the form of an easy-to-use, high-level language.

"We changed our whole philosophy of how we did development," says David H. Nordby, director of Research Services at Searle. "We build a prototype DATATRIEVE system after a very quick analysis. This lets users try something very quickly and then change it as their ideas evolve. With a few iterations, we have the final system.

"You can't do this with COBOL because programs are so much harder to change after they're written," he says. "So you go through time-consuming analyses to develop systems that won't need change later.

"Most user applications never stay the way they started. Their needs change. In a formalized development effort, users never got to change their mind."

DATATRIEVE offers many more advantages. "Documentation is not the big headache it was. You can read a DATATRIEVE program and understand what it's doing," Nordby observes. "You don't normally have to spend much time testing the systems either," since they are built on familiar, tested DATATRIEVE commands.

As an example, in one week Nordby and his staff finished a DATATRIEVE program that replaced a COBOL application system that took two years to develop. Today, Searle's Research Services group does much of its programming in DATATRIEVE.

"We have half the people we had then and do two or three times as much work," Nordby says. "My guess is that we get ten times the productivity now."[1]

- How has the query language used by Searle proven superior to their previous use of COBOL? Why has this occurred?
- Would COBOL be better for other applications? Explain.

[1] Source: "Searle's Research and Development Division Cuts Budget, Improves Service with DATATRIEVE," *Insight,* June 1981, p. 1.

8-2   Automobile Club of Michigan

"Our goal was to enable end users to design and perform their specialty in their own way and to keep smaller, low priority job requests out of this department," says Charles L. Cone, director of data processing for Automobile Club of Michigan, Dearborn.

"To achieve this we gave terminals to a number of nonprogrammer accountants, actuaries and others. They learned to use APL on those terminals, and within three months one of them even wrote a program that we sold.

You can see, we began realizing our goal right from the start," he adds, "and today our end users do a range of work that could not be accomplished through conventional data processing operations."

"Typically, we would get requests from our actuaries to revise new rating programs," says Cone. "We'd assign an analyst who studied the need, developed program specifications and send them to the actuaries for agreement. They would come back with new requirements. The process would continue back and forth until we could finally agree on exactly what was needed.

"Now, we still run new rating programs because COBOL handles them more efficiently, but the actuaries develop and refine their own specs and formats through APL" he continues. "They come to us with a job that's ready for coding, and we save countless hours all around."[2]

• How are APL and COBOL being used in the example above? What are the benefits of such use?

[2] Source: "Proof of the Pudding . . . ," *Data Processer,* September/October 1980, pp. 17–18. Reprinted with permission.

8-3   The Department of Defense

Confronted with a costly and at times chaos-producing array of more than 1,000 computer languages, the Pentagon several years ago decided to develop a single tongue for the thousands of computers in the Department of Defense that aim weapons, watch for Soviet ballistic missles, guide patrolling submarines and bombers, and relay critical information to battlefield commanders. The language has now made its debut, and the Pentagon hopes it will eventually spell the end of computer babel.

As at the Tower of Babel, however, this single language is already under fire. Some academicians who perform research for the Pentagon feel that mandatory use of a single language will hamper their creativity. And the Navy is resisting introduction of the single language.

Called Ada, in honor of Augusta Ada Byron, considered the world's first computer programmer and the only legitimate daughter of English poet Lord Byron, the language will cut the Pentagon's

cost of developing and maintaining computer programs and will increase the reliability and speed of computer networks.

Pentagon experts say that Ada, unlike many other languages, is simple to use since it mimics human languages by incorporating common words and phrases in its programming and printed answers. Further, it has the functional richness for a diverse and demanding set of applications and can be used on almost any computer. Ada is a "high-order" language, one in which a single command initiates a series of low-level computer operations. In most applications, a high-order language such as Ada is easier to use than a low-order one. Ada and the unique characteristics that make it so attractive to the military are the result of a 2-year international competition held by the Pentagon, the first of its kind. It resembles an extension of the Pascal programming language and was submitted by Jean Ichbiah of Honeywell Bull in Paris and of the Honeywell Systems and Research Center in Minneapolis.

8–3 *(continued)*

The Army soon expects to have 13,000 computers, the Navy 33,000 and the Air Force 40,000. The software bill for military computers last year came to more than $3 billion. One study estimates that the introduction of Ada will result in savings of more than $24 billion by the end of the century.

Ada should also result in less electronic chaos. During the past 20 years the electronic links among the Pentagon's computers have greatly increased in number, bringing serious problems in networking, similar to having speakers of French and Farsi struggling to communicate with one another on the telephone. A Pentagon-inspired computer language is not new. The Pentagon was the driving force behind the development of COBOL (Common Business-Oriented Language), which was introduced in 1959 and is today used extensively around the world.

While technical, or even random, considerations have often accounted for the use of different computer languages, their use has also been motivated by the turf-consciousness that often characterizes the branches of the armed forces. For example, the Air Force in some cases may not want the Navy to have unlimited access to its computers, and vice versa. Ada, on the other hand, will facilitate this exchange of information, which may be why the Navy has taken a wait-and-see attitude toward the introduction of Ada and is now basing its standardization efforts around the continued use of CMS-2, its own standard computer language.

Because of this type of resistance, and because of the service-wide benefits that are expected, a recent study by the General Accounting Office suggests that the introduction of Ada be made mandatory in the U.S. military. For the moment, however, the Pentagon says introduction will be voluntary.

The Pentagon hopes to entice all computer users—not just the military. It wants universities to use Ada for teaching computer programming and software engineering, wants companies to exploit Ada in the commercial marketplace, wants foreign vendors to adopt Ada, and wants the NATO allies to accept it. The benefits for the U.S. military would be many, including easier hiring of programmers and easier purchasing of program-compatible equipment. The Pentagon even chose the name of the new language with enticement in mind. When development first began, the language was dubbed DOD-I, a name that many observers felt, in the aftermath of Vietnam, would inhibit the use of the language by universities and industry. Instead, the name Ada was eventually chosen, after the Countess of Lovelace.

It remains to be seen whether the Pentagon's drive for language unification will be thwarted by academies, with their desire for freedom to choose which language to use for computer research, or by the Navy, with its apparent desire to keep secrets from the other services. If developments are similar to those described by the Biblical Patriarchs, the outlook for continued proliferation of computer languages is good.[3]

- What benefits are expected from the use of the Ada programming language by the Department of Defense? By other computer users?
- Do you think that Ada should become a standard computer language like COBOL? Explain.

[3] Source: William J. Broad, "Pentagon Orders End to Computer Babel," *Science*, vol. 211, January 1981, pp. 31–33. Copyright 1981 by the American Association for the Advancement of Science. Reprinted with permission.

Modern Data and Information Processing Systems

9

CHAPTER OUTLINE

Electronic Data Processing Concepts

LEARNING OBJECTIVES

The purpose of this chapter is to promote a basic understanding of electronic data processing by analyzing essential data organization concepts and the types and capabilities of electronic data processing systems.

After reading and studying this chapter, you should be able to:

1. Identify the components and functions of electronic data processing as a system.
2. Outline the types of input and output and the storage, processing, and control functions that are typical of business EDP systems.
3. Provide examples to illustrate each of the common data elements.
4. Differentiate between the following EDP concepts:
   a. Physical versus logical data elements.
   b. Sequential versus random file organization.
   c. Sequential-access versus direct-access file processing.
   d. Batch processing versus real time processing.
   e. Interactive processing versus time sharing.
5. Provide several reasons for the use of batch processing and realtime processing systems.
6. Use examples to illustrate several levels of real-time processing systems.

ELECTRONIC DATA PROCESSING AS A SYSTEM

Electronic data processing, or EDP, is the use of computers to process data automatically. However, it is important to view EDP as a *data processing system* which performs the basic functions of *input, processing, output, storage,* and *control,* using computer *hardware, software,* and *personnel.* Thus, we could define an electronic data processing system as a system of computer hardware, software, and personnel that processes data into information. See Figure 9–1.

We have already defined hardware as computer equipment and media, and software as the various types of programs which direct the computer to perform its data processing functions. The third important component of an electronic data processing system is the *personnel* required for its operation.

FIGURE 9–1   Electronic Data Processing as a System

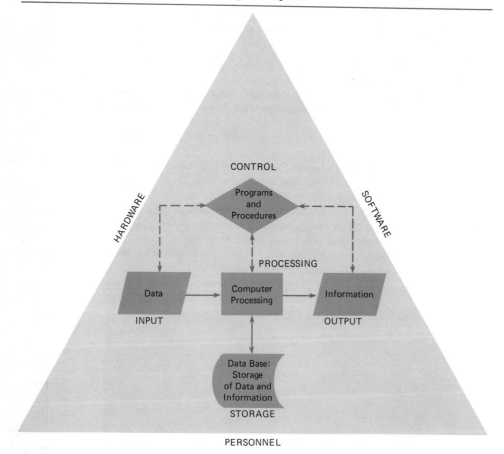

The categories of personnel that are required are systems analysts, programmers, computer operators, and other managerial, technical, and clerical personnel. Basically, *systems analysts* design information systems and data processing systems based on the information requirements of an organization, *programmers* prepare computer programs based on the specifications of the systems analyst, and *computer operators* operate the computer. Such computer personnel should be differentiated from ''computer users.'' A *computer user* or *end user* is anyone who uses a computer system or its output, whether he or she be an accountant, salesperson, engineer, clerk, or manager. The job activities of EDP personnel are discussed in the *Careers in Computer Services* section of Chapter 17.

Business EDP Systems

The use of electronic data processing in business can also be considered in a systems context. Each application of computers and EDP for the solution of a specific business problem, or the performing of a particular business data processing assignment should be viewed as a *system,* with input, processing, output, control, and storage components. Figure 9–2 outlines the types of input and output and data base functions

FIGURE 9–2   Typical Input, Processing, Output, Storage, and Control Components of Business EDP Systems

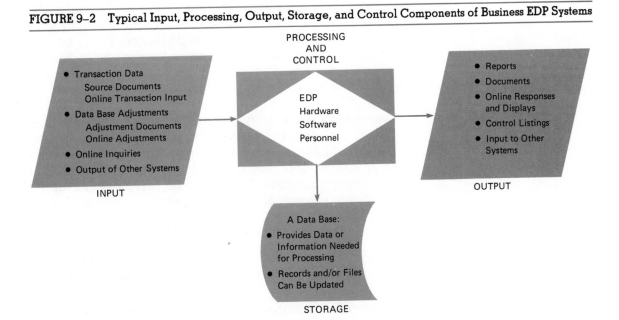

typical of many applications of computers and EDP in business.

You should note the following system components and examples:

Input. Input is frequently collected from *source documents* (such as payroll time cards) and converted to machine-sensible data by a *data entry* process (such as keypunching and key-to-tape). Other input data may be generated by online terminals (such as POS terminals). Input into the system consists of:

- *Transactions data.* Example: A sales transaction.
- *Data base adjustments.* Example: Change a customer's credit balance, using an online terminal in the credit department or by processing a "credit increase request form" mailed in by a customer.
- *Inquiries.* Example: What is the balance owed on a customer's account?
- *Output of other systems.* Example: The output of a sales order/transaction processing system includes data needed as input to an inventory control system to correctly reflect transactions that change the amount of inventory on hand.

Storage. Additional data or information is supplied from the records and/or files contained in the **data base** of the system, which can also be *updated* to reflect the new transaction input. For example: Current credit balances of customers are supplied as a result of inquiries from sales personnel. Completed sales transactions on credit will then change a customer's credit balance.

Processing. Computer system hardware, software, and EDP personnel *process* the data, resulting in an updated data base and output of information. For example: The equipment, computer programs, and computer specialists of a regional computer center connected to POS terminals in retail stores supply the processing power for the EDP system.

Output. Output can take the form of:

- *Reports.* Example: A sales analysis report outlining the sales made during a period by sales territory, product, and salesperson.
- *Documents.* Example: A paycheck or sales receipt.

- *Responses or displays.* Example: A CRT terminal displays the balance owed on a customer's account. Or the same information is transmitted to a telephone by a computer audio-response unit.
- *Control listings.* Example: Each time an employee paycheck is printed, a listing known as a "payroll register" is also printed and written on magnetic tape. This helps provide an "audit trail" for control purposes.
- *Input to other systems.* Example: Part of the output of a payroll system serves as input to a labor cost accounting system and the general accounting system of the firm.

Control. Input, processing, output, and storage *controls* are provided by the hardware, software, and personnel of the EDP system. For example, computer hardware contains *error checking* circuitry; software includes *diagnostic program routines;* and output includes *control listings.*

DATA ORGANIZATION IN ELECTRONIC DATA PROCESSING

A basic understanding of the electronic data processing depends to a large measure on an understanding of several basic concepts of *data organization.* In all electronic data processing systems, data must be organized and structured in some logical manner so that it can be processed efficiently. *Data structures* ranging from simple to complex have been devised to logically organize data in electronic data processing.

Common Data Elements

A *hierarchy* of several levels of data has been devised which differentiate between the most simple elements of data and more complex data elements. Thus, data is organized into *characters, fields, records,* and *files,* just as writing may be organized in letters, words, sentences, and paragraphs. Examples of these *common data elements* are shown in Figure 9–3.

Character. The most basic data element is the "character," which consists of a single alphabetic, numeric, or other symbol.

Field. The next higher level of data is the "field" which consists of a grouping of characters, such as the grouping

**FIGURE 9–3
The Common Data Elements**

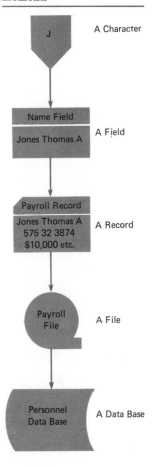

of alphabetical characters in a person's name which forms a *name field,* or the grouping of numerical characters in a sales amount which forms a *sales amount field.* The field is sometimes also called an *item* or *word.* A data field represents an *attribute* (a characteristic or quality) of some *entity* (objects, people, places or events). For example, a person's age could be a data field that represents one attribute of an individual.

Record. Related fields of data are grouped to form a "record," such as the *payroll record* for a person, which consists of data fields such as his or her name, Social Security number and rate of pay. *Fixed-length* records contain a fixed number of data fields, whereas *variable length* records may contain a variable number of fields.

File. A group of related records is known as a "file" (or *data set*). Thus a *payroll file* would contain the payroll records for all of the employees of a firm. Files are frequently classified by the data processing application for which they are primarily used, such as a *payroll file* or an *accounts receivable file.* Files are also classified by their permanence. For example, a *payroll master file* as opposed to a payroll *weekly transaction file.* A **transaction file** would therefore contain records of all transactions occuring during a period and would be used periodically to update the permanent records contained in a **master file.** A *history file* is an obsolete transaction or master file retained for *backup* purposes, or for long-term historical storage called *archival storage.*

Data Base. In the early years of electronic data processing, the data file was the most complex data element in the data hierarchy. However, a level of data organization known as the *data base* has now become an important data element in modern electronic data processing. A data base is a *nonredundant* collection of logically related records or files. A data base consolidates records previously stored in separate files so that a common pool of data records serves as a single *central file* or *data base* for many data processing applications. Thus a *personnel data base* consolidates data formerly segregated in separate files, such as a payroll file, personnel action file, employee skills file, etc. The term **data bank** is sometimes used to describe a collection of several data bases.

Logical and Physical Data Elements

A distinction should be made between "logical" and "physical" data elements. The common data elements just discussed are *logical* data elements, not *physical* data elements.

- *Physical data elements* are related to the individual physical data media or devices on which logical data elements are recorded. For example, a single punched card is a *physical record,* while a single reel of magnetic tape represents a frequently used *physical file* or "volume."

- *Logical data elements* are independent of the data media on which they are recorded. Thus, a punched card can contain several logical records, while several reels of magnetic tape may be used to store a single logical file. *For example,* a punched card may contain payroll data concerning two different employees (two logical records), while several reels of magnetic tape may be needed to store the payroll data file (one logical file) of a large business firm. See Figure 9–4.

Another example: A magnetic tape or disk file may contain blank spaces (*gaps*) between groups **(blocks)** of logical records. A *block* of logical records on magnetic tape or disk is considered a *physical record.* Interrecord or interblock gaps are required since a certain amount of blank space between records or blocks is needed to allow for such mechanical operations as the start/stop time of a magnetic tape unit. Most

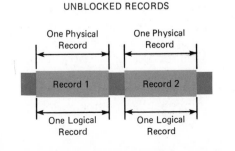

Jones Thomas A
575 32 3874
$10,000 etc.

Jones Mary C
624-79-4012
$12,000 etc.

One Physical Punched Card Record

Two Logical Payroll Records

Payroll File Volume I

Payroll File Volume II

Two Physical Magnetic Tape Reel Files

One Logical Payroll File for the Firm

FIGURE 9–4   Logical versus Physical Data Elements

FIGURE 9–5   Unblocked and Blocked Records

UNBLOCKED RECORDS

One Physical Record   One Physical Record

Record 1   Record 2

One Logical Record   One Logical Record

BLOCKED RECORDS

One Physical Record

Record 1   Record 2   Record 3

Three Logical Records

files group logical records into blocks to conserve file space instead of leaving gaps between each logical record. See Figure 9–5.

File Organization

The records in a file can be organized in two basic ways, *sequential file organization* and *random file organization*. Other methods of file organization which are based on the sequential and random file organizations are the *indexed sequential* and the *list* file organizations. In addition, there is another important method of file organization called the *inverted file*. Before outlining these major types of file organization, three basic aids used in data organization should be explained.

Key. Each record in a file or data base contains one or more *identification fields* or *keys* which are used when searching or sorting a file. For example: A Social Security number might be used as the *key* for identifying each employee's data record in a payroll file.

Pointer. Records may contain other identifying fields (called *pointers*) which help in cross-referencing the contents of a file or data base. Thus, each record could contain a *pointer field* which contains the storage location address of a related record in the file or data base. For example, the payroll record of an employee could include the address of the payroll record for another employee who works on the same project.

Index or Directory. A file or data base may contain an *index or directory*. This is an ordered reference listing of record keys and their associated storage location addresses which helps locate records in the file or data base.

Sequential versus Random File Organization

Sequential File Organization. One of the basic ways to organize the data in a file is to use a *sequential* methodology. Records can be physically stored in a predetermined sequence. Records are arranged in a specified order according to a *record key*. For example, payroll records could be placed in a payroll file in a *sequential* manner according to a numeric order based on employees' Social Security numbers or an alphabetical order based on employees' last names.

The sequential file organization is a simple method of data organization which is fast and efficient when processing large volumes of data that do not need to be processed except on a periodic basis. However, the sequential file organization requires that all records be sorted into the proper sequence before processing, and the entire file must be searched in order to locate, store, or modify even a small number of data records. Thus this method is too slow to handle applications which require immediate updating or responses.

Random File Organization. This method is also called *direct, nonsequential* or *relative* file organization. Records are physically stored in a file in a *random* manner, that is, they are not arranged in any particular sequence. However, the computer must keep track of the storage location of each record in the file using **data organization aids** such as *keys, pointers, indexes,* and other methods so that data can be retrieved when needed. For example, payroll records could be placed in a payroll file in no particular sequence. The computer system could use each record's *key field* to assign and keep track of the storage locations of each record in the file. In the random file organization, input data does not have to be sorted, and processing which requires immediate responses or updating is easily handled.

There are a number of ways to assign storage locations and locate the records in the random file organization. One common technique uses a *transform algorithm* (also called a *randomizing* or *hashing* algorithm) which involves performing some arithmetic computation on a record key and using the result of the calculation as an address for that record. Thus the process is also known as a *key transformation* since an arithmetic operation is applied to a key to transform it into a storage location address. To use a simple example, the transform algorithm might involve dividing the key field of a record (such as an employee number) by the maximum number of records that might be stored in a file, and using the resulting number as the storage location address for that record. Thus in the random file organization, the computer uses record keys and a key transformation process to randomly store and directly locate the data records in a file.

Sometimes the transformation computation results in the same address (the same answer) for two different keys. This occurrence is called a *collision,* and the keys with the same address are called *synonyms.* One method of handling such collisions is to place the record in the next available storage location. In order to minimize collisions, randomly organized files are usually kept only 60 to 70 percent full. Thus the speed of the random file organization must be balanced with the file space that is wasted. Another basic technique used to store and locate records in the random file organization involves the use of an index or directory of record keys and storage addresses. A new record is stored at the next available location and its key and address are placed in the directory so that a list of occupied and available storage locations is maintained.

Other File Organization Methods

Indexed Sequential File Organization. This method is also called the indexed sequential access method (ISAM). In this method, records are stored sequentially on a direct access storage device (such as a magnetic disk) based upon the key field of each record. However, each file also contains an index (like the index in a book) which references the key field of each data record to its storage location address. Thus, any individual record can be directly located by using its key to search and locate its address in the file index. See Figure 9–6.

FIGURE 9–6 Example of an Index

Record Key (employee number)	Record Address
28541	101
35879	102
47853	103
50917	104

The indexed sequential file organization combines the advantages of both the sequential and random file organizations. The sequential organization provided by this method is used when large numbers of records must be processed periodically. However, if a few records must be processed quickly, the file index is used to directly access the records needed. The index sequential organization does have several disadvantages. It is slower than the direct organization because the index is usually stored on secondary storage devices and not in main memory. Another disadvantage is the cost of creating, storing, and maintaining the indexes, including the extra storage space this requires.

List Organization. This method uses **pointers** to locate related records stored in a nonsequential manner. This data structure is called a *list* (or *linked list*) because pointers (also called *link fields*) are used to express data relationships as *lists* of data records. Each data record contains a pointer field which gives the address of the next logical record. Thus, all logically related records can be linked together by means ot pointers. A grouping of records related by pointers is called a *list* or *chain*. Since the records in a file can have many possible relationships (for example, employees' ages, sex, department, etc.), each record can contain several pointers. These pointers form *chains* throughout the file or data base. This allows records with the same particular attributes (such as all male employees over age 55) to be located. In many cases, an index containing the addresses of the first record in each list is used. The pointer in the first record will point to the address of the next logical record in the list, thus allowing the computer to follow the chain of pointers in each record throughout the file.

A pointer field may also indicate the address of a related record in another file. For example, the payroll record for an employee in the *payroll file* might include a pointer linking it to the same employee's record in a *personnel action file*. Figure 9–7 demonstrates how pointers can link an employee record in a personnel file with the same employee's record in the payroll file. It also shows a pointer linking two records in the payroll file for employees who belong to the same department. In summary, the list organization uses pointers to easily access records having multiple logical data relationships. A disadvantage of this method is that pointers may become too numerous and the lists or chains may become

FIGURE 9–7 Pointers Linking Records in Files

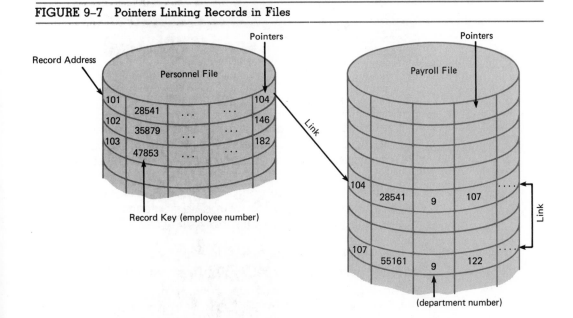

too long, thus increasing access time and storage requirements.

Inverted Files. This approach employs the *inverted file* (also called an *inverted index* or *inverted directory*) which is a table similar to the index of a book. Each inverted file lists the addresses or keys for all records having the same attribute. For example, an inverted index might indicate the record addresses of all employees between the ages of 18 to 25, 26 to 30, 31 to 35, and so forth. Several inverted files would be needed if we wish to locate the records for multiple alternatives (such as age, sex, marital status, etc.). Thus, inverted files allow efficient access to records having multiple logical relationships. This greatly facilitates searching a file for records sharing one or more attributes. However, it must be emphasized that these advantages are attained at the cost of creating, storing, and continually updating multiple large inverted files. The data needed to express relationships and addresses of the records referenced by inverted files is known as *overhead data.* Such overhead data may be several times as great as the original data it describes! Figure 9–8 provides an example of an inverted file.

FIGURE 9–8 Inverted File Example

Portion of Personnel File			Inverted File by Age	
Record Address	Employee Number	Age	Age	Record Address
101	28541	43	18–25	104, . . .
102	35879	27	26–35	102, 103, . . .
103	47853	32	36–45	101, . . .
104	50917	24		

Sequential Access File Processing

Sequential access files store data on sequential access media (such as magnetic tape) using the sequential method of file organization. Data records are sequentially stored and located when such *sequential access method* (SAM) files are used. For example, the computer must search an entire reel of magnetic tape in order to update a record near the end of the reel. (Refer back to Figure 4–19.)

Sequential Access File Processing. Figure 9–9 illustrates sequential access file processing. In this example:

● The input data from source documents (such as sales invoices) is captured and edited for correctness using a key-

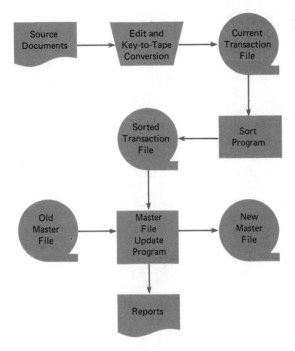

FIGURE 9-9 Sequential Access File Processing

to-tape device which records the data on a magnetic tape *transaction file.* Editing is important in insuring that incorrect data is not entered into the processing system. (Remember GIGO—Garbage In Garbage Out).

- The current transaction file is then sorted into the same sequence as the master file (such as a sales order master file).
- A master file update program uses the transactions data from the sorted transaction file to update the records in the old master file. This requires sequentially reading the entire master file.
- A new updated master file is produced which incorporates all the changes to records that were affected by the data in the transaction file. *Updated master files* are then usually stored *offline* (away from the computer) until the next time transactions are scheduled for processing. The old master file may also be stored offline for backup purposes. Usually, three **generations** of master files are kept for control purposes. Thus, for example, if the sequential access file processing is being done on a weekly basis, master files from the three most recent weeks' processing (known as the *child, parent, grandparent files*) are kept for backup purposes.
- Various reports are also produced such as control listings, activity reports and analytical reports for management.

Direct Access File Processing

Direct access files store data in direct access storage devices (DASDs) such as magnetic disks which allow the direct storage and retrieval of any record in a file. Therefore, the computer does not have to search an entire file in order to find a data record that is needed. Direct access files may take the form of removable magnetic disk packs or cartridges that can be stored offline until the next time the files are needed. However, direct access storage equipment such as magnetic disk units are usually *online* devices. Thus, they are electronically connected to the central processor of a computer system so that they can respond instantly to data processing assignments.

FIGURE 9–10 Direct Access File Processing

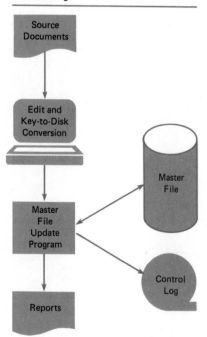

Direct Access File Processing. Figure 9–10 illustrates direct access file processing.

- Input source documents such as sales orders or sales invoices are edited and entered into the system by a key-to-disk conversion process using a **data entry** terminal with a keyboard and CRT display.
- Since a direct access master file is used, there is no need to sort input data before updating the master file. Thus, the master file is immediately updated.
- The master file update program also produces several reports such as control listings, summary reports, exception reports, and analytical reports for management.
- Direct access file processing does not result in old master files that can be used for backup purposes. Therefore, **backup copies** of the direct access files are obtained by periodically copying or *dumping* the contents of a direct access file to a magnetic tape file. This backup file is then stored for *control* purposes. Another control method is to keep a magnetic tape *control log* which records all transactions.

Data Base Structures

The data bases of modern computer-using organizations are collections of integrated files and complex record relationships. They may use many variations of the data organization methods we have just described in order to support a *quick-response* capability for data processing and information retrieval and reporting. The complex relationships between the many individual records stored in large data bases can be expressed by several basic **logical data structures** or **models.** The *data base management systems* (DBMS) discussed in Chapter 5 are designed to use specific data structures to provide computer users with quick and easy access to information stored in large data bases. The three fundamental **data base structures** or models are *hierarchical, network,* and *relational.* Simplified illustrations of these three data base structures are shown in Figure 9–11.

Hierarchical Structure. In this model, the relationships between records form a *hierarchy* or *tree* structure. In this structure, all records are dependent and arranged in multilevel structures consisting of one *root* record and any number of *subordinate* levels. Thus, all of the relationships between records are *one-to-many,* since each data element is related to several records below it, but only one data element above it. The data element or record at the highest level of the hierarchy (the *department* data element in this illustration) is called the *root* and is the point of entry into the hierarchy. Data elements are stored and located by moving progressively downward from a root and along the *branches* of the tree until the desired record (for example, the *employee* data element) is located.

Network Structure. This model can represent more complex logical relationships between records by allowing *many-to-many* relationships between records. Thus, the network structure allows entry into a data base at multiple points because any data element or record can be related to any number of other data elements. For example, in Figure 9–11, departmental records can be related to more than one employee record and employee records can be related to more than one project record. Thus one could locate all employee records for a particular department, or all project records related to a particular employee. The network structure is also called the CODASYL model, because the Conference On Data Systems Languages formed a subcommittee which developed specifications and standards in 1973 for a network data base structure. (CODASYL is the same group which developed the COBOL programming language.)

Relational Structure. The relational model is the most recent of the three data base structures. It was developed in an attempt to simplify the representation of complex relationships between data elements in large data bases. In this approach, all data elements within the data base are viewed as being

FIGURE 9–11   Three Fundamental Data Base Structures

HIERARCHICAL STRUCTURE

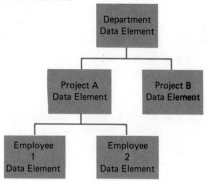

NETWORK STRUCTURE

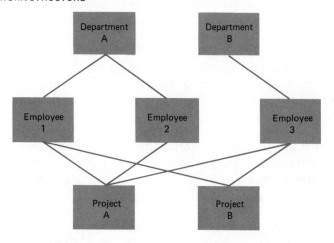

RELATIONAL STRUCTURE

Departmental Records

Dept No	D Name	D Loc	Emp Cnt
Dept A			
Dept B			
Dept C			

Employee Records

Emp No	E Name	E Title	E Salary	Dept No
Emp 1				Dept A
Emp 2				Dept B
Emp 3				Dept A
Emp 4				Dept B
Emp 5				Dept C
Emp 6				Dept B

stored in the form of simple tables. Figure 9–11 shows two such tables (called **relations**) representing departmental and employee records. Other relations might represent the data element relationships between projects, divisions, product lines, etc. Data base management system programs are needed to link data elements from various tables.

TYPES OF ELECTRONIC DATA PROCESSING SYSTEMS

There are two basic types of electronic data processing: **batch processing** and **realtime processing**. All EDP systems in use today have characteristics that fall into one or both of these two categories, though many other terms may be used to describe them. For instance, batch processing is also known as *sequential, serial,* or *offline,* while realtime processing may also be called *online, in-line, direct access, random access, interactive, transaction,* or even *online, realtime* processing! Though even experts disagree in using these terms, in this book **batch processing systems** are those in which *data is accumulated in batches and processed periodically,* while **realtime processing systems** are those which *process data immediately after it is generated and provide immediate output to users.* As you will see in this text, many forms of EDP systems possess both batch processing and realtime processing capabilities. Figure 9–12 outlines some of the important concepts, capabilities, and terms that differentiate batch processing and realtime processing.

Batch Processing Systems

In a batch processing system, data is accumulated over a period of time in batches and then processed periodically. Batch processing usually involves:

- Gathering source documents such as sales orders or invoices into groups called *batches.*
- Recording transaction data on an *input medium* such as floppy disks, punched cards, or magnetic tape.
- Sorting the transactions in a *transaction file* into the same sequence as the records in a sequential *master file.*
- Computer processing which results in an updated master file and a variety of *documents* (such as customer invoices or paychecks) and *reports* (such as control and management reports).

FIGURE 9–12 Batch versus Realtime Processing

CHARACTERISTICS	BATCH PROCESSING	REALTIME PROCESSING
Processing of transactions	Transaction data is recorded, accumulated into batches, sorted, and processed periodically	Transaction data is processed as generated
File update	When batch is processed	When transaction is processed
Response time/turnaround time	Several hours or days after batches are submitted for processing	A few seconds after each transaction is captured
Processing mode	Periodic processing of batches when scheduled	Interactive processing
Access to processor	Primarily local access Some remote access	Primarily remote access using data communications Some local access
File access method	Sequential access	Direct access
File organization method	Sequential Indexed sequential	Random Indexed sequential
File storage medium	Magnetic tape Some magnetic disk	Magnetic disk
File status between processing	Offline	Online
Control logs and backup files	Created as part of processing	Capability must be added to the system

In batch processing, not only are the data for a particular application or job accumulated into batches, but usually a number of different jobs are accumulated into batches and *run* (processed) periodically (daily, weekly, monthly). The rationale for batch processing is that data and jobs should be grouped into batches and processed periodically according to a planned schedule in order to efficiently use the computer system, rather than allowing data and jobs to be processed in an unorganized, random manner. Of course, this efficiency, economy, and control is accomplished by sacrificing the immediate processing of data for computer users. In a typical example of batch processing, the banking industry usually accumulates all checks that are deposited at banks during the day into batches for later processing each evening. Thus, customer bank balances are updated on a daily basis and many management reports are produced daily.

Figure 9–13 illustrates a batch processing system where batches of data, computer programs, and master files for several different jobs are processed periodically according to a schedule set up by the computer operations department of an organization. The master files are updated by making any

FIGURE 9-13   A Batch Processing System Example

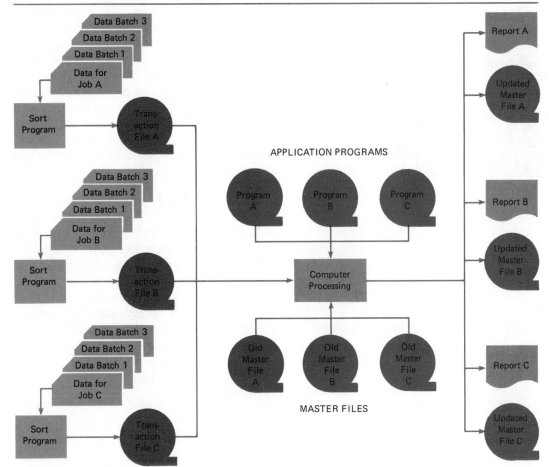

necessary changes to the records in the files based on the contents of the batches of input data. Output takes the form of required reports and updated master files. *For example,* the data could be in the form of batches of sales transactions, income and expense figures, or units of production. Reports produced could be reports required by management such as sales analysis reports, income and expense reports, or production status reports.

Remote Access Batch Processing.   Batch processing systems can have a *remote access capability,* frequently called "remote job entry" (RJE). Batches of data can be collected and converted into an input medium at "remote" locations that

Courtesy Harris Corporation.

are far away from the computer. Input/output devices at these locations (called RJE stations) are then used to transmit data over communications circuits to a distant computer. The batches of data are then processed, thus producing updated master files as well as information that is transmitted back to the remote terminal. Remote access batch processing can also involve "remote offline input/output." For example, data can be transmitted from the keyboard of a terminal to an offline magnetic tape unit where they are accumulated for subsequent batch processing. Part of a remote job entry station, including a minicomputer, CRT terminal, and magnetic tape and disk drives, is shown in Figure 9–14.

Advantages and Disadvantages.   Batch processing is an economical method when large volumes of data must be processed. It is ideally suited for many applications where it is not necessary to update files as transactions occur, and documents and reports are required only at scheduled intervals. For example, customer statements may be prepared on a monthly basis while payroll processing might be done on a weekly basis. Many batch processing systems still make heavy use of magnetic tape, which is a low-cost medium for simple sequentially organized files. A final advantage of batch processing is the fact that transaction files and old master files which are created as part of regular processing also serve as excellent control and backup files.

Batch processing has some real disadvantages. Much of them stem from the use of sequentially organized files stored on sequential access media such as magnetic tape. Transactions must be sorted and an entire file must be processed, even if only a few records are affected. Also, master files are frequently out-of-date between scheduled processing, and immediate updated responses to inquiries cannot be made. For these reasons, more and more computer applications use realtime processing systems. However, batch processing systems are still widely used and some of their disadvantages are overcome by using direct-access files and realtime processing for some data processing functions. For example, many EDP systems with large volumes of transactions use the indexed sequential method of file organization (ISAM) to store data sequentially on direct access storage devices such as magnetic disks. They then use batch processing to update the files on a periodic basis, but can give immediate responses to user inquiries concerning information stored in the file.

Realtime Processing Systems

In full-fledged realtime processing systems, data is processed as soon as it is originated or recorded without waiting to accumulate batches of data. Data is fed directly into the computer system from *online terminals* without having to be sorted and is always stored *online* in *direct access files.* The master files are always up-to-date since they are updated whenever data is originated, regardless of its frequency. Responses to user inquiries are immediate, since information in the direct-access files can be retrieved almost instantaneously. Heavy use is made of *remote terminals* connected to the computer using *data communications* links. The realtime processing system concept is illustrated in Figure 9–15.

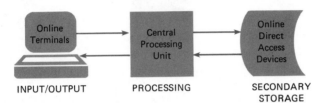

FIGURE 9–15   Realtime Processing System Concept

An example of a realtime processing system is shown in Figure 9–16. Notice how POS terminals are connected by data communications links for immediate entry of sales data and control responses (such as customer credit verification). The online, direct-access customer, inventory, and sales master files are all immediately updated to reflect the effect of sales transactions. The application programs required for sales transactions processing, file updates, and inquiry/response processing are brought into the CPU from a direct-access program file as needed. Finally, management personnel use data communication links to terminals located throughout the organization to make inquiries and receive displays concerning customer sales potential, inventory status, and salesperson performance.

Realtime processing is frequently called *online,* or *direct access* processing, since both of these capabilities are required of realtime processing systems. However, use of such terms can be misleading because we have seen that *batch processing systems* can use online direct-access files in the processing of batches of data. As a compromise, experts may use the term *online realtime* (OLRT) processing. Others use

FIGURE 9-16 Example of a Realtime Processing System

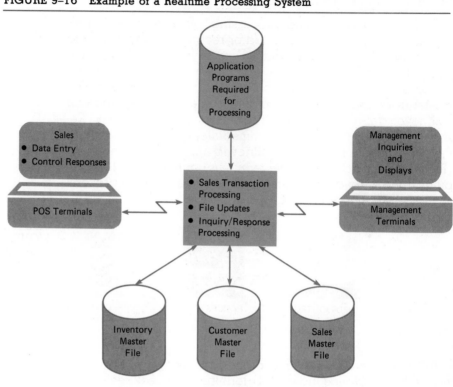

the term *interactive processing* to emphasize the interactive capability of many realtime systems, or the term *transaction processing* to emphasize that individual transactions are processed as they occur and are not accumulated into batches in realtime processing systems.

Some of the semantic confusion arises from the fact that there can be different levels of realtime processing systems depending on the data processing functions to be performed. In fact, many current EDP systems are combinations of batch and realtime processing subsystems. Again, a typical example is the banking industry which updates checking accounts on a daily batch basis, but uses realtime processing to allow immediate response to inquiries concerning customer bank balances stored on online direct-access files. Realtime processing systems can be subdivided into the five levels illustrated in Figure 9-17 and summarized below.

● **Inquiry Systems.** The main function of an inquiry system is information retrieval. The user of a realtime inquiry system

FIGURE 9-17 **Levels of Realtime Processing Systems, with Examples**

Level of Realtime Processing	Business Examples
Inquiry	Request customer balance in bank checking accounts, utilizing online audio-response terminals. Request number of parts on hand in inventory, utilizing on-line visual display terminals.
Data Capture	Collect sales data with online terminals and record on magnetic tape for later processing. Capture checking account transactions handled by bank tellers and record on temporary file for control purposes.
File Processing	Update customer files due to sales transaction data captured by online terminals. Update work-in-process inventory files due to production data captured by data recording terminals on the factory floor.
Full Capability	Process airline reservations, utilizing online terminals and update online flight reservation files. Process data arising from the purchase or sale of securities, utilizing on-line terminals and update on-line securities transaction files.
Process Control	Control petroleum refinery process with online sensing and control devices. Control of electric power generation and transmission.

wishes a quick response to a request for information; *for example,* the current balance in a particular bank checking account.

● **Data Capture Systems.** The main function of a data capture system is the immediate but temporary collection and recording of data until it can be processed at a later date. Thus, the realtime data capture system is designed to perform only the collection, conversion, and storage functions of data processing, leaving the manipulation function to a batch processing system. *For example,* some retail stores utilize online "point-of-sale" terminals to capture and record sales data on magnetic tape or disk during the day for subsequent remote batch processing at night.

● **File Processing Systems.** File processing realtime systems perform all of the functions of data processing except the communication function. Thus, data is collected, converted, manipulated, and then stored—resulting in an immediate and continual updating of files. The communication function is performed by subsequent batch processing which produces reports and other output, or by a realtime inquiry system which interrogates the files. *For example,* customer files could be updated immediately by POS terminals, but customer statements and credit reports could be done only on a periodic basis.

- **Full Capability Systems.** The full capability realtime processing system provides immediate and continuous performance of all of the functions of data processing. It can perform the services of any of the other levels of realtime systems, along with the immediate processing of assignments that require only data manipulation and communication of results. *Example:* The reservation systems of the major airlines are full capability systems, since they process passenger reservations in realtime utilizing online terminals at airline offices and airports. Realtime processing systems with a full data processing capability are being installed or developed by almost all users of large or medium-scale computers.

- **Process Control Systems.** A particular type of full capability realtime processing system is the process control system, which not only performs all of the data processing functions but, in addition, uses its information output to control an ongoing physical process. *Examples* are industrial production processes in the steel, petroleum, and chemical industries.

Advantages and Disadvantages. Realtime processing systems provide immediate updating of files and immediate responses to user inquiries. Realtime processing is particularly important for applications where there is a high frequency of changes which must be made to a file during a short period of time to keep it updated. Nonsequential methods of file organization are used and data is stored on direct-access storage devices. Thus, input data does not need to be sorted, and only the specific records affected by transactions or inquiries need to be processed. Also, several files can be processed or updated concurrently since transaction data does not have to be sorted into the sequence of any particular file.

Realtime processing has its disadvantages. Direct-access storage devices such as hard magnetic disks are still more expensive than the magnetic tape used in many batch processing applications. Because of the online, direct access nature of realtime processing, special precautions must be taken to protect the contents of data files. Thus many realtime systems have to use magnetic tape files as *control logs* (to record all transactions being made) or as *backup files* (by periodically making a magnetic tape copy of a file). Also, more controls have to be built into the software and data processing procedures to protect against unauthorized access or accidental destruction of data. Thus the many advantages of realtime processing must be balanced with the extra costs and security precautions that are necessary. However, most computer-using firms are willing to pay this price since the use of realtime processing continues to increase in modern EDP systems.

Interactive Processing Systems

Realtime processing systems provide an **interactive processing** capability in which users at online terminals can interact with a computer on a realtime basis. This may take the form of:

- **Inquiry/response** applications, where a request for information is entered through the keyboard and the answer is immediately displayed on the screen.
- **Conversational computing** which uses *interactive packaged programs* to carry on a dialogue and help a user solve a problem or accomplish a particular job on the computer.
- **Online data entry,** which provides sophisticated data entry assistance to operators. For example, a data entry system is usually a *menu-driven* approach which *prompts* and guides the data entry operator with menu-selecting choices, specialized formats which help an operator with prompting messages, and sophisticated editing with error-control reminders.
- **Interactive programming** where a programmer uses a terminal to develop and test the instructions for a program with the realtime assistance of the computer. It is an important form of interactive processing which has become the primary form of programming for professional programmers.

Most interactive processing systems are *menu oriented* or **menu driven.** They provide *menu* displays and operator *prompting* to support use by clerical staff and even the *casual user* or manager. They usually display a menu of available options from which operators can select the functions they wish to perform. Each time the operator makes a choice, another more specific menu from which to choose may be displayed until the selected processing function is performed. At this point, many terminals provide operator *prompts* which are helpful messages which assist the operator in performing a particular job. This would include error messages, correction suggestions, prompting questions and other messages which guide an operator through the work in a series of structured steps. Thus the computer uses the logic of a computer program and its memory capability to make the task as easy and as *friendly* as possible for the operator. See Figure 9–18.

FIGURE 9–18 An Example of Menu-Driven Interactive Processing

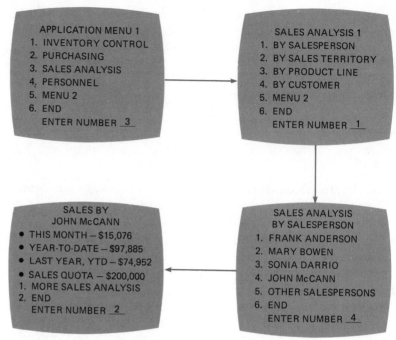

Time-Sharing Systems

Time-sharing systems are a major type of realtime processing systems. **Time-sharing** is the sharing of a computer system by many users in different locations at the same time through the use of online input/output terminals. Time-sharing systems "interleave" the data processing assignments of many users by giving each user a small, frequently repeated "slice" of time. Time-sharing systems operate at such fast speeds that each user has the illusion that he or she alone is using the computer because of the seemingly instantaneous response. The ability of time-sharing systems to service many users simultaneously is sometimes hard to comprehend. However, one must remember that a computer operating in nanoseconds speeds can process millions of instructions per second.

Remote batch processing and *realtime processing* can be accomplished utilizing time-sharing systems. A time-sharing user could accumulate batches of data and periodically process them, utilizing a time-sharing device. Users could use input/output devices ranging from small terminals, to larger batch processing stations, to small satellite computer systems. However, time-sharing systems are currently used primarily for realtime processing applications. Time-sharing systems can easily handle the inquiry, data capture, and file processing types of realtime processing assignments. Time sharing thus relies heavily on data communications hardware and software in order to provide instantaneous responses to many users using remote terminals.

Types of Time-Sharing. Special-purpose time-sharing systems exist which have been designed for a specific application such as an airline reservation system. More prevalent, however, are general-purpose time-sharing systems which can be used internally within an organization, such as a large business firm or university, where many remote time-sharing terminals allow simultaneous use of the computer by many users throughout the organization.

The other major form of general-purpose time sharing is the time-sharing service offered by data processing service centers and national time-sharing companies. Time sharing services are provided to many subscribers, representing various business firms and organizations. Subscribers pay for time sharing by paying an initial installation charge, basic monthly charges, and transaction charges which vary according to the amount of computer resources used. Firms which offer such time sharing services are sometimes referred to as computer or information "utilities." Nation-wide time-sharing services are offered to business firms by companies such as General Electric, Control Data, Tymeshare, and Telenet. Time-sharing services are also available to personal computer users from networks such as *The Source* and CompuServe.

SUMMARY

- An electronic data processing system is a system of hardware, software, and personnel that processes data into information. EDP personnel include systems analysts, programmers, computer operators, and other managerial, technical, and clerical personnel. Each business EDP system has input, processing, output, control, and storage components that can take a variety of common forms.

- Data must be organized in some logical manner so that it can be efficiently pro-

cessed. Thus, data is commonly organized into characters, fields, records, files, and data bases, and can be described as either physical or logical elements. Data files can be organized in either a sequential or random manner and files can be processed by either sequential access or direct-access file processing methods.

- Variations of the two basic file organization methods include the indexed sequential method in which records are organized sequentially but referenced by an index; the list file organization, which uses pointers to locate related records stored in a nonsequential manner; and the inverted file method. Data base structures are used to organize the complex relations between the individual records stored in large data bases. Three fundamental data base structures are the hierarchical, network, and relational models.

● The two basic categories of EDP systems are batch processing systems, in which data is accumulated and processed periodically, and realtime processing systems which process data immediately. Realtime processing systems can be subdivided into several levels: inquiry, data capture, file processing, full capability, and process control systems.

● Realtime processing systems provide an interactive processing capability in which users at online terminals can interact with a computer on a realtime basis. This may take the form of inquiry/response, conversational computing, online data entry, or interactive programming. Most interactive processing systems are menu-driven to assist users. Time-sharing systems are a major form of realtime processing systems which allow many users in different locations to share a computer system at the same time through the use of online input/output terminals.

KEY TERMS AND CONCEPTS

EDP system

Business EDP system components

Common data elements: character, field, record, file, data base

Logical and physical data elements

Data organization aids: key, pointer, index

File organization: random, sequential, indexed sequential, list, inverted file

Sequential access file processing

Direct access file processing

Data base structures: hierarchical, network, relational

Batch processing systems

Realtime processing systems

Interactive processing

Menu driven

Time-sharing

REVIEW AND DISCUSSION QUESTIONS

1. What are the major components of electronic data processing as a system?

2. What are the basic categories of computer personnel and what roles do they play in the operation of EDP systems?

3. What are some of the typical forms of input, output, and storage functions of business EDP systems? Give an example of each.

4. Provide examples to illustrate each of the common data elements.

5. Can a single physical record contain more than one logical record? Explain.

6. What is the difference between sequential and random methods of file organization, and sequential access and direct access file processing?

7. What are the functions of keys, pointers, and indexes? How are these data organization aids used in the indexed sequential, list, and inverted file methods of file organization?

8. Why are data base structures necessary? Use the concepts of the hierarchical, network, and relational data structure models to illustrate your answer.

9. What is the difference between batch processing and realtime processing? Use examples to illustrate your answer.

10. Realtime processing can be subdivided into several levels of processing. What examples can you think of to illustrate this concept?

11. What is interactive processing? Explain the use of interactive processing for inquiry/response, conversational computing, online data entry, and interactive programming.

12. Why are most interactive processing systems menu driven? What are several characteristics of a menu-driven system?

13. What is time-sharing? Can time-sharing be used for remote batch processing as well as realtime processing?

14. What are the major types and sources of time-sharing services? Can individuals as well as business firms make use of nationwide time-sharing networks?

REAL WORLD APPLICATIONS

9-1 Commercial Office Products Company

Commercial Office Products (COPCO) is a large distributor of office supplies in the Midwest. Based in Denver, the firm handles receiving, order processing, and distribution from four different locations. With the business growing at over 35 percent per year, David Elliott, president, noticed that his batch system could not keep pace with the demands of his business. After extensive investigation, Mr. Elliott chose an HP 3000 system along with an application package, developed in conjunction with Information Resources of Denver to solve his data processing needs.

"We chose the HP 3000 because of its data base capability, QUERY, virtual memory for multi-programming, in general for the capabilities of the entire system. The system is able to do multiple tasks such as batch and transaction processing at

the same time. It also has the ability to do multiple language processes.

"We use the system interactively in every area of our business. Twenty eight terminals are distributed in order entry, purchasing, receiving, will-call department, cash receipts, collection, program development, and in the executive offices. We even have two customers who have terminals in their offices. They simply phone into the system and place the orders themselves. This saves us considerable cost.

The system has benefitted COPCO in a number of ways. Orders are taken and entered into the system over the telephone. Within seconds our customers can get information on stock and price as well as getting definitive answers about the status of their

9–1 *(continued)*

orders. The system has given us the flexibility to get immediate departmentalized reports, allowing me to keep better track of the business. With the HP 3000 I am now able to predict nearly 100 percent of our annual purchases and sales.

"QUERY (the data base enquiry language) is fantastic. We do all of our reporting with it. QUERY gives me instant access to all of the information relating to my company. Sales, total sales per salesman, per market, by zip code, whatever. QUERY makes it easy to do. And it takes but a few hours on instruction at the most to learn to use.

"Our programmers love the system. Because it is an interactive system they have access to all of the capabilities of the machine at every terminal. The

system is easy to use and the capabilities proved unreal. The software and data base components have great flexibility in allowing users to develop their own applications.

"The HP 3000 has been the solution for COPCO. We can now process an order in a matter of minutes and send the bill out with the order. Because of this, accounts receivable has dropped from 48 days to 38 days. At the same time, inventory turnover has climbed from about five to eight times per year. In addition, we have saved money by reducing our inventory from 21,000 to 7,000 items while, at the same time, our order fill efficiency has gone up to 96 percent. With the new system we are beating our competition by responding quicker to customer needs."[1]

- Why did COPCO switch from a batch processing system to a realtime, interactive system? What benefits have occurred?
- What levels of realtime systems and types of interactive processing are demonstrated in this example?

[1] Source: Courtesy Hewlett-Packard.

9–2   The Reserve Fund

Mutual funds require an extraordinary degree of transaction processing and information control. The Reserve Fund, Inc. is no exception. This 2 billion dollar money market fund handles more than 5,000 transactions a day. Brokers and customers are calling constantly to check the status of their accounts to make certain that their temporary cash balances are always working.

In order to meet this demand for data, Reserve Fund has turned to Honeywell's transaction processing system, TPS-6. Together with four Level 6 computers, TPS-6 makes it possible to do immense amounts of production work while simultaneously developing new programs. Their four Level 6 systems give Reserve Fund all the flexibility and backup they need. Information flows easily.

For example, terminals are used to enter pur-

chase orders and to provide quick answers to customer inquiries. At the same time, the system is also maintaining an ongoing record of all transactions.

As you'd expect, security is a great concern. But thanks to features built into TPS-6, Reserve Fund has developed effective safeguards. Every operator has an ID number, a password, and a specific security clearance. Access is carefully regulated. As a further precaution, the system has a built-in time-out feature that automatically clears the screen after a specified period.

Thanks to capabilities like screen data formatting and multiple key access to files, Reserve Fund has been able to tailor a system that's both effective and efficient. Current information is always available. When it's needed. Where it's needed.[2]

- Why does the Reserve Fund need a realtime transaction processing system?
- What capabilities and controls are features of this system?

[2] Source: Courtesy Honeywell.

9–3   The University of Iowa

The University of Iowa began offering free access to instructional computing in 1962 when it opened the University Computing Center, renamed the Weeg Computing Center in 1978. By 1977, with over 23,000 graduate and undergraduate students, the University had run out of computing capacity, and was purchasing 20 percent of its computing time from outside services at a cost that was stifling, according to James Johnson, director.

"Because our systems were overloaded, turnaround time was six times longer than it should have been. As a result, outside resources were used to get quicker service, but this drove our costs up beyond what we could afford.

According to Johnson, the University needed a system that was interactive and could provide state of the art software, a data management facility, and interactive data analysis and development capabilities. The system also had to be compatible in an IBM environment that included an IBM 370/168 system. Because the University has a heavy investment in software development and trained users on the IBM system, Johnson had to find a system that would protect that investment.

The University of Iowa purchased four Prime 750 systems to replace a CDC Cyber 70/71 that had been used in-house for four years. The Prime systems are connected to each other in a local ring network and to the IBM 370/168. The innovative network enables file transfer among systems and access to software on the other computers.

Each Prime system is configured with two million bytes of main memory, three 300 M byte storage module disk drives, and two additional 300M byte disk drives for system back-up. In addition, the four Prime systems are connected to two line printers, two tape drives, and other peripheral equipment accessed through the IBM 370/168.

The University has over 300 terminals—clustered and individual—located throughout the 15-square-mile campus, and plans to increase that number to 500 by the end of 1982. Users are assigned to individual Prime systems in order to balance the computing load and access them using a communications switch. Each Prime 750 system can support up to 63 users simultaneously running different applications.

According to Johnson, the Prime network is unique in another way. "It's the only network facility that really delivers what it promises," said Johnson. "In many cases it's totally transparent to the user. If a student logs-onto one Prime system and later has to change over to another, the network performs the file transfer easily. This multi-access capability significantly increases the ease-of-use and reliability of the systems.[3]

- Why does the University of Iowa need a time-sharing system?
- Could student, faculty, and administrative users be served by some other combination of batch and realtime processing systems? Explain.

[3] Source: "Prime Computer 750 Systems Help the University of Iowa Double Its Computing Capacity," *Primeworld*, November/December 1980, pp. 4–5.

10

CHAPTER OUTLINE

Data Communications Systems

LEARNING OBJECTIVES

The purpose of this chapter is to promote a basic understanding of data communications and the role it plays in electronic data and information processing systems.

After reading and studying this chapter, you should be able to:

1. Identify the functions and components of a data communications system.
2. Explain the functions of data communications hardware and software.
3. Identify the major types of communications channels, carriers, and networks.
4. Use examples to illustrate the benefits and limitations of data communications for electronic data and information processing.

Data communications systems (also called **telecommunications** or **teleprocessing** systems) combine the capabilities of the computer with high-speed electronic communications. Data communications systems provide for the transmitting of data over electronic communication links between one or more computer systems and a number of input/output terminals at some physical distance away from the computer. This can range from simple telephone communication links to complex communications networks involving earth satellites and many communications control computers.

Today, data communications is used for *remote-access* batch processing systems and all realtime processing systems (except when the input/output device used is near the computer). Therefore, all types of realtime processing systems (*transaction processing, online data entry, interactive processing, inquiry/response,* and *time-sharing systems*) as well as *distributed processing systems* and *data base systems* rely heavily on data communications. Also, many *word processing systems* and other office communication systems (such as *electronic mail*) require a telecommunications capability. Thus, modern use of computers is heavily dependent on data communication systems.

DATA COMMUNICATIONS SYSTEM COMPONENTS

A basic data communications system consists of five major components which are illustrated in Figure 10–1.

- **Terminals,** such as CRT or printing terminals. (Remember, a *terminal* can be any input/output device that uses communications channels to transmit or receive data.)
- **Data communications interface units** (such as *modems, communications controllers, front-end processors,* etc.) enable data to be transmitted between terminals and computers. They convert data from digital form to analog and back, code and decode data, and control the communications flow between the computers and the terminals in a data communications network.
- **Communications channels** (or links) over which data is transmitted and received. Communications channels can be telephone lines, coaxial cables, fiber optic cables, microwave systems, or earth satellite systems.
- **Computers** of all sizes and types use data communications to carry out their data processing assignments. Many times

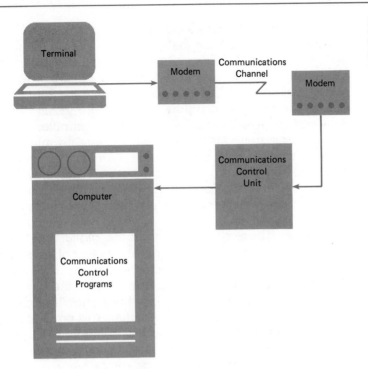

FIGURE 10–1 Basic
Components of a Data
Communications System

there is one larger general-purpose computer which serves
as the *host* computer and contains the main data communications control programs (software) which control the data
communications network.

- **Communications control software** are control programs
which reside in the host computer system and other communications control computers in the data communications system. They control input/output activities involving the data
communications system, and manage the functions of communications networks.

DATA COMMUNICATIONS HARDWARE

Data communications hardware consists of a variety of computer terminals, several types of data communication interface
units, communications channel equipment and media, and
the computers that operate in the data communications network. Let us examine these hardware devices more closely.

Terminals. In Chapter 4 we discussed the many types of
computer terminals which can be used in data communications systems. These included *CRT terminals, printing termi-*

nals, transaction terminals and *intelligent terminals.* However, any input/output device that has data communications capabilities is a terminal. Even small dedicated computer systems can act as terminals in a data communications network. Such *remote job entry* (RJE) *stations* are used for *remote-access batch processing* where they collect and transmit batches of data and receive the output of the host computer in a batch processing system. Many RJE stations are really minicomputer systems which might include CRT terminals, magnetic disk and tape drives, and punch card units. Thus they can also act as a *stand-alone* computer system and perform a variety of data processing assignments at their own *local* site.

Modems. These devices convert the *digital* signals from a computer or transmission terminal at one end of a communications link into *analog* frequencies which can be transmitted over ordinary telephone lines. A modem at the other end of the communications line converts the transmitted data back into digital form at a receiving terminal. This process is known as modulation and demodulation, and the word modem is a combined abbreviation of these two words. Modems are necessary because ordinary telephone lines were primarily designed to handle continuous analog signals, such as the human voice. Since data from computers is in digital form, devices are necessary to convert digital signals into appropriate analog transmission frequencies and vice versa. However, *digital* communications channels which transmit digital signals are rapidly developing. Modems are not required when such channels are used.

Intelligent modems are capable of supporting simultaneous data and voice transmission, automatic dialing and answering of calls to and from remote terminals, and automatic testing and selection of transmission lines. Modems can vary in their data communications speed capacity. Typically, speeds vary from 300 *bits per second* (BPS or *baud*) for connecting low-speed printing terminals to 1,200 BPS for use with medium-speed video terminals, and up to 9,600 BPS or higher for high-speed peripheral devices.

One special type of low-speed modem that is widely used is the **acoustic coupler.** They are used to connect portable and movable terminals (including microcomputer systems) to a telephone line by cradling the telephone receiver in a special holder. The person using the portable terminal dials the telephone number used for data communications, receives

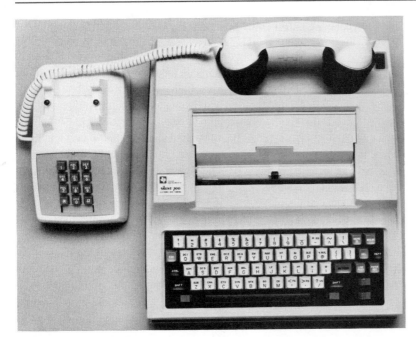

FIGURE 10–2 Terminal with an Acoustic Coupler Modem

Courtesy Texas Instruments, Inc.

a special tone signal, and then places the telephone receiver (handset) into the cradle of the acoustic coupler. The acoustic coupler converts the digital signals generated by the terminal into audible tones (*acoustic* signals) and then converts them into digital signals for data transmission. In the reverse process an acoustic coupler will convert analog signals transmitted over telephone lines into digital signals for a receiving terminal. See Figure 10–2.

Communications Control Units. Other data communications interface devices are needed to code and decode data, to control data communications equipment and to allow many terminals to use the same data transmission channel. See Figure 10–3.

- A **multiplexer** is an electronic device which allows a single communications channel to carry simultaneous data transmission from many terminals by dividing a higher-speed channel into multiple slow-speed channels.
- A **concentrator** is a special-purpose mini or micro computer which accepts information from many terminals using slow-speed lines and transmits data to a main computer system over a high-speed line. The concentrator uses an internally

FIGURE 10-3 Communications Control Units in a Data Communications Network

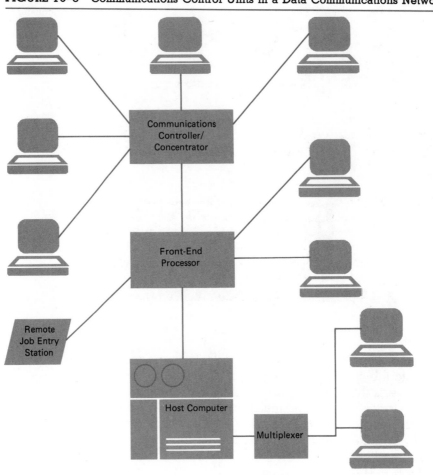

stored program to carry out its functions. It also serves as a *buffer* by temporarily storing data received from many terminals until it can be transmitted to the host computer.

- A **communications controller** is another data communications interface device that is evolving into a special-purpose mini or micro computer which can control a data communications network containing many terminals. The communications controller has its own memory which is used to store its data control programs and to provide temporary buffer storage. Its functions include coding and decoding data, error detection, recovery, recording, interpreting, and processing control information which is transmitted (such as characters which indicate the beginning and end of mes-

sages). A communications controller can *poll* remote terminals to determine if they have a message to send or are
ready to receive a message. It serves as an interface between a computer and many communications lines thus relieving the main computer of many data communications
control functions.

- A **front-end processor** is typically a smaller general-purpose
computer which is dedicated to handling the data communications control functions of large EDP systems. It can perform
many of the functions of other data communications interface
devices and can be programmed to perform additional necessary functions. It controls access to a network and allows
only authorized users to utilize the system, assigns priorities
to messages, logs all data communications activity, computes statistics on network activity, and routes and reroutes
messages among alternative communication links. Thus the
front-end processor can relieve the host computer of its data
communications control functions. It has been estimated that
the use of front-end processors and other advanced data
communications interface devices can provide up to 30 percent additional processing time for a host computer system.

DATA COMMUNICATIONS SOFTWARE

Data communications software consists of computer programs stored in the *host computer* or in *front-end computers*
and other communications processors which control and support the communications occuring in a data communications
network. Data communications systems software includes *communications access programs* which establish the connection
between terminals and computer systems and the link between
user application programs and the communications network.
Data communications control programs also include *network
control programs* (also called teleprocessing or TP monitors)
which manage the functions of the communications network.
They may reside in the host computer or in front-end computers or other communications processors. Their functions include:

- Connecting and disconnecting communications links.
- Detecting and correcting errors.
- Polling the terminals in a network.
- Forming "waiting lines" *(queuing)* and routing messages
in the network.
- Logging statistics of errors and other network activity.

DATA COMMUNICATIONS CARRIERS

Common Carriers. Data communications and other telecommunications services are provided by many companies including American Telephone and Telegraph (AT&T) and its affiliated companies in the Bell system, General Telephone, ITT, many independent telephone companies, Telenet, World Communications, American Satellite, and Satellite Business Systems (SBS). Most computer-using firms and individuals use the communications channels provided by these communications *common carriers* which are authorized by government agencies to provide public communications services.

Specialized Carriers. Private communications networks used by major government agencies and business firms have also been developed. However, most data communications activity is carried by the public networks. This includes companies known as *specialized common carriers* which sell high-speed data communications services in selected high-density areas of the country. In addition, there are companies called *value-added carriers* which lease communications facilities from the common carriers and combine messages from customers into groupings called *packets* for transmission. These **packet switching** networks (also known as **value-added** networks—VAN) add "value" to their communications facilities by adding advanced hardware and software to provide packet switching and other data communication services. Examples of value-added companies include Telenet and Tymeshare.

Besides data communications, many communications carriers provide voice and video communications, *facsimile* (FAX) and *teleconferencing*. **Facsimile** involves the transmission of images for reproduction in a permanent form, so that copies of photographs, documents, and reports can be transmitted and received in *hard copy* form. **Teleconferencing** is the use of video communications to allow business conferences to be held with participants who are scattered across a country, continent, or the world. Figure 10–4 illustrates the services offered by major communications carriers.

DATA COMMUNICATIONS CHANNELS

Modern data communications systems make use of *communications channels* such as ordinary telephone lines, coaxial cables, fiber optic cables, microwave systems, and earth satel-

FIGURE 10–4   A Guide to Communications Services

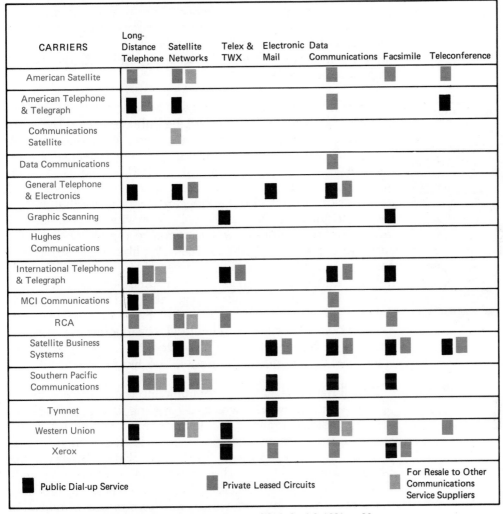

Source: "The Gold Mine in Satellite Services," *Business Week*, April 6, 1981, p. 90.

lite systems to transmit and receive data. Let us briefly explore the major data communications channels in use today.

Communication Lines.   Ordinary telephone lines are widely used for data communications since they provide an established communications network throughout the world. This includes privately leased lines which can be *conditioned* to reduce distortion and error rates and thus allow faster transmission rates. Coaxial cables are high-quality high-speed cables that have been laid underground or under the ocean. They are also being used in office buildings and other work sites for *local* communications networks. Microwave systems transmit high-speed radio signals in a line-of-sight path between relay stations spaced approximately 30 miles apart. Microwave antennas are usually placed on top of buildings, towers, and mountain peaks.

FIGURE 10–5 A Fiber Optic Cable

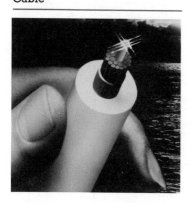

Fiber Optics. *Fiber optic* cables consist of very thin filaments of glass fibers which can conduct the light generated by **lasers** at transmission frequencies that approach the speed of light. *Lasers* are very concentrated high-frequency beams of light that are capable of transmitting about 100,000 times as much information as microwaves. Fiber optics has demonstrated transmission speeds about a thousand times faster than microwave transmission. Fiber optic cables provide substantial size and weight reductions as well as increased speed and greater carrying capacity. A half-inch diameter fiber optic cable can carry up to 50,000 channels compared to about 5,500 channels for a standard coaxial cable. In another comparison, a one and one-half pound fiber optic cable can transmit as much data as 30 pounds of copper wire. Fiber optic cables are already being installed on a limited basis in a few major cities. Lasers and fiber optics are expected to seriously compete with other communications media. See Figure 10–5.

Digital Networks. Many communications carriers are developing digital networks which do not need the modems of present voice-oriented analog communications networks. Even the Bell System is slated to provide digital data service to more than 200 cities in the United States. However the same channels that carry digital data can carry voice as well. Voice signals can be *digitized* before transmission and then reassembled on the receiving end. This is the opposite of present data transmission over voice channels which uses modems to change digital signals to analog frequencies for transmission over voice-oriented communications lines. Digital networks provide high quality, high-speed data communications at low error rates and eliminate the need for modems.

AT&T has proposed an advanced digital data communications service called Advanced Communication Service (ACS). If approved by the FCC, ACS will significantly reduce communication costs and increase data communications capabilities and services. It will serve as an interface between terminals and computers having different data communications characteristics. It will provide an *intelligent* data communications network because it will make heavy use of communications processors and computer systems for communications control and network management.

Communication Satellites. The most promising data communications development at the present time is the use of communications satellites. There are several dozen communication satellites from several nations placed into stationary "parking orbits" approximately 22,000 miles above the equator. Most

FIGURE 10–6 Communications Satellite Systems

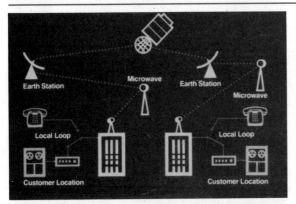 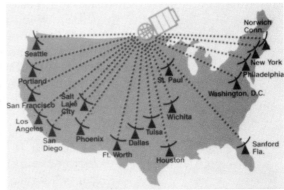

Courtesy American Satellite Company.

Top row, left to right: typical intercity network; typical nationwide network. Bottom row left to right: Westar communications satellite; earth station dish antenna.

satellites are launched by NASA, weigh several thousand pounds, are powered by solar panels, and can transmit signals at a rate of several hundred million bits per second. They serve as relay stations for communication signals transmitted from *earth stations*. Earth stations beam signals to the satellites which amplify and retransmit the signals to other earth stations thousands of miles away. While communication satellites were used initially for voice and video transmission, they are capable of high-speed transmission of large volumes of data. See Figure 10–6.

Present communication satellite systems are operated by AT&T, Western Union, RCA, and Satellite Business Systems (SBS), which is owned jointly by IBM, Aetna Insurance, and the Communications Satellite Corporation (COMSAT). SBS is launching a series of domestic communication satellites during the 1980s to service large corporations and government agencies. These satellites are part of an all-digital communications network and transmit more than 40 million bits-per-second from each of eight transmitters. The SBS system will substantially reduce the time and cost of communications compared to ground networks. This is one of the primary factors behind estimates of tremendous growth in all communications services including data communications and *electronic mail* systems.

DATA COMMUNICATIONS NETWORKS

Data communications systems rely on one or more **data communications networks**, which consist of interconnected hardware, software, and communications channels which support data communications activity. Thus we can speak of *public* data communications networks open to everyone, *private* networks dedicated to support the data communications activity of one particular business organization, *international* networks which span the globe, etc. Let us now look at several examples of modern data communications networks in business. (Technical network characteristics are discussed in the supplement at the end of this chapter.)

Business Networks. Data communications systems are becoming more and more prevalent in carrying out business and individual activities. Commercial and savings banking is a good example. Bank data communications systems support teller terminals in all branch offices, *automated teller ma-*

chines (ATMs) at remote locations throughout a city or state, and *pay-by-phone* services which allow bank customers to use their touchtone telephones as computer terminals to electronically pay their bills.

Airline and hotel reservation systems are another example. Computer terminals are installed all over the world at airline offices and ticket counters, in the offices of travel agents, rental car agency offices and hotels and motels. These national and international data communications systems provide realtime inquiries and responses concerning the status of travel reservations and realtime file updating to reflect reservations made or other transactions. In other examples, data communications systems allow insurance agencies across the country to access and update insurance policy files in realtime, retail stores to use *point-of-sale* terminals to capture sales data when a sale is made, and national and multinational corporations to communicate with all of their branch offices, manufacturing plants and distribution centers throughout the country and the world. See Figure 10–7.

FIGURE 10–7   A Worldwide Communications Network

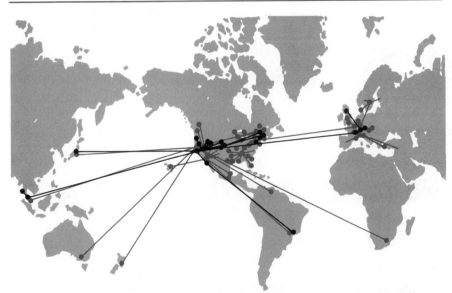

Courtesy Hewlett-Packard.

HP's internal communications network has 110 nodes linking manufacturing plants and sales offices to corporate centers in Palo Alto and Geneva. Most lines are dial-up facilities, and so communications line costs are held under $50,000 per month even though message volume averages 140 million characters per day.

Local Networks. Most data communications facilities are provided by common carriers or value-added carriers. However, the use of privately owned **local networks** is growing rapidly. Local networks use coaxial cable to connect computers, word processors, terminals, and electronic copying machines and dictation systems within a limited physical area such as an office building, manufacturing plant, or other work site. Local networks were originally developed to interconnect word processing terminals but have been expanded to include computer terminals for electronic data processing and other office information systems. Examples of local networks include *Ethernet* by Xerox, *ARC* by Datapoint, and IIPS by Harris Corporation. See Figure 10–8.

Personal Computer Networks. Another fast-growing group of communications networks are the personal computer networks which were discussed in Chapter 6. They are provided by public value-added carriers such as *Micronet* by Compuserve and *The Source* by Telenet. These networks offer a

FIGURE 10–8 A Local Communications Network

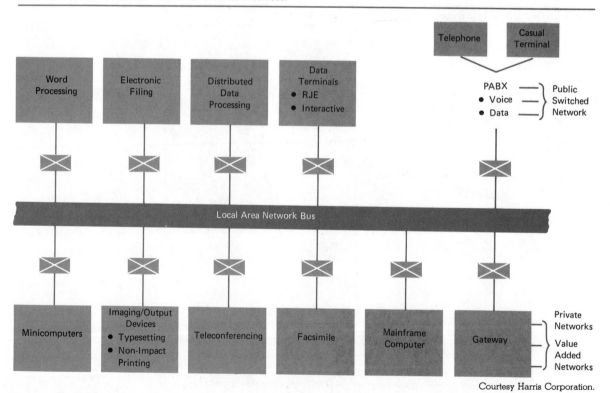

Courtesy Harris Corporation.

FIGURE 10-9   Services of Personal Computer Networks

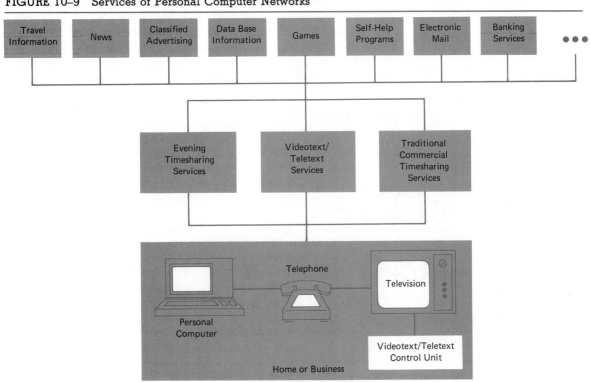

Source: Stephen A. Caswell, "Microcommunications: An Evolving Bazaar," *Mini-Micro Systems,* September 1980, p. 112.

wide variety of information services to personal computer users who have installed inexpensive modems to connect their computers to the telephone system. See Figure 10–9.

Distributed Processing Networks.   As has been mentioned several times previously in this text, distributed processing involves dispersing smaller computers throughout an organization rather than relying on one central computer facility. These distributed computers are typically interconnected by data communications links to form a *distributed processing network.* We will discuss these networks in the next chapter.

Communication Network Architectures.   Until quite recently, there was a lack of sufficient standards for the interface between the hardware, software, and communications channels of data communication networks. Therefore it is quite common to find a lack of compatibility between the data communications hardware and software of different manufacturers. This situation has hampered the use of data communications, increased its costs, and reduced its efficiency and effectiveness. Since the mid-1970s, computer manufacturers and national and international organizations have developed standards called **protocols** and have been working on master plans called **network architectures** to support the development of

FIGURE 10–10 A Communications Network Architecture

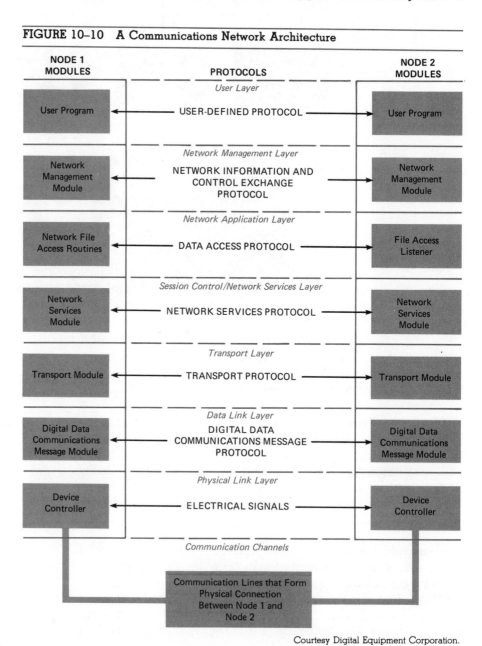

Courtesy Digital Equipment Corporation.

advanced data communications networks. (A *protocol* is a set of rules and procedures for the control of communications in a network.)

The goal of network architectures is to promote an *open, simple, flexible,* and *efficient* data communications environment. This will be accomplished by the use of standard protocols, standard communications hardware and software interfaces, and the design of a *standard multilevel interface* between end users and computer systems. Network architectures currently being developed include IBM's System Network Architecture (SNA), Univac's Distributed Communication Architecture (DCA) and Honeywell's Distributed Systems Architecture (DSA). Figure 10–10 illustrates the multilevel interface of the Digital Network Architecture (DNA) of the Digital Equipment Corporation.

ADVANTAGES AND DISADVANTAGES

Data communications systems of one kind or another are used by many business organizations, and this usage will continue to increase in the future. Data communications allows:

- *Quick response systems* since data and inquiries are transmitted electronically to and from a realtime processing system thus providing up-to-date information for business operations and management.

- *Online data entry and remote job entry* in which data is captured and entered into the computer system immediately after it is generated at its point of origin. Terminals in retail stores, business offices, and on factory floors minimize manual data processing thus cutting costs and reducing errors.

- *Remote computer use* is provided by linking users, terminals, and computer systems spread over a large geographic area. This may include *teleconferencing* which makes possible meetings and conferences between employees in different parts of a large region. Thus data communications can reduce energy consumption, travel, shipping, and postage costs.

- *Centralized or distributed processing* is made possible. Users can be linked to a central computer system or serviced by a *distributed* network of computers dispersed throughout the organization. The choice depends on the philosophy of management and the needs of the organization for control of computer use and costs, and the quality and flexibility of service to user departments.

Data communications systems do have several significant limitations. Unauthorized persons can gain access to the data that is transmitted over communications lines or stored in secondary storage devices of computer systems tied into communications networks. Many instances of tampering and theft of data from data communications systems have been reported over the years. Significant control methods and measures must be taken to protect the integrity and security of data communications systems. For example, complex coding techniques called **encryption** are applied to data by special communications control circuitry and decoded upon arrival at a receiving terminal. Many data communications systems use the national Data Encryption Standards (DES) as the basis for the encryption of data.

Data communications systems are subject to a small degree of error, and do cause additional costs for required hardware, software, and communications channel use. However, the benefits of data communications outweigh its costs and limitations. The use of data communications networks is expected to accelerate in the future as more data communications terminals move into business offices, warehouses, factories, retail stores, banks, and other organizations.

SUMMARY

- Data communications systems provide for the transmitting of data over electronic communications links between one or more computer systems and a number of input/output terminals at some physical distance away from the computer. Modern use of computers is heavily dependent on data communications systems for remote-access batch processing, most realtime processing, and many word processing and office communication systems.

- The major components of a data communications system consists of (1) terminals, (2) data communications interface units, (3) communications channels, (4) computers, and (5) communications control software. Data communications hardware consists of a variety of computer terminals, modems, and various communica-

tions control units and processors. Data communications software consists of computer programs which control and support the communications occurring in a data communications network.

- Communications channels include ordinary telephone lines, coaxial cables, fiber optic cables, microwave systems, and earth satellite systems. Use of these channels is provided by companies called common carriers and specialized carriers. Communications network architectures are being developed which will provide standard protocols and standard communications hardware and software interfaces beween end users and computers systems.

- Data communications systems are becoming more prevalent in carrying out business and individual activities. They range from the worldwide networks of multinational operations, to local networks in office buildings and other worksites, and personal computer networks. Data communications make quick response systems, online data entry and remote job entry, remote computer use, and either centralized or distributed processing possible. Data communications systems also require controls over unauthorized use such as data encryption.

KEY TERMS AND CONCEPTS

Data communications

Communications interface

Modems

Communications controllers

Front-end processors

Communications channels

Fiber optic cables

Communications satellites

Communications control software

Communications carrier

Communications network architecture

Digital networks

Local networks

Personal computer networks

Encryption

Protocol

Packet switching

Facsimile

Teleconferencing

REVIEW AND DISCUSSION QUESTIONS

1. What are data communications systems? Why are they necessary in today's computer environment?

2. What are the major components and functions of a data communications system?

3. What are the major types and functions of data communications hardware and software?

4. What are communications carriers? What services do they provide?

5. What are the major types of communications channels? Will communication satellite systems become the primary channel for data communications?

6. What role does a *protocol* play in data communications?

7. Are communication network architectures necessary? Why or why not?

8. What are local networks? How do they differ from other data communications networks?

9. What are some examples of the use of data communications by business firms and individuals? Can personal computers utilize data communications?

10. What are some of the advantages and disadvantages of data communications systems? Do you expect the use of data communications to increase in the future? Why or why not?

REAL WORLD APPLICATIONS

10-1   First Interstate Bank Corporation

First Interstate Bank Corporation has developed and now operates what *Business Week* has described as "the most sophisticated network of interstate electronic terminals yet built," the Teller Item Processing System (TIPS) which connects more than 825 banking offices in 11 western states. This system currently processes more than 300,000 account inquiries every day by means of IBM 3604 terminals located at teller work stations.

The terminals work during the daytime into a distributed data processor. At night, that whole data base is turned around by satellite channels into the Los Angeles facility to update the central data base and then transmit the data back.

An American Satellite Company network, consisting of three 5-meter stations and one 10-meter station, connects the three largest regional computer processing centers with the TIPS center in Los Angeles where the larger station is located. A total of eight satellite channels are being used, and the satellite network now handles about 40 million of the 60 million bits transmitted over the entire network every day. The sensitive financial information transmitted is protected by cryptographic equipment which codes and decodes data before and after transmission.

Over a three-year period, First Interstate expects to save nearly $1 million in communications costs.[1]

• Why did First Interstate Bank Corporation develop a communications satellite network? Explain the advantages (and disadvantages) of this approach.

[1] Source: "Satellite Data Exchange Service," *American Satellite Capabilities and Service,* American Satellite Company.

10-2   IBM Corporation

Business was great. But administrative costs soared as branch offices beefed up their ranks to help with the flood and complexity of new paperwork. Customers waited for weeks for delivery confirmation. This set of events spurred IBM's Data Processing Division, riding high in the mid-1960s on the success of the System/360 computer line, to create a streamlined administrative system.

That system, known as the Advanced Administrative System (AAS), has become the keystone of IBM's business systems. It encompasses order entry and accounts receivable as well as the maintenance of customer records and the inventory of installed equipment numbering in the millions. It's also used for hundreds of other applications. Today, terminals in IBM locations across the country are online to central computers that process and confirm orders,

relay information to plants, and store and update pertinent information on virtually all customer data processing installations.

The AAS network includes some 2,400 display terminals in more than 200 branch offices, with 12,000 users. The average response time to 750,000 inputs per day is five seconds. Two network-connected IBM System/370 Model 168s, one each at White Plains, N.Y., and Bethesda, Md., share the workload and provide mutual backup capability.

When an order is entered, AAS expands the order into system components for manufacturing, processes the system component numbers for inventory control, and summarizes the order for both sales and manufacturing management control.

10–2   *(continued)*

Today there are approximately 850 AAS applications, supported by some 10,000 application programs. Many aspects of payroll, personnel, and financial support are provided by the system: the processing of a marketing representative's commissions; education activity, such as computer-assisted instruction and education center enrollments; daily business register and general accounting are also included.[2]

- What role does data communications play in IBM's advanced administrative system?
- What capabilities and benefits are evident in this system?

[2] Source: "IBM's Administrative System," *Data Processor,* January 1977, p. 13. Reprinted with permission.

10–3   Chase Manhattan Bank

"Our objective is to become the premier bank in service quality in the marketplace," says Chase Manhattan's Senior Vice President and retail banking department executive Frederick S. Hammer. "In a fiercely competitive environment, COMETS (Community Electronic Teller System) has allowed us to provide far more service at the teller window. It is a signal to our people that we believe in the market and we believe in them."

The banking giant has clearly underscored that belief by moving in recent years to a leadership position in the field of teller automation. As recently as early 1977, Chase's retail branch network had not been automated. Tellers were still using outdated bookkeeping machines, not unlike those at other banks where automation was slow to take hold. But during 1978 Chase installed one of the largest IBM 3600 Finance Communication Systems in the United States—nearly 1,600 teller terminals in some 10 downstate branches.

The system links keyboard display teller and platform terminals via telephone lines with computers in the Lake Success, Long Island, Retail Operations Center. Among other things, it has boosted teller productivity and customer service, slashed paperwork, increased interbranch responsiveness and provided a framework for a range of customer-convenience services.

Says vice president and division executive Stephen P. Hirsch: "With a system like COMETS, we can track more activity. If a Visa cardholder takes cash from an ATM, goes next door to the bank for a cash advance, then to a merchant and uses the credit card, we can track each transaction against a common data base."[3]

- Why did Chase switch to a data communications-based realtime teller system?
- What communications capabilities and benefits are evident in the Chase system?

[3] Source: "Fine-tuning the Chase Advantage," *Data Processor,* April/May 1980, p. 19. Reprinted with permission.

CHAPTER SUPPLEMENT

DATA COMMUNICATIONS—TECHNICAL CHARACTERISTICS

Data communications is a highly technical, rapidly developing field of computer technology. Most business computer users will not become involved in decision-making concerning data communications alternatives, and therefore do not need a detailed knowledge of its technical characteristics. However, it is important that business computer users who wish to become better managers of the computer resources of their organizations become familiar with the basic characteristics of data communications channels and networks. This supplement should help such computer users achieve that goal.

Transmission Speed. The communication capabilities of communication channels can be classified by *bandwidth* which is the frequency range of the channel and which determines its maximum transmission rate. Data transmission rates are typically measured in bits per second (BPS), also called **baud.**

- *Narrowband* or *low-speed* channels allow transmission rates up to 300 bits per second (BPS) and are used primarily for teletypewriters and other low-speed printing terminals.
- *Voiceband* or *medium-speed* channels are "voice grade" communication lines commonly used for voice communications. Data transmission rates up to 4,800 BPS are attainable while rates up to 9,600 BPS are achieved with the use of specially conditioned leased lines. These medium-speed lines are typically used for CRT terminals and medium-speed printers.
- *Broadband* or *high-speed* channels allow transmission rates at specific intervals from about 20,000 BPS to more than 200,000 BPS and typically use microwave or satellite transmission. These channels are primarily used for high-speed data transmission between computer systems.

Transmission Mode. The two modes of transmitting data are called *asynchronous* and *synchronous* transmission. **Asynchronous** transmission transmits one character at a time with each character preceded by a *start bit* and followed by a *stop bit.* Asynchronous transmission is normally used for low-speed transmission at rates below 2,000 BPS. **Synchronous** transmission transmits groups of characters at a time with the beginning and ending of a character determined by timing circuitry of a modem or other data communications control unit. Synchronous transmission is normally used for high-speed transmission exceeding 2,000 BPS.

Transmission Direction. Communications channels can provide for three types of data transmission direction. A **simplex** channel allows data to be transmitted in only one direction, such as just receiving transmissions or just sending transmissions. A *half-duplex* channel allows transmission in either direction, but in only one direction at a time. This is usually sufficient for many low-speed terminals (such as transaction terminals) where alternating sending and receiving is characteristic of normal communications activities. The **full duplex** channel allows data to be transmitted in both directions at the same time. It is used for high-speed communications between computer systems. See Figure S10–1.

Packet Switching. *Packet switching* involves subdividing communications messages into groups called packets, typically 128 characters long. The packet switching network carrier uses minicomputers and other communications processors to control the packet switching process and transmit the packets of various users over its leased lines. Packet switching networks are also known as *X.25 networks* which is the international standard or *protocol* governing the operations of public packet switching networks. Protocols frequently establish the communications control information needed for *handshaking* which is the process of exchanging predetermined signals and characters in order to establish a connection between two data communications terminals or stations.

Point-to-Point versus Multidrop Lines. The two basic types of communication links in data communications networks are *point-to-point* and *multidrop*. When point-to-point lines are used, each terminal is connected by its own individual line to the computer system. When multidrop lines are used, several terminals share each data communications line to a computer system. Obviously, point-to-point lines are more expensive than multidrop lines because all of the communications capacity and interface equipment of a data communications line is being used by a single terminal. Thus a multidrop line decreases communications costs because each line is shared by many terminals. Thus point-to-point lines are used only if there will be continuous communications between a computer and a terminal or other computer system.

Multidrop lines allow more than one terminal on the line

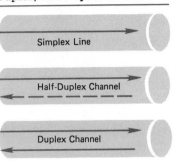

FIGURE S10–1   Simplex, Half-Duplex, and Duplex Channels

Simplex Line

Half-Duplex Channel

Duplex Channel

to receive data at the same time, but only one terminal at a time can transmit data to the computer system. There are several ways to get around this limitation. In the **contention** approach, line use is on a first-come, first-served basis where a terminal can transmit data if the line is not in use, but must wait if it is busy. In the **polling** approach, the computer or communications processor polls (contacts) each terminal in sequence to determine which has a message to send. The sequence in which the terminals are polled is based upon the communications traffic expected from each terminal. Thus the transmissions of each terminal is based on a "roll call" of each terminal on the line. Polling is widely used because the speed of computers allows them to poll and control transmissions by many terminals sharing the same line without any apparent slowdown in response time. The typical terminal user would not be aware that many terminals were using the same line. Thus, users at many terminals can share the same line if their typical communications consists of brief messages and inquiries. See Figure S10–2.

Leased versus Switched Lines. Multidrop lines are usually *leased lines* (or *direct lines*) in which a specific communications circuit is leased (or acquired) and used to connect terminals with a computer system. Typically, a user can be using a terminal on a leased line by merely turning it on and entering appropriate identification messages. Point-to-point lines may

FIGURE S10–2 Multidrop versus Point-to-Point Lines

Multidrop Lines   Point-to-Point Lines

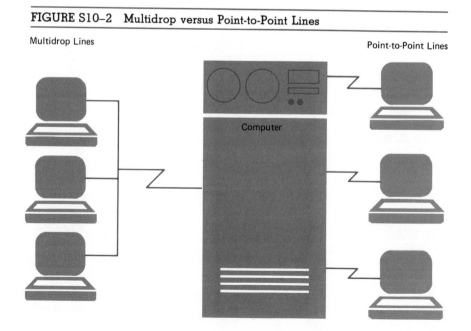

Computer

use leased lines or a *switched line* which uses the telephone lines and switching service of the regular telephone system. A user wanting to begin using a terminal on a switched line must dial the telephone number assigned to the communications processor which establishes contact with the computer system.

Communications Codes. Data communications systems typically use the American Standard Code for Information Interchange (ASCII) to represent the characters of data being transmitted. Since most computers use the Extended Binary Coded Decimal Interchange Code (EBCDIC), the ASCII code is typically translated into the EBCDIC code by communications control units prior to entry into a computer system. These computer codes were illustrated in Chapter 3.

Communications Control Information. Communications control units and processors control errors in transmission by several processes including *parity checking.* As described in Chapter 3, parity checking involves determining whether there is an odd or even number of *binary one* digits in a character being transmitted and received. If a transmission error is detected, it is usually corrected by retransmitting the message. Besides parity bits, additional *control information* is usually added to the message itself. This includes information which indicates the destination of the data, its priority, the beginning and ending of the message, plus additional error detecting and correcting information. For example, in packet switching networks, packets are preceded and followed by control information which is necessary to manage their routing through the network and to detect transmission errors. Thus a *protocol layer,* or *envelope* of control information "packages" the user data being transmitted. See Figure S10–3.

FIGURE S10–3   An Envelope of Protocol Layer Control Information

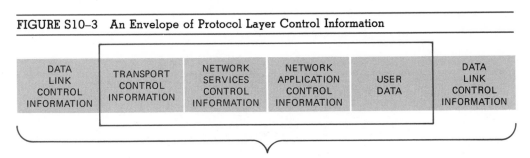

Complete Envelope Transmitted
from One Node to an Adjacent Node

Courtesy of Digital Equipment Corporation.

11

CHAPTER OUTLINE

Modern Information Processing Systems

LEARNING OBJECTIVES

The purpose of this chapter is to promote a basic understanding of modern information processing systems by analyzing the basic concepts, functions, and capabilities of distributed processing, data base processing, and word processing systems.

After reading and studying this chapter, you should be able to:

1. Explain the concepts of distributed processing and data base processing, and the reasons for their importance in today's computer environment.
2. Identify the major types of distributed processing networks and applications.
3. Differentiate between file processing systems and data base processing systems.
4. Discuss the development and use of data base processing systems.
5. Identify the functions and components of word processing as a system, and the major types of word processing systems.
6. Identify the advantages and disadvantages of distributed processing, data base processing, and word processing systems.
7. Discuss the trend toward automated office systems.

The use of computers for information processing began when manual data processing systems were replaced by electronic data processing systems which relied on *batch processing* methods. In the late 50s and early 60s *realtime* EDP systems began to appear, along with *remote-access* batch processing systems. This trend accelerated with third and fourth generation developments which made possible **distributed processing systems** of microcomputers, minicomputers, intelligent terminals and other computers dispersed throughout an organization and interconnected by *data communication networks*. Other developments included **data base processing systems** which integrate the use and storage of data, and computerized **word processing systems,** where computers automate typing and other office communications. These developments emphasize the mutual dependence of data and information processing, storage and communications. **Modern information processing systems** have integrated *data processing* and *word processing* (which is why the term *information processing* is used), and with the help of advanced **telecommunications systems** have begun to integrate the transmission and processing of data, words, images and voices. Therefore, in this chapter we will analyze three basic systems which underly modern information processing: *distributed processing systems, data base processing systems*, and *word processing systems*. See Figure 11–1.

FIGURE 11–1 Modern Information Processing Systems

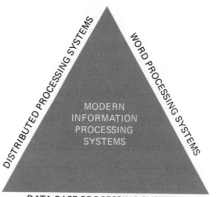

DISTRIBUTED PROCESSING SYSTEMS

WORD PROCESSING SYSTEMS

MODERN INFORMATION PROCESSING SYSTEMS

DATA BASE PROCESSING SYSTEMS

SECTION I: DISTRIBUTED PROCESSING SYSTEMS

Distributed processing, also called *distributed data processing* (DDP) is a new form of decentralization of information processing made possible by a network of computers "dispersed" throughout an organization. Processing of user applications is accomplished by several computers interconnected by a data communications network, rather than relying on one large centralized computer facility, or on the decentralized operation of several completely independent computers. Computers may be dispersed over a wide geographic area if necessary, or may be distributed to various user departments of an organization in a limited *local network* at a major user location such as a large building or manufacturing plant. Distributed processing systems rely heavily on a network composed of microcomputers, minicomputers, and intelligent terminals controlled by computer users throughout an organization. These computer users can perform many of their own data processing and word processing tasks with their own *local processors,* and can communicate with similar computers *(processing nodes)* in the network if necessary. See Figure 11–2.

Distributed processing systems are a major fourth generation computer development. Computer power can be brought more effectively to the people in an organization through distributed processing systems with computer processors in branch offices, retail stores, factories, warehouses, remote locations, and other work sites. A business firm or other organization may still have a large central computer facility, but it is no longer the sole source of computer power in the organization.

Reasons for Distributed Processing

In the early years of computer development, a *decentralized* approach was taken to the use of computers. Computer-using departments throughout an organization replaced manual methods or old punched-card systems with computer systems. Typically, large computers were installed at a corporations's headquarters location, while smaller computers were installed in manufacturing plants, distribution centers, scientific laboratories, engineering departments, and in regional offices. However as larger and more efficient computers were developed, many organizations concluded that decentralized data processing was inefficient and expensive. Therefore organizations

FIGURE 11–2 Centralized, Decentralized, and Distributed Data Processing

CENTRALIZED DATA PROCESSING

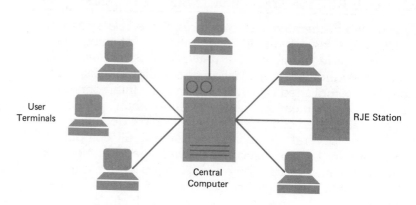

User Terminals

RJE Station

Central Computer

DECENTRALIZED DATA PROCESSING

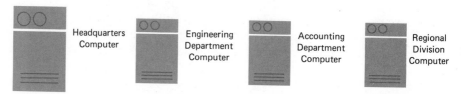

Headquarters Computer

Engineering Department Computer

Accounting Department Computer

Regional Division Computer

DISTRIBUTED DATA PROCESSING

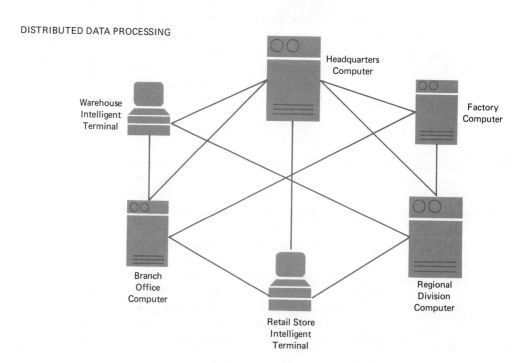

Headquarters Computer

Warehouse Intelligent Terminal

Factory Computer

Branch Office Computer

Retail Store Intelligent Terminal

Regional Division Computer

began to swing toward the use of a *centralized* approach using large computer systems and a centralized data processing department. Large centralized computer systems were more cost-effective due to economies of scale. A centralized data processing department increased management's control of business operations and costs, as well as data processing costs and activities.

The move toward centralized data processing continued with the growth of data communications capabilities and the development of the *centralized data base* concept. Data communications networks tied to a large central computer system provided *time-sharing systems* where many users at remote locations could interactively share the services of the central computer at the same time, as well as allowing *remote job entry* for batch processing from geographically dispersed user locations. The data base concept also seemed to favor centralization as organizations decided that a centralized data base would reduce costs and duplications in data processing and increase the efficiency and effectiveness of computer-based information systems. It was felt that if data and information were in a centralized *data bank,* it would be used as a valuable resource to help manage business operations and support management decision making.

With the development of minicomputers in the early 1970s, another change began which shifted the focus of computing to the *end user.* Large central computer installations were becoming overloaded with work and were unable to respond satisfactorily to the data processing needs of the end users in the organization. The lack of sufficient data processing support became intolerable since the management of end user departments were still expected to attain specific productivity and profitability objectives. Since the price of minicomputers and small computers continued to decline while their performance continued to increase, it became easier for user departments to argue that small computers of their own could handle their data processing assignments in a cost-effective manner.

Thus a dispersion of small computers to process end user applications at the users' sites began to spread. This trend accelerated with continued price/performance improvements in minicomputers and data communications facilities, and with the development of intelligent terminals and microprocessor and microcomputer systems. It has become even more feasible to provide users with computers to handle a significant part of their information processing requirements. Dispersion is achieved while still providing a significant degree of integration and interdependency among the computers at corporate headquarters and user sites due to the use of data communications networks to form **distributed processing systems.**

Distributive processing systems place data as well as computer power where they are needed within an integrated *systems architecture.* Data communications networks interconnect multiple levels of processing power and multiple levels of data storage. Computer power can be provided by central or *host* computers, local or *subhost* computers, *satellite* computers, *personal* computers, and intelligent terminals. Distributed processing also requires organizing and coordinating the data required for processing in *distributed data bases* which can be a combination of central and local data bases.

The cost-effectiveness of distributed data processing is not based on the economies of scale of large central computers but on the *economies of specialization* provided by tailoring computer processing to the specific requirements of local operations and management. This cost-effectiveness makes it more feasible to distribute processing power as a business firm becomes more geographically or organizationally distributed. Many business firms have *geographically distributed* branch offices, retail outlets, distribution centers, factories, and so forth. Also, many businesses are *organizationally distributed* into various departments such as engineering, accounting, and marketing. Therefore, distributing processing power can become operationally and economically feasible. This is especially true since the economies of scale of large computer systems begin to lessen as more different applications and uses are added to a central computer facility and it becomes unresponsive to users, hard to manage, and expensive to operate. Thus *offloading* some user data processing to distributed computers becomes a natural solution to an organization's information processing problems.

Though distributed processing is a move away from centralized data processing and toward a more decentralized approach, it is not the same as traditional *decentralized data processing.* That would involve completely independent user computer systems with independent data bases, programs, applications, budgets, and information system development efforts. Instead, distributed data processing constitutes a *system* of user department and headquarters computers which are *interconnected* by a data communications network, *integrated* by a common data base-oriented approach, and *coordinated* by an organization-wide *information resource management* philosophy. Thus distributed processing systems provide the best of both the centralized and decentralized approaches to using computers. Information processing tasks take place wherever they can be performed most efficiently and effectively, either at user departments or at a central site. Thus the goal of distributed processing systems is to meet the diverse information needs of all end users while maximizing the use of the information resources of the organization.

Distributed Processing Networks

Figure 11–3 illustrates the two basic structures of distributed processing networks: a **star network** with end user computers tied to a large central computer, and a **ring network** where local computer processors are tied together on a more equal basis. In many cases, star networks take the form of *hierarchical networks* with a large headquarters computer at the top of the company's hierarchy connected to medium-sized computers at the divisional level which in turn are connected to smaller computers at the departmental or local level. Ring networks are also called *peer networks* because in most cases computers operate autonomously for local processing and are connected to each other on an equal *peer* relationship on which the computers cooperate as partners or *colleagues.* A variation of the ring network is the *mesh network,* where

FIGURE 11–3 Distributed Processing Network Structures

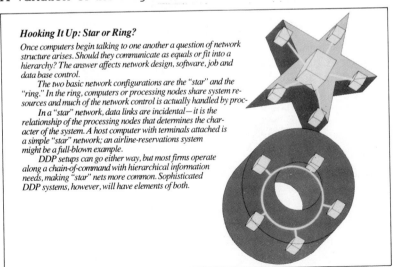

Hooking It Up: Star or Ring?

Once computers begin talking to one another a question of network structure arises. Should they communicate as equals or fit into a hierarchy? The answer affects network design, software, job and data base control.

The two basic network configurations are the "star" and the "ring." In the ring, computers or processing nodes share system resources and much of the network control is actually handled by proc-

In a "star" network, data links are incidental—it is the relationship of the processing nodes that determines the character of the system. A host computer with terminals attached is a simple "star" network; an airline-reservations system might be a full-blown example.

DDP setups can go either way, but most firms operate along a chain-of-command with hierarchical information needs, making "star" nets more common. Sophisticated DDP systems, however, will have elements of both.

Courtesy International Data Corporation, reprinted from *Fortune* magazine of March 1977.

direct communication lines are added to connect some or all of the computers in the ring to each other. In most cases, distributed processing systems use a combination of star and ring approaches. Figure 11–4 illustrates a simple combination of star and ring approaches, while Figure 11–5 outlines a ring and star DDP network of a large manufacturing firm.

Obviously, the star network appears to be more centralized while the ring network is a more decentralized approach. However, this is not always the case. For example, the central computer in a star configuration may be acting only as a

FIGURE 11–4 A Typical Distributed Processing Network

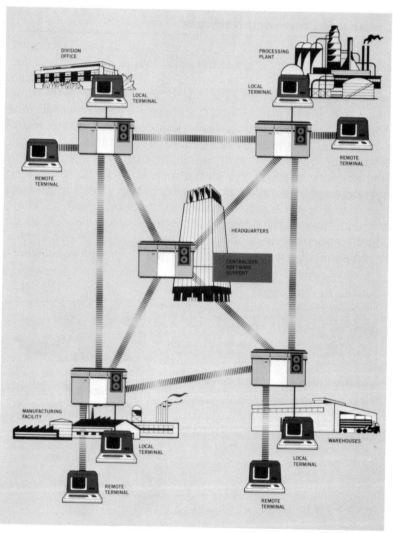

Courtesy of Formation, Inc.

FIGURE 11-5 A Manufacturing Distributed Processing Network

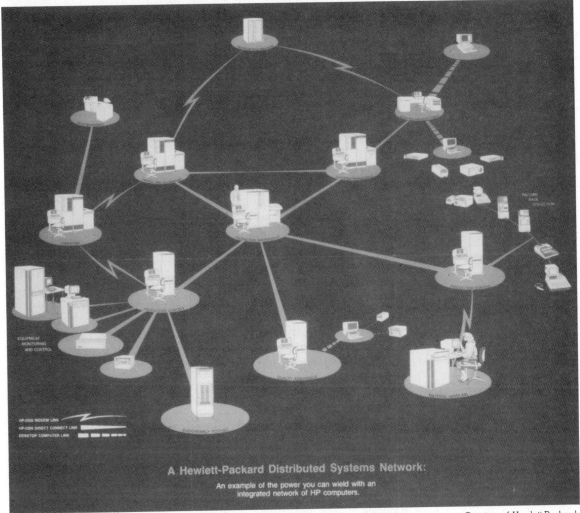

A Hewlett-Packard Distributed Systems Network:

An example of the power you can wield with an
integrated network of HP computers.

Courtesy of Hewlett-Packard.

switch or message switching computer which handles the data
communications between primarily autonomous local computers. Star and ring networks differ in their performance, reliability, and cost depending on the type of organization structure
and information processing required. There is no simple answer to which type of network will provide the best performance. A pure star network is considered less reliable than
a ring network since the other computers in the star are heavily
dependent on the central host computer. If it fails, there is

no backup processing and communications capability and the local computers will be cut off from the corporate headquarters and each other. Therefore, it is essential that the host computer be highly reliable, including having some type of *multiprocessor architecture* to provide a backup capability.

Star network variations are most common because they can support the *chain-of-command* and hierarchical structure of most organizations. Ring networks are most common in the form of *local networks* which tie together several computers at one local site. Ring networks are considered more reliable and less costly if there is a minimum of communication between the computers in the ring. Also, if one computer in the ring *goes down,* the other computers can continue to process their own work as well as communicating with each other. If there is a lot of communications within a distributed processing network, computers in a ring network will have to have sophisticated communications control hardware and software compared to the local computers in a star network, where the host computer or switching computer handles communications control assignments. Thus if most communication is with a central site, a star network is the most simple and practical approach. In any event, the performance, reliability, and cost of each type of network is dependent on the organizational structure, geographic dispersion and information processing needs of each computer-using organization.

Distributed Processing Applications

The use of distributed data processing systems can be subdivided into six application categories: (1) distributed data processing, (2) central site processing, (3) distributed data entry, (4) distributed data base processing, (5) distributed word processing, and (6) distributed communications networks.

- **Distributed Data Processing.** Local users can handle a broad range of information processing tasks ranging from data entry processing, to local data base inquiry and response systems, to fully independent transaction processing, which includes updating local data bases and generating necessary output reports. One rule of thumb states that if 70 percent to 80 percent of the information needed by users can be produced locally, then users should have their own computer systems. Thus data can be completely processed locally, where most input and output (and errors and problems) must be handled anyway. This should provide computer processing more tailored to the needs of users, and increase information processing efficiency and effectiveness as users become more responsible for their own application systems.

- **Central Site Processing.** With DDP, large central site computers can be applied to those jobs they can best handle, like large highly structured and repetitive batch applications, communications control for the entire distributed processing network, maintaining large corporate data bases, and providing sophisticated planning and decision making support for corporate management. Users at local sites might typically access a central computer to receive corporate-wide management information or transmit summary transaction data reflecting local site activities.

- **Distributed Data Entry.** Data entry using intelligent terminals (or dumb terminals connected to a local computer) help generate *clean data* from source documents at their point of origin for local processing or transmittal to a central site. Data which contains errors and requires editing and preprocessing *(dirty data)* can usually be cleaned up better at the site from which it originated. Local personnel are more familiar with the local conditions which may have caused the errors and feel more responsible to having them corrected.

- **Distributed Data Base Processing.** There are many kinds of data that may be of interest to only one local site. Thus specialized *local data bases* containing data unique to user departments can be *distributed* to local sites. In such *distributed data base processing systems,* all transaction data, or just summary data may be sent to a central computer for storage in a common data base. Distributed data base systems can provide faster response times, better user control of data structures and access, and lower communication costs because data is closer to users.

- **Distributed Word Processing.** Computerized word processors or terminals connected to a local computer with word processing software can easily automate the preparation of internal and external correspondence, business documents and management reports. Such *local word processing* can improve productivity and timeliness, while providing the flexibility to make last-minute changes to official documents and reports.

- **Distributed Communications Networks.** Several computers and many terminals can typically be interconnected by local communications networks at each large local site such as

FIGURE 11–6   A Local Distributed Processing Network

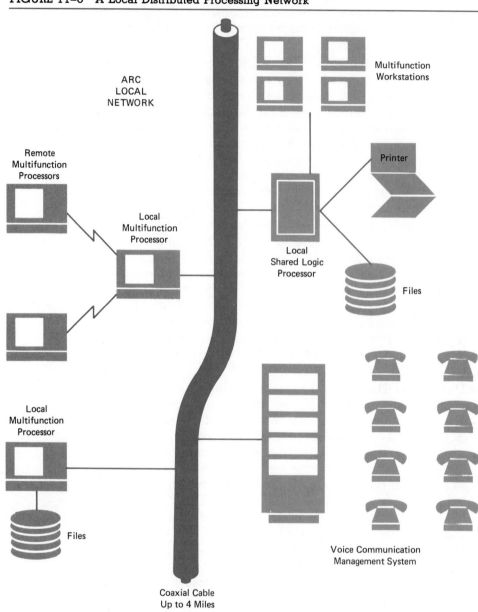

ARC
LOCAL
NETWORK

Multifunction
Workstations

Remote
Multifunction
Processors

Local
Multifunction
Processor

Printer

Local
Shared Logic
Processor

Files

Local
Multifunction
Processor

Files

Voice Communication
Management System

Coaxial Cable
Up to 4 Miles

Source: Reproduced by permission of Datapoint Corporation. Copyright Datapoint Corporation, February 1981.

a large building or plant facility. See Figure 11–6. End-
user computers are also connected to each other and headquarters computers by data communications to form various
types of distributed processing networks. The processing

power and communications capability of local computers allows user-oriented applications to be *offloaded* from a headquarters computer while still providing for company-wide communications and control from corporate headquarters to user departments.

Advantages and Disadvantages

What are the advantages and disadvantages of the distributed processing approach? First let us summarize the advantages of distributed processing systems.

- Communication costs can be reduced by the reduction in the amount of data that must be transmitted to a central site. There is also a more efficient transmission of data since local computers can preprocess data after it is captured—cleaning it and condensing it (by such techniques as removing blank spaces in transmitted data). Also, interactive inquiry of local data bases can substantially reduce the requirements for communication with a central data base.

- Response time and turnaround time to the users are improved because processing is carried out at the user's location.

- Input errors are minimized because computerized data entry supports and controls user input and simplifies the capture of clean data. Some users report an input error rate of less than one tenth of one percent.

- Productivity of end users can be increased by shortening and reducing the need for communications links, improving the accessibility of data, and providing interactive computing power for user applications that had been performed manually or handled by a central batch processing system.

- Computer applications can be more flexible and tailored to a user's requirements since hardware and software can be developed in modular units to fit the user's organizational and operational requirements.

- Reliability and availability are improved because malfunctions do not have to affect the information processing operations of the entire organization. Unaffected local computers can act as backup systems and function as *stand-alone* systems since they are not totally dependent on a large central computer.

- User pressure on the central computer installation is reduced by offloading user applications to local computer systems.

Reducing the workload of the central main frame computer will reduce the need for expensive upgrades and expansion of its capabilities, and free it to handle company-wide batch applications and provide more sophisticated data analysis and decision support applications for corporate management.

- Providing computer processing at user sites has significantly lessened the flow of paperwork between users and home offices thus decreasing clerical costs and increasing productivity. This advantage is reinforced since most modern distributed processing systems make heavy use of video display units and interactive inquiry and response systems to further decrease the flow of paper. Some users have reported that this aspect along has returned enough savings to cover the cost of the distributed systems.
- Computer processing at user locations bring users into a closer and more responsible relationship with their work activities. It allows users to feel more involved and responsible and more in control of their computer-based systems.
- Managerial decision-making effectiveness can be improved because both corporate and user management should have more convenient and immediate access to information tailored to support their decisions.

Several disadvantages and limitations should be considered in order to design more effective distributed processing systems.

- Building a complete distributed processing network for an entire organization is a complex task. Attempting to integrate separate computer systems at many user sites is a complicated problem requiring much advance planning. Hardware, software, data communications facilities, data base design, data processing methods, and application systems will tend to become incompatible between computer-using sites unless advance planning and coordination is emphasized. In addition, hardware devices, software packages, and data communication services can be acquired from different suppliers creating a multivendor *mixed shop* situation which can result in further incompatibility and loss of control.
- Distributed processing has the potential for a loss of consistency in the data and information needed to run the organization. Additional controls and security measures are required to preserve the integrity of the distributed data bases in the organization.

- Inadequately trained user personnel may result unless there are adequate training methods and good documentation of all data processing procedures. On the other hand, if user departments hire EDP personnel, a costly and unnecessary increase in personnel may result. Solving such potential problems requires (1) providing temporary help when user systems are implemented, (2) training users to run their own systems, and (3) designing applications which are tailored to user needs and easy to use, but which meet company-wide guidelines and standards. In many cases, companies continue to centralize much of their systems development and applications programming staff.

- Inefficient use and unnecessary duplication of information processing resources may make it difficult to achieve the economies of specialization which are possible in distributed systems. Avoiding this problem requires holding user management strictly responsible for the use and resulting costs of their information processing resources.

Distributed processing systems can provide many benefits to the new generation of computer users by providing them with efficient and effective information processing systems to help them control and manage their operations. The additional problems arising from the use of distributed processing systems can be solved if managing information processing functions and resources is made a major responsibility of the managers of user departments. Since distributed processing allows information processing resources to follow an organization's functional and geographic structure, user managers should be able to integrate the management of information processing with their other management responsibilities.

SECTION II: DATA BASE PROCESSING SYSTEMS

Reasons for Data Base Processing

For many years, electronic data processing had a *file processing* orientation. Data needed for each user application was stored in independent data files. Data processing consisted of using separate computer programs which updated these independent data files and used them to produce the documents and reports required by each separate user application. This file processing approach had several major problems which limited the efficiency and effectiveness of electronic data processing.

Data Redundancy. Independent data files include a lot of duplicated data. The same data (such as a customer's name, address, etc.) was recorded and stored in several files. This caused problems when data had to be updated, since separate file *maintenance* programs had to be developed and coordinated to insure that each file was properly updated. This was a time consuming and costly process which increased the secondary storage space requirements of computer systems.

Unintegrated Data. Independent data files made it difficult to provide users with information which required processing data stored in several different files. Special computer programs would have to be written to retrieve data from each independent file. This was so difficult, time consuming, and costly for some organizations that it was impossible to provide users or management with such information. Some users had to manually extract the required information from the various reports produced by each separate application.

Program/Data Dependence. Computer programs typically contained references to the specific *format* of data stored in the files that they used. Thus any changes to the format and structure of data and records in a file required that changes be made to all of the programs that used that file. This *program maintenance* effort due to changes to the format of data is a major burden of file processing systems.

The Data Base Concept

The concepts of **data bases** and **data base processing** were developed to solve the problems of file processing systems.

In Chapter 9, we defined a data base as a nonredundant collection of logically related records or files which consolidates records previously stored in independent files, so that it serves as a common pool of data which can be accessed by many different application programs. The data stored in a data base is independent of the computer programs which use it and the type of secondary storage devices on which it is stored.

Data base processing systems are a major type of modern information processing systems. They consist of electronic data processing systems which use a *data base orientation* for both the *storage* and *processing* of data.

Data Base Storage. The data needed by many different data processing applications in an organization is consolidated and integrated into several *common data bases* instead of being stored in many *independent data files. For example:* customer records and other data needed for several different applications in banking such as check processing, automated teller systems, bank credit cards, savings accounts, and installment loan accounting can be consolidated into a common *customer data base* rather than being kept in separate files for each of those applications.

Data Base Processing. Electronic data processing no longer consists of updating and using independent data files to produce information needed by each user's application. Instead, electronic data processing with a data base orientation consists of three basic activities:

● Updating and maintaining a comon data base.
● Providing information needed for each user's application by using computer programs that share the data in the common data base.
● Providing an inquiry/response capability so that users can easily interrogate the data base and receive quick responses to their requests for information.

Example. Traditionally, an individual computer program for each banking application mentioned above would be used to update a special data file for each application, as well as producing desired reports and documents. Thus Figure 11–7 illustrates the use of separate computer programs and independent data files in a file processing approach to the savings, installment loan, and checking account applications.

FIGURE 11–7 **Examples of
Banking File Processing Systems**

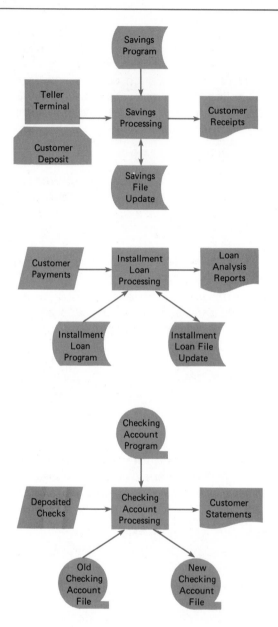

However, in a data base processing system, the computer programs needed for each banking application would be designed to use a common *customer data base* to produce information in a variety of forms. In addition, special *data base management systems* programs would be used to control the updating of the data base and to provide an inquiry/response capability for users. Thus Figure 11–8 illustrates how the sav-

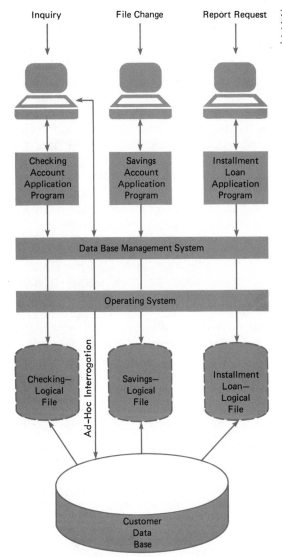

FIGURE 11–8   **A Banking Data Base Processing System Example**

ings, checking, and installment loan programs use a DBMS to share a customer data base, as if it were organized into separate *logical files*. Note also that the DBMS allows a user to make a direct *ad-hoc interrogation* of the data base without using an application program.

Developing a Data Base

Developing a data base is a complex task, which is the responsibility of users, programmers and systems analysts. In many companies, developing and managing the data base is the primary responsibility of a *data base administrator* (DBA). Users and EDP professionals must determine what data should be included in the data base and what structure or relationships exist between the data elements. Defining the structure of the logical relationships between data in a data base results in the development of a data base **schema**. The schema is an overall *conceptual* or *logical* view of the relationships between the data in the data base. For example, the schema would describe what types of data elements (fields, records, files, etc.) are in the data base, the relationships between the data elements (pointer fields, linking records, etc.) and the structure of data relationships (hierarchical, network, or relational data base structures).

Once the schema is designed and documented, the data base administrator must define a **subschema** for each user application program that will access the data base. A subschema is a subset or transformation of the logical view of the data base schema which is required by a particular user application program. Obviously, each program does not have to access the entire data base, but only a portion (subschema) of its logical data elements and relationships. For example, the subschema for a bank's checking account program would not include all of the record types and relationships in a customer data base, but only those records and files that were related to the operation and management of the checking account activity. Of course, the schema and subschema must be designed to meet the information processing needs of all users within the limits of the hardware, software, personnel, and financial resources of the organization.

It must be emphasized that both the schema and subschema are *logical* views of the data and relationships of the data base. The *physical* view of the data (also called the internal view) describes how data is physically arranged and stored on secondary storage devices of the computer system. The actual physical arrangement of data in the data base may be quite different from the logical data relationships defined in the schema and subschema (frequently called *user's views*). The physical arrangement and placement of data on secondary storage devices is one of the primary tasks performed by the data management control programs of an operating system. See Figure 11–9.

DATA BASE ENVIRONMENT

FIGURE 11-9   Multiple Data Base Views

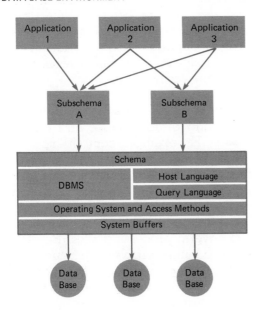

STEPS OF LOGICAL DATA BASE DESIGN

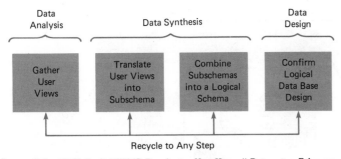

Source: Robert H. Holland, "DBMS: Developing User Views," *Datamation,* February 1980, p. 142. Reprinted with permission of *Datamation* magazine. Copyright by Technical Publishing Company, a Dun & Bradstreet Company, 1980; all rights reserved.

The concept of **distributed data bases** is a major consideration when developing data bases for an organization which uses *distributed processing systems.* As we mentioned in the previous section, data as well as computing power must be distributed to the user departments in the organization. Thus, data that needs to be used and processed only at a user's site (called *local data*) is stored in *local data bases,* while data needed by all or several of the local and central computer systems (called *global data*) is frequently stored in a *common data base.* However, parts or all of the common data base can be duplicated at one or more local sites. Thus, global data can be *centralized* in one common data base, or *partitioned* into *segments* which are distributed to several processing sites. However, all or part of the global data in the common data base can be duplicated (also called *replicated*) and distributed to various processing sites.

Obviously, any of these methods of distributing data bases has its advantages and disadvantages and requires careful planning and design. For example, centralizing all global data is the simplest arrangement but may involve potential problems of performance and reliability since all computers in the network are dependent on the computer system where the common data base is stored. These problems can be eliminated if the global data is replicated and copies of the data are distributed to several processing sites. However, this arrangement involves potential problems in insuring that all copies of the global data are properly and concurrently updated every time they are affected by transactions or other changes. Thus developing a distributed data base system frequently requires tradeoffs between service to users, processing and

FIGURE 11–10   Example of a Distributed Data Base System

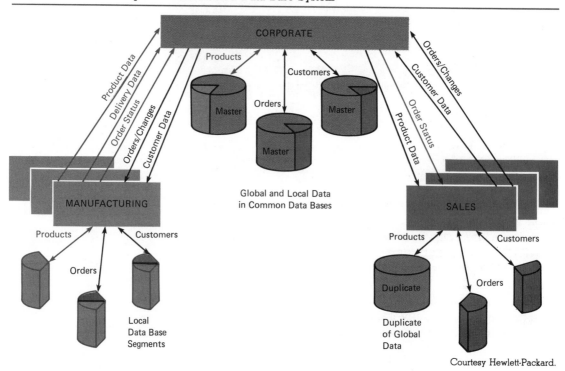

Courtesy Hewlett-Packard.

communications costs, and processing performance and control. See Figure 11–10.

Using a Data Base

Data base processing systems supported by DBMS software are being used by more and more organizations with large computers, minicomputers, and even some microcomputer systems. We have already discussed how data base processing differs from traditional file processing. The superior service and performance of data base processing is a result of the integration of data required by the data base concept, the

FIGURE 11–11   Some of the External Data Bases Available to Computer-Using Organizations

ADP Network Services	A large distributor offering computational data banks in: Agriculture, Autos, Commodities, Demographics, Economics, Finance, Insurance and International Business. Its main suppliers are Chase Econometric Associates and Standard & Poor's.
CompuServe Network	A large distributor offering bibliographic data banks in: Agriculture, Business, Education, Environment, General News Publications, Science and Social Science. Its suppliers are various trade associations and governmental groups.
Data Resources	A large vendor offering (primarily computational) data banks in: Agriculture, Banking, Commodities, Demographics, Economics, Energy, Finance, Insurance, International Business, and the Steel and Transportation Industries. DRI economists maintain a number of these data banks; Standard & Poor's is also a source.
General Electric Information Services	A computational data-bank vendor covering: Economics, Energy, Finance and International Business. Its suppliers include the University of California and Value Line.
Interactive Data Corporation	A large computational data-bank distributor covering: Agriculture, Autos, Banking, Commodities. Demographics, Economics, Energy, Finance, International Business, and Insurance. Its main suppliers are Chase Econometric Associates, Standard & Poor's, and Value Line.
Lockheed Information Systems	The largest bibilographic distributor, offering over 75 different data banks in: Agriculture, Business, Economics, Education, Energy, Engineering, Environment, Foundations, General News Publications, Government, International Business, Patents, Pharmaceuticals, Science and Social Sciences. Its economic source is Predicasts Terminal Systems, Inc.; it relies on many trade associations and governmental groups for other data bases.
National CSS	A financial vendor of computational data banks covering: Autos, Commodities, Economics and Finance. Its main suppliers are Merrill Lynch Economics and Value Line.
Rapidata	A statistical data-bank vendor covering: Economics and Finance. Rapidata compiles some of its own data banks, and uses Citibank, Telrate and the Federal Reserve Board as additional suppliers.
SDC Search Service	One of the largest bibliographic distributors, offering over 50 different data banks in: Agriculture, Business, Education, Energy, Engineering, Environment, Foundations, General News Publications, Government, Industry, Science and Social Science. Its suppliers are various trade associations and governmental groups.
Service Bureau Co.	A statistical data-bank distributor covering: Agriculture, Banking, Demographics, Economics, Engineering, Finance and Insurance. Its suppliers include Standard & Poor's, Data Resources, Inc., and Telstat.

Source: Donna S. Stein, "Data Banks: How to Know Everything," *Output*, June 1980, pp. 66–67.

availability of fast and high capacity direct-access storage devices, and the use of powerful data base management systems which greatly facilitate the control and use of data bases. Thus the integrated nature of common data bases stored on direct-access storage devices and the use of DBMS software provides computer users with easy access to specific information derived from manipulating the data in an updated data base. Updating and maintaining the data base, producing documents and reports required by various user application programs, and responding to user inquiries, all require access and search of an organization's data bases and are easily handled by modern data base processing systems. Even **external data bases** provided by time sharing companies and other data base service organizations can be accessed by data base processing systems to obtain external data needed by management. See Figure 11–11.

The data base processing capability of most benefit to ordinary end users is the **query language** feature which reduces their reliance on information provided by periodic reports produced by a traditional EDP system. (We discussed this DBMS feature in Chapters 5 and 8.) Managers and other computer users do not have to write complete programs in order to easily obtain immediate responses to spontaneous inquiries concerning the operations and management of their organization. Instead, they can key in a few short statements on a computer terminal using a simple, English-like query language provided by most data base management systems. For example, a request by a sales manager for the amount of sales made by a particular salesperson might take the following form on a video display terminal:

A realtime data base management system would respond almost instantly to such an ad hoc inquiry by providing the sales manager with the requested information:

CURRENT SALES
FOR J. THOMPSON IS
$372,516

Advantages and Disadvantages

Several advantages of data base processing systems have already been mentioned. Data base processing systems reduce the duplication of data and integrate data so it can be accessed by multiple programs and users. Programs are not dependent on the format of data and the type of secondary storage hardware being used. Users are provided with an inquiry/response capability which allows them to easily obtain information they need without having to write computer programs. Computer programming is simplified because programs are not dependent on either the logical format of data or its physical storage location. Finally, control and security of the data stored in data bases is significantly increased since all access to data is controlled by the data base management system.

Disadvantages and limitations of data base processing systems arise from the increased complexity of the data base concept. Developing a data base and installing a DBMS can be difficult and expensive. More hardware capability is required since storage requirements for the organization's data, *overhead control data*, and the DBMS programs are greater. Finally, if an organization relies on one central data base, its vulnerability to errors and failures is increased.

In most cases, the benefits of data base processing systems far outweigh their limitations. Data base processing systems increase the productivity of users by providing information more efficiently and effectively than file processing systems. Users can more easily get the data they need in less time using the data base approach. Thus the use of data base processing is increasing in modern information processing systems.

SECTION III: WORD PROCESSING SYSTEMS

Word processing is the automation of the transformation of ideas and information into a readable form of communication. It involves the manipulation of characters, words, sentences, and paragraphs in order to produce office communications in the form of letters, memos, messages, documents, and reports. **Word processing systems** are information processing systems which rely on automated and computerized typing, dictation, copying, filing, and telecommunication systems that are used in many offices and other work areas of modern organizations. Word processing systems are a primary component of *office automation* in which the application of computer and communications technology to most office activities is supposed to result in the development of the **automated office,** also known as the *electronic office* or *office of the future.*

Word processing began with the automation of typing activities. One of the first major developments was the introduction of the IBM magnetic tape selectric tape typewriter (MTST) in 1964. It had electronic circuitry and used magnetic tape to store what was being typed. Changes could be made electronically without retyping and the finished copy could be typed automatically on paper. Other automatic typewriter systems began to appear, including some which used CRT units to display keyed-in material so it could be visually edited before typing a final copy. Finally, *electronic typewriters* with video displays, computerized features, and even telecommunications capabilities were developed. Today, many **word processors** are full fledged minicomputers or computer terminals although there is still a big market for "dumb" *electric* typewriters and "smart" *electronic* typewriters which are not full fledged computers.

Word Processing as a System

Like data processing, the activities of work processing can be viewed as a *system* of input, processing, output, storage, and control components. This is illustrated in Figure 11–12 and outlined below.

- **Input** activities include the *creation* or *origination* of ideas expressed in words—by writing on paper or by using the keyboard of the typewriter/word processor. One may also dictate ideas to a secretary who records them in *shorthand* coding, or more commonly by speaking into *dictation* equipment which records spoken words on magnetic media.

CONTROL

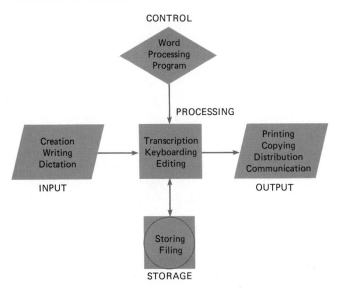

PROCESSING

INPUT

OUTPUT

STORAGE

FIGURE 11–12   Word
Processing System Concept

Some word processing systems use remote, pooled dictation in which users dial a central transcription service and dictate into a magnetic recorder by telephone. One technology that is being introduced to automate word processing input is the use of OCR (Optical Character Recognition) devices that can read typewritten text material and convert it into electronic input and enter it into the word processing CPU. Thus the printed paper output of ordinary typewriters and computer printers promises to be another source of automated input for word processing systems.

- **Processing** activities include the *transcription* (conversion) of words recorded on written material or magnetic media using the keyboard of the typewriter/word processor. This *keyboarding* activity converts words into electronic impulses in the circuitry of the word processor, records them on electronic media such as floppy disks and simultaneously displays them on a CRT screen. At this point, the *editing* activity is performed in which the displayed material is visually checked or proofed by the operator or electronically proofed by the word processor and corrections and other changes are made. Errors can be corrected by electronically typing over the error, and characters, words, sentences, paragraphs, and pages can be inserted, moved around, and deleted.

Automatic *text editing* includes a *global editing* feature which searches through the entire recorded text material for a particular word or phrase and allows the operator to automatically correct or replace it wherever it is used in the text material. For example, every occurrence of a particular word or phrase can be changed automatically throughout an entire document with a single instruction from the operator. Some word processors also include a *spelling dictionary* to automatically correct the spelling of all words in the typed material. For example, the IBM Displaywriter has a 50,000-word spelling dictionary which checks for misspelled words by comparing words being keyed against the dictionary and highlighting them on the video display so they can be corrected by the operator. Some word processors even include multilingual dictionaries which can be used to help translate from one language to another!

Other *text processing* activities include the automatic typing of letters and documents according to a predetermined format. The word processor stops at predetermined places for the manual or electronic insertion of variable information such as names and addresses on a *form letter* sent to a firm's customers. Standard phrases and paragraphs (nicknamed *boilerplate*) stored on floppy disks are retrieved and automatically typed. The operator then inserts names, dates, and other information at appropriate points in the text to produce form letters, legal documents, and all types of reports. Text processing also includes *hyphenation,* which automatically hyphenates words and adjusts word spacing and line endings, as well as many other features, such as automatic margins, spacing and indentation.

Advanced word processing systems include *list processing* capabilities which allow long mailing lists of names and addresses (and other lists) to be automatically merged with previously created standard text (such as form letters). They also may include a built-in math program package which lets the operator do on-the-spot arithmetic calculations on data as it is entered into the system and inserts the resulting figures in the appropriate spot on the document being typed.

- **Storage** activities include (1) *storing* typed material on magnetic floppy diskettes for temporary storage before printing, and (2) *filing* which involves storing material in a structured and organized manner so that it can be retrieved easily when needed. For example, the typed material might be given a *document number* which describes the location of the *physical file* where it will be stored (typically on magnetic media) and describes it as a *record* which can be stored *(filed)* by subject matter, title, author, document category, or other descriptive or identifying characteristic.

The storage and retrieval of office records is called **records processing** or *records management* and allows a typed document to be stored and retrieved under several different categories as if there were several copies stored in multiple files. Some word processing systems use **micrographics** equipment which can store a microfilm (or microfiche) copy of a document, display a full-size image on a screen, prepare a full-size paper copy, and transmit an electronic image to another terminal in the word processing system. Micrographic media are frequently used for long term *archival* storage.

- **Control.** All word processing activities are directed by a word processing program residing in the main memory of the word processor. However, the logic of some control and processing functions can be *hardwired* in the electronic circuitry of the processor, or be stored as *firmware* in ROM modules. Word processing software is usually stored in secondary storage such as floppy disks and other magnetic media until it is needed for processing. A great number of word processing software packages are available for word processors as well as general-purpose microcomputers, minicomputers, and full-size computer systems.

- **Output** activities involve printing the typed material on paper and transmitting it or an electronic image to a recipient or destination. This may involve making copies of the material, either electronically or on paper using copying machines. Paper copies can be physically distributed to several persons or communicated in electronic form over telecommunications lines to other word processing or computer terminals as a form of *electronic mail.*

Figures 11–13 and 11–14 illustrate many word processing activities. These figures show how a personnel department responds to inquiries concerning employment opportunities with a personal letter composed of variable information and standard paragraphs. The following word processing activities take place:

1. A member of the personnel department (called the *principal*) dictates a listing of names and addresses of persons applying for employment and also indicates the appropriate standards paragraphs which should be selected from those stored in the system.

FIGURE 11-13 Steps in a
Word Processing Application

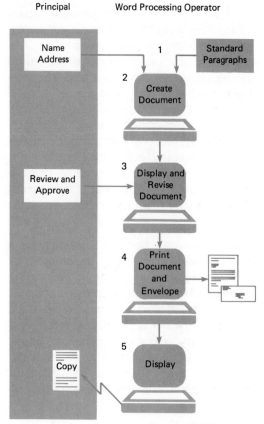

Courtesy IBM Corporation.

2. The word processing *operator* creates a *document* (letter) from the variable information and the chosen standard paragraphs.

3. If this was a more complex document, the operator could visually and electronically proof the letter, print out a *draft copy* for the principal to review and approve, and make all necessary revisions electronically.

4. A personalized letter and an envelope are printed for each applicant. (If an *electronic mail* system was in use, an electronic version of the letter could be sent to each applicant!)

5. A copy of each letter is transmitted to the word processing terminal of the personnel department which can electronically store the letter on a magnetic disk file, print a paper copy if requested, or electronically store and display a short message that tells the principal that this particular letter was sent.

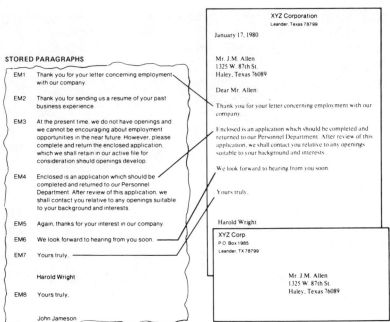

Courtesy IBM Corporation.

FIGURE 11–14 A Personalized Letter Produced by Word Processing

Types of Word Processing Systems

The hardware of a typical word processing system is pictured in Figure 11–15. Notice that a CRT terminal serves as the **work station** and is electronically connected to a CPU. The visual display unit may be larger than many CRT units so that it can display a full page (8½ x 11 inches or larger) of text. Floppy disks are used for secondary storage. Typically, a floppy disk unit with at least two disk drives is included, so that one floppy disk contains the word processing programs and space for documents that are currently being processed, while the second disk holds documents recorded for storage. Floppy disks can hold over 120 pages of typed material. Large capacity and more expensive hard disk cartridges can also be used, and can hold over a thousand pages of documents.

Word processing systems typically include a *letter quality* printer which provides better quality printing than most printing terminals or high-speed computer printers. *Daisy wheel* or *dot matrix* printing elements in a variety of print styles are often used. Larger word processing systems may use an *inkjet printer* or an **intelligent copier** as output devices. These copying machines use microprocessor intelligence and can

FIGURE 11-15   A Word Processing System: The IBM Displaywriter

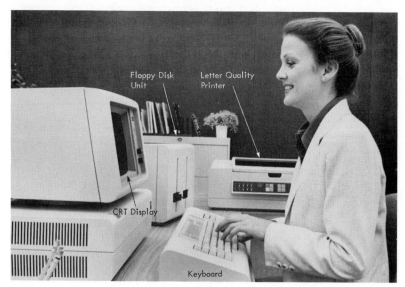

Courtesy IBM Corporation.

be linked by communication lines to the CPU and terminals of a word processing system. Thus, though they can still make copies from paper documents, they also provide a **facsimile** capability since they can receive documents electronically from word processing terminals and print them on paper in multiple copies.

There are five major categories of computerized word processing systems.

- **Intelligent Electronic Typewriters.** These smart typewriters use microprocessors to perform many basic word processing functions at a lower cost than full-fledged computerized word processors. They can have built-in electronic memory, small video *minidisplays*, and even built-in minidiskette drives. Intelligent typewriters are typically priced from $2,000 to $3,000.

- **Stand-Alone Word Processors** consist of a keyboard, CRT screen, floppy disk or hard disk storage, and a printer. Stand-alone word processing systems sell for between $5,000 to $15,000 depending on the capabilities required. It should be emphasized that most microcomputer and minicomputer systems (including personal computers and small business computers) can act as word processing computers when they use readily available word processing program packages.

- **Shared Logic Systems** consist of several CRT terminals which share the processing power and storage capacity of a minicomputer. These minicomputer systems include printers for hard copy output and magnetic disk units for secondary storage, and are quite similar to the key-to-disk data entry computer systems used in electronic data processing.

- **Distributed Processing Systems** use intelligent terminals as word processing *work stations* which are part of a distributed local network in a large building or other large work site. The work stations are essentially small minicomputers that are part of a distributed processing network which includes a *host computer* which can act as a communications control processor (a *switch*), or can be a powerful host processor using a variety of software packages to manage the workload, communications, peripherals and file storage systems of the network.

- **Time-Sharing Systems** consist of computer terminals connected by telecommunications lines to a central computer which has word processing software as well as programs for other applications. Many users can share the computer at the same time for both word processing and data processing jobs. Thus any computer system with data communications and time-sharing capabilities can use word processing program packages to provide word processing services to its users.

Figure 11–16 illustrates a word processing system in a large office building which combines the features of shared logic and time-sharing systems. The number of word processing computers and terminals is expected to grow rapidly during the 1980s. However, many experts predict that most will eventually be replaced by general-purpose computer systems and terminals which can integrate both *word processing* and *data processing*. These predictions seem accurate since word processing software packages are now readily available for most microcomputer, minicomputer and full-sized computer systems.

Advantages and Disadvantages

Word processing systems significantly improve the simplicity and efficiency of typing and other written office communication processes. Correcting errors and making revisions and changes no longer mean long hours of mechanically typing the same text over and over again. Word processing makes

FIGURE 11–16 A Word Processing System with Shared Logic and Time-Sharing Features

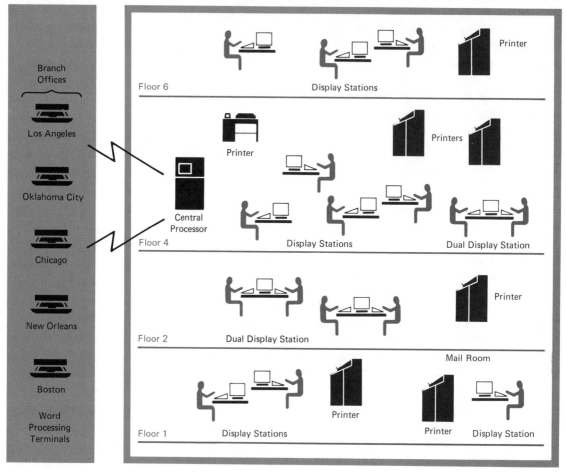

Courtesy IBM Corporation.

it easy to correct typographical errors, make changes and revisions, and automatically type standard paragraphs and pages while allowing insertion of variable information. Studies have shown that word processing reduces typing time by about 50 percent. This allows growth in typing work loads to be handled by fewer typists and frees secretaries for more productive work. Besides improving typing productivity, word processing has also upgraded the quality of the typing task by reducing the drudgery in error correction, revisions, proofing, and typing long sections of standard text material. In addition, word processing can increase the productivity of executives and other "knowledge workers" by significantly reducing the time and effort needed to produce, access, and receive office communications. In summary, word processing can:

- Increase the productivity of secretarial personnel and reduce the costs of creating, reviewing, revising, and distributing written office communications.
- Shorten the turnaround time between the preparation and receipt of a document by moving information quickly and efficiently to the people who need it.
- Reduce the frustration, expense, and errors involved in typing or retyping variable or standard text material.
- Store, retrieve, and transmit documents and other written office communications quickly and efficiently.
- Increase the productivity of executives and professionals who are heavy users of office communications.

Of course, all of these advantages are not acquired without some negative effects. First, the cost of word processing hardware is significantly higher than the equipment it replaces. Another limitation is less obvious. Word processing disrupts traditional office work roles and work environments. For example, some word processing systems have caused employee dissatisfaction by giving some secretaries nothing but typing to do, while removing typing duties completely from other secretaries, and eliminating private secretaries for some executives. Problems such as these must be overcome in order to increase the economy and efficiency of word processing systems and their extension into other forms of office automation.

Automated Office Systems

Word processing systems are the forerunner of other automated office systems which many experts predict will lead to the *automated office,* the *electronic office* or the *office-of-the-future.* Word processing systems will be joined by a number of major automated systems which combine word processing, data processing, telecommunications, and information systems technologies. These systems will develop computerized *administrative work stations* and *management work stations* in the office and other work places. Figure 11–17 illustrates some of the important components of automated office systems. A brief outline of the major systems which will be integrated in future automated office systems include:

- **Advanced word processing systems** include communicating word processors and the interconnection of intelligent office machines such as intelligent copiers, printers, micrographics systems, OCR systems, and photocomposition systems.
- **Electronic mail and message systems** allow for the transmission and distribution of text material in electronic form over computerized data and communication networks. This practice would drastically reduce the present flow of paper messages, letters, memos, documents, and reports which flood our present interoffice and postal systems. Voice and video message systems will be another part of this development.
- **Electronic audio/visual systems** will make heavy use of communications satellite systems for electronic facsimile (printed

FIGURE 11–17 Major Components of Automated Office Systems

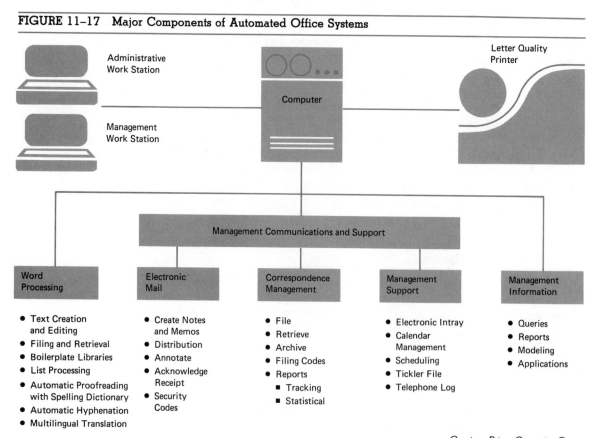

Courtesy Prime Computer Corp.

image) transmission, but more importantly for **teleconferenc-ing** which integrates video and voice communications so that geographically separated users can conduct ordinary business meetings.

- **Office support systems** will provide support services to managers such as electronic calendars, scheduling, *tickler files*, telephone logs, and even an *electronic intray*.

Figure 11–18 illustrates how the Exxon Corporation has invested in subsidiary firms which are developing products needed by the office of the future.

Other computer-based information systems which serve businesses and other organizations as well as homes and individuals will interface with these automated office systems. This will significantly affect the environment of the office and work place. The term **enterprise systems** has been used to describe a systems concept that merges electronic data processing, automated office systems, telecommunications systems, management information systems, and other computer-based information systems. The additional major information systems that would be involved are:

- **Electronic information service systems** will provide information in audio/visual, text, and image form, using electronic audio/visual and micrographic data bases and time-sharing public networks. Computer terminals in homes, businesses, and other locations will be connected to this network.

- **Electronic transaction systems** include computer-based transaction processing and communications systems such as point-of-sale systems and other electronic funds transfer (EFT) systems, pay-by-phone systems, banking transfer systems, credit checking systems, and so forth.

- **Management information and decision support systems** which use computer-based telecommunications, data base, and decision model systems to provide managers with both structured information and interactive information to support their decision making on a realtime basis.

Many of the components of the automated office systems mentioned above are *technically* and *economically* feasible for larger business firms and organizations. It is only a matter of time before further technological developments will lower costs so automated office systems become economically feasible for many business firms and organizations. Technologi-

374

FIGURE 11–18 The Pieces Exxon Is Assembling for the Office of the Future

The pieces Exxon is assembling for the office of the future

WORD PROCESSOR

Vydec: The first Exxon venture in information to launch a product, in 1973, it took an early lead with its word processor coupled to a display screen. But new products have not kept pace

MICROPROCESSOR

Zilog: Started in 1974 with Exxon backing, it has become a major competitor in microprocessors, with 1979 sales of $25 million—double the previous year's

VOICE-TO-DATA TRANSLATOR

Dialog Systems: It enjoys a unique marketing niche with a system to translate spoken words into data to flow over normal telephone lines, developed since a 1971 startup

VOICE SYNTHESIZER

Periphonics: Funded in 1971 and 100% acquired in 1980, it builds voice-response systems that store a vocabulary in code and make it possible for a computer to respond to users

TELEPHONE FACSIMILE

Qwip Systems: A low-cost model propelled it to No. 1 in 1979 shipments from a 1973 start as an in-house project. A new unit, more expensive but easier to use, is aimed at the executive's desk

'VERBAL TELEGRAPH'

Delphi Communications: Its products include a redundant-computer system and a telephone answering-switching system. It is expected to use its computer to transmit and deliver synthesized voice messages. First funding: 1974

INTELLIGENT TYPEWRITER

Qyx: A head-to-head rival of IBM, it has a modular line ranging from an electronic typewriter to a communicating word processor. It was the fastest growing Exxon venture last year but reportedly lost millions

DATA TRANSMITTER

Optical Information Systems: Started by Exxon in 1977, it builds semiconductor lasers that will be used to transmit data over optical fiber networks

SWITCHING NETWORK

InteCom: This company, first funded in 1979, is expected to announce its first product this year: a switching network for both voice and data to connect all the Exxon products for the office

Ventures that will add future products (now in research and development)

| Summit: Micro-computer systems | Xonex: An advanced work station capable of word and data processing, accessing a data base, and electronic filing and mail | Danbury Systems: A high-resolution ink-jet printer capable of receiving facsimile transmission | EPID: A low-cost, flat-panel display to replace cathode-ray tubes | Magnex: Thin-film recording heads that will allow much more data to be stored, more cheaply, on such devices as magnetic disks | Star Systems: New devices for storing data |

cal and economic feasibility affect the *environmental, communication,* and *processing* factors as illustrated in Figure 11–19. However, the primary *management* and *people* factors shown in Figure 11–19 are the major limitations to the attainment of *operational feasibility* for the integrated electronic office. This means that much more research and development needs to be done before managers and other employees will accept and cooperate with a technology that significantly changes their work roles, processes, and environment. Only then will the promises of increased productivity, improved decision making, and job satisfaction be fulfilled.

FIGURE 11–19   Development Issues in the Integrated Electronic Office

Management Factors
- System Economics
- Management Planning Support
- Management Monitoring Support
- Management Control Support
- Positive Personal I.D.
- Impact on Organization
- Impact on Pace of Change

Environment Factors
- Space Planning
- Aesthetics
- Access to Electronics for Maintenance
- System Power Availability/ Consumption
- Power Protection
- Heat Dissipation
- Noise Control
- Physical Security

Communication Factors
- Channel and Switch Loading
- Data Transmission Protocols
- Code Selection
- Text File Transmission Protocols
- Data Compression
- Directory Maintenance
- Line Security

People Factors
- Ergonomics
- Fatigue
- Adaptation
- Isolation/Socialization
- Job Enrichment/Job Content Change
- Privacy
- Pace of Information Flow

Processing Factors
- Word Processing
- Graphics
- Calculation and Computation
- Remote Processor Links
- Local Applications
- Archival Filing and Retrieval
- Reliability and Back-up
- Media Conversion
- Data Security and Confidentiality
- Software Updates and Maintenance

Source: Robert B. White, "A Prototype of the Automated Office," *Datamation*, April 1977, p. 88. Reprinted with permission of *Datamation* magazine. Copyright by Technical Publishing Company, a Dun & Bradstreet Company, 1977; all rights reserved.

MULTISYSTEM INFORMATION PROCESSING

We shall conclude this chapter by stressing the concept of *multisystem information processing*. We have discussed many different types and levels of information processing systems in the last three chapters. This multisystem diversity is the cause of some of the confusion concerning the use of computers. However, such diversity is really the key to the

FIGURE 11–20 Multisystem Information Processing

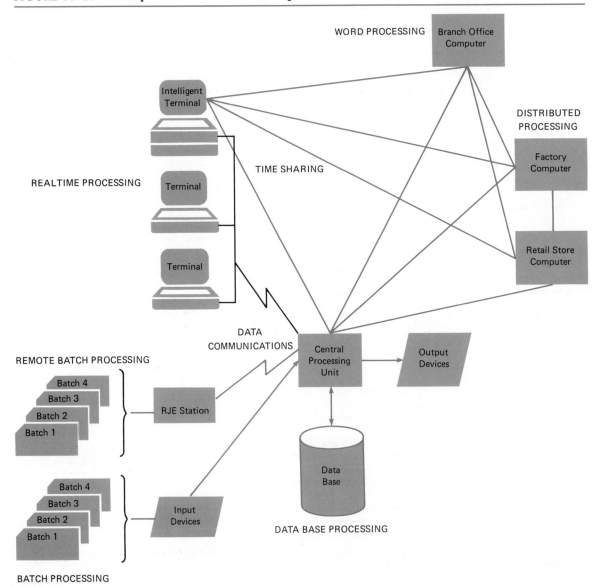

amazing versatility of the computer and the wide range of problems that it can handle. Therefore modern information processing must be understood in a multisystem context; that is, that several varieties of information processing systems may be needed to meet the information requirements of an organization.

Figure 11–20 illustrates the concept of multisystem information processing. It reveals an information processing environment composed of several types of systems, including batch processing, remote batch processing, realtime processing, time sharing, distributed processing, data communications, data base processing, and word processing systems. Multisystem information processing is a concept that is being implemented in the information processing systems of many computer-using organizations.

SUMMARY

- Modern information processing systems use distributed processing systems, data processing systems, and word processing systems to integrate data processing and word processing with the help of advanced telecommunications systems.

- Distributed processing is a new form of decentralization of information processing made possible by a network of computers dispersed throughout an organization. Processing of user applications is accomplished by several computers interconnected by a data communications network, rather than relying on one large centralized computer facility, or on the decentralized operation of several completely independent computers. Distributed data processing constitutes a system of user department and headquarters computers which are interconnected by a data communications network, integrated by a common data base-oriented approach, and coordinated by an organization-wide information resource management philosophy.

- The two basic types of distributed processing networks are the star network and the ring network. Distributed data processing systems are found in six major application areas: (1) distributed data processing, (2) central site processing, (3) distributed data entry, (4) distributed data base processing, (5) distributed word processing, and (6) distributed communications networks. Distributed processing systems can reduce communication costs, improve response time, minimize input errors, and improve user productivity. Computer reliability and availability are improved, and there is a reduction in user pressure on the central computer installation and of the flow of paper work between users and corporate headquarters. However, building a complete distributed processing network for an organization is a complex task. It requires significant additional planning and controls by both corporate and user management.

- For many years, electronic data processing had a file processing orientation in which separate computer programs were used to update independent data files and produce the documents and reports required by each user application. This caused problems of data redundancy, unintegrated data, and program/data dependence. The concepts of data bases and data base processing were developed to solve these problems. Data base processing systems use a data base orientation for both the storage and processing of data. The data needed by different data processing applications is consolidated and integrated into several common data bases instead of being stored in many independent data files. Also, electronic data processing consists of updating and maintaining a common data base, having users application programs share the data in the data base, and providing an inquiry/response capability so users can easily receive quick responses to requests for information from the data base.

- Developing a data base is a complex task, which is the responsibility of users, programmers, systems analysts, and the data base administrator. The schema or structure of the logical relationships between data elements in the data base must be developed, as well as the subschema which is a subset of the schema required for a particular user application. Developing distributed data bases requires tradeoffs between service to users, processing and communications costs, and processing performance and control. Security of the data stored in data bases can be significantly improved. However, vulnerability to errors and failures may be increased unless stringent controls and security are developed.

- Word processing automates the transformation of ideas and information into readable forms of communication, such as let-

ters, memos, messages, documents, and reports. Word processing systems are information processing systems which rely on automated and computerized typing, dictation, copying, filing, and telecommunication systems. The activities of word processing can be viewed as a system of input, processing, output, storage, and control components. Ideas are expressed in words and recorded (input); keyed into a word processor (processing); stored and filed electronically, or on magnetic, micrographic, or paper media (storage); under the direction of a word processing program (control); and communicated electronically or on paper to a recipient (output).

- The five major types of computerized word processing systems include intelligent electronic typewriters, stand-alone word processors, shared logic systems, distributed processing systems, and time-sharing systems. Word processing systems increase the productivity of secretarial personnel and reduce the costs of written office communications. They shorten the turnaround time between the preparation and receipt of a document, reduce the expense and errors involved in typing standard text material, and increase the productivity of executives and professionals who are heavy users of office communications. However, the cost of word processing hardware is significantly higher than the equipment it replaces, and word processing may disrupt traditional office work roles and work environments.

- Automated office systems combine word processing, data processing, telecommunications, and information systems technologies to develop computerized administrative and management work stations in the office and other work places. The automated office systems that are being developed will include advanced word processing systems, electronic mail and message systems, electronic audio/visual systems, and advanced office support systems. Other computer-based information systems will interface with automated office systems to produce enterprise systems which will include electronic information service systems, electronic transaction systems, and management information and decision support systems.

- The different types, levels, and capabilities of modern information processing systems must be understood in a multisystem context. Many different types of data and information processing systems may be required to meet the information needs of an organization.

KEY TERMS AND CONCEPTS

Distributed processing	Distributed data bases
Data base processing	Word processing system
Word processing	Word processors
Information processing	Automated office systems
Star and ring networks	Electronic mail
Schema, subschema	Multisystem information processing

REVIEW AND DISCUSSION QUESTIONS

1. How are modern information processing systems related to data processing and word processing systems? Do you think that the trend toward the integration of the transmitting and processing of data, words, images, and voices will continue into the future?

2. What is distributed processing? How does it differ from centralized data processing? From traditional decentralized data processing?

3. Why did the trend toward distributed data processing develop? Do you expect this trend to continue? Why or why not?

4. What are the major types of distributed processing networks? What are their advantages and disadvantages?

5. What are several major types of distributed processing applications? Use examples to illustrate how these applications use the distributed processing concept.

6. What are several advantages and disadvantages of the distributed processing approach? Do you expect the trend toward distributed processing to continue?

7. "Problems arising from the use of distributed processing systems can be solved if managing information processing functions and resources is made a major responsibility of the managers of user departments." Do you agree with this statement? Why or why not?

8. What are data base processing systems? Are they superior to file processing systems? Explain.

9. Explain how data base processing systems use a data base approach for both the storage and processing of data.

10. What are a schema and subschema? What role do they play in the development of a data base?

11. Should data bases be centralized or distributed? Explain.

12. What data base processing capability is of most benefit to ordinary end users? Use an example to substantiate your answer. What are several advantages and disadvantages of data base processing systems? Do the benefits of data base processing outweigh its limitations? Explain.

13. What is word processing? How has the computer become involved in word processing systems?

14. What are the major functions and components of a word processing system? How do these system functions differ from those of a data processing system?

15. What are the major types of word processing systems? Select one of these systems and explain which type of office could best use its capabilities.

16. What are some of the advantages and disadvantages of word processing? What solutions do you have for some of the problems arising from word processing systems?

17. What capabilities will be available in automated office systems? Do you think that electronic mail and teleconferencing can be cost-justified in present business organizations?

18. Do you believe that the enterprise sytems concept which merges electronic data processing, automated office systems, telecommunications, management information systems, and other computer-based information systems will become a reality? Explain.

19. What is meant by the concept of multisystem information processing? Does this concept represent a typical approach found in many computer using organizations?

REAL WORLD APPLICATIONS

11–1 Hewlett-Packard Company

Most Hewlett-Packard North American manufacturing plants and regional offices have HP 3000s to handle their local data processing needs, reducing the burden on the company's central computers. Major offices are linked with HP headquarters in Palo Alto by computer based communications systems. These are powerful enough to give the smaller sales offices plenty of EDP capability for such things as order processing and maintaining customer files.

In Brazil, the Campinas manufacturing plant is linked by computer to the main office in Sao Paulo. This in turn communicates with headquarters in California. Sales offices in Venezuela and Mexico have computer-based communications systems with sufficient computer power to handle local accounting and inventory management.

Most data from Europe is funneled through the European headquarters in Geneva. Data from sales

11–1 *(continued)*

offices is generally "queued" in the Geneva computers, waiting for the twice daily call from the United States. All three manufacturing facilities in France, Germany, and Scotland also use HP computers for accounting, order processing, management information, and the like.

The two major factories in Southeast Asia (more than 2000 people), reduce communications costs by linking the Penang plant with the Singapore facility. Here data is consolidated for transmission to the U.S. Accounting, payroll and inventory is handled locally by HP computers. A similar situation exists in Japan, with the plant in Hachioji connected with the main sales office in Tokyo. In Australia and New Zealand, HP sales offices are equipped with computers for both local data processing and long distance communications.[1]

- Would you say that Hewlett-Packard has a worldwide distributed processing network? Explain.
- What are the benefits and limitations of this approach?

[1] Source: Courtesy Hewlett-Packard.

11–2 **The Veterans Administration**

The Veterans Administration is the largest independent agency of the United States Government, providing service to 30 million veterans and their families. In one year alone, the portion of the VA responsible for compensation, pensions and educational benefits will disburse over 14 billion dollars. One would expect an operation this big to be a bureaucratic nightmare. But the truth is it runs like clockwork. A Honeywell distributed processing system with a data-base orientation provides instant control of the work flow and nearly 15 million records. Online access now enables VA people to answer in seconds questions that once took weeks. As a result of this new system, the efficiency with which veterans receive their benefits has been enhanced. And taxpayers are saving millions.

The VA's data base oriented, distributed processing system is called TARGET. And it includes four Honeywell large-scale host computers, 100 small computers, 3,000 terminals, and 800 printers.

Naturally, the system is spread throughout the country, operating in 57 cities in the United States. There are data bases in Chicago and Austin, and regional data processing centers are located in Philadelphia, Chicago and Los Angeles. But from the user's point of view, it's all a single system with a single data base. The VA wants to protect its data base. And sophisticated Honeywell security technology is doing the job.

A veteran's file stored in Chicago can be on a CRT in Miami faster than Claims Developers could pull it from a stack on their desks. Providing quick, uncomplicated service is TARGET's prime function. Currently, the system is processing 200,000 complex transactions a day. Response time per transaction? A few seconds. TARGET was designed this way so veterans could be served quickly and easily from whatever VA regional office they walk into.[2]

- Is the VA's TARGET system a distributed processing system? A data base processing system? Explain.
- Do you agree that TARGET is the best approach for the VA? Explain.

[2] Source: Courtesy Honeywell Information Systems.

11-3 Eastman Kodak

At Eastman Kodak's Rochester headquarters, word processing equipment is helping to streamline the time-consuming job of text preparation and is providing for significant increases in the volume of work completed, without significant increases in labor.

Kodak's Central Correspondence and Reprographics Department (CC&R) is currently using multiple word processing systems from Wang Laboratories, Inc. Yet, the word processing equipment has been in application at Kodak's corporate headquarters since the 1940s when typing devices which utilized paper tape were installed in the central correspondence area to supplement the existing typing staff and help automate the work flow. Magnetic media typing equipment with more sophisticated editing capabilities was installed during the late 1960s.

In late 1976, a study was undertaken to review the editing and typing needs in the CC&R Department. Although the whole range of potential solutions to the text-editing problem was studied, three basic approaches to word processing were scrutinized most carefully: "stand-alone" systems, the broad range of shared-logic systems, and large-scale, computerized, text-editing systems.

The feasibility study ruled out the stand-alone approach as offering little more text-editing flexibility than the magnetic media equipment. Large-scale, computerized systems could not be justified in terms of the hardware support and software development required for such an operation. Shared-resource, multiterminal systems, the study reasoned, seemed best suited to handle Kodak's immediate applications because of their self-contained power, modularity, and flexibility. Numerous minicomputer-based, multiterminal systems were investigated by the study group. Of the units judged appropriate to handle Kodak's applications, three Wang word processing systems were recommended as the best-suited.

The Central Correspondence and Reprographics Department is currently using one Wang System 20 and one Wang System 30. The System 20 supports one CRT-based workstation. The System 30 supports seven workstations and three daisy wheel printers. A Wang System 10A has also been installed as an offline editing station for use by the Business and Technical Personnel Department.

Another System 10A is being used by the Business Systems Markets Division (BSMD), one of the six markets divisions within the Kodak organization. Storage of data on the 10A and the larger Wang System 20 word processing systems is on floppy diskettes, while the Wang System 30 uses a larger-capacity fixed disk. Thus, BSMD often will use the three daisy wheel printers in the CCR Department to prepare documents it has "stacked up" in a background mode on System 10A disks. This playout process is typically done at night, unattended.[3]

- How does the capabilities of Eastman Kodak's present word processing system compare to what they have used in the past? To the other two basic WP approaches they considered?
- Identify each of the basic system components in Kodak's word processing system.

[3] Source: *Word Processing—At Kodak*, Wang Laboratories, Inc.

Computer Applications and Information Systems in Business

12

CHAPTER OUTLINE

Management Information and Decision Support Systems

LEARNING OBJECTIVES

The purpose of this chapter is to promote a basic understanding of the role of management information and decision support systems by analyzing (1) the business firm as a system, (2) the information requirements of the business firm and its management, (3) the role of management information and decision support systems, and (4) the trends in business applications and information systems.

After reading and studying this chapter, you should be able to:

1. Identify the components of computer-based information systems.
2. Identify the functions of the basic subsystem components of the business firm as a system.
3. Explain how the information requirements of management are affected by *(a)* the functions of management, *(b)* programmed decisions, *(c)* management by exception, *(d)* levels of management, and *(e)* internal versus external information.
4. Identify the functions of the major components of a management information system, and discuss the reasons for the development of the MIS concept for computer use in business.
5. Explain the decision support system concept and how it differs from traditional operational and management information systems in the support of managerial decision making.
6. Discuss how and why information systems should be integrated.
7. Identify the trends in the growth of computer applications in business.

INFORMATION SYSTEMS

What is an *information system?* An information system is a system which uses personnel, operating procedures, and data processing subsystems to collect and process data and disseminate information in an organization. When such information systems make extensive use of computer hardware, software, data bases, personnel, and procedures, they are called *computer-based information systems.*

Figure 12–1 illustrates the components of modern computer-based information systems. Notice the following system components:

Input—Data, information requests and organizational resources are entered into the system.

FIGURE 12–1 Components of Computer-Based Information Systems

ORGANIZATION ENVIRONMENT

INFORMATION PROCESSING TECHNOLOGY

INPUTS

- Data
- Requests for Information
- Resources

HARDWARE   SOFTWARE

PERSONNEL

DATA BASE   PROCEDURES

OUTPUTS

- Transaction Processing (OIS)
- Management Reporting (MIS)
- Decision Support (DSS)
- Programmed Decisions (PDS)

INFORMATION RESOURCE MANAGEMENT

Feedback-Control for
- Efficiency
- Effectiveness

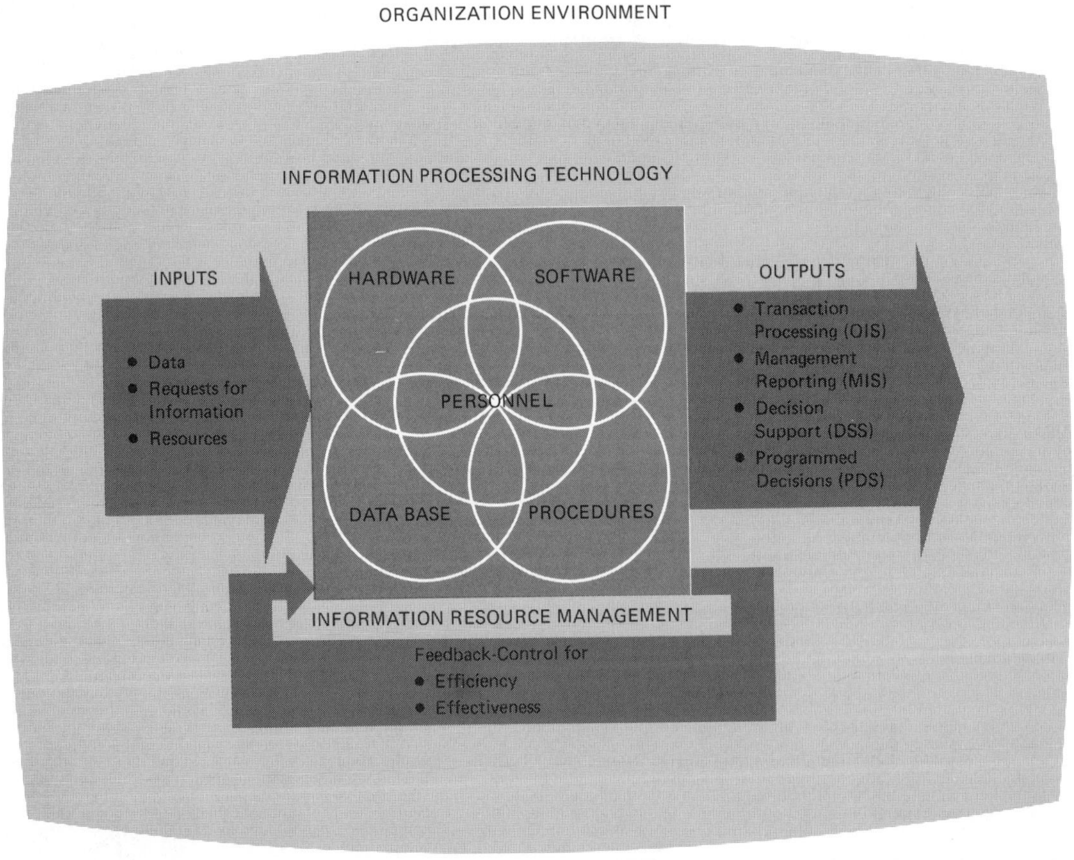

Source: Adapted and reprinted by special permission from the *MIS Quarterly,* from "Toward a Comprehensive Framework for MIS Research," by Richard L. Nolan and James C. Wetherbe, vol. 4, no. 2, published June 1980. Copyright by the Society for Management Information Systems and the Management Information Systems Research Center.

Processing—Information processing technology uses computer hardware, software, personnel, data bases, and procedures to convert inputs into outputs.

Output—Transaction processing is accomplished by *operational information systems* (OIS).

—Management reporting is accomplished by *management information systems* (MIS).

—Managerial decision support is accomplished by *decision support systems* (DSS).

—Automatic programmed decision making is accomplished by *programmed decision systems* (PDS).

Feedback and Control—The *information resource management* function monitors and adjusts information system performance for optimum efficiency and effectiveness.

In this chapter we will explore the various types of information systems mentioned above. Understanding such systems is necessary if you are to effectively use computers in business management.

THE BUSINESS FIRM AS A SYSTEM

It is important to understand management information and decision support systems in terms of their unique role in the business organization. However, this is not possible until we first learn to understand the business firm as a *system.*

There are many ways to view the business firm as a system. We can view the business firm as (1) a *social system* composed of people and their interrelationships, (2) an *information system* which relies on information to support decision making, (3) a *financial system* that emphasizes the flow of funds that occurs in the operation of a business, or (4) an *economic system* which utilizes economic resources to produce economic welfare. However, let us concentrate on a model of the business firm that emphasizes (1) the *feedback-control* nature of the business system, and (2) the *feedback-control* role played by management information and decision support systems within the business system.

Figure 12–2 illustrates the business firm as a *business system* which consists of interrelated components which must be controlled and coordinated toward the attainment of organizational goals such as profitability and social responsibility. In this simple model of the business system, *economic resources*

FIGURE 12–2   The Business
Firm as a System

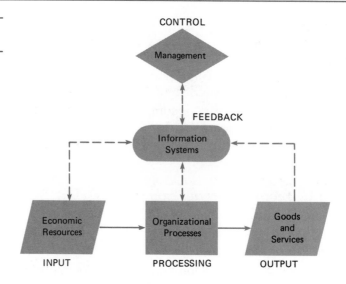

(input) are transformed by various *organizational processes* (processing) into *goods and services* (output). *Information systems* provide information on the operations of the system (feedback) to *management* for the direction and maintenance of the system (control).

We can also view the business firm as a subsystem of society, and as a system composed of several basic *subsystems*. Figure 12–3 illustrates these attributes of the business firm as a system. We should analyze the components of the *operational, information,* and *management* subsystems of the business firm and of the *business environment,* so that we can better understand the role of management information and decision support systems in business.

Operational Systems: Input—Processing—Output

The most basic components of the business firm are its *operational systems.* They constitute the input, processing, and output components of the business system as illustrated in Figure 12–3 and summarized below.

- *Input.* Employs people, money, material, machines, land, facilities, energy, and information.
- *Processing.* Utilizes various kinds of organizational processes, including production, marketing, finance, personnel, etc., known as the *"functions of business,"* and other pro-

FIGURE 12-3   The Business Firm as a System; Basic Subsystems, Components, and Environment

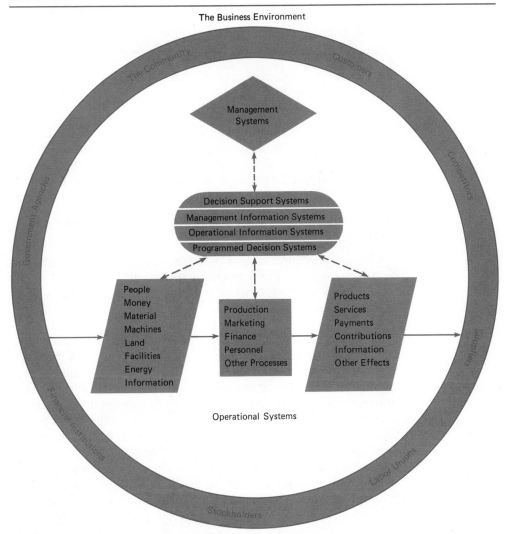

cesses that help transform input into output (such as engineering, research and development, and legal services).

- *Output.* Produces products, services, payments (such as employee benefits, dividends, interest, taxes, and payments to suppliers), contributions, information, and other effects.

The types of input, processing, and output utilized by operational systems depend on the particular business activities of each business firm. *For example,* one of the operational sys-

FIGURE 12–4 The Basic
Operational System of a
Manufacturing Firm

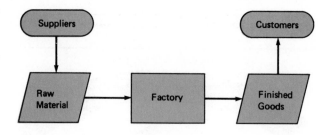

tems of an oil company would include the physical system
of oil fields, pipe lines, tankers, and refineries that transforms
oil into various petroleum products. The basic operational system of a manufacturing firm is shown in Figure 12–4.

Operational Information and Programmed Decision Systems: Feedback for Operations

Operational information systems (OIS) and *programmed
decision systems* (PDS) perform information *feedback* functions as well as producing information and decisions as *output*
of the business system.

An *operational information system* collects, processes, and
stores data generated by the operational systems of the business and produces data and information for *input* into a programmed decision or management information system. Programmed decision systems accept operational information
and produce decisions that *control* an operational process.
Operational information systems process data that is generated by business operations (sales transactions, production
results, employee payroll, etc.) but do not produce the kind
of information that can best be used by management. Further
processing by a management information system is usually
required. Figure 12–5 illustrates an integrated group of operational, programmed decision, and management information
systems for a manufacturing firm built upon a manufacturing
operational system.

Management Information and Decision Support Systems: Feedback for Management

Figure 12–3 showed that *management information systems*
(MIS) and *decision support systems* (DSS) play a vital *feedback* role in support of the management of a business firm.

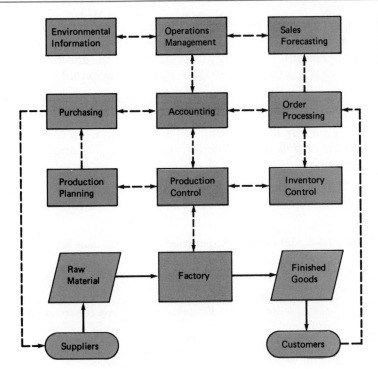

FIGURE 12-5 Selected Information Systems of a Manufacturing Firm

They refine the data and information provided by the *operational information systems* of the firm, gather information from the business environment, and provide structured and unstructured information to support management decision making.

Management Systems: Control of the Firm

Figure 12-3 showed that the *management systems* of a business firm constitute the *control* component of the business. The management of an organization can be viewed as a subsystem of managers at all organizational levels who are engaged in planning, organizing, staffing, directing, and controlling activities (called the *functions of management*) that control the operations of the business system.

The Business Environment: The Firm as a Subsystem

The business firm is a *subsystem* of society and is surrounded by the other systems of the *business environment*. Figure 12-3 showed that the business firm exchanges inputs and outputs with its environment. Such a system is called an "open system." In addition, the business firm is an "adaptive system," i.e., it has the ability to adjust to the demands of its environment. This is very important, for it means that a business firm can utilize its *feedback-control* component in two ways:

- It monitors and regulates its operations to achieve its predetermined goals.
- It monitors the environment and can change both its operations *and its goals* in order to survive in a changing environment.

The business firm must maintain proper interrelationships with the other economic, political, and social subsystems in

---

FIGURE 12–6 Information Requirements of the Business Environment

Customer Systems. Information systems should help the business firm understand what consumers want and why they want it, so *consumers* can be converted into *customers*. Such "marketing information systems" support marketing activities such as advertising, selling, pricing, distribution, product development, and market research.

Competitor Systems. Information systems must provide management with information on present and potential *competitors*, why they are competitors, and what their competitive activities are and will be. Such information helps management shape its competitive strategy.

Supplier Systems. *Suppliers* provide a business firm with goods and services. Information systems must support the purchasing function so that the business firm can minimize its purchasing cost and maximize the value of goods and services that it procures.

Labor Union Systems. Though employees are a vital component of the business firm they are frequently represented by an environmental system—the *labor union*. Information systems must provide management, employees, and labor unions with information on employee compensation and labor productivity within the firm and competing business systems.

Stockholder Systems. Though *stockholders* are the owners of business firms that are organized as corporations, they can be considered as an environmental system because many business firms are owned by many different and distant stockholders. Information systems must provide information concerning dividends and financial and operating performance to management and stockholders.

Financial Institution Systems. Financial institutions (such as banks) provide the business system with money, credit and various financial services. Information systems must provide management and financial institutions with information on the financial and operating performance of the firm, and the state of the financial markets.

Governmental Systems. Business firms are governed by laws and regulations of *government agencies* at the city, county, state, federal, and foreign government levels. The information systems of a business firm must supply a wide variety of information to various governmental agencies concerning many aspects of the operations of the firm. Management also needs information on political, legal, and legislative developments so that it can effectively deal with changes in laws and regulations.

Community Systems. The business firm resides in local, regional, national, and world *communities*. Information systems must provide the management of business firms with information concerning how well they are meeting their responsibilities as "good citizens" of these communities.

its environment, including customers, suppliers, competitors, stockholders, labor unions, financial institutions, governmental agencies, and the community. How *information systems* must be developed to help the business firm shape its relationships to each of these *environmental systems* is summarized in Figure 12–6.

INFORMATION REQUIREMENTS OF MANAGEMENT

The Functions of Management

Before we discuss the information requirements of management we should define what the term **management** means. Management is traditionally described as a process of leadership involving the functions of **planning, organizing, staffing, directing,** and **controlling.** These traditional functions can be used in response to the question, "What does a manager do?" A manager should *plan* the activities of the organization, *staff* it with required personnel, *organize* its personnel and their activities, *direct* the operations of the organization, and *control* its direction by evaluating feedback and making necessary adjustments.

Planning involves the development of long- and short-range plans which requires the formulation of goals, objectives, strategies, policies, procedures, and standards. It also involves the perception and analysis of opportunities, problems, and alternative courses of action, and the design of programs to achieve selected objectives. *Organizing* involves the development of a structure which groups, assigns, and coordinates activities by delegating authority, offering responsibility, and requiring accountability. *Staffing* involves the selecting, training, and assignment of personnel to specific organizational activities. *Directing* is the leadership of the organization through communication and motivation of organizational personnel. *Controlling* involves observing and measuring organizational performance and environmental activities and modifying the plans and activities of the organization when necessary.

Management as a System

Figure 12–7 illustrates management as a system. Information from management information and decision support systems is the *input* to this system. Information is subjected to *analysis and synthesis,* utilizing data and techniques from the

FIGURE 12–7 Management as
a System

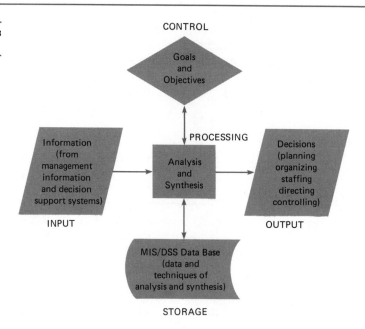

CONTROL

Goals
and
Objectives

PROCESSING

Information
(from
management
information
and decision
support systems)

Analysis
and
Synthesis

Decisions
(planning
organizing
staffing
directing
controlling)

INPUT

OUTPUT

MIS/DSS Data Base
(data and
techniques of
analysis and synthesis)

STORAGE

MIS/DSS data base. Alternative decisions are evaluated in the light of the *goals and objectives* of the firm. *Output* is in the form of planning, organizing, staffing, directing, and controlling *decisions*. The management decision output is then transmitted to the appropriate components of the business or to the business environment.

Figure 12–7 emphasizes why information is an indispensable ingredient in management. Each of the management functions requires *the analysis and synthesis of information* before a specific decision can be made. This information must be accurate, timely, complete, concise, and relevant or the quality of the decisions being made will suffer. Of course, even the best information cannot guarantee good decisions if managers do not have the ability to use it effectively. This is why information must be presented in a form which is easy to understand and use. Figure 12–7 also emphasizes the importance of information systems since they supply management with the *feedback* and *data base* required for decision making.

Management Information Requirements

What information does management need? First of all it must be emphasized that management cannot possibly absorb all of the information that can be produced by an information system. Therefore, systems developers must determine not only (1) what information management *wants,* but (2) what information management *needs.* Several concepts which guide the determination of the information needed by management are outlined below.

Decision Networks. The analysis of management information requirements must begin with an analysis of management decisions. Developers of information systems which support management must focus on the flow of decision information between "decision centers" where decisions are made to "action points" where decisions are implemented. It must be emphasized that the "decision network" of an organization may not be identical to the formal organizational structure of the firm. Thus, the organization chart of a firm may differ with a decision network that outlines the decision centers and action points of the organization. See Figure 12–8.

The factors that are important in making each decision must be identified. *What* decisions must be made, *who* should make them, and *when, where,* and *how* they should be made in the organization must be determined. Only then can we identify the types of information required to support each decision.

Programmed Decisions. Another important consideration is the presence or potential for *programmed decisions.* Programmed decisions are decisions that can be automated (programmed) by basing them on a "decision rule" which outlines the steps to take when confronted with the need for a specific decision. A programmed decision does not have to be part of a computer program, though this is usually the case since the computer is the usual method for automating information systems. Therefore, a study of management should be made to determine if any decisions can be programmed.

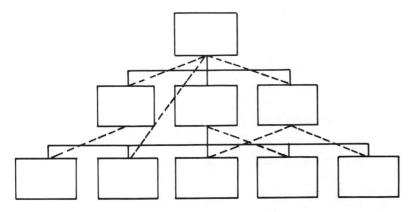

FIGURE 12–8 **Traditional Organization Chart Showing Actual Decision Network**

Management by Exception. "Exception reporting" or *management by exception* is another important concept which is utilized by system designers to avoid "drowning managers in a sea of information." Information is provided to managers only when exceptional conditions occur which require management decision making. For example, credit managers might only be notified of the account status of delinquent customers, rather than giving them a report listing the account balances of all customers of the firm.

Levels of Management. The information requirements of management depend on the management level involved. Figures 12–9 and 12–10 illustrate how a management system can be subdivided into three major subsystems: (1) strategic management, (2) tactical management, and (3) operational management. These subsystems are related to the traditional management levels of top management, middle management, and operating management. The activities and results of each management subsystem are summarized, as well as the types of information required by each subsystem.

Figure 12–10 emphasizes that the *information requirements of management are directly related to the types of activities that predominate in each level of management.* For example, the strategic management level requires more special one-time reports and forecasts to support its heavy planning and policymaking responsibilities. The operational management level on the other hand, may require more regular internal reports emphasizing current and historical data comparisons which support its control of day-to-day operations.

FIGURE 12–9 Levels of Management Information Needs

FIGURE 12–10   Management Activities and Information Requirements

Management Levels	Primary Activities	Activity Results	Activity Examples	Information Requirements
Strategic management	Long-range planning Determine organizational resource requirements and allocations	Goals Objectives Policies Long-range plans and other strategic decisions	Policy on diversification Social responsibility policy Major capital expenditure policy	Forecasts Simulations Inquiries External reports One-time reports Condensed internal reports
Tactical management	Allocate assigned resources to specific tasks Make rules Measure performance Exert control	Budgets Procedures Rules and other tactical decisions	Personnel practices Capital budgeting Marketing mix	Forecasts and historical data Regular internal reports Exception reports Simulations Inquiries
Operational management	Direct the utilization of resources and the performance of tasks in conformance with established rules	Directions Commands Actions and other operational decisions	Production scheduling Inventory control Credit management	Regular internal reports Detailed transaction reports Procedures manuals Current and historical data Programmed decisions

Based in part on: Sherman C. Blumenthal, *Management Information Systems: A Framework for Planning and Development* (Englewood Cliffs, N.J.: Prentice-Hall, 1969), p. 29.

Internal versus External Information

Management should be provided with information (and *information analysis techniques*) about the internal operations of the business system as well as the developments in the business environment. Figures 12–11 and 12–12 summarize such information needs.

FIGURE 12–11   Internal Information Needs of Management

Activity information.   Information techniques that summarize, analyze, and evaluate the activities taking place in the operation of the business.

Status information.   Information on the performance status of various aspects of the business, such as customer accounts, work in process, or project completion reports.

Resources information.   Information about the resources of the business system, such as personnel, material, and facilities.

Resource allocation information.   Information and techniques for cost/benefit analysis which allow management to make "trade-offs" between competing proposals and thus allocate scarce resources among the competing needs of the business.

Planning and control information.   Information and techniques required to produce plans, budgets, schedules, project specifications, forecasts, and standards. Mathematical models help provide such planning and control information. Simulation techniques allow managers to ask "what if" questions and review the results of alternative proposed decisions.

FIGURE 12–12 External Information Needs of Management

Politics and government. Information on political, legal, and legislative developments, laws and regulations, monetary and fiscal policies, etc.

Society. Information on demographic, cultural, and social trends.

The economy. Information on the components of the Gross National Product and other economic indicators.

Competition. Information on trends in the industry and in competing firms.

Technology. Information on the development of new products and processes.

Resources. Information on past and present status and expected trends in the supply of necessary resources such as labor, materials, financing, energy, etc.

MANAGEMENT INFORMATION SYSTEMS

When information systems are designed to provide information needed for effective decision making by managers, they are called **management information systems.** The concept of management information systems (MIS) originated in the 1960s and became the byword (and the "buzzword") of almost all attempts to relate computer technology and systems theory to data processing in business. During the early 1960s, it became evident that the computer was being applied to the solution of business problems in a piecemeal fashion, focusing almost entirely on the computerization of clerical and record-keeping tasks. The concept of management information systems was developed to counteract such *inefficient* development and *ineffective* use of the computer.

The MIS concept is vital to efficient and effective computer use in business for two major reasons:

- It serves as a *systems* framework for organizing business computer applications. Business applications of computers should be viewed as interrelated and integrated *computer-based information systems*, and not as independent data processing jobs.
- It emphasizes the *management* orientation of electronic data processing in business. The primary goal of computer-based information systems should be the support of *management decision making*, not merely the processing of data generated by business operations.

Effective management information systems are needed by all business organizations because of the increased complexity and rate of change that are characteristics of our present civilization. Management information systems must help management cope with the "future shock" caused by the accelerated pace of social and technological changes which has drastically shortened the life cycle of products, production methods, personnel practices, organizational relationships, and "proven facts"—to name a few. These changes have triggered an "information explosion." Management needs effective information systems that can cope with the rapidly expanding production and accumulation of information and knowledge and that can provide selective and strategic information to support their decision-making responsibilities.

The Management Information System Concept

Figure 12–13 illustrates that the management information system concept includes the system components summarized below:

- *Input.* Collects data generated by the other subsystems of the business system and the business environment.
- *Processing.* Utilizes data processing systems to transform data into information, or to process information into a more suitable form for decision making.
- *Storage.* Maintains a data base containing data and information in the form of historical records, forecasts, plans, standards, decision rules, models, and other managerial and analytical techniques.
- *Output.* Provides information needed to support the decision-making activities of management (1) *on demand,* (2)

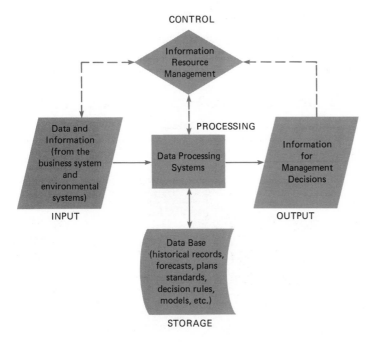

FIGURE 12–13 The Management Information System Concept

according to a predetermined schedule, or (3) *when exceptional conditions occur.*

● *Control.* Utilizes a continual process of *information resource management* to control the performance of the MIS.

DECISION SUPPORT SYSTEMS

Decision support systems (DSS) are a natural progression from management information systems and earlier operational information systems. Decision support systems are interactive, computer-based information systems that use decision models and a management data base to provide information tailored to support specific decisions faced by individual managers. They are thus different from operational information systems which focus on processing the data generated by business transactions and operations. They also differ from management information systems which have primarily been focused on providing managers with structured information (reports) which could be used to help them make more effective, structured types of decisions. They also are not programmed decision systems, since they do not make decisions for management. Figure 12–14 illustrates the place of decision support systems among the major types of computer-based information systems.

The Decision Support System Concept

Decision support systems help managers solve the *semistructured* and *unstructured* problems typically faced by decision makers in the real world. They are flexible, adaptable, quick response systems which are user initiated and controlled, and support the personal decision-making style of a

FIGURE 12–14 Decision Support Systems and Major Types of Computer-Based Information Systems

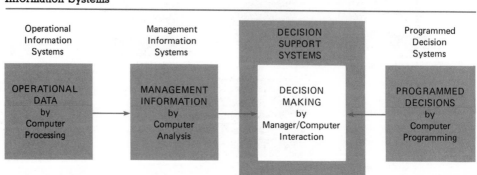

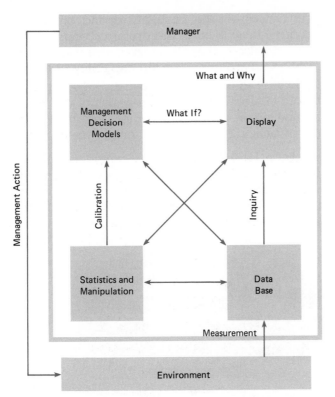

Source: Adapted from David B. Montgomery and Glen L. Urban, *Management Science in Marketing*, © 1969, p. 18. Adapted by permission of Prentice-Hall, Inc., Englewood Cliffs, N.J.

manager. DSS are designed to use a decision maker's own insights and judgments in an interactive computer-based process leading up to a specific decision. Figure 12–15 illustrates the decision support system concept.

An effective DSS should attain the following performance objectives:

• Support semistructured and unstructured decision making and problem solving at all levels of organizations where they occur.

• Enhance the coordination between decision makers, especially when several people must cooperate in a decision making task, or work on related decision making tasks.

• Support all phases of the decision making task instead of just data gathering, analysis, comparative evaluation, or implementation.

• Be process independent and user controlled so that the

user can direct the problem solving or decision making in accordance with his or her preferred cognitive style. This characteristic also makes DSS responsive to changes in task, organization environment, or the capability of the user over time.

● Be easy to use. DSS will usually have "discretionary users" who can elect not to use the system if it is more trouble than it is worth. A DSS, unlike most information systems, has a major built-in market test—it must earn its user loyalty.[1]

Figure 12–16 illustrates the capabilities of a DSS **generator** or software package called EIS (Executive Information System) which integrates various business decision models with a specialized data base management system. Figure 12–17 lists some of the benefits experienced by users of another DSS

FIGURE 12–16   Capabilities of a DSS Generator

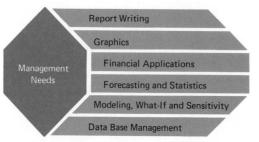

Courtesy Boeing Computer Services.

FIGURE 12–17   Benefits of a DSS Generator

People-Oriented Benefits

● Easy to learn and easy to use
● "What-if?" capability
● Low hurdle entry—speed of being effective
● Flexibility of use
● Complete, accurate output in a few minutes
● Communication with management
● Model itself readable in English
● Ability to respond quickly to user requests
● Decision makers can easily build own models

Feature-Oriented Benefits

● Quantify risk in a sensible manner
● Goal-seeking (reverse what-if)
● Consolidation of levels of data
● Sensitivity analysis
● Power, simplicity, and flexibility of report writing
● Variety of functions and applications
● Quick updates

Source: Adapted from P. G. Keen and G. R. Wagner, "DSS: An Executive Mind-Support System" *Datamation* (November 1979), p. 122. Reprinted with permission of *Datamation* magazine. Copyright by Technical Publishing Company, a Dun & Bradstreet Company, 1979; all rights reserved.

---

[1] Ralph H. Sprague, Jr., "Selected Papers on Decision Support Systems," *Data Base,* Fall 1980, p. 4.

generator called IFPS (Interactive Financial Planning System). Several other DSS software packages such as EXPRESS and FOCUS are available from independent consulting firms and computer manufacturers.

INTEGRATED INFORMATION SYSTEMS

Most business firms agree that *integration* and *coordination* should exist between the various information systems of the organization and are working toward that goal in their information systems development. Integrated management information systems promise many benefits such as economy, efficiency, effectiveness, and control. Integration can avoid duplication, simplify operations, and produce an *efficient* information system. However, some duplication is necessary in order to insure *effective* information systems. For example, duplicate copies of reports may be required if several users require "hard copy" output, or duplicate storage files may be necessary if a "back-up" capability is required. *Carrying systems integration to an extreme* could result in systems that are costly, cumbersome, or unreliable and which do not effectively meet the information needs of users. Therefore, some duplication and "redundancy" is usually required in systems design.

Business Information Systems

Business information systems support the traditional *functions of business,* such as marketing, finance, and production. Many current business information systems are "integrated" combinations of *management information systems* and *operational information systems.*

Example. A payroll system that processes employee time cards and produces employee paychecks is an *operational* information system. An information system which utilizes payroll data to produce labor analysis reports, which show variances and trends in labor cost and utilization is a *management* information system. However, in most cases, these functions are combined in an integrated *management-operational information system* which not only processes employee time cards and produces paychecks but also furnishes management with labor analysis reports.

Example. Sales order/transaction processing is typically considered to be an operational information subsystem, while sales analysis is considered a management information subsystem. However, both are subsystems of the marketing information system. The sales order processing system collects and records sales transaction data and provides input to the sales analysis system which produces management reports concerning sales generated by each salesperson, sales territory, customer, product, etc.

Example. Production and sales activity data generated by manufacturing and marketing operational information systems are utilized by the marketing MIS for sales forecasts, which are then used by the production MIS for production scheduling. See Fig 12–18.

FIGURE 12–18
Interelationships of Business
Information Systems

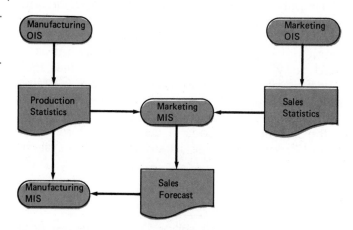

Common Data Flows and Data Bases

An important feature of integrated information systems is "common data flows," which is the use of common input, processing, and output procedures and media whenever possible or desirable. Systems analysts try to design systems which capture data only once and as close to its original source as possible. They then try to use a minimum of data processing procedures and subsystems to process the data and strive to minimize the number of output documents and reports produced by the system. *For example,* many payroll systems try to capture as much data as possible from an employee's time card while sales, accounts receivable, and inventory systems try to capture as much data as possible at the time and place a sales order is received. This eliminates much duplication in data collection documents and procedures.

Another major characteristic of integrated information systems is *common data bases* which avoid duplication in the

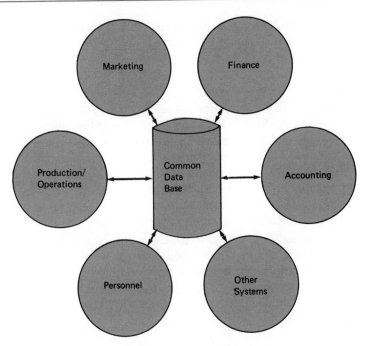

FIGURE 12–19   A Common Data Base

storage and retrieval of data and information. These common data bases can be viewed as integrated collections of data and information which are used by most of the information subsystems of the organization. See Figure 12–19.

Advanced Integrated Systems

Advanced integrated information systems are being developed by many computer-using organizations which will have the important characteristics summarized below.

- *Common data flows.* Common source documents, common input media, and a common data base are utilized so that unnecessary processing activities, storage files, input data, and output information are eliminated.
- *Immediate data entry.* Data created from transactions and operations are entered directly into the computer system from the point of origin, which may be a local or remote terminal.
- *Common data base.* Current and historical data, forecasts, plans, standards, decision rules, mathematical models, and other analytical techniques are stored in direct-access data base for use by all subsystems.

- *Integrated information subsystems.* The major categories of business information systems are integrated into a single information system which provides an efficient and effective flow of information to management.
- *Decision support orientation.* The computer system utilizes decision rules and models, and other tools and techniques, to evaluate the data being processed, the information produced, and the contents of data bases. As a result, the computer may make programmed decisions, specify decisions that must be made, specify actions to be taken, notify users of unusual conditions requiring decision making, or may integrate the decision maker's insights and judgments into an interactive decision-making process.
- *Conversational computing.* Data communications terminals, data base management software, and other computer system capabilities encourage conversational computing. Computer users can simply and instantly direct the computer to solve problems, answer questions, process data, update files, and produce output in any format desired.

Advanced completely integrated "total" information systems do not exist. Major considerations make such systems economically unfeasible for most organizations. For example, many large business firms have offices and plants throughout a nation and various foreign countries. The cost of a totally integrated system with "fail-safe" controls to prevent errors, loss or destruction of data, and unauthorized use, and which also provides instant response capabilities from a common data base may be prohibitive. However, the concept of integrated information systems must be understood by computer users since it indicates the direction being taken and the goal being sought by many developers of computer-based information systems.

TRENDS IN BUSINESS COMPUTER APPLICATIONS AND INFORMATION SYSTEMS

Computer-based information systems and subsystems are frequently called *computer application systems* or simply, *computer applications.* For example, a computer-based *payroll* information system would typically be called a *payroll application.* Thus we should view all computer applications in business as *computer-based business information systems or subsystems.* As computer users, we should develop the capability to analyze, design, and improve the *input, process-*

ing, output, storage, and *control* components of business application systems.

In the early years of computer use, the computer was applied to the solution of business problems in a piecemeal fashion to meet specific problems. In addition, most computer applications involved the computerization of clerical and record-keeping tasks. The trend of computer applications since that time has been away from such *operational information systems* and toward the concept of *management information and decision support systems.* The modern trend is to develop integrated computer applications whose main purpose is to provide information to support management decision making. Figure 12–20 illustrates that the trend in computer applications can be viewed as a change from the *clerical record-keeping* functions of operational information systems to the *decision-making support* functions of management information and decision support systems.

Why were computers applied to record-keeping functions before being applied to the managerial functions of planning and control?

- In many businesses, the computer replaced electromechanical data processing systems which had been used primarily for clerical types of applications.
- Controlling the sheer volume and growth of data processing required by many record-keeping functions made it imperative to use computers for such applications at an early stage. The banking industry's pioneering use of computers for check processing is an example.
- Computerizing record-keeping applications is a lot easier and cheaper than developing computer-based management information systems. Record-keeping applications are simpler, more familiar, and more formalized than managerial applications, thus making it easier and cheaper to develop (or purchase) the systems design and computer programs that are required.
- Direct and immediate cost reductions could usually be shown when the cost of EDP was compared against the cost of the clerical personnel and data processing equipment that would be replaced by the computerized system. Therefore, even today, many business firms begin their use of computers by computerizing record-keeping applications.

FIGURE 12–20   The Trend in Business Computer Applications

THE PAST

THE FUTURE

Adapted from John Diebold, "Bad Decisions on Computer Use," *Harvard Business Review* (January/February 1969), pp. 14–28.

Stage	Function Involved	Benefits	Payoff
1	RECORDKEEPING	Reduced clerical cost Reduced marginal cost of increased volume Improved speed Improved accuracy	Immediate upon introduction of effective, working system
2	OPERATIONS	Improved service Improved product design Improved production scheduling Improved production control Reduced inventory Reduced cost of product	One to three years after introduction of system
3	STRATEGIC PLANNING	Improved information Improved predictions Improved decisions by top management	Five to ten years after introduction of system

FIGURE 12–21 Three Stages of Computer Applications in Business

Source: John E. Cooke and Ted Kuchta, *Cost and Management,* September–October, 1970, p. 12. *Cost and Management* is the official journal of the Society of Industrial Accountants of Canada.

Figure 12–21 illustrates three stages of computer applications in computer-using business firms. Computers are (1) applied to *record-keeping* functions where the payoff is frequently an immediate reduction in costs; then (2) the computer is applied to *operational* functions which have a less immediate payoff and whose benefits are less tangible. Larger firms with many years of computer experience move to a third stage where (3) computers are used to support the *strategic planning* functions of top management but whose payoff may take many years to occur. Thus, as the use of the computer moves from "paper work automation" to "operations control" and then to "strategic planning" applications, the benefits of computer use change from tangible *cost reductions* to less tangible benefits such as operating improvements and improved decision making, which are frequently described as *profit producing* benefits.

Figure 12–22 outlines a six-stage growth trend in computer applications in business firms. This analysis shows that computer-using business firms go through six stages of growth. Notice the following trends:

Applications Portfolio Trends

● The types of computer applications in a firm's *applications portfolio* changes from functional cost-reduction applications

FIGURE 12-22 Six Stages of Growth in Computer Applications

	Stage 1 Initiation	Stage 2 Contagion	Stage 3 Control	Stage 4 Integration	Stage 5 Data Administration	Stage 6 Maturity
APPLICATIONS PORTFOLIO TRENDS	Functional Cost Reduction Applications	Proliferation	Upgrade Documentation and Restructuring of Existing Applications	Retrofitting Existing Applications using Data Base Technology	Organization Integration of Applications	Application Integration "Mirroring" Information Flows
	There is a concentration on labor-intensive automation, scientific support, and clerical replacement.			Applications move out to user locations for data generation and data use as distributed processing begins.	Balance is established between centralized shared data/common system applications and decentralized user-controlled applications.	
EDP TECHNOLOGY TRENDS	100 Percent Batch Processing	80 Percent Batch Processing / 20 Percent Remote Job Entry Processing	70 Percent Batch Processing / 15 Percent Data Base Processing / 10 Percent Inquiry Processing / 5 Percent Time-Sharing Processing	50 Percent Batch and Remote Job Entry Processing / 40 Percent Data Base and Data Communications Processing / 5 Percent Personal Computing / 5 Percent Minicomputer and Microcomputer Processing	20 Percent Batch and Remote Job Entry Processing / 60 Percent Data Base and Data Communications Processing / 5 Percent Personal Computing / 15 Percent Minicomputer and Microcomputer Processing	10 Percent Batch and Remote Job Entry Processing / 60 Percent Data Base and Data Communications Processing / 5 Percent Personal Computing / 25 Percent Minicomputer and Microcomputer Processing
USER INVOLVEMENT	"Hands off"	Superficially Enthusiastic	Arbitrarily Held Accountable	Accountability Learning	Effectively Accountable	Acceptance of Joint User and Data Processing Accountability
	Reactive: End user is superficially involved. The computer provides more, better, and faster information than manual techniques.		Driving force: End user is directly involved with data entry and data use. End user is accountable for data quality and for value-added end use.		Participatory: End user and data processing are jointly accountable for data quality and for effective design of value-added applications.	

Source: Adapted and reprinted by permission of the *Harvard Business Review*, from "Managing the Crisis in Data Processing," by Richard L. Nolan (March/April 1979, pp. 117–21). Copyright 1979 by the President and Fellows of Harvard College, all rights reserved.

(e.g., payroll, accounts receivable, etc.) to a proliferation of applications in all functional areas (e.g., inventory, sales, capital budgeting, personnel, etc.) until it is curtailed and brought under management control in the third stage. In these early stages there is a concentration on applications which provide labor-intensive automation, scientific support, and clerical replacement.

● In the next two stages, existing applications are "retrofitted" and integrated with new applications using a data base orientation and data base management systems as *data base processing systems* are developed. Also, applications move out to user locations as *distributed processing systems* are developed to provide for user-controlled local data processing.

● Finally, computer applications are integrated so that they "mirror" the organization's information flows that they automate. At this stage of computer-using maturity a balance is established between centralized and shared data base/data communications applications and the decentralized user-controlled applications of distributed processing systems.

EDP Technology Trends

● In their early stages, computer applications are primarily *batch processing systems*. Then *realtime processing begins* to develop in the form of time-sharing inquiry/response and data base processing systems.

● Much of the batch processing applications begin to take the form of RJE (remote job entry) processing since such applications can use the data communications networks that are required by the realtime processing applications. *Personal computing* applications using microcomputer and minicomputer systems also begin to develop.

● Finally, applications requiring data base and data communications processing make up the majority of computer applications, while distributed processing and personal computing systems (with user-owned minicomputers and microcomputers) make up a sizable part of the firm's computer applications.

User Involvement Trends

● Notice how there is minimal user involvement in the early stages of computer applications as a "hands off" policy is enforced by DP management. User involvement is "reactive," since the end user is only superficially involved. However, users accept this situation because the computer is providing them with more, better, and faster information than manual techniques.

● In the middle stages, users become "the driving force" behind the development of computer applications since they are being held accountable for their share of DP costs, the quality of data being processed, and the value of their use of computer resources.

● Finally, there is an acceptance of joint user and DP accountability for the quality of data and information produced by computer applications. User involvement is highly "participatory," since users are held jointly accountable for the effective design of "value-added" applications.

Figure 12-22 and its analysis should emphasize and clarify the dynamics of computer applications in business, and the need for effective management of the use of computer and information resources in business operations and management.

SUMMARY

● An information system is a system which uses personnel, operating procedures, and data processing subsystems to collect and process data and disseminate information in an organization. Computer-based information systems such as operational information systems (OIS), management information systems (MIS), decision support systems (DSS), and programmed decision systems (PDS) make extensive use of computer hardware, software, data bases, personnel, and procedures.

● The business firm should be viewed as a system in which economic resources (input) are transformed by various organizational processes (processing) into goods and services (output). Information systems provide information on the operation of the business (feedback) to management for the direction and maintenance of the firm (control). Business firms are composed of "operational systems" which perform the input, processing, and output functions, "management systems" which constitute the control component of the

business system, and "information systems" which perform the feedback function.

● The business firm is a subsystem of society and is surrounded by other systems of the "business environment." Therefore, business firms must maintain proper interrelationships with the other economic, political, and social subsystems in their environment. These include customers, competitors, suppliers, labor unions, stockholders, financial institutions, government agencies, and the community.

● Management receives information from management information systems as input and relies on the data and techniques from the MIS data base to support a process in which alternative decisions are evaluated in the light of the goals and objectives of the organization. Output of a management system is in the form of planning, organizing, staffing, directing, and controlling decisions.

● Management information systems are systems that provide information needed for effective management decision making. Information needed by managers is provided on demand, according to a schedule, or on an exception basis. The concept of management information systems (MIS) was developed to provide a systems framework and management orientation for the development of efficient and effective computer applications in business.

- Decision support systems are interactive, computer-based information systems that use decision models and a management data base to provide information tailored to support specific decisions faced by individual managers. They are designed to use a decision maker's own insights and judgments in an interactive computer-based process leading up to a specific decision.

- A major concept of modern information systems is the concept of "integrated information systems." In its most advanced form, this concept would involve combining the various management and operational information systems of an organization and transforming them into integrated subsystems of a single "total system." For most business firms, however, the concept of integrated information systems is a goal which emphasizes that integration and coordination should exist between the various information systems of the organization.

- The trend in the growth of business computer applications has been away from the computerization of operational information systems and toward the use of computer-based management information and decision support systems. The use of computers in a business firm usually goes through several growth stages, which can be measured in terms of changes in the firm's applications portfolio, use of EDP technology, and user involvement.

KEY TERMS AND CONCEPTS

Information system

The business firm as a system

Operational systems

Management as a system

Operational information systems

Environmental systems

Functions of management

Management information systems

Decision support systems

Computer-based information systems

Programmed decision systems

Management by exception

Management levels

Business information systems

Integrated information systems

Common data flows

Common data base

Computer application trends

REVIEW AND DISCUSSION QUESTIONS

1. What are information systems? Computer-based information systems?

2. How does the concept of computer-based information systems, tie together the functions of operational, programmed decision, management information, and decision support systems?

3. Identify the basic system components of the business firm as a system and their functions as components of this system.

4. What are some of the typical input, processing, and output components of the operational systems of business firms?

5. What is the difference in the role of operational and management information systems?

6. What is the role of the management systems of the firm?

7. How can a business firm utilize its feedback-control component as an "adaptive system"?

8. What are the functions of management? How do they affect the concept of management as a system?

9. Is the decision network of an organization identical to its formal organizational structure?

10. Can decisions be programmed? Explain.

11. Explain what is meant by management by exception.

12. Why do the information requirements of management depend on the management level involved?

13. What are management information systems? Identify the components of a management information system.

14. Why is the MIS concept vital to efficient and effective computer use in business?

15. What are decision support systems? How do they differ from management information systems?

16. What are several performance objectives and benefits that can be gained from the use of decision support systems?

17. Is a single integrated "total system" for an organization a realistic goal?

18. Explain how many current business information systems are integrated combinations of management and operational information systems.

19. What are the advantages and disadvantages of common data flows?

20. What is a common data base? Does it have to be a centrally located data base or can it consist of a grouping of distributed data bases?

21. What has been the historical trend in the types of business applications being computerized? What are several reasons for such trends?

22. What are several of the stages of computer applications in computer-using business firms? What are some of the reasons that computer-using firms go through these stages?

REAL WORLD APPLICATIONS

12–1   Glass Containers Corporation

Loren Karabin is the manufacturing vice president in charge of the Western area plant operations for Glass Containers Corporation of Fullerton, California. He arrives at his office early every weekday morning, sifts through the messages on his desk, and sorts out the appointments on his daily calendar. Then, before the telephones start ringing and the office gets busy, he swivels his chair about and fixes his attention on the CRT terminal display screen on the cabinet behind him. "About seven thirty, I turn it on and call up information I never used to have before mid-morning. I can pinpoint major problems and develop questions or suggestions before I talk with my plant managers."

Karabin is no computer expert, he's never had a training course, he doesn't even have a keyboard on his terminal, so he does no programming on his own. But using the selector pen attached to his IBM 3270, he can get up-to-date production information from the three plants in his area. Those figures include tonnage of raw material melted, total bottles formed, and total bottles packed. The computer also provides efficiency quotients and compares those figures to a set of standards established from historical data.

"We used to wait until my secretary got in," says Karabin. "She would call the plant locations to get the performance figures for the preceding day. But even at that, it didn't give me all the information I wanted. I didn't get the complete picture until it was mailed in from the plant two or three days later."

Now, that information is entered in what the company has named the Common Operating Information Network (COIN) at the end of each shift. COIN is anchored by an IBM 4341 host computer in the Glass Containers Corporate Offices in Fullerton. A total of 102 terminals, including CRTs and printers, are linked across the country by high speed phone lines. The company's 13 sales offices and 12 manufacturing facilities all operate in an online environment.

"It's very difficult to directly attribute cost saving to the use of COIN," says Senior Vice President for Operations Andrew Mauro, "But we do know early problem identification is basic to any cost improvement." Like Karabin, Mauro spends the early part of his morning going over the production figures for the preceding day. "I'm able to generate a series of questions before I telephone my vice president for manufacturing in the east, who is responsible for nine plants. COIN allows us to focus on items of production that require attention. We are both looking at the same sort of data and it eases the communication tremendously. We can discuss what happened yesterday, by plant, by shift, and get an indication of trends.

"Before the installation of COIN," Mauro continues, "I would receive gross figures by furnace and that information would generate more questions than it would answer. We use to run the gamut of information for every plant because all I had were total figures. With COIN, we don't discuss certain plants or furnaces if the data is satisfactory and the performance appears to be acceptable."[1]

- What capabilities does the COIN system have that identifies it as a management information system?
- What are the benefits of this system to management?

[1] Source: "Information in a Bottle," *Data Processor*, September/October 1980, pp. 10–11. Reprinted with permission.

12–2 GTE Electronic Components Group

Six months before the fiscal year begins, financial analysts at GTE start to prepare the operating budget for the Electronic Components Group. To organize and store the data, they use the Planning Control and Decision Evaluation (PLANCODE) system: an IBM program product comprising an easy-to-use, English-like planning language. "We can revise the figures at any time by making an entry at a terminal," John J. Nugent, vice-president-controller, says, "because PLANCODE automatically recalculates all the affected variables."

At its Seneca Falls, New York, headquarters, the Electronic Components Group makes Sylvania cathode ray tubes for television sets and data systems. Analysts there use PLANCODE on an IBM 4341 Processor in order to forecast sales and budget its manufacturing and marketing operations. "A complete budget represents literally millions of calculations," Nugent observes. "Suppose we want to revise a sales forecast, expected selling price, or standard direct cost assumption. Each of these affects a lot of dependent variables. Changing the sales forecast, for example, has an impact on the extrapolation of cash discounts, defective returns, and transportation costs. With PLANCODE, we can revise any of these major parameters and the system automatically makes the necessary adjustments.

"PLANCODE lets us look at several variables and measure their effect. We can test the sensitivity of a forecast to the variables we're certain of. The plan is better initially, and is easier to revise." Budgeting has taken on added importance, Nugent points out, as the economy has become more complex. "Knowing our capital needs in advance is critical today," he notes, "so we can decide how to go to the capital market.

"And with PLANCODE we can react faster—if, for example, a major cost item takes an unexpected jump. We have confidence in our results, since we know the math is accurate. The users control the structure of the budget and of the forecasting models, as well as the format of each printed document. This self-service by the users frees the professional programmers to work on the company's primary computer systems, and gives us the flexibility we need for effective financial planning."[2]

- Does PLANCODE provide GTE with a MIS? A DSS?
- How has PLANCODE benefitted the financial management of the Electronic Components Group?

[2] Source: "PLANCODE Displays the Financial Picture for CRT Maker." Reprinted by permission from *DP Dialogue*. © 1981 by International Business Machines Corporation.

12–3 Shaklee Corporation

The Shaklee Corporation is headquartered in Emeryville, California, and is a major producer of vitamins, food supplements, cosmetics, and household cleaners. Their sales grew from 10 million to 350 million dollars in ten years and are still growing. The company grew so fast that its data base was in poor condition, and management had resorted to making decisions on a subjective and political basis. Shaklee management decided to develop a comprehensive data base and a decision support system (DSS). It took six months and $250,000 to develop the data base and to design and program a DSS model of business operations. Thus Shaklee had the two key ingredients for a successful DSS: a software model of the process to be managed, and a data base of both historical and projected information, concerning both internal operations and external factors.

Shaklee's decision support system was first used to find the best way to reduce delivery times to customers without increasing production or distribution costs. The DSS calculated the impact that various delivery requirements would have on transportation costs, the cost of operating distribution centers, and the cost of carrying inventories. Says Charles D. Fry, manager of materials analysis and planning, "For the first time, management is able to understand the financial impact associated with various service-level decisions." Without the DSS model, he says, "there is no quantifiable way to determine the cost. And decisions become political issues between the sales side of the company, which would like a warehouse in any town where there is a reasonable demand, and the distribution side, which wants to minimize costs." Now, Shaklee Corporation expects that by using its decision support system, it will be able to cut delivery time to customers by one third and save $850,000 in operating costs this year.[3]

- How are decision support systems used by Shaklee? How has it helped their management?
- Would the DSS have taken as much time and money to develop if Shaklee already had a good corporate data base? Explain.

[3] "What If Help for Management," *Business Week,* January 21, 1980, pp. 73–74.

13

CHAPTER OUTLINE

HOW ARE COMPUTERS USED IN BUSINESS?

SECTION ONE: COMPUTER APPLICATIONS IN MARKETING
Marketing Information Systems
Computer Applications in Retailing
The Point-of-Sale Revolution

SECTION TWO: COMPUTER APPLICATIONS IN PRODUCTION/OPERATIONS
Manufacturing Information Systems
Process Control
Numerical Control and Robotics
Physical Distribution

SECTION THREE: COMPUTER APPLICATIONS IN FINANCE AND ACCOUNTING
Financial Information Systems
Financial Performance Models
Accounting Information Systems
Applications in Banking
Applications in Investments

SECTION FOUR: OTHER COMPUTER APPLICATIONS IN BUSINESS
Personnel Information Systems
Operations Research Applications
Other Business Applications
Airlines. Agribusiness. Construction. Insurance. Real Estate

SUMMARY

KEY TERMS AND CONCEPTS

REVIEW AND DISCUSSION QUESTIONS

REAL WORLD APPLICATIONS
Gould Instrument Division
Citizens Fidelity Bank
GE Plant Services Division

Computer Applications
in Business: Overview

LEARNING OBJECTIVES

The purpose of this chapter is to promote a basic understanding of how computers are used in business by analyzing computer applications in marketing, production/operations, finance, accounting, personnel, and other areas.

After reading and studying this chapter you should be able to identify several ways that the computer is used to support the functions of business (marketing, production/operations, finance, accounting, and personnel), or a particular industry (such as retailing, banking, investments, airlines, agribusiness, construction, insurance, and real estate).

HOW ARE COMPUTERS USED IN BUSINESS?

This chapter will attempt to answer questions concerning specific uses of the computer in business. What do computers do in business? How are computers used in business operations? How is the computer applied to business management? This chapter and the one that follows will explore the answers to such questions by providing an overview as well as focusing on specific applications of the computer in business firms and other computer-using organizations.

There are as many computer applications in business as there are business activities to be performed, business problems to be solved, and business opportunities to be pursued. It is therefore impossible to acquire a complete understanding of all computer applications in business. However, a business person should not have a *vague, unorganized* idea of business computer applications. As a present or future computer user, you should have a *basic* but *organized* understanding of the major ways the computer is used in business. You should also have a *specific* understanding of how computers affect a *particular business function* (marketing, for example) or a *particular industry* (banking, for example) that is directly related to your *career objectives*. Thus, someone whose career objective is a *marketing* position in *banking* should acquire a basic understanding of how computers are used in banking and how computers support the marketing activities of banks and other business firms.

Figure 13–1 illustrates how major computer applications can be grouped into business function and management level categories. Figure 13–2 gives examples of computer applications in a variety of industries. Applications in this chapter will thus be discussed according to the *"business function"* they support (marketing, production/operations, finance, accounting, and personnel) or according to the *industry* in which they are utilized (retailing, banking, insurance, etc.). The next chapter will take a closer look at several common business applications. This should help you acquire a *basic, organized,* and *specific* understanding of how computers support the management and operations of modern business firms.

FIGURE 13-1 Computer Applications by Business Function and Management Level

STRATEGIC PLANNING SYSTEMS

Strategic and Operating Plan	Economic Forecasting	Manpower Planning	Sales and Profit Planning

MANAGEMENT CONTROL SYSTEMS

Manufacturing Control	Marketing Control	Financial Control	Accounting Control
Purchasing Time Series Planning Order Point Planning Inventory Control Plant Loading Master Production Scheduling Demand Forecasting	Product Introduction Advertising/ Sales Promotion Sales Management Product Requirements Planning Sales Forecasting and Analysis Market Research	Pricing and Profitability Analysis Portfolio Analysis Capital Investment Analysis Capital Requirements Forecasting and Planning Cash Requirements Forecasting	Inventory Valuation Estimating Cost Analysis Budgeting Standard Costing

OPERATIONAL SYSTEMS

Manufacturing	Marketing	Distribution	Finance	Accounting	Personnel	Administration
Facilities and Environmental Protection and Control Testing and Quality Control Machine Control Plant Maintenance Time Reporting Receiving Stores Control Material Movement Control Plant Scheduling	Order Release Order Tracking and Inquiry Order Processing Order Entry Dealer/ Branch Operations	Distribution Center Operation Shipping Document Preparation Vehicle Scheduling Freight Routing and Tracking Freight Bill Rating and Audit Distribution Planning	Cash Management Tax and Government Reporting Auditing	Billing and Accounts Receivable Credit Payroll Asset Accounting Accounts Payable General Ledger	In-house Education Government Reporting Employee Services Wage and Salary Administration	Library Services Stockholders Relations Legal

Source: Adapted and reprinted by permission of the *Harvard Business Review*, from "Managing the Crisis in Data Processing," by Richard L. Nolan (March/April 1979, pp. 117–21). Copyright 1979 by the President and Fellows of Harvard College; all rights reserved.

FIGURE 13–2 Computer Applications by Industry Categories

Industry Segment	Basic Applications	Advanced Applications
Discrete Manufacturing	Accounting Order processing Purchasing Inventory control	Forecasting Numerical control Production scheduling Design automation
Process Manufacturing	Accounting Order processing Purchasing Inventory control	Mix formulation Process control Simulation Revenue models
Business and Personnel Service	Service bureau functions Tax preparation Accounting Client records	Econometric models Time sharing Engineering analysis Data base
Banking and Finance	Demand deposit accounting Check processing Proof and transit operations Cost control	Online savings Centralized life systems Portfolio analysis Cash flow analysis
Federal Government	Accounting and administration Tax-reporting and auditing Order processing Census analysis	Information retrieval Intelligence Command and control Pollution control
Education	Attendance accounting Grading and scoring School administration Alumni records	Student scheduling Computer aided instructions Library cataloging Student counseling
Insurance	Premium accounting Customer billing External reports Reserve calculation	Actuarial analysis Investment analysis Policy approval Cash flow analysis
Utilities	Customer billing Accounting Meter reading Inventory control	Rate analysis Line and generator loading Operational simulation Financial models
State and Local Government	Utility billing Tax recordkeeping Payroll School administration	Traffic analysis Budget preparation Police identification City planning
Distribution	Order processing Inventory control Purchasing Warehouse control	Vehicle scheduling Merchandising Forecasting Store site selection
Transportation	Rate calculation Vehicle maintenance Cost analysis Accounting	Traffic pattern analysis Automatic rating Tariff analysis Reservation systems

FIGURE 13-2 *(continued)*

Industry Segment	Basic Applications	Advanced Applications
Health Care	Patient billing Inventory accounting Health care statistics Patient history	Lab/operation scheduling Nurses' station automation Intensive care Preliminary diagnosis
Retail	Customer billing Sales analysis Accounting Inventory reporting	Point of sale automation Sales forecasting Merchandising Cash flow analysis
Printing and Publishing	Circulation Classified ads Accounting Payroll	Automatic typesetting Home finder Media analysis Page layout

Source: Adapted from Jerome Kanter, *Management Oriented Management Information Systems*, 2d ed., © 1977, p. 40. Reprinted by permission of Prentice Hall, Inc., Englewood Cliffs, New Jersey.

SECTION I: COMPUTER APPLICATIONS IN MARKETING

The business function of **marketing** is concerned with the planning, promotion, and sale of existing products in existing markets and the development of new products and new markets to better serve present and potential customers. Thus, marketing performs a vital function in the operation of a business enterprise. Performing the marketing function in business has become a much more difficult assignment because of the dynamic environment of today which includes:

- Rapidly changing market demands.
- Steadily increasing consumer pressures.
- Shortened product life spans.
- Proliferation of new products.
- Intensified competition.
- Growing government regulations.[1]

Business firms have increasingly turned to the computer to help them perform the vital marketing function in the face

[1] Some of the material in this section has been adapted from *Consumer Goods Information System—Marketing* (White Plains, N.Y.: IBM Corporation, 1973), pp. 8–9.

of the rapid changes of today's environment. The computer has been the catalyst in the development of *marketing information systems* which integrate the information flows required by many marketing activities. We shall now briefly analyze marketing information systems and several computer applications in marketing. This should provide you with a basic understanding of how computers help business firms perform their marketing activities.

Marketing Information Systems

Marketing information systems provide information for the planning and control of the marketing function. *Marketing planning information* assists marketing management in product planning, pricing decisions, planning advertising and sales promotion strategy and expenditures, forecasting the market potential for new and present products, and determining channels of distribution. *Marketing control information* supports the efforts of management to control the efficiency and effectiveness of the selling and distribution of products and services.

The information flows in a marketing information system are illustrated in Figure 13-3. The following major computer applications constitute a marketing information system:

- *Sales order processing.* A basic form of this application will be analyzed in the next chapter. It captures and processes customer orders and produces invoices for customers and data needed for sales analysis and inventory control. In many firms, it also keeps track of the status of customer orders until goods are delivered.

- *Marketing planning.* Computers assist marketing management in developing short and long-range plans outlining product sales, profit, and growth objectives. They also provide information feedback and analysis concerning performance-versus-plan for each area of marketing. Mathematical marketing models may be utilized to investigate the effects of various alternative plans.

- *Sales forecasting.* The basic functions of sales forecasting can be grouped into the two categories of "short-range forecasting" and "long-range forecasting." Short range forecasting deals with forecasts of sales for periods up to one year, while long-range forecasting is concerned with sales forecasts for a year or more into the future.

FIGURE 13–3   Information and Decision Flows in Marketing Management

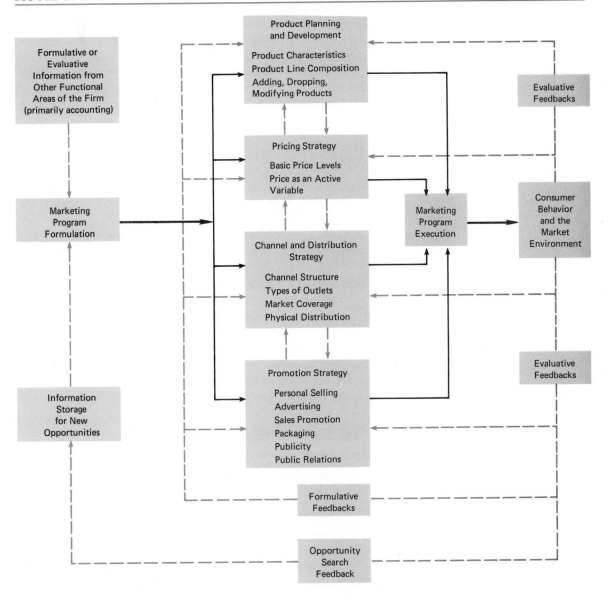

Source: Smith, Brien, and Stanford, *Readings in Marketing Information Systems*. (Boston: Houghton Mifflin, 1968), p. 3.

- *Sales management.* This application provides information to help sales managers plan and monitor the performance of the sales organization. The *sales analysis* application described in the next chapter is a basic form of this system.
- *Product management.* Management needs information to plan and control the performance of specific products, product lines, or brands. Revenue, cost, and growth information is required for existing products and new product development.
- *Advertising and promotions.* Management needs information to help it achieve sales objectives at the lowest possible costs for advertising and promotion. Information and analytical techniques are utilized to select media and promotional methods, allocate financial resources, and control and evaluate results.
- *Market research.* The market research information subsystem provides "marketing intelligence" to help management make more effective marketing decisions. It also provides marketing management with information to help plan and control the market research projects of the firm. The computer helps the market research activity collect, analyze, and maintain an enormous amount of information on a wide variety of market variables which are subject to continual change. The information input and output of the market research information system for a large corporation is shown in Figure 13–4.

Computer Applications in Retailing

The computer has traditionally been utilized by many retailers for one or more of the basic applications such as customer billing, accounts receivable, inventory control, general accounting, and payroll. The basic form of such applications will be analyzed in the next chapter and will not be repeated here. However, the computer is also being utilized for more advanced applications in retailing, such as management information systems and point-of-sale systems. Figure 13–5 illustrates the basic components of a retail management information system (MIS). Figure 13–6 depicts the kind of "customized" management report that could be provided on demand to the online terminals of retail executives.

The Point-of-Sale Revolution

Computer-based retail information systems with online *point-of-sale terminals* in retail outlets are a major new com-

FIGURE 13–4   A Market Research Information System

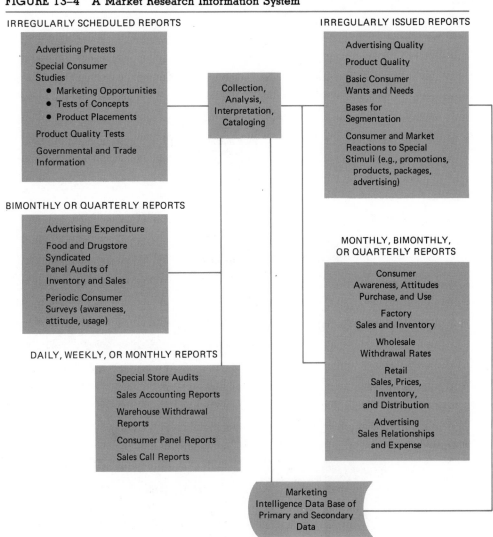

IRREGULARLY SCHEDULED REPORTS

Advertising Pretests

Special Consumer
Studies
- Marketing Opportunities
- Tests of Concepts
- Product Placements

Product Quality Tests

Governmental and Trade
Information

Collection,
Analysis,
Interpretation,
Cataloging

IRREGULARLY ISSUED REPORTS

Advertising Quality

Product Quality

Basic Consumer
Wants and Needs

Bases for
Segmentation

Consumer and Market
Reactions to Special
Stimuli (e.g., promotions,
products, packages,
advertising)

BIMONTHLY OR QUARTERLY REPORTS

Advertising Expenditure

Food and Drugstore
Syndicated
Panel Audits of
Inventory and Sales

Periodic Consumer
Surveys (awareness,
attitude, usage)

MONTHLY, BIMONTHLY,
OR QUARTERLY REPORTS

Consumer
Awareness, Attitudes
Purchase, and Use

Factory
Sales and Inventory

Wholesale
Withdrawal Rates

Retail
Sales, Prices,
Inventory,
and Distribution

Advertising
Sales Relationships
and Expense

DAILY, WEEKLY, OR MONTHLY REPORTS

Special Store Audits

Sales Accounting Reports

Warehouse Withdrawal
Reports

Consumer Panel Reports

Sales Call Reports

Marketing
Intelligence Data Base of
Primary and Secondary
Data

Source: Adapted from Lee Adler, "Systems Approach to Marketing," *Harvard Business Review* 45, no. 3 (1967): 111.

puter application in retailing. Figure 13–7 is an example of a retail POS (Point-of-Sale) system. Most POS systems consist of several cash-register-like terminals which are online to a data controller or data concentrator located somewhere in the store. The data controller could be a minicomputer with peripherals, or it can merely be a unit for storing transactions from 'the POS registers on magnetic tape and transmitting data over communication lines to a regional computer center.

FIGURE 13-5 A Retail
Management Information
System

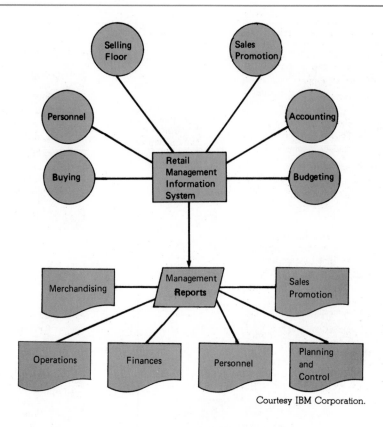

Courtesy IBM Corporation.

FIGURE 13-6 A Customized
Retail Management Report

EXPENSE CONTROL
PERFORMANCE   12 WEEKS ENDED 4/30/19

   SALES PROMOTION
       NEWSPAPER LINAGE UP 21.0%
       DOLLAR COST UP 14.0%
   INITIAL ADVERTISING SCHEDULE CREATED 60% OF
   FORECASTED DEMAND IN PERIOD ENDED 2/28.
   REINSERTED DURING PERIOD ENDED 3/28. DEMAND
   WAS 115% OF REVISED FORECAST.

   OPERATIONS
       RECEIVING EXPENSE UP 12.7%
       RECEIPTS 48% OF FORECAST DURING PERIOD ENDED
       2/28.
       OVERTIME EXPENSE $40,000 REQUIRED TO HANDLE
       INCREASED RECEIPTS DURING 6 WEEKS ENDED 4/16.

Courtesy IBM Corporation.

FIGURE 13–7   A Retail POS System

Form Follows Function: J.C. Penney Company

A nationwide chain of 2,000 stores and a company that believes in local store autonomy, J.C. Penney Co. is a prime target for DDP, as are many other big retail outfits with point-of-sale operations.

The POS installations are built around an in-store controller hooked to POS terminals (registers). For each credit transaction the customer's account number is keyed on the register, transmitted to the controller, and from there sent to a regional minicomputer with files on bad or overdrawn accounts. If the transaction is approved, it is rung up and recorded on the in-store system. Nightly the store's transactions are polled by the regional mini and transferred to a regional mainframe for actual processing of customer accounts. The mini's files are updated nightly. Meanwhile, back at the store, the in-store controller is producing reports for the store manager—sales analysis, commission reporting, merchandise control.

While Penney's justified its system on the basis of "hard" savings in labor reduction and bad-debt costs, improved customer satisfaction has added to sales and identification of slow-moving items has helped improve profit margins.

Courtesy International Data Corporation; reprinted from *Fortune* magazine of March, 1977.

In many POS systems, the "cash register" is an *intelligent terminal* which can guide the operator through each transaction, step by step. These terminals can also perform necessary arithmetic operations, such as tax, discount, and total calculations. Some terminals permit on-line credit verification for credit transactions. Most POS terminals can automatically read information from tags or merchandise labels. Hand-held "wands" or other optical reading devices are utilized by some terminals to scan the merchandise label and capture price and stock data. Data may be printed on the merchandise labels and tags in OCR or MICR characters or may utilize various optical bar-coding methods. The grocery industry has agreed on a "universal product code" utilizing bar-coding on merchandise labels which can be scanned by optical reading devices in automated checkout counters. (See Figures 4–5 and 4–34 of Chapter 4).

Benefits of POS systems. What are the benefits of retail POS systems? Obviously, POS terminals, data controllers, and other data communications hardware are expensive devices. Figure 13–8 summarizes the results of tests by a large retail chain which compared a POS system and the previously used cash register system.

Large manufacturers of consumer products (such as food products, household products, and appliances) are counting

FIGURE 13–8   Comparison of POS System and Traditional Cash Register System

- The POS terminals cost 20 percent more than the cash registers they replaced.
- It took only 40 seconds to complete a sales transaction on a POS terminal as opposed to 160 seconds on a conventional cash register.
- The number of checkout registers could be reduced by 20 percent to 25 percent with a POS system. Checkout personnel requirements can also be reduced.
- The POS terminal can perform functions either impossible or uneconomical on the conventional cash register (such as credit verification). It is estimated that more than 80 percent of the input data required by retail information systems can be captured by POS terminals.
- Use of a minicomputer as a communications controller allowed store managers to make online inquiries concerning merchandise availability and customer credit and to receive much faster reports on sales activity, merchandise replinishment, customer billing, clerk productivity, and store traffic.
- POS terminals demonstrated greater accuracy, increased customer service, and a 50 percent reduction in personnel training time.

Source: Adpated from "The Terminal Takeover," *Infosystems* (March 1972), pp. 22–28.

on information systems utilizing POS terminals and online management terminals to reduce costs, increase efficiency, and improve management decisions. Figure 13–9 shows the computer-based management information system of a large consumer products manufacturer. One of the major benefits of such systems is their ability to produce advanced types of *sales and advertising impact analysis* by quickly providing a detailed analysis of sales by store and product, as well as such vital merchandising facts as shelf life, shelf position, displays, and the promotions and displays of competitors.

Figure 13–10 summarizes several typical marketing applications and provides examples of the benefits which can result when the computer is applied to marketing.

FIGURE 13–9   An MIS for a Consumer Products Manufacturer-Retailer

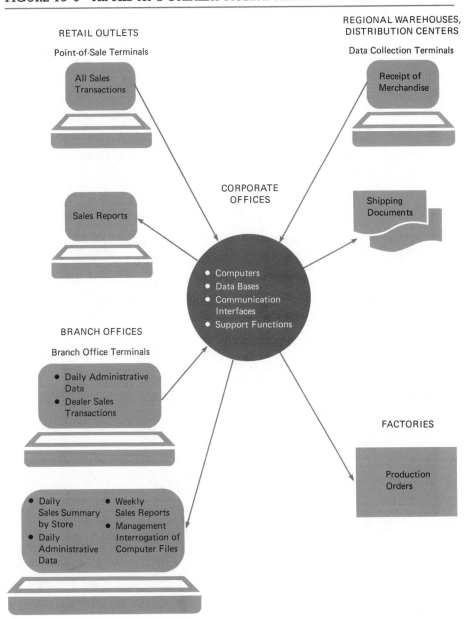

FIGURE 13–10 Benefits of Computer-Based Marketing Information Systems

	Typical Applications	*Benefits*	*Examples*
CONTROL SYSTEMS	Control of marketing costs	More timely computerized reports	Undesirable cost trends are spotted more quickly so that corrective action may be taken sooner.
	Diagnosis of poor sales performance	Flexible online retrieval of data.	Executives can ask supplementary questions of the computer to help pinpoint reasons for a sales decline and reach an action decision more quickly.
	Management of fashion goods.	Automatic spotting of problems and opportunities.	Fast-moving fashion items are reported daily for quick reorder, and slow-moving items are also reported for fast price reductions.
	Flexible promotion strategy	Cheaper, more detailed, and more frequent reports.	Ongoing evaluation of a promotional campaign permits reallocation of funds to areas behind target.
PLANNING SYSTEMS	Forecasting	Automatic translation of terms and classifications between departments.	Survey-based forecasts of demand for complex industrial goods can be automatically translated into parts requirements and production schedules.
	Promotional planning and corporate long-range planning.	Systematic testing of alternative promotional plans and compatibility testing of various divisional plans.	Complex simulation models both developed and operated with the help of data bank information can be used for promotional planning by product managers and for strategic planning by top management.
	Credit management.	Programmed executive decision rules can operate on data bank information.	Credit decisions are automatically made as each order is processed.
	Purchasing	Detailed sales reporting permits automation of management decisions.	Computer automatically repurchases standard items on the basis of correlation of sales data with programmed decision rules.
RESEARCH SYSTEMS	Advertising strategy.	Additional manipulation of data is possible when stored for computers in an unaggregated data base.	Sales analysis is possible by new market segment breakdowns.
	Pricing strategy.	Improved storage and retrieval capability allows new types of data to be collected and used.	Systematic recording of information about past R&D contract bidding situations allows improved bidding strategies.
	Evaluation of advertising expenditures.	Well-designed data banks permit integration and comparison of different sets of data.	Advertising expenditures are compared to shipments by county to provide information about advertising effectiveness.
	Continuous experiments.	Comprehensive monitoring of input and performance variables yields information when changes are made.	Changes in promotional strategy by type of customer are matched against sales results on a continuous basis.

Source: Donald Cox and Robert Good, "How to Build a Marketing Information System," *Harvard Business Review* 45, no. 3 (1967): 146.

SECTION II: COMPUTER APPLICATIONS IN PRODUCTION/OPERATIONS

The **production/operations** function includes all activities concerned with the planning, monitoring, and control of the processes that produce goods or services. Thus, the production/operations function is concerned with the management of the operational systems of all business firms. Computers are used for such *operations management* functions not only by manufacturing companies but also by all other firms which must plan, monitor, and control inventories, purchases, and the flow of goods and services. Therefore, firms such as transportation companies, wholesalers, retailers, financial institutions, and service companies must utilize production/operations information systems to plan and control their operations.

In this section, we will concentrate on manufacturing and physical distribution to illustrate the application of the computer to the production/operations function. A few examples of such applications should spotlight the dramatic impact of computers.

Manufacturing Information Systems

Computer-based manufacturing information systems consist of both *operational* and *management* computer applications. *Management* applications in manufacturing are concerned with (1) production planning (including *material requirements planning*—MRP), (2) production control, (3) production inventory control, (4) purchasing, (5) physical distribution management, (6) production engineering management, and (7) facilities planning. *Operational* computer applications in manufacturing include plant floor operations, plant communications, and process and numerical control.

A computer-based manufacturing information system may typically include several major application categories:

- *Production planning.* The computer assists in the development of a master production schedule and in the determination of long-range resource requirements such as cash, plant capacity, and material requirements. The master production schedule is based on many factors, including long-range forecasts of sales and required production resources. Other applications in production planning are facilities planning, manpower planning, and material requirements planning.

- *Production inventory management.* This application "explodes" the master production schedule to determine specific material requirements. It also coordinates the purchasing, receiving, accounting, and storage activities required for proper production inventories.
- *Production scheduling.* The computer provides information required for the detailed scheduling of production which consists of assigning production starting dates, making short-range capacity adjustments, allocating materials from production inventories, and "releasing" production orders to the plant floor.
- *Production control.* This important "realtime" application provides continuous information feedback to production management concerning labor, production, and maintenance by such reporting activities as labor reporting, machine-downtime reporting, and production counts. Production control also includes "process control," which involves the direct monitoring and control of an ongoing production process, and "quality control," which involves the detection and analysis of deviations from production standards.
- *Plant maintenance.* This subsystem provides management with information for maintenance planning, work order dispatching, maintenance costing, and preventive maintenance scheduling.

Figure 13–11 illustrates some of the activities of several subsystems of a manufacturing information system. Figure 13–12 emphasizes the concept of "computer-aided manufacturing" (CAM) in which a central computer and several "sub-host" minicomputers are utilized to automate the operational systems of a manufacturing plant. Some of the benefits of computer-based manufacturing information systems are:

- Increased efficiency due to better production schedule planning and better balancing of production workload to production capacity.
- Improved utilization of production facilities, higher productivity, and better quality control resulting from continuous monitoring, feedback, and control of plant operations.
- Reduced investment in production inventories through better planning and control of production and finished goods requirements.
- Improved customer service by reducing out-of-stock situations and producing products that better meet customer requirements.

FIGURE 13–11   Subsystems of a Manufacturing Information System

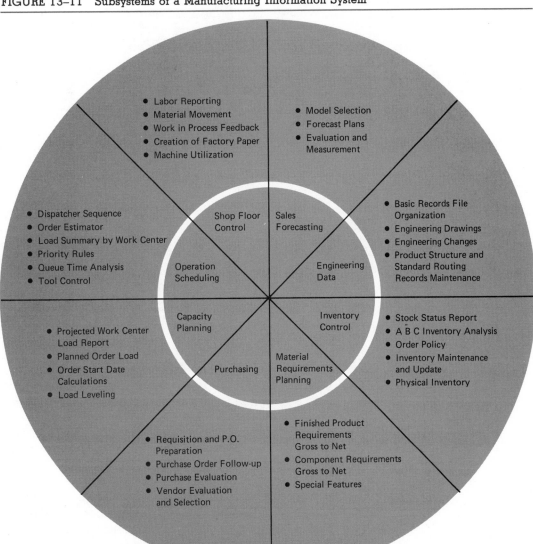

Courtesy IBM Corporation.

Process Control

Process control is the use of computers to control an ongoing physical process. Process control computers are utilized to control physical processes in petroleum refineries, cement plants, steel mills, chemical plants, food product manufacturing plants, pulp and paper mills, electric power plants, etc.

FIGURE 13–12 Computer-Aided Manufacturing (CAM) System

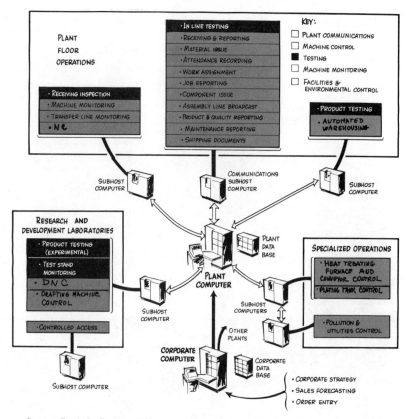

Source: Frank L. Stadulis, "Computers in Production—How to Get Started," *Automation*, October 1971, p. 24.

Many process control computers are special-purpose or dedicated general-purpose minicomputer systems.

A process control computer system requires the use of special sensing devices that measure physical phenomena such as temperature or pressure changes. These continuous physical measurements are converted to digital form by analog-to-digital converters and relayed to computers for processing. Process control computer programs utilize mathematical models to analyze the data generated by the ongoing process and compare it to standards or forecasts of required results. Output of a process control system can take three forms:

- Periodic reports analyzing the performance of the production process.
- Messages and instructions which allow a human operator to control the process.

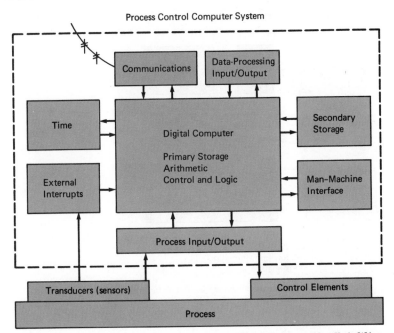

Process Control Computer System

FIGURE 13–13 **A Process Control Computer System**

Source: Thomas Harrison, *Handbook of Industrial Control Computers* (New York: Wiley-Interscience, 1972), p. 12.

- Direct control of the process by the use of control devices which control the process by adjusting thermostats, valves, switches, etc. See Figure 13–13.

Numerical Control and Robotics

Numerical control is the use of a computer to control the actions of a machine. **Robotics** is the technology of building machines with computer "intelligence" and "human-like" physical capabilities (dexterity, movement, vision, etc.). The control of machine tools in factories is a typical numerical control application, though numerical control can also be used for typesetting machines, weaving machines, and other "industrial robots." Numerical control computer programs for machine tools convert geometric data from engineering drawings, and machining instructions from process planning into a numerical code of commands which controls the actions of a machine tool. See Figure 13–14. Numerical control can be accomplished offline by using a special paper tape or

FIGURE 13–14   A Numerical Control System

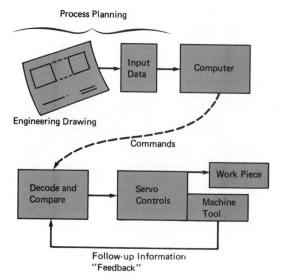

Process Planning

Engineering Drawing

Input Data

Computer

Commands

Decode and Compare

Servo Controls

Work Piece

Machine Tool

Follow-up Information
"Feedback"

Source: From *Digital Computer Principles and Applications*
by A. Favret. © 1972 by Litton Educational Publishing, Inc.

FIGURE 13–15   Computer Controlled Machine Tool

Courtesy Cincinnati Milacron, Inc.

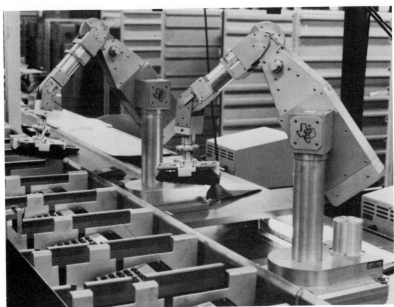

FIGURE 13–16 Robot Arms at Work on a Calculator Assembly Line; Overhead TV Cameras Help Them "See" Their Work

Courtesy Texas Instruments.

magnetic tape units which utilize the output of a computer to direct a machine. "Direct numerical control" is a type of numerical control involving the online control of machines by a computer. The development of the microcomputer is creating a new breed of "smart machines" and **robots** which directly control their own activities with the aid of "built-in" microcomputers. See Figures 13–15 and 13–16.

Physical Distribution

A major activity of the production/operations function is known as *physical distribution*. Physical distribution is concerned with moving raw materials to the factory and moving products from the production floor to the ultimate consumer. Physical distribution involves a "distribution network" which connects raw material sources, manufacturing plants, warehouses, middlemen, wholesale and retail outlets, and customers. It also involves the storage, transfer and transportation of goods from manufacturer to customer.

Physical distribution information systems are frequently computerized. The major computer applications of a physical distribution information system include:

- *Physical distribution planning.* This information subsystem provides information for the planning of the physical distribution system of a business firm. Mathematical models may be used to analyze alternative distribution networks by considering such factors as customer characteristics, manufacturing locations and capabilities, the number and location of warehouses, processing and inventory management policies, and alternative transportation arrangements.

- *Inventory control.* Inventory data is processed and information is provided to assist management in minimizing inventory costs and improving customer service. Figure 13–17 illustrates an advanced inventory control information system for large retail firms. This system uses mathematical decision rules, forecasting models, and simulation techniques to generate inventory replenishment decisions and various management reports.

FIGURE 13–17 An Advanced Inventory Control Information System

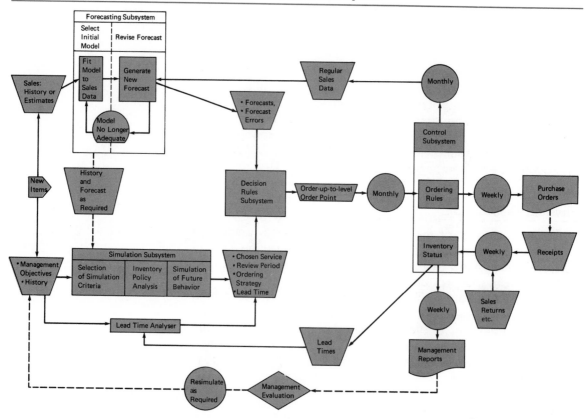

Courtesy IBM Corporation.

- *Distribution center management.* Supports the management and operations of "distribution centers" which consist of warehouses, shipping and receiving terminals, and other distribution support facilities. The objective of this system is to process data and provide information to assist management in the effective utilization of warehousing, shipping, and receiving personnel, facilities, and equipment, while maintaining a high level of customer service.
- *Traffic management.* Supports the daily planning and control of the movement of the products within the distribution network of a firm. It must provide information required for

FIGURE 13–18 A Purchasing/Receiving Information System

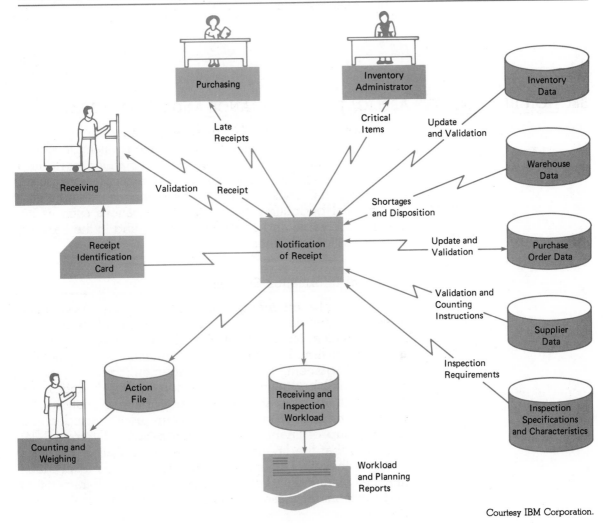

Courtesy IBM Corporation.

the scheduling of transportation requirements, the tracking of freight movement, the audit of freight bills, and the determination of efficient and economical methods of transportation.

- *Purchasing and receiving.* Provides information to ensure availability of the correct quantity and quality of the required materials at the lowest possible price. The purchasing subsystem assists in the selection of suppliers, placement of orders, and the follow-up activities to ensure on-time delivery of materials. The receiving subsystem identifies and validates the receipt of materials and routes the received material to its proper destination in storage or on the production floor. Figure 13–18 illustrates a computerized purchasing information system.

SECTION III: COMPUTER APPLICATIONS IN FINANCE AND ACCOUNTING

Computer applications in **finance** *and* **accounting** involve the use of computers in financial information systems, accounting information systems, and in industries which perform a financial function in our economy. For example, computers are utilized in financial applications such as cash management and capital budgeting, accounting applications such as accounts receivable and accounts payable, and in the banking and securities industries.

Financial Information Systems

Computer-based *financial information systems* support management in decisions concerning the financing of the business and the allocation and control of financial resources within the business firm. Major financial information systems include cash management, portfolio management, credit management, capital budgeting, financial forecasting, financing requirements analysis, and financial performance analysis. *Accounting information systems* are also frequently included as a major group of financial information systems. Figure 13–19 illustrates that the financial performance analysis system ties together the other financial information systems to produce financial planning and control information. The characteristics and functions of these computer-based systems are summarized below.

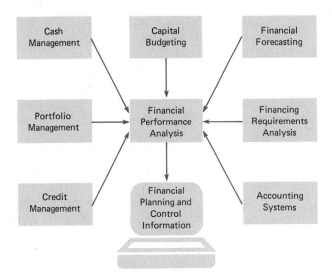

FIGURE 13-19 Financial Information Systems

- *Cash management.* The computer collects information on all cash receipts and disbursements throughout a company on a realtime or periodic basis. Such information allows business firms to deposit or invest excess funds more quickly and thus increase the income generated by deposited or invested funds. The computer also produces daily, weekly, or monthly forecasts of cash receipts or disbursements (cash flow forecasts) which are utilized to spot future cash deficits or cash surpluses. Mathematical models may be utilized to determine optimum cash collection programs and to determine alternative financing or investment strategies for dealing with forecasted cash deficits or surpluses.

- *Portfolio management.* Many business firms invest their excess cash in short-term marketable securities (such as U.S. Treasury bills, commercial paper, or certificates of deposit) so that investment income may be earned until the funds are required. The "portfolio" of such securities must be managed by buying, selling, or holding each type of security so that an optimum "mix" of securities is developed which minimizes risk and maximizes investment income.

- *Credit management.* Computerized credit management information systems plan and control the extension of credit to the customers of a firm. It provides information which is utilized to control credit policies in order to minimize bad-debt losses and investment in accounts receivable while maximizing sales and profitability. Advanced information systems of this type utilize the computer to automate the "screening" of credit applications and the decision to accept or reject a credit application.

- *Capital budgeting.* The computer is utilized to evaluate the profitability and financial impact of proposed capital expenditures. Large, long-term expenditure proposals can be analyzed utilizing a variety of computer-based analytical techniques such as present value analysis and probability analysis.

- *Financial forecasting.* This application provides information and analytical techniques which result in economic or financial forecasts such as national and local economic conditions, wage levels, price levels, and interest rates. It is heavily dependent on data gathered from the external environment and the utilization of various mathematical models and forecasting techniques.

- *Financing requirements analysis.* The computer supports the analysis of alternative methods of financing the business. Information concerning the economic situation, business operations, the types of financing available, interest rates, and stock and bond prices are utilized to develop an optimum financing plan for the business.

- *Accounting systems.* Several types of accounting systems will be discussed in an upcoming section and in the next chapter.

- *Financial performance analysis.* This application utilizes data provided by accounting systems and other financial information systems to evaluate and control present financial performance and to formulate short and long-range plans based upon their effect on projected financial performance. Advanced systems utilize "financial performance models" which allow management to evaluate the effect of various proposals on the revenues, cost, and profitability of the business firm.

Financial Performance Models

Advanced computer applications in finance utilize mathematical techniques and models for such applications as cash management, portfolio management, and capital budgeting. A more recent development is the use of computerized financial models which analyze the financial performance of the entire business firm or one of its divisions or subsidiaries. Figure 13–20 illustrates the components of a *financial performance model* of a business firm. Computerized financial performance models are used for the following purposes:

- To control the present performance by analyzing and evaluating current operations in comparison to budgeted objectives.

- To plan the short- and long-range operations of the firm by evaluating the effect of alternative proposals on the financial performance of the firm.

- To determine the future financing requirements and the optimum types of financing required to finance alternative proposals.

FIGURE 13–20   A Financial Performance Model

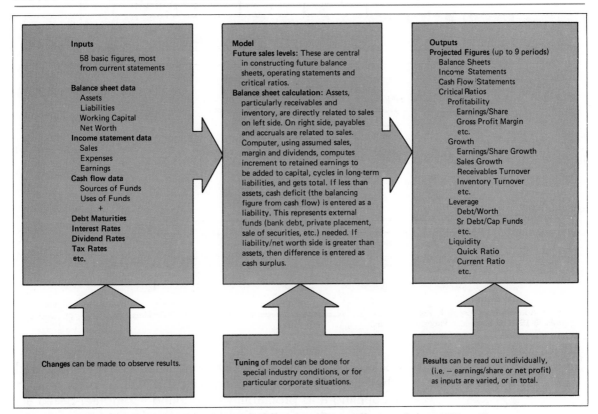

Source: "Successes Turn Detractors to Computer-Methods Converts," *Computer Decisions,* January 1972, p. 40.

Accounting Information Systems

Accounting information systems are the oldest and most widely used business information systems. They record and report business transactions and other economic events. Accounting information systems are based on the double-entry

FIGURE 13–21   Computer-Based Accounting Information Systems

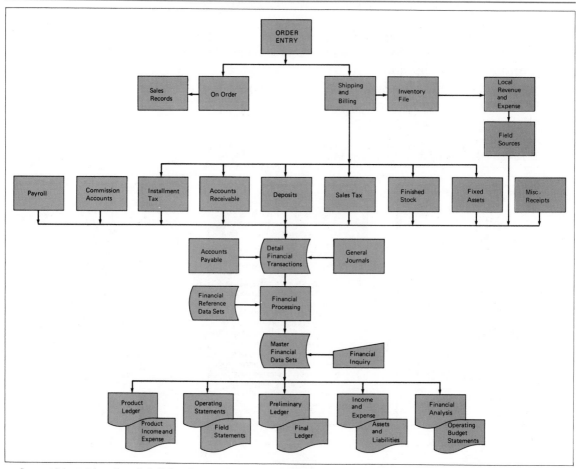

Source: Adapted from Joseph F. Kelly, *Computerized Management Information Systems* (New York: Macmillan, 1970), pp. 200–201. Copyright © 1970 by Macmillan Publishing Co., Inc.

bookkeeping concept, which is hundreds of years old, and other more recent accounting concepts such as responsibility accounting and profitability accounting. Computer-based accounting systems record and report the flow of funds through the organization on a historical basis and produce financial statements such as the balance sheet and income statement. Such systems also produce forecasts of future conditions such as projected financial statements and financial budgets.

Operational accounting systems emphasize legal and historical recordkeeping and the production of accurate financial statements. *Management accounting systems* focus on the planning and control of business operations through the development of financial budgets and projected financial statements. In the next chapter, we will analyze several operational accounting applications such as accounts receivable, accounts payable, and general ledger. Other major computer applications in accounting are summarized below.

- *Fixed asset accounting.* Involves the physical control and the financial recordkeeping caused by the use and depreciation of fixed assets.
- *Cost accounting.* Involves the accumulation and apportionment of costs within a business firm. For example, costs must be grouped into specific cost categories and attributed to specific products, projects, departments, etc.
- *Tax accounting.* Involves the recording and payment of business taxes such as income taxes, and inventory taxes.
- *Budgeting.* Involves the development of budgets which contain revenue and expense projections and other estimates of expected performance for the firm.

Figure 13–21 provides an overview of the relationships of various accounting information systems.

Applications in Banking

Computers have had a major impact on the *banking industry.* The computer has not only affected the accounting and reporting operations required by traditional bank services but has influenced the form and extent of all such services and made possible a variety of new "computer services." The computer is playing an even more decisive role in the operation of many banks through its use in financial models and other management science applications.

Traditional and new bank services that are computerized include:

- *Demand deposit accounting.* This application involves the automation of checking account processing. This was the first and most widely used computer application in banking. It depends heavily on the use of MICR-coded checks and deposit slips and the use of MICR reader-sorters to automate the capture of input data. Output of this system includes special reports concerning checking account activity and monthly customer statements.
- *Savings.* Most banks utilize data communications terminals at teller windows and automated remote "cash machines" which are electronically linked to the computers in the bank. Such machines are really special-purpose minicomputers

or "intelligent terminals," which automatically update a customer's balance on the computer and perform various banking services for the bank customer. Mutual savings banks and savings and loan associations are other major users of computers for realtime banking applications. See Figure 13–22.

- *Consumer, commercial, and mortgage loans.* Banks have computerized many aspects of the data processing required by their lending activities to consumers and business firms. The widespread development of bank credit card plans has greatly increased the use of computers to process the multitude of transactions generated by millions of bank credit card holders. Output of this application includes monthly customer statements, interest and tax reports, and various loan analysis reports.

- *Trust applications.* The trust function of banks involves the management of corporate trusts, personal trusts, pension funds, and health and welfare funds. The computer is utilized to handle a wide variety of accounting chores and produce management reports and legal documents. Advanced trust applications involve the use of computerized security analy-

FIGURE 13–22 Automated Teller Machine (ATM)

Courtesy Fidelity Mutual Savings Bank.

sis and portfolio selection applications which will be discussed shortly.

- *Computer services.* Many banks are offering computer services to other banks and financial institutions, business and professional firms, government and public organizations, and individuals. Some banks have "spun off" their EDP departments into separate EDP service subsidiaries that compete with independent computer service bureaus.

- *Advanced applications.* Many large banks use computerized financial performance models for internal planning and control and to evaluate the financial condition and financing requirements of bank customers. Banks are utilizing many other tools of operations research that require the computational power of the computer.

The computer is the primary component of future *electronic funds transfer* (EFT) systems which will replace cash and checks as the primary method of payment. The banking industry is in the forefront of efforts to develop the hardware,

FIGURE 13-23   An Electronic Funds Transfer System

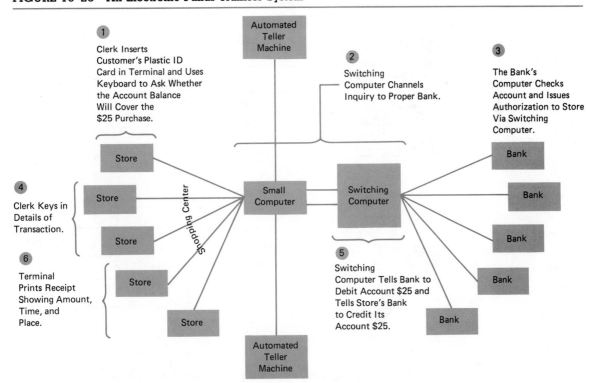

Source: Adapted with permission from *Changing Times* Magazine, © 1975 Kiplinger Washington Editors, Inc., October 1975.

software, and procedures required by EFT systems. Automated teller machines (ATMs), POS terminals, and computerized pay-by-phone systems are evidences of this development. See Figure 13–23.

Applications in Investments

Computers have been used by firms in the *investment industry* for many years to perform "back office operations," that is, recording transactions, billing customers, preparing monthly statements, etc. More recent applications of the computer in the investment industry are summarized below.[2]

- *The stock market.* Under the prodding of the SEC (Securities and Exchange Commission), the stock exchanges and other organizations in the investment industry are developing a computerized "central market" that will automate and centralize securities trading. Realtime computer-based information networks are currently used to facilitate the exchange

FIGURE 13–24 The NASDAQ Stock Quotation System

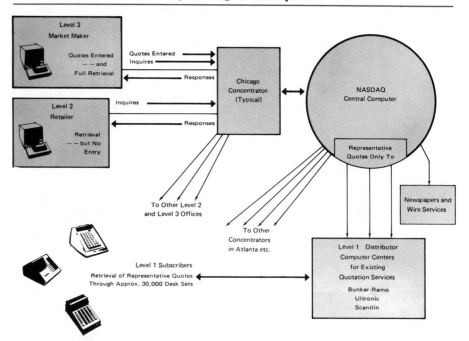

Source: Information Services Division, Bunker-Ramo Corporation.

---

[2] Some of the material in this section is adapted from Jerome B. Cohen, Edward D. Zinberg, and Arthur Zeikel, *Investment Analysis and Portfolio Management*, rev. ed. (Homewood, Ill.: Richard D. Irwin, 1973), pp. 66–67, 106–8, 134–38, and 837–41.

of information between securities brokers, dealers, and large institutional investors. The National Association of Securities Dealers (NASD) operates a nationwide realtime computer-based information network for over-the-counter (OTC) stocks called NASDAQ. See Figure 13–24.

- *Financial information retrieval.* Investment advisory service companies now provide the investment industry with computerized data banks, computer developed reports, and specialized time-sharing services. See Figure 13–25.

- *Security analysis.* Security analysis involves the analysis and evaluation of the value of an individual security. This type of analysis focuses on the financial position and prospects of a corporation in order to forecast the market price of its securities. Computerized security analysis utilizes data on selected corporations provided by financial advisory ser-

FIGURE 13–25 Financial Data Bases for Investment Analysis

ON-LINE DATA BASES & SYSTEMS

Interactive specializes in providing its subscribers with large scale, on-line data bases and proprietary processing programs to enable them to monitor, access, and display this information.

The on-line data bases and processing programs are oriented primarily to the financial and economic communities. They are used by Finance, Acquisition, and Treasury Departments within Banks, Brokerage Houses, Insurance Companies, and other financial institutions, and by Economists and Economic Business Forecasting Departments – to assist them in making better business decisions and in reducing related costs.

An *Interactive* Account Representative will be pleased to discuss these data bases and processing programs in more detail.

DATA BASES

The Securities' Price Data Base
- Daily since January 1968, price and volume data for all New York and American Stock Exchange Common Stocks and 1800 Over-the-Counter Stocks. Split factors resulting from capitalization changes are also indicated.
- Daily market indexes on — New York Stock Exchange — Dow Jones Industrial, Transportation & Utilities — American Stock Exchange — Standard & Poor's 425 and 500

The Corporate Financial Data Base [1]
- Sixty annual items from balance sheets, income statements and company ratios for the past twenty years on 1800 key industrial companies and utilities.
- Sixteen quarterly financial items plus monthly price information for the past ten years for 1800 key industrial companies.

The Financial XSPERT[sm] **Data Bases**
- all daily stock return from the New York and American Stock Exchanges for the past eight years
- monthly returns for 230 mutual funds for the past ten years

The XTICK[2] **Data Base**
Provide data on trading throughout the day with summary and transaction data for the current trading day for every security listed on the New York and American Stock Exchange tickers (15 minutes delayed per Exchange regulations). Closing prices are available shortly after 4:00 PM each day.

The Bond Data Base
Daily price and volume information on over 1800 bonds traded on the New York and American Stock Exchanges.

The Split and Dividend Data Base
Daily information on all New York and American Stock Exchange stocks and 1800 Over the Counter stocks.
- Accessible by stock symbol or ex-date
- Ex-date, record date, payable date and type of distribution available

The Economic Data Base [3]
- Weekly, monthly, quarterly, and annual time-series describing more than six thousand separate economic variables. This data, which highlights a wide variety of U.S. economic indicators, is grouped as follows:
  - National Income and Product Accounts
  - Gross National Product and Components by Industry
  - U.S. Balance of International Payments Accounts
  - New Plant and Equipment Expenditures
  - Retail and Wholesale Trade and Inventory by Type of Store
  - Manufacturers Shipments, Inventories, and Orders
  - Profit and Loss Statements and Balance Sheet Data for Manufacturing Corporations
  - Measures of Economic Activity in 475 Manufacturing Sectors
  - Selected Business Indicators and Product Line Statistics
  - Federal Reserve Board Production Indexes
  - Population, Labor Force, Employment, Hours, and Earnings by Industry
  - Consumer and Wholesale Prices Indexes
  - Monetary Statistics
  - Weekly Statistics

Private Data Bases
- Subscribers may create their own private data bases containing any information which they wish to enter. This data can then be analyzed independently or in conjunction with data maintained in the above data bases.

Interactive Data Corporation
486 Totten Pond Road
Waltham, Massachusetts 02154

Courtesy Interactive Data Corporation.

vices and time-sharing companies. Various types of financial, economic, and market analyses are then made in order to forecast alternative values for the security being analyzed. See Figure 13–26.

- *Portfolio management.* Portfolio management involves the management of a combination of securities by holding, selling, or buying selected securities in order to minimize the risk and maximize the return of the entire "portfolio" of investments. Computerized portfolio management utilizes a computer program that contains mathematical models which can select one or more portfolios which minimize risk for specific levels of investment return and which also satisfy various investment constraints. In most cases the portfolio selection process produces a list of acceptable portfolios which are reviewed by a "portfolio manager" who then makes the final hold, buy, and sell decisions for each portfolio managed. Figure 13–27 illustrates an integrated portfolio management system.

FIGURE 13–26 Output of a Security Analysis Application

MINNESOTA MINING AND MANUFACTURING

YEAR	HIGH	LOW	EPS	OFFICE EQUIPMENT DIVIDEND
71	33.000	19.000	0.780	0.400
72	38.000	24.000	0.860	0.400
73	60.000	37.000	1.250	0.500
74	88.000	53.000	1.380	0.580
75	87.000	66.000	1.460	0.650
76	70.000	41.000	1.610	0.800
78	73.000	52.000	1.730	0.900
79	70.000	54.000	1.920	1.000
80	71.000	54.000	2.180	1.100
81	86.000	61.000	2.590	1.200

83.880 (CURRENT)   2.750 (EST)   1.450 (EST)

MINNESOTA MINING AND MANUFACTURING
PROJECTED AND CURRENT PRICE

		OFFICE EQUIPMENT 10 YEARS OF DATA EARNINGS GROWTH RATES	
1-10	108.08	1-4	23.19
6-1	90.10	4-7	8.07
8-10	88.82	7-10	14.31
CURRENT	83.88		

PROJECTED 5 YEAR PRICE

		EARNING GROWTH RATES	
1-10	176.52	1-10	13.05
6-10	144.57	6-10	12.55
8-10	161.62	8-10	16.14

FIGURE 13–27   Integrated Portfolio Management System

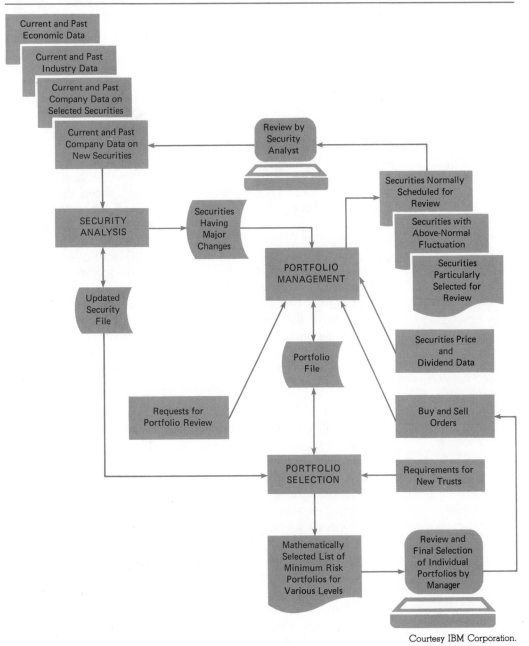

Courtesy IBM Corporation.

SECTION IV: OTHER COMPUTER APPLICATIONS IN BUSINESS

In this section we will briefly explore several major computer applications that should contribute to a well rounded understanding of the use of computers in business.

Personnel Information Systems

The **personnel** function involves the recruitment, placement, evaluation, compensation, and development of the employees of an organization. *Personnel information systems* are traditionally used by business firms to (1) produce paychecks and payroll reports, (2) maintain personnel records, and (3) analyze the amounts, types, and costs of labor utilized in business operations. Many firms have gone beyond these traditional functions and have developed personnel information systems which support (1) recruitment, selection, and hiring, (2) job placement, (3) performance appraisals, (4) employee benefits analysis, (5) training and development, and (6) health, safety, and security. Personnel information systems support the concept of *human resource management,* which emphasizes *planning* to meet the personnel needs of the business and the *control* of all personnel policies and programs, so that effective and efficient use is made of the *human resources* of the company. The major computer applications in personnel are summarized below and illustrated in Figure 13–28.

- *Payroll and labor analysis.* Computers process data concerning employee compensation and work activity and produce paychecks, payroll reports, and labor analysis reports.
- *Personnel record-keeping.* This application is concerned with additions, deletions, and other changes to the records in the personnel data base. Changes in job assignments and compensation, or hirings and terminations are examples of information that would be utilized to update the personnel data base.
- *Employee skills inventory.* The computer is utilized to locate specific human resources within a company and to maximize their use. The employee skills inventory system utilizes the employee skills data from the personnel data base to locate employees within a company who have the skills required for specific assignment and projects. See Figure 13–29.
- *Training and development analysis.* Computers help personnel management plan and control employee recruitment, training, and development programs by analyzing the success history of present programs. They also analyze the ca-

FIGURE 13–28   Integrated Personnel Systems Concept

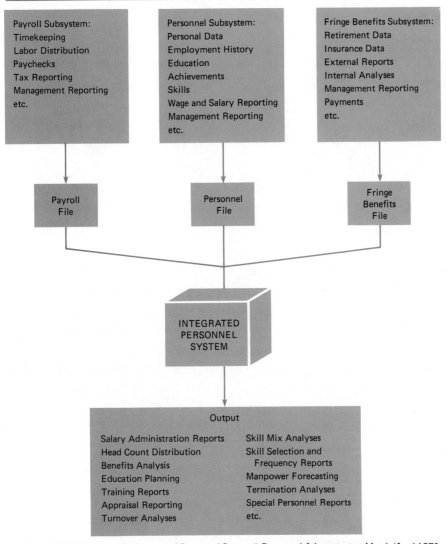

Source: Rolf E. Rogers, "An Integrated Personnel System," *Personnel Administration*, March/April 1970.

reer development status of each employee to determine whether development methods such as training programs or performance appraisals should be recommended.

- *Compensation analysis.* This application analyzes the range and distribution of employee compensation (wages, salaries, incentive payments, and fringe benefits) within a company and makes comparisons with compensation paid by similar firms or with various economic indicators. This

FIGURE 13–29 Skills Inventory Profile Report

		Confidential	SKILLS INVENTORY PROFILE	
JAMESON	JAMES L	626	05/8X	342971
MANAGEMENT/PROJECT LDR EXPERIENCE				
MANAGER		3.0		AC105
MANAGER			FIRST PREFERENCE	96 AC105
ENGINEERING/SCIENTIFIC/TECH FIELDS				
ELECTRICAL–ELECTRONICS ENGINEER		10+		BC001
CIRCUIT DESIGN–GENERAL		8.0		BC145
CIRCUIT DESIGN–GENERAL			FIRST SPECIALTY	91 BC145
CIRCUIT DESIGN–SOLID STATE		5.5		BC150
INTEGRATED CIRCUITS		3.5		BC280
COMPONENTS EXPERIENCE – BB				
CORE CIRCUITS			DESIGN	08 CL090
DDTL			QUALITY ENGR	28 CL160
INSTRUMENTS EXPERIENCE				
ELECTROMETERS		4.0		CO140
			RESEARCH OR DEV ENGR	21 TB100
			RESEARCH OR DEV ENGR	21 TD060
			RESEARCH OR DEV ENGR	21 TD070
			PRODUCT TEST ENGR	26 TD220
			RESEARCH OR DEV ENGR	21 TG140
			RESEARCH OR DEV ENGR	21 TG160
FOREIGN LANGUAGE PROFICIENCY				
GERMAN			INTERPRET	87 VE260
RUSSIAN			SUMMARIZE IN ENGLISH	88 VE510

Courtesy IBM Corporation.

information is useful for planning changes in compensation, especially if negotiations with labor unions are involved. It helps keep the compensation of a company competitive and equitable, while controlling compensation costs.

- *Personnel requirements forecasting.* Short- and long-range planning is required to assure a business firm of an adequate supply of high-quality human resources. This application provides information required for forecasts of personnel requirements in each major employment category for various company departments or for new projects and other ventures being planned by management. Such long-range planning may use a computer-based simulation model to evaluate alternative plans for recruitment, reassignment, or retraining programs.

Operations Research Applications

Operations research (or *management science*) represents a major area of computer use. Operations research is the application of scientific techniques to organizational problems, utilizing a methodology based on the concepts and techniques of mathematics and the natural, physical, and social sciences. Operations research techniques usually involve the formulation of "mathematical models" of the system being investigated. Mathematical models can be used for problem solving, utilizing either "mathematical analysis" or "mathematical simulation." Therefore, most computer applications in operations research involve the use of computer programs containing mathematical models which are then solved or "manipulated," using various types of mathematical analysis or simulation. Figure 13–30 outlines the function, effect, and software requirements of several operations research techniques.

A more detailed example of a computer application in operations research is shown in Figure 13–31. Operations research techniques such as linear programming and simulation and the processing power of the computer are utilized by a shipping company for the scheduling of tankers. The computer provides management with alternative feasibile monthly schedules which outline the effects of each alternative. Such information dramatically increases the effectiveness of management decisions.

Other Business Applications

A quick glance at how the computer is used in several industries should be sufficient to emphasize the amazing versatility of the computer and the variety of its applications in business.

- **Airlines.**   Airline reservation systems were the earliest major realtime application of computers in business. Real-time computer systems are on-line to terminals in airline offices both nationwide and overseas. Besides such real-time passenger reservation systems and traditional business applications, computers provide information for such functions as: (1) flight plan preparation, (2) fuel loading, (3) meal catering, (4) air cargo routing, and (5) freight, supplies, and spare parts inventory control.
- **Agribusiness.**   Agriculture has become a big business—

FIGURE 13–30 Analysis of Selected Operations Research Applications

Operations Research Technique	Function	Effect	Software Tools Available
MATHEMATICAL ANALYSIS	Utilize complex mathematics for solving engineering/research problems.	Computational processing is performed at electronic speeds. Special languages and subroutines facilitate expression and solution of problems.	Math library-precoded routines, e.g., numerical analysis, interpolation, exponential and log functions and matrix analysis.
STATISTICAL ANALYSIS	Analysis of quantitative and statistical data for such applications as market research, sales forecasting, inventory control, research, and quality control.	Improves accuracy and validity of decision making by providing more sophisticated analysis.	Statistics library, e.g., variance, T-ratio, standard deviation, binomial distribution, random number generator, regression analysis, etc.
LINEAR PROGRAMMING	Mathematical technique for solving problems of competing demands for limited resources where there are a great number of interacting variables.	Resolves complex problems that can only be approximated or guesstimated by conventional means. Increases accuracy and improves decision making in broad class of decisions.	Linear programming (LP) packages assist in problem structuring and formulation and then provide high-speed computing power to efficiently produce solutions based on alternate decision rules.
NETWORK ANALYSIS	Scheduling, costing and status reporting of major projects.	Improves planning, scheduling, and implementing of complex projects comprising multiple events and activities. Permits continuous evaluation of projects' progress to increase probabilities of on-time, on-cost performance.	PERT (program evaluation and review technique) and CPM (critical path method) software systems for processing large networks of events and activities producing a variety of computer reports to pinpoint schedule slippages, critical events, and action needed to get back on schedule.
QUEUEING THEORY	Solving problems where it is desirable to minimize the costs and/or time associated with waiting lines or queues.	Improves management ability to improve operations like checkout counters, receiving docks, machine centers or turn-toll stations.	General-purpose simulators aid the construction and development of complex simulation models. The simulator has the ability to produce random numbers to test various activity patterns and optimize the use of resources.
SIMULATION	Determines the impact of decisions using hypothetical or historical data in lieu of incurring the expense and risk of trying out decisions in actual operations.	Business managers can test and project the effects of decisions on a wide variety of operational areas thus ensuring optimal results when the decisions and policies are put into practice.	General-purpose simulators as above.

Source: Adapted from Jerome Kanter, *Management-Oriented Management Information Systems*, 2d ed., © 1977, p. 168. Reprinted by permission of Prentice-Hall, Inc., Englewood Cliffs, New Jersey.

"Agribusiness." Many corporate and family farms and ranches are now using the power of the computer. Major applications include (1) farm and crop record-keeping and analysis, (2) financial and tax accounting, and (3) optimal feed-blending, fertilizing, and crop-rotation programs. Com-

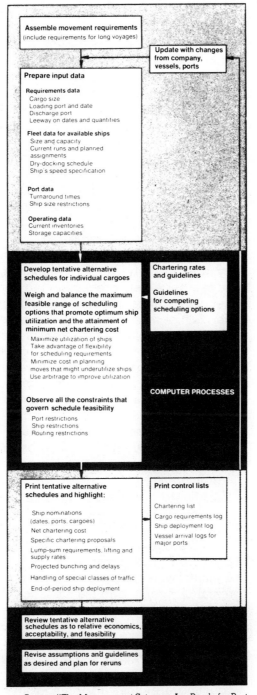

FIGURE 13–31 Scheduling Ships: A Computer Application of OR

Assemble movement requirements
(include requirements for long voyages)

Update with changes from company, vessels, ports

Prepare input data

Requirements data
Cargo size
Loading port and date
Discharge port
Leeway on dates and quantities

Fleet data for available ships
Size and capacity
Current runs and planned assignments
Dry-docking schedule
Ship's speed specification

Port data
Turnaround times
Ship size restrictions

Operating data
Current inventories
Storage capacities

Develop tentative alternative schedules for individual cargoes

Weigh and balance the maximum feasible range of scheduling options that promote optimum ship utilization and the attainment of minimum net chartering cost
Maximize utilization of ships
Take advantage of flexibility for scheduling requirements
Minimize cost in planning moves that might underutilize ships
Use arbitrage to improve utilization

Observe all the constraints that govern schedule feasibility
Port restrictions
Ship restrictions
Routing restrictions

Chartering rates and guidelines

Guidelines for competing scheduling options

COMPUTER PROCESSES

Print tentative alternative schedules and highlight:

Ship nominations (dates, ports, cargoes)
Net chartering cost
Specific chartering proposals
Lump-sum requirements, lifting and supply rates
Projected bunching and delays
Handling of special classes of traffic
End-of-period ship deployment

Print control lists

Chartering list
Cargo requirements log
Ship deployment log
Vessel arrival logs for major ports

Review tentative alternative schedules as to relative economics, acceptability, and feasibility

Revise assumptions and guidelines as desired and plan for reruns

Source: "The Management Sciences Are Ready for Business." Reprinted from *Computer Decisions* (January 1972), p. 34. © 1972, Hayden Publishing Company.

puter services are provided by government agricultural extension agencies, commercial banks, EDP service bureaus, and farm cooperatives. Microcomputer-based devices to automatically control farm machinery for planting, fertilizing, irrigating, and harvesting are a recent development.

- **Construction.** Large construction companies have been using computers for many years for traditional business applications such as payroll and general accounting. Scientific applications requiring mathematical computations for design engineering analysis have also been utilized. The most recent major application, however, is the use of network analysis techniques like PERT (Program Evaluation and Review Technique) and CPM (Critical Path Method) for construction planning and scheduling. The computer can utilize such techniques to produce plans and schedules (in terms of time, men, money, and materials) for each stage of complex construction projects.

- **Insurance.** Like the banking industry, the insurance industry was an early user of computers. Insurance companies have a huge data processing job because of the large number of insurance policies, claims, premium notices, and dividends that must continually be processed. Large numbers of customers and complex insurance policy provisions require the maintenance of a large data base. Complex actuarial computations (such as life expectancy statistics) must also be performed. A major recent application is the use of real-time inquiry systems that allow branch offices to interrogate the central data base for customer policy information. Another application is the use of the computer to perform part of the "underwriting" function by preparing detailed insurance coverage proposals for presentation to prospective customers.

- **Real Estate.** Real estate applications fall into several major categories. Real estate investment applications analyze financial, tax, marketing, and physical requirements data to compute rate-of-return alternatives for proposed real estate projects. Property management applications assist the management of rental property by processing rental statements, rental payments, and maintenance and utility disbursement, and by providing various management reports, such as income and expense analysis. Property listing applications (also called a multiple listing service) maintain up-to-date listings of all properties registered for sale with participating realtors. Mortgage loan accounting and property title accounting are other applications in the real estate category that are usually performed by banks and title companies, respectively.

SUMMARY

- Business computer users should have an understanding of how the computer supports the basic functions of business, and especially how computers affect a particular business function or a particular industry that is directly related to their career objectives.

- In this chapter, we briefly described many important applications in business according to the business function they support (marketing, production/operations, finance, accounting, and personnel) and according to the industry in which they are utilized (retailing, banking, investments, airlines, agribusiness, construction, insurance, and real estate). Refer back to Figures 13–1 and 13–2 for summaries of major business computer applications by functional and industry categories.

KEY TERMS AND CONCEPTS

Marketing information systems

Computer applications in retailing

The point-of-sale revolution

Manufacturing information systems

Process control

Numerical control

Robotics

Physical distribution applications

Financial information systems

Financial performance models

Accounting information systems

Computer applications in banking

Computer applications in investments

Personnel information systems

Operations research applications

REVIEW AND DISCUSSION QUESTIONS

1. How are computers used in business? Is there a simple answer to this question?
2. What kind of understanding of computer use in business should a computer user have?
3. Discuss several computer applications in marketing and retailing.
4. What effect will the use of point-of-sale terminals have on computer applications in marketing?
5. Discuss several computer applications in production/operations and manufacturing.
6. What effect will computer-aided manufacturing have on computer applications in production? What impact will robotics have?
7. Discuss several computer applications in finance and accounting.
8. What are several traditional and new computer applications in banking?

9. What do you think will be the impact of electronic funds transfer (EFT) systems on computer applications in banking?

10 Identify several computer applications in investments. How will these applications be affected by an "electronic stock market"?

11. Identify several computer applications in personnel.

12. Can computer applications in operations research be applied to any business function or industry? Explain.

13. Identify the use of computers in one of the following industries: airlines, agribusiness, construction, insurance, and real estate.

14. Prepare a "computer applications report" which describes and evaluates how the computer is utilized by a specific business firm or industry. Do the research for this report by contacting a computer-using business firm, the local office of a computer manufacturer, or by reviewing books and articles on specific business firms, industries, or business computer applications in your library.

REAL WORLD APPLICATIONS

13–1 Gould Instrument Division

It's the difference between charting a course and bailing the ship," said Roy Tottingham. "Bringing our manufacturing operation under control has had a favorable effect on all aspects of our business—from managerial productivity right on down to the bottom line. And COPICS is part of the synergism that has achieved it." (COPICS is IBM's Communications Oriented Production Information and Control System software package.) Tottingham is president of the Santa Clara, California, operation of Gould Instrument Division, Gould, Inc., a producer of state-of-the-art electronic test and measurement instruments. Getting IBM's COPICS online and on-the-air with a minimal staff, and doing it just four months after installation of the firm's first in-house computer, was a major achievement for the company.

"We have gone from 130 days inventory on hand in 1977, to 117 in 1979, to about 89 days on hand now, and the quantity is still dropping. At the same time, our annual sales volume has increased three fold," said Robert A. Nazarenus, vice president of finance. We have saved on the tremendous cost of 'flooring' unneeded inventory at today's high cost of money," he said. "The cost of carrying inventory is one of the most significant expenditures in any company, but the cost of *not* hav-

ing inventory when it's needed can be even greater in terms of lost production," declared Rich Anderson, vice president, manufacturing. "However, COPICS solves that problem, too, because it has the ability to alter Material Requirements Planning (MRP) at any level of detail we require. This allows us, for example, to determine weekly exactly how many of what type of subassembly we want to process. We also have a new capability to plan manpower usage and cope with other manufacturing problem areas."

In the past, 25 percent of the dollar volume of inventory went out as "unplanned" issues; the firm's inventory shortage report used to be 20 pages long; unfavorable cost variance against standards in both labor and materials ran around (−) 25 percent and in 1978 profitability declined for the first time in the division's history. Now, the number of unplanned issues is miniscule; the inventory shortage report is less than 1½ pages long; materials have leveled to standard; and labor and overhead variances hit a favorable plus 50 percent, so the standards were changed. Finally, the percentage of before-tax profits has doubled since 1978.

"Improved inventory management has also held the unit cost of an item to what it was 1½ years ago, despite inflation, because of planned purchasing from vendors instead of the short-term crisis buys from distributors in the past," said Hal Erpenbeck, director of management information systems. "When we initially submitted a capital expense proposal to install COPICS, we said it would pay off in just 4.3 months after it went into operation. Instead, establishing the COPICS discipline in April, 1979, radically reduced unplanned issues from the first. So the project began paying for itself even before the first modules were up and running."

The COPICS modules at Gould include: online Bills of Material (BOM); Bill of Material Batch Utilities; Advanced Function MRP; Inventory Planning and Forecasting; Inventory Accounting; Product Cost Calculation; Shop Order Release, and Routing Data Control.[1]

● How has COPICS benefitted manufacturing operations and management at the Gould Instrument Division?

[1] Source: "To Have or Have Not," *Data Processor,* September/October 1980, pp. 13–14. Reprinted with permission.

13-2 Citizens Fidelity Bank

A bank in Louisville, Kentucky, believes that more depositor transactions will soon be performed in nonbanking locales. Says Frank M. Knego, senior vice president of Citizens Fidelity Bank & Trust Company: "We need some fundamental changes if we are to offer consumers the convenience they expect. It costs too much to build new branches and to extend banking hours. We chose the alternative—customer-operated services off-premises, through an online banking system—and we haven't had to increase the number of branches since 1975. We've also cut back hours in 33 branches. We had been feeling pressure for Saturday banking, but we've been able to meet that demand with electronic funds transfer (EFT) instead."

In addition to the 16 IBM 3614 ATMs (automated teller machines) online to its IBM 3033 Processor, Citizens Fidelity worked closely with local merchants to develop point-of-sale (POS) service. Depositors can now withdraw and deposit money, as well as pay for purchases, through instore IBM 3608 Point-of-Sale Terminals. The customer inserts a plastic card and keys in the dollar amount, Knego explains. The terminal produces a printed slip that the depositor hands the store clerk, who then accepts the deposit or pays out the withdrawal.

"Everyone gains," Knego points out. "We pay merchants to handle our EFT service, although we charge them to process paper checks. The funds are transferred to the stores' accounts immediately, rather than after a check clears. Surveys show that EFT users make significantly higher average purchases than they did before. The merchants gain in goodwill by offering the service. And withdrawals help them dispose of surplus cash. For the depositor, there is the convenience of one-stop banking and shopping. Banking hours are more flexible. And we've found that many depositors prefer to do their banking in neighborhood convenience stores.

"The bank has avoided new construction and longer hours. The cost per transaction is declining steadily as the volume of EFT activity increases. And a survey showed that our best EFT customers maintain higher balances and write 35 percent fewer checks. And, most importantly, implementing the EFT program has allowed us to be innovative in our approach to the distribution of banking services. Rather than bring people to the bank, we are bringing banking to the people."[2]

● How does Citizens Fidelity Bank's EFT program extend banking service hours and locations? What benefits have resulted?

[2] Source: "A Louisville Bank Goes Where the People Are." Reprinted by permission from *DP Dialogue.* © 1981 by International Business Machines Corporation.

13–3   GE Plant Services Division

Everything about the General Electric Co. plant in Erie, Pa., is imposing. It sprawls across 400 acres, a bustling agglomeration of 11,000 people who produce industrial machinery—locomotives, mining equipment, and the like. The scale of GE's operation there is exemplified by the $30-million budget of the plant services division—which covers construction, maintenance, utilities, and so forth—a sum large enough to run a fair-sized town.

Industrial engineer Lyn Brawn, manager of maintenance and construction planning and scheduling, is responsible for producing weekly forecasts of the plant services division's labor and construction needs—reports of shop orders, materials lists, job descriptions, and man-hour specifications for nine trades on three different shifts. Until a year ago, Brawn would process this information at the end of each week on GE's own giant Mark III mainframe time-sharing computer network and wait until Monday morning for the results. Now, thanks to the installation of a $7,000 desktop Apple III—a microcomputer system no bulkier than a tabletop stereo yet complete with two 5-inch disk drives, a Panasonic color monitor, and a Texas Instruments printer—he produces daily reports.

"The DP people were resistant at first to the idea of getting a micro," says Brawn. "They were concerned about having to provide support for it." So Brawn took matters into his own hands and, with the computer literacy gained from courses offered at the plant (and some previous experience with a home computer), was able to write his own software, customized for his division's needs.

What made true believers of the micro skeptics in the plant services division was the efficiency gained with VisiCalc—an off-the-shelf financial-planning software package developed by Personal Software, Inc., of Sunnyvale, Calif. "VisiCalc gave us speed in recalculating budgets and long-range forecasts," explains Brawn. "We had to make budget projections in over 70 different categories, including personnel and billing. Often, a shift in the inflation rate would be enough to change all our projections, so we would have 12 staff people recalculating numbers and an accountant consolidating their figures. The time we saved in the first month with VisiCalc paid for our first Apple." The success of VisiCalc in the plant services division has since led to the installation of a half dozen Apple microcomputers throughout the plant—each equipped with the financial software.

"Plant policy is to treat desktop computers as disposable assets—like calculators," notes Bill Bovee, advanced applications systems analyst at the plant. For this reason, the plant's DP department adheres to a philosophy of servicing only mainframes and minicomputers. "It's up to the user to buy micro hardware and software once the finance department has approved the purchase," says Bovee. This lack of micro software support is Lyn Brawn's greatest source of annoyance. He has had to resolve problems with many prepackaged programs, getting "no more than vocal encouragement from our local microcomputer dealer: 'When you solve the problem, let me know' is the attitude. Fortunately, I have enough expertise to fix it."

Despite such snags, Brawn is bullish on micros bringing greater productivity to Fortune 500 manufacturing firms. He points to the three Apple microcomputer systems that have found their way into the plant services division. "We had to lease an additional Apple II with Apple Plot graphics software so our graphics people could draw up [as many as] 150 charts for a management report." The $4,500 Apple II with which Brawn first introduced micro efficiency to his operation—since replaced with the more sophisticated $7,000 system—now gets constant use in the division's accounting department. "Once they saw what software like VisiCalc could save in hand calculations, they wanted their own [system]. One procedure alone—liquidating monthly accounts for our power house—now takes them only minutes instead of hours."[3]

- How are microcomputer systems used by the plant services division?
- What role does the VisiCalc software package play in these applications? What benefits have occurred?

[3] Source: Steve Ditlea, "At a Pennsylvania G.E. Plant, Progress in Planning by Micro," *Output,*" June 1981, p. 44.

14

CHAPTER OUTLINE

Common Business Applications

LEARNING OBJECTIVES

The purpose of this chapter is to promote a basic understanding of how the computer is used in business by analyzing seven common computer applications in business.

After reading and studying this chapter, you should be able to summarize the objectives, input, data base, and output of several of the common business applications.

OVERVIEW

Out of all of the possible applications of the computer in business, several basic applications stand out because they are common to most business computer users. Most of these applications exist in both large and small computer-using business firms, whether they are experienced computer users or are utilizing the computer for the first time. These *common business applications* are summarized below and illustrated in Figure 14–1.

Sales Order/Transaction Processing. Processes orders received from customers and produces receipts for customers and data needed for sales analysis and inventory control.

Inventory Control. Receives data concerning customer orders, prepares shipping documents if the ordered items are available, and records all changes in inventory.

Billing and Sales Analysis. Receives filled-orders data from the inventory control system and produces customer invoices and management reports analyzing the sales generated by each salesperson, customer, product, etc.

Accounts Receivable. Receives data concerning customer invoices and payments and produces monthly customer statements and credit management reports.

Accounts Payable. Receives data concerning purchases from suppliers and produces checks in payment of outstanding invoices and cash management reports.

Payroll and Labor Analysis. Receives data from employee time cards and other records and produces paychecks, payroll reports, and labor analysis reports.

General Ledger. Receives data from accounts receivable, accounts payable, payroll and labor analysis, and many other business information subsystems. Produces the general ledger trial balance, the income statement and balance sheet of the firm, and various income and expense reports for management.

The description of each common computer application that follows has been simplified since our purpose is to understand computer applications from the viewpoint of a *business computer user* rather than that of *computer specialist.* Therefore, no attempt is made to describe all of the variations that are possible for each common computer application, since the particular form of an application will vary depending upon the type of business firm involved. For example, the sales order processing system that will be described is most often utilized by business firms whose customers are other business firms rather than consumers. Another example is the inventory control system which we will describe. It is most widely used to control the inventory of wholesale or retail firms or the finished goods inventory of manufacturing firms. However, in all cases the applications we describe represent a basic form that should be understood by all business computer users.

Figure 14–2 illustrates some of the many possible variations of the common business applications. It represents a video

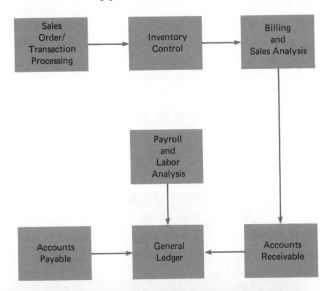

FIGURE 14–1 How the Common Computer Applications in Business Are Related

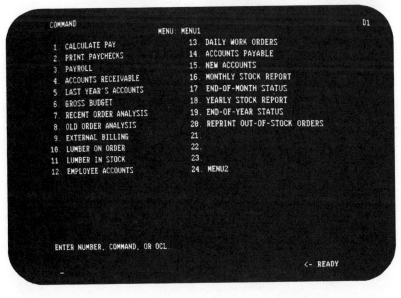

FIGURE 14–2 A Menu of Common and Specialized Business Computer Applications

display of a "menu" of common and special computer applications from which a user at a CRT terminal would select an application for processing.

THE SALES ORDER/TRANSACTION PROCESSING APPLICATION

Objectives

The objectives of the *sales order/transaction processing* application are:

- To provide a fast, accurate, and efficient method of recording and screening customer orders and sales transactions.
- To provide the inventory control system with information on accepted orders so that they can be filled as quickly as possible.

Figure 14–3 is a general systems flowchart that summarizes the components of the sales order/transaction processing system that should be understood by computer users.

FIGURE 14–3 A Sales Order/ Transaction Processing System

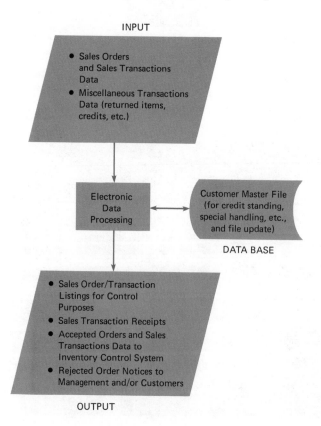

INPUT

- Sales Orders and Sales Transactions Data
- Miscellaneous Transactions Data (returned items, credits, etc.)

Electronic Data Processing

Customer Master File (for credit standing, special handling, etc., and file update)

DATA BASE

- Sales Order/Transaction Listings for Control Purposes
- Sales Transaction Receipts
- Accepted Orders and Sales Transactions Data to Inventory Control System
- Rejected Order Notices to Management and/or Customers

OUTPUT

Input

Sales transactions and sales orders from customers or salespersons are received by mail, telephone or telegraph, or are made in person. They can be recorded on sales receipt or sales order forms and then converted into punched cards, paper tape, or magnetic tape form unless OCR documents are utilized. Alternatively, *point-of-sale terminals* and other types of remote terminals may be utilized to enter sales order and sales transaction data directly into the computer system. Though such data is the primary form of input into the system, other types of input data must also be captured. Data from "miscellaneous transactions" such as returned items, credits for damaged goods, etc., are also entered into the system.

Data Base

The sales order/transaction processing system utilizes a "customer master file" as its data base. The customer master file contains data on each customer such as (1) name, number, address, and phone number, (2) codes indicating sales tax liability, eligibility for discounts, etc., and (3) other information such as location, line of business, credit limits, and assigned salespersons. This file provides information on the credit standing of customers, special handling requirements, and other information which is utilized to decide which orders should be accepted. The file can also be updated to reflect changes in credit standing, new customers, address changes, etc.

Output

Like most business computer applications, the output of the sales order/transaction processing system includes listings (also called logs or registers) of each sales order transaction which allow control totals and other types of data processing controls to be accomplished. The purpose of such controls is to guard against errors or fraud in the input or processing of the data and to provide an "audit trail" to facilitate the auditing of the system.

One of the primary outputs of the system consists of data describing accepted sales orders and completed sales transactions. This data becomes input for the inventory control system. Figure 14–4 illustrates the types of output data required to describe a single sales item.

FIGURE 14–4 Sales Transaction Record

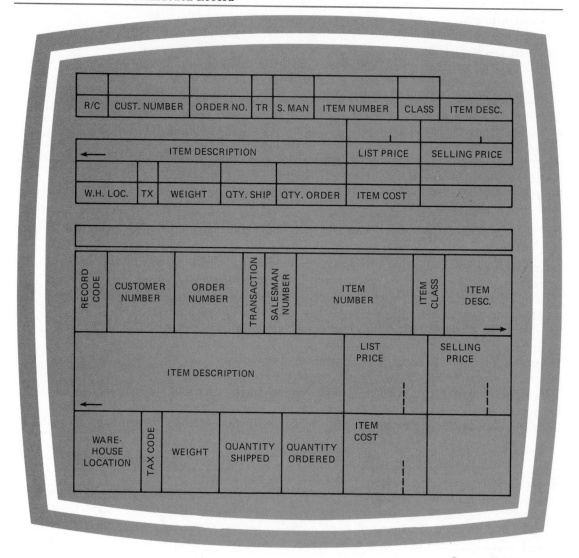

Courtesy IBM Corporation.

The output of many sales order/transaction processing systems also includes notices or receipts to customers acknowledging completed sales transactions or receipt of their orders. In most nonretail business firms, sales invoices ("bills") describing filled and shipped sales orders are produced by a "billing" system which will be described shortly. Orders not accepted by the system because of inaccurate information are corrected by EDP personnel after consultation with salespersons or customers and reentered into the system. Orders rejected for exceeding credit limits or other reasons are usually referred to operating management (such as credit management or sales managers) for corrective action or may be returned to the customer.

THE INVENTORY CONTROL APPLICATION

Objectives

The objectives of the *inventory control* application are:

- To provide high quality service to customers by utilizing a fast, accurate, and efficient method of filling customer orders and avoiding "stock outs."
- To minimize the amount of money invested in inventory and required to cover inventory "carrying costs."
- To provide management with information needed to help achieve the two preceding objectives.

Figure 14–5 is a general systems flowchart that summarizes the major components of the inventory control system.

Input

Input into the inventory control system consists of accepted order data, sales transaction data, as well as data describing stock received by the receiving department of the business firm. Input may also include "miscellaneous inventory transactions" such as adjustments for lost or damaged stock.

Data Base

The data base of this application consists of an "inventory master file" which is checked for item availability and updated to reflect changes in inventory caused by filling sales orders or receipt of new stock. A "back order file" is also updated for sales orders that cannot be filled because of stock outs. Some customers are willing to wait until new stock is received. The back-order file provides data on outstanding back orders that must be filled when stock receipt notices are received for back-ordered items.

Output

The output of the inventory control system includes inventory transactions listings for control purposes. Data describing

FIGURE 14–5 An Inventory
Control System

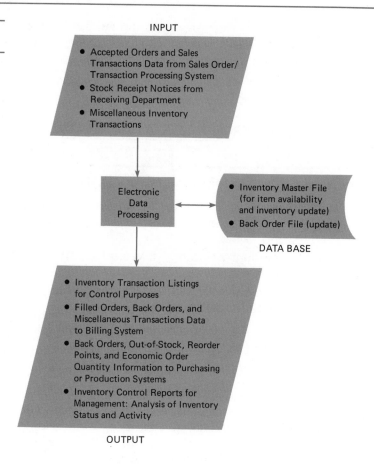

INPUT

- Accepted Orders and Sales
  Transactions Data from Sales Order/
  Transaction Processing System
- Stock Receipt Notices from
  Receiving Department
- Miscellaneous Inventory
  Transactions

Electronic
Data
Processing

- Inventory Master File
  (for item availability
  and inventory update)
- Back Order File (update)

DATA BASE

- Inventory Transaction Listings
  for Control Purposes
- Filled Orders, Back Orders, and
  Miscellaneous Transactions Data
  to Billing System
- Back Orders, Out-of-Stock, Reorder
  Points, and Economic Order
  Quantity Information to Purchasing
  or Production Systems
- Inventory Control Reports for
  Management: Analysis of Inventory
  Status and Activity

OUTPUT

filled orders, back orders, and miscellaneous sales order transactions is a major system output and becomes the primary input into the billing and sales analysis system. Information concerning back orders, out-of-stock items, reorder points, and economic order quantities is sent to the purchasing or production departments for entry into their information subsystems. The purchasing department will utilize such information to procure more inventory, while a manufacturing firm would utilize this information to schedule the production of additional finished goods inventory.

A final major category of output consists of inventory control reports for management. These reports analyze inventory status and activity in order to help management meet the objectives of inventory control. Management must determine (1) whether the items being reordered and the amounts being

FIGURE 14–6   Inventory Control Reports for Management

Stock No.	Description	Opening Balance	+ Receipts	- Issue	= On Hand	PLANNING			OP
						+ On Order	= Available	Order Point	
11398	TRANSFORMER	210			210	300	510	400	
11402	MOTOR ASM 50	1205	500		1705	1500	3205	2000	
11610	CAM	10341		1423	8918		8918	9000	*
11682	LEVER	433	3500	1255	2678	500	3178	2750	

Item No.	Cumulative Count		Annual Units	Unit Cost	Annual $ Sales	Cumulative Sales	
	Number	%				$	%
T 7061	1	.01	51,553	3.077	158,629	158,629	.5
–	–	–	–	–	–	–	–
S 6832	13	.12	243,224	.317	77,102	1,652,385	5.0
K 5322	110	1.0	8,680	3.286	28,522	5,882,489	17.8
S 5678	549	5.0	244,690	.045	11,011	13,252,124	40.1
S 6121	2,198	20.0	7,239	.490	3,547	23,662,146	71.6
–	–	–	–	–	–	–	–
–	–	–	–	–	–	–	–
S 6219	6,593	60.0	15,360	.050	768	31,395,306	95.0
–	–	–	–	–	–	–	–
–	–	–	–	–	–	–	–
M 3742	10,988	100.0	0	.073	0	33,047,690	100.0

Courtesy IBM Corporation.

reordered require adjustment, (2) the amount of unfilled orders that are occurring, (3) whether any items are becoming obsolete, (4) unusual variations in inventory activity, and (5) the items which account for the majority of the sales of the business. Figure 14–6 illustrates several inventory control reports.

Fixed order points and order quantities may be arbitrarily set by management and utilized by the inventory control system. However, the computer can be programmed to utilize mathematical techniques to calculate optimum order points and economic order quantities for use by the inventory control system. Such calculations take into account the cost of an item, its carrying cost, its annual sales, the cost of placing an order, and the length of time it takes to process, procure, and receive an item.

Too little stock may mean lost sales or excessive rush orders for stock replenishment. Too much stock may mean increased carrying costs, higher interest on invested capital, additional warehousing expenses, and greater loss to obsolescence. In many cases, carrying costs can run as high as 25 percent.[1]

THE BILLING AND SALES ANALYSIS APPLICATION

Objectives

The objectives of the *billing and sales analysis* application are:

- To prepare customer invoices (bills) quickly and accurately and thus maintain customer satisfaction and improved cash flow into the business.
- To provide management with sales analysis reports which provide information concerning sales activity and trends which is required for effective marketing management.

Figure 14–7 summarizes the important components of the billing and sales analysis system.

Input

The input into the billing and sales analysis system consists of data from the inventory control system which describes the filled orders, back orders, and miscellaneous transactions.

Data Base

The data base for this system consists of the "customer master file" which is utilized to provide additional information about a customer that is required by a billing operation. Examples are customer "ship to" addresses, shipping instructions, special handling, etc. A "sales summary file" is updated with current sales order data and provides information concerning previous sales for the sales analysis reports.

Output

The output of the billing and sales analysis system includes a "billing register" which is a summary listing of all invoices that is utilized for control purposes. A major output of the system is customer invoices such as that shown in Figure 14–8. (The computer calculates all required invoice amounts.)

---

[1] *Management Reports in Today's Business* (White Plains, N.Y.: IBM Corporation, 1973), p. 12.

Other output of the system includes shipping documents such as "picking slips," shipping labels, bills of lading, and delivery receipts. The computer frequently lists the items on the invoice in a warehouse-location sequence so that a copy of the invoice can be used as a "picking slip" by warehouse personnel

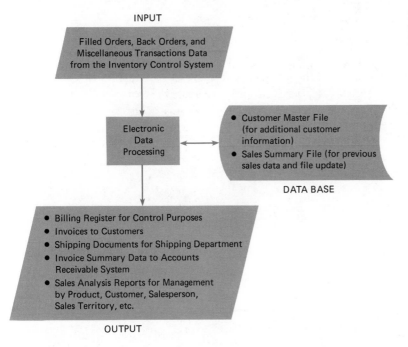

INPUT

Filled Orders, Back Orders, and Miscellaneous Transactions Data from the Inventory Control System

Electronic Data Processing

- Customer Master File (for additional customer information)
- Sales Summary File (for previous sales data and file update)

DATA BASE

- Billing Register for Control Purposes
- Invoices to Customers
- Shipping Documents for Shipping Department
- Invoice Summary Data to Accounts Receivable System
- Sales Analysis Reports for Management by Product, Customer, Salesperson, Sales Territory, etc.

OUTPUT

FIGURE 14–7 A Billing and Sales Analysis System

FIGURE 14–8 Customer Invoice

LAURENTIAN INDUSTRIES, INC.

SOLD TO
S. W. STAPLES
498 RIVERVIEW STREET
SAN JOSE, CALIF.   94067

SHIP TO
RODRIGUEZ DESIGN HOMES
DIVISION OF S. W. STAPLES
8363 OLIVE STREET
SUNNYVALE, CALIF.   95117

CUSTOMER NO.
430875

DATE 09/15/--	INV. NO. 138265	ORDER NO. 717690	SHIPPING INSTRUCTIONS VIA SMITH TRANSPORT	STATED TERMS 2% 15 DAYS NET 30	SALESMAN G. PEREZ

QUANTITY ORDERED	QUANTITY SHIPPED	QUANTITY B/O	DESCRIPTION	UNIT PRICE	EXTENDED AMOUNT	DISCOUNT AMOUNT	NET AMOUNT	TAX-ABLE
40	40		8500 TWINLITE SOCKET B	.60	24.00	1.20	22.80	
350	100	250	8506 SOCKET ADAPTER BRN	.32	32.00	3.20	28.80	
200	150	50	C151C SILENT SWITCH IVORY	1.20	180.00	9.00	171.00	•
175	175		A210 PULL CORD GOLD	.42	73.50		73.50	•
60		60	1436 LAMP ENTRANCE	.50				
175	105	70	A200 FIXTURE 5 LIGHT	20.13	2113.65	211.37	1,902.28	
			FREIGHT CHARGE				18.95	
			PACKING CHARGE				45.00	

TAXABLE 244.50	TAX 12.23	FREIGHT 18.95	MISC. SPECIAL CHARGE 45.00		INVOICE AMOUNT 2,274.56

Courtesy IBM Corporation.

FIGURE 14–9 Sales Analysis Reports for Management

LAURENTIAN INDUSTRIES, INC.

SALES BY ITEM CLASS

MONTH ENDING 03/31/--

ITEM CLASS	CLASS DESCRIPTION	SOLD THIS MONTH	GROSS PROFIT	PROFIT PERCENT	SOLD THIS YEAR	GROSS PROFIT	PROFIT PERCENT
1	ABRASIVES	2,720.19	271.36	10	9,900.17	907.60	9
2	ACIDS AND CHEMICALS	1,216.27	170.27	14	3,139.68	408.07	13
3	BRASS	6,220.83	435.45	7	16,341.47	1,143.87	7

LAURENTIAN INDUSTRIES, INC.

COMPARATIVE SALES ANALYSIS BY CUSTOMER

FOR EACH SALESPERSON

PERIOD ENDING 07/31/--

SLP. NO.	CUST. NO.	SALESPERSON/CUSTOMER NAME	THIS PERIOD THIS YEAR	THIS PERIOD LAST YEAR	YEAR-TO-DATE THIS YEAR	YEAR-TO-DATE LAST YEAR
10		A R WESTON				
	1426	HYDRO CYCLES INC	3,210.26	4,312.06	10,010.28	9,000.92
	2632	RUPP AQUA CYCLES	7,800.02	2,301.98	20,322.60	11,020.16
	3217	SEA PORT WEST CO	90.00CR	421.06	900.00	593.10
		SALESPERSON TOTALS	10,920.28	7,035.10	31,732.88	20,614.18
12		H T BRAVEMAN				
	0301	BOLLINGER ASSOCIATES	100.96	0.00	100.96	0.00

Courtesy IBM Corporation.

when assembling an order for shipment. Summarized data for each invoice is the major category of input to the accounts receivable system.

The final major output of the billing and sales analysis system is sales analysis reports for management such as those shown in Figure 14–9. Sales analysis reports can analyze sales by product, product line, customer, type of customer, salesperson, sales territory, etc. Such reports help marketing management determine the sales performance of products, customers, and salespeople. They can determine whether a firm is expending too much sales effort on low-volume customers or low-profits products.

. . . one distributor discovered he had 1,300 accounts, representing 32 percent of all customers, who purchased less than 1 percent of his total volume. Looking at the other end of the report, he found that he had more than 1,700 accounts who bought at least $1,000 annually and accounted for 95 percent of the volume.[2]

THE ACCOUNTS RECEIVABLE APPLICATION

Objectives

"Accounts receivable" represents the amounts of money owed to a company by its customers (accounts). The objectives of the *accounts receivable* application are:

- To stimulate prompt customer payments by preparing accurate and timely monthly statements to credit customers.
- To provide management with the information required to control the amount of credit extended and the collection of money owed, in order to maximize profitable credit sales while minimizing losses from bad debts.

Figure 14–10 illustrates a typical accounts receivable system.

Input

Input into the system consists of invoice summary data from the billing system and source documents showing payments received from customers. The usual customer payment document is the return portion of an invoice or statement which the customer returns by mail along with a check in payment of the account. Another type of input into this system is "miscel-

---

[2] *Management Reports in Today's Business* (White Plains, N.Y.: IBM Corporation, 1973), p. 10.

FIGURE 14–10 An Accounts
Receivable System

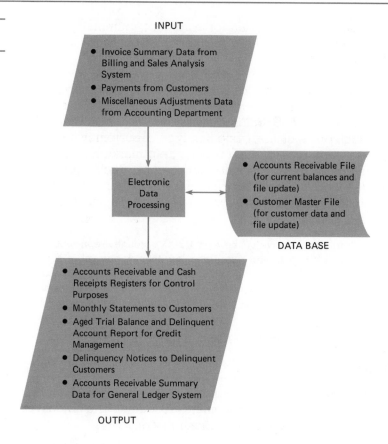

FIGURE 14–10 An Accounts
Receivable System

INPUT

- Invoice Summary Data from Billing and Sales Analysis System
- Payments from Customers
- Miscellaneous Adjustments Data from Accounting Department

Electronic Data Processing

- Accounts Receivable File (for current balances and file update)
- Customer Master File (for customer data and file update)

DATA BASE

- Accounts Receivable and Cash Receipts Registers for Control Purposes
- Monthly Statements to Customers
- Aged Trial Balance and Delinquent Account Report for Credit Management
- Delinquency Notices to Delinquent Customers
- Accounts Receivable Summary Data for General Ledger System

OUTPUT

laneous adjustments" which are prepared by the accounting department to adjust customer accounts for mistakes in billing, the return of goods, bad debt write-offs, etc.

Data Base

The data base for the accounts receivable application includes the "accounts receivable file" which provides current balances for each customer account and which is also updated by the new billing, payments, and adjustments input data. The "customer master file" is utilized to provide data needed for customer statement preparation. The customer credit standing information in this file is also updated as a result of changes in accounts receivable balances.

Output

Proper data processing control requires that listings and control totals be prepared for all cash received and for each

FIGURE 14–11 Customer Monthly Statement

LANG COMPANY

STATEMENT

CUSTOMER NO. 554386 — HITTON CORPORATION, 138 MARSHALL DR., PO BOX 851, LONG PORT CALIF 94134 — DATE 9/30/--

DATE MO	DY	YR	INVOICE NUMBER	REFERENCE NUMBER	DESCRIPTION	AMOUNT
					PRIOR BALANCE	$2,565.46
09	08	--	185163		INVOICE	1,685.91
09	10	--	075126		PAYMENT	1,856.00CR
09	15	--		091531	LC ADJUSTMENT	13.00CR
09	30	--			LATE CHARGES	8.00

CURRENT AMOUNT	30 DAYS	60 DAYS & OVER	BALANCE DUE
$1,693.91	$696.46		$2,390.37

LANG COMPANY

STATEMENT

CUSTOMER NO. 554386 — HITTON CORPORATION, 138 MARSHALL DR, PO BOX 851, LONG PORT CALIF 94134 — DATE 9/30/--

DATE MO	DY	YR	INVOICE NUMBER	REFERENCE NUMBER	DESCRIPTION	AMOUNT
					PRIOR BALANCE	$2,565.46
09	08	--	185163		INVOICE	1,685.91
09	10	--	075126		PAYMENT	1,856.00CR
09	15	--		091531	LC ADJUSTMENT	13.00CR
09	30	--			LATE CHARGES	8.00

CURRENT AMOUNT	30 DAYS	60 DAYS & OVER	BALANCE DUE
$1,693.91	$696.46		$2,390.37

RETAIN THIS PORTION FOR YOUR RECORDS

Courtesy IBM Corporation.

customer account in the accounts receivable file. Thus, the output of the accounts receivable system includes an accounts receivable register and a cash receipts register. Monthly statements are also prepared for each customer which show recent charges and credits as well as the present balance owed. See Figure 14–11. Notice that this customer statement also indicates amounts that are overdue.

The accounts receivable system can also be programmed to automatically produce delinquency notices which are sent

FIGURE 14–12 Accounts Receivable Aged Trial Balance

ACCOUNTS RECEIVABLE AGED TRIAL BALANCE

DATE 6/30/1

CUSTOMER NUMBER	CUSTOMER NAME	SALESMAN'S NUMBER	BALANCE	CURRENT	OVER 30 DAYS	OVER 60 DAYS	90 DAYS & OVER	CREDIT LIMIT	EXCEEDS CREDIT LIMIT
13985	ANDERSON CORP.	27	1324 35	1200 00	121 50		2 85	3500 00	
14007	ARMSTRONG INTL.	27	3896 68	439 61	1911 25	499 00	1046 82	3000 00	-
37243	CONTI RENTAL	27	379 80	379 80				500 00	
48277	DELTA LIGHTING	27	241 28	65 98	175 30			500 00	
63365	FOXBORO CORP.	27	222 18	222 18				2000 00	
72466	HINDS ELECTRIC	27	2767 15	1632 09	1135 06			15000 00	
78144	INNSBRUCK ELEC.	27	861 70	27 50	54 40	127 23	652 57	1000 00	
85433	MILLER SUPPLY	27	457 90	202 60	50 70	120 70	83 90	500 00	
87542	PALMER APPL.	27	40 24	40 24				500 00	
93421	SMYTHE CO.	27	336 05	260 40		75 65		1500 00	
95642	WELLS HARDWARE	27	3195 98	469 76	325 01	151 63	2249 58	3000 00	-

Courtesy IBM Corporation.

to customers whose accounts are seriously overdue. Management reports produced by the system include a delinquent account report and an "aged trial balance" report (also called an "aged accounts receivable report"). Figure 14–12 illustrates an aged trial balance which helps the credit manager identify accounts which are seriously overdue and require special collection efforts. The final output of the accounts receivable system consists of accounts receivable summary data which is utilized as input by the general ledger system.

THE ACCOUNTS PAYABLE APPLICATION

Objectives

"Accounts payable" refers to the amounts of money that a business firm owes to its suppliers. The primary objectives of the *accounts payable* application are:

- Prompt and accurate payment of suppliers in order to maintain good relationships, insure a good credit standing, and secure any discounts offered for prompt payment.
- Provide tight financial control over all cash disbursements of the business.
- Provide management with information needed for the analysis of payments, expenses, purchases, and cash requirements.

Figure 14–13 illustrates the accounts payable application.

Input

Input into the accounts payable system consists of invoices (bills) from suppliers and others who have furnished goods or services to the business firm. Input may also be in the form of expense "vouchers" for various business expenses and miscellaneous payments and adjustments from the accounting department. (A *voucher* is an accounting form which records the details of a transaction and authorizes its entry into the accounting system of a firm.) For example, expense vouchers may be prepared to reimburse employees for authorized expenditures. Typically, salespersons and managerial personnel request reimbursement by completing an "expense account" statement and submitting it to the accounting department.

Payments from "petty cash" or adjustments from suppliers for billing errors are other types of miscellaneous input. Receiving reports from the receiving department acknowledge the

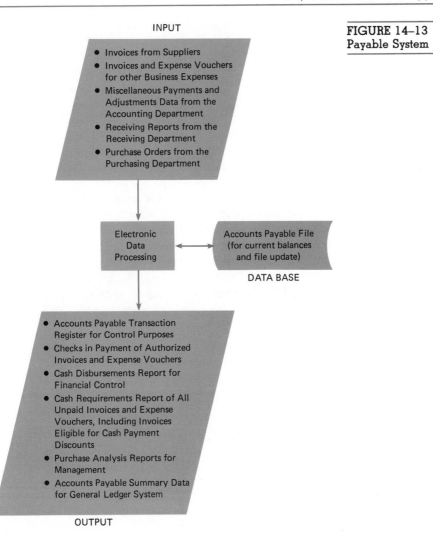

INPUT

- Invoices from Suppliers
- Invoices and Expense Vouchers for other Business Expenses
- Miscellaneous Payments and Adjustments Data from the Accounting Department
- Receiving Reports from the Receiving Department
- Purchase Orders from the Purchasing Department

Electronic Data Processing

Accounts Payable File (for current balances and file update)

DATA BASE

- Accounts Payable Transaction Register for Control Purposes
- Checks in Payment of Authorized Invoices and Expense Vouchers
- Cash Disbursements Report for Financial Control
- Cash Requirements Report of All Unpaid Invoices and Expense Vouchers, Including Invoices Eligible for Cash Payment Discounts
- Purchase Analysis Reports for Management
- Accounts Payable Summary Data for General Ledger System

OUTPUT

FIGURE 14–13   An Accounts Payable System

receipt of goods from suppliers and are required before payment can be authorized. A copy of purchase orders from the purchasing department provides data describing purchase orders that have been sent to suppliers. This data is utilized to record "pending payables" and to help determine whether the business firm has been accurately billed by its suppliers.

Data Base

The data base for the accounts payable application is the "accounts payable file" which provides current balances for all accounts and is updated by the new input data.

484

As in previous applications, data processing control requires that an "accounts payable transaction register" be produced. This output document lists all system transactions and computes various control totals. A major form of output of the system are checks in payment of authorized invoices and expense vouchers. A "cash disbursements report" provides a detailed record of all checks written and contributes to proper financial control of the cash disbursements of the firm.

An important output of the system for management is the "cash requirements report" which lists and/or summarizes all unpaid invoices and expense vouchers and identifies all invoices eligible for cash payment discounts during the current period. The computer can also be programmed to analyze unpaid invoices and expense vouchers so that forecasts of the cash requirements for several future periods can be included in the cash requirements report. See Figure 14–14.

FIGURE 14–14 Purchase Analysis and Cash Requirements Reports

PURCHASE ANALYSIS BY VENDOR

VENDOR'S NO.	VENDOR'S NAME	AMOUNT THIS MONTH	RETURNS YEAR TO DATE	NET AMOUNT YEAR TO DATE	NET AMOUNT LAST YEAR TO DATE	INCREASE OR DECREASE
27	ABBOT MACHINE CO	1286|44		3194|26	3010|42	183|84
58	ACE TOOL CO			1975|15	1859|76	115|39
66	ACME ABRASIVE CO	342|86		1505|93	1482|50	23|43
324	ALLAN ALLOYS CO		95|10	4675|22	4410|15	265|07
367	AMERICAN TOOL CO			986|74	1293|84	307|10 CR
425	ANGUS METAL WORKS			842|89	795|22	47|67
475	APEX CORPORATION	2316|84	245|73	10476|79	9473|65	1003|14
502	ARCO STATIONERY CO			319|42	445|93	126|51 CR

KRAUSZ MANUFACTURING COMPANY
ACCOUNTS PAYABLE
CASH REQUIREMENTS STATEMENT

DATE APR 1 2 19-- SHEET 1 OF 2

ROUT TO *Mr. J. R. Crossin - Dept 00*

VENDOR	VENDOR NUMBER	DUE DATE	INVOICE AMOUNT	DISCOUNT	CHECK AMOUNT
SOLVAY GEN SUP	1016	4/16	$ 773.30	$ 15.47	$ 757.83
ROCHESTER PR CO	1021	4/16	1,620.18	32.40	1,587.78
CALABRIA CONT	1049	4/16	143.65	2.87	140.78
ONONDAGA STL CO	1077	4/16	5,982.82	119.66	5,863.16
BLACK & NICHOLS	1103	4/16	14.25	.71	13.54
AUSTERHOLZ INC	1240	4/16	624.77	12.50	612.27
AUSTERHOLZ INC	1240	4/16	1,833.19	36.66	1,796.53
CHRISTIE & CO	1366	4/16	745.54		745.54
WILSON & WILSON	2231	4/16	2,936.12	58.72 .	2,877.40
CLAR. HIGGINS	2590	4/16	1,000.00		1,000.00
HONOUR BROS	3101	4/16	97.36	1.95	95.41
BASTIANI & SON	3112	4/16	3,580.85	71.62	3,509.23
DRJ WIRE CO	3164	4/16	256.90	5.14	251.76
HASTING-WHITE	3258	4/16	1,144.42	22.89	1,121.53
DARONO ART MET	3427	4/16	32.75	.66	32.09
DARONO ART MET	3427	4/16	127.52	2.55	124.97
DARONO ART MET	3427	4/16	96.60	1.93	94.67

Courtesy IBM Corporation.

The accounts payable system can also produce "purchase analysis reports" for management which summarize the purchases and payments made to each supplier of the firm. (This report is sometimes produced by a separate *purchasing* system.) The final category of output consists of summarized accounts payable transaction data which becomes input data for the general ledger system.

THE PAYROLL AND LABOR ANALYSIS APPLICATION

Objectives

The primary objectives of the *payroll and labor analysis* application are:

- Prompt and accurate payment of employees.
- Prompt and accurate reporting to management, employees, and appropriate agencies concerning earnings, taxes, and other deductions.
- Providing management with reports analyzing labor costs and productivity.

The payroll and labor analysis application is widely computerized because it involves many complex calculations and the production of many types of reports and documents, many of which are required by government agencies. Besides earnings calculations, many types of taxes and fringe benefit deductions must be calculated. Payroll processing is also complicated because many business firms employ hourly paid employees and salaried personnel and may have several kinds of incentive compensation plans. Figure 14–15 illustrates the payroll and labor analysis application.

Input

The input into the payroll and labor analysis system consists of employee time cards or other records of time worked or attendance. Time cards are normally utilized by hourly paid employees while some type of attendance record is usually kept for salaried personnel. Additional input includes records of employee incentive compensation such as factory piecework or salesperson commissions. Input may also be in the form of miscellaneous payroll adjustments from the personnel or accounting departments such as changes in wage rates, job classifications, and deductions.

FIGURE 14–15 A Payroll and
Labor Analysis System

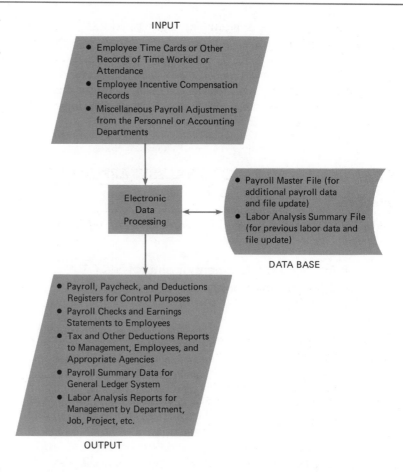

INPUT

- Employee Time Cards or Other Records of Time Worked or Attendance
- Employee Incentive Compensation Records
- Miscellaneous Payroll Adjustments from the Personnel or Accounting Departments

Electronic Data Processing

- Payroll Master File (for additional payroll data and file update)
- Labor Analysis Summary File (for previous labor data and file update)

DATA BASE

- Payroll, Paycheck, and Deductions Registers for Control Purposes
- Payroll Checks and Earnings Statements to Employees
- Tax and Other Deductions Reports to Management, Employees, and Appropriate Agencies
- Payroll Summary Data for General Ledger System
- Labor Analysis Reports for Management by Department, Job, Project, etc.

OUTPUT

Data Base

The data base for the payroll and labor analysis application includes a "payroll master file" which provides additional payroll data needed for payroll calculations and reports. This file is updated by the new input data. A "labor analysis summary file" provides previous labor analysis data and is also updated each time new input data is processed.

Output

All payroll transactions, all paychecks written, and all deductions made are listed and totaled on control registers. Of course, the primary output of the system consists of payroll checks and earning statements for employees of the firm. See Figure 14–16. In addition, tax and other deductions reports are prepared periodically for management, employees, and appropriate agencies. These include quarterly tax reports to

FIGURE 14–16 Paycheck and Earnings Statement

					90–1211		
					0519		

CHECK DATE 4/30/69

J. R . SMITH & CO.

CHECK NUMBER

1303

PAY ***136 DOLLARS AND 35 CENTS**   ****136.35**

TO
THE
ORDER   A H ANKSTER
OF

SPECIMEN

COMMERCIAL TRUST BANK

⑈0 2ⅼ0ⅲ098 7⑉ Ⅼⅼ2ⅼ 00360ⅲ

EMPLOYEE NUMBER	EMPLOYEE NAME		DEPT.	PAY PERIOD	PAY PERIOD ENDED	CHECK NO.	CHECK DATE
0123	A H ANKSTER		03	8	4/30/69	1303	4/30/69

EARNINGS AND STATUTORY DEDUCTIONS								
HOURS	RATE	REGULAR PAY	OVERTIME PAY	OTHER PAY	GROSS PAY	FED.W/TAX	F.I.C.A. TAX	STATE TAX
5C.0	2.75	137.50	11.25	12.80	161.55	7.75	8.70	1.62

VOLUNTARY DEDUCTIONS							
MEDICAL INS.	LIFE INS.	CREDIT UNION	UNION DUES	CHARITY	SAVINGS BONDS	ALL OTHERS	NET PAY
2.00		4.13	1.00				136.35

SOCIAL SECURITY AND W–2 INFORMATION						
SOCIAL SECURITY NO.	EXEMPT	Y.T.D. GROSS	Y.T.D. FED. W/TAX	Y.T.D. F.I.C.A.	Y.T.D. STATE TAX	NOT NEGOTIABLE
312-32-1337	X	2,105.92	222.98	101.08	21.06	

Courtesy IBM Corporation.

the Internal Revenue Service such as Form 941a and the annual W–2 form which must be sent to employees before January 31 of each year. Reports listing and summarizing other tax and deduction information are prepared for management and agencies such as school districts, city, county, and state agencies, labor unions, insurance companies, charitable organizations, credit unions, etc.

"Labor analysis reports" for management are another major form of output of the payroll and labor analysis system. See Figure 14–17. These reports analyze the time, cost, and personnel required by departments of the firm or by jobs and projects being undertaken. They assist management in planning labor requirements and controlling the labor cost and productivity of ongoing projects. The final output of the payroll and labor analysis system is "payroll summary data" which is utilized as input by the general ledger system.

FIGURE 14-17 Labor Analysis Report

```
DATE  8/08/--                        WORK IN PROGRESS REPORT
                                        FOR JULY 19--

JOBNO   FINISH    PROGRESS   WORK   EMPNO   EST JOB   ACT JOB   % HRS   EST JOB    ACT JOB   % $
         DATE       DATE     DEPT            HOURS     HOURS    USED    DOLLARS    DOLLARS   USED

11111  10/30/70   6/30/--                   120.0      30.0    25.0     635.00    190.00-   30.0
                  7/05/--    360   00508                 8.0                        40.00
                  7/10/--    360   00508                 8.0                        40.00
                  7/11/--    360   00604                 6.0                        24.00
                  7/30/--    360   00501                10.0                        60.00

TOTAL JOB 11111 TO DATE STATUS              120.0      62.0    51.7     635.00    354.00    55.7

23468   9/30/70   4/30/--                   100.0      80.0    80.0    1000.00    700.00    70.0
                  7/06/--    400   10105                 8.0                        80.00
                  7/28/--    506   36350                 4.0                        80.00
                  7/29/--    506   36350                 4.0                        80.00
                  7/30/--    506   36350                 5.0                       100.00

TOTAL JOB 23468 TO DATE STATUS              100.0     101.0   101.0    1000.00   1040.00   104.0

33335   7/15/70   6/30/--                    40.0      42.0   105.0     160.00    200.00   125.0
                  7/14/--    500   40608                 4.0                         8.00
                  7/18/--    360   00508                 8.0                        40.00

TOTAL JOb 33335 TO DATE STATUS               40.0      54.0   135.0     160.00    248.00   155.0

40608  11/30/70   4/30/--                   200.0     120.0    60.0    1600.00    960.00    60.0

TOTAL JOB 40608 NO CURRENT ACTIVITY
```

Courtesy IBM Corporation.

THE GENERAL LEDGER APPLICATION

The general ledger application consolidates financial data from all of the other accounting subsystems and produces the monthly and annual financial statements of the firm. The many financial transactions of a business are first recorded in chronological order in *journals,* then transferred ("posted") to *subsidiary ledgers* where they are organized into "accounts" such as cash, accounts receivable, and inventory. The summary of all accounts and their balances is known as the *general ledger.*

At the end of each accounting period (at the end of each month or fiscal year) the balance of each account in the general ledger must be computed, the profit or loss of the firm during the period must be calculated, and the financial statements of the firm (the balance sheet and income statement) must be prepared. This is known as "closing the books" of the business. The income statement of the firm presents its income, expenses, and profit or loss for a period, while the balance sheet shows the assets, liabilities, and net worth of the business as of the end of the accounting period.

Objectives

The primary objective of the *general ledger* application is to utilize the power of the computer to accomplish the many accounting tasks mentioned in the preceding paragraph in

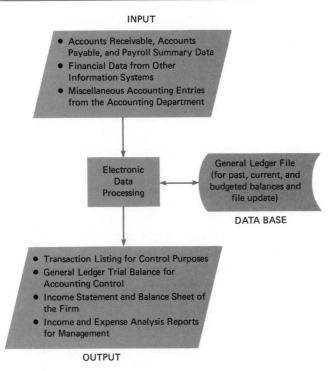

FIGURE 14–18   A General Ledger System

an accurate and timely manner. Using the computer for general ledger can result in greater accuracy, earlier closings, and more timely and meaningful financial reports for management. The computer can frequently accomplish this with less personnel and at a lower cost than manual bookkeeping and accounting methods. Figure 14–18 is a general systems flowchart of the general ledger application.

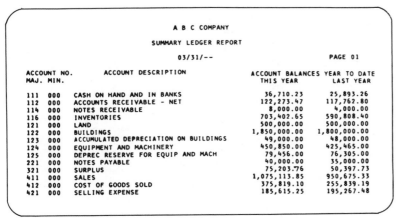

FIGURE 14–19   General Ledger Summary Report

Courtesy IBM Corporation.

Input

Input into the general ledger system consists of summary data from the accounts receivable, accounts payable, and payroll systems, as well as financial data from other information systems (such as production control, purchasing, engineering, etc.) that we have not described in this chapter. Another form

FIGURE 14–20 Comparative Income Statement and Balance Sheet

HASTING-WHITE TOOL COMPANY
COMPARATIVE BALANCE SHEET

PERIOD ENDING JUNE 30, 19—

MAJOR ACCOUNT	DESCRIPTION	PREVIOUS PERIOD THIS YEAR	CURRENT PERIOD		OVER* OR UNDER-	% OVER* OR UNDER-
			THIS YEAR	LAST YEAR		
	ASSETS					
	CASH AND RECEIVABLES					
111	CASH	$ 15,673.38	$ 16,739.73	$ 15,248.61	$ 1,491.12 *	9.8 *
112	ACCOUNTS RECEIVABLE	32,967.21	33,291.18	32,968.32	322.86 *	.9 *
113	RESERVE FOR BAD DEBTS	329.67-	332.91-	329.68-	3.23 *	.9 *
114	NOTES RECEIVABLE	1,000.00		1,500.00	1,500.00 -	100.0 -
115	MARKETABLE SECURITIES	2,164.30	5,898.13	3,673.21	2,224.92 *	60.6 *
	TOT	$ 51,475.22*	$ 55,596.13*	$ 53,060.46*	$ 2,535.67***	
	INVENTORIES					
116	INVENTORIES	$ 183,621.83	$ 161,298.67	$ 149,238.61	$ 12,060.06 *	8.1 *
	TOT	$ 183,621.83*	$ 161,298.67*	$ 149,238.61*	$ 12,060.06***	
	LAND AND BUILDINGS					
121	LAND		$ 50,238.96		$ 50,238.96 *	*
122	BUILDINGS					
123	RES. FOR DEPREC.	$ 2,116.45-	2,363.74-	$ 1,767.88-	595.36 *	33.7 *
	TOT	$ 2,116.45-	$ 47,875.22*	$ 1,767.88-	$ 49,643.10***	
	EQUIP. AND MACHINERY					
124	EQUIP. AND MACHINERY	$ 10,873.98	$ 8,339.61	$ 16,298.38	$ 7,958.77 -	48.8 -
125	RES. FOR DEPREC.	3,245.67-	3,469.22-	2,975.12-	494.10 *	16.6 *
	TOT	$ 7,628.31*	$ 4,870.39*	$ 13,323.26*	$ 8,452.87*-*	

SOUTH LAKE SAND COMPANY
COMPARATIVE INCOME STATEMENT

Routing
☐ President's Office
☑ Treasurer
☐ Comptroller
☐ Accounting
☐ Sales Manager
☐ Plant Superintendent

PERIOD ENDING MAY 31, 19—

ACCOUNT NUMBER	DESCRIPTION	CURRENT PERIOD		YEAR-TO-DATE		INCREASE* OR DECREASE-
		THIS YEAR	LAST YEAR	THIS YEAR	LAST YEAR	
411	SALES					
411-100	GROSS SALES	$ 1,223,195.85	$ 1,083,474.02	$ 4,739,999.14	$ 3,415,174.67	$ 1,324,824.47 *
411-200	LESS RETURNS & ALLOW	1,726.40	1,912.71	3,245.97	3,464.22	218.25 -
	NET SALES	$ 1,221,469.45	$ 1,081,561.31	$ 4,736,753.17	$ 3,411,710.45	$ 1,325,042.72 *
412-100	LESS COST OF SALES	581,786.15	541,950.16	2,852,146.73	2,008,762.23	843,384.50 *
	GROSS PROFIT	$ 639,683.30*	$ 539,611.15*	$ 1,884,606.44*	$ 1,402,948.22*	481,658.22 *
421	SELLING EXPENSES					
421-100	SALARIES & COMMISSIONS	$ 184,373.27	$ 179,264.48	$ 705,623.06	$ 541,579.46	$ 164,043.60 *
421-200	TRAVELING EXPENSE	14,425.15	13,790.80	53,726.92	42,968.21	10,758.71 *
421-300	DELIVERY EXPENSE	6,140.20	5,956.00	28,364.15	16,428.19	11,935.96 *
421-400	ADVERTISING EXPENSE	1,582.00	1,450.25	18,250.00	5,225.75	13,024.25 *
421-500	OFFICE SALARIES	27,684.35	25,829.15	94,342.18	79,415.14	14,927.04 *
421-600	STATIONERY & SUPPLIES	1,380.60	1,295.00	4,982.76	3,576.82	1,405.94 *
421-700	TELEPHONE	1,315.85	1,305.62	4,148.15	3,381.26	766.89 *
421-800	BUILDING	6,725.00	6,215.10	25,175.00	18,634.55	6,540.45 *
421-900	MISCELLANEOUS	1,460.38	1,385.75	4,965.48	3,519.47	1,446.01 *
	TOTAL SELLING EXPENSE	$ 245,086.80*	$ 236,492.15*	$ 939,577.70*	$ 714,728.85*	224,848.85 *

Courtesy IBM Corporation.

of input is "miscellaneous accounting entries" from the accounting department that record changes to accounts such as cash, marketable securities, and plant and equipment.

Data Base

The data base of the general ledger application is the "general ledger file" which is updated by the new input data and provides information on past, current, and budgeted balances for each general ledger account.

Output

The output of the general ledger system includes a listing of all transactions for control purposes and a general ledger "trial balance" report which provides accounting control by summarizing and balancing all general ledger accounts. See Figure 14–19. The *income statement* and *balance sheet* of the firm for an accounting period are major outputs of the system and are of primary importance to financial management and the top management of the firm. See Figure 14–20. A final important output of the general ledger system is "income and expense analysis reports" which can be produced for all levels of management. Such reports analyze the financial performance of a department or the business firm by comparing current performance to past and forecasted (budgeted) figures. The difference ("variance") between actual and budgeted amounts show managers in what area their performance is falling short or surpassing their financial objectives for a period. See Figure 14–21.

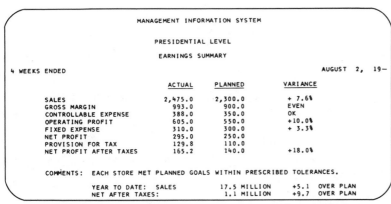

FIGURE 14–21 Income and Expense Analysis Report for Management

```
                    MANAGEMENT INFORMATION SYSTEM


                        PRESIDENTIAL LEVEL

                        EARNINGS SUMMARY

4 WEEKS ENDED                                          AUGUST  2,   19—

                        ACTUAL      PLANNED       VARIANCE

     SALES              2,475.0     2,300.0       + 7.6%
     GROSS MARGIN         993.0       900.0       EVEN
     CONTROLLABLE EXPENSE  388.0      350.0       OK
     OPERATING PROFIT      605.0      550.0       +10.0%
     FIXED EXPENSE         310.0      300.0       + 3.3%
     NET PROFIT            295.0      250.0
     PROVISION FOR TAX     129.8      110.0
     NET PROFIT AFTER TAXES 165.2     140.0       +18.0%


  COMMENTS:   EACH STORE MET PLANNED GOALS WITHIN PRESCRIBED TOLERANCES.

           YEAR TO DATE:  SALES        17.5 MILLION    +5.1   OVER PLAN
                          NET AFTER TAXES:  1.1 MILLION  +9.7  OVER PLAN
```

Courtesy IBM Corporation.

SUMMARY

Several common business applications exist in both large and small computer-using business firms, whether they are experienced computer users or are utilizing the computer for the first time. The objectives, input, data base, and output of the following seven common business applications were described in this chapter: (1) *sales order/ transaction processing*, (2) *inventory control*, (3) *billing and sales analysis*, (4) *accounts receivable*, (5) *accounts payable*, (6) *payroll and labor analysis*, and (7) *general ledger*.

KEY TERMS AND CONCEPTS

Common business applications

Sales order/transaction processing

Inventory control

Billing and sales analysis

Accounts receivable

Accounts payable

Payroll and labor analysis

General ledger

REVIEW AND DISCUSSION QUESTIONS

1. Why are the computer applications discussed in this chapter called the "common business applications"?
2. Briefly describe each of the seven common computer applications discussed in this chapter.
3. Summarize the objectives, input, data base, and output of one of the common business applications.
4. How are the common business applications related to each other?
5. Prepare a computer applications report which describes and evaluates how a specific business firm or industry utilizes one of the common business applications.

REAL WORLD APPLICATIONS

14–1   W. H. Shurtleff Co.

For more than five years, W. H. Shurtleff Company, Portland, Maine, used an online service bureau which helped them double their business. But when the bureau announced an increase in fees, without an increase in service, Shurtleff management decided an inhouse Commercial System CS/40 computer would provide more and better data processing power for the dollar. The resulting Chemical Management Information System (CHEMIS) was developed jointly by Shurtleff and the Computer Center of Falmouth, Maine. The hardware and software perfectly match Shurtleff's distributor data processing needs, and is equally suitable for any chemical distributor.

The computer system handles a number of typical business applications, but the programs were expanded to supply employees with a wide range

14-1   *(continued)*

of comprehensive information. For example, the Order Entry program provides immediate data on credit checking; automatic pricing; bills of lading; hazardous materials classifications; priced and unpriced orders; inventory levels; and reorder points. The Invoicing program can update inventory; compute line items and total invoices, gross profit margins and percentages; automatically handle credit memos and cash transactions; and track returnable

deposit cylinders by serial number. Sales Analysis is accomplished item by customer; customer by item; customer by item by sales territory; and more. The Inventory Control program handles 10 different locations and supplies data on hazardous material codes; automatic inventory expense for year-end tax reporting; unit and dollar turns; as well as pickup and delivered dollar and volume.[1]

- What common business applications are included in the CHEMIS system?
- What information is supplied by this system?

[1] Source: *The Sensible Way to Use Computers*, Data General Corporation.

14-2   Hamilton/Avnet

Nobody distributes more electronic components and computer products, or delivers them faster, than Hamilton/Avnet. It's company policy that every order is to be shipped within 24 hours. Last year, Hamilton/Avnet turned its enormous inventory four times, distributing more than $700 million worth of components. By any standard, they are one of the world's most efficient distributors. And no wonder, Hamilton/Avent uses a finely-tuned network of computers to keep its operation running smoothly. Their Honeywell system includes a large-scale mainframe and 54 small computers. These are distributed among Hamilton/Avnet's 43 stocking locations.

On an average day the system will process 150,000 transactions. Hamilton/Avnet expects to process 300,000 transactions a day next year.

600,000 a day by 1985. To handle this load they're envisioning an all-electronic paperless operation. Besides orders, there are many accounting jobs to do. Shipments are billed the day they go out. Receivables updated. Obviously, inventory control is also essential. And with more than 600,000 items on the shelves, this is no easy task. Hamilton/Avnet will soon use its Honeywell system to process about 55,000 purchase orders a month.

The system also provides an administrative message system and an interface to key suppliers. Customers are also tying into the system for online order entry. With the help of a distributed network of Honeywell computers, Hamilton/Avnet can serve its thousands of customers as responsively as any Mom and Pop distributor can serve a handful.[2]

- Why does Hamilton/Avnet need such a large sales order processing system?
- What other common business applications are also processed?

[2] Courtesy Honeywell Information Systems.

14–3   Rockford Paper Mills

The business of manufacturing and selling paperboard and folding cartons has two characteristics that have an impact on cost control and, ultimately, on profitability: lead times and production cycles are quite short; and all orders are "custom" with regard to stock, size, printing requirements and, in some instances, even to the design of the carton itself. Production scheduling, then, is of critical importance. Along with that scheduling, the proper allocation of both direct and indirect costs must be made with great precision.

A management information system of considerable sophistication and flexibility becomes, therefore, a virtual necessity. Computerization is the answer, but the range of approaches is wide, and the wrong choice can invite disaster. Payroll processing was the logical first step toward computerization. Accounts receivable and payable followed at intervals of several months, followed in turn by general ledger. The entire process was relatively painless, although at the beginning it was necessary to make certain compromises about the amount and level of detail of historical data that could be included.

Each application includes a set of registers, recaps, schedules and summaries to our specifications. They are now the basis for the financial management information system. In addition, there are a number of more specialized reports that have been derived from the same accounting source data. These have been added over the past three years as the need for them was determined. Some of these reports are standard, such as a monthly balance sheet and a corporate P&L statement. Also produced are detailed income and expense statements that compare month's actual operations and year-to-date operations with budget. The statements show the dollar and percentage variance from budget.

Aside from the benefits of fast turnaround and great accuracy, how does this kind of automated processing provide a superior management information capability? There are really two answers to this question. In contrast to the conventional manual accounting system where the source data is most accessible at the time of entry and progressively less accessible thereafter, a properly designed automated system not only retains source data accessibility but also tends to make it more accessible as data accumulates. Why? Simply because with more source data it becomes more practical to restructure it into more useful forms.

The second answer may appear somewhat paradoxical at first: A great deal of the value of a computerized management information system lies not so much in the answers it provides but, rather, in the questions it permits a manager to ask. These questions may be directed to subordinates, superiors, or to the manager himself. In order to ask them, the manager needs to be able to review historical data, of course, but he must also be able to make comparisons of budget to actual for this month, quarter, or year to last, this activity or entity to that one, and so forth. And the manager needs to make those comparisons in terms of percentages, ratios, and dollar amounts. Not infrequently, such comparisons must be made after the fact and on short notice, if they are to be of any value.

Getting this kind of information requires more than just access to the raw data. It takes a great many routine computations that can be ordered and carried out quickly and inexpensively. Only a very powerful and flexible system has the built-in capability to do this.[3]

- Why did Rockford Paper Mills computerize the common business applications?
- What benefits has this provided to management?

[3] Source: Marvin Weingard, "The Rockford Files: A Case for the Computer," *Management Accounting*, April 1979, pp. 36–38.

15

CHAPTER OUTLINE

ORIGINS OF SYSTEMS ANALYSIS AND DESIGN
  Methods and Procedures
  Systematic Analysis and Operations Research
  The Systems Approach
  The Systems Development Cycle
INFORMATION SYSTEMS DEVELOPMENT
SYSTEMS INVESTIGATION
  System Survey and Selection
  Feasibility Studies
SYSTEMS ANALYSIS
  Structured Analysis
  Analysis of the Organization
  Requirements Analysis
  System Requirements
SYSTEMS DESIGN
  Structured Design
  Logical System Design
  Physical System Design
  System Specifications
PROGRAMMING
SYSTEMS IMPLEMENTATION
SYSTEMS MAINTENANCE
USER INVOLVEMENT IN SYSTEMS ANALYSIS AND DESIGN
TECHNIQUES OF SYSTEMS ANALYSIS AND DESIGN
CHECKLIST FOR SYSTEMS ANALYSIS AND DESIGN
SUMMARY
KEY TERMS AND CONCEPTS
REVIEW AND DISCUSSION QUESTIONS
REAL WORLD APPLICATIONS
  Mattel Toys
  Farmers Insurance Group
  Armco Incorporated

Systems Analysis and Design

LEARNING OBJECTIVES

The purpose of this chapter is to promote a basic understanding of the development of information systems by analyzing the origins, activities, and major considerations of systems analysis and design.

After reading and studying this chapter, you should be able to:

1. Briefly explain how systems analysis and design is related to other problem-solving methodologies.
2. Explain what "the systems approach" means in terms of a systems *viewpoint* and a systems *process*.
3. Outline the stages of the information systems development cycle.
4. Describe the purpose and content of a feasibility study.
5. Outline some of the potential costs and benefits of a computer-based information system.
6. Explain the purpose and activities of systems analysis and systems design.
7. Identify the purpose and activities of systems implementation and maintenance.
8. Explain why and how users should be involved in systems analysis and design.
9. Identify several tools and techniques of systems analysis and design.
10. Identify several input, processing, output, storage, and control considerations of systems analysis and design, and illustrate them with examples based on the business computer applications discussed in Chapters 13 and 14.

Who develops the business computer applications and information systems discussed in the previous chapters? Such computer-based information systems do not just happen. They must be conceived, designed, and implemented. This developmental process is known as *information systems development, applications development,* or more popularly, *systems analysis and design.* **Systems analysis and design** is the process in which users and systems analysts **design** information systems and data processing systems based on an **analysis** of the information requirements of an organization. Effective systems analysis and design is vital to the development of computer applications and computer-based information systems, since ineffective and inefficient use of computers in business is frequently attributed to a failure to understand and apply the *systems concept* to the information requirements of the business firm. To a great extent, therefore, successful use of the computer in business requires that "every computer user should learn to be his or her own systems analyst."

ORIGINS OF SYSTEMS ANALYSIS AND DESIGN

Methods and Procedures

The systems analysis and design function in many business firms originated in "methods and procedures" groups and may still exist in "systems and procedures" departments. *Methods and procedures* departments applied the techniques of "scientific management" to the data processing and communications functions of a business. Thus, systems analysis is related to scientific management and industrial engineering.

The founder of scientific management was Frederick W. Taylor (1856–1915), who proved that industrial processes could be significantly improved if (1) production was segmented into individual tasks, (2) alternative ways of accomplishing these tasks were developed, and (3) the best sequence of operations was adapted as a standard for all workers. Though Taylor concentrated on factory operations, he maintained that *all* work could be improved if the techniques of scientific management were utilized. By the early 1900s, scientific management techniques spread from the factory to the office. For example, techniques such as time and motion studies, which had been used to improve the efficiency of "blue collar" manufacturing personnel, were used to improve the efficiency of "white collar" office personnel.

The increase in paperwork and shortage of clerical employees during World War II encouraged the development of specialists in "office procedures" or "methods and procedures" in government agencies and large business firms. These specialists engaged in such activities as *forms design, forms control, work simplification, time and motion studies, work sampling, office layout design, procedure writing,* etc. Methods and procedures departments composed of specialists suchs as "methods analysts," "procedures analysts," and "forms designers" began to emerge. Some of these specialists are still utilized today by large organizations.

Systematic Analysis and Operations Research

The term "systems analysis" is frequently used to describe a type of systematic analysis of problems which was popularized by the U.S. Department of Defense during the 1960s. This type of systems analysis is really a modification of the "scientific method" which has long been used by scientists and scholars to analyze problems and develop alternative solutions. The scientific method was modified to apply more specifically to the solution of management problems.

Systems analysis is sometimes considered as one of the tools of "operations research," which is also known as "management science," or "decision science." *Operations research* can be defined as the application of scientific techniques to organizational problems, utilizing a methodology based on the concepts and techniques of mathematics and the natural, physical, and social sciences. The definition can also be applied to management science and decision science, though these terms emphasize the decision-making and scientific orientation of the theories and techniques that are utilized.

Operations research (OR) stresses the systems approach since it looks at an organization "as a whole" before analyzing the problems of organizational components. OR stresses the "team approach" by utilizing teams of specialists with expertise in different scientific and technical fields to develop *feasible* (not optimal) solutions to complex organizational problems. Operations research strives to provide management with "decision aids" or *"decision rules"* to help managers make better decisions. Finally, OR places great emphasis on the development of "models" of the problem being investigated. Figure 15–1 summarizes the steps in the scientific method, systematic analysis and operations research approaches to problem solving.

FIGURE 15–1   The Scientific Method, Systematic Analysis, and Operations Research Approaches

Scientific Method	Systematic Analysis	Operations Research
• Recognize a problem.	• Define the problem.	• Define the problem.
• Develop a hypothesis.	• Define the objectives.	• State the criteria.
• Gather data.	• Define the alternatives.	• Construct the model.
• Test the hypothesis through experimentation.	• Make assumptions concerning the system	• Manipulate the model.
• Reach conclusions about the hypothesis.	• Define the constraints.	• Evaluate and modify the model.
	• Define the criteria.	• Test the solution in the real world.
	• Collect the data.	• Implement the solution.
	• Build the model.	• Periodically review the solution.
	• Evaluate the alternatives.	

Sources: Richard L. Shell and David F. Steltzer, "Systems Analysis: Aid to Decision Making," *Business Horizons,* December 1971, p. 68, and Kalman J. Cohen and Frederick S. Hammer, *Analytical Methods in Banking* (Homewood, Ill.: Richard D. Irwin, Inc., 1966), pp. 5–14.

The Systems Approach

The "systems approach" is a term which describes the use of the systems concept in studying a problem and formulating a solution. The systems approach has two basic characteristics:

• "Using the systems approach" means using a **viewpoint** which tries to find systems, subsystems, and components of systems in the phenomena we are studying so that all important factors and their interrelationships are considered. Therefore, the systems approach encourages us to look for the components and relationships of a *system* as we analyze a specific problem and formulate its solution.

For example, we have used a system's viewpoint throughout this text as we analyzed data processing, computers, information flows, and business firms as **systems** of **input, processing, output, storage,** and **control** components.

• The systems approach also refers to the **process** by which we study a problem and formulate a solution. Studying a problem and formulating a solution can be considered as an organized *system* of interrelated activities (frequently called the **systems development cycle**) composed of investigation, analysis, design, programming, implementation, and maintenance activities.

The Systems Development Cycle

Figure 15–2 illustrates the systems approach as a "recycling" process of systems development. This model summarizes the stages of the *systems development cycle* (or *systems*

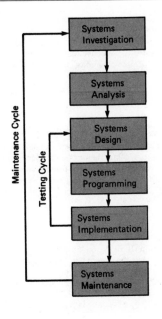

- Identify the Objectives, Problems, and Opportunities of Present or Proposed Systems and Analyze the Feasibility of Developing New or Improved Systems

- Identify the Environment, Subsystems, Components, and Requirements of a Specific Present or Proposed System

- Design a Model of the New or Improved System
  Design the System

- Construct (program) a Model of the System
  Construct (program) the System

- Test the Model and Redesign If Tests Are Not Satisfactory
  Test, Document, Install, and Operate the System

- Monitor, Evaluate, and Modify the System

FIGURE 15–2 The Systems Development Cycle

life cycle) and can be applied to *all systems,* not just information systems. It incorporates concepts of systems theory, operations research, and scientific management. Notice that the systems development cycle consists of two distinct cycles. The "testing cycle" involves testing the model or system and performing any necessary redesign, reprogramming, and retesting activities. The "maintenance cycle" involves performing the systems development activities required to improve an established system.

INFORMATION SYSTEMS DEVELOPMENT

Developing an information system requires a process called *information systems development* (or systems analysis and design) which includes the steps of (1) **investigation,** (2) **analysis,** (3) **design,** (4) **programming,** (5) **implementation,** and (6) **maintenance,** each of which is summarized in Figure 15–3. It is a systematic process based on the systems development cycle and systems life cycle concepts. Let us now take a closer look at what goes on in each stage of this process.

SYSTEMS INVESTIGATION

The systems analysis and design process begins with the **systems investigation** phase which results in the selection and

FIGURE 15-3 The Stages of Information Systems Development

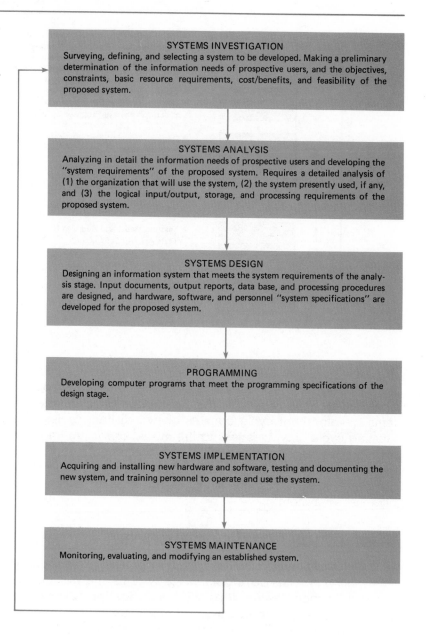

SYSTEMS INVESTIGATION
Surveying, defining, and selecting a system to be developed. Making a preliminary determination of the information needs of prospective users, and the objectives, constraints, basic resource requirements, cost/benefits, and feasibility of the proposed system.

SYSTEMS ANALYSIS
Analyzing in detail the information needs of prospective users and developing the "system requirements" of the proposed system. Requires a detailed analysis of (1) the organization that will use the system, (2) the system presently used, if any, and (3) the logical input/output, storage, and processing requirements of the proposed system.

SYSTEMS DESIGN
Designing an information system that meets the system requirements of the analysis stage. Input documents, output reports, data base, and processing procedures are designed, and hardware, software, and personnel "system specifications" are developed for the proposed system.

PROGRAMMING
Developing computer programs that meet the programming specifications of the design stage.

SYSTEMS IMPLEMENTATION
Acquiring and installing new hardware and software, testing and documenting the new system, and training personnel to operate and use the system.

SYSTEMS MAINTENANCE
Monitoring, evaluating, and modifying an established system.

definition of the particular system that will be developed. Systems investigation is the stage which answers the question: "Should we develop new or improved systems?" Because the process of developing a new or improved system can be a costly one, this stage requires that a preliminary study called a **feasibility study** be made. Systems investigation should include the steps shown in Figure 15–4.

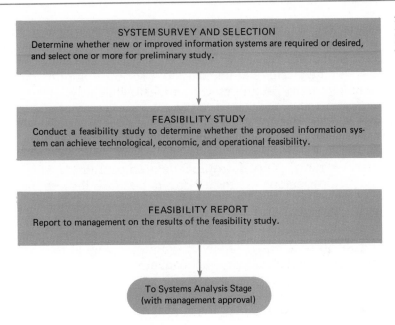

FIGURE 15–4   The Systems Investigation Stage

System Survey and Selection

Requests for the development of new information systems may come from present and potential computer-using departments of an organization. They should also be identified by continually surveying the information needs of the organization in order to identify the need for possible new information systems. Projects should also be identified by a formal *systems maintenance* activity which involves the monitoring and evaluating of established information systems in order to identify the need for modifying or replacing systems. In any case, *most business firms will have more proposed systems projects than it is possible for them to develop.* Limitations of money, personnel, time, and technology require the selection of information systems development projects which best utilize the resources of the firm. The systems investigation phase should therefore include a survey of possible information systems development projects, and the selection of projects for further investigation.

Feasibility Studies

Systems selected for further investigation are subjected to feasibility studies. A *feasibility study* determines the information needs of prospective users and the objectives, constraints, basic resource requirements, cost/benefits, and feasibility of proposed projects. The findings of such a feasibility study are usually formalized in a written report which is submitted to the management of the firm for approval. Let us now briefly discuss the basic characteristics of proposed information systems that must be analyzed in a feasibility study.

Defining Problems and Opportunities. Problems and opportunities must be identified in a feasibility study. *Symptoms* must be separated from *problems.* For example, the fact that "sales are declining" is not a properly defined problem. A statement that "salespersons are losing orders because they cannot get current information on product prices and availability" gets closer to the facts of the problem. *Opportunities* are indicated by statements such as: "We could increase sales 20 percent if salespersons could receive instant response to requests for price quotations and product availability."

Determining Information Needs. The feasibility study should make preliminary determination of the *information needs* of prospective users. *Who* wants *what* information and *when, where,* and *why* they want it are the basic questions that must be answered. Users may express their information needs by describing a problem that has developed. For example: "We are not receiving production information early enough in our shipping department." Such statements are symptoms of an underlying information system problem which must be identified and defined with the help of users, systems analysts, and management.

Information needs should also be stated specifically. For example: "Get me all the facts" or "Give me the same information I am getting now" are not specific statements of information needs. A request for "immediate notification on any products that have fallen below the minimum inventory level" is a better statement of information needs.

Determining System Objectives. Feasibility studies should determine the objectives of the system. Objectives should not be stated in vague terms. For example, compare the statement, "Improve efficiency," with more specific statements, such as— "Pay all invoices before the due date," or "Provide production status information to the shipping department within one hour of the end of each shift but without disturbing the production process."

Such specific objectives bring "the real world" into the system development process since they emphasize that the purpose of an information system is to *improve the effectiveness of the users of the system in the performance of their business activities.*

Identifying System Constraints and Criteria. The feasibility study must identify the "constraints" of the proposed system, also known as the "restrictions" or "boundaries" of a system. *Constraints* are restrictions which limit the form and content of the system design. Constraints can be *internal* or *external* to the business organization. For example, an external constraint, also called an "environmental" constraint, might restrict the format and size of a source document or output document to specifications required by law or industry agreement. The checks of the banking industry and the "W-2" forms of the Internal Revenue Service are specific examples.

Internal constraints may arise due to a scarcity of organizational resources or due to the conflicting information needs and objectives of departments and personnel within an organization. *For example,* the objective of providing timely production status information to the shipping department may be restricted by constraints that specify: "Don't impose new duties on production personnel," or "Operating costs of any new system must not exceed the costs of the present system."

An important step in systems investigation is defining the *criteria* to be used in evaluating the feasibility of the alternative systems being proposed. Criteria must also be ranked in order of their importance because a criterion such as "low cost" may conflict with a criterion such as "instant response." Figure 15–5 summarizes many of the criteria which can be used to specify the performance required of a system.

FIGURE 15–5 System Performance Criteria

- Cost—Operating, maintenance, unit.
- Time—Response, access, elapsed, cycle, process, turnover.
- Accuracy—Frequency and number of errors, significance of errors.
- Reliability—Stability, durability, life.
- Security—Legal, safety, secrecy.
- Quality—Appearance, tolerance.
- Flexibility—Variability, sensitivity.
- Capacity—Volume of transactions, inquiries, computations, etc.
- Efficiency—Performance ratios.
- Acceptance—Customer, employee, management, stockholder.

Source: Adapted from *Management Systems,* 2d ed., by Thomas B. Glans, Burton Grad, David Holstein, William E. Meyers, and Richard N. Schmidt. Copyright © 1979 by Holt, Rinehart and Winston, Inc. Reprinted by permission of Holt, Rinehart and Winston, Inc.

Economic, Technological, and Operational Feasibility. The goal of feasibility studies is to evaluate alternative systems through cost/benefit analysis and other methods of evaluation so that the most feasible and desirable system can be selected for development. The "feasibility" of a proposed system can be evaluated in terms of:

Economic feasibility—whether expected cost savings, increased profits, and other benefits exceed the costs of developing and operating the system.

Technological feasibility—whether reliable hardware and software required by a proposed system is available or can be acquired by the business firm.

Operational feasibility—the willingness and ability of the management, employees, customers, suppliers, etc., of an organization to operate, use, and support a proposed system. See Figure 15–6.

Cost/Benefit Analysis. Feasibility studies should include a *cost/benefit analysis* of the proposed system. *Costs* must include the costs of computer hardware and software, CPU time, systems analysis and design, programming, personnel, training, installation, and operations. Such **tangible costs** are comparatively easily to quantify compared to the analysis of **intangible costs** such as the loss of customer goodwill or employee morale caused by errors and disruptions arising from the installation of a new system.

Tangible benefits are comparatively easy to estimate, such as the decrease in payroll costs caused in a reduction in personnel or a decrease in inventory carrying costs caused by

FIGURE 15–6 Economic, Technical, and Operational Feasibility

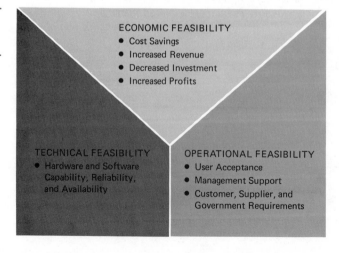

ECONOMIC FEASIBILITY
- Cost Savings
- Increased Revenue
- Decreased Investment
- Increased Profits

TECHNICAL FEASIBILITY
- Hardware and Software Capability, Reliability, and Availability

OPERATIONAL FEASIBILITY
- User Acceptance
- Management Support
- Customer, Supplier, and Government Requirements

TANGIBLE BENEFITS

- Increase in sales or profits. (Improvement in product or service quality.)
- Decrease in data processing costs. (Elimination of unnecessary procedures and documents.)
- Decrease in operating costs. (Reduction in inventory carrying costs.)
- Decrease in required investment. (Decrease in inventory investment required.)
- Increased operational ability and efficiency. (Improvement in production ability and efficiency; for example, less spoilage, waste, and idle time.)

INTANGIBLE BENEFITS

- New or improved information availability. (More timely and accurate information, and new types and forms of information.)
- Improved abilities in computation and analysis. (Mathematical simulation.)
- Improved customer service. (More timely service.)
- Improved employee morale. (Elimination of burdensome and boring job tasks.)
- Improved management decision making. (Better information and decision analysis.)
- Improved competitive position. (Faster and better response to actions of competitors.)
- Improved business and community image. ("Progressive" image as perceived by customers, investors, other businesses, government, and the public.)

FIGURE 15–7   Benefits of Computer-Based Information Systems

a reduction in inventory of the proposed system. **Intangible benefits** are much harder to estimate. Such benefits as "better customer service" or "faster and more accurate information for management" fall into this category. In any event, a determined effort must be made to detail the costs and benefits that are expected from a proposed system. Figure 15–7 lists typical tangible and intangible benefits (with examples).

It is not a simple task to determine whether the dollar value of benefits exceeds the dollar value of development and operating costs. It may be difficult to answer this basic but vital question of management: "Will investing in a new or improved system produce a satisfactory rate of return?" This question must be answered, though many times it can never be adequately answered by numbers alone. One way to answer this question is to compute a percentage **rate of return on investment** for new or improved systems proposals.

$$\text{Return on Investment} = \frac{\text{Increased profits due to cost savings and/or increased revenue}}{\text{New investment required less reductions in investment}}$$

The return-on-investment (ROI) concept emphasizes three potential methods of achieving economic feasibility for proposed systems:

- Cost reduction (such as lower operating costs).
- Increased revenue (such as an increase in sales).
- Decreased investment (such as a decrease in inventory requirements).

The Feasibility Study Report. The results of systems investigation are recorded in written form in a *feasibility study report*. This report *documents* and *communicates* the findings of the feasibility study to management and other users. Management uses the information in the feasibility report as the basis for a decision to approve or disapprove the proposal. Figure 15–8 outlines the contents of such a report.

The feasibility study report should include:

- Preliminary specifications of the proposed new or improved system.
- An evaluation of the economic, technical, and operational feasibility of the proposed system.
- A plan for the development of the proposed system.

FIGURE 15–8 Feasibility Study Report Outline

Introduction
   Statement of the problem or opportunity
   Objectives of the proposed information system
   Estimates of benefits, limitations, life, and costs
   Constraints and priorities

Systems Description
   The present system
   Information requirements, present and future
   Estimate of hardware, software, and personnel required
   Cost/benefit analysis of alternatives

Development Plan
   Budget and schedule estimates for the project
   Techniques of data gathering and analysis
   Personnel assignments
   Project control reports

Conclusion
   Summary of proposal
   Request for management action

SYSTEMS ANALYSIS

Systems analysis involves analyzing in detail the information needs of prospective users and developing the **system requirements** of a proposed system. This stage follows the stage of systems investigation in which a feasibility study for a proposed system is accomplished. Assuming a "go ahead" decision by management, the stage of systems analysis can begin. (This stage is also known as a "systems study," "functional requirements analysis," or "logical requirements analysis.") *The goal of systems analysis is to produce the system requirements* of the proposed information system. The system requirements describe the data processing and information requirements of the proposed information system and are developed by a detailed analysis of (1) the organization that will use the system, (2) the information requirements of the user organization, and (3) the information system presently used, if any.

Structured Analysis

The systems analysis stage is a **top-down** and **structured** series of activities using much of the philosophy and methodology of **structured programming** discussed in Chapter 7. Instead of first focusing on the basic requirements of the proposed system (from the *bottom-up*), **structured analysis** begins with an analysis of the organization's requirements (from the *top down*). It then moves in a structured series of steps to the analysis of major *subsystems* or *modules* affected, then to an analysis of the information system presently used, and then finally to an analysis of the information requirements of the proposed system. See Figure 15–9.

Analysis of the Organization

Organization system analysis views a business organization as a *system* and requires that a broad "background study" of the business firm be undertaken to analyze factors and characteristics such as those outlined in Figure 15–10.

Why is such a background study important to systems analysis and design? The answer is obvious. Information systems must be tailored to the organizational background of a business. The information systems of business firms differ because business firms are different. Each business may have its own unique objectives, organization, management style, products, technology, financial status, customers, employees, and suppliers.

Example. Let us examine the importance of knowing "goals, objectives, and strategies." If we wished to develop an information system to support the sales activity of a business, we would surely discover that business objectives and marketing strategy would significantly affect the design of the proposed system. For example, a decision by a business firm to enter the consumer goods market utilizing a marketing strat-

FIGURE 15–9   The Systems
Analysis Stage

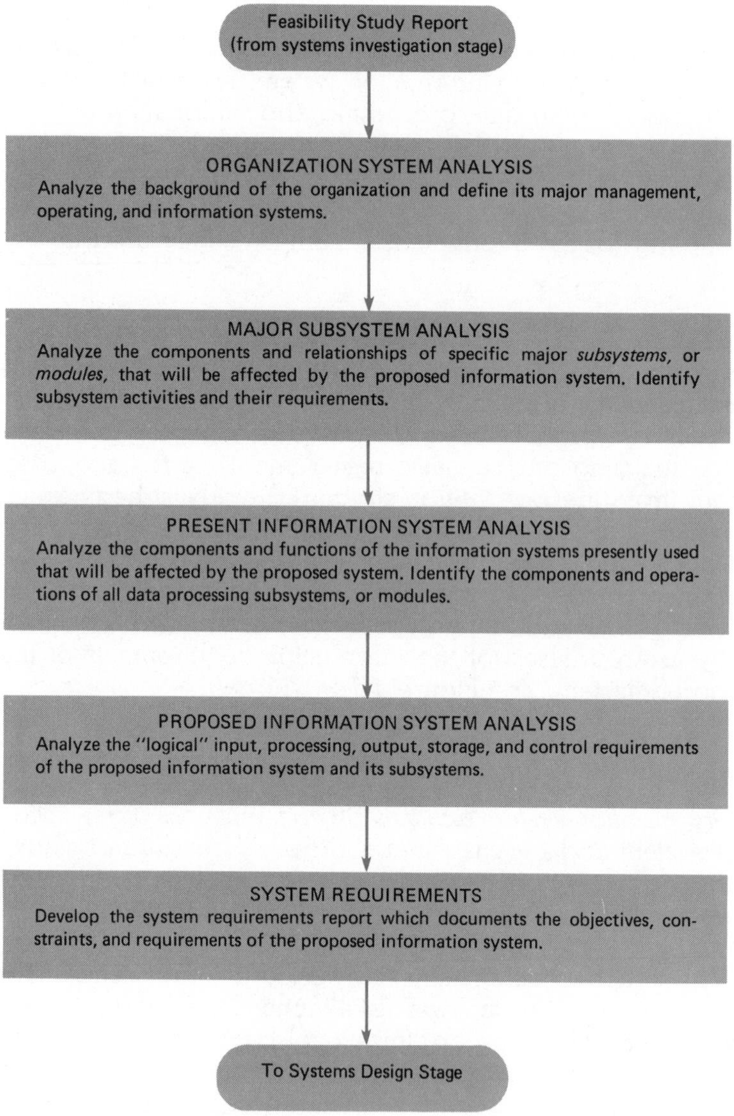

Feasibility Study Report
(from systems investigation stage)

ORGANIZATION SYSTEM ANALYSIS
Analyze the background of the organization and define its major management, operating, and information systems.

MAJOR SUBSYSTEM ANALYSIS
Analyze the components and relationships of specific major *subsystems,* or *modules,* that will be affected by the proposed information system. Identify subsystem activities and their requirements.

PRESENT INFORMATION SYSTEM ANALYSIS
Analyze the components and functions of the information systems presently used that will be affected by the proposed system. Identify the components and operations of all data processing subsystems, or modules.

PROPOSED INFORMATION SYSTEM ANALYSIS
Analyze the "logical" input, processing, output, storage, and control requirements of the proposed information system and its subsystems.

SYSTEM REQUIREMENTS
Develop the system requirements report which documents the objectives, constraints, and requirements of the proposed information system.

To Systems Design Stage

FIGURE 15–10   Factors in
Organization System Analysis

- History of the organization, its performance and prospects
- Background of the industry and competition
- Government regulation and other environmental factors
- Goals, objectives, and strategies
- Policies and practices
- Resources, products, and services
- Organizational structure and management systems
- Major operational systems
- Present information systems

egy of door-to-door selling would greatly affect the design of a new or improved marketing information system.

Requirements Analysis

Each subsystem of a business organization that will be affected by a proposed information system should be identified. Then the major functions or activities of each subsystem are analyzed as individual modules. Each module is then analyzed as an individual subsystem which has specific *logical requirements* in the form of required inputs, operations, outputs, and resources. See Figure 15–11.

FIGURE 15–11   Logical Requirements of an Order Processing System

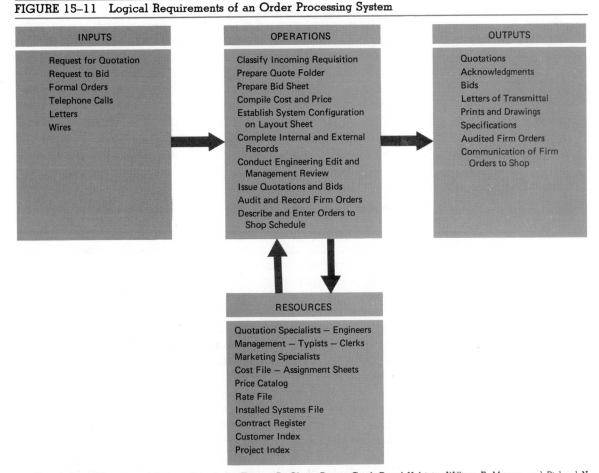

INPUTS	OPERATIONS	OUTPUTS
Request for Quotation	Classify Incoming Requisition	Quotations
Request to Bid	Prepare Quote Folder	Acknowledgments
Formal Orders	Prepare Bid Sheet	Bids
Telephone Calls	Compile Cost and Price	Letters of Transmittal
Letters	Establish System Configuration on Layout Sheet	Prints and Drawings
Wires	Complete Internal and External Records	Specifications
	Conduct Engineering Edit and Management Review	Audited Firm Orders
	Issue Quotations and Bids	Communication of Firm Orders to Shop
	Audit and Record Firm Orders	
	Describe and Enter Orders to Shop Schedule	

RESOURCES

Quotation Specialists — Engineers
Management — Typists — Clerks
Marketing Specialists
Cost File — Assignment Sheets
Price Catalog
Rate File
Installed Systems File
Contract Register
Customer Index
Project Index

Source: From *Management Systems,* 2d ed., by Thomas B. Glans, Burton Grad, David Holstein, William E. Meyers, and Richard N. Schmidt. Copyright © 1979 by Holt, Rinehart and Winston, Inc. Reprinted by permission of Holt, Rinehart and Winston, Inc.

In many cases, systems analysis requires the analysis of the data media and data processing procedures of existing information systems. Present systems may be computer-based and may include manual methods. It may be a highly structured formalized system or be informal and unorganized. In any case, systems analysis must focus on what information system components *should be,* rather than what they *are* at the present. In particular, the information requirements of the prospective users of the new system must be determined. Users must answer the question: "What information is *really needed* for decision making or other purposes?" Thus, users and systems analysts must distinguish between the information *requirements* and the information *preferences* of the users of the proposed system; between *essential* information and *unwanted* or *unnecessary* information.

The development of *management information and decision support systems* requires that systems analysis focus on the information requirements of decisions that must be made within the organization. Of course, the information requirements of an organization cannot be limited to just a decision-making focus. Organizations also require information for historical, legal, and operational purposes. *For example,* payroll tax information must be supplied to government agencies, financial information to stock holders, and sales information to customers.

System Requirements

Whether analyzing the information requirements of the organization, the data processing activities of present information systems, or the logical requirements of proposed systems, systems analysis must reveal the **input, output, processing, storage,** and **control** requirements of the information system. (See the section entitled "Checklist for Systems Analysis and Design" at the end of this chapter.) These requirements are documented in a *system requirements report* that is the final step of systems analysis. Such a report should provide a detailed description of the logical input/output, processing, storage, and control requirements of the proposed system, utilizing written descriptions, general system flowcharts, input/output and storage descriptions, and other tools. The kinds of input data available, the contents of present or proposed data bases or files, the control considerations required, the types of information required, and processing requirements such as volumes, frequencies, and turnaround times must be

System Description
Overview of the system and its relationship with other systems, system objectives, constraints and criteria.

Input Requirements
Source, format, media, organization, volume (average and peak), frequency, codes, and conversion requirements.

Output Requirements
Format, media, organization, volume (average and peak), frequency, copies, destination, codes, and conversion required.

Processing Requirements
The data processing hardware, software, people, and procedures required to transform input into output.

Storage Requirements
Organization, content, and size of the data base, types and frequency of updating and inquiries, and the length and rationale for record retention or deletion.

Control Requirements
Control requirements for system input, output, processing, and storage which promote the accuracy, validity, safety, and adaptability of the system.

FIGURE 15–12 Contents of a System Requirements Report

described and illustrated. These **system requirements** are then transformed into **system specifications** in the design stage. See Figure 15–12.

SYSTEMS DESIGN

Systems design involves the development of a *logical* and *physical* design for an information system that meets the *system requirements* developed by the systems analysis process. Systems design involves the detailed design of input documents, output reports, data base, and processing procedures. Personnel, data media, equipment, and programming specifications are also developed for the proposed system. Designing an efficient, economical, and effective system is a challenging assignment.

Structured Design

Structured systems design uses a *top-down structured* approach in designing a new system. Structured systems design moves in a top-down process from (1) the development of alternative *logical design concepts,* to (2) the development of a *logical system design,* to (3) the design of the components of the *physical system,* and finally to (4) the development of **systems specifications** for the developed system. This process is applied to each of the major *subsystems* or *modules* that make up the system being developed. Several tools are used to describe how available data will be transformed into re-

FIGURE 15–13 The Systems Design Stage

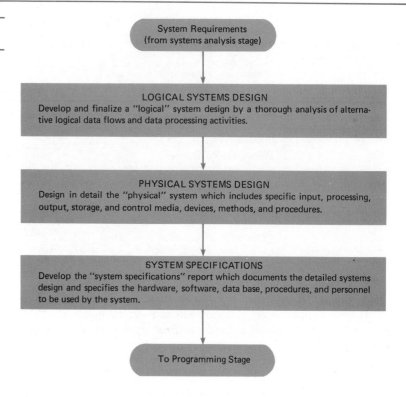

quired information by the new system. They include general and detailed system flowcharts, data flow diagrams, hierarchical systems structure and HIPO charts, decision tables and input/output and data base layout forms. Many of these tools are described in the discussion of structured programming in Chapter 7 and in a later section of this chapter entitled "Techniques of Systems Analysis and Design." Detailed written descriptions of personnel, equipment, manual procedures, and programming specifications are developed that outline the *input, processing, output, storage, control,* and *hardware, software,* and *personnel* components of the proposed system. The systems design stage can be structured into the three major steps illustrated in Figure 15–13.

Logical System Design

Early in the systems investigation stage, **logical design concepts** were developed which were a *rough* or *general* idea of the basic components and flows of the proposed information system. Several alternative logical design concepts may have been developed before a single basic concept was tentatively selected. In the systems design stage, the logical design concepts are refined and finalized by a thorough analysis of alternative design concepts and their effect on the system's requirements. See Figure 15–14.

Logical systems design should also include the consideration of an "ideal system" and alternative "realistic systems." Developing general specifications of an **ideal system** encourages users and systems analysts to be creative and emphasizes that meeting the information requirements of the organization is the primary goal of systems analysis and design. On the other hand, the development of **alternative realistic systems** encourages users and analysts to be flexible and realistic and emphasizes the several ways must be found to meet systems requirements while taking into account the limited financial, personnel and other resources of most organizations.

Trade-offs may have to be made between various system criteria. *For example,* management may demand that inventory "stockouts" never occur, which would override the criterion of minimizing inventory costs. Some criteria on the other hand, can be adjusted to accommodate the requirements of other criteria. *For example,* the criterion of low fuel costs may be adjusted to accommodate the criterion of a low level of environmental pollution.

Physical System Design

Users and systems designers utilize their knowledge of business operations, data processing, and computer hardware and software to develop the **physical design** of an information system that meets the *system requirements* developed during the systems analysis stage. Obviously, they must relate their design to the **input, processing, output, storage,** and **control** requirements of the proposed information system. Examples of such considerations are outlined in the section entitled "Checklist for System Analysis and Design" at the end of this chapter. They must decide what types of input/output and storage media and equipment are required and the processing procedures and hardware that are necessary. If electronic data processing systems are to be used, they must decide the requirements of batch processing and realtime processing systems, including the use of sequential access of direct-access files, direct data-entry devices, data communications terminals, a data base orientation, and distributed processing networks. See Figure 15–15.

FIGURE 15–14   Analysis of the Physical versus the Logical System

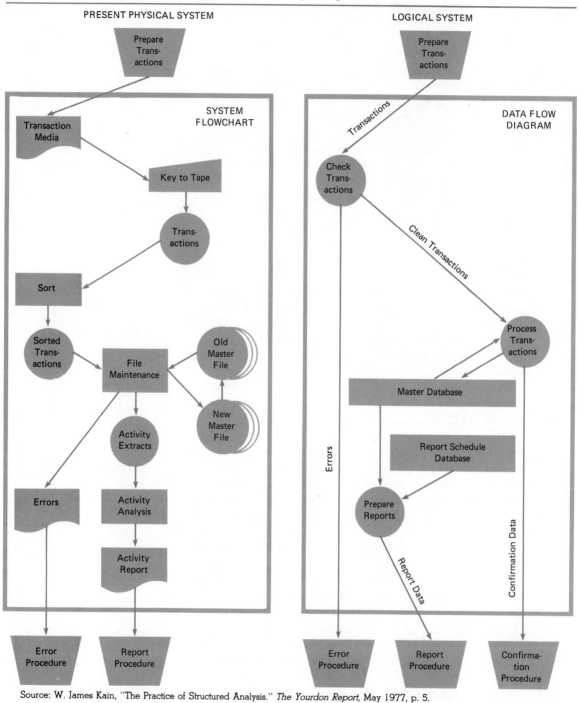

Source: W. James Kain, "The Practice of Structured Analysis." *The Yourdon Report,* May 1977, p. 5.

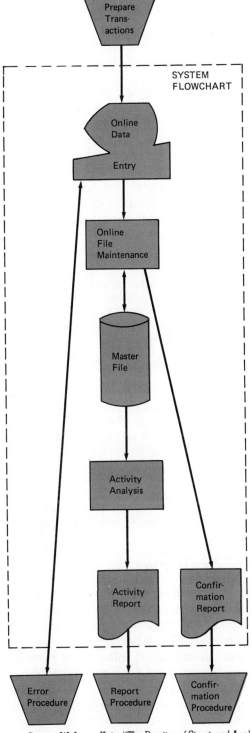

FIGURE 15–15 A Physical
System Design

Source: W. James Kain, "The Practice of Structured Analysis," *The Yourdon Report,* May 1977, p. 5.

System Specifications

The final step of the systems design stage is the development of a document called the *system specifications* report or the *systems definition*. It provides a description of the objectives and scope of the proposed system and a detailed description of the systems design. It includes specifications for source documents, the data base, and output media, procedures for data preparation and collection, and data processing procedures, both manual and electronic. It includes specifications for the hardware and software that will be utilized by the new system, including *programming specifications* which outline the computer programming requirements of the new system. See Figure 15–16.

FIGURE 15–16 Contents of a System Specifications Report

System Description
The objectives, constraints, structure, and flows of the system, utilizing written descriptions, system flowcharts, and other documentation methods.

Software Specifications
The required software components and the computer programming specifications of the proposed system.

Data Media Specifications
The content, organization, and format of input/output media, such as forms, documents, reports.

Data Base Specifications
Content, organization format, media, distribution, and access, response, maintenance, and retention capabilities.

Hardware and Facilities Specifications
The physical and performance characteristics of the equipment and facilities required by the proposed system.

Personnel Specifications
Job descriptions of persons who will operate the system.

Procedures Manuals
Specific instructions for the personnel who will operate or use the proposed system.

PROGRAMMING

The **programming** stage should be a top-down structured process which results in programs which meet the specifications of the design stage. (Described in detail in Chapter 7.) However, it must be emphasized that the programming stage requires continual interaction between computer users, systems analysts, and programmers who may be part of a "systems development project team." The system specifications and system design developed by the project team can be considered as a model of the "real world" which must be continually refined and revised during the programming, implementation, and maintenance stages of systems development. Programmers may have to confer frequently with the other members of the project team as they dig deeper into the processing procedures and logic required by the programming specifications and when they attempt to debug and test programs.

SYSTEMS IMPLEMENTATION

The activities of *systems implementation* involve the testing, documenting, acquiring, installing, and operation of a newly designed system, and the training of personnel to operate and use the system. See Figure 15–17.

Planning. This activity involves the development of plans, procedures, and schedules for training, testing, acquisition, and installation. Such planning is usually part of a "project management" effort which plans and controls the progress of information systems development projects.

Acquisition. The first step of the *acquisition* process is an evaluation of the proposals of manufacturers and other suppliers who furnish the hardware and software components required by the system specifications. (The software to be acquired are programs that will not be developed by the computer-users' own programmers.) The computer user must choose from among many different models and suppliers of hardware and software components. The evaluation and acquisition of such computer resources is discussed in the next chapter.

Training. Implementation of a new system involves *orientation* and training of management, users, and operating personnel, and the "selling" of the new system to each of these groups. Users and operating personnel must be trained in specific skills in order to operate and use the system. If an adequate job of management and user involvement in systems development has been accomplished, the "shock effect" of transferring to a new system should be minimized. If user representatives participated in the development of the system, the problems of installation, conversion and training should be minimized.

Testing. Systems implementation requires the *testing* of the newly designed and programmed system. This involves not only the testing and debugging of all computer programs but the testing of all other data processing procedures, includ-

520

FIGURE 15–17 The Systems
Implementation Stage

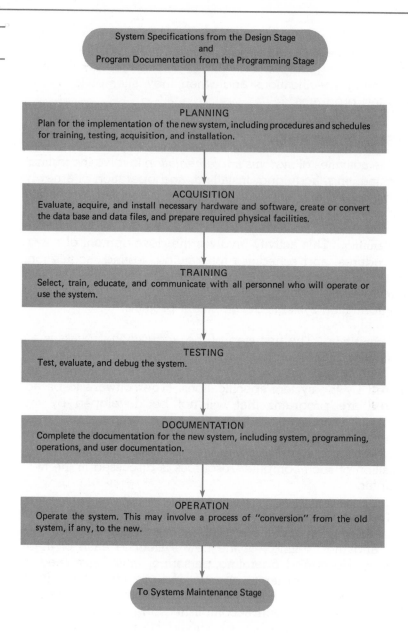

ing the production of test copies of reports and other output
which should be reviewed by the users of the proposed systems for possible errors. System modules can also be tested
by using methods such as *structured walkthroughs* discussed
in Chapter 7. Testing does not only occur during the system's
implementation stage, but should occur throughout the sys-

tem's development process. *For example,* input documents and procedures can be tested before their final form is determined by allowing them to be examined and critiqued by users and operators of the proposed system.

Documentation. *Systems documentation* is an important process that utilize the tools and techniques of systems analysis and design to *record* and *communicate* the activities and results of each stage of information system development. Proper documentation allows management to monitor the progress of the project and minimizes the problems that arise when changes are made in systems design.

Documentation serves as a method of communication between the personnel that are responsible for a project. It not only helps to eliminate duplication and redundancy of effort but serves to stimulate the systems development process. Documenting a proposed system "in black and white" for the first time frequently reveals the "holes" in the system caused by incorrect or missing procedures. It is also vital for proper implementation and maintenance, since installing and operating a newly designed system or modifying an established system requires a detailed record of the systems design. Figure 15–18 outlines the types of documentation needed by systems analysts and users that can be consolidated into "documentation manuals."

Operation. The initial operation of a new computer-based system can be a difficult task. Such an operation is usually a *conversion process* in which the personnel, procedures, equipment, input/output forms, and data base of an old information system must be converted to the requirements of a new system. However, conversion problems should be minimized if an adequate job of systems analysis and design has been performed.

SYSTEM MANUAL	USER MANUAL
System summary	System summary
Organizational requirements	Operating schedule
Hardware and software specifications	Operating procedures
Input data definition	Input/output descriptions
Output data definition	Job descriptions
Data base definition	System controls
Index of computer programs	Sample forms and reports
Computer operations summary	
Manual processing procedures	
Sample forms and reports	

FIGURE 15–18 Outlines of System Documentation Manuals

Conversion can be done on a *parallel* basis, whereby both the old and the new system are operated until the project development team and user management agree to switch completely over to the new system. It is during this time that the operations and results of both systems are compared and evaluated. Errors can be identified and corrected, and operating problems can be solved before the old system is abandoned. Installation can also be accomplished by a direct *cut over* to the newly developed system, or on a *phased* basis where only one department, branch office, or plant location at a time is converted. A phase conversion allows a gradual implementation process to take place within an organization.

SYSTEMS MAINTENANCE

Systems maintenance is the monitoring, evaluating and modifying of a system in order to make desirable or necessary improvements. This includes monitoring the progress of the other stages of systems development to insure that the development plan and objectives are being accomplished. For example, errors in the development, operation, or use of the system must be corrected by the maintenance activity. Installation of a new system usually results in the phenomenon known as the *learning curve*. Personnel who operate and use the system will make mistakes simply because they are not familiar with it. However, such errors diminish as experience is gained with a new system. Maintenance is also necessary for unexpected failures and problems that arise during the operation of a system. Systems maintenance personnel must then perform a *trouble shooting* function to determine the causes and solutions to a particular problem.

The systems maintenance activity requires a periodic review or *audit* of a system to ensure that it is operating properly and meeting its objectives. This activity is in addition to a continual monitoring of a new system. Systems maintenance also includes making modifications to a system due to changes within the business organization or in the business environment.

USER INVOLVEMENT IN SYSTEMS ANALYSIS AND DESIGN

The focus of systems analysis and design must be *user-oriented* or *people-oriented* rather than *hardware-oriented* or *software-oriented.* Thus, **user involvement** in systems analysis and design should be considered in three different contexts:

- *People* will use the product of the information system. The analysis of the information requirements of an organization and the design of an information system to meet those requirements must take into account the needs and capabilities of the human users of the information produced.

- *People* will help process the information. The designers of an information system must take into account the fact that people are an integral component of most information systems. Many information systems include manual data processing subsystems which require a significant amount of human involvement. Even electronic data processing systems require much human effort, especially in the input preparation activity. Computer hardware and software must be "human engineered" using the concepts of **ergonomics,** which strive to produce systems that are "user-friendly," ie., safe, comfortable and easy to use.

- *People* will be involved in information systems development. The fact that people are both *producers* and *users* of information makes it essential that persons representing the users who will be affected by a proposed system be included in the development of the system. The formation of information systems development "project teams" composed of systems analysts, computer programmers, and affected computer users is recommended for all but the smallest projects. This approach is contrasted to the "us versus them" approach, where a team of systems analysts and computer programmers meet periodically with affected computer users.

Figure 15–19 outlines the important responsibilities that users and systems analysts should assume in each stage of the information systems development process. Notice how deeply users should be involved from inception to final installation and operation of a new computer application. Such a participatory approach results in a people-oriented and a user-oriented information system, which has several distinct advantages. First, the new system should better reflect the true information requirements of the organization and the true capabilities of the people who operate the new system. Thus, the new system should be an effective "user-oriented" system. Secondly, *user involvement* helps insure the acceptability of the new system since it is a result of a joint effort rather than a system developed by a group of "outsiders." This involve-

FIGURE 15–19
Responsibilities during
Information Systems
Development

Stages	Responsibilities of	
	Users	Information Services Staff
INCEPTION	Initiate study, suggest application, sketch information needs, describe existing processing procedures.	Listen to requirements, respond to questions, devise alternatives, assess using rough estimates, prepare preliminary survey
FEASIBILITY STUDY	Help evaluate existing system and proposed alternatives, select alternative for design	Evaluate alternatives using agreed-upon criteria
SYSTEMS ANALYSIS	Help describe existing system, collect and analyze data	Conduct analysis, collect data, and document findings
DESIGN	Design output, input, processing logic; plan for conversion and forecast impact on users, design manual procedures; remain aware of file structures and design	Present alternatives and tradeoffs to users for their decisions
SPECIFICATIONS	Review specifications, help develop specifications for manual procedures	Combine user needs with technical requirements to develop specifications, develop technical conversion plan
PROGRAMMING	Monitor progress	Organize programming, design modules, code programs
TESTING	Generate test data and evaluate results	Test program modules individually and in entire system
TRAINING	Develop materials, conduct training sessions	Aid in preparation of materials and train operations staff
CONVERSION AND INSTALLATION	Phase conversion, provide resources, conduct postimplementation audit	Coordinate conversion, perform conversion processing tasks, help in postimplementation audit
OPERATIONS	Provide data and utilize output, monitor system use and quality, suggest modifications and enhancements	Process data to produce output reliability, respond to enhancement requests, suggest improvements, monitor service

Source: Adapted from Henry Lucas, *Information Systems Concepts for Management.* (New York McGraw-Hill 1978), p. 333. Copyright © 1978 by McGraw-Hill Book Company. Used with the permission of McGraw-Hill Book Company.

ment is also vital in the systems implementation and systems maintenance stages since it ensures that users will cooperate in the solution of problems that arise when any new system is installed and operated.

User involvement in systems development is also important in reducing the threat that new systems, especially computer

FIGURE 15–20   Systems Development without User Involvement

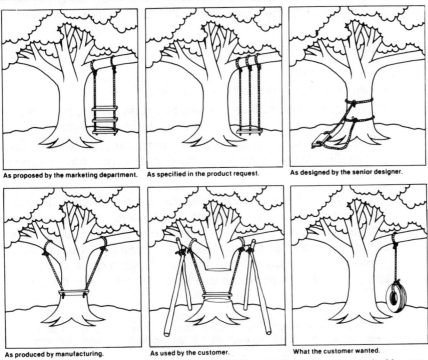

As proposed by the marketing department.   As specified in the product request.   As designed by the senior designer.

As produced by manufacturing.   As used by the customer.   What the customer wanted.

Courtesy Educational Exploration Center Inc., Minneapolis, Minnesota.

systems, may pose to the affected members of an organization. The users on the systems development project team can help plan and carry out programs of *consultation, orientation, education,* and *training* which may be required in the system implementation phase. User involvement also helps identify organizational conflicts which might otherwise escape the notice of an outside systems analyst. Conflicts between groups of people such at the departments of an organization, can have a major effect on the design and implementation of a new system. A tongue-in-cheek reminder of what happens to a systems development project when users are not involved is illustrated in Figure 15–20.

TECHNIQUES OF SYSTEMS ANALYSIS AND DESIGN

We have discussed *what* systems analysis and design is, but we have not emphasized *how* it is accomplished. Information about the present and proposed system must be collected and analyzed, and a new or improved system must be designed. How is this accomplished? First of all, information must be gathered from present and prospective users and operators of the system to be developed. This information is collected by:

- Personnel interviews.
- Questionnaires.
- Personal observation of the system.
- Examination of documents, reports, data media, procedures manuals, and other methods of systems documentation.
- Inspecting accounting and management reports to collect operating statistics and cost data of data processing operations.

The types of information that should be collected describe the characteristics of the **input, processing, output, storage,** and **control** components of the system being studied. After this information has been collected, it must be "analyzed and synthesized," using several tools and techniques of systems analysis and design which are summarized in Figure 15–21.

FIGURE 15–21 Tools and Techniques of Systems Analysis and Design

System Flowcharts. Graphically portray the flow of data media and the data processing procedures that take place in an information system. See many figures in previous chapters.

Structure Charts. Show the flow of data and data processing tasks in a hierarchical "tree" structure of data processing "modules." See Chapter 7, Figure 7–4.

HIPO Charts. Show the input/processing/output characteristics of various system modules. See Chapter 7, Figure 7–6.

Decision Tables. Identify the conditional decision logic of the information system. See Chapter 7, Figure 7–16.

Layout Forms. Show the content and format of input/output and storage media. See Chapter 7, Figures 7–7 and 7–8.

Data Flow Diagrams. Portray the logical flow of data in a system without specifying the media, hardware, or procedures involved. See Figure 15–15.

Entity Diagrams. Define the *application context* of an information system by highlighting the entities, transactions, and objectives of the business system it serves. See Figure 15–22.

Grid Charts. Identify each type of data element and information in the system and whether it is present in the form of input, output, and/or storage media. They are often utilized to identify redundant data elements and can result in the consolidation and elimination of forms, files, and reports. See Figure 15–23.

Mathematical Models. Represent in mathematical form the components, constraints, relationships, and decision rules of an information system. Techniques of simulation and mathematical analysis can then be used to provide valuable information for systems analysis and design.

Statistical Analysis. The systems development team may collect *samples* of data concerning important characteristics and components of a system instead of trying to analyze *all* of the information about a system. Statistical techniques such as probability distribution analysis, regression analysis, and tests of statistical significance and confidence are then used to analyze the relationships within the system.

Other Tools and Techniques. Many other types of graphic and written analysis can be used, such as organization charts, position descriptions, financial statements and reports, work distribution charts, and forms which describe the content and format of data records, data files, documents, and reports.

Remember that such tools and techniques are used in every stage of system development as analytical tools, design tools, and as documentation methods. For example, a flowchart can be used to *analyze* an existing system, express the *design* of a new system, and provide the *documentation* method for a newly developed system.

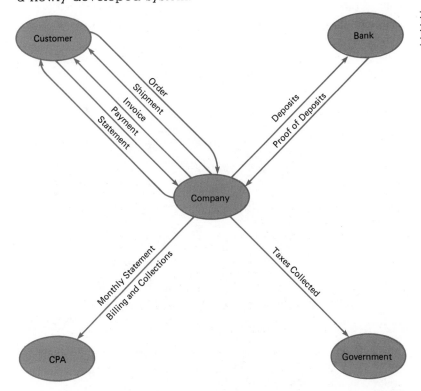

FIGURE 15–22 An Entity Diagram

FIGURE 15–23 A Grid Chart

Data Items \ Reports, Documents, and Files	Order Acknowledgment	Shipping Papers	Invoice	Sales by Customer Report	Customer Credit Report	Customer Master File	Etc.
Customer Number	√	√	√	√	√	√	
Customer Name	√	√	√	√	√	√	
Customer Address	√	√	√			√	
Discount Code			√			√	
Credit Code				√	√	√	
Salesperson Name	√			√		√	
Etc.							

CHECKLIST FOR SYSTEMS ANALYSIS AND DESIGN

Systems analysis and design should focus on the **input, processing, output, storage,** and **control** functions of proposed information systems. Users and systems analysts must determine how these data processing functions are being accomplished by present systems and should be accomplished by proposed systems. Figure 15–24 is a useful *checklist* which outlines in more detail some of the typical input, processing, output, storage and control questions that must be answered in the systems analysis and design process.

FIGURE 15–24 Checklist for Systems Analysis and Design

Input Considerations:

- How is data captured? Will the input be in the form of source documents, turnaround documents, or is it entered directly into the computer system by a keyboard or other device?
- Will the source documents be in machine-readable form (MICR, OCR, punched card) or must they be converted into another data medium such as punched cards or magnetic tape?
- Will input data be accumulated into batches or will it be processed in realtime?
- Is sorting of input data required?
- What effect will variations in volume of input data, speed of data entry, and size of input data elements have on the system?
- Are input preparation procedures and input media designed to facilitate correct data entry by the people who will operate and use the system?
- Will coding, classifying, and editing procedures be necessary?
- What control procedures will be used to ensure accurate input?
- Have input format and procedures been designed to accommodate changes due to growth, organizational policy, or environmental demands?

Processing Considerations:

- What types of processing activities (sorting, calculating, comparing, summarizing, etc.) are required?
- Should any processing activities be performed manually or mechanically instead of by the electronic computer?
- Is a batch processing or realtime processing system required?
- What levels of EDP (batch, remote batch, realtime: inquiry, data capture, file processing, full capability, and process control, distributed processing, timesharing, etc.) will be required to process input into output?
- Can the processing procedures and methods produce accurate and timely output, given the types and volumes of input and output that are required and the financial, hardware, software, and personnel resources of the organization?
- Are processing procedures designed to achieve the turnaround time, response time, and throughput requirements expected of the system even if growth and changes occur?
- How much human intervention will be required during processing?
- Are processing procedures designed and documented to facilitate the operation of the system by its users?
- What controls are built into the processing procedures?

Output Considerations:

- Will output be in the form of printed documents and reports or is information to be displayed on devices such as CRT terminals?

FIGURE 15-24   *(continued)*

- Should output be in a machine-readable form such as punched cards or magnetic tape which require additional conversion to a human-readable document?
- Will output of the system become the input to another system? (Such as turnaround documents)
- Will output be accumulated in batches or is realtime output required?
- Does output have to report every transaction or activity, or should only exceptional items be reported (exception reporting), or is summarized information acceptable?
- Must output be generated on demand, on schedule, or on exception?
- Are output support procedures such as editing, copying, microfilming, sorting, and distributing required?
- Is output for external users (such as invoices, statements, and reports for customers, suppliers, or government agencies) or for internal users such as reports for operating and management personnel?
- Are output support procedures and output media formats designed to ensure accurate, timely, and usable information to the users of the system?
- Can certain output reports and documents be standardized, consolidated, or eliminated?
- What control procedures are necessary to ensure the accuracy and timeliness of output?
- Have output format and procedures been designed to accommodate growth or possible changes in organizational policy or the environment?

Storage Considerations:
- Can the information system utilize an integrated data base instead of several separate data files?
- If multiple files are to be used, are procedures designed to update all files that are affected by a particular item of data or information?
- Will data and information be stored in sequential access files or direct access files?
- Will the data base be used to support realtime or batch processing?
- How should the data base or data files be organized? What should be the design of the data elements (characters, fields, records) that will be included?
- Can multiple keys, pointers, and directories be provided for direct access files so that data and information can be easily retrieved and updated?
- Are the files or data base designed to facilitate interactive processing by users of the system? Will data base management software be utilized in this regard?
- What are the criteria for retention or deletion of data records?
- Are controls built into file processing and inquiry procedures in order to limit the possibility of unauthorized entry into the files, loss of data and information, or incorrect recording or transmittal of data or information?
- Is storage design flexible? Does it take into account possible changes in the type, size, volume, and frequency of data elements, inquiries, and file processing due to growth, organizational changes, or external environment developments?

Control Considerations:
- Are input/output control methods which detect invalid and inaccurate input data or output information included in this system? (Examples are batch control totals, check digits, and reasonableness checks.)
- Are processing control procedures which detect invalid and incorrect processing of data included in the system? (For example, checkpoints can be designed into a computer program.)
- What procedures have been devised to monitor input, output, processing, and storage files so that the computer system will provide instant notification of unusual conditions or results which require investigation or action by the computer user?

FIGURE 15–24 *(concluded)*

- Are storage control procedures which protect the accuracy and confidentiality of the data base or data files included in the system? (For example, identification codes which limit file updating and inquiries to authorized personnel and programs.)
- Are "backup" file procedures which limit the loss of data caused by physical breakdowns or incorrect processing included in this system? ("Dumping" the contents of direct access files onto magnetic tape is an example.)
- Are data processing control forms required for this system? (Input batch tickets and output transmittal sheets are examples.)
- Are feedback-control procedures included in the systems design so that fraudulent use of the system can be detected or prevented?
- Are "audit trails" which allow the flow of an item of data or a document to be traced through the entire information system included in the system design?
- Have the control procedures of the system been designed to avoid "over control"? (This condition may be caused by conflicting control procedures.)
- Have control procedures been provided which facilitate and control the systems maintenance activity? (The system is monitored, evaluated, and modified when corrections and changes are necessary.)

SUMMARY

- Systems analysis and design is a systems development process utilized by systems analysts who design information systems and data processing systems based on the information requirements of an organization. It embodies some of the principles and techniques of scientific management, systematic analysis, operations research, and the "systems approach."

- Information systems development is a process that results in the creation of computer-based information systems. Information systems development, also known as the "systems life cycle," can be subdivided into the six stages of systems investigation, analysis, design, programming, implementation, and maintenance.

- The systems investigation stage includes the conducting of a "feasibility study" to determine the economic, technological, and operational feasibility of a proposed information system. The determination of economic feasibility requires a cost/benefit analysis which focuses on the tangible and intangible costs and benefits that would result from the implementation of a proposed system.

- Systems analysis involves an in-depth analysis of the information needs of users. Its objective is to determine the information requirements and other "logical system requirements" of a proposed information system after analyzing the organization and its information requirements.

- Systems design is a stage of information systems development which involves the logical and physical design of an information system that meets the systems requirements developed in the systems analysis stage. It develops the "system specifications" for a proposed system which specifies the hardware, software, data base, procedures, and personnel to be used by the system.

- Once the steps of system analysis, systems design, and programming are accomplished, a system is implemented by: (1) evaluating, acquiring, and installing necessary hardware and software, (2) Selecting and training required personnel, (3) testing the new system, (4) completing the documentation for the new system, and (5) operating the new system, which may include converting from a previous system to the new system. Finally, the systems maintenance activity assures the continual monitoring, evaluating, and improvement of established systems.

- A major consideration in systems analysis and design is the "human factor." This aspect must be stressed because people (1) utilize the product of information systems, (2) help process data into information, and (3) are involved in information systems development. Thus, the focus of information systems development must be user-oriented, rather than hardware-oriented or software-oriented.

- Information about present and proposed information systems is collected by personal interviews, questionnaires, personal observations, and examination of documents and reports. This information is then "analyzed and synthesized" utilizing various tools and techniques of systems analysis and design such as system flowcharts, decision tables, layout forms, and grid charts.

KEY TERMS AND CONCEPTS

Methods and procedures	Tangible and intangible costs
Scientific management	Tangible and intangible benefits
Systematic analysis	Return on investment
Scientific method	Cost/benefit analysis
Operations research	Systems analysis
Systems approach	Systems design
Systems development cycle	Structured analysis
Information systems development	Structured design
Systems investigation	Logical versus physical systems design
Feasibility study	Organization analysis
Economic feasibility	Requirements analysis
Technological feasibility	System requirements
Operational feasibility	System specifications
Techniques of systems analysis and design	User involvement
Systems implementation	Human factors in systems analysis and design
Systems maintenance	

REVIEW AND DISCUSSION QUESTIONS

1. What is systems analysis and design? Why is it necessary to the development of computer-based information systems?

2. How did the field of "methods and procedures" contribute to the origin of systems analysis and design?

3. How does one use the systems "approach" as a systems "viewpoint," and as a systems "process"?

4. How is the systems development cycle related to the scientific method, systematic analysis, and operations research?

5. Outline the stages of the information systems development cycle. Are all of these steps really necessary?

6. What is the purpose of the systems investigation stage of systems development? What activities are involved in this stage?

7. What is a feasibility study? What are some of the basic characteristics of information systems that must be analyzed in a feasibility study?

8. What are some of the potential costs and benefits of computer-based information systems?

9. What methods of achieving economic feasibility are emphasized by the return-on-investment concept of cost/benefit analysis?

10. What are the purpose and the activities of systems analysis? Utilize examples to illustrate several of these activities.

11. Explain the difference between a "physical" system and a "logical" system.

12. What are the purpose and the activities of systems design?

13. What is the difference in the purpose and content of the system requirements and the system specifications?

14. What are the purpose and the activities required by the systems implementation stage of information systems development?

15. What is systems maintenance? Why is it important to the development of effective information systems?

16. In what three ways should the human factor be considered in systems analysis and design? Provide examples to illustrate your answer.

17. Why is user involvement important in systems analysis and design?

18. How is information required for systems analysis and design gathered?

19. What are some of the tools and techniques of systems analysis and design?

20. Can the tools and techniques of systems analysis and design be used as analytical tools, design tools, and documentation methods? Explain.

21. Utilize the checklist in Figure 15–24 to identify several input, processing, output, storage, and control considerations of systems analysis and design. Use examples drawn from the business computer applications outlined in Chapters 13 and 14 to illustrate such considerations.

   For example, what do you think would be some input, processing, output, storage, and control considerations for a retail POS system, a manufacturing process control system, an automated bank teller machine system, a payroll system, etc.?

REAL WORLD APPLICATIONS

15-1   Mattel Toys

Mattel Toys, a division of Mattel, Inc., is a major toy manufacturer with headquarters in Hawthorne, California. When the management information services department at Mattel makes a detailed study of a user request, the system analyst is expected to look at the problem in an overall context. The analyst assumes that the system will be built the way the customer has requested it, but still looks to see if there is a better way. The analyst is expected to make a basic problem identification and definition. What is the business problem? What is user department management trying to accomplish

with the new system? Is this a one-time problem or a recurring one?

Next, the analyst develops a preliminary design of the new system, including sample output reports, just as would be produced by the new system. The analyst goes over these reports with the users, to find out how the users will actually use them. This step usually uncovers more new requirements and more changes in design. With the preliminary design developed, the analyst is then in a position to estimate development costs, operating costs, and maintenance costs.[1]

- How does Mattel want system analysts to approach and implement the analysis and design of a computer-based information system?

[1] Source: Adapted from "Getting the Requirements Right," *EDP Analyzer*, July 1977, pp. 1–2.

15-2   Farmers Insurance Group

"The simplicity of operation and maintenance of the 8100 is important to us," says Lewis J. Bohache of the Farmers Insurance Group of Companies. "Clerical employees in our regional offices have learned to operate it with only one or two days of training. "The 8100 is easy to install—it plugs into a standard wall outlet. In fact, we were able to set up and start our system by ourselves. Since it does not require a special computer room, it is located in the policy service area."

Farmers uses IBM 8100 intelligent terminals in a distributed data processing (DDP) network to provide better service to its property and casualty insurance customers. It has meant much quicker response and a much lower error rate. In each of Farmers' 11 regional offices, operators enter the details of new and revised policies into an 8100. Preparing the specifics of insurance coverage for

entry requires the use of a complex code, which clerks formerly consulted in a printed manual. Today, the 8100 prompts the operator through the terminal display, providing guidance in the coding of input. "The result," Bohache notes, "has been improved productivity as well as much greater accuracy. The prompting system has enabled us to reduce the operator training period to three to four weeks, from a previous three to four months."

Each 8100 operates as a stand-alone processor for data entry during the day, and then batches the policy data over a WATS line to an IBM 3033 Processor at Farmers' Los Angeles headquarters at night. The next day, the 3033 transmits the formatted policy data back to the regional office, and a printer there produces the complete policy under the control of an IBM 4331 Processor. "We're in-

534

15-2 *(continued)*

stalling an online inventory control system to run on an 8100 here at headquarters, to manage supplies and equipment," Bohache adds. "This is feasible only because the 8100 is simple and 'user-friendly' for online applications. We can train people from the purchasing department to use it."[2]

- Does the IBM 8100 seem like a user-oriented system?
- What features in particular seem user-friendly?
- What have been the benefits of this system to Farmers?

[2] Source: "Good Policy for Farmers Insurance." Reprinted by permission from *DP Dialogue.* © 1981 by International Business Machines Corporation.

15-3 Armco Incorporated

Armco, Inc., is a major manufacturer of steel and building products with headquarters in Middletown, Ohio. Its special products division uses the PRIDE system development methodology. PRIDE is a structured methodology for developing computer-based applications including both systems design and project management methods. It includes nine phases: the first three cover the system study, system design, and subsystem design, the next three cover the design of the manual system, program design and program test, and the final three cover system testing, system operation, and system audit. There are numerous check points and user sign-off points in these nine phases.

The division has used PRIDE for a variety of projects. They have used it to help install purchased application software, and for small projects, such as improvements to existing applications. They have also used it for major projects, such as developing a manufacturing order entry system for a steel plant. As compared with other methods they have used previously, Armco feels that PRIDE provides more comprehensive documentation at earlier stages of a project, provides better communication among the involved parties, encourages greater user involvement at all levels and all stages of a project, and leads to better definition and planning of requirements and resources.[3]

- How has Armco used PRIDE for information system development projects?
- How has the use of this systems development methodology benefitted Armco?

[3] Source: Adapted from "The Production of Better Software," *EDP Analyzer,* February 1979, pp. 4–5.

Managing Information
Resources

16

CHAPTER OUTLINE

THE COMPUTER-BASED BUSINESS ENVIRONMENT
THE COMPUTER INDUSTRY
   Hardware Suppliers
   Software Suppliers
   EDP Service Suppliers
   Benefits and Limitations of EDP Services
EVALUATING COMPUTER ACQUISITIONS
   Hardware Evaluation Factors
   Software Evaluation Factors
   Evaluation of Vendor Support
FINANCING COMPUTER ACQUISITIONS
   Rental
   Purchase
   Leasing
THE COST OF COMPUTER RESOURCES
   Systems Development Costs
   Operations Costs
   Administrative Costs
   Controlling Computer Costs
SUMMARY
KEY TERMS AND CONCEPTS
REVIEW AND DISCUSSION QUESTIONS
REAL WORLD APPLICATIONS
   Spaulding Division
   Merrimack Valley Pet Supply
   Yorx Electronics

Acquiring Computer Resources

LEARNING OBJECTIVES

The purpose of this chapter is to promote a basic understanding of how computer resources should be acquired by business firms by analyzing (1) the role of the computer industry, (2) the evaluation of computer acquisitions, and (3) the financing and cost of computer resources.

After reading and studying this chapter you should be able to:

1. Identify several types of firms in the computer industry and the products or services they supply.
2. Identify several benefits and limitations of using external EDP services.
3. Discuss several evaluation factors that should be considered in evaluating hardware, software, and vendor support.
4. Summarize the benefits and limitations of the rental, leasing, and purchase of computer resources.
5. Describe several major categories of EDP costs and identify several specific costs in each category.
6. Identify several methods of controlling the cost of systems development and computer operations.

Computer-using business firms must acquire **computer resources** (hardware, software, and personnel) and **computer services** from many sources in the computer industry. Therefore, business computer users should have a basic understanding and appreciation of the role of the computer industry. In this chapter we shall explore the important segments and services of the computer industry and discuss how computer users should evaluate the acquisition of computer resources and services. In the next two chapters, we will discuss how such resources should be managed. Thus the last three chapters of this text are dedicated to the concept of **information resource management** (IRM) which views information and computer hardware, software, and personnel as valuable organizational resources which should be efficiently, economically, and effectively managed for the benefit of the entire organization.

THE COMPUTER-BASED BUSINESS ENVIRONMENT

The use of computers in business does not take place in a vacuum. The business firm is a system that interacts with many other systems in its environment. The computer operations of a business firm should thus be viewed as taking place in a "computer-based business environment." See Figure 16–1.

The computer hardware, software, and personnel resources of a business firm provide computer services to *internal computer users,* that is, the departments in the firm that require electronic data processing. Outside of the business firm is the *computer industry,* which includes computer manufacturers, other hardware and software companies, and the suppliers of other computer-related services such as EDP service bureaus and time-sharing service companies. The computer services department of a business firm relies heavily on the *hardware, software, and services* supplied by the computer industry. Beyond this ring of computer support organizations are *external computer users in society,* such as customers, other business firms, governmental units, and the general public. These external groups provide input or utilize output produced by the computer-based information systems of the business firm or are affected in some way by the business uses of the computer.

FIGURE 16–1   The Computer-Based Business Environment

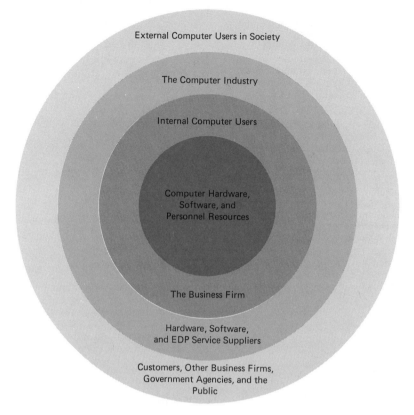

External Computer Users in Society

The Computer Industry

Internal Computer Users

Computer Hardware,
Software, and
Personnel Resources

The Business Firm

Hardware, Software,
and EDP Service Suppliers

Customers, Other Business Firms,
Government Agencies, and the
Public

THE COMPUTER INDUSTRY

Business managers cannot effectively use their computer resources unless they have a basic understanding of the computer industry. Business computer users should view the computer industry as a vital source of **computer hardware, software, and EDP services.** Effective and efficient use of the computer by computer users requires the continual support of firms within the computer industry. Figure 16–2 groups the major types of firms within the computer industry into the three major categories of hardware suppliers, software suppliers, and EDP service suppliers.

Though the computer industry consists of over 5,000 companies, only a few firms are considered *major computer manufacturers.* They include the International Business Machines Corporation (IBM, which has a major share of the market for computers—defined as the dollar value of computers installed in the United States), Honeywell Information Systems,

FIGURE 16–2   The Computer
Industry

Hardware Suppliers
Computer manufacturers
Independent peripheral manufacturers
Original equipment manufacturers
Data processing supplies companies
Computer retailers
Computer leasing companies
Used-computer-equipment companies

Software Suppliers
Computer manufacturers
Computer retailers
Independent software companies
User-developed software suppliers

EDP Service Suppliers
Computer manufacturers
Computer service centers
Time-sharing service companies
Telecommunications service suppliers
Data base service suppliers
Facilities management companies
Independent EDP consultants
Other EDP service suppliers
   Computer time rental, systems design services,
   contract programming, EDP education,
   hardware maintenance, turnkey systems

the Univac Division of the Sperry Rand Corporation, Control Data Corporation (CDC), National Cash Register (NCR), Burroughs Corporation, and Digital Equipment Corporation (DEC).

Of course, the development of minicomputers and microcomputers has greatly increased the number of companies manufacturing computers. Companies such as Intel, National Semiconductor, and Motorola are examples of large companies that produce microprocessors and microcomputers. Minicomputers and small business computers are manufactured by the major computer manufacturers as well as many other companies, including Hewlett-Packard, Datapoint, Data General, Wang Laboratories, General Automation, and Prime Computer. Important manufacturers in the microcomputer system and personal computer market include Apple Computer Corporation, the Radio Shack Division of Tandy Corporation, Texas Instruments, and Commodore Business Machines, along with larger firms such as IBM, Hewlett-Packard, and Xerox. Figure 16–3 lists many of the major firms in the computer industry.

FIGURE 16–3   The Top 50 Firms in the Computer Industry—Ranked by Revenue from Computer Products and Services

Rank and Company	Major Source of Revenue	Rank and Company	Major Source of Revenue
1 IBM	Systems	26 Mohawk Data Sciences	Peripherals
2 NCR	Systems	27 Prime Computer	Systems
3 Control Data	Systems	28 Harris Corp.	Systems
4 Digital Equipment Corp.	Systems	29 Teletype Corp.	Peripherals
5 Sperry Corporation	Systems	30 ITT Corporation	Peripherals
6 Burroughs	Systems	31 Dataproducts	Peripherals
7 Honeywell	Systems	32 National Semiconductor	Systems
8 Hewlett-Packard	Systems	33 Perkin-Elmer	Systems
9 Xerox	Peripherals	34 Raytheon Company	Peripherals
10 Memorex	Peripherals	35 Tandy Corporation	Systems
11 Wang Laboratories	Systems	36 Northern Telecom	Systems
12 Data General	Systems	37 Racal Electronics Ltd	Peripherals
13 Storage Technology	Peripherals	38 Tymeshare	Services
14 Texas Instruments	Systems	39 3M Company	Supplies
15 Computer Sciences	Services	40 Four-Phase Systems	Systems
16 Automatic Data Processing	Systems	41 Computervision	Systems
17 General Electric	Systems	42 C. Itoh Electronics	Peripherals
18 Electronic Data Systems	Systems	43 System Development Corp	Peripherals
19 Amdahl Corporation	Systems	44 Motorola	Peripherals
20 TRW	Systems	45 General Instruments	Peripherals
21 Datapoint	Systems	46 Ampex Corporation	Peripherals
22 Triumph-Adler	Peripherals	47 Apple Computer	Systems
23 Management Assistance Inc.	Systems	48 Bunker Ramo	Peripherals
24 Tektronix	Peripherals	49 Sanders Associates	Peripherals
25 McDonnell-Douglas	Software	50 Bradford National	Services

Source: Adapted from Peter Wright, "The Datamation 100," *Datamation*, June 1981, pp 102–92. Reprinted with permission of *Datamation* magazine. Copyright by Technical Publishing Company, a Dun & Bradstreet Company, 1981; all rights reserved.

Hardware Suppliers

The primary sources of computer hardware are the major computer manufacturers, who manufacture many sizes of computer systems, as well as peripheral equipment, and data processing supplies. Other computer manufacturers may produce microcomputers, minicomputers, small computer systems, special-purpose computers, and a few types of peripheral devices. Other hardware suppliers can be primarily classified as *independent peripheral manufacturers*. These firms confine themselves to the production of peripheral computer equipment such as input, output, storage, and data preparation devices.

Two other categories of computer hardware manufacturers are the *original equipment manufacturer* (OEM) and the *plug compatible manufacturer* (PCM). OEMs manufacture and sell computers by assembling components produced by other hardware suppliers. PCMs manufacture computer mainframes and peripheral devices that are specifically designed to be compatible (by just "plugging in") to the mainframes or peripherals of major computer manufacturers, especially IBM. Such firms claim that their hardware is similar to that produced by IBM or other major manufacturers, but provide better performance at lower cost. For example the Amdahl Corporation and the National Advanced Systems Division of Intel produce large mainframe computers that are marketed as lower priced versions of IBM mainframes.

Computer retailers who sell microcomputers and peripherals to individuals and small businesses are an important form of hardware supplier resulting from the development of microcomputer systems used as personal computers and small business computers. Thousands of retail computer stores include primarily independent retailers, national chains, such as Computerland and The Computer Store, and some outlets owned by computer manufacturers, including Radio Shack, Control Data, IBM, and Digital Equipment Corporation.

Other important sources of computer hardware are computer leasing companies who purchase computers from computer manufacturers and lease them to computer users at rates that may be 10 to 20 percent lower than the manufacturer's rental price. Leasing companies are able to offer lower prices because they are willing to gamble that they can recover their costs and make a profit at the lower rates before their computers become obsolete. A final source of computer hardware is used-computer-equipment companies which purchase used computers and peripheral equipment from computer users and sell them at substantial discounts.

Software Suppliers

System software and *application software* can be obtained from several sources if computer users do not wish to develop their own software. Computer manufacturers are the largest source of software in the computer industry. They supply most of the system software (such as operating systems and other control programs and service programs) for computer users and are the major source of application packages. However, independent software companies which specialize in the development of software packages have become major software suppliers. Software can also be obtained from computer retailers and from other computer users. "User-developed software suppliers" are computer users who have developed application programs or service programs that are marketed to other computer users.

EDP Service Suppliers

The five major sources of external EDP services are computer manufacturers, computer service centers, time-sharing companies, facilities management companies, and independent EDP consultants. They and other types of firms in the computer industry offer a variety of *EDP services.* For example: Off-premise computer processing of customer jobs, time-sharing services, computer-time rental, systems design services, contract programming, EDP consulting, "turnkey" systems, EDP education, and hardware maintenance are offered. Many companies, especially computer manufacturers, supply several or almost all of these services. The following is a summary of three of these EDP services.

- *Computer service centers* (or service bureaus) provide a variety of EDP services. They process the jobs of many small firms who do not wish to acquire their own computer systems. Larger computer users also use service bureaus to handle specialized applications (such as computer-output-microfilm) or when problem situations occur, such as peak volume periods or during periods of computer "down time."
- *Time-sharing service companies* provide realtime processing services to many subscribers utilizing remote terminals and a central computer system. Time-sharing service companies are utilized by many computer users who have specialized data processing needs which require realtime processing and a large computer system.
- *Facilities management companies* are firms which take over complete responsibility for a computer user's EDP operation. Thus, a business firm may "subcontract" all EDP service needs to an outside contractor. The facilities management firm might take over all computer facilities at the user's site, utilizing its own hardware, software, and EDP personnel.

External services are widely used by small firms and firms which are using computer processing for the first time. However, the majority of computers in the United States are purchased or leased by organizations for their own use. The advent of economical and easy-to-use micro- and minicomputer systems should accelerate this development. To counteract this trend, computer service centers and EDP consultants have begun to sell computer hardware, software and systems development services to their customers. This includes the offering of *turnkey systems,* where all of the hardware, software, and systems development needed by a user are provided by the EDP service supplier. Ideally, the user should merely have to "turn the key" to begin operating and using the system.

Benefits and Limitations of EDP Services

The major benefit of using EDP service suppliers is that computer users pay only for the data processing services that they need. Purchasing or leasing computer hardware or software and employing a staff of data processing professionals creates fixed costs, such as minimum machine rental payments, depreciation charges, and the salaries of professional and managerial data processing personnel. The use of external services also eliminates the personnel and management problems caused by the employment of a group of highly paid technical professionals in a rapidly changing and highly technical field such as computers and data processing.

The management of many organizations use external EDP sources to avoid the problems that arise from having to manage computer hardware, software or personnel. They may also turn to external EDP services in order to avoid the problems of obsolescence caused by major changes in computer technology, or user needs. In some cases the cost of external services may be lower than if the computer-using firm performed its own data processing services. This may be due to "economies of scale" since a large data processing service company may utilize larger and more efficient computer hardware and software to serve its many customers.

External services do have several limitations. The loss of control over data processing procedures and confidential information is one limitation. Off-premise computer processing may be inconvenient. The cost of external services may be significantly higher in some cases because the data processing service company must not only meet expenses but must include a profit in its fee to computer users. Many firms are unwilling to depend on an outsider to provide vital data processing services. They want to have more control over data processing procedures, report deadlines, and changes in computer programming, hardware and software, and processing schedules.

EVALUATING COMPUTER ACQUISITIONS

The evaluation and selection of computer resources should require manufacturers and suppliers to present bids and proposals based on *systems specifications* developed during the design stage of systems development. Minimum acceptable physical and performance characteristics for all hardware and software requirements should have been established. A formal evaluation process reduces the possibility of buying unnecessary computer hardware or software. This sometimes happens because computer users or computer specialists want to keep up with their competitors and with the latest developments in computing. Badly organized computer operations, inadequate systems development, and poor purchasing practices may also cause unnecessary acquisitions.

Whatever the claims of hardware manufacturers and software suppliers, the *performance* of hardware and software must be demonstrated and evaluated. Independent hardware and software information services (such as Datapro Reports) should be used to gain detailed specification information and evaluations. Hardware and software should be demonstrated and evaluated either on the premises of the computer user or by visiting the operations of other computer users who utilize similar types of hardware or software. Other users are frequently the best source of information needed to evaluate the claims of manufacturers and suppliers. Vendors should be willing to provide the names of such users.

Large computer users frequently evaluate proposed hardware and software by requiring the processing of special "benchmark" test programs and test data. Users can then evaluate test results to determine which hardware device or software package displayed the best performance characteristics. Special simulators have also been developed which simulate the processing of typical jobs on several computers and evaluate their performances.

Computer users may use a "scoring" system of evaluation when there are several competing proposals for a hardware of software acquisition. Each evaluation factor is given a certain number of maximum possible points. Then each compet-

Factor	A	B	C	D	E
CPU					
Word size	40	20	0	0	40
Cycle time	6	12	18	6	12
Instruction set	15	0	10	10	15
Arithmetic	4	2	0	2	4
Addressing	12	8	16	16	8
Registers	12	0	24	18	18
Communications ports	28	7	21	7	21
Input/output channels	32	24	8	16	24
Environmental requirements	4	4	4	4	4
Product life cycle	26	26	19	16	19
Subtotal	179	103	120	95	165
Vendor					
Delivery time	14	21	28	28	28
Past performance	12	12	8	8	16
Maintenance	9	6	3	12	9
Location	4	0	8	8	8
Business position	2	4	2	2	2
Number installed	12	16	4	16	16
Training	20	15	5	10	15
Subtotal	73	74	58	84	94
Total	252	177	178	179	259

FIGURE 16–4 A Scoring System of Evaluation

ing proposal is assigned part or all of the possible points for each factor, depending on how well it meets the specifications of the computer user. Scoring each evaluation factor for several proposals helps organize and document the evaluation process and spotlights the strengths and weaknesses of each proposal. See Figure 16–4.

Hardware Evaluation Factors

The evaluation of computer *hardware* includes a technical analysis of specific physical and performance characteristics for each hardware component to be acquired. For example, some of the factors that should be considered in the evaluation of the central processing unit of a computer system were shown in Figure 16–4.

Evaluating hardware acquisitions should also involve the analysis of several general categories of hardware performance. These hardware evaluation factors are summarized in Figure 16–5.

Software Evaluation Factors

Software should be evaluated according to many factors that are similar to those used for hardware evaluation. Thus,

FIGURE 16–5   Hardware Evaluation Factors

Performance
    What is its speed, capacity, and throughput?

Cost
    What is its lease or purchase price? What will be its cost of operation and
    maintenance?

Reliability
    What is the risk of malfunction and its maintenance requirements? What are its
    error control and diagnostic features?

Availability
    When is the firm delivery date?

Compatibility
    Is it compatible with existing hardware and software? Is it compatible with hardware
    provided by competing suppliers, including PCM's?

Modularity
    Can it be expanded and upgraded by acquiring modular "add on" units?

Technology
    In what year of its product life cycle is it? Is it "ahead of its time" or does it run
    the risk of obsolescence? Has it been recently developed or is it due to be replaced
    by a new technology?

Ergonomics
    Has it been "human engineered" with the user in mind? Is it a "friendly" system,
    designed to be safe, comfortable, and easy to use?

Environmental Requirements
    What are its electrical power, air conditioning, and other environmental
    requirements?

Software
    Is system and application software available that can best utilize this hardware?

Support
    Are the services required to support and maintain it available?

the factors of *performance, cost, reliability, availability, compatibility, modularity, technology, ergonomics, and support* mentioned above should also be used to evaluate the acceptability of proposed software acuisitions. In addition, however, the factors summarized in Figure 16–6 must also be evaluated.

Evaluation of Vendor Support

Vendor support services which assist the computer user during the installation and operation of hardware and software must be evaluated. Assistance during installation or conversion of hardware and software, employee training, and hardware maintenance are examples of such services. Some of these services are provided without cost by hardware manufacturers and software suppliers. Other types of services can

---

FIGURE 16–6 Additional Software Evaluation Factors

Efficiency
Is the software a well-written system of computer instructions that does not utilize much storage space or CPU time?

Flexibility
Can it handle its data processing assignment easily without major modification?

Security
Does it provide control procedures for errors, malfunctions, and improper use?

Language
Is it written in a programming language that is used by our computer programmers and users?

Documentation
Is the software well-documented?

Hardware
Does existing hardware have the features required to best utilize this software?

---

be contracted for at a negotiated price. Evaluation factors for vendor support services are summarized in Figure 16–7.

FINANCING COMPUTER ACQUISITIONS

Computer hardware can be rented, purchased, or leased, while software is usually purchased, leased, or is sometimes made available without charge by the hardware manufacturer. Computer manufacturers offer all three methods of financing, while peripheral equipment manufacturers usually offer purchase or lease arrangements. Independent computer-leasing companies use long-term lease arrangements, while used-computer-equipment companies offer used equipment for purchase. The benefits and limitations of each method of financing computer acquisitions are analyzed below.

Rental

Computer users may favor the rental arrangement for several reasons. For example, the rental price includes the cost of maintenance, and the rental agreement can be cancelled without penalty by the user with only a few months' notice. Thus, computer users do not have to arrange for the maintenance of the equipment and do not have to commit to a long series of lease payments or to the financing of a large purchase price. Renting computer hardware provides greater flexibility in changing equipment configurations and greatly reduces

FIGURE 16-7   Vendor Support Evaluation Factors

Performance
What has been their past performance in terms of their past promises?

Systems development
Are systems analysts and programming consultants available? What are their quality and cost?

Maintenance
Is equipment maintenance provided? What is its quality and cost?

Conversion
What systems development, programming, and hardware installation services will they provide during the conversion period?

Training
Is the necessary training of personnel provided? What is its quality and cost?

Documentation
Are the necessary hardware, software, and applications manuals available?

Backup
Are several similar computer facilities available for emergency backup purposes?

Proximity
Does the vendor have a local office? Are sales, systems development, programming, and hardware maintenance services provided from this office?

Business position
Is the vendor financially strong, with good industry market prospects?

Hardware
Do they have a wide selection of compatible hardware and accessories?

Software
Do they have a wide variety of useful system software and application programs?

the risk of technological obsolescence since users are not "locked in" to a purchased computer that has become obsolete due to major technological developments. The monthly rental price is commonly based on 176 hours of use per month (8 hours per day for 22 working days in an average month). Use of rented computers for second and third shifts result in additional charges which are much lower than the rate for the first 176 hours.

The major disadvantages of equipment rental is the higher total cost incurred if equipment is rented for more than four or five years. Hardware manufacturers usually base their rental prices on a two to four year life, during which they will recover the cost of the equipment as well as substantial profit. Therefore, if computer hardware is going to be used for a longer period (especially if it is going to be used for more than 176 hours per month) the cost of rental is higher than the cost of purchase.

Purchase

The number of computer users *purchasing* their equipment has grown in recent years for several reasons. First the prices of microcomputers, minicomputers, and small computers are low enough to make outright purchase affordable for many computer users. Secondly, computer users feel that the increased capabilities and cost savings of fourth generation computer equipment is worth the risk of technological obsolescence.

Also, more computer users are using their computers for more than one shift per working day. If they purchase their computers, they do not have to pay additional charges for such "overtime" use. Purchase also has a tax advantage since buying a computer is considered a capital investment and thus allows computer users to qualify for an investment tax credit which reduces their income tax liability.

One of the major disadvantages of the purchasing arrangement is that equipment maintenance is not included in the purchase price and therefore must be arranged separately with the computer manufacturer, an independent computer maintenance company, or be maintained by the computer user's own personnel. Two other major disadvantages have been previously mentioned: (1) the risk of technological obsolescence and (2) the necessity to finance a large purchase price.

Leasing

Leasing computer hardware from independent computer-leasing companies was a major development of the third generation of electronic data processing. So successful did such "third-party" leasing become that computer manufacturers themselves now offer long-term lease arrangements. Leasing companies typically purchase specific equipment desired by a user and then lease it to the user for a long-term period such as five years. Leasing arrangements include a maintenance contract, purchase and trade-in options, no charges for extra shift operation, and a reduction in lease charges after a minimum period of time. However, a cancellation charge is assessed if a lease is terminated before the end of the minimum lease period.

The leasing method combines some of the advantages and disadvantages of rental and purchase. Leasing does not require the financing of a large purchase price and is less expensive than renting equipment for the same period of time. The decline of lease charges after a minimum period, the inclusion of maintenance in the lease charges, and the absence of additional charges for overtime usage are other benefits. The major disadvantage is the long-term period of the lease contract which cannot be terminated without the payment of a substantial cancellation charge.

THE COST OF COMPUTER RESOURCES

Acquiring computer resources may involve substantial expenditures. **Hardware costs** were once the largest part of EDP costs but have been steadily decreasing compared to **software costs** (which include salary costs of systems and programming personnel, plus the cost of external software packages). Figure 16–8 shows how software costs have outstripped hardware costs.

Another way to look at the costs of computer resources spotlights the size of **personnel costs** which include salaries of systems analysts, programmers, and operations personnel. Figure 16–9 illustrates (based on 1981 estimates) that personnel costs are now the major cost category in providing computer services.

The growth in software and personnel costs is related to a growth in the cost of developing and maintaining new computer applications. See Figure 16–10. The salaries of systems analysts and programmers who develop and maintain applica-

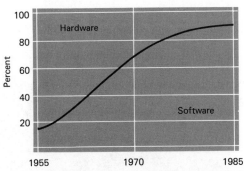

FIGURE 16–8   The Growth of Software Costs

Source: Reprinted by special permission from the *MIS Quarterly,* from "The Systems Development Dilemma—A Programming Perspective," by Jack Ewers and Iris Vessey, in vol. 5, no. 2, published June 1981. Copyright by the Society for Management Information Systems and the Management Information Systems Research Center.

FIGURE 16–9 The Costs of Computer Resources and Services

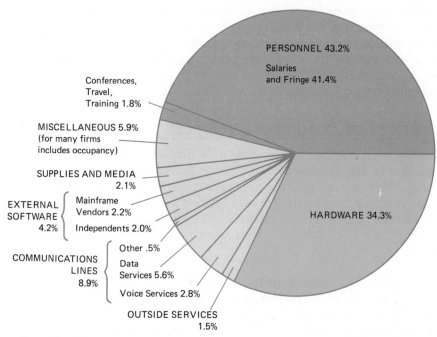

FIGURE 16–10 Growth in the Cost of Developing and Maintaining Computer Applications

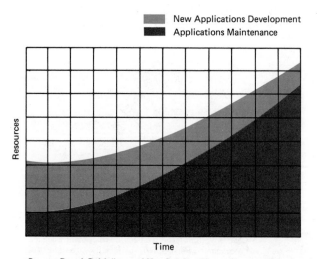

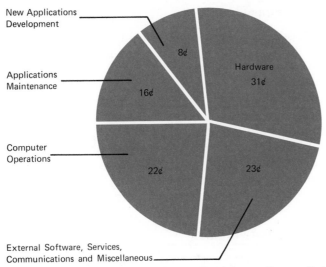

New Applications Development — 8¢

Applications Maintenance — 16¢

Computer Operations — 22¢

Hardware 31¢

23¢

External Software, Services, Communications and Miscellaneous —

FIGURE 16–11 Costs of Applications Development and Maintenance Compared to Other EDP Costs

Source: David C. Mollen and Van Bakshi, "How to Support Company End Users," *Data Processor*, May/June 1981, p. 7. Reprinted with permission.

tion systems and software make up a sizeable portion of the costs of computer services. See Figure 16–11. These figures illustrate the high cost of application systems and software maintenance. Another way to analyze the cost of providing computer services is to group costs into the functional categories of (1) systems development, (2) operations, and (3) administration. A summary of costs based on these categories is shown in Figure 16–12.

Systems Development Costs

Systems development costs includes the costs of the systems development process, such as (1) the salaries of systems analysts and computer programmers who design and program the system, (2) the cost of converting and preparing data files, documents and other media, (3) the costs of preparing new or expanded computer facilities, and (4) the costs of testing and documenting the system, training employees, and other *startup* costs. Other costs may also be included under the systems development category—such as the cost of financing the development of a new system. The facilities preparation and furnishing cost may be substantial for large systems. Large computers require environmental considerations such as air conditioning, humidity control, dust control, false flooring under which interconnecting electric cables can be laid, fire prevention systems, and auxiliary generating equipment.

FIGURE 16–12 Computer Cost Categories

Systems Development Costs
Systems development personnel
Computer program testing
Systems development supplies
Facilities preparation and furnishing
Personnel training
Other installation and conversion costs

Operations Costs
Hardware
Supplies
Software
Program maintenance
Operations personnel
Occupancy and utilities
Communications and external services

Administrative Costs
Management personnel
Administrative staff
Secretarial and clerical personnel
Miscellaneous costs
Organizational overhead

Operations Costs

Operating costs include (1) hardware and software rental or depreciation charges, (2) the salaries of computer operators and other data processing personnel who will operate the new system, (3) the salaries of systems analysts and computer programmers who perform the systems maintenance and programming maintenance functions, (4) the cost of data preparation and control, (5) the cost of data processing supplies, (6) the cost of maintaining the proper physical facilities including power, light, heat, air conditioning, building rental, security services, and equipment and building maintenance charges, and (7) overhead charges of the business firm.

Administrative Costs

Salary and other compensation expense for management personnel, administrative staff, and secretarial and clerical personnel is the major category of *administrative costs*. Organizational overhead is a major cost category for business firms who insist that the computer services department bear its share of administrative and general expenses of the company. Miscellaneous costs may include such items as employee travel and training that cannot be attributed to specific systems development projects.

Controlling Computer Costs

The cost of providing computer services has become a major operating expense of computer-using business firms. Therefore, an extensive cost control program is necessary if computer costs are to be controlled. Some of the major *cost control techniques* that are utilized by computer users are summarized below.

Systems Development. The costs of systems development must be controlled by a formal *project management* program in which a combination of plans, budgets, schedules, and reporting techniques are utilized to control the cost and direction of a systems development project. Some computer users also find it cheaper to utilize contract programming or systems design services from external sources rather than hire the additional personnel required for such systems development effort. Other firms find that buying or leasing software packages provide a cheaper method of systems development for some applications.

Computer Operations.   Several techniques are used to control computer operations costs. A formal *cost accounting system* is a major cost control technique. All costs incurred must be recorded, reported, allocated, and charged to specific computer users. Under this arrangement the computer services department becomes a "service center" whose costs are charged directly to computer users rather than being lumped together with other administrative and service costs and treated as an overhead cost.

The use of *financial budgets* is another method of managing computer costs. Financial budgets should be required for computer operations as well as for systems development. Cost control is exercised by identifying and investigating the reasons for deviations from the budget. Finally, *external EDP services* such as facilities management and EDP service bureaus have been found to be a cheaper method of computer operations for some computer-using firms. Many computer users have found such services to be a decisive method of identifying and reducing the cost of computer operations.

SUMMARY

- Information resource management (IRM) views information and computer hardware, software, and personnel as valuable organizational resources which must be managed for the benefit of the entire organization.

- The computer-using business firm must acquire computer resources from many sources in the computer industry. Therefore, business computer users should have a basic understanding of the computer industry since it is a vital source of computer hardware, software, and EDP services. The U.S. computer industry consists of a few major computer manufacturers and many smaller suppliers of hardware, software, and EDP services. Effective and efficient use of the computer by business firms requires the continual support of many firms within the computer industry.

- Information systems development and data processing services can be acquired from sources outside the business firm instead of developing such capabilities within the organization. Many business firms utilize the "external EDP services" provided by computer service centers, time-sharing companies, facilities management companies, etc. The major benefit of using external EDP services is that computer users pay only for the specific services needed and do not have to acquire or manage EDP hardware, software, and personnel. Loss of control over the data processing function, inconvenience, and higher costs are limitations that are attributed to some forms of external EDP services.

- Computer users should have a basic understanding of how to evaluate the acquisition of computer resources. Manufacturers and suppliers should be required to present bids and proposals based on systems specifications developed during the design stage of systems development. A formal evaluation process reduces the possibility of incorrect or unnecessary purchases of computer hardware or software. Several major "evaluation factors" such as performance, cost, and reliability should be utilized to evaluate computer hardware, software, and vendor support. The use of rental, purchase, or lease arrangements in financing computer acquisitions must also be evaluated.

- A major concern of computer users is the control of the cost of computer resources. Acquiring computer resources usually involves substantial expenditures for hardware, software, EDP services, supplies, and EDP personnel compensation. Major cost control programs are necessary in order to control the cost of systems development, computer operations, and EDP administration.

KEY TERMS AND CONCEPTS

Information resource management

Computer-based business environment

Computer industry

EDP service bureau

Facilities management

EDP services

Hardware evaluation factors

Software evaluation factors

Evaluation of vendor support

Financing computer acquisitions

Computer cost categories

Computer cost control

REVIEW AND DISCUSSION QUESTIONS

1. How does the information resource management concept view the role of information and computer hardware, software, and personnel in an organization?
2. Why should the computer operations of a business firm be viewed as taking place in a "computer-based business environment"?
3. Identify several types of firms in the computer industry and the products or services they supply.
4. What are some of the benefits and limitations of using EDP services provided by computer industry firms?
5. Are speed and capacity the most important factors in evaluating hardware?
6. What factors are important in evaluating software?
7. Why is the evaluation of vendor support an important consideration for computer users?
8. Should computers be rented, leased, or purchased? Explain.
9. Is hardware, software, or personnel the most important component of the costs of electronic data processing? Explain. What changes have been occurring in this area?
10. What are some of the typical costs incurred in developing and operating computer-based information systems?
11. Can the costs of electronic data processing be controlled? Explain.

REAL WORLD APPLICATIONS

16–1 Spalding Division

Spalding, a division of Questor Corporation, is a manufacturer of a general line of sporting goods with manufacturing, sales, and distribution facilities worldwide. Their annual sales of over 15,000 items approaches $200 million. Spalding's previous batch mainframe could not provide timely solutions to the company's financial and manufacturing needs. After a lengthy feasibility and design study, Spalding decided to go with the HP online distributed data processing approach.

Says Joseph Mitchel, MIS director: "We chose the HP 3000 for a couple of reasons. First, we chose the Hewlett-Packard Company for its record of profitability and stability. We also chose the HP 3000 because its marketing and support orientation is geared toward the end-user and the manufacturing environment rather than being strictly an OEM machine. Another reason was Hewlett-Packard's reputation for service and all around excellence in terms of documentation and training and for not misrepresenting the capabilities of the products provided."

"We knew what we wanted. What HP has given us can best be measured in light of what we didn't have with our previous computer systems. Noteably among them are a data base management capability, online processing, and the in-house redundancy provided by DS/3000. HP was the only vendor we could find with computer to computer network control software that was not custom, that we could just buy and use. We also picked the HP 3000 because we felt that the IMAGE data base system was easy to use and best suited to the needs of our environment.

"We presently have four HP 3000 systems connected together with DS/3000. One system is used strictly for program development. Another is used for sales and marketing type work and scientific data processing. The third system is used for order processing and accounts receivable while the last system is used for financial applications and our manufacturing control system. Active communication takes place between all of these systems over the DS lines."

"Approximately 145 online terminals of various types are distributed in all areas of the company. We perform online data entry, inquery, retrieval, editing and transaction processing. We are also doing continuous program development and batch processing."

"The users are unilaterally pleased because the system makes existing information more available in terms of timeliness. We now get instant reports on operating data without having to wait for a printed batch output. With our previous batch processing system, the reports were often out of sync with our business needs. Most of these problems have gone away as a result of the online capabilities of the HP 3000.

"HP support has been very good. We haven't required much support because our computer downtime has been less than 2 percent. As for price/performance, when we made this decision we saw a price/performance advantage over a general purpose mainframe of anywhere from 5 to 10 to 1. This advantage for the HP 3000 has held true, perhaps improved.

"The primary reason that I selected HP and would recommend it to others is that it works as advertised. The HP 3000 also essentially eliminates some of the pontetially troublesome variables that all DP managers face: hardware reliability and operating system reliability and capability. It is also important to know that the HP organization that is here today will be around tomorrow. By selecting HP you can eliminate these as potential problems and be better able to focus your efforts on developing information systems."[1]

- Why did Spalding select the HP 3000 system?
- What criteria seemed most important?
- What benefits have resulted?

[1] Source: Courtesy Hewlett-Packard.

16–2 Merrimack Valley Pet Supply

Merrimack Valley Pet Supply's experience reflects many of the difficulties and the benefits of putting a computer in a small business. Merrimack Valley operates a national distributorship, plus they are exclusive suppliers to six Harmon-family-owned retail pet stores in New Hampshire and Massachusetts. With the business expanding, owner and president, Richard Harmon, made the decision to computerize in 1979. He and general manager, Chuck Theroux, originally believed they could get a computer to do their job—they were most interested in order entry and inventory control—for about $1,500. "We ended up buying a $5,000 system," says Theroux. "We bought it as a business system, but it was really a home computer. We bought every option you could hang on the system, but after six months we knew it didn't fill our needs. We got all our money back, which says a lot for the integrity of the people we bought it from, but we had lost six months. It was just before Christmas, and we were already committed to computerizing, so we had to move fast."

Based on recommendations, they went to an independent computer retailer and bought a Data General microNOVA system. "Our first experience was valuable because we never could have been convinced we needed a computer as powerful as the microNOVA if we hadn't seen for ourselves that even a $5,000 home computer wasn't enough."

Their second effort has been far more successful. "Basically, the computer has let us keep up with the business," says Theroux. "Compared to doing everything manually, it saves times all around. We also get a lot more information than we could manually. For example, it helps when we order. We get year-to-date sales figures by item, so we know how well something is selling, and we get an up-to-date inventory level, without having to take the time to make a physical check."

One of the basic decisions Merrimack Valley made was to buy standard software packages. Says Theroux, "We had already lost six months, Christmas was coming up, and we didn't want to wait another six months to develop custom software." They haven't regretted the decision. The standard packages, plus a little imagination, have done the job. "For example," says Theroux, "we don't have an order form program per se, but we use the inventory control package to generate order forms. We stock over 6,000 items, and prices change all the time, so that's a valuable capability." Similarly, they've set up their order entry program to printout picking orders in the same sequence in which the warehouse is organized physically, reducing order picking time by 70 percent. "We've bent a little to fit the software," says Theroux, "but basically we've been able to make the system do all the things we want it to."[2]

- Why did Merrimack have to replace their first microcomputer system after only six months?
- What acquisition criteria and methods should be emphasized in order to avoid such situations?
- Was buying standard software a good decision? Explain.

[2] Source: *The Insider's Guide to Small Business Computers* (Westboro, Mass.: Data General Corporation, 1980), p. 52.

16-3   Yorx Electronics

Smart companies realize that successful automation entails more than acquiring computers. Software, training, staffing, and support are also crucial.

Take Yorx Electronics. When the company was founded in 1977 to distribute radios, tape players, and low-priced stereos from the Far East to the United States, management knew right away in what business it wanted to be. Running a computer wasn't it. So Yorx turned to Automatic Data Processing Inc. (ADP), a firm with both financial stability and on-site equipment for local report generation in its services repertoire. Successively, Yorx computerized its accounts receivables, order entry, invoicing, and inventory control. Over the years Yorx's collection of inhouse equipment—owned, maintained, and programmed by ADP, not Yorx—has grown from a single terminal to a full minicomputer system. The result: Yorx has been able to grow 25 percent to 30 percent a year without increasing clerical staff.

At first, service bureaus viewed small computers as a threat. Now they see opportunity, too, and companies like ADP, Computer Sciences, GE, or NCSS offer on-site equipment that can do stand-alone processing as well as tie into bureau mainframes. If on-site hardware helps solve a customer's need—so be it. Service bureaus sell solutions.[3]

- Why does Yorx Electronics use a facilities management service, rather than having their own computer installation?
- How are computer service bureaus meeting the competition from user-owned small business systems?

[3] Source: International Data Corporation, "Computer Systems and Services for Business and Industry," special advertising section, *Fortune,* April 20, 1981, p. 46.

17

CHAPTER OUTLINE

ORGANIZING FOR COMPUTER SERVICES
    Systems Development
    Operations
    Administration
    Organizational Location and Structure

CAREERS IN COMPUTER SERVICES
    Careers in Systems Development
    Careers in Programming
    Careers in Computer Operations
    Careers in EDP Administration

COMPUTER RESOURCE MANAGEMENT
    Managing Systems Development
    Managing Computer Operations
    EDP Personnel Management

COMPUTER SECURITY AND CONTROL
    EDP Controls
    Data Processing Controls
    Organizational Controls
    Facility Controls
    Auditing EDP

SUMMARY

KEY TERMS AND CONCEPTS

REVIEW AND DISCUSSION QUESTIONS

REAL WORLD APPLICATIONS
    Wang Laboratories
    Citibank, N.A.
    Martin Marietta Corporation

Managing Computer Resources

LEARNING OBJECTIVES

The purpose of this chapter is to promote a basic understanding of how business firms must manage their computer resources by analyzing (1) the organization and staffing of a computer services department, (2) the management of systems development and computer operations, and (3) the control of electronic data processing.

After reading this text and studying, you should be able to:

1. Identify several activities that are involved in each of the three basic functions of a computer service organization, i.e., systems development, operations, and administration.
2. Outline the job responsibilities of several types of careers in computer systems development, programming, and operations.
3. Identify several methods for managing the systems development function, including the concept of project management.
4. Identify some of the planning and control activities of the operations management function.
5. Outline several types of (1) data processing controls, (2) organizational controls, and (3) facility controls that can be used by a computer-using organization.

The **information resource management** concept emphasizes that managing the computer and information resources of a business firm has become a major new responsibility of business management. However, inadequate management of computer performance by many business firms is well-documented. Thus there is a real need for business people to understand how to manage these vital organizational resources. In this chapter, we will first analyze the basic functions performed by computer services groups within a computer-using firm. We will then discuss methods of managing these functions, with special emphasis given to the *planning, organizing, staffing, and controlling* activities that are required.

ORGANIZING FOR COMPUTER SERVICES

Computer services groups in large organizations are usually given departmental or divisional status. We will use the name "computer services department," though other names such as "information systems," "information processing," "information services," "data processing," or "EDP" department are

FIGURE 17–1   A Functional Organizational Structure for a Computer Services Department

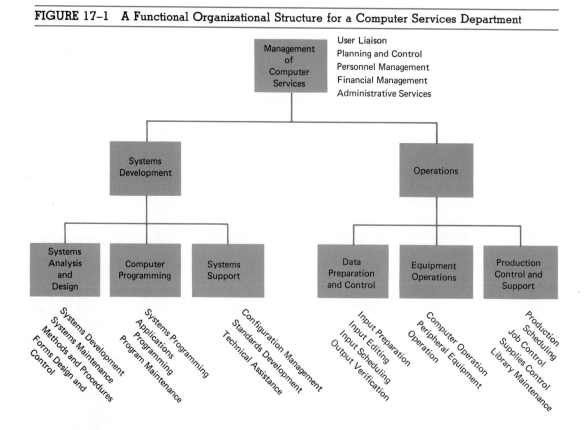

also used. However, no matter what name is utilized, computer services organizations perform several basic functions and activities which can be grouped into three basic functional categories: (1) *systems development,* (2) *operations,* and (3) *administration.* Figure 17–1 illustrates this grouping of computer service functions and activities into a functional organizational structure.

Systems Development

Systems development activities include the investigation, analysis, design, programming, implementation, and maintenance of information systems within the computer-using organization. These activities were discussed in detail in Chapter 15. In addition, the systems development function frequently includes the activities of system programming, data base administration, configuration management, development of data processing standards, and technical assistance. These additional systems development activities are summarized below.

- *Systems Programming.* Design and maintenance of system software such as operating systems and other control programs and service programs.
- *Data Base Administration.* Design and maintenance of data bases and data base management software.
- *Configuration Management.* Planning and evaluating present and proposed hardware and software systems, i.e., "configurations." Results in recommendations for hardware and software modifications or acquisitions.
- *Development of Data Processing Standards.* Development, publication, distribution, and maintenance of standards and procedures that govern the performance of all data processing activities.
- *Technical Assistance.* Assist computer users and computer personnel by providing information, consulting assistance, training programs, and other technical resources.

Operations

The operations function of the computer services department is concerned with the processing of data into information through the use of hardware, software, and EDP personnel. The operations function includes the major activities of data preparation, equipment operation, production control, and production support. The content of these activities is summarized below.

- *Data Preparation and Control.* Includes converting input source documents into machine-sensible form by keypunching, key-to-tape or key-to-disk operations, utilizing a variety of data entry equipment. The data control aspect of this activity refers to the continual checking and monitoring of input data and output reports to insure their accuracy, completeness, and timeliness.

- *Equipment Operation.* Includes the operation of the computer system, including the computer console, on-line peripheral equipment, and data communications terminals and control equipment. It also includes the operation of off-line equipment such as offline magnetic tape units and printers, and other types of offline data conversion or output support equipment.

- *Production Control.* Includes the scheduling, monitoring, and control of facilities and data processing jobs. It includes the scheduling of equipment, data files, and necessary data processing supplies, scheduling and logging job input and output, and communicating with users on scheduling requirements and the status of specific jobs.

- *Production Support.* Activities which support data processing operations include acquisition and maintenance of data processing supplies, maintaining a library of data files on magnetic tape, magnetic disk, or punched cards, maintaining a library of operations documentation, providing for the physical security of the computer facilities, and distribution of computer output.

Administration

The administration of computer services requires the performance of several specific managerial activities. These activities include planning, controlling, managerial liaison, personnel management, financial management, and administrative services. The content of these activities is summarized below.

- *Planning.* Includes long- and short-range planning of computer operations, systems development projects, hardware, software, and facilities acquisitions.

- *Controlling.* Includes the monitoring and evaluating of computer operations, systems development projects, and hardware, software, facilities, and personnel utilization. Reporting systems are developed to compare performance with plans.

- *Managerial Liaison.* This activity involves communicating and reporting to computer users and management concerning the plans and performance of the computer services department. Managerial liaison also includes meeting and maintaining proper relationships with hardware and software vendors and suppliers.

- *Personnel Management.* Includes defining personnel requirements, recruiting, and selection of personnel, employee training and development, performance evaluation, and personnel recordkeeping.
- *Financial Management.* Includes developing and maintaining methods of financial record-keeping and financial analysis so that the cost of computer operations and systems development projects can be analyzed and controlled. This activity also includes billing computer users for EDP costs, providing cost estimates for planning purposes, and purchasing required hardware, software, and services.
- *Administrative Services.* Includes the supply of services such as secretarial and clerical assistance, hardware maintenance scheduling, and custodial services.

Organizational Location and Structure

The location of computer services within the structure of a business firm depends on the type and size of computer operations and the emphasis given to computer services by management. Large-scale operations usually become independent departments or divisions whose managers may have vice-presidential status in the firm. The use of large computers with centralized data bases and many remote data communications terminals support such **centralization** of computer services. However, the use of microcomputers, minicomputers, intelligent terminals, and data communications in distributed processing networks supports **decentralization** of computer services since computer power is dispersed among the user departments of an organization.

The extent to which business firms should centralize or decentralize computer services depends on many factors. *Centralized* computer facilities may be *more economical* and *efficient* in terms of hardware, software, and personnel cost and utilization. This is especially true of firms with a high volume of repetitive business data processing. In addition, centralization fosters integration and standardization of information systems wihin an organization. However, *decentralized* computer services are usually *more responsive* to user needs, encourage greater utilization of the computer, and reduce the risks of computer errors and malfunctions.

FIGURE 17–2   Medium-Scale Organization Structure

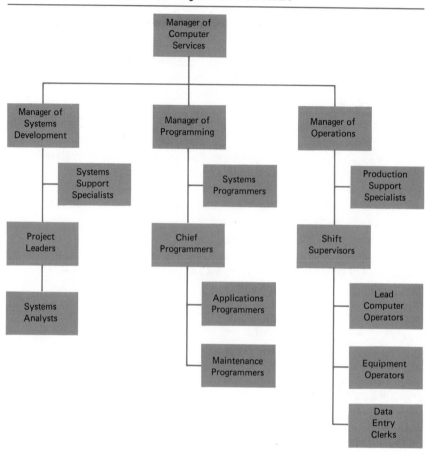

The internal organizational structure of a computer services organization must reflect its major functions and activities. However, the particular structure utilized depends on many factors, including organizational location, centralization or decentralization of data processing, and the size of the computer services organization. Figure 17–2 illustrates the organizational structure of a medium-scale computer services organization, including job titles commonly used in such organizations.

CAREERS IN COMPUTER SERVICES

The success or failure of a computer services organization rests primarily on the quality of its personnel. Many computer users consider recruiting, training, and retaining qualified personnel as their greatest single problem. Millions of persons are employed in the computer services organizations of computer users. National employment surveys continually forecast shortages of qualified services personnel (especially programmers and systems analysts) that range into the hundreds of thousands. Employment opportunities in the computer field are excellent since the need for systems analysts, programmers, and managerial personnel is expected to expand significantly as business firms continue to expand their use of computers. Therefore, it is important to analyze the types of jobs and the managerial problems associated with computer services personnel.

Figure 17–3 presents an organization chart which illustrates the wide variety of job types that are possible in a computer

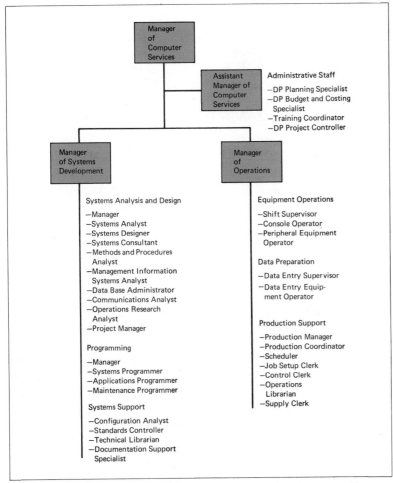

FIGURE 17–3   Job Titles in a Large-Scale Computer Services Organization

Source: This chart and the job descriptions in this section are based in part on *Organizing the Data Processing Activity* (White Plains, N.Y.: IBM Corporation, 1973), pp. 29–38.

services organization. However, the positions available in a computer services department can be grouped into four occupational categories: (1) *systems development*, (2) *programming*, (3) *operations*, and (4) *administration*. The types of jobs and the number of persons required for each job type depends on the size of the computer services organization. Large-scale computer operations allow more specialization of job assignments and thus create more types of jobs.

Figure 17–4 gives valuable insight into the high salaries commanded by many computer services personnel. Of course, these figures are national averages, and actual salaries

FIGURE 17–4 Annual Salaries for Computer Services Personnel

Job Title	1981 Average	Job Title	1981 Average
1. Vice President of MIS	$40,753	DATA COMMUNICATIONS	
2. Director of Communications	41,120	22. Manager	39,794
		23. Analyst	29,862
DIVISION OR DEPARTMENTAL STAFF		24. Technical Control Specialist	21,834
3. Director of DP	32,125		
4. Business Manager	27,073	COMPUTER OPERATIONS	
		25. Manager	23,838
SYSTEMS ANALYSIS		26. Shift Supervisor	19,255
5. Manager	31,005	27. Lead	15,085
6. Senior	27,251	28. Operator	13,254
7. Analyst	24,454	29. Magnetic Media Librarian	13,254
APPLICATIONS PROGRAMMING		PRODUCTION AND I/O CONTROL	
8. Manager	28,550	30. Supervisor	19,695
9. Senior	22,991	31. Lead Production Control Clerk	14,585
10. Applications Programmer	18,611	32. Clerk	11,613
11. Trainee	15,795	33. Liaison	14,729
SYSTEM ANALYSIS/PROGRAMMING		DATA ENTRY	
12. Manager	31,071	34. Supervisor	14,524
13. Senior	26,343	35. Operator	11,162
14. Analyst/Programmer	21,806		
15. Trainee	16,787	OTHER	
		36. Word Processing Supervisor	18,214
OPERATING SYSTEMS PROGRAMMING		37. Word Processing Operator	14,028
16. Manager	30,569	38. Account Executive	27,056
17. Senior	28,237	39. User Services Staff	16,502
18. Systems Programmer	23,959	40. Technical Writer	17,264
19. Trainee	16,880	41. Librarian	17,964
		42. Remote Site Administrator	25,029
DATA BASE ADMINISTRATION		43. Remote Terminal Operator	12,288
20. Manager	31,686	44. Minicomputer Specialist	18,068
21. Administrator	27,513	45. Training and Education Specialist	23,646
		46. Computer Security Specialist	28,086
		47. Field Service Engineer	18,050

Source: Adapted from Janet Crane, "1981 DP Salary Survey," *Datamation*, May 1981, p. 104. Reprinted with permission of *Datamation* magazine. Copyright by Technical Publishing Company, a Dun & Bradstreet Company, 1981; all rights reserved.

can range much higher and lower, depending on such factors as the size and geographic location of the computer services organization.

Careers in Systems Development

The most common type of job in this category is the job of "systems analyst." Larger computer service operations expand this job operation into several specialized job types. Job descriptions for several jobs in this category are summarized in Figure 17–5.

FIGURE 17–5 **Systems Development Job Descriptions**

Systems Analyst. Gathers and analyzes information needed for the development or modification of information systems. Develops a statement of systems requirements and prepares detailed system specifications on which computer programs will be based. Supervises installation of new systems and evaluates existing systems for possible improvements.

Systems Designer. Translates systems requirements prepared by the systems analyst into alternative systems designs. Develops detailed systems specifications for the system being developed.

Management Information Systems Analyst. Plans, designs, and installs information systems which utilize integrated data bases and advanced processing systems to provide management with information for decision making.

Data Base Administrator. Designs and maintains the data bases of the organization. Prepares and enforces standards for the use and security of information in the data bases.

Communications Analyst. Plans, designs, and installs data communications networks, including the specification and selection of software, terminals, and communications control equipment.

Operations Research Analyst. Applies mathematical techniques to the solution of difficult problems in systems analysis and design as well as in other areas of the business.

Methods and Procedures Analyst. Develops and installs improved clerical methods, procedures, and forms as part of the development of new or improved systems.

Systems Consultant. Assists computer users in the development and installation of new computer systems and the maintenance of existing systems. Frequently serves as a liaison between computer users and the computer services department.

Other systems development job categories are frequently classified as "systems support" occupations. These include: (1) a *configuration analyst* who is responsible for evaluating and improving hardware and software performance, (2) a *standards controller* who develops and maintains data processing standards and procedures for the organization, (3) a *technical librarian* who develops and maintains a library of system documentation and technical information, and (4) a *documentation support specialist* who assists systems analysts and programmers in developing detailed system, programming, and operations documentation.

Careers in Programming

Careers in programming involve job responsibilities for the development of computer programs. The most common job title is "programmer," but several other job titles are also used that reflect the specialization in particular types of programming effort. See Figure 17–6.

FIGURE 17–6 Job Descriptions in Programming

Programmer.   Develops program logic and codes; tests and documents computer programs.

Applications Programmer.   Develops programs required for specific applications of computer users.

Maintenance Programmer.   Modifies and improves existing programs.

Systems Programmer.   Develops, modifies, and maintains the operating system and other system software utilized by a computer services organization.

Analyst Programmer.   A systems analyst who does his or her own application programming, or vice versa, an applications programmer who does his or her own systems analysis and design.

Chief Programmer.   Leads a team of programmers all working on the same programming project. Recommended for structured programming.

Careers in Computer Operations

Operations personnel are responsible for operating or controlling the operation of electronic data processing equipment. Operations job types can be grouped into the categories of (1) *equipment operations*, (2) *data preparation*, and (3) *production support*. See Figure 17–7.

FIGURE 17–7 Job Descriptions in Computer Operations

Computer Operator.   Monitors and controls the computer by operating the central console. Adjusts the configuration of the computer system in response to messages from the operating system or instructions contained in the operations documentation. Operates peripheral equipment in smaller installations.

Peripheral Equipment Operator.   Assists the computer operator by setting up and operating tape drives, magnetic disk drives, printers, etc. Also operates offline input/output equipment.

Data Entry Equipment Operator.   Converts data on source documents into machine-sensible form by use of a keyboard-driven machine, such as a keypunch, key-to-tape, or CRT terminal.

Production Coordinator.   Coordinates and controls the mix of data processing jobs to achieve optimum equipment utilization and service to users. Prepares and maintains schedules for data processing jobs and maintains records of job and equipment performance.

Careers in EDP Administration

Administrative personnel manage and supervise the activities of the computer services organization. They include administrative staff positions which support management in administrative planning and control. See Figure 17–8.

FIGURE 17–8   Job Descriptions in EDP Administration

Manager of Computer Services.   Plans and directs the activities of the entire computer services organization.

Manager of Systems Development.   Directs the activities of the systems development process.

Operations Manager.   Directs the operation of all data processing equipment and the production of all data processing jobs.

Data Processing Planning Specialist.   Prepares long- and short-range plans for application selection, systems development, and acquisition of hardware, software, and personnel resources.

Project Controller.   Develops and administers a planning, control, and reporting system for systems development projects.

Training Coordinator.   Develops and administers training programs for computer services personnel and computer users.

Budget and Costing Specialist.   Develops budgets for the computer services organization and evaluates performance against the budget. Develops and administers a system for allocating the cost of computer services to computer users.

Other administrative positions include the managers of systems analysis and design, programming, systems support, production support, and "shift supervisors" who supervise equipment operations during each shift of a working day. Additional administrative job classifications exist in many computer services organizations due to the recognition of seniority and the assignment of supervisory responsibilities. Thus, titles such as "Lead Systems Analyst," "Lead Programmer," and "Lead Computer Operator" recognize the assignment of supervisory responsibilities to these positions. Another widely used administrative job type is the position of "project manager" or "team leader." This person is frequently a senior systems analyst or programmer who supervises the activities of a systems development project team.

COMPUTER RESOURCE MANAGEMENT

Managing Systems Development

Planning, organizing, and controlling the systems development function of a computer services department is a major managerial responsibility. Important methods used to manage

·systems development include *long-range planning* and *project management.*

Long-Range Planning. The "master information systems development plan" for managing the computer resources of a business firm is a description of the information systems development projects that the business firm intends to accomplish in the future, i.e., in the next two to five years. The plan indicates a tentative timetable for the projects and provides "ball park" estimates of the resources required and the benefits to be obtained. In some large firms, long-range planning groups at the corporate level or in the information systems division are employed to gather data and formulate the alternatives required in the planning process. These alternatives are presented to top management for review and final decision making. Figure 17–9 illustrates the major activities and outputs in long-range and annual MIS planning.

Project Management. This is the term used to describe the management of the development work required by a pro-

FIGURE 17–9 Major Activities and Outputs in MIS Planning

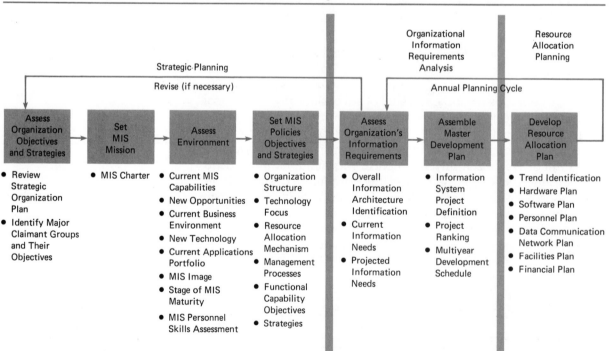

posed information system project. The concept of project management requires that each information system be developed by a "project team" according to a specific "project plan" that is formulated during the systems investigation stage. Assigning systems analysts and programmers to specific projects headed by a project leader allows better control of the progress of systems development. The alternative is to assign personnel to work on projects on a "when available" basis. This method usually results in a lack of project control and a waste of human and financial resources.

The Project Plan. Descriptions of the tasks involved and the assignment of responsibility for each task are included in the project plan. Estimated startup and completion dates for the entire project, as well as for major checkpoints or "milestones" in the development of the project must also be included. Specified amounts of time, money, and staff should be allocated to each segment of the project.

The project plan should include provisions for handling suggested changes to the proposed system, including a "design freeze" policy. Such a policy prohibits changes in systems design after specified project deadlines unless the change is formally approved by management. Provisions must also be made for revision of the project schedule due to major unforeseen developments. Record-keeping forms which report the progress of individual members of a systems development project are also used in many project management systems. Good project management also requires that each phase of systems development be properly documented before new stages are begun.

Project Management Techniques. All information systems development projects should be planned and controlled by several types of project management techniques. For example, many firms use special reporting forms to ensure that all systems development projects are properly authorized and controlled. The use of financial and operating budgets is another method of managing systems development projects. Budgets serve as a short-range planning device as well as a method of control. Deviations from budgeted amounts identify projects which need closer management attention. Several types of charts are used to plan and control projects such as the Gantt chart, which specifies the times allowed for the various activities required in information systems development. See Figure 17–10. The PERT system (Program Evaluation and Review

574

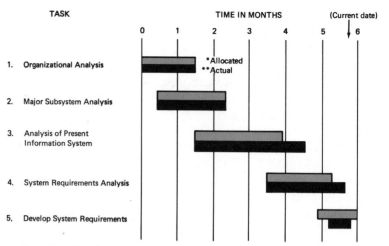

FIGURE 17–10 Gantt Chart Showing Progress of a Systems Development Project

TASK

TIME IN MONTHS

(Current date)

0   1   2   3   4   5   6

1. Organizational Analysis
   *Allocated
   **Actual

2. Major Subsystem Analysis

3. Analysis of Present Information System

4. System Requirements Analysis

5. Develop System Requirements

Note: Steps 3 and 4 have exceeded their allocated time, and therefore step 5 is behind schedule.

Technique), which involves the use of a network diagram of required events and activities is also used by some computer users. See Figure 17–11.

Managing Computer Operations

Planning and controlling the operations of the computer services department is a major management responsibility. "Operations management" refers to the major areas of responsibility of the manager of computer operations that require planning and control activities such as those outlined in Figure 17–12.

Production planning and control methods are necessary for effective management of EDP operations. Information must be gathered concerning:

- The hardware, software, and personnel utilized by each data processing job.
- Job-processing times, equipment utilization, time spent by operating personnel, and the production status of each job.
- Computer malfunctions, the number and type of reruns, processing delay and errors, and other evidences of unsatisfactory or unusual conditions.

Such information is used to produce reports on computer system utilization, costs, and performance. These reports are

FIGURE 17–11 PERT Network for a Systems Development Project

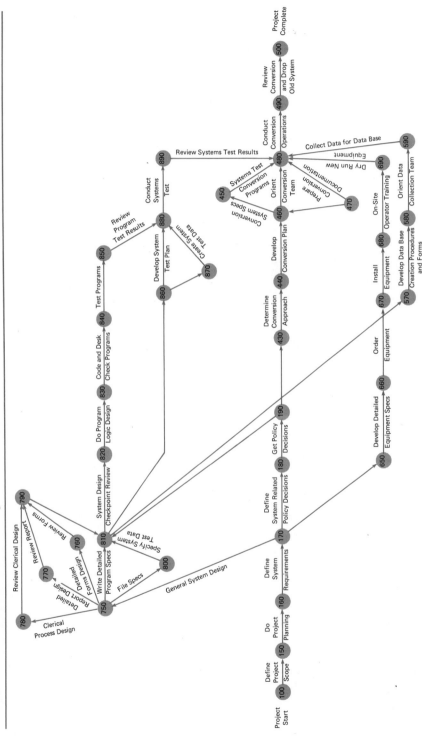

Source: From Dick H. Brandon and Max Gray, *Project Control Standards* (New York). © Mason/Charter Publishers, Inc., 1970, p. 111. Reprinted by permission of Mason/Charter.

FIGURE 17–12 Computer Operations Management Functions

Operations Planning. Forecasting changes in the volume and type of computer applications and their effect on future hardware, software, and personnel requirements.

Production Planning. Formulating daily, weekly, and monthly forecasts which schedule specific systems and applications for computer processing.

Operating and Financial Budgets. Developing budgets for EDP operations and comparing performance to budget.

Computer System Utilization. Analysis of computer system utilization by computer users and types of applications. Determination of any excess capacity or need for additional capacity.

Computer System Performance. Analysis of computer "downtime," aborted jobs, returns, input/output errors, late reports, etc.

Computer Operations Costs. Analysis of the cost of computer hardware, software, and operating personnel.

Computer User Service and Assessments. Evaluating the quality of user service and assessing users for the costs of computer operations.

Computer Systems Acquisition. Evaluating plans and negotiations for hardware and software changes and their effect on EDP operations.

Systems Implementation. Planning and supervising the effect on ongoing operations of the installation and conversion of information systems or computer systems.

Controls and Security. Control of data preparation, input, processing, and output. Control of storage files and computer facilities. Fraud control.

then used as the basis for production planning, distribution of computer costs to users, control of computer system performance, and quality control of service to computer users.

Software packages known as *system performance monitors* are available which monitor the processing of computer jobs and help develop a planned schedule of computer operations which can optimize the use of a computer system. Advanced operating systems use performance monitors to monitor computer system performance and produce detailed statistics that are invaluable for effective production planning and control. *For example,* a system performance monitor could automatically generate the reports shown in Figure 17–13.

EDP Personnel Management

Management of computer services requires the management of managerial, technical, and clerical personnel. One of the most important jobs of computer service managers is to recruit qualified personnel and to develop, organize, and direct the capabilities of the existing personnel. Employees must be continually trained to keep up with the latest developments in a fast-moving and highly technical field. Employee job performance must be continually evaluated, and outstand-

FIGURE 17-13 Operations and Reports Produced by a Computer System Performance Monitor

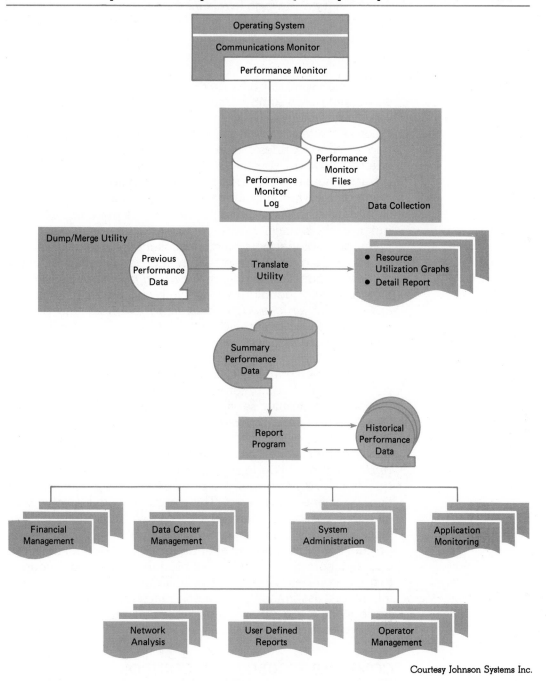

Courtesy Johnson Systems Inc.

ing performance rewarded with salary increases or promotions. Salary and wage levels must be set, and "career paths" must be designed so that individuals can move to new jobs through promotion and transfer as they gain in seniority and expertise.

The management and development of computer services personnel poses some unique problems for management. For example, systems analysts and computer programmers are creative, professional personnel who cannot be managed with traditional work rules or evaluated by traditional performance criteria. How do you measure how well a system analyst or programmer is doing? This question has plagued the management of many computer-using business firms. However, it should be emphasized that this question is not unique to computer professionals, but is common to the management of many professional personnel, especially the scientists and engineers employed in the research and development activities of many organizations. Effective *project planning, controlling,* and *reporting* techniques (especially the modular and team approach of *structured programming, analysis, and design*) are available, which provide information required for the evaluation of systems development and programming personnel.

Another personnel management problem area is the professional loyalty of computer services personnel. Like other professionals, computer services personnel may have a greater loyalty to the "data processing profession" than to the organization which employs them. Thus, computer programmers consider themselves programmers *first,* and employees, *second.* When this attitude is coupled with the shortages of many qualified EDP personnel, a serious problem in retaining qualified personnel may arise. This problem can be solved by effective personnel management. Providing computer services personnel with opportunities for merit salary increases, promotions, transfers, and attendance at professional meetings and seminars provides the flexible job environment needed to retain competent personnel. Challenging technological and intellectual assignments and a congenial atmosphere of fellow professionals are other major factors in retaining computer services personnel.

COMPUTER SECURITY AND CONTROL

Does electronic data processing increase or decrease the probability of errors, fraud, and destruction of data processing facilities? Computers have proven that they can process huge volumes of data and perform complex calculations more accurately than manual or mechanical data processing systems. However, we know that (1) errors do occur in EDP systems, (2) computers have been used for fraudulent purposes, and (3) computers and their data files have been accidentally or maliciously destroyed. There is no question that computers have had some detrimental effect on the detection of errors and fraud. Manual and mechanical data processing systems utilize data processing media that can be visually checked by data processing personnel. Several persons are usually involved in such systems and, therefore, crosschecking procedures are easily performed. These characteristics of manual and mechanical data processing systems facilitate the detection of errors and fraud.

Electronic data processing systems, on the other hand, utilize machine-sensible data processing media and accomplish data processing manipulations within the electronic circuitry of a computer system. The ability to check visually the progress of data processing activities and the contents of data processing files is significantly reduced. In addition, a relatively small number of EDP personnel may effectively control all of the data processing activities of the entire organization. Therefore, the ability to detect errors and fraud can be reduced by computerization, and requires the development of "EDP controls."

EDP Controls

EDP controls are methods utilized to insure **computer security,** i.e., the *accuracy, integrity,* and *safety* of the electronic data processing activities and resources of computer users. They attempt to minimize *errors, fraud,* and *destruction* in a computer services organization. Effective EDP controls can make an electronic data processing system more free of errors and fraud than other types of data processing. There are three major types of electronic data processing controls: (1) data processing controls, (2) organizational controls, and (3) facility controls. Figures 17-14 and 17-15 illustrate and summarize the EDP controls needed to achieve computer security. Let's take a closer look at each of them.

Data Processing Controls

Data processing controls are methods and devices which attempt to ensure the accuracy, validity, and propriety of data processing functions and activities. Controls must be developed to ensure that all proper input data is collected, con-

FIGURE 17–14 Protecting Computer-Based Information Systems with Adequate EDP Controls

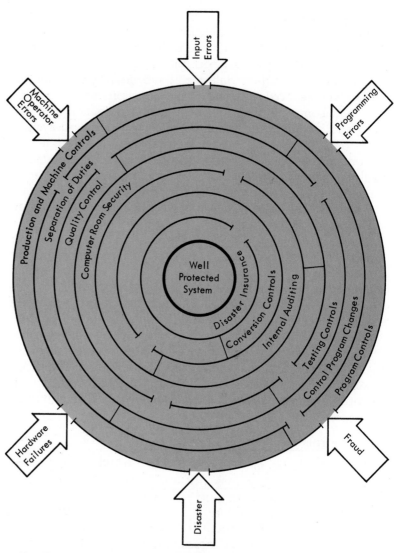

Note: The attack arrows have as their objectives destruction of the "Well-Protected System." If the system is properly controlled, each of the factors represented by an arrow will be interrupted and negated by applicable control elements as it attempts to penetrate the control maze.

Source: Joseph J. Wasserman, "Plugging the Leaks in Computer Security," *Harvard Business Review*, September–October 1969, p. 124.

FIGURE 17–15 Electronic Data Processing Controls

Data processing controls utilize the speed and accuracy of the computer to monitor itself and all its data processing activities. They include input controls, processing controls, output controls, and storage controls.

Organizational controls can be developed for the computer services organization to maintain proper methods of systems development and computer operations. They include production control, separation of duties, standard procedures, documentation, authorization requirements, conversion scheduling, and EDP auditing.

Facility controls can be developed to protect the facilities of the computer services department. They include data base controls, data communications controls, computer failure controls, physical protection controls, and insurance.

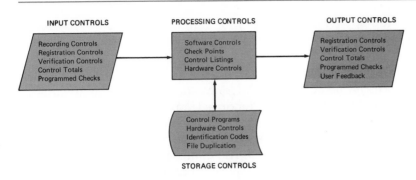

FIGURE 17–16 Types of Data Processing Controls

verted into a form suitable for processing, and entered into the computer system. Thus, data processing controls can be organized according to the *input, processing, output,* and *storage* components of any data processing system. See Figure 17–16.

Input Controls. Examples of input controls that are frequently utilized are summarized below.

- *Recording Controls.* Input recording aids help reduce the chance for error. Examples: Prepunched cards, templates over the keys of key-driven input devices, and prenumbered forms.
- *Registration Controls.* Source documents can be registered by recording them in a logbook when they are received by data preparation personnel. External labels attached to the outside of magnetic tapes or disks are another method of registering the contents and disposition of input data. Realtime systems that utilize direct access files frequently record all inputs into the system on magnetic tape "control logs." Such logs preserve evidence of all system inputs and are utilized to develop "control totals" which can be compared to control totals generated during processing.
- *Verification Controls.* Visual verification of source documents or input media by clerical personnel and machine verification as performed by intelligent data entry terminals are examples.
- *Control Totals.* A "record count" is a control total which consists of counting the total of source documents or other input records and comparing this total to the number of records counted at other stages of input preparation. If the totals do not match a mistake has been made. "Batch totals" and "hash totals" are other forms of control totals. A *batch total* is the sum of a specific item of data within a batch of transactions, such as the sales amount in a batch of sales transactions. *Hash totals* are the sum of data fields which

are added together only for control comparisons. For example, employee Social Security numbers could be added together to produce a control total in the input preparation of payroll documents.

- *Programmed Checks.* Computer programs can include instructions to identify incorrect, invalid, or improper input data as it enters the computer system. Computers can be programmed to check input data for invalid codes, data fields, and transactions. The computer may be programmed to conduct "reasonableness checks" to determine if input data exceeds certain specified limits or is out of sequence.

Processing Controls. Processing controls are developed to identify errors in arithmetic calculations and logical operations. They are also used to ensure that data is not lost or does not go unprocessed. Processing controls can be categorized as *software controls* and *hardware controls* and are summarized below.

Software Controls. Validity checks, reasonableness checks, sequence checks, and control total checks similar to the programmed checks on input mentioned above are also utilized during the processing stage. The computer can also be programmed to check the "internal file labels" at the beginning and end of magnetic tape and disk files. These labels contain information identifying the file as well as providing control totals for the data in the file. These internal file labels allow the computer to ensure that the proper storage file is being used and that the proper data in the file has been processed.

Another major software control is the establishment of *checkpoints* during the processing of a program. Checkpoints are intermediate points within a program being processed where intermediate totals, listings, or "dumps" of data are written on magnetic tape or disk or listed on a printer. Checkpoints minimize the effect of processing errors or failures since processing can be restarted from the last checkpoint rather than from the beginning of the program. They also help build an "audit trail" which allows transactions being processed to be traced through all of the steps of processing.

Hardware Controls. Hardware controls are special checks built into the hardware to verify the accuracy of computer processing. Hardware checks include:

- Multiple read-write heads on certain hardware devices.
- Parity checks (described in Chapter 3) and echo checks, which require that a signal be returned from a device or circuit to verify that it was properly activated.
- Malfunction detection circuitry within the computer. This may include a microprocessor which is used to support remote diagnostics and maintenance.
- Switches and other devices. Switches can be set which prohibit writing on magnetic tapes or disks. On magnetic tape reels, a removable plastic or metal ring can be removed to prevent writing on a tape.
- Miscellaneous hardware controls. There are many other kinds of hardware controls such as duplicate arithmetic load checks, overflow checks, sign checks, and CPU timing and voltage checks.

Output Controls. Output controls are developed to ensure that output information is correct and complete and is transmitted to authorized users in a timely manner. Several types of output controls are similar to input control methods. For example, output is frequently logged, identified with route slips, and visually verified by input/output control personnel. Control totals on output are compared with control totals generated during the input and processing stages. Prenumbered output forms are utilized to control the loss of important output documents such as stock certificates or payroll check forms. Distribution lists help input/output control personnel ensure that only authorized users receive output. Access to the output of realtime processing systems is controlled by hardware or software which identifies who can receive output and the type of output they are authorized to receive. Finally, persons who receive output should be contacted on a regular basis for feedback on the quality of output.

Storage Controls. Many data files are protected from unauthorized or accidental use by control programs which require proper identification before a file can be used. Hardware devices and software routines are utilized to protect the data base of realtime processing systems from unauthorized use or processing accidents. "Lock words" (also called "pass words") and other identification codes are frequently used to restrict access to authorized users. A catalog of authorized users enables the computer system to identify eligible users and determine which types of information they are authorized to receive.

Organizational Controls

Organizational controls are methods of organizing and performing the functions of the computer services organization that facilitate the accuracy and integrity of computer operations and systems development activities. Some of these controls are discussed below.

- *Production Control.* A production control section should monitor the progress of data processing jobs, data preparation activities, and the quality of input/output data.

- *Separation of Duties.* A basic principle of organizational control in EDP is to assign the duties of systems development, computer operations, and control of data and program files to separate groups. For example, systems analysts and computer programmers are not allowed to operate the computer console or make changes to data or programs being processed. In addition, the responsibility for maintaining a library of data files and program files is assigned to a "librarian" or "data base administrator."

- *Standard Procedures.* Manuals of standard procedures for systems development, computer programming, and computer operations should be developed and maintained. Following standard procedures promotes uniformity and minimizes the chances of errors and fraud.

- *Documentation.* System, program, and operations documentation must be developed and kept up-to-date to ensure the correct processing and maintenance of each computer application.

- *Authorization Requirements.* Requests for systems development, program changes, or computer processing must be subject to a formal process of review before authorization is given. *For example,* program changes generated by maintenance programmers should be approved by the manager of programming after consultation with the manager of computer operations and the manager of the affected user department.

- *Conversion Scheduling.* Conversion to new hardware and software, installation of newly developed information systems, and changes to existing programs should be subjected to a formal notification and scheduling procedure to minimize their detrimental effects on the accuracy and integrity of computer services.

- *Auditing of EDP.* The computer services organization and its EDP activities must undergo periodic examinations or "audits" to determine the accuracy, integrity, and safety of all computer-based information systems. We will discuss this important aspect of organizational control shortly.

Facility Controls

Facility controls are methods which protect the computer service facility and its contents from loss or destruction. Computer centers are subject to such hazards as accidents, natural disasters, sabotage, vandalism, industrial espionage, and theft. Therefore, physical safeguards and various control procedures are necessary to protect the hardware, software, and, most importantly, the vital information and records of computer-using organizations. Several important facility controls are described below.

Data Base Controls. Control over files of computer programs and data must be maintained. A librarian or data base administrator is responsible for maintaining and controlling access to the libraries and data bases of the organization. Many firms utilize "backup" files which are duplicate files of data or programs. Such files may be stored "off premise," that is, in a location away from the computer center, sometimes in special storage vaults in remote locations. Many realtime processing systems utilize duplicate files that are updated by data communication links. Files are also protected by "file retention" measures which involves storing copies of master files and transaction files from previous periods. If current files are destroyed, the files from previous periods are used to reconstruct new current files.

Data Communications Controls.. The communications control hardware and software described in Chapter 10 play a vital role in the control of data communications activity. In addition, data can be transmitted in "scrambled" form and unscrambled by the computer system only for authorized users. This process is called **encription.** It transforms digital data into a secret code before it is transmitted and then decodes the data when it is received. Special hardware and software must be utilized for the encription process.

Computer Failure Controls. A variety of controls are needed to prevent computer failure or minimize its effects. Computers fail or "go down" for several reasons, such as power failure, electronic circuitry malfunctions, mechanical malfunctions of peripheral equipment, hidden programming errors, and computer operator errors. Therefore, the computer services department must take steps to prevent equipment failure and to minimize its detrimental effects. Computers with automatic and remote maintenance capabilities should be acquired. A program of "preventive maintenance" of hardware must be developed. Adequate electrical supply, air conditioning, humidity control, and fire prevention standards must be set. A "backup" computer system capability should be arranged with other computer-using organizations. Major hardware or software changes should be carefully scheduled and implemented. Finally, computer operators must have adequate training and supervision.

Physical Protection Controls. Providing maximum security and disaster protection for the computer installation requires many types of controls. Only authorized personnel are allowed access to the computer center through such techniques as identification badges for EDP personnel, electrical door locks, burglar alarms, security policy, closed-circuit TV, and other detection systems. The computer center should be protected from disaster by such safeguards as fire detection and extinguishing systems; fireproof storage vaults for protection of files; emergency power systems; electromagnetic shielding; and temperature, humidity, and dust control.

Insurance. Adequate insurance coverage must be secured to protect the business firm from substantial financial losses in the event of accidents, disasters, fraud, and other risks. Several insurance companies offer special EDP policies which include insurance against fire, natural disasters, vandalism and theft, liability insurance for data processing errors or omissions, fidelity insurance for the bonding of EDP personnel as a protection against fraud, etc. The amount of such insurance should be large enough to replace computer equipment and facilities. Insurance is also available to cover the cost of reconstructing data and program files.

Auditing EDP

The computer service organization should be periodically examined or *audited* by internal auditing personnel of the business firm or by external auditors from professional accounting firms. Such audits should review and evaluate whether proper and adequate *data processing controls, organizational controls,* and *facility controls* have been developed and implemented. There are two basic approaches for testing the data processing activities of a computer application. They are known as (1) "auditing around the computer," and (2) "auditing through the computer."

Auditing around a computer involves verifying the accuracy and propriety of computer input and output without evaluating the computer programs utilized to process the data. This is a simpler and easier method which does not require auditors with EDP or programming experience. However, since this auditing method does not trace a transaction through all of its stages of processing and does not test the accuracy and integrity of the computer program, it should not be the only method used for large-volume, sophisticated computer applications.

Auditing through the computer involves verifying the accuracy and integrity of the computer programs that process the data, as well as the input and output of the computer system. Auditing through the computer requires a knowledge of EDP operations and computer programming. Some firms employ special "EDP auditors" for this assignment. Special *test data* may be used to test processing accuracy and the control procedures built into the computer program. The auditors may develop a special *test program* or use **audit software packages** (such as that illustrated in Figure 17–17) to process the data of the business firm. They then compare the results produced by their audit program with the results generated by the computer users' own programs. One of the objectives of such testing is to detect the presence of unauthorized changes or "patches" to computer programs. Unauthorized program patches may be the cause of "unexplainable" errors or may

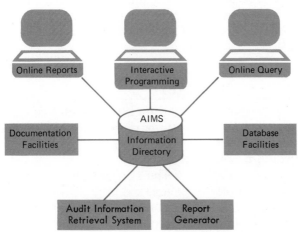

FIGURE 17–17 Audit Information Management System

Courtesy Cullinane Data Base Systems, Inc.

be utilized by an unscrupulous programmer for fraudulent purposes.

Auditing through the computer may be too costly for some computer applications. Therefore, a combination of both auditing approaches is usually employed. However, both auditing approaches must effectively contend with the changes caused by electronic data processing to the **audit trail**. The "audit trail" can be defined as the presence of data processing media and procedures which allow a transaction to be traced through all stages of processing, beginning with its appearance on a source document and ending with its transformation into information on a final ouput document.

The audit trail of manual data processing systems was quite visible and easy to trace. However, EDP has changed the form of the audit trail. Information formerly available to the auditor in the form of visual records is no longer available or is recorded on media which can be interpreted only by machines. Real-time processing systems have increased the "invisibility" of the traditional audit trail. Paper documents and historical files are frequently eliminated when remote terminals and direct access files are utilized.

Such developments make the auditing of EDP systems a complex but vital assignment. Therefore, auditing personnel should be included on the project team of all major systems development projects and consulted before smaller systems projects are implemented. In addition, auditing personnel should be notified of all changes to computer programs caused by the program maintenance activity. Such procedures give the auditor the opportunity to suggest methods of preserving the audit trail and providing adequate data processing controls in systems that are being developed or modified.

SUMMARY

- Managing the computer resources of a business firm has become a major new responsibility of business management. Business computer users must learn how to plan, organize, staff, and control the activities of their computer service departments. The major activities of a computer services department can be grouped into three basic functional categories: (1) systems development, (2) operations, and (3) administration.

- The organizational structure, location, and staffing of a computer services department must reflect these three basic functions and activities. However, many variations exist, which reflect the attempts of business computer users to tailor their organizational and staffing arrangements to their particular business activities and management philosophy, as well as to the capabilities of centralized or distributed EDP.

- There is a wide variety of career choices and job types in many computer-using organizations. However, computer services personnel can be grouped into four occupational categories: systems development, programming, operations, and administration. Managing the wide variety of technical personnel in a computer services department is a major personnel management assignment of business computer users.

- Another major managerial responsibility in computer-using business firms is the management of systems development. It requires long-range planning and project management techniques. Managing computer operations requires many applications of "operations management,"

including various production planning and control techniques.

- One of the most important responsibilities of the management of computer-using business firms is the security and control of its EDP activities. "EDP controls" are methods which insure the accuracy, integrity, and safety of the electronic data processing activities and resources of computer users. Such controls attempt to minimize errors, fraud, and destruction in the computer services department. EDP controls can be grouped into three major categories: (1) data processing controls, (2) organizational controls, and (3) facility controls.

- The computer services department should be periodically audited to review and evaluate whether proper and adequate data processing controls, organizational controls, and facility controls have been developed and implemented. EDP auditing, therefore, plays a vital role in ensuring proper managerial control of computer resources and EDP activities.

KEY TERMS AND CONCEPTS

Organizational functions of computer services

Centralization or decentralization of computer services

Careers in computer services

Job categories of computer services personnel

Project management

Operations management

Computer security and control

EDP controls

Data processing controls

Organizational controls

Facility controls

Auditing EDP

Audit trail

REVIEW AND DISCUSSION QUESTIONS

1. Why do you think that managing the computer and information resources of a business firm has become a major responsibility of management?

2. What are some of the activities that are involved in the functions of systems development, operations, and administration in a computer services organization?

3. Where do you think the computer services department should be located within the business firm?

4. Should computer services be centralized or decentralized within a business firm?

5. What are some of the career choices and job responsibilities of computer services personnel? Which job type is most appealing to you? Why?

6. Why does the management and development of computer services personnel pose some unique problems for management?

7. What are some of the solutions to the personnel management problems in electronic data processing?

8. Identify several methods for managing the systems development function.

9. What is project management? How can it be applied to systems development projects?

10. Identify some of the planning and control activities of operations management.

11. Does electronic data processing increase or decrease the probability of errors, fraud, and destruction of data processing facilities? Explain.

12. Distinguish between data processing controls, organizational controls, and facilities controls. Provide several examples of each type of control.

13. Is "auditing through the computer," always superior to "auditing around the computer"? Explain.

14. What is meant by the "audit trail"? How has it been affected by electronic data processing?

REAL WORLD APPLICATIONS

17–1   Wang Laboratories

Computers were supposed to put people out of work. But contrary to the dire predictions of gross unemployment, the data processing business has itself become a labor intensive industry. It's a boom job market out there and likely to stay the way for a long time, say the personnel and recruiting experts. It's not uncommon for companies to "raid" competitor turf for new employees, like a recent well-publicized foray into computer-rich Dallas by Wang Laboratories Inc. of Boston.

Wang recruiters set themselves up in a hotel barely a couple of miles from the 20,000 employees at the sprawling main plant of Texas Instruments and just down the road from Electronic Data Systems, Mostek, University Computing Co., Harris, and Moore Business Systems. They ran newspaper and radio ads and gave interviews to the press. "If TI is here, in Dallas, it has to be a viable market," said Steve Eldridge, a Wang recruiter. And business was "pretty good," he said.

17–1   *(continued)*

With jobs offering salaries ranging from $20,000 to over $40,000, the trek resulted in about 35 prospects visiting with Wang. Wang's biggest selling point, according to Eldridge, was "more flexibility, a more casual structure, and one in which you can be visible and yet still move around."

"That's what attracted me," admitted one TI software manager who'd been out of school only 18 months. "It looks like more career opportunities and even though you can move up fast at TI, I'm pretty sure you can move up faster at Wang. "It's all part of the game," he said. "When you go to another company in this business, you move up a notch on the totem pole, and you boost your salary up a notch also."

"Jumping around is the only way to get ahead," added an electronics engineer. "Many engineers spend their first five to 10 years doing this, looking around, going from one job to another."

Wang's recruiter said that, of the people interviewed, about seven will get offers and about four will end up accepting a job at Wang. The hardest to find, he said, are skilled software experts, like systems analysts. According to about everyone's survey, topping the "most wanted" lists are applications and systems programmers. According to the Bureau of Labor Statistics, there are 534,000 programmers and systems analysts in the United States,

an increase by 25 percent over two years ago. And that, by far, isn't enough.

Data processing professionals in all categories are in demand and getting top salaries. Why? Demand has something to do with supply and another important factor called "turnover." DP people are creating their own job market to a very large extent. Long gone is the 25-year pin and the gold watch because DP people have discovered that they can get ahead faster, either financially or technically, by jumping from job-to-job and/or company-to-company.

Scott Upp, president of Data Base Consultants, a Chicago recruiting firm, said that contrary to popular belief, one of the last reasons members of the DP community change positions is money. DP people are simply more career-plan oriented today, quick to switch jobs to enhance their resume on the way to the top. "Keeping up with the state of the art," is the reason many DP professionals move on to larger, more sophisticated departments, Upp said. "In the DP industry, technology changes so quickly that keeping up with the lastest equipment, software and various software interfaces is an important career goal. If a present employer is neither entering into these areas nor keeping up with the state of the art, or if the employees aren't exposed to it by their company; they'll look for it elsewhere."[1]

- Why did Wang go to Dallas to recruit computer specialists?
- What motivates computer professionals to change jobs?
- Why are computer professionals "in demand and getting top salaries"?
- What categories top the most wanted list?

[1] Source: Steve Stibbens, "The Movement Is Up, Up and Away," *Infosystems*, December 1980, p. 74. Copyright 1980, Hitchcock Publishing Co. Reprinted with permission.

17–2   Citibank, N.A.

- "It was four to five months of the worst chaos I've ever been involved in," complains a former executive of Citibank, N.A.
- "It got worse week after week," says a manager at an Eastern branch office of Fireman's Fund Insur-

ance Companies. "The performance just kept deteriorating and we couldn't find the problem."
- "They tried to mix and match incompatible components," says a DP consultant about one of his client firms on the West Coast. "It was a classic

17–2 *(continued)*

case of 'I saved a lot of money . . . but I'm out of business.' "

Although these three rueful reflections refer to incidents that took place several years and several thousand miles apart, they have one thing in common. They express the feelings of executives who have experienced the advent of distributed data processing (DDP)—and the turmoil that accompanied it.

Because, theoretically, distributed data processing can solve many of the problems associated with centralized operations, managers everywhere are clamoring for a taste of this new method of organizing an information system. "A computer on every desk" sometimes seems the cry of the technologically aware executive. But when the equipment arrives, these same managers often find that DDP has created some problems as well as solutions. Here's the difficulty in a nutshell: When companies distribute processing power without concurrently distributing the know-how to use this capability, the result can be havoc. Users discover that they don't have the nuts-and-bolts knowledge required to make their new toys perform. Subsequently, they run into a second problem: with computers cropping up everywhere, there's no longer enough technical talent to go around.

To make matters worse, general management can no longer blame the DP department for all its processing problems. The reason: distributed data processing leads to distributed responsibility. When the problems start—incompatible components, mysterious failures, mass confusion—users themselves must often take charge of making the new systems work.

Citibank experienced all these kinds of problems when it first started putting processing power in the hands of its nontechnical executives. "We never realized we'd have to tell our MBA's and middle managers that you can't just turn on the machine and forget it," says John Lee Hughes, former vice president of data systems at Citibank. Now a division vice president with Automatic Data Processing, the big computer services company in Clifton, N.J., Hughes recalls how it was when DDP arrived at Citibank four years ago: "These managers were smart people, and when we passed out the minicomputers, our project leader assumed they could keep things running. He insisted the computers were just another piece of office equipment."

But computers simply aren't the same as typewriters and copying machines. General managers competent in other areas must be retrained before they're given DP responsibilities—as Citibank discovered. All the commonsense things that "weren't written down because everybody knew how to do them" proved to be a major problem. Simple housekeeping chores were neglected, and as a result, continuous problems turned the next few months into a nightmare. Users and technical personnel alike were soon screaming for help. The solution turned out to be what Hughes calls DP 101. "We taught managers commonsense techniques to help them make use of their new DP resources. This time we took nothing for granted."

These kinds of glitches often represent only the tip of the iceberg. If DDP is allowed to run its course without being monitored and controlled by top management, the result may well be chaos. For example, while taking a belated inventory of its DDP efforts, one big Boston concern discovered it had a dozen vendors and several hundred small computers that senior management wasn't even aware of. And at Citibank, where managers were able to pick out their own minicomputers—many of which were incompatible—the bank subsequently had to spend thousands of dollars per computer model so that the various minis could communicate with each other.[2]

- How has distributed processing affected the management of computers in business?
- What problems did Citibank experience in their movement to DDP?
- What solutions are needed to solve such problems? Is centralization the answer?

[2] Source: Jesse Burst, "How to Get the Bugs out of DDP," *Output*, March 1981, pp. 60–62.

17-3   Martin Marietta Corporation

"It's like having a chain link fence charged with electricity around your files." Jim Elliott is talking about data security at Martin Marietta Data System's massive computer center in Orlando, Florida, one of the world's largest. More precisely, he's talking about the Resource Access Control Facility, or RACF, an IBM program product designed to protect data files from unauthorized disclosure, modification or destruction. Basically an access control mechanism, RACF controls who may use a system, what parts of the system they may access, and how each user may access those resources. In effect, the customer defines users, groups, and resources and builds profiles to verify them, check authorizations, and provide an audit trail.

Formed in 1970 to provide data processing support in the commercial marketplace, as well as to the aerospace and other divisions of Martin Marietta Corp., Data Systems focused on company business during its early years. Data security was not a concern, notes Chuck Elliott, director of quality assurance and security. However, Sam Waddill, quality assurance administrator, says, "We moved into more sophisticated online systems, with more data moving from manual control to computer control. It was no longer a hands-on environment. People began to rely on computer output as authoritative, to depend more on audit and edit routines. They started to worry more about data protection."

Adds Chuck Elliott, "A consciousness developed about security in the DP environment. More than one company raised questions that went beyond the classic physical, personnel, and administrative forms of security. This awareness spread to our risk management people, internal audit end users, our accounting firm, our board of directors, and third party audit firms. And the Privacy Act of 1974 raised concerns about personal data handled for the government, a key source of business for Data Systems."

"Expanding our customer and application base increased our legal liabilities on the protection of customer data," notes Mr. Waddill. "Smaller companies did not want other users on our systems to have access to their data. We clearly needed account or company separation of data."

"For the past three years, we've doubled our sales volume," says Mr. Elliott, who is director of Orlando host operations for this $90 million Information Services division of the Martin Marietta Corporation. "With the continuing rapid expansion of our business from commercial customers," he says, "it's more important than ever to protect the data assets of the facility and our clients. In the past, an analyst or programmer could have broken into those files. RACF has helped to plug that loophole."

It also has helped the division serve government customers who require data protection, such as the Department of Agriculture, Bureau of Indian Affairs, HUD and the office of the Comptroller of the Currency. That agency recently awarded the company a nine-plus rating following its periodic audit. "Anything above a five from a bank examiner is considered good," Mr. Elliott says.

Notes Rick Walters, vice president of computer services, "One of the top eight CPA firms has given us an endorsement, saying the Orlando data center carries no undue business risks. That's an overwhelming vote of confidence and we feel RACF helped us earn it."

Protecting data is, of course, just one aspect of security for the division. But it is an area in which the Orlando facility has done more than most. "Overall security is something we have to live with, part of the job," says Mr. Elliott. "There are all kinds of things that can be done, from palm prints to cipher locks. We've always been on the leading edge, with closed-circuit TV, fire and smoke detection, and redundant diesel-powered generators for our own uninterruptable power supply. RACF has helped make us state-of-the-art in the security of data as well—for anyone who wants to use the service."

Perhaps the greatest impact at Martin Marietta Data Systems has been the growing confidence level in data security. All involved have a new appreciation of what it takes to protect data in today's environment. "There's always skepticism, often with good reason, on the part of technicians in adding attributes like data security software, Mr. Elliott says. "It's the burglar-alarms-are-only-for-the-burglarized syndrome. With management's blessing we have

17-3 *(continued)*

turned that around. The skepticism is gone. People here are believers."

This belief has helped to foster new relationships at the Data Systems Division—particularly between DP auditing and security. These two areas are combined in the division's quality assurance function under Chuck Elliott. "Quality assurance here functions in a number of capabilities," he explains. "Among other things, we are a form of substitute for DP auditing. We interface with the corporation's internal and external auditors. Now, through this interface, our internal auditors have an avenue to DP they never had before. Our outside CPA firm recognizes both the interface and RACF utilization as desirable and has recommended to the internal audit staff that they assess how our corporate customers are using RACF. Quality assurance is being more formally aligned with the corporate internal audit team. The services complement each other."

"It goes all the way to the board of directors level," adds Jim Elliott. "Security is not a one-man show here. Everybody is concerned about it. Protection and control are the key to this whole operation. We want to protect ourselves as well as our customers."[3]

- What types of EDP controls are used by Martin Marietta for computer security?
- What control functions are provided by the RACF software package?
- What are its benefits to Martin Marietta and its customers?

[3] Source: "Getting a Lock on Data Security," *Data Processor*, December 1979, pp. 9–12. Reprinted with permission.

18

CHAPTER OUTLINE

Computers, Management, and Society

LEARNING OBJECTIVES

The purpose of this chapter is to promote a basic understanding of the major challenges that computers present to business management by analyzing (1) the challenge of computer performance, (2) the challenge to management performance, and (3) the social challenge of the computer.

After reading and studying this chapter, you should be able to:

1. Explain how the problem of poor computer performance can be solved by management involvement in planning and control.
2. Identify several reasons for user resistance to computerization.
3. Discuss how and why solving the problems of user resistance requires meaningful user involvement.
4. Explain how the computer can support either the centralization or decentralization of *(a)* data processing, *(b)* management, and *(c)* operations.
5. Discuss how the computer can be a "catalyst" for the systems approach to management.
6. Identify several ways that the computer can enlarge and enrich the job of management.
7. Discuss the impact of computers on society in terms of several socioeconomic effects.
8. Identify several social applications of the computer which have helped to solve human and social problems.

598

FIGURE 18–1 The Challenges of the Computer

PERFORMANCE CHALLENGE

SOCIETAL CHALLENGE

THE CHALLENGES OF THE COMPUTER

MANAGEMENT CHALLENGE

The preceding chapters of this text should have emphasized that the computer is a valuable and powerful resource that presents a major challenge to business management. Figure 18–1 illustrates that we will conclude our study of computers in business management by focusing on three major challenges of the computer:

- The challenge of computer performance.
- The challenge to management performance.
- The social challenge of the computer.

THE CHALLENGE OF COMPUTER PERFORMANCE

Computers are utilized by business firms to reduce costs, increase profits, provide better service to customers, and provide better information to management. Computers should reduce the cost of doing business by automating the processing of data and the control of operations. Better customer service and improved management information is supposed to result from the speed and accuracy of the computer. Thus, computers should improve the competitive position and profit performance of business firms. However, this has not occurred in many documented cases. Studies by management consulting firms, computer-user groups, and others have shown that many business firms moved too far and too fast into computer processing without adequate personnel resources and management involvement, and that many computer users and computer professionals have not yet learned how to manage this vital but expensive business resource.

Poor Computer Performance

There can be no doubt that the computer has become an indispensable tool for modern business management. Without computers, management could not plan, operate, and control the operations of most of the businesses of today. However, it is obvious that the management of many computer-using business firms have not yet learned to plan, organize, and control the operations of their own computers and computer service departments. The valuable resource of the computer is not being effectively, efficiently, and economically utilized by such business firms. For example:

- The computer is not being used *effectively* by companies which use the computer primarily for record-keeping applications.

- Computers are not being used *efficiently* by computer service departments which provide inadequate service to users while failing to properly utilize their computing capacity.
- Many computer systems are also not being used *economically*. Data processing costs have risen faster than other costs in many business firms, even though the cost of processing each unit of data is decreasing due to improvements in hardware and software technology.

Poor computer performance can take many forms, as illustrated by the list of "symptoms" of a "sick" computer services department show in Figure 18–2. Further, poor computer performance is not limited to small business firms with limited financial and human resources. Many large business firms have openly admitted their failure to manage the computer effectively.

FIGURE 18–2 Symptoms of a Sick Computer Services Department

Computers not used, when applicable, in key business areas.

Poor establishment of project priorities.

Inability to provide management with information needed to make decisions.

Dissatisfied users.

Spiraling costs.

Inability to establish the payback on investments in systems development.

Low productivity of people or equipment.

Schedules not being met.

High turnover of personnel, including management.

Low morale.

Poor internal communications.

Source: "How to Spot the Ailing EDP Department," *Bank Automation Newsletter*, May 1972, p. 4

What is the solution to the problem of poor computer performance? Is more hardware, software, and sophisticated computer systems the answer? Or does the solution lie in the emotional reaction of some business computer users who have "pulled the plug" and "disintegrated their integrated information systems" by "decomputerizing"? The solution to poor computer performance does not lie in either extreme position. There are no quick and easy answers to this problem. Solutions such as "better management of computer resources and services" are obvious but much too vague. However, the experiences of successful computer users reveal that the basic ingredient of high-quality computer performance is *extensive and meaningful management and user involvement* in the development and operation of computer-based information systems. This should be the key ingredient in shaping the response of management to the challenge of improving the quality of computer services.

Management Involvement

Proper management involvement requires the knowledgeable and active participation of managers in the planning and control of computer-based information systems. Being an involved manager means knowing the answers to questions such as:

- How do our computer resources contribute to the short- and long-term profitability of this company?
- Have we invested too little or too much in computer resources?
- Do we have realistic long-range plans for information systems development and acquisition of computer resources that will improve the efficiency of business operations and the quality of management decisions?
- Are information systems development projects and our computer operations being properly managed?
- To sum it all up, are computer resources being utilized efficiently, effectively, and economically in every part or activity of this organization?

Without a high degree of management involvement, managers will not know the answer to such questions and thus will not be able to control the quality of computer performance. Management can no longer claim that acquiring knowledge about computer fundamentals and computer use in business is too difficult or time-consuming. (It is hoped that this book has shown that this is not the case.) Such knowledge should be sufficient to allow managers to become active participants in the development and management of computer-based information systems. Such participation will provide a form of "on-the-job training" which will further reinforce their ability to manage the computer resource effectively, and not be baffled by the EDP "snow job." See Figure 18–3.

Several studies have shown that companies which are successfully using computers view the development and management of computer-based information systems as a responsibility of both top management and operating management. These companies have come to understand that systems ana-

I've seen the ablest and toughest of executives insist on increased productivity by a plant manager, lean on accounting for improved performance, and lay it on purchasing in no uncertain terms to cut its staff. But when these same executives turn to EDP they stumble to an uncertain halt, baffled by the snow job and the blizzard of computer jargon. They accept the presumed sophistication and differences that are said to make EDP activities somehow immune from normal management demands. They are stopped by all this nonsense, uncertain about what's reasonable to expect, what they can insist upon. They become confused and then retreat, muttering about how to get a handle on this blasted situation.

Source: Harry T. Larson, "EDP, a 20-Year Ripoff," *Infosystems*, November 1974, p. 27. Copyright 1974, Hitchcock Publishing Co. Reprinted with permission.

FIGURE 18–3 Managers and the EDP Snow Job

lysts cannot design information systems that effectively support the decision needs of management without management involvement in the systems design process. Systems development projects will not "manage themselves." They need the planning and control activities of management personnel. The computer services department needs the active support of top management and user management to improve and maintain the quality of computer services. Figure 18–4 illustrates several levels of management involvement which are indicated below:

- Many business firms utilize an "Executive EDP committee" of top management to develop long-range plans and coordinate the development of information systems. This committee includes the senior management of the major divisions of the firm, as well as the manager of the computer services organization.
- A "steering committee" of middle managers, operating managers, and management personnel from the computer services department may be created to oversee the progress of project teams. The committee meets on a regular basis during the existence of systems projects to review progress made, settle disputes, and change priorities if necessary.
- Development of major strategic information systems requires management involvement through active participation in systems development as members of systems development project teams.

Information Resource Management

Figure 18–5 illustrates how the management of computer resources is moving from variations of *EDP management* to **Information Resource Management** (IRM). Notice how the organization, planning, and control of a computer-using organi-

FIGURE 18–4 Levels of Management Involvement

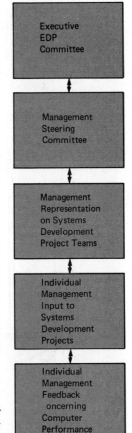

Executive EDP Committee

Management Steering Committee

Management Representation on Systems Development Project Teams

Individual Management Input to Systems Development Projects

Individual Management Feedback concerning Computer Performance

FIGURE 18–5 From EDP Management to Information Resource Management

	Stage 1 Initiation	Stage 2 Contagion	Stage 3 Control	Stage 4 Integration	Stage 5 Data Administration	Stage 6 Maturity
EDP ORGANIZATIONAL ROLE	Specialization for Technological Learning	User-oriented Programmers	Middle Management	Establish Computer Utility and User Account Teams	Data Administration	Information Resource Management
	Data processing is centralized and operates as a "closed shop."		Data processing becomes data custodian. Computer utility established and achieves reliability.		There is organizational implementation of the information resource management concept. There are layers of responsibility for data processing at appropriate organizational levels.	
EDP PLANNING AND CONTROL	Lax	More Lax	Formalized Planning and Control	Tailored Planning and Control Systems	Shared Data and Common Systems	Information Resource Management
	No formal planning or control.		Internal planning and control is installed to manage the computer. Included are standards for programming, responsibility accounting, and project management.		External planning and control is installed to manage information resources. Included are value-added user chargeback, steering committee, and data base administration.	

Source: Adapted and reprinted by permission of the *Harvard Business Review*, from "Managing the Crisis in Data Processing," by Richard L. Nolan (March/April 1979, pp. 117–21). Copyright 1979 by the President and Fellows of Harvard College; all rights reserved.

zation's EDP effort changes as the organization moves through six stages of growth in computer applications. In early stages, EDP management is *data processing-oriented* as the computer services effort moves from a "closed-shop" to a *computer utility* role, with centralized internal planning and control. In later stages, computer and information resources are managed by an organization-wide *information resource management* philosophy, which is *user-oriented* and uses decentralized but integrated planning and control methods. Thus, information resource management views information and computer hardware, software, and personnel as valuable organization resources which can be effectively, efficiently, and economically managed for the benefit of the entire organization. It is thus an application of the functions of management (planning, organizing, staffing, controlling, etc.) to the role of information resources and technology in a firm.

The User Generation

As each succeeding generation of computer systems is developed, it becomes exceedingly difficult for management and computer professionals to pacify computer users with past excuses based on untried applications, inexperienced EDP personnel, or inadequate equipment. Most computer users rightly feel that the "experimental" stage of EDP has passed and expect high-quality computer services. Both management and computer professionals must realize that we are in a "user generation" of computer usage which will continue indefinitely into the future.

The attitudes of computer users are accentuated by an increased awareness of the current state-of-the-art of the computer industry. The public news media, computer industry propaganda, and company publications have touted the speed, power, and sophistication of modern computer systems. The microcomputer revolution, with its promise of computer power for every person and product will only add to the rising expectations of computer users. It is hoped that microcomputers, minicomputers, and the distributed data processing they make possible will do much to meet the increasing expectations of the user generation.

Computer users are demanding economical, efficient, and effective computer-based information systems. They are becoming impatient with the rising costs of EDP, the inefficiencies and "downtimes" of computer operations, and the long lead times of information systems development. They want more consistent accuracy, flexibility, and timeliness in the information produced by current information systems. Management users want new information systems that provide information which more effectively supports their planning and decision-making functions. They want these new systems to integrate the information produced by the organization and disperse it wherever and whenever needed throughout the organization.

Computer-using business firms want information systems which allow management and operating personnel without any technical sophistication to easily utilize an information system in carrying out their assignments. They want flexible, well-planned information systems that can keep pace with the growth in volume and complexity of the business system without the disruptions of major systems conversions every few years. What the new generation of computer users want is a new generation of *user-oriented information systems*.

User Resistance

The coming of the user generation has intensified the potential for resistance by computer users. Any "new way of doing things" generates some resistance by the people affected. However, computer-based information systems can generate a significant amount of fear and reluctance to change. There

FIGURE 18–6 Reasons For User Resistance

Ignorance. Computer users do not have a sufficient knowledge of EDP, while computer professionals do not have a sufficient knowledge of the operations and problems of the business.

Performance. Poor computer performance, resulting in broken promises and inadequate service.

Participation. Users have not been made active participants in systems development and systems maintenance.

Ergonomics. Hardware and software are not designed for ease of use, safety, and comfort of end users; not "user-friendly."

Communication. Computer users may not understand the technical jargon of computer professionals, and EDP personnel may not understand the unique terminology of each group of computer users.

Personnel problems. Some computer users resent the influence of computer professionals on their work activities. EDP personnel are viewed as "technical types" with different work assignments, different working conditions, and different promotion and other personnel policies.

Organizational conflict. The computer services department is viewed as trying to gain too much influence and control within the organization, getting involved in too many operations of the company, and receiving a disproportionate share of the financial resources of the company.

are many reasons for this state of affairs, some of which we will explore in later discussion concerning the impact of computers on society. Whatever the reasons for user resistance, it is the responsibility of business management and computer professionals to find ways of reducing the conflict and resistance that arises from the use of computers. A brief summary of several reasons for user resistance is outlined in Figure 18–6.

User Involvement

Solving the problems of *user resistance* requires meaningful *user involvement* based on formal methods of (1) *education,* (2) *communication,* and (3) *participation.* Like management, user personnel must be educated in the fundamentals of computer technology and their application to business information systems. This basic knowledge should be supplemented by specific programs of orientation, education, and training concerning computer-based information systems.

We have discussed several methods of increasing user participation and communication. We have emphasized, in particular, the necessity of including user representatives on project teams charged with the development of new information systems. We stressed that direct user participation should provide the type of user involvement required to improve the quality of computer services and reduce the potential for user resistance. Such user involvement helps assure that computer-based information systems are "user oriented" in their design. Systems that tend to inconvenience or frustrate their users cannot be effective systems, no matter how efficiently they process data. *Systems must be designed to appear more responsive to the user, rather than appear to force users to be responsive to the system.*

Several methods of "user liaison" are utilized by successful computer users. The manager of the computer services department should meet frequently with the heads of user departments on an individual basis to discuss the status of new and existing systems. In addition, some firms have created "user liaison" positions. Computer-user departments are assigned representatives from the computer services department who perform a vital role by "troubleshooting" problems, gathering and communicating information, and coordinating educational efforts. These activities improve communication and coordination between the user and the computer services department because all questions and problems that arise are referred to one individual. This avoids the "runaround" effect that can frustrate computer users and is an important reminder of the user-orientation of the computer services department.

THE CHALLENGE TO MANAGEMENT PERFORMANCE

The Impact of Computers on Management

When computers were introduced into business, predictions were made that there would be significant changes in management because the data processing power and programmed decision-making capability of the computer would cause drastic reductions in employees, including middle management and supervisory personnel. A centralized computer system would process all of the data for the organization, control most of its operations, and make most of its decisions. This has not proven to be the case. Changes in organizational structure and types of personnel have occurred, but they have not been as dramatic as has been predicted. Naturally, highly automated systems do not require as many people as manual methods. Therefore, there have been significant reductions in the amount of people required to perform certain manual tasks in certain organizations. However, this has been countered to some extent by the need for increased data processing personnel and computer professionals to run the computer-based systems of the organization.

In the previous chapter we concluded that modern computer systems could support either the *centralization* (with a large central computer) or *decentralization* (with a distributed processing network) of *electronic data processing* within a business firm. The same concept can be applied to the centralization and decentralization of *operations* and *management* within a computer-using organization.

- *Centralization.* Large central computer systems allow top management to centralize decision making formerly done at lower levels of the organization and reduce the number of branch offices, manufacturing plants, and warehouses needed by the firm.
- *Decentralization.* Computers and data communication networks allow top management to delegate more responsibility to middle managers and to increase the number of branch offices or other company units while still providing top management with the ability to control the organization.

Thus whether the computer encourages centralization or decentralization of business operations and management depends on the philosophy of top management and the nature of the operations of the specific business firm.

The Systems Approach to Management

The challenge of the computer to business management can be considered in a positive sense if the computer is viewed as a "catalyst" for applying the systems concept to business management. Computerizing information systems requires huge commitments of time, money, and personnel. It requires intensive studies of the various operations and information requirements of the business. It puts management "eyeball to eyeball" with the highly sophisticated technology of computer hardware, software, and personnel. It forces painful decisions that change "the way we always used to do things."

Faced with these pressures, management can take the easy way out by computerizing information systems in the traditional "piecemeal" approach, i.e., the information requirements of each department in the firm is computerized, one after the other, as resources permit. Instead, management should welcome the computer as a *catalyst* for *the systems approach.* If the business firm is a business "system" rather than just a series of departments which perform various functions, the piecemeal approach can be disastrous. Management must use the systems approach when confronted with the need to introduce computers into the business firm. Managing a business firm becomes a form of systems development as illustrated in Figure 18–7.

Systems investigation. Survey the subsystems of the business firm and the business environment for problems and opportunities. Separate symptoms from problems. Select the most urgent and most feasible problems to be solved or opportunities to be pursued.

Systems analysis. Gather and analyze information about the selected problem or opportunity in terms of the systems and subsystems that are involved.

Systems design. Develop alternative courses of action by designing and testing models of the systems that affect the problem or opportunity.

Programming. Choose a single course of action and develop plans, programs, budgets, policies, and necessary procedures.

Systems implementation. Put the decision into effect by implementing the plans developed in the programming stage.

Systems maintenance. Monitor and evaluate the results of the decision, since the subsystems of the business firm and the business environment are subject to continual change. Modify the decision as necessary.

FIGURE 18–7 A Systems Approach to Management

Enlarging the Job of Management

A major challenge to management arises from the ability of the computer to handle clerical details and simple decisions which can be programmed, thus freeing management from these routine tasks. Many managers can no longer use the excuse that "I'm too tied up with details and paper work," or "I can't get the right information at the right time in the right form in the right place." Management must develop new and creative activities including the use of the computer to support high-level decisions.

Letting the computer take over routine decisions should not be viewed as a threat by management but as an opportunity to engage in more activities that are beneficial to the business firm. Many managers have reported that the computer has finally given them the time to "get out of the office and into the field." They can finally spend enough time pursuing their *marketing responsibilities* with customers and salespersons, their *personnel management responsibilities* with subordinates, and their *societal responsibilities* with various public and governmental groups. Managers can spend more time on *planning* activities instead of spending much of their time "putting out fires." Thus, the computer can enable many managers finally to become "managers" rather than "paper shufflers."

Another aspect of the management challenge lies in the ability of the computer to help management make strategic planning and control decisions. The use of the computer must rise above the "paper shuffling" level to a higher level which utilizes simulation and other mathematical and statistical techniques to analyze the important factors that must be considered in management decisions and to test the possible results of proposed decisions. The computer requires only a few seconds to process business data using many of these techniques. The challenge to management is to become acquainted with such *decision support systems* so that they can intelligently use them in planning and control decisions.

THE SOCIAL CHALLENGE OF THE COMPUTER

We are in the midst of a "computer revolution" that experts expect to continue for many years. There can be no doubt that the computer has significantly magnified our ability to analyze, compute, and communicate, thereby greatly improving our ability to plan and control many varieties of human endeavor. However, several social commentators have become alarmed at the "ubiquitous" nature of the computer. They note that computers seem to be present everywhere in all the activities of daily life in our present society. Such commentators worry about our continually increasing dependence on the computer and have identified many adverse social effects of computer usage. What should our attitude be toward the widespread use of the computer in business and society? In order to answer this question, we shall analyze some of the major social and economic effects of computers and the computer industry.

The Impact of Computers on Society

The impact of computers on society can be analyzed in terms of social applications and social-economic effects. The *social applications* of the computer include its use to solve human and social problems such as crime and pollution. *Socioeconomic effects* of the computer refer to the impact on society of the use of computers. For example, computerizing a production process may have the *adverse* effect of a decrease in employment opportunities and the *beneficial* effect of providing consumers with products of better quality at lower cost. Business managers must understand the beneficial and adverse effects of computer usage on society. Such an understanding will help them plan and control the development and operation of computer-based information systems within their organizations. We will therefore analyze several major aspects of the impact of computers on society. See Figure 18–8.

Impact on Employment and Productivity

The Industrial Revolution of the 18th century saw the development of *mechanization* in which machines replaced muscle power. The term *automation* began to be used around the middle of this century and refers to the automatic transfer and positioning of work by machines or the automatic operation and control of a production process by machines. The assembly line operations of an automobile manufacturer or the petroleum refinery operations of an oil company are examples of automation. Thus, automation is the use of machines to control other machines and physical processes and replaces some of the human "brain power" and manual dexterity formerly required. The term *cybernation* then came into use to

FIGURE 18–8 Major Aspects of the Computer's Impact on Society

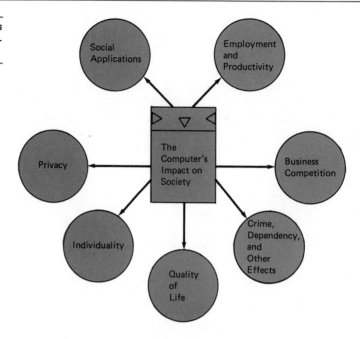

emphasize the automatic control aspect of automation, especially automatic self-regulating "process control" systems. The increasing use of computers to control automatically all types of production processes as well as traditional clerical tasks ("office automation") are major developments of the second half of the 20th century.

The impact of computers on employment and productivity is therefore directly related to the use of computers to achieve automation and cybernation. There can be no doubt that the use of computers has created new jobs and increased productivity, while also causing a significant reduction in some types of job opportunities. Computers utilized for office data processing or the numerical control of machine tools are accomplishing tasks formerly performed by many clerks and machinists. Also, jobs created by the computer within a computer-using organization require different types of skills and education than the jobs eliminated by the computer. Therefore, specific individuals within an organization may become unemployed unless they can be retrained for new positions or new responsibilities.

However, the productivity of an individual worker is significantly increased by computerization. One worker can now do the work of several, and the length of time required to perform certain tasks has been drastically shortened. Increased productivity may lead to lower costs and lower prices which may increase demand for a product and thus generate increased employment. The higher profits caused by increases in productivity may also stimulate more investment to expand productive facilities, resulting in increased employment. These positive effects on employment have been characteristic of the "mass production" of goods and services in our economy.

Another point to remember is that the higher standard of living caused by increased productivity generates *more* rather than *less* demand for more types and amounts of goods and services. "Yesterday's luxuries become today's necessities" is a statement which emphasizes the almost limitless demands for goods and services that our society seems to exhibit. This phenomenon should be related to the impact of computers on employment since an increased standard of living seems to lead to expansion of demand for goods and services which must result in an increase in employment opportunities.

There can be no doubt that the computer industry has created a host of new job opportunities for the manufacture, sale, and maintenance of computer hardware, software, and other services. Many new jobs such as systems analysts, computer programmers, and computer operators have been created in computer-using organizations. Many new jobs have been created in service industries which provide services to the computer industry and computer-using firms and the people that work for them. Additional jobs have been created because the computer makes possible the production of complex industrial and technical goods and services which would otherwise be impossible to produce. Thus, jobs have been created by activities that are heavily dependent upon the computer in such fields as space exploration, microelectronic technology, and scientific research.

The controversy over the effect of computers on employment will continue as long as activities formerly performed by people are computerized. *Unemployment is more than a statistic;* office and factory workers whose jobs have been eliminated by computerization are real people with real employment needs. Such persons will take little comfort in the fact that computers have many beneficial effects upon employment. Business firms and other computer-using organizations, labor unions, and government agencies must continue to provide job opportunities for people displaced by computers. This includes transfers to other positions, relocation to other facilities, or training for new responsibilities. Only if society continues to take positive steps to provide jobs for people displaced by computers can we take pride in the increase in employment caused by computer usage. The effect of computers on employment can be a positive one if new job opportunities and incentives are provided that offset specific instances of unemployment caused by the computer.

Impact on Competition

The impact of computers on *competition* concerns the effect that computer systems have on the size of business organizations. Computers allow large firms to become more efficient. This can have several anticompetitive effects. Small business firms that could exist because of the inefficiencies of large firms are now driven out of business or absorbed by the larger firms. The efficiency of the larger firms allows them to continue to grow and combine with other business firms and thus create the large corporations that exist today. The previously high cost of most computer systems (which only larger firms could afford) accentuated this trend toward bigness.

It is undoubtedly true that computers allow large organizations to grow larger and become more efficient. Organizations grow in terms of people, productive facilities, and geographic locations such as branch offices and plants. Only a computer-based information system is capable of controlling the complex activities and relationships that occur. However, it should be noted that the cost and size of computer systems continues to *decrease* due to the development of microcomputers and minicomputers, and the availability of computer services continues to *increase* due to the activities of computer service bureaus and time-sharing companies. Therefore, even the small firm can take advantage of the productivity and efficiency generated by computer-based systems.

It should also be noted that the computer is changing the *nature* of competition as well as the size of the competing units. As business firms possess better information on their own internal position and their business environment and as they utilize new analytical techniques such as mathematical stimulation, the competition between business firms will become very keen and their response to each other's competitive moves will become more accurate and more rapid. Thus, only firms with effective computer-based information systems will be able to survive this type of dynamic competition.

Impact on Individuality

A frequent criticism of computers concerns their negative effect on the *individuality* of people. Computer-based systems are criticized as impersonal systems which dehumanize and depersonalize activities which have been computerized, since they eliminate the human relationships present in noncomputer systems. Because it is more efficient for a data processing system to deal with an individual as a number than as a name, many people feel the loss of identity that seems inherent in systems where they seem to be "just another number."

Another aspect of the loss of individuality is the regimentation of the individual that seems to be required by some computer-based systems. These systems do not seem to possess any flexibility. They demand strict adherence to detailed procedures if the system is to work. "Do not fold, spindle, or mutilate" is the statement on punched card documents that has become a popular symbol of the regimentation and inflexibility of computer-based systems. The negative impact of computers on individuality is reinforced by "horror stories" which describe how inflexible and uncaring computer-based systems are when it comes to rectifying their own mistakes. Many of us are familiar with stories of how computerized customer billing and accounting systems have continued to demand payment and send warning notices to a customer whose account has already been paid, despite repeated attempts by the customer to have the error corrected.

Are there any rational arguments against the charges that the computer robs people of their individuality? One major fact that must be considered is summed up by the statement "computers don't make mistakes, people do." That is to say that the errors and inflexibility of computer-based systems are primarily caused by poor systems design or mistakes in computer programming or operations. Thus, the computer can be blamed only for occasional hardware malfunctions. Systems analysts, computer programmers, and other EDP personnel must accept the responsibility for errors in systems design, computer programming, and data processing operations.

Another point to emphasize is that computer-based systems can be designed to minimize depersonalization and regimentation. "People-oriented" and "user-friendly" information systems can be developed. The computer hardware, software, and systems design capabilities that make such systems possible are increasing rather than decreasing. The use of microcomputers promises to dramatically improve the development of people-oriented information systems (through personal computing and distributed processing) and even of everyday products and services (through microcomputer-powered "smart" products).

The computer is frequently blamed for the "bigness" of business firms and other insitutions in which the individual is treated as no more than a statistic. However, it must be remembered that though computers may help make bigness possible, computers alone are not responsible for the growth in size and complexity of our institutions. We live in a society which is attempting to provide *all people,* rather than a small elite, with food, clothing, shelter, employment, education, medical care, and other "necessities" of life while continuing to protect the freedom of the individual. This is an awesome task, accomplished by no previous civilization. Much of the bigness and complexity of modern institutions is caused by our attempt to provide the necessities and amenities of life to vast numbers of people in an efficient and effective manner, rather than reserving them for a small aristocracy. In this regard, the computer is *helping* rather than *hindering* our attempts to provide the "good life" to each individual.

It can also be argued that computers can help promote greater personalization and attention to the individual than would otherwise be possible, given the large size of organizational units, the complexity of individual and organizational relationships, and the volume of individual activities. Computer systems can easily handle large masses of routine transactions, thus allowing *more personal attention* to important transactions. Computer systems can provide information and analytical techniques that allow individuals a *diversity* of choice so that the *individual preferences* of the users of the system can be accommodated in the operation of the system. This is the goal of *people-oriented* and *user-friendly* systems.

Impact on the Quality of Life

The impact of the computer on the quality of life is directly related to its impact upon employment and productivity. For example, computerized business systems increase productivity and allow the production of better quality goods and services at lower costs. Thus, the computer is partially responsible for the high standard of living we enjoy. In addition, the computer has eliminated monotonous or obnoxious tasks in the office and the factory that formerly had to be performed by people. In many instances, this allows people to concentrate on more challenging and interesting assignments, has upgraded the skill level of the work to be performed, and created challenging jobs requiring highly developed skills in the computer industry and within computer-using organizations. Thus, computers can be said to upgrade the quality of life because they can upgrade the quality of working conditions and the content of work activities.

Of course, it must be remembered that some jobs created by the computer, keypunching, for example, are quite repetitive and routine. Also, to the extent that computers are utilized in some types of automation, they must take some responsibility for the criticism of assembly line operations which require the continual repetition of elementary tasks, thus forcing a worker to "work like a machine" instead of like a skilled craftsperson. Many automated operations are also criticized for relegating people to a "do nothing" standby role where workers spend most of their time waiting for infrequent opportunities to "push some buttons." Such effects do have a detrimental effect on the quality of life, but they are more than offset by the less burdensome and more creative jobs created by the computer.

Computers have also contributed to the increased availability of leisure time. The increase in productivity provided by computer usage has helped to allow the average worker to produce more goods and services in less time. We have gone from the six-day week to the five-day week to the four-day week in some industries. The working day has decreased from 12 hours to 8 hours or less. The number of holidays and the length of vacations have increased, as well as the types and length of personal and professional leaves. Young people tend to stay in school longer before seeking permanent employment, while workers can now retire at an earlier age. Thus, the quality of life is improved because people have more time for recreation, entertainment, education, and creative activities. This development in itself has created more employment since many new jobs have been created in the "leisure industry" to serve the leisure time activities of people.

Impact on Privacy

Modern computer systems make it technically and economically feasible to collect, store, integrate, interchange, and retrieve data and information quickly and easily. This characteristic has an important beneficial effect on the efficiency and effectiveness of computer-based information systems. However, the power of the computer to store and retrieve information can have a negative effect on *the right to privacy* of every individual. Confidential information on individuals contained in centralized computer data bases by credit bureaus, government agencies, and private business firms could be misused and result in the invasion of privacy and other injustices. Unauthorized use of such information would seriously invade the privacy of individuals, while errors in such data files could seriously hurt the credit standing or reputation of an individual. Such developments were possible before the

FIGURE 18–9 The Scope of U.S. Government Personal Data Bases

Department of Health and Human Services: 693 data systems with 1.3 billion personal records including marital, financial, health, and other information on recipients of Social Security, social services, medicaid, medicare and welfare benefits.

Treasury Department: 910 data systems with 853 million records that include files on taxpayers, foreign travelers, persons deemed by the Secret Service to be potentially harmful to the President, and dealers in alcohol, firearms and explosives.

Justice Department: 175 data systems with 181 million records including information on criminals and criminal suspects, aliens, persons linked to organized crime, securities-laws violators and "individuals who relate in any manner to official FBI investigations."

Defense Department: 2,219 data systems with 321 million records pertaining to service personnel and persons investigated for such things as employment, security or criminal activity.

Department of Transportation: 263 data systems with 25 million records including information on pilots, aircraft and boat owners, and all motorists whose licenses have been withdrawn, suspended, or revoked by any state.

Department of Commerce: 95 data systems with 447 million records, primarily Census Bureau data, but including files on minority businessmen, merchant seamen, and others.

Department of Housing and Urban Development: 58 data systems with 27.2 million records including data on applicants for housing assistance and federally guaranteed home loans.

Veterans Administration: 52 data systems with 156 million records, mostly on veterans and dependents now receiving benefits or who got them in the past.

Department of Labor: 97 data systems with 23 million records, many involving people in federally financed work and job-training programs.

Civil Service: 14 data systems with 103 million records, mostly dealing with government employes or applicants for government jobs.

Source: Reprinted from *U.S. News and World Report*, April 10, 1978, p. 45. Copyright 1978, U.S. News and World Report, Inc.

advent of the computer. However, the speed and power of a large computer with centralized direct-access data bases and remote terminals greatly increases the potential for such injustices. The trend towards nationwide integrated information systems with integrated data bases by business firms and government agencies substantially increases *the potential* for misuse of computer-stored information. See Figure 18–9.

The Federal Privacy Act of 1974 strictly regulates the collection and use of personal data by governmental agencies (except for law enforcement investigative files, classified files, and civil service files). The law specifies that individuals have the right to inspect their personal records, make copies, and correct or remove erroneous or misleading information. It also specifies that federal agencies (1) must annually disclose the types of personal data files they maintain, (2) cannot disclose personal information on an individual to any other individual or agency except under certain strict conditions, (3) must inform individuals of the reasons for requesting personal information from them, (4) must retain personal data records only if it is "relevant and necessary to accomplish" an agency's legal purpose, and (5) must "establish appropriate *administrative, technical,* and *physical safeguards* to ensure the security and confidentiality of records." Such legislation should emphasize and accelerate the efforts of systems designers to utilize hardware, software, and procedural controls to maintain the accuracy and confidentiality of computerized data bases.

Other Effects

Computer usage creates the *potential* for several other *negative societal effects* which have not been previously mentioned. The potential for fraud and embezzlement by "electronic criminals" has been proven by many widely publicized instances of *computerized crime.* Incriminating personal information in computerized files can be used to blackmail individuals. Fraud or errors in election vote-counting systems can occur. Integrated information systems which allow greater centralization in the control of an organization may give some individuals too much power over other people. In the political sphere, this centralization of power is viewed as a potential threat to democracy if centralized government planning and control robs people of their individual freedoms. Computers can also be misused to distort information about candidates in political campaigns.

Our great and increasing dependence upon computers in the operations of our economy and society is seen as a potential threat by some social observers. Such observers worry about "computers taking over," since we have become so dependent upon their use. They also worry that computer malfunctions might have disastrous consequences if military weapons systems, industrial control systems, and financial information systems are involved. Such potential negative effects pose serious challenges to the *control* aspects of systems design.

Social Applications

Computers can have many direct *beneficial effects* on society when they are used to solve human and social problems through *social applications* such as medical diagnosis, computer-assisted instruction, governmental program planning, environmental quality control, and law enforcement. Computers can be used to help diagnose an illness, prescribe necessary treatment, and monitor the progress of hospital patients. Computer-assisted instruction (CAI) allows a computer to serve as a "tutor" since it utilizes conversational computing on remote terminals to tailor instruction to the needs of a particular student. This is a tremendous benefit to students, especially those with learning disabilities.

Computers can be used for crime control through various law enforcement applications which allow police to identify and respond quickly to evidences of criminal activity. Computers have been used to monitor the level of pollution in the air and in bodies of water in order to detect the sources of pollution and to issue early warnings when dangerous levels are reached. Computers are also utilized for the program planning of many government agencies in such areas as urban planning, population density and land use studies, highway planning, and urban transit studies. Computers are being used in job placement systems to help match unemployed persons with available jobs. These and other applications illustrate that the computer can be used to help solve the problems of society.

Systems Design and Social Responsibility

It should be obvious that management must insist that the social and economic effects of computer usage be considered when a computer-based system is being developed. A major management objective should be to develop systems which can be easily and effectively utilized by the individual system user. The objectives of the system must also include the protection of the privacy of the individuals, and the defense of the system against fraudulent use. Control hardware, software, and procedures must be included in the systems design. The potential for misuse and malfunction of a proposed system must be analyzed with respect to the impact on computer-using organizations, individuals, and society as a whole.

Many of the potential negative effects of computer usage mentioned previously have or would result from errors in systems design and programming. Increased emphasis on the control capabilities of computer-based systems would protect us from many of these potential effects. Computer-based systems can be designed to prevent their own misuse and remedy their own malfunctions. Computers make it possible for us to monitor the activities of computer-based systems and thus prevent computerized crime and correct systems malfunctions. Management must recognize that the *design and maintenance of systems controls* is the key to minimizing the negative effects of computer misuse and malfunction.

However, the elimination of some adverse effects of computer usage may require *government regulation* or *a greater evidence of social responsibility* on the part of the management of computer-using organizations. For example, many business firms have been able to assure their employees that no person would be laid off because of a conversion to computer systems, though some employees have had to accept changes in assignments. Business firms are frequently able to make such a guarantee (and stay in business) because their long-term employment needs have continued to increase due to the growth of the business and the normal attrition of other employees. Such a policy also improves employee morale and productivity and enhances the long-run position of the business firm in society.

It should be obvious that many detrimental effects of the computer on society are caused by improperly designed systems or by individuals and organizations who are not willing to accept the social responsibility for their actions. Like other powerful tools, the computer possesses the potential for great good or evil. Managers, computer users, and computer professionals must accept the responsibility for its proper and beneficial use.

SUMMARY

- Poor computer performance in many business firms is well documented and reveals that many computer users and computer professionals have not learned how to manage this vital but expensive business resource. The computer is not being used effectively, efficiently, and economically by many business firms.

- The experiences of successful computer users reveal that the basic ingredient of high-quality computer performance is extensive and meaningful management and user involvement in the development and operation of computer-based information systems. This should be the key ingredient in shaping the response of management to the challenge of improving the quality of computer services. Information resource management, which views information and computer technology as resources which must be managed is another useful concept for management.

- The challenge of the computer to management performance is based on its role as a catalyst for a systems approach to management. Computer-based information systems challenge management to utilize systems concepts of decision making, and frees them from routine tasks, while allowing them more time for marketing, personnel, and planning activities.

- Computers have had a major impact on society and thus impose serious responsibilities upon the management of computer-using business firms. Computers have had a major effect on employment, productivity, and competition in the business world. Computers have had both beneficial and detrimental effects on individuality, the quality of life, and privacy. Social applications of computers provide a direct beneficial effect to society when they are used to solve human and social problems.

- Business management must accept the responsibility for the proper and beneficial use of computers in business. They must insist that effective measures be utilized to ensure that the social and economic effects of computer usage are considered during the development and operation of computer-based information systems.

KEY TERMS AND CONCEPTS

Poor computer performance	Systems approach to management
Management involvement	
The user generation	Management job enlargement
User resistance	Socioeconomic effects of computers
User involvement	
Centralization versus decentralization	Social applications of computers
	Systems design and social
The computer as a catalyst	responsibility

REVIEW AND DISCUSSION QUESTIONS

1. What is meant by inadequate computer performance? What have been some of the causes of such inadequate performance?

2. How can management involvement in the planning and control of

computer-based information systems be implemented? What role does the information resource management concept play in this regard?

3. What is the user generation? What does this new generation of computer users expect?

4. What are some of the causes of user resistance to computerization?

5. How and why does solving the problems of user resistance require meaningful user involvement?

6. Does the computer support the centralization or decentralization of electronic data processing, business operations, and management within a computer-using firm? Explain.

7. How can the computer be a catalyst for the systems approach to management?

8. Why can the computer enlarge and enrich the job of management?

9. What are some of the beneficial and adverse effects of computer usage on society?

10. Do computers create unemployment? Explain.

11. Does the use of computers rob people of their individuality? Explain.

12. What has been the effect of computers on the quality of life?

13. Why is the impact of computers on personal privacy an important issue?

14. What are some of the social applications of the computer which have helped to solve human and social problems?

15. What can managers, computer users, and computer professionals do to ensure the proper and beneficial use of computers?

REAL WORLD APPLICATIONS

18-1 Cumberland Farms Dairy

Cumberland Farms Dairy is a chain of almost 1,200 convenience food stores and 400 gas stations throughout the eastern United States with headquarters in Canton, Massachusets. We heard about Query-by-Example (QBE) from IBM, a software tool that operates in conjunction with our present computer system. QBE works like this: After computer files are converted from batch applications to the system's columnar, tabular format, the user can access information by keying in English-language commands on a CRT terminal. The data will then appear on the screen in a series of rows and columns. The user can then either select data from these columns or sort, group, average, accumulate, summarize, define, and modify the information as desired—all without the DP department having to write a single program.

As you can imagine, QBE represented a radical change to our employees. But what sold us on the system was the ease with which it could be implemented and understood by our people. Within three months after the first terminal was installed, we had established a user information center and a four-day course to educate our employees. One out of every five employees has taken the course; about 30 of these are department heads and executives, composing 85 percent of the management team at our headquarters site.

Today, a total of 40 terminals are installed in 13 departments throughout headquarters, including accounting, finance, sales, security, and data processing—as well as in four executive offices. Approximately 150 of our non–DP-oriented managers

18–1 *(continued)*

and support personnel use QBE to access information from approximately 100 computer files in minutes—hundreds of times faster than with our former system—which means that we can react to customer and market needs now, not months from now. This flexibility has allowed every department within the company to reap substantial benefits, both tangible and intangible.

The Data Processing Department, for example, reports that requests for special programming have dropped by 30 percent, freeing these employees to concentrate on developing new internal control systems and improving existing ones. Other departments, as well, have benefitted dramatically from our use of the system. The Security Division, for instance, uses QBE to single out stores with unusually high inventory losses and link them with personnel statistics to curb dishonest employees. In this way, we have been able to cut these losses by one fourth.

However, the real worth of QBE cannot actually be measured in dollars or percentages. Because department heads and executives are as involved as our other employees with this data access program, the entire management style of our company has changed—for the better. In this competitive field, our upper-level personnel now have all corporate financial and sales information at their fingertips. Using this timely data, they can, for instance, zero in on developing sales trends and refine the company's marketing tactics accordingly. QBE's general ledger system allows them, in a matter of minutes, to call up any information, from source documentation to financial statements—thus providing them with full control over any division in the company. Within the next year, we will be adding at least six more terminals in selected remote regional offices, giving some of our other managers the same advantages we now have at headquarters.[1]

- Why do you think managers are willing and able to use QBE?
- How does it benefit them?
- How has it changed the jobs of management?

[1] Source: Francis N. Alger, "Execs Access DP Info via Online Query System," *Office Products News,* May 1981, p. 24.

18–2   Computer Crimes

Dramatic Crimes the Computer Helped Commit[2]

The case: Wells Fargo.
The date: 1979–1981.
The take: $21.3 million.
The modus operandi: L. Ben Lewis, an operations officer for the 11th largest U.S. bank, allegedly produced bogus deposits in an account at one branch belonging to a boxing promotion outfit. He did this by using the bank's computerized interbranch account settlement process to withdraw funds from a different branch. To keep the computer from flagging the imbalance, Lewis created new fraudulent credits to cover the withdrawal—and allegedly kept the rollover going for two years. Lewis denies the charges.

The case: Morgan Guaranty
The date: 1980
The take: Zero
The modus operandi: The New York bank reportedly accepted as legitimate a bogus telex from the Central Bank of Nigeria transferring $21 million. In response to subsequent instructions, the money was routed electronically to three banks. When an attempt was made to wire the funds to a new $50,

18-2   *(continued)*

account in a Santa Ana (Calif.) bank, the transfer was refused. This triggered inquiries by the other banks. The Nigerian bank branded the first message as fraudulent, and the funds were never collected.

The case: Dalton School
The date: 1980
The take: Zero
The modus operandi: Using a classroom terminal, teenage students at Manhattan's private Dalton School allegedly dialed into a Canadian network of corporate and institutional data systems. No funds were diverted—but damage was done to data files.

The case: Security Pacific
The date: 1978
The take: $10.3 million
The modus operandi: Stanley Mark Rifkin, who had been a computer consultant for the Los Angeles bank, visited the bank's wire transfer room, where he obtained the electronic funds transfer code. Later, posing as a branch manager, he called from a public telephone and used the code to send money to a Swiss account. By the time the bank's computers flagged the fraud, he had flown to Swit-

zerland, converted the funds into diamonds, and returned to the United States. Only when he boasted of the feat was he identified, convicted, and sentenced to prison.

The case: Union Dime
The date: 1973
The take: $1.2 million
The modus operandi: A teller at the New York City savings bank skimmed money from large new accounts by making a simple computerized correction entry. His embezzlement was discovered when police investigated a gambling parlor he frequented and questioned the source of his betting money.

The case: Equity Funding
The date: 1973
The take: $27.25 million
The modus operandi: The insurance holding company used computers to create phony insurance policies that were later sold to reinsurers. Of the company's assets, $143.4 million were found to be fictitious, of which an estimated 19 percent was the result of computer fraud.

- What role did the computer play in each of the crimes summarized above?
- Why is it that several banks are involved in these crimes?
- How could such crimes be prevented?

[2] Source: "The Spreading Danger of Computer Crime," *Business Week*. Reprinted from the April 20, 1981, issue of *Business Week* (p. 88) by special permission. © 1981 by McGraw-Hill, Inc., New York, N.Y. 10020. All rights reserved.

18-3   The Rocky MIS Horror Show

Scene I:

What was supposed to be a look at the future of MIS at the annual Society for Management Information Systems (SMIS) conference turned out instead to be a review of the present. It wasn't pleasant, the picture portrayed by three panelists and the moderator (Jim Emery of The Wharton School) on a beautiful fall day in Philadelphia the last full week of September, 1980.

George Glaser—a long-time McKinsey consultant, professional society leader, and entrepreneur—told a horror story about a friend of his who has inherited a DP shop that features a 370/168 with 600 terminals, 500 of them remote. It provides a response time of 30 seconds. The shop is run by a former systems programmer who has a staff of eight applications programmers, one systems an-

18–3 *(continued)*

alyst, and zero systems programmers. Personnel turnover has been running at 60 percent. There are 700 programs, 15 of them major ones, with one assembly language program that has 50 pages of code. There are no useful comments, no more registers available, and the people who wrote the program are all gone. There is a backlog of 278 change requests going back to 1976, with 208 of them dated 1979.

Glaser wondered if this installation is atypical, then suggested that it is not. He had opened his comments with a remark that MIS has "severe maintenance problems, a shortage of people and the people we have are sinking into a quagmire of undocumented, obsolete systems that are unmaintained and unmaintainable." Makes you feel warm all over?[3]

Scene II:

Who in the first place suggested the wonders of MIS to management? Some of the vendors, of course. And justifiably so. The technology was available to produce the results. And vendors sell technology. Accomplishing those advertised results was another thing. And who promised the results would actually happen? Was it not the members of SMIS and their counterparts in systems management? They bought the vendor pitch. They sold management on the expectations of MIS. Management bought the MIS story, put up the dollars and sat back and awaited the payoff. Is management to blame, or the soothsayers, including consultants who pied pipered management down the primrose path?

Herb Schwartz states, "Today, we're online, with networks to complicate our lives. We've conquered the relatively mundane, structured applications. Now we get the 'tough' jobs requiring distributed processing, shared data bases and special, one-of-a-kind, unstructured problems, including ad hoc questions and 'what-if' games . . . requested by unsophisticated, but demanding end users." His comments are a sort of self indictment of the systems profession. The "unsophisticated, demanding end users" didn't discover online, networks, distributed processing, shared data bases and what-if games. They were led to them by MIS practitioners and vendors. They were sold on the concepts and they now await the promised benefits. According to the panel, the users have little hope of reaching the promised land.

We don't share the pessimism of the SMIS panel. For all the horror stories that have emerged from this history of data processing, there are many, many more untold stories involving effective, efficient operations. As we move into the era of Information Resource Management (IRM), the systems profession has a new challenging opportunity to provide management with the ability to manage information as a major resource. We can benefit from past mistakes. To our mind, most failures in management information systems can be attributed to the following: Too many systems practitioners are limited by a punched-card, data processing mentality; too many management people still think of computer systems as little more than extensions of the accounting department; and all too many top management people and their systems managers are willing to allow vendors to do their systems thinking for them.[4]

- Who is responsible for poor computer performance: Computer professionals? Computer users? Management? Explain.
- How can such situations be improved?
- How can the concept of information resource management (IRM) help?

[3] Source: Robert Forest, "The Rocky MIS Horror Show," *Infosystems*, November 1980, p. 91. Copyright 1980, Hitchcock Publishing Co. Reprinted with permission.

[4] Source: Arnold Keller, "MIS: The Pot and the Kettle," *Infosystems*, November 1980, p. 34. Copyright 1980, Hitchcock Publishing Co. Reprinted with permission.

Integrative Cases

These integrative cases describe the problems and opportunities faced by actual computer-using organizations. They are designed to give you an opportunity to integrate the knowledge gained from reading and studying the text material, and to apply it to situations faced by real world business firms and other organizations.

In order of their appearance, the cases are:

- HAMBURGER HEAVEN
- PROGRESSIVE ELECTRONICS
- HILLTOP COLLEGE
- METROPOLITAN MOTORS

There are several approaches that can be used in analyzing cases. One suggested approach is as follows:

1. Read the case quickly to get an overall feel for the situation faced by the computer-using organization.
2. Go over the case material slowly, underlining or taking written notes which identify major problems, opportunities, and other facts which you think may have a major bearing on the case.
3. Develop several alternative solutions that would help the computer-using organization solve the problems it faces.
4. Evaluate the alternative solutions and select the best solution, explaining why you feel it should be implemented.
5. Prepare a written or oral report summarizing the results of your analysis as outlined in the previous steps. This case report may include or consist primarily of written or oral answers to the discussion questions at the end of each case.

HAMBURGER HEAVEN

Background

Hamburger Heaven is a chain of fast-food restaurants in which regional franchises are granted by the corporate headquarters to selected individuals who have adequate capital, management training, and experience.

The franchisee in the Southeast region is Sally Flynn, an aggressive, energetic entrepreneur with a college degree in business and perhaps more experience than she would have liked as a part-time order taker in other fast-foods establishments. She had "smart" cash registers installed at her three existing Hamburger Heaven restuarants. These registers have keys labeled with the names of food products rather than with dollar amounts, so that even an order taker with no training can ring up a sale accurately. The registers generate automatic daily totals of sales by dollar amount and by units, along with the estimated dollar cost of input raw materials comprising the products. Thus, a hamburger with one ounce of cheese and two ounces of lettuce on a bun would be costed at the current rate (previously input) for each of those items.

Sally pays her accountant $300 per month to prepare the financial statements which she is obliged to forward to Hamburger Heaven's corporate headquarters. While her relationship with the accounting firm is generally good, Sally feels that she might obtain considerably more management control information in addition to her financial statements for the same dollar outlay per month. She is also concerned because the financial statements do not arrive until approximately two weeks after the books are closed.

Data Processing Problems

Sally's three restaurants are very successful at this time. Another restaurant is under construction and, if all goes well, three more are targeted for completion within the next two years. If the accounting firm multiplies its fee by the anticipated increase in the number of restaurants, Sally would be paying $700 per month for her financial statements.

Sally is confronted almost daily with the need to record earnings for, and to pay a crew of minimum-wage, part-time service employees. The employee turnover is very high. Maintenance of payroll data and preparation of paychecks, government documents and union reports is tedious and time-consuming already. Often the checks are late, causing justifiable employee consternation. With seven restaurants the paperwork burden would be enormous!

Wastage and spoilage of raw materials is a constant concern to Sally. With a low profit margin on each item sold, any substantial wastage, spoilage, or pilferage might easily "eat up" profits. Sally wonders whether and how accurate records of these factors, categorized by ingredient, by the vendor who sold the ingredient, and by the cook on duty, could be kept.

When vendor prices for individual ingredients at different locations fall (and there is variation almost daily), Sally would like to offer customer-enticing specials which would leave her percentage of profit unchanged for each final product. This would involve recomputing the prices of each product, weighting each input ingredient by its new cost, and by the quantity of each contained in the final product. This is impossible to do for each product, at each location, daily on a manual basis.

Alternatives

The accounting firm is about to install a large business microcomputer system. Sally is considering several possibilities to reduce her current costs for the financial statements and to augment the quality and quantity of management information she receives:

a. Continuing as at present.
b. Using the microcomputer installed by the accounting firm.
c. Purchasing her own microcomputer.
d. Using an established EDP service or bank for all or part of the desired applications.
e. Using a service until she has two more restaurants in operation, then switching to her own computer system.

Questions

1. What kinds of information are essential for Sally to decide among these alternatives?

2. Suppose Sally's good fortune does not continue, and she is forced to continue with only four restaurants indefinitely. Which alternative offers the best protection against this contingency?

3. Suppose, on the other hand, that she fares exceptionally well and has 10 restaurants within five years. How might she provide for this possibility in terms of data processing?

PROGRESSIVE ELECTRONICS

Background

Progressive Electronics manufacturers and assembles computer components to order for many large and small companies who sell computer systems to the general public. Over the past seven years the company has risen from obscurity to the third-largest employer in its metropolitan area, counting the most famous names in the data processing industry among its faithful clientele. The principal impetus to Progressive's success has been its founder and president, Jim Saraceno, who came out of retirement with the idea for the business. Jim and his son, Leonard, have backgrounds in diverse industries, but it was Jim's 20-year stint with a major electronics manufacturer which provided much of the technological foundation for the processes to be used. Jim and Leonard carefully chose a group of well-trained young executives to manage the major functions of the organization—marketing, accounting, production, research, finance, and engineering—on a relatively autonomous basis.

Within two years of its inception, Progressive was backlogged with orders for lots of hundreds of custom keyboards and circuit boards. The fledgling company was full of enthusiasm but inundated with paperwork. It was virtually impossible to find out where, in the two-block-square assembly facility, the lot ordered by a particular customer might be, or how soon it would be completed. Quality control was done by cursory visual inspection and tedious testing of every tenth unit in a lot. Whenever a customer wished to add to an existing order or reorder a previous item, a new bill of materials had to be handwritten, repriced, and reextended before the customer could be given a firm quotation. Some customers elected not to wait for the recalculation, while others received bargain prices, to Progressive's chagrin, because of the long and inflation-plagued lead time between placing the order, sending the quotation to the customer, purchasing the raw materials, paying for them, and ultimately delivering the finished product to the customer. Although many customers ordered according to a fairly predictable pattern, Progressive did not have the facilities to forecast the timing and quantity of new orders from established accounts. Since many of the persons employed in the manufacturing and assembly areas were low-paid unskilled workers, turnover was high and the paperwork costs of maintaining payroll records equally so. New requirements by the U.S. government requiring all employers in Progressive's size class to maintain statistics and prepare periodic reports showing the job class, wage or salary history, promotion history, and minority group status of each employee precipitated the decision to obtain a computer system.

Despite the fact that Progressive had always been closely tied to the EDP industry because of the nature of its products, its management knew virtually nothing about the procedure for selecting and implementing a computer system. Jim used a local placement agency to hire a data processing manager, to whom he gave free rein in choosing a computer system for Progressive. The data processing manager had considerable previous experience in programming but little background in systems analysis and none at all in equipment and software acquisition. He was persuaded to rent one of the largest systems in the product line of a major EDP systems manufacturer, on the grounds that, if Progressive continued to grow at the rate it had for the past two years, a smaller system would be outgrown in a matter of a year or two.

The circle of executives responsible for the major functional areas soon realized that the newly hired data processing manager was not conversant with their problems and did not have the systems analysis skills requisite to remedying them. As a result the large computer system was scarcely used at all, and when the one-year trial rental period had elapsed, Jim fired the data processing manager and returned the computer to the vendor.

The Current Situation

In spite of having been badly burned in the EDP area, Jim acknowledged that his paperwork problems could not feasibly be corrected using a manual system. He decided that the conservative strategy, consistent with his policy of autonomy on the part of the functional area managers, would be to install the smallest possible business computer system that would handle basic accounting functions, and then to permit the managers of the various functional areas to order their own small computers to handle their own specific data processing problems.

The engineering manager purchased a microcomputer which created patterns for printed circuits via an analog-digital conversion device. The production manager purchased a small minicomputer which performed very rudimentary quality control on a go-no go basis for every item in every lot, a big improvement over the previous selective quality control system in terms of reliability. The controller, who is the chief accounting officer of the firm, supervised the small business computer system and the single programmer/analyst/operator who served as Progressive's data processing staff. The vendor of the small business computer system also rented an accounting package to Progressive: This package permitted the company to perform accounts receivable, accounts payable (but without forecast of cash requirements by due date, which the finance manager felt was the reason discounts were rarely taken), simple sales analysis, simple inventory control, and payroll. The package did not contain any manufacturing software such as Material Requirements Planning or Critical Path Scheduling programs, but the other applications occupied a full shift on the small business computer, including data entry time. Payroll could not be accommodated on the small business computer system because of lack of time, so that application was farmed out to a local data processing service.

Within the accounting department a clerk responsible for each specific function would perform data entry on the computer for that function as well as run reports pertaining to that application. Thus, for example, the accounts receivable clerk went daily to the data processing room, selected a diskette from an open tub file, placed the diskette in the computer, and posted payments and new charges; monthly she ran an aged trial balance, compared it against the daily invoice and payments registers, and ran customer statements. Since the computer was too small to support terminals, the clerks had to be present in the data processing area in order to perform these necessary functions. On any particular day, perhaps half a dozen clerks representing half a dozen subsidiary accounting tasks might come to the data processing room and access the computer to perform their tasks. Although the manufacturing and assembly areas of the building were open for second- and third-shift work, the data processing facility was closed.

Approximately one year after the installation of the small business computer, the accounting workload became too heavy for the single-shift operation of the data processing system. In order to minimize conversion problems, Jim and Leonard decided to rent a second, identical small business computer and place it in the data processing room next to the original system. The tub file containing the diskettes which could be used equally well by either system was placed between them, in the aisle used by the clerks, for convenience. The service bureau continued to process the payroll.

During this period the programmer/analyst/operator perceived his role as speaking only when spoken to. He was acutely aware of the untimely demise of his predecessor and confined himself to dealing with the operating system and utilities, diagnosing hardware problems and contacting the service representative, diagnosing and repairing bugs in the software packages, supervising operations, and writing short special programs on demand. One such program which was requested by the controller was a comparative analysis of the actual expenditure versus the budgeted expenditure for each account in the chart of accounts, using both absolute and percentage amounts for each quarter, year-to-date, the same quarter last year, and by last year to this date. While this information might have appeared on a single line of 132-column-width computer paper for each account, the controller insisted that the report give each account a separate page in the report. There were 1,903 accounts in the chart of accounts, the report was to be printed monthly, and a copy was to be distributed to each of the functional managers and to the Saracenos. Needless to say, none of these individuals found the time to peruse a report of roughly 2,000 pages on a monthly basis. Running the report on expensive eight-part paper required about 12 hours of computer time.

Conclusion

At this point all of the functional managers as well as top management are chagrined because they recognize that they continue to suffer a number of problems which might be alleviated by a computer. Yet they neither have the expertise to determine which applications might best be computerized, or how, nor do they want to relinquish their power and authority once again to a potentially incompetent stranger.

Files which reside on the fixed disk of one of the small business computer systems are inaccessible to the other system unless the file is first copied onto diskette and transported manually to the second system. There is no possibility of inquiry into files from remote locations. Payroll records maintained by the EDP service are not accessible by any medium except paper reports. Since a variety of individuals have access to the data processing room during the course of a day, there are many opportunities for unobserved sabotage and fraud. Also, no single individual is capable of interfacing several applications into an innovative management report, as would be possible in a data base management environment.

Discussion Questions

1. Suppose you could convince the controller that he should consider the principle of management by exception. You recommend an alternative to the 2,000-page comparative expense report as follows: print one line per account *only* for those accounts in which one or more of the differences exceeds 20 percent. Suppose that such accounts comprise 1/10 of all accounts, that it is possible to print 50 lines to a page, and that the speed of the printer is 150-lines-per-minute. How long will it take to print the exception report? Contrast this with the time required for the original report as the controller suggested it. Comment.

2. "Since even today the majority of data processing applications in business pertain to accounting, the only reasonable supervisor for a data processing center is the chief accounting officer of the company." Discuss.

3. "The proper role of a programmer/analyst is to execute the desires of the users of data processing who pay his/her salary. The analyst should not suggest alternatives." Do you agree? Why or why not?

4. "The managers of the functional areas know their own applications best and therefore, are best equipped to choose hardware and software which will perform these applications adequately." Discuss.

5. What arguments support the choice of Jim and Leonard to install two identical small business computer systems. What are the contrary arguments?

6. The first small business computer system installed by Progressive actually was idle during two thirds of its possible usage time (i.e., on the second and third shifts). Should this time have been fully utilized before considering a second system? Discuss.

7. Is it rational for one or more applications to be performed by an EDP service bureau when the company has an installed computer system? Comment.

HILLTOP COLLEGE

Background

Hilltop College, with an enrollment of about 10,000 students and a faculty of 400, occupies a pleasant location 20 miles from a medium-sized city. Many of the students commute from the city in the early morning by car or by bus, returning to their homes or jobs typically in the early afternoon. Another significant student population does not come to the campus at all, but attends evening classes at a downtown location. Bachelor's and Master's degree programs are offered in the liberal arts and sciences as well as in professional specializations such as business, education and social work.

Fifteen years ago Hilltop tried to use IBM punched card equipment to handle the major administrative functions of the college; included were admissions, registration, financial aid, payroll and personnel, planning and budgeting, and alumni relations. The punched card equipment was not adequate for the volume and complexity of the applications, so about 10 years ago, the college installed a very small IBM computer. The presence of a computer on the campus enabled the academic departments to begin to offer classes in programming and computer usage and also enabled faculty members to attempt some research projects which would be impossible without a computer. The small computer, too, was soon overloaded.

Coincidentally, a major computer vendor decided to discontinue its data processing manufacturing operations and closed out its existing computer inventory and base of installed accounts in a sale to another large vendor. This event enabled the college to lease at a rock-bottom cost a high-quality, medium-sized computer with a virtual memory operating system and the capacity to serve about 50 terminals as well as a large number of batch users. Although the hardware and the operating system were quite advanced for that time, the compilers, assemblers, and applications software available were of average quality. Since the vendor had assumed merely custodial care over this line of systems which would no longer be produced, the vendor did not find it cost effective to invest in upgrading the existing software. Thus, as the years went by, the system compared less and less favorably with others. In the meantime administrative users continued to request the development of new applications; and student and faculty users vastly increased in numbers, amount of computer time used, and sophistication of applications desired. Terminal ports and disk capacity on the system soon became scarce.

The campus data processing manager decided to deal with the situation in what he believed was the most expeditious manner: He negotiated a contract with the vendor to return the old system and substitute a larger system made by the new vendor which was, nevertheless, almost totally compatible with the software used on the old system. He did not perform a feasibility study nor solicit competitive bids in any systematic and rational way. Conversion to the new system was accomplished in a two-week period between summer session and the beginning of classes in the Fall. Almost no reprogramming was required, and the presence of the new system was transparent to users. When the new system was installed, however, it became clear that many of the preexisting problems would not automatically disappear. Disk space was soon in short supply again. Terminal capacity had not increased, and terminals actually seemed to run more slowly under the new operating system. There was little, if any, improvement in software on the new system.

Since the vendor with whom the college dealt was "bundled," that is, software and some services were included in the lease price of the hardware, the data processing manager urged administrative users to take advantage of a data base management system available for the new computer, as an alternative to batch reports which took several days to prepare, which had high paper costs, and which were relatively inconvenient for clerks and managers to reference in processing inquiries. At this point a school year ended and the data processing manager retired.

User Problems

When Steve Montague took over as data processing manager for Hilltop College, he knew from prior experience as a systems analyst that his first task should be to contact users of Hilltop's computer system and solicit their views on its current status, as well as their plans and desires for the future. He was surprised at the wealth of unforeseen problems which he had inherited! For example:

- Students who were taking a class in a programming language such as COBOL, RPG, BASIC, or FORTRAN found that the version of these languages available on Hilltop's system often compared unfavorably with that described in their textbooks in terms of versatility, compatibility, clarity of error diagnostics, and freedom from compiler bugs.

- Computer Services retained only one full-time programmer/analyst for academic purposes. This person was expected to schedule and perform design and coding of new computer programs for research and classroom use, modify existing programs for those purposes, assist with the design and execution of statistical studies using the computer, advise on operating system instructions, and teach individuals and small groups to use specific system features. Those who sought his advice came from disciplines as diverse as biology, sociology, business, and industrial technology. There was no way he could have sufficient time or expertise to cope with his assigned workload.

- Since the installed mainframe computer was used by very few four-year colleges and universities with research as a principal endeavor, much of the software desired for research purposes was not available, or would have to undergo extensive modification to run on the installed system. Computer Services refused to consider this in recommending the transition from the old system to the new. Many faculty members felt that a thorough market search and feasibility study would have shown that software superiority of equipment from other vendors should have outweighed ease of conversion in the choice of a new system.

- In spite of the burgeoning popularity of microcomputers and their increasing presence around the campus in various departments, Computer Services did not attempt to facilitate the use of these systems not just as small stand-alone systems but as intelligent terminals which could perform information transfers to and from the mainframe at high speed and which could enable offline editing and utility operations. It was nearly impossible to discern the telecommunications hardware and software which would make such a network practical.

- Batches of records sent by administrative offices to Computer Services were returned with an inordinately high frequency of erroneous changes, failures to add records, and failures to delete records.

- Faculty, student, and administrative computer users voiced complaints that:

    1. There was no organized and consistent vehicle for communicating and resolving problems between Computer

Services management, staff, and users; user input was never solicited.

2. Computer Services often did not follow through on the solution of problems called to its attention.

3. Computer Services' hiring practices were mysterious, although occasionally college faculty were asked to review applications for selected positions.

4. Computer Services seemed to take the attitude that users were ignorant nuisances who should be made to conform to the convenience of the data processing staff, rather than equal partners in a venture of great importance.

After accumulating the above points of view, Steve returned, with some trepidation, to his office to speak with his staff and decide how to proceed.

Discussion Questions

1. Compare the situation at Hilltop College with conditions at your college or university, to the extent that you have such information. You might consider issues such as:
    a. Turnaround time for the typical student job.
    b. Apparent quality and quantity of software.
    c. Accessibility of computer time, file storage space, and terminals to students.
    d. Quality and quantity of consulting services.

2. Define the tasks of a data processing manager. Would these vary depending on whether the organization were profit oriented, such as a business, or service oriented, such as a college? Discuss.

3. Many colleges have separate computer facilities for academic (i.e., faculty and student) and administrative usage. To what extent do you feel that such an arrangement would improve or worsen conditions at Hilltop College? Explain.

4. Consider each problem mentioned in the case discussion on a separate basis and attempt to formulate one or more possible approaches to solving it. Be prepared to justify your recommendations. Then examine the list. Are any solutions in conflict with each other? If so, attempt to resolve them.

METROPOLITAN MOTORS

Background

Metropolitan Motors is a well-established dealership selling American-made automobiles in a fast-growing, progressive suburban area of a medium-sized city. Eighteen months ago the dealership was bought by Dave Allison. Since childhood, Dave has loved to work with cars. After completing a bachelor's degree in management, he was hired by a major oil company to travel to company stations and franchises to train service personnel in newly developed techniques, to demonstrate new parts and equipment, and to mediate disputes between customers and station managers regarding service. In this capacity Dave became adept not only at solving technical problems but also at interacting effectively with people.

Eventually Dave decided that he would prefer not to spend so much time on the road, so he opened a service station of his own. This was sufficiently successful that he soon had enough capital to start a diagnostic repair center at another location. As both businesses prospered, Dave became aware of the opportunity to acquire the Metropolitan Motors dealership. This transaction taxed his financial resources to the limit, and when Dave assumed the presidency of Metropolitan Motors, he was forced immediately to seek ways to cut costs, improve efficiency, and increase sales volume.

Data Processing Problems

Metropolitan Motors' previous owner had a long-term contract with one of only five nationwide data processing service companies which specialize in automobile dealership accounting. Dave's office staff entered transactions via a CRT which enabled the service to produce accounts receivable documents, including customer statements, a trial balance, and daily registers, as well as financial reports in the general ledger system, such as a balance sheet and an income statement. For this service Dave's contract called for a payment of $1,400 per month. The service center was located in a distant city, so several days elapsed between closing the books each month and receipt of statements to be verified and mailed to customers. Also, balancing entries to general ledger accounts had to be posted separately, leading to data entry errors and eventual out-of-balance controls.

While accounts payable consisted primarily of payments to the parent automobile manufacturer and payroll accounting involved only 15 employees, inventory control represented a very real cost problem which potentially might be alleviated by an expanded use of data processing. Dave carried about 10,000 different types of parts and final products in inventory. He often found himself out of stock of what he needed, thus losing a sale or incurring customer displeasure and mechanic idle time while awaiting a special order of the part, at higher unit cost. Similarly, Dave unwittingly carried some very expensive parts which remained unsold for long periods, occasionally until they were rendered obsolete by an improved version. Sales slips for parts customers were handwritten by the parts clerk who had to look up the price of each item sold, calculate the extensions, sales tax, and total manually. This procedure was time-consuming and error-prone.

Dave believed that a computer could provide him with valuable information on the relationship between new and used-car inventory levels and sales, so that he could optimize his expenditure on flooring costs (opportunity cost of capital invested in cars in stock plus cost of space to store and display the cars). He also felt that the service reminders routinely mailed by other dealers at three-month intervals after the sale of a car would generate a great deal of service business.

Metropolitan Motors often obtained financing for new car customers through the auto manufacturer's credit subsidiary. A clerk prepared each installment contract individually, taking pains to change the variable parameters of customer name, type of vehicle, down payment, length of contract, nominal interest rate, actual interest paid over the life of the contract, and trade-in, if any. Similar contracts were prepared for the customer who elected to lease rather than buy his or her vehicle. The clerk was forced to obtain portions of this information from installment payment tables or through use of a hand calculator, with a very high error rate on a legally binding contract. Dave hoped that the word processing, table lookup, and calculation capabilities of a computer might alleviate this burdensome paperwork.

Evaluation of Alternatives

Dave was acutely aware of his lack of knowledge of data processing, but he was equally aware that Metropolitan's current EDP situation exhibited a number of deficiencies which were costing him lost sales, clerical time, and cash tied up in receivables and inventories, as well as the out-of-pocket cost of the EDP service. He had an acquaintance, Joe Meade, who had spent several years as a systems analyst with a large local bank but who had recently decided to retire to his farm. In lieu of a consulting fee, Dave agreed to permit Joe to use the computer or service to do the minimal recordkeeping needed by the farm. Also, Dave accepted the condition that Joe would be available for consulting only during the farming off-season, October through March. Dave resolved to concern himself as little as possible with the computer situation. He insisted, "My business is cars, not computers!"

Three months after taking control of Metropolitan, Dave reviewed his EDP options with Joe. They considered the use of a local EDP service for either batch or online input and output. The batch option was discarded because it would not permit the preparation of the purchase and lease financing agreements and the printing of sales slips for parts customers. The online option was also eliminated because Dave feared that his competitors might find a way to acquire online access to his privileged information despite the precautions taken by the EDP service.

The only alternative remaining was the acquisition of an in-house computer system. Joe was not particularly familiar with microcomputers, minicomputers, and small business computers, since the bank used a large mainframe with intelligent terminals. He did suggest to Dave that he contact several of the largest computer manufacturers with offices in his city, as well as a local microcomputer store and three minicomputer companies. The systems proposed by the large manufacturers all were beyond the price which Dave had decided he could afford, while the microcomputers did not have adequate direct-access capacity to keep his parts inventory online at all times for potential parts sales, and they were quite slow at retrieval of price information. The minicomputer vendors told Dave and Joe that they sold and serviced equipment exclusively, and that lease arrangements were to be made through a third-party leasing agent, while software was to be custom-written or procured and installed by someone else. However, the minicomputer vendors introduced Dave and Joe to an "OEM," a vendor-licensed original equipment manufacturer's representative who was based locally. The OEM representative was conversant with the details of the vendor's hardware, had access to software packages, and had some programming expertise. (In this limited search Dave never made contact with the vendor of minicomputers with the largest market share both nationally and locally because Joe had not heard of it.)

Although Dave was a member of an auto dealers' association, he was unable to determine the relative frequency of installation of computers within the group or their degree of satisfaction with various computer systems. Most dealers seemed to use their parent manufacturer's computer systems and packages or those of the five national service bureaus. Few had in-house computer systems.

Selection of a Vendor

One of the OEMs contacted was fairly new to the business. He offered Dave a bargain price for installation of a software package in exchange for his patience and, later, for his referrals. The minicomputer itself was to be a system with one CRT, one 30-character-per-second serial printer, 64K words of memory, one fixed hard-disk unit, and one diskette unit, at a price of $30,000. Over a five-year lease period the estimated monthly cost of hardware would be $500, while a single-shift, five-day-a-week service contract would cost an additional $250 per month. The OEM offered a complete standard billing, accounts receivable, accounts payable, payroll, inventory, sales analysis and general ledger accounting package for $10,000, with modifications to be made on-site by the OEM to meet the specific requirements of the dealership. The operating system, BASIC interpreter, and utility programs were provided at nominal cost by the mainframe manufacturer.

Dave was thrilled with the potential savings compared with the service bureau fee! He further envisioned usage of the computer for the accounting work of his service station and repair facility.

The system was ordered in late November, with an anticipated delivery date of April 1. Dave was anxious to get the new system into operation, discontinue the service bureau, and proceed with the service reminder and forecasting application development. Furthermore, he was concerned that Joe would be busy with farm work just at the time when the system was due to be installed. He asked the OEM to expedite delivery of the system, but that was not possible due to previous commitments by the manufacturer.

Since the OEM did not own a computer system nor have access to one, new program development and modification of the software package had to be deferred until Dave's system arrived. Although he had never before installed a business data processing system (his only prior customer was a medical partnership), he assured Dave that the modifications would be minor and the system completed very quickly.

Preinstallation Site Planning

Since the profit-making areas of the dealership were the showroom floor, and the parts and the service departments, those areas were quite expansive while the office space was very limited. For purposes of control Dave and Joe thought it was desirable not to have the computer located in the show-room, where sales representatives and customers might be tempted to access files without proper authorization or disrupt operations by pushing random buttons. Dave and Joe originally decided to locate the system in a corner of the service department. They did not envision the downtime of the system and destruction of files potentially generated by a dirty environment in which spray painting, soldering and welding were commonplace. Likewise, they did not consider installing separate supplementary electrical wiring and air conditioning to enhance the prospects for smooth operation of the system.

The CRT terminal remaining from the service bureau system was to be placed in the parts department to handle customer inquiries, with the printer adjacent to prepare on-the-spot parts invoices for customers.

Arrival of the Computer

On April 1 the manufacturer delivered the computer system as promised. Even during the initial setup and diagnostic checking of the system by the manufacturer's service representatives it became apparent that the service area chosen to house the computer would not be at all satisfactory. After some hasty reorganization and remodeling the system was moved to the office. Only the CRT and printer were left in the parts department since this was absolutely necessary.

When the OEM attempted to install the accounting package, he found that the programs had many bugs and those which did run often operated differently than the operating manual (obtained from the software house) indicated they should run. He spent about two months attempting to repair these deficiencies, only to find that the software house had made an error; they had shipped an obsolete version of the program package along with the latest operating manual. The latest version of the package was shipped and ran much the same as the version modified at great pains by the OEM.

The OEM was proud and happy to demonstrate the package to Dave (by this time Joe was in the fields planting his Spring crops). Dave was dismayed to find that the package had been designed for a wholesaler, whereas his operations were much more similar to those of a retailer (auto and parts sales) or a manufacturer (service department pricing of custom jobs and maintenance of raw materials, in-process, and finished goods inventories). The parts manager complained that the package did not provide space for alternative parts prices for different classes of customers (e.g., retail, wholesale to service stations and other dealerships, internal for used-car renovation, internal for new-car-warranty work, and internal for in-house service for retail customers). Furthermore, he argued, there were quite a few items which could be sold as a broken set on rare occasions, such as one brake shoe, but the computer inventory carried the items as units of pairs. The OEM estimated that provision for the extra prices and extra items would require 400K of extra disk space as well as substantial modification to the programs which accessed the inventory file.

Dave also discovered that it was impossible to create parts invoices on demand whenever a customer or a Metropolitan service employee needed parts, and still use the computer for printing of reports, checks, or other documents. The problem was that forms for parts invoices had to be in the printer at all times in anticipation of the arrival of a customer. Batch runs such as printing of payroll checks required other forms and their control totaling mechanisms dictated that they could not be interrupted to process a parts order. Similarly, the CRT in the parts department was very inconvenient for input of other data or usage by the OEM for program debugging or development. While program debugging and development could feasibly take place on a second shift, the production of sensitive reports or negotiable documents after hours should have the attention of an operator. It was apparent that a second terminal with printing capability was the best solution to these problems.

The OEM found that the manufacturer of the computer system did not have any printing terminals in stock at this time.

Since the problem was an immediate one, he ordered a different brand of terminal from a local supplier. When he attempted to interface this terminal with the existing computer system, he found that it did not operate properly. The terminal supplier's service representative claimed that the terminal was in perfect working order, and that the defect was in the computer system hardware or software. The service representative of the computer company retorted that it was the fault of the new terminal. After weeks of delays it was found that the existing version of the operating system would not support a multiprogrammed environment with more than one terminal. An augmented version of the operating system was ordered, and when it would not run, it became necessary to order an additional 32K of memory to accommodate it.

At this point the OEM had spent far more time than he had anticipated would be necessary to install Metropolitan's applications successfully. He was eager to begin the search for new prospects to alleviate his own cash problems. On the other hand Dave wanted the OEM to continue working at his location until all problems were resolved. The fixed fee paid to the OEM had been paid many months before. The OEM wanted more money and Dave was adamant about making no further payments. An appeal to the computer manufacturer drew the reply that it had no responsibility for problems with software which it did not provide. Nevertheless, when Dave threatened to announce his dissatisfaction with that company's operating system—and licensed OEM—to auto dealers nationwide via their trade publications, and to all local businesses through meetings of the Chamber of Commerce, the vendor relented and sent its own systems engineer to interface the terminals, main memory, and operating system properly. It further advised the OEM that his license would be revoked unless he completed Metropolitan's applications packages within a reasonable time.

Ongoing Operations

After making lease payments on an installed system for nine months with little productive output, Metropolitan finally could boast an accurate parts inventory system, customer statements and financial reports. The national EDP service was discontinued. However, the auto manufacturer sent Metropolitan an updated price list for parts every three months. It required about five working days to enter the new prices, excluding correction of any data entry errors detected later, and tied up the office terminal for the duration. An inquiry to the headquarters of the auto manufacturer produced the response that the prices could be provided on magnetic tape as an alternative to the printed list. Metropolitan's computer system did not have a tape drive, though, and acquisition of a single drive would cost $12,000.

Dave contacted several local data processing services to find out whether they could convert magnetic tape records to diskette records for input to his computer system. Most did not have that capability, and the two which responded affirmatively said a special program would have to be written to handle this rare application. Dave also would have to engage a programmer to write a program to read the diskettes and update the parts master file. Unfortunately, Dave corresponded with the auto manufacturer's headquarters at this time was informed that no one expect the five national services and the dealerships themselves was permitted to handle the parts price updates. The manual updating system remains in effect.

Security and Backup

Metropolitan backs up its data files by copying all records on the fixed disk onto diskettes once a week. All documents which caused the updating of files during the week are preserved until the following week's backup is completed. The process of copying records onto diskettes is slow and tedious—it degrades the operation of the terminals during prime system time or necessitates overtime and requires a dozen diskettes to complete the process. For that reason backup at more frequent intervals has not been considered. When a system "crash" occurs and the backup/restart process has to be initiated, an average of one day has been required to return the system to its status just prior to the crash. The magnetic tape drive which was contemplated to read the parts updates would expedite backup considerably. The only other alternative is to install a second hard-disk unit with removable packs, a much more expensive alternative than the tape unit but also more versatile one.

The Present and Future

As of this time Dave has learned a great deal about data processing. He supervises computer activities closely and performs some programming and operations himself. With the assistance of a part-time programmer he is developing the service reminder and financing applications which were not part of the original package obtained and modified by the OEM. Dave hopes to advertise and sell the extensively modified package with the additional applications to other auto dealers to defray his development costs, but he is still unsure of his legal right to do so.

In addition to the $30,000 of computing equipment originally proposed to him by the OEM, Dave had bought a printing terminal and associated coupling devices at a cost of $3,000 and 32K of additional memory at a cost of $5,000. He has spent $5,000 for a part-time programmer and paid an additional $5,000 to the OEM over and above the original $10,000 in the contract in order to induce him to spend the time to modify the package properly. The accounting system and operations have been in disarray for about a year, and he has invested virtually every weekend of his own time in attempts to make the computer system work. He has come to realize why most auto dealers use the national services and very few have in-house computer systems, but he is confident that he has the resources to provide them that option now. He will soon embark on the automation of the record-keeping systems of the service station and the diagnostic repair facility, this time with a wealth of data processing experience behind him.

Discussion Questions

1. Should Dave have been more thoroughly acquainted with the automobile dealership business before deciding to abandon the data processing service? Discuss.

2. What sources of data processing information might Dave have explored before making his decision to acquire the computer?

3. What activities should have been undertaken by the staff of Metropolitan Motors before selecting a computer system?

4. How do you feel about Dave's desire to concern himself as little as possible with the computer?

5. What activities should have taken place between the time the system was ordered and when it was delivered?

6. What questions should Dave have asked the data processing equipment vendor? the OEM?

7. Discuss the advantages and disadvantages of a data processing system comprised of components manufactured by more than one vendor.

8. Would you accept Dave's solution to the parts update problem? Discuss.

9. Dave keeps his backup diskettes on the shelf next to the computer

for convenience. Do you approve of this procedure? Why or why not?

10. Are you as skeptical as Dave about the privacy provided by a local data processing service? What types of system controls might be implemented to ensure privacy?

11. Many microcomputer and minicomputer systems are advertised on a "turnkey" basis. That is, the vendors claim that once a package is installed, no further programming is needed and only a clerk/operator is required to implement the system. Do you agree? Why or why not?

Bibliography of Recommended Reading

The Computer Revolution and Society

Arbib, Michael A. *Computers and the Cybernetic Society*. New York: Academic Press, 1977.

Forester, Tom. *The Microelectronics Revolution*. Cambridge: MIT Press, 1981.

Osborne, Adam. *Running Wild: The Next Industrial Revolution*. Berkeley, Calif.: Osborne/McGraw-Hill, 1979.

Sanders, Donald H., and Stanley J. Birkin. *Computers and Management in a Changing Society*. 3d ed. New York: McGraw-Hill, 1980.

Toffler, Alvin. *The Third Wave*. New York: William Morrow, 1980.

Microcomputer Systems

Givone, Donald D., and Robert P. Roesser. *Microprocessors/Microcomputers: An Introduction*. New York: McGraw-Hill, 1980.

McGlynn, Daniel R. *Personal Computing: Home, Professional and Small Business Applications*. New York: John Wiley & Sons, 1979.

Sippl, Charles J. *Microcomputer Handbook*. New York: Petrocelli/Charter, 1977.

Zaks, Rodney. *An Introduction to Personal and Business Computing*. Berkeley, Calif.: Sybex, 1978.

Software and Programming Languages

Brady, Alan H., and James T. Richardson. *BASIC Programming Language*. rev. ed. Homewood: Learning Systems Company, 1981.

Bux, William E. and Edward C. Cunningham. *RPG and RPG II Programming: Applied Fundamentals*. Englewood Cliffs, N.J.: Prentice-Hall, 1980.

Freeman, Peter. *Software Systems Principles*. Chicago: Science Research Associates, 1975.

Graham, Neill. *Introduction to Pascal*. St. Paul: West Publishing, 1980.

Grauer, Robert T. *COBOL: A Vehicle for Information Systems*. Englewood Cliffs, N.J.: Prentice-Hall, 1981.

Hughes, Joan K. *PL/1 Programming*. New York: John Wiley & Sons, 1973.

Peterson, W. Wesley. *Introduction to Programming Languages*. Englewood Cliffs, N.J.: Prentice-Hall, 1974.

Khailany, Asad. *Business Programming in FORTRAN IV and ANSI FORTRAN 77: A Structured Approach*. Englewood Cliffs, N.J.: Prentice-Hall, 1981.

Stair, Ralph M. Jr. *Programming in BASIC*. Homewood, Ill.: Richard D. Irwin, 1979.

Wiedmann, Clark. *Handbook of APL Programming*. New York: Petrocelli Books, 1974.

Data Communications

Chorafas, Dimitris N. *Computer Networks for Distributed Information Systems*. New York: Petrocelli, 1980.

Sherman, Kenneth. *Data Communications: A User's Guide*. Reston, Va.: Reston Publishing, 1981.

Techo, Robert. *Data Communications: An Introduction to Concepts and Design*. New York: Plenum Press, 1980.

Distributed Processing

Catzan, Harry Jr. *Distributed Information Systems*. New York: Petrocelli, 1979.

Breslin, Judson, and C. Bradley Tashenberg. *Distributed Processing Systems: End of the Main Frame Era?* New York: ANACOM, 1978.

Thierauf, Robert J. *Distributed Processing Systems*. Englewood Cliffs, N.J.: Prentice-Hall, 1978.

Data Base Systems

Cardenas, Alfonso F. *Data Base Management Systems*. Boston: Allyn & Bacon, 1979.

Kroenke, David. *Database Processing*. Chicago: Science Research Associates, 1977.

Martin, James. *An End-User's Guide to Data Base*. Englewood Cliffs, N.J.: Prentice-Hall, 1981.

Word Processing Systems

Bergerud, Marly, and Jean Gonzalez. *Word/Information Processing Concepts: Careers, Technology, and Applications*. New York: John Wiley & Sons, 1981.

Cecil, Paula P. *Word Processing in the Modern Office*. 2d ed. Menlo Park, Calif.: Benjamin/Cummings Publishing, 1980.

Kleinschrod, Walter A. *Managements Guide to Word Processing.* Chicago: The Dartnell Corporation, 1981.

Management Information and Decision Support Systems

Alter, Steven. *Decision Support Systems: Current Practice and Continuing Challenges.* Menlo Park, Calif.: Addison-Wesley Publishing, 1980.

Burch, John G. Jr.; Felix R. Strater; and Gary Grudnitski. *Information Systems: Theory and Practice.* 2d ed. New York: John Wiley & Sons, 1979.

Davis, Gordon B. *Management Information Systems: Conceptual Foundations, Structure, and Development.* New York: McGraw-Hill, 1974.

Keen, Peter, and Michael Scott Morton. *Decision Support Systems: An Organizational Perspective.* Menlo Park: Addison-Wesley Publishing, 1978.

Lucas, Henry C. Jr. *Information Systems Concepts for Management.* New York: McGraw-Hill, 1978.

Murdick, Robert G. *MIS Concepts and Design.* Englewood Cliffs, N.J.: Prentice-Hall, 1980.

Systems Analysis and Design

Awad, Elias M. *Systems Analysis and Design.* Homewood, Ill.: Richard D. Irwin, 1979.

Demarco, Tom. *Structured Analysis and System Specification.* Englewood Cliffs, N.J.: Prentice-Hall, 1981.

Fitzgerald, Jerry; Ardra F. Fitzgerald; and Warren D. Stallings, Jr. *Fundamentals of Systems Analysis.* New York: John Wiley & Sons, 1981.

Lucas, Henry C. Jr. *The Analysis, Design, and Implementation of Information Systems.* New York: McGraw-Hill, 1981.

Business Computer Applications

Bodnar, George H. *Accounting Information Systems.* Boston: Allyn & Bacon, 1980.

Eliason, Alan L., and Kent D. Kitts. *Business Computer Systems and Applications.* 2d ed. Chicago: Science Research Associates, 1979.

Meek, Brian L., and Simon Fairthorne. *Using Computers.* London: Ellis Horwood, Limited, 1977.

Managing Computer Resources

Johnson, James R. *Managing For Productivity in Data Processing.* Wellesley, Mass.: Q.E.D. Information Sciences, 1981.

Norton, David, and Kenneth Rau. *A Guide to EDP Performance Management.* Wellesley, Mass.: Q.E.D. Information Sciences, 1979.

Perry, William F. *Computer Control and Security: A Guide for Managers and Systems Analysts.* New York: John Wiley & Sons, 1981.

Glossary for
Computer Users

The following extensive glossary includes terms which are fundamental to effective understanding and communication between *business computer users* and *computer specialists*. Most definitions used are consistent with those published by several official sources. However, the form of such definitions is *not* designed to express exact standards for computer professionals, but to assist the beginning computer user in business.

Two major standard glossaries are:

- American National Standards Institute, *American National Dictionary for Information Processing* (New York: Computer and Business Equipment Manufacturers Association, 1977).
- Martin H. Weik, *Standard Dictionary of Computers and Information Processing,* rev. 2d ed. (Rochelle Park, N.J.: Hayden Book, 1977).

Absolute Address. An address that is permanently assigned by the computer designer to a particular physical storage location.

Access Method. A technique for moving data between primary storage and input/output and secondary storage devices.

Access Time. The time interval between the instant that the CPU requests a transfer of data to or from a storage device and the instant such an operation is completed.

Accumulator. A register in which the results of arithmetic or logic operations are formed.

Acoustic Coupler. A modem which converts digital data into a sequence of tones which are transmitted by a conventional telephone hand set to a receiving modem which transforms the data back to digital form.

Ada. A programming language named after Augusta Ada Byron, considered the world's first computer programmer. Developed in 1980 for the U.S. Department of Defense as a standard high-order language. It resembles an extension of Pascal.

Address. A name, number, or code that identifies a particular location in storage or any other data source or destination.

Address Modification. The process of altering the address portion of a machine instruction.

ADP. Automatic Data Processing. Data processing performed by electronic or electrical machines with a minimum of human assistance or intervention. The term is applied to both electro-mechanical punched card data processing and electronic data processing.

ALGOL. ALGOrithmic Language. An international procedure-oriented language that is widely used in Europe. Like FORTRAN it was designed primarily for scientific-mathematical applications.

Algorithm. A set of well-defined rules or processes for the solution of a problem in a finite number of steps.

Alphanumeric. Pertaining to a character set that contains letters of the alphabet, numeric digits, and special characters such as punctuation marks. Also called alphameric.

Analog Computer. A computer that operates on data by measuring changes in continuous physical variables, such as voltage, resistance, and rotation. Contrast with Digital Computer.

APL. A Programming Language. A mathematically oriented language originated by Kenneth E. Iverson of IBM. Real-time and interactive versions of APL are being utilized in many time-sharing systems.

Application Development System. A system of computer programs which provides interactive assistance to programmers in the development of application programs.

Arithmetic-Logic Unit (ALU). The unit of a computing system that contains the circuits that perform arithmetic and logical operations.

Array. An arrangement of elements in one or more dimensions.

Artificial Intelligence (AI). The capability of a computer to perform functions that are normally associated with human intelligence such as reasoning, learning, and self-improvement.

ASCII. American Standard Code for Information Interchange. A standard code used for information interchange among data processing systems, communication systems, and associated equipment. The coded character set consists of seven-bit coded characters (eight-bits including a parity check bit.)

Assemble. To translate a symbolic language program into a machine language program by substituting absolute operation codes for symbolic operation codes and absolute or relocatable addresses for symbolic addresses.

Assembler. A computer program that assembles.

Assembler Language. A programming language that utilizes symbols to represent operation codes and storage locations. Also called a symbolic language.

Associative Storage. A storage device in which storage locations are identified by their contents, not by names or positions.

Asynchronous. Involving a sequence of operations without a regular or predictable time relationship. Thus, operations do not happen at regular timed intervals, but an operation will begin only after a previous operation is completed. In data transmission, involves the use of start and stop bits with each character to indicate the beginning and end of the character being transmitted.

Audio-Response Unit. An output device of a computer system whose output consists of the spoken word. Also called a voice synthesizer.

Audit Trail. The presence of data processing media and procedures which allow a transaction to be traced through all stages of data processing, beginning with its appearance on a source document and ending with its transformation into information on a final output document.

Automated Office Systems. Automated systems which combine word processing, data processing, telecommunications, and information systems technologies which automate much office activity. Also called electronic office or office-of-the-future systems.

Automatic Teller Machine (ATM). A special purpose intelligent terminal used to provide remote banking services.

Automation. The automatic transfer and positioning of work by machines or the automatic operation and control of a work process by machines, i.e., without significant human intervention or operation.

Auxiliary Operation. An off-line operation performed by equipment not under control of the central processing unit.

Auxiliary Storage. Storage that supplements the primary storage of the computer. Same as Secondary Storage.

Backend Processor. Typically a smaller general-purpose computer which is dedicated to data base processing using a data base management system (DBMS). Also called a data base machine.

Background Processing. The automatic execution of lower-priority computer programs when higher-priority programs are not using the resources of the computer system. Contrast with Foreground Processing.

Backup. Standby equipment or procedures for use in the event of failure, damage, or overloading of normally used equipment and facilities.

Bar Codes. Vertical marks or bars placed on merchandise, tags, or packaging which can be sensed and read by optical character reading devices. The width and combination of vertical lines are used to represent data.

Base Address. A given address from which an absolute address is derived by combination with a relative address.

BASIC. Beginners All-purpose Symbolic Instruction Code. A programming language developed at Dartmouth College which is widely utilized by time-sharing systems.

Batch Processing. A category of data processing in which data is accumulated into "batches" and processed periodically. Contrast with Realtime Processing.

Baud. A unit of measurement used to specify data transmission speeds. It is a unit of signaling speed equal to the number of discrete conditions or signal events per second. In many data communications applications it represents one bit per second.

Binary. Pertaining to a characteristic or property involving a selection, choice, or condition in which there are two possibilities, or pertaining to the number system which utilizes a base of two.

Bit. A contraction of "binary digit" which can have the value of either 0 or 1.

Block. A grouping of contiguous data records or other data elements which are handled as a unit.

Blocking. Combining several data records or other data elements into blocks in order to increase the efficiency of input, output, or storage operations.

Bootstrap. A technique in which the first few instructions of a program are sufficient to bring the rest of itself into the computer from an input device. Contrast with Initial Program Loader (IPL).

Branch. A transfer of control from one instruction to another in a computer program that is not part of the normal sequential execution of the instructions of the program.

Bubble Memory. See Magnetic Bubble Memory.

Buffer. Temporary storage used to compensate for a difference in rate of flow of data or time of occurrence of events when transmitting data from one device to another.

Bug. A mistake or malfunction.

Bundling. The inclusion of software, maintenance, training, and other EDP products or services in the price of a computer system.

Bus. A set of conducting paths for movement of data and instructions which interconnects the various components of the CPU. It may take the form of a cable containing many wires or of microscopic conducting lines on a microcomputer chip.

Business Data Processing. Use of automatic data processing in accounting or management.

Business Information System. Information systems within a business organization that support one of the traditional "functions of business," such as marketing, finance, production, etc. Business information systems can be either operational or management information systems.

Byte. A sequence of adjacent binary digits operated upon as a unit and usually shorter than a computer word. In many computer systems, a byte is a grouping of eight bits which can represent one alphabetic or special character or be "packed" with two decimal digits.

Cache Memory. A high-speed temporary storage area in the CPU for storing parts of a program or data during processing.

CAD. Computer Assisted Design. The use of computers and advanced graphics hardware and software to provide interactive design assistance for engineering and architectural design.

Calculator. A data processing device suitable for performing arithmetical operations which requires frequent intervention by a human operator.

Call. To transfer control to a subroutine.

CAM. Computer Aided Manufacturing. The use of minicomputers and other computers to automate the operational systems of a manufacturing plant.

Cathode Ray Tube (CRT). An electronic vacuum tube (television screen) which displays the output of a computer system.

Central Processing Unit (CPU). The unit of a computer system that includes the circuits which control the interpretation and execution of instructions. In many computer systems, the CPU includes the arithmetic-logic unit, the control unit, and primary storage unit. The CPU is also known as the central processor or the main frame.

Chain. A list of data records which are linked by means of pointers. Though the data records may be physically dispersed, each record contains an identifier by which the next record can be located.

Chaining. The use of a pointer in a record to indicate the address of another record that is logically related to the first.

Channel. A path along which signals can be sent. More specifically, a small special-purpose processor which controls the movement of data between the CPU and input/output devices.

Charge-Coupled Device (CCD). A slower serial access form of semiconductor memory which uses a silicone crystal's own structure to store data.

Check Bit. A binary check digit; for example, a parity bit.

Check Digit. A digit in a data field which is utilized to check for errors or loss of characters in the data field as a result of data transfer operations.

Check Point. A place in a program where a check or a recording of data for restart purposes is performed.

Clock. (1) A device that generates periodic signals utilized to control the timing of a synchronous computer. (2) A register whose content changes at regular intervals in such a way as to measure time.

COBOL. COmmon Business Oriented Language. A business data processing language.

CODASYL. COnference on DAta SYstems Languages. The group of representatives of users and computer manufacturers who developed and maintain the COBOL language.

Coding. Developing the programming language instructions which direct a computer to perform a data processing assignment.

Collate. To combine items from two or more ordered sets into one set having a specified order not necessarily the same as any of the original sets.

Communications Carrier. An organization which supplies communications services to other organizations and to the public as authorized by government agencies.

Communications Channel. That part of a communication system that connects the message source with the message receiver. It includes the physical equipment used to connect one location to another for the purpose of transmitting and receiving information. Frequently used as a synonym for communication link or communication line.

Communications Control Program. A computer program which controls and supports the communications between the computers and terminals in a data communications network.

Communications Controller. A data communications interface device (frequently a special-purpose mini or microcomputer) which can control a data communications network containing many terminals.

Communications Satellite. Earth satellites placed in stationary orbits above the equator which serve as relay stations for communications signals transmitted from earth stations.

Compile. To translate a high-level programming language into a machine language program.

Compiler. A program that compiles.

Computer. (1) A data processing device that can perform substantial computation, including numerous arithmetic or logic operations without intervention by a human operator during the processing. (2) An electronic device that has the ability to accept data, internally store, and execute a program of instructions, perform mathematical, logical, and manipulative operations on data, and report the results.

Computer Application. The use of a computer to solve a specific problem or to accomplish a particular job for a computer user. For example, common business computer applications include sales order processing, inventory control, and payroll.

Computer Assisted Instruction (CAI). The use of computers to provide drills, practice exercises, and tutorial sequences to students.

Computer Industry. The industry composed of firms which supply computer hardware, software, and EDP services.

Computer Program. A series of instructions or statements, in a form acceptable to a computer, prepared in order to achieve a certain result.

Computer Specialist. A person whose occupation is related to the providing of computer services in computer-using organizations or in the computer industry. For example, a systems analyst, programmer, computer operator, etc.

Computer System. Computer hardware and software as a system of input, processing, output, storage, and control components. Thus, a computer system consists of input and output devices, primary and secondary storage devices, the central processing unit, and the control units within the CPU and other peripheral devices. Computer software can also be considered as a system of programs concerned with input/output, storage, processing, and control.

Computer User. Anyone who uses a computer system or its output. Same as end user.

Concentrator. A special-purpose mini or microcomputer which accepts information from many terminals using slow-speed lines and transmits data to a main computer system over a high-speed line.

Conditional Transfer. A transfer of control in the execution of a computer program that occurs if specified criteria are met.

Console. That part of a computer used for communication between the operator and the computer.

Control. (1) The systems component that evaluates "feedback" to determine whether the system is moving toward the achievement of its goal and then makes any necessary adjustments to the input and processing components of the system to insure that proper output is produced. (2) Sometimes synonymous with feedback-control. (3) A management function that involves observing and measuring organizational performance and environmental activities and modifying the plans and activities of the organization when necessary.

Control Card. A punched card that contains input data required for a specific application of a general routine. For example, "job control cards" are a series of cards coded in "job control language" (JCL) which direct an operating system to load and begin execution of a particular program.

Control Program. A program that assists in controlling the operations and managing the resources of a computer system. It is usually part of an Operating System.

Control Unit. A subunit of the central processing unit which controls and directs the operations of the entire computer system. The control unit retrieves computer instructions in proper sequence, interprets each instruction, and then directs the other parts of the computer system in the implementation of a computer program.

Conversational Computing. A type of real-time processing involving frequent man-machine interaction. A dialogue occurs between a computer and a user, in which the computer directs questions and comments to the user in response to the questions, comments, and other input supplied by the user.

Counter. A device such as a register or storage location used to represent the number of occurrences of an event.

Cryogenics. The study and use of devices utilizing the properties of materials near absolute zero in temperature. The superconductive nature of such materials provide ultra high-speed computer logic and memory circuits.

Cursor. A moveable point-of-light displayed on most video display screens to assist the user in the input of data. The cursor may look like a dot or short underline or other shape that indicates the position of data to be entered or changed.

Cybernetic System. A system that uses feedback and control components to achieve a self-monitoring and self-regulating capability.

Cylinder. An imaginary vertical cylinder consisting of the vertical alignment of data tracks on each surface of magnetic disks which are accessed simultaneously by the read/write heads of a disk storage device.

Data. A representation of facts, concepts, or instructions in a formalized manner suitable for communication, interpretation, or processing by humans or machines.

Data Bank. (1) A comprehensive collection of libraries of data utilized by an organization. (2) A centralized common data base which supports several major information systems of an organization.

Data Base. A nonredundant collection of logically related records or files. A data base consolidates many records previously stored in separate files so that a common pool of data records serves as a single central file or data bank for many data processing applications.

Data Base Management System (DBMS). A generalized set of computer programs which control the creation, maintenance, and utilization of the data bases and data files of an organization.

Data Base Processing System. An electronic data processing system that uses a common data base for both the storage and processing of data.

Data Communications. Pertaining to the transmitting of data over electronic communication links between a computer system and a number of terminals at some physical distance away from the computer.

Data Communications System. An electronic data processing system that combines the capabilities of the computer with high-speed electrical and electronic communications.

Data Entry. The process of converting data into a form suitable for entry into a computer system. Also called data capture or input preparation.

Data Management. Control program functions which provide access to data sets, enforce data storage conventions, and regulate the use of input/output devices.

Data Medium. The material in or on which a specific physical variable may represent data.

Data Processing. The execution of a systematic sequence of operations performed upon data.

Data Processing System. A system which accepts data as input and processes it into information as output.

Debug. To detect, locate, and remove errors from a program or malfunctions from a computer.

Decision Support System (DSS). A management information system which utilizes decision rules, decision models, a comprehensive data base, and a decision maker's own insights in an interactive computer-based process leading to a specific decision by a specific decision maker.

Decision Table. A table of all contingencies that are to be considered in the description of a problem, together with the actions to be taken.

Dedicated Computer. Typically, a general purpose computer that has been "dedicated" or committed to a particular data processing task or application.

Diagnostics. Messages transmitted by a computer during language translation or program execution which pertain to the diagnosis or identification of errors in a program or malfunctions in equipment.

Digital Computer. A computer that operates on digital data by performing arithmetic and logical operations on the data. Contrast with Analog Computer.

Direct Access. Pertaining to the process of obtaining data from or placing data into storage where the time required for such access is independent of the location of the data. Synonymous with random access. Contrast with Serial Access.

Direct Access Storage Device (DASD). A storage device that can directly access data to be stored or retrieved. For example, a magnetic disk unit.

Direct Address. An address that specifies the storage location of an operand.

Direct Memory Access (DMA). A type of computer architecture in which intelligent components other than the CPU (such as a channel) can directly access data in main memory.

Disk Pack. A removable unit containing several magnetic disks which can be mounted on a magnetic disk storage unit.

Display. A visual presentation of data.

Distributed Data Bases. The concept of distributing data bases or portions of a data base at remote sites where the data is most frequently referenced. Sharing of data is made possible through a network which interconnects the distributed data bases.

Distributed Processing. Also called distributed data processing (DDP). A major form of decentralization of information processing made possible by a network of computers dispersed throughout an organization. Processing of user applications is accomplished by several computers interconnected by a data communication network rather than relying on one large centralized computer facility or on the decentralized operation of several completely independent computers.

Distributed Processing Network. A network of computers and intelligent terminals distributed throughout an organization. Basic network structures include the *star network,* in which end user computers are tied to a large central computer, and the *ring network,* where local computers are tied together on a more equal basis.

Document. A medium on which data has been recorded for human use, such as a report or invoice.

Documentation. A collection of documents or information which describes a computer program, information system, or required data processing operations.

Double Precision. Pertaining to the use of two computer words to represent a number.

Down Time. The time interval during which a device is malfunctioning or inoperative.

Dump. To copy the contents of all or part of a storage device, usually from an internal device onto an external storage device.

Duplex. In communications, pertaining to a simultaneous two-way independent transmission in both directions.

Duplicate. To copy so that the result remains in the same physical form as the source. For example, to make a new punched card with the same pattern of holes as an original punched card.

Dynamic Relocation. The movement of part or all of an active computer program and data from one part or type of storage to another without interrupting the proper execution of the program.

EBCDIC. Extended Binary Coded Decimal Interchange Code. An eight-bit code that is widely used by current computers.

Echo Check. A method of checking the accuracy of transmission of data in which the received data are returned to the sending device for comparison with the original data.

Edit. To modify the form or format of data; for example, to insert or delete characters such as page numbers or decimal points.

Effective Address. The address that is derived by applying indexing or indirect addressing rules to a specified address to form an address which is actually used to identify the current operand.

EFT. Electronic Funds Transfer. The development of banking and payment systems which transfer funds electronically instead of using cash or paper documents such as checks.

Electromechanical Data Processing. The use of electromechanical devices such as typewriters and calculators to process data into information.

Electronic Data Processing (EDP). The use of electronic computers to process data automatically.

Electronic Mail. The transmission, storage, and distribution of text material in electronic form over communications networks.

Emulation. To imitate one system with another so that the imitating system accepts the same data, executes the same programs, and achieves the same results as the imitated system. Contrast with Simulation.

Encription. To scramble data or convert it, prior to transmission, to a secret code that masks the meaning of the data to unauthorized recipients. Similar to encipher.

End User. See Computer User.

Enterprise System. An integrated system which merges electronic data processing, word processing, automated office systems, telecommunication systems, management information systems, and other computer-based information systems which support the modern organization or enterprise.

Ergonomics. The science and technology which emphasizes the safety, comfort, and ease of use of human-operated machines, such as computer video display terminals. The goal of ergonomics is to produce systems which are user friendly, i.e.

safe, comfortable, and easy to use. Ergonomics is frequently called human engineering.

Executive Routine. A routine that controls the execution of other routines. Synonymous with supervisory routine.

Facilities Management. The use of an external service organization to operate and manage the electronic data processing facilities of an organization.

Facsimile. The transmission of images and their reconstruction and duplication on some form of paper at a receiving station.

Feedback. (1) Information concerning the components and operations of a system. (2) The use of part of the output of a system as input to the system.

Feedback-Control. A systems characteristic that combines the functions of feedback and control. Information concerning the components and operations of a system (feedback) is evaluated to determine whether the system is moving toward the achievement of its goal, with any necessary adjustments being made to the system to insure that proper output is produced (control).

Fiber Optics. The technology which uses cables consisting of very thin filaments of glass fibers which can conduct the light generated by lasers at transmission frequencies that approach the speed of light.

Field. A subdivision of a data record that consists of a grouping of characters which describe a particular category of data. For example, a "name field" or a "sales amount field." Sometimes also called an item or word.

File. A collection of related data records treated as a unit. Sometimes called a data set.

File Label. A unique name or code that identifies a file.

File Maintenance. The activity of keeping a file up-to-date by adding, changing, or deleting data.

File Processing. Utilizing a file for data processing activities such as file maintenance, information retrieval, or report generation.

Firmware. The use of microprogrammed read-only memory modules in place of "hardwired" logic circuitry. See also microprogramming.

Fixed-Length Record. A data record that always contains the same number of characters or fields. Contrast with Variable-Length Record.

Fixed-Point. Pertaining to a positional representation in which each number is represented by a single set of digits, the position of the radix point being fixed with respect to one end of the set, according to some convention. Contrast with Floating-Point.

Fixed Word-Length. Pertaining to a computer word or operand that always has the same number of bits or characters. Contrast with Variable Word-Length.

Flag. Any of various types of indicators used for identification.

Flip-Flop. A circuit or device containing active elements, capable of assuming either one or two states at a given time. Synonymous with toggle.

Floating-Point. Pertaining to a number representation system in which each number is represented by two sets of digits. One set represents the significant digits or fixed-point "base" of the number, while the other set of digits represents the "exponent," which indicates the precision of the radix point.

Floppy Disk. A small plastic disk coated with iron oxide which resembles a small phonograph record enclosed in a protective envelope. It is a widely used form of magnetic disk media which provides a direct access storage capability for microcomputer and minicomputer systems.

Flowchart. A graphical representation in which symbols are used to represent operations, data, flow, logic, equipment, etc. A "program flowchart" illustrates the structure and sequence of operations of a program, while a "system flowchart" illustrates the components and flows of data processing or information systems.

Foreground Processing. The automatic execution of the computer programs that have been designed to preempt the use of the computing facilities. Contrast with Background Processing.

Format. The arrangement of data.

FORTRAN. FORmula TRANslator. A high-level procedure-oriented programming language widely utilized to develop computer programs that perform mathematical computations for scientific, engineering, and selected business applications.

Front-End Processor. Typically a smaller general-purpose computer which is dedicated to handling data communications control functions in a communications network, thus relieving the host computer of these functions.

Function.   A specific purpose of an entity or its characteristic action.

General Purpose Computer.   A computer that is designed to handle a wide variety of problems. Contrast with Special Purpose Computer.

Generate.   To produce a machine-language program by selecting from among various alternative subsets of coding the subset that embodies the most suitable methods for performing a specific data processing task based upon parameters supplied by a programmer or user.

Generator.   A computer program that performs a generating function.

Gigabyte.   One billion bytes. More accurately, 2 to the 30th power, or 1,073,741,824 in decimal notation.

GIGO.   A contraction of "Garbage In, Garbage Out," which emphasizes that data processing systems will produce erroneous and invalid output when provided with erroneous and invalid input data or instructions.

Graphics.   Pertaining to symbolic input or output from a computer system, such as lines, curves, geometric shapes, etc., using video display units or graphic plotters and printers.

Handshaking.   Exchange of predetermined signals when a connection is established between two communications terminals.

Hard Copy.   A data medium or data record that has a degree of permanence and that can be read by man or machine. Similar to Document.

Hardware.   Physical equipment, as opposed to the computer program or method of use, such as mechanical, magnetic, electrical, or electronic devices. Contrast with Software.

Hash Total.   The sum of the numbers in a data field which is not normally added, such as account numbers or other identification numbers. It is utilized as a "control total," especially during input/output operations of batch processing systems.

Header Card.   A card that contains information related to the data in cards that follow.

Header Label.   A machine-readable record at the beginning of a file containing data for file identification and control.

Heuristic.   Pertaining to exploratory methods of problem solving in which solutions are discovered by evaluation of the progress made toward the final result. It is an exploratory trial-and-error approach guided by rules of thumb. Contrast with Algorithmic.

Hexadecimal.   Pertaining to the number system with a radix of 16. Synonymous with sexadecimal.

High-Level Language.   A programming language that utilizes macro instructions and statements that closely resemble human language or mathematical notation to describe the problem to be solved or the procedure to be used. Also called a compiler language.

HIPO Chart.   (Hierarchy + input/processing/output). Also known as an IPO Chart. A design and documentation tool of structured programming utilized to record input/processing/output details of the hierarchical program modules.

Hollerith.   Pertaining to a particular type of code or punched card utilizing 12 rows per column and usually 80 columns per card. Named after Herman Hollerith, who originated punched card data processing.

Host Computer.   Typically a larger central computer that performs the major data processing tasks in a computer network.

Hybrid Computer.   A computer for data processing which utilizes both analog and digital representation of data.

Index.   An ordered reference list of the contents of a file or document together with keys or reference notations for identification or location of those contents.

Index Register.   A register whose contents may be added to or subtracted from the operand address prior to or during the execution of a computer instruction.

Index Sequential.   A method of data organization in which records are organized in sequential order and also referenced by an index. When utilized with direct access file devices, it is known as index sequential access method or ISAM.

Indexing.   The use of index registers for address modification in stored-program computers.

Information.   (1) Data that has been transformed into a meaningful and useful form for specific human beings. (2) The meaning that a human assigns to data by means of the known conventions used in their representation.

Information Processing. The integration of data processing and word processing. With the help of advanced telecommunications systems, the integration of the transmission and processing of data, words, images, and voices.

Information Resource Management (IRM). A management concept which views data, information, and computer resources (computer hardware, software, and personnel) as valuable organizational resources which should be efficiently, economically, and effectively managed for the benefit of the entire organization.

Information Retrieval. The methods and procedures for recovering specific information from stored data.

Information System. A system which uses personnel, operating procedures, and data processing subsystems to collect and process data and disseminate information in an organization.

Information Theory. The branch of learning concerned with the likelihood of accurate transmission or communication of messages subject to transmission failure, distortion, and noise.

Initialize. To set counters, switches, addresses, and variables to zero or other starting values at the beginning of or at prescribed points in a computer program.

Input. Pertaining to a device, process, or channel involved in the insertion of data into a data processing system. Opposite of output.

Input/Output (I/O). Pertaining to either input or output, or both.

Input/Output Control System (IOCS). Programs which control the flow of data into and out of the computer system.

Inquiry. A request for information from a computer system.

Installation. (1) The process of installing new computer hardware or software. (2) A data processing facility such as a computer installation.

Instruction. A grouping of characters that specifies the computer operation to be performed and the values or locations of its operands.

Instruction Cycle. The phase in the execution of a computer instruction during which the instruction is called from storage and the required circuitry to perform the instruction is readied.

Integer. A whole number as opposed to a real number which has fractional parts.

Integrated Circuit. A complex microelectronic circuit consisting of interconnected circuit elements which cannot be disassembled because they are placed on or within a "continuous substrate" such as a silicon chip.

Intelligent Terminal. A terminal with the capabilities of a microcomputer or minicomputer which can thus perform many data processing and other functions without accessing a larger computer.

Interactive Processing. A type of realtime processing in which users at online terminals can interact with the computer on a realtime basis. This may take the form of inquiry/response, conversational computing, online data entry, or interactive programming.

Interactive Program. A computer program that permits data to be entered or the flow of the program to be changed during its execution.

Interactive Programming. Designing and coding the processing logic of a computer program with substantial realtime assistance from a computer system. Interactive programming has become feasible through the use of software tools such as application development systems which provide interactive assistance to programmers in their development of application programs.

Interface. A shared boundary, such as the boundary between two systems. For example, the boundary between a computer and its peripheral devices.

Interpreter. A computer program that translates and executes each source language statement before translating and executing the next one.

Interrupt. A condition that causes an interruption in a data processing operation during which another data processing task is performed. At the conclusion of this new data processing assignment, control may be transferred back to the point where the original data processing operation was interrupted or to other tasks with a higher priority.

Inverted File. A method of data organization in which a data element identifies a record in a file instead of the original identifier or key.

Iterative. Pertaining to the repeated execution of a series of steps.

Job. A specified group of tasks prescribed as a unit of work for a computer.

Job Control Cards. See Control Card.

Job Control Language (JCL). A language for communicating with the operating system of a computer to identify a job and describe its requirements.

Justify. (1) To adjust the printing positions of characters toward the left- or right-hand margins of a data field or page. (2) To shift the contents of a storage position so that the most or the least significant digit is at some specified position.

K. An abbreviation for the prefix "kilo," that is 1,000 in decimal notation. When referring to storage capacity it is equivalent to 2 to the 10th power, or 1,024 in decimal notation.

Key. One or more characters within an item of data that are used to identify it or control its use.

Keyboarding. Using the keyboard of a typewriter, word processor, or computer terminal.

Keypunch. (1) A keyboard actuated device that punches holes in a card to represent data. Also called a card-punch. (2) The act of using a keypunch to record data in a punched card.

Key-to-Disk. Data entry using a keyboard device to record data directly on a magnetic disk.

Key-to-Tape. Data entry using a keyboard device to record data directly on magnetic tape.

Label. One or more characters used to identify a statement or an item of data in a computer program or the contents of the data file.

Language. A set of representations, conventions, and rules used to convey information.

Language Translator Program. A program which can convert the programming language instructions of computer programs into machine language instructions. Also called language processors. Major types include assemblers, compilers, and interpreters.

Large-Scale Integration (LSI). A method of constructing electronic circuits in which thousands of circuits can be placed on a single semiconductor chip.

Library. A collection of related files or programs.

Library Routine. A proven routine that is maintained in a program library.

Light Pen. A photo-electronic device which allows data to be entered or altered on the face of a video display terminal.

Line Printer. A device that prints all characters of a line as a unit. Contrast with Character Printer.

Linear Programming. In operations research, a procedure for locating the maximum or minimum of a linear function of variables that are subject to linear constraints.

Linkage. In programming, the coding that connects two separately coded routines.

List. (1) An ordered set of items. (2) A method of data organization which uses indexes and pointers to allow for nonsequential retrieval.

List Porcessing. A method of processing data in the form of lists.

Load. In programming, to enter data into storage or working registers.

Local. Connected to a computer by regular electrical wires. In close proximity to a computer. Contrast to remote access.

Local Network. A communications network which typically uses coaxial cable to connect computers, word processors, terminals, and electronic copying machines and dictation systems within a limited physical area such as an office building, manufacturing plant, or other work site.

Location. Any place in which data may be stored.

Log. A record of the operations of a data processing system.

Logical Data Elements. Data elements that are independent of the physical data media on which they are recorded.

Loop. A sequence of instructions that is executed repeatedly until a terminal condition prevails.

Machine Cycle. The timing of a basic CPU operation as determined by a fixed number of electrical pulses emitted by the CPU's timing circuitry or internal clock.

Machine Instruction. An instruction that a computer can recognize and execute.

Machine Language. A programming language where instructions are expressed in the binary code of the computer.

Macro Instruction. An instruction in a source language that is equivalent to a specified sequence of machine instructions.

Mag Stripe Card. A plastic wallet-size card with a strip of magnetic tape on one surface; widely used for bank credit cards.

Magnetic Bubble. An electro-magnetic storage device which stores and moves data magnetically as tiny magnetic spots which look like bubbles under a microscope as they float on the surface of a special type of semiconductor chip.

Magnetic Card. A card with a magnetic surface on which data can be stored.

Magnetic Core. Tiny rings composed of iron oxide and other materials that are strung on wires which provide electrical current that magnetizes the cores. Data is represented by the direction of the magnetic field of groups of cores. Widely utilized as the primary storage media in second- and third-generation computer systems.

Magnetic Disk. A flat circular plate with a magnetic surface on which data can be stored by selective magnetization of portions of the flat surface.

Magnetic Drum. A circular cylinder with a magnetic surface on which data can be stored by selective magnetization of portions of the curved surface.

Magnetic Ink. An ink that contains particles of iron oxide which can be magnetized and detected by magnetic sensors.

Magnetic Ink Character Recognition (MICR). The machine recognition of characters printed with magnetic ink. Contrast with Optical Character Recognition.

Magnetic Tape. A tape with a magnetic surface on which data can be stored by selective magnetization of portions of the surface.

Mainframe. (1) Same as central processing unit. (2) A larger size computer system, typically with a separate central processing unit, as distinguished from microcomputer and minicomputer systems.

Management Information System (MIS). An information system that provides the information needed to support management functions.

Manual Data Processing. (1) Data processing requiring continual human operation and intervention which utilizes simple data processing tools such as paper forms, pencils, filing cabinets, etc. (2) All data processing that is not automatic, even if it utilizes machines such as typewriters, adding machines, calculators, etc.

Mark-Sensing. The electrical sensing of manually recorded conductive marks on a nonconductive surface.

Mass Storage. (1) Devices having a large storage capacity, such as magnetic disks or drums. (2) Secondary storage devices with extra large storage capacities (in the hundreds of millions of bytes) such as magnetic strip and card units.

Master File. A data file containing relatively permanent information which is utilized as an authoritative reference and is usually updated periodically. Contrast with Transaction File.

Mathematical Model. A mathematical representation of a process, device, or concept.

Matrix. A two-dimensional retangular array of quantities.

Megabyte. One million bytes. More accurately, 2 to the 20th power or 1,048,576 in decimal notation.

Memory. Same as Storage.

Menu. A displayed list of items (usually the names of data processing jobs) from which a video terminal operator makes a selection.

Menu Driven. A characteristic of most interactive processing systems which provide menu displays and operator prompting which assist a video terminal operator in performing a particular job.

Merge. To combine items from two or more similarly ordered sets into one set that is arranged in the same order.

Message. An arbitrary amount of information whose beginning and end are defined or implied.

Microcomputer. A very small computer, ranging in size from a "computer on a chip" to a small typewriter-size unit.

Micrographics. The use of microfilm, microfiche, and other microforms to record data in greatly reduced form. The use of computers in the field of micrographics involves computer-output-microfilm or COM, in which microfilm is used as a computer output medium, computer-input-microfilm or CIM, where microfilm is used as an input medium, or computer-assisted-retrieval or CAR, in which special-purpose computer terminals or minicomputers are used as micrographics terminals to locate and retrieve a document stored on microfilm.

Microprocessor (MPU). A microcomputer central processing unit (CPU) on a chip and without input/

output or primary storage capabilities in most types.

Microprogram. A small set of elementary control instructions called microinstructions or microcodes.

Microprogramming. The use of special software (microprograms) to perform the functions of special hardware (electronic control circuitry). Microprograms stored in a read-only storage module of the control unit interpret the machine-language instructions of a computer program and decode them into elementary microinstructions which are then executed.

Minicomputer. A small (for example, desk-top size) electronic, digital, stored-program, general purpose computer.

Mnemonic. The use of symbols which are chosen to assist the human memory, which are typically abbreviations or contractions, such as "MPY" for multiply.

Modem. MOdulator-DEModulator. A device converts the digital signals from input/output devices into appropriate frequencies at a transmission terminal and converts them back into digital signals at a receiving terminal.

Module. A unit of hardware or software that is discrete and identifiable and designed for use with other units.

Monitor. Software or hardware that observes, supervises, controls, or verifies the operations of a system.

Multiplex. To interleave or simultaneously transmit two or more messages on a single channel.

Multiplexor. An electronic device which allows a single communications channel to carry simultaneous data transmission from many terminals by dividing a higher-speed channel into multiple slow-speed channels.

Multiprocessing. Pertaining to the simultaneous execution of two or more instructions by a computer or computer network.

Multiprocessor Computer System. Computer systems which use a multiprocessor architecture in the design of their central processing units. Instead of having one CPU with a single control unit, arithmetic-logic unit, and primary storage unit (called a uniprocessor design), the CPU of a multiprocessor computer contains several types of processing units, such as support microprocessors or multiple arithmetic-logic and control units.

Multiprogramming. Pertaining to the concurrent execution of two or more programs by a computer by interleaving their execution.

Nanosecond. One billionth of a second.

Natural Language. A programming language which is very close to human language. Also called very high-level language.

Nest. To embed subroutines or data in other subroutines or data at a different hierarchical level such that the different levels of routines or data can be executed or accessed recursively.

Network. An interconnection of computers, terminals, and communications channels and devices.

Network Architecture. A master plan designed to promote an open, simple, flexible, and efficient data communications environment through the use of standard protocols, standard communications hardware and software interfaces, and the design of a standard multilevel data communications interface between end users and computer systems.

Node. A terminal point in a communications network.

Noise. (1) Random variations of one or more characteristics of any entity such as voltage, current, or data. (2) A random signal of known statistical properties of amplitude, distribution, and special density. (3) Any disturbance tending to interfere with the normal operation of a device or system.

Numeral. A discrete representation of a number.

Numeric. Pertaining to numerals or to representation by means of numerals. Synonymous with numerical.

Numerical Control. Automatic control of a process performed by a device that makes use of all or part of numerical data generally introduced as the operation is in process.

Object Program. A compiled or assembled program composed of executable machine instructions. Contrast with Source Program.

Octal. Pertaining to the number representation system with a radix of eight.

OEM. Original Equipment Manufacturer. A firm which manufactures and sells computers by assembling components produced by other hardware manufacturers.

Offline. Pertaining to equipment or devices not under control of the central processing unit.

Online. Pertaining to equipment or devices under control of the central processing unit.

Operand. That which is operated upon. That part of a computer instruction which is identified by the address part of the instruction.

Operating System. Software that controls the execution of computer programs and that may provide scheduling, debugging, input/output control, accounting, compilation, storage assignment, data management, and related services.

Operation. A defined action, namely, the act of obtaining a result from one or more operands in accordance with rules that specify the result for any permissible combination of operands.

Operation Code. A code that represents specific operations. Synonymous with instruction code.

Operational Information System. An information system that collects, processes, and stores data generated by the operational systems of an organization and produces data and information for input into a management information system or for the control of an operational system.

Operational System. A basic subsystem of the business firm as a system which constitutes its input, processing, and output components. Also called a physical system.

Operations Research (OR). The use of the scientific method to provide criteria for decisions concerning the actions of people, machines, and other resources in a system.

Optical Character Recognition (OCR). The machine identification of printed characters through the use of light-sensitive devices.

Optical Scanner. A device that optically scans printed or written data and generates their digital representations.

Output. Pertaining to a device, process, or channel involved with the transfer of data or information out of a data processing system.

Overflow. That portion of the result of an operation that exceeds the capacity of the intended unit of storage.

Overlapped Processing. Pertaining to the ability of a computer system to increase the utilization of its central processing unit by overlapping input/output and processing operations.

Overlay. The technique of repeatedly using the same blocks of internal storage during different stages of a program. When one routine is no longer needed in storage, another routine can replace all or part of it.

Pack. To compress data in a storage medium by taking advantage of known characteristics of the data in such a way that the original data can be recovered.

Packet. A group of data and control information in a specified format transferred as an entity.

Packet Switching. A data transmission process that transmits addressed packets such that a channel is occupied only for the duration of transmission of the packet.

Page. A segment of a program or data, usually of fixed length, that has a fixed virtual address but can in fact reside in any region of the internal storage of the computer.

Paging. A process which automatically and continually transfers pages of programs and data between primary storage and direct access storage devices. It provides computers with advanced multiprogramming and virtual memory capabilities.

Parallel. Pertaining to the concurrent or simultaneous occurrence of two or more related activities in multiple devices or channels.

Parity Bit. A check bit appended to an array of binary digits to make the sum of all the binary digits, including the check bit, always odd or always even.

Parity Check. A check that tests whether the number of ones or zeros in an array of binary digits is odd or even.

Pascal. A high-level general-purpose structured programming language named after Blaise Pascal. It was developed by Niklaus Wirth of Zurich in 1968.

Pass. One cycle of processing a body of data.

Patch. To modify a routine in a rough or expedient way.

Pattern Recognition. The identification of shapes, forms, or configurations by automatic means.

PBX. Private Branch Exchange. An office telephone switchboard device.

PCM. Plug Compatible Manufacturer. A firm which manufactures computer equipment which can be plugged into existing computer systems without requiring additional hardware or software interfaces.

Peripheral Equipment. In a data processing system, any unit of equipment, distinct from the central processing unit, that may provide the system with outside communication.

Personal Computing. The use of microcomputers as personal computers by individuals for educational, recreational, home management, and other personal applications.

PERT. Program Evaluation and Review Technique A network analysis technique utilized to find the most efficient scheduling of time and resources when developing a complex project or product.

Physical Data Element. The physical data medium which contains one or more logical data elements. For example, a punched card is a single physical record which may contain several logical records.

Picosecond. One trillionth of a second.

PL/1 (Programming Language 1). A procedure-oriented high-level general purpose programming language designed to combine the features of COBOL, FORTRAN, ALGOL, etc.

Plot. To map or diagram by connecting coordinate values.

Plotter. A hard-copy output device that produces drawings and graphical displays on paper or other materials.

Point-of-Sale (POS) Terminal. A computer terminal used in retail stores that serves the function of a cash register as well as collecting sales data and performing other data processing functions.

Pointer. A data item associated with an index, a record, or other set of data which contains the address of a related record.

Port. (1) Electronic circuitry which provides a connection point between the CPU and input/output devices. (2) A connection point for a communication line on a CPU or other front-end device.

Position. In a string, each location that may be occupied by a character or binary digit and may be identified by a serial number.

Precision. The degree of discrimination with which a quantity is stated.

Privileged Instruction. A computer instruction whose use is restricted to the operating system of the computer and is not available for use in ordinary programs.

Problem-Oriented Language. A programming language designed for the convenient expression of a given class of problems.

Procedure. The course of action taken for the solution of a problem.

Procedure-Oriented Language. A programming language designed for the convenient expression of procedures used in the solution of a wide class of problems.

Process. A systematic sequence of operations to produce a specified result.

Process Control. The use of a computer to control an ongoing physical process such as industrial production processes.

Processor. A hardware device or software system capable of performing operations upon data.

Program. (1) A series of actions proposed in order to achieve a certain result. (2) An ordered set of computer instructions which cause a computer to perform a particular process. (3) The act of developing a program.

Program Library. A collection of available computer programs and routines.

Programmed Decision. A decision that can be automated by basing it on a decision rule which outlines the steps to take when confronted with the need for a specific decision.

Programmer. A person mainly involved in designing, writing, and testing computer programs.

Programming. The design, writing, and testing of a program.

Programming Language. A language used to prepare computer programs.

Protocol. A set of rules and procedures for the control of communications in a communications network.

Pseudocode. An informal design language of structured programming which expresses the processing logic of a program module in ordinary English-language phrases.

Punched Card. A card punched with a pattern of holes to represent data.

Punched Tape. A tape on which a pattern of holes or cuts is used to represent data.

Query. A request for specific data or information.

Query Language. A high-level, English-like language provided by a data base management system which enables users to easily extract data and information from a data base.

Queue. (1) A waiting line formed by items in a system waiting for service. (2) To arrange in or form a queue.

Random Access. Same as Direct Access.

Random Access Memory (RAM). One of the basic types of semiconductor memory used for temporary storage of data or programs during processing. Each memory position can be directly sensed (read) or changed (write) in the same length of time, irrespective of its location on the storage medium.

Random Data Organization. A method of data organization in which logical data elements are distributed randomly on or within the physical data medium. For example, logical data records distributed randomly on the surfaces of a magnetic disk file.

Read. To acquire or interpret data from a storage device, a data medium, or any other source.

Read-Only Memory (ROM). A basic type of semiconductor memory used for permanent storage. Can only be read, not "written," i.e., changed. Variations are Programmable Read-Only Memory (PROM) and Eraseable Programmable Read-Only Memory (EPROM).

Realtime. Pertaining to the performance of data processing during the actual time a process transpires in order that results of the data processing can be used in guiding the process.

Realtime Processing. Data processing in which data is processed immediately rather than periodically. Contrast with Batch Processing.

Record. A collection of related items or fields of data treated as a unit.

Register. A device capable of storing a specified amount of data such as one word.

Relative Address. The number that specifies the difference between the absolute address and the base address.

Remote Access. Pertaining to communication with the data processing facility by one or more stations that are distant from that facility.

Reproduce. To prepare a duplicate of stored data or information.

Remote Job Entry (RJE). Entering jobs into a batch processing system from a remote facility.

Robotics. The technology of building machines (robots) with computer intelligence and human-like physical capabilities.

Rounding. The process of deleting the least significant digits of a numeric value and adjusting the part that remains according to some rule.

Routine. An ordered set of instructions that may have some general or frequent use.

RPG. Report Program Generator. A problem-oriented language which utilizes a generator to construct programs that produce reports and perform other data processing tasks.

Run. A single continuous performance of a computer program or routine.

Scan. To examine sequentially, part by part.

Schema. An overall conceptual or logical view of the relationships between the data in a data base.

Secondary Storage. Storage that supplements the primary storage of a computer. Synonymous with auxiliary storage.

Segment. (1) To divide a computer program into parts such that the program can be executed without the entire program being in internal storage at any one time. (2) Such a part of a computer program.

Sequence. An arrangement of items according to a specified set of rules. Contrast with Random.

Sequential Access. A sequential method of storing and retrieving data from a file. Contrast with Random Access.

Sequential Data Organization. Organizing logical data elements according to a prescribed sequence.

Serial. Pertaining to the sequential or consecutive occurrence of two or more related activities in a single device or channel.

Serial Access. Pertaining to the process of obtaining data from or placing data into storage, where the access time is dependent upon the location of the data most recently obtained or placed in storage. Contrast with Direct Access.

Service Bureau. A firm offering computer and data

processing services. Also called a computer service center.

Service Program. A program that provides general support for the operation of a computer system, such as input/output, diagnostic, and other "utility" routines.

Set. (1) A collection. (2) To place a storage device into a specified state, usually other than that denoting zero or space character.

Set up. To arrange and make ready the data or devices needed to solve a particular problem.

Setup Time. The time required to set up the devices, materials, and procedures required for a particular data processing application.

Sign Position. A position, normally located at one end of a numeral, that contains an indication of the algebraic sign of the number.

Signal. A time-dependent value attached to a physical phenomenon which conveys data.

Significant Digit. A digit that is needed for a certain purpose, particularly one that must be kept to preserve a specific accuracy or precision.

Simplex. Pertaining to a communications link that is capable of transmitting data in only one direction. Contrast with Duplex.

Simulation. The representation of certain features of the behavior of a physical or abstract system by the behavior of another system. Contrast with Emulation.

Skeletal Coding. Sets of instructions in which some addresses and other parts remain undetermined. These addresses and other parts are usually determined by routines that are designed to modify them in accordance with given parameters.

Small Business Computer. A small computer used primarily for business applications.

Smart Products. Industrial and consumer products with "intelligence" provided by built-in microcomputers or microprocessors which significantly improve the performance and capabilities of such products.

Software. A set of computer programs, procedures, and possibly associated documentation concerned with the operation of a data processing system. Contrast with Hardware.

Software Package. A computer program supplied by computer manufacturers, independent software companies, or other computer users. Also known as canned programs, proprietary software, or packaged programs.

Solid State. Pertaining to devices whose operation depends on the control of electric or magnetic phenomenon in solids, such as transistors, diodes, etc.

Sort. To segregate items into groups according to some definite rules.

Source Document. The original written record of an activity, such as a purchase order or sales invoice.

Source Program. A computer program written in a language that is an input to a translation process. Contrast with Object Program.

Special Character. A graphic character that is neither a letter, a digit, nor a space character.

Special Purpose Computer. A computer that is designed to handle a restricted class of problems. Contrast with General Purpose Computer.

Spooling. Simultaneous peripheral operation online. Storing input data from low-speed devices temporarily on high-speed secondary storage units which can be quickly accessed by the CPU. Also, writing output data at high speeds onto magnetic tape or disk units from which it can be transferred to slow-speed devices such as a card punch or printer.

Statement. In computer programming, a meaningful expression or generalized instruction in a source program, particularly in high-level programming languages.

Storage. Pertaining to a device into which data can be entered, in which they can be held, and from which they can be retrieved at a later time.

Storage Allocation. The assignment of blocks of data to specified blocks of storage.

Storage Protection. An arrangement for preventing access to storage for either reading or writing, or both.

Store. To enter or retain data in a storage device. Sometimes synonymous with storage device.

Stored Program Computer. A computer controlled by internally stored instructions that can synthesize, store, and in some cases alter instructions as though they were data and that can subsequently execute these instructions.

String. A linear sequence of entities such as characters or physical elements.

Structure Chart. A design and documentation technique used in structured programming to show the purpose and relationships of the various modules in a program.

Structured Programming. A programming methodology which involves the use of a "top-down" program design and uses a limited number of control structures in a program to create highly structured "modules" of program code.

Structured Walk-Throughs. A structured programming methodology which requires a peer review by other programmers of the program design and coding to minimize and reveal errors in the early stages of programming.

Subroutine. A routine that can be part of another routine.

Subschema. A subset or transformation of the logical view of the data base schema which is required by a particular user application program.

Subsystem. A system that is a component of a larger system.

Supercomputer. A category including the largest, fastest, and most powerful computers available.

Supervisor. The main control program of an operating system.

Switch. (1) A device or programming technique for making a selection. (2) A computer that controls message switching among the computers and terminals in a data communications network.

Symbol. A representation of something by reason of relationship, association, or convention.

Symbolic Address. An address expressed in symbols convenient to the computer programmer.

Symbolic Coding. Coding that uses machine instructions with symbolic addresses.

Synchronous. A characteristic in which each event, or the performance of any basic operation, is constrained to start on, and usually to keep in step with, signals from a timing clock. Contrast with Asynchronous.

Synergism. A system characteristic where the whole of the system is equal to more than the sum of its component parts.

System. (1) A group of interrelated or interacting elements. (2) A group of interrelated components that seeks the attainment of a common goal by accepting inputs and producing outputs in an organized process. (3) An assembly of methods, procedures, or techniques united by regulated interaction to form an organized whole. (4) An organized collection of people, machines, and methods required to accomplish a set of specific functions.

Systems Analysis. (1) Analyzing in detail the components and requirements of a system. (2) Analyzing in detail the information needs of an organization, the characteristics and components of presently utilized information systems, and the requirements of proposed information systems.

Systems Development. (1) Conceiving, designing, and implementing a system. (2) Developing information systems by a process of investigation, analysis, design, programming, implementation, and maintenance.

Table. A collection of data in which each item is uniquely identified by a label, by its position relative to the other items, or by some other means.

Tabulate. To form data into a table or to print totals.

Telecommunications. Pertaining to the transmission of signals over long distances, including not only data communications but also the transmission of images and voices using radio, television, and other communications technologies.

Teleconferencing. The use of video communications to allow business conferences to be held with participants who are scattered across a country, continent, or the world.

Teleprocessing. See Data Communications.

Terabyte. One trillion bytes. More accurately, 2 to the 40th power, or 1,009,511,627,776 in decimal notation.

Terminal. A point in a system or communication network at which data can either enter or leave. Also, an input/output device at such a point in a system.

Throughput. The total amount of useful work performed by a data processing system during a given period of time.

Time-Sharing. Providing computer services to many users simultaneously while providing rapid responses to each.

Top-Down Design. A methodology of structured programming in which a program is organized into "functional modules," with the programmer designing the main module first and then the lower-level modules.

Track. The portion of a moving storage medium,

such as a drum, tape, or disk, that is accessible to a given reading head position.

Transaction File. A data file containing relatively transient data to be processed in combination with a master file. Synonymous with detail file.

Transducer. A device for converting energy from one form to another.

Transform Algorithm. Performing an arithmetic computation on a record key and using the result of the calculation as an address for that record. Also known as key transformation.

Translator. A device or computer program that transforms statements from one language to another, such as a compiler or assembler.

Transmit. To send data from one location and to receive the data at another location.

Truncate. (1) To terminate a computational process in accordance with certain rules. (2) To remove characters from the beginning or ending of a data element, especially digits at the beginning or ending of a numeric quantity. Contrast with Rounding.

Turnaround Time. The elapsed time between submission of a job to a computing center and the return of the results.

Turnkey Systems. Computer systems where all of the hardware, software, and systems development needed by a user are provided.

Unbundling. The separate pricing of hardware, software, and other related services.

Unconditional Transfer. Pertaining to an unconditional departure from the normal sequence of execution of instructions in a computer program.

Unit Record. Pertaining to a single physical record that contains a single logical record.

Universal Product Code (UPC). A standard identification code using bar coding, printed on products which can be read by the optical supermarket scanners of the grocery industry.

Update. To incorporate into a master file the changes required to reflect the most current status of the records in the file.

User-Friendly. A characteristic of human-operated equipment and systems which makes them safe, comfortable, and easy to use.

Utility Program. A standard set of routines which assists in the operation of a computer system by performing some frequently required process such as sorting, merging, etc.

Variable. A quantity that can assume any of a given set of values.

Variable-Length Record. Pertaining to data records which contain a variable number of characters or fields.

Variable Word-Length. Pertaining to a machine word or operand that may consist of a variable number of bits or characters. Contrast with Fixed Word-Length.

Verify. To determine whether a transcription of data or other operation has been accomplished accurately.

Virtual Machine. Pertaining to the simulation of one type of computer system by another computer system.

Virtual Memory. The use of secondary storage devices as an extension of the primary storage of the computer, thus giving the "virtual" appearance of a larger "virtually unlimited" main memory than actually exists.

Voice Recognition. Direct conversion of spoken data into electronic form suitable for entry into a computer system. Also called voice data entry.

Volatile Memory. Memory (such as electronic semiconductor memory) which loses its contents when electrical power is turned off.

Wand. A hand-held optical character-recognition device used for data entry by many transaction terminals.

Word. (1) A character string or bit string considered as an entity. (2) An ordered set of characters handled as a unit by the computer.

Word Processing. The automation of the transformation of ideas and information into the readable form of communication. It involves the manipulation of characters, words, sentences, and paragraphs in order to produce office communications in the forms of letters, memos, messages, documents, and reports.

Word Processing Systems. Information processing systems which rely on automated and computerized typing, dictation, copying, filing, and telecommunication systems that are used in modern offices.

Write. To record data on a data medium.

Zero Suppression. The elimination of nonsignificant zeros in a numeral.

Index

This book has been set CAP VideoComp in 11 and 9 point Stymie Light, leaded 2 points. Part numbers, part titles, and chapter titles are 24 pt. Roma; chapter numbers are 64 pt. Roma Semi-Bold. The size of the type page is 37 by 48 picas.

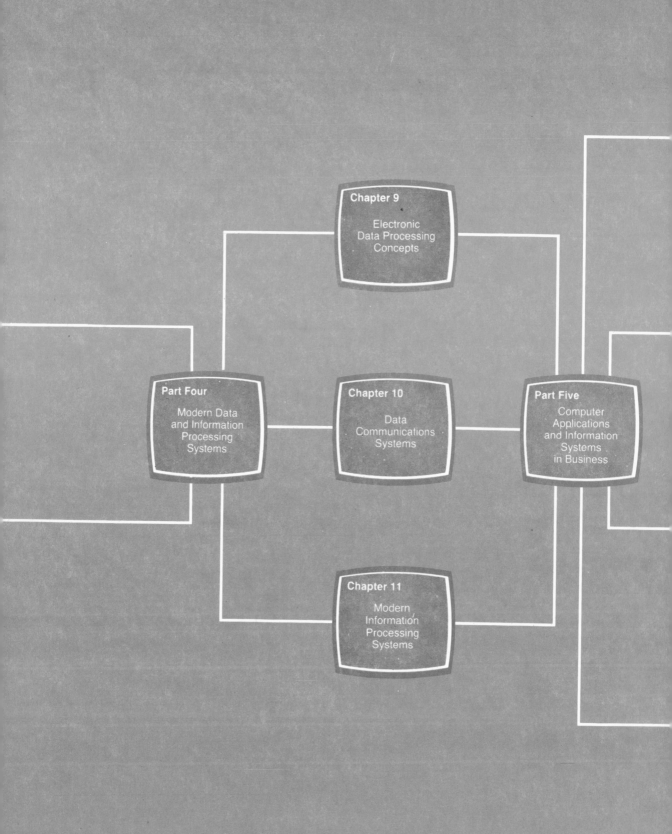

Chapter 9

Electronic
Data Processing
Concepts

Part Four

Modern Data
and Information
Processing
Systems

Chapter 10

Data
Communications
Systems

Part Five

Computer
Applications
and Information
Systems
in Business

Chapter 11

Modern
Information
Processing
Systems